THE AUTHORIZED
P-FUNK
SONG REFERENCE

THE AUTHORIZED
P-FUNK
SONG REFERENCE

OFFICIAL CANON OF PARLIAMENT-FUNKADELIC
1956 ★ 2023

DANIEL BEDROSIAN

ROWMAN & LITTLEFIELD
Lanham • Boulder • New York • London

Published by Rowman & Littlefield
An imprint of The Rowman & Littlefield Publishing Group, Inc.
4501 Forbes Boulevard, Suite 200, Lanham, Maryland 20706
www.rowman.com

86-90 Paul Street, London EC2A 4NE

British Library Cataloguing in Publication Information Available

Library of Congress Cataloging-in-Publication Data

Names: Bedrosian, Daniel, 1981- author.
Title: The authorized P-Funk song reference : official canon of Parliament-Funkadelic, 1956-2023 / Daniel Bedrosian.
Identifiers: LCCN 2023028287 (print) | LCCN 2023028288 (ebook) | ISBN 9781538183427 (cloth) | ISBN 9781538183434 (ebook)
Subjects: LCSH: P-Funk All Stars—Discography. | Parliament (Musical group)—Discography. | Funkadelic (Musical group)—Discography. | Funk (Music)—Discography. | Clinton, George, 1940—Discography. | LCGFT: Discographies.
Classification: LCC ML156.7.P46 2023 (print) | LCC ML156.7.P46 2023 (ebook) | DDC 016.78242164—dc23/eng/20230621
LC record available at https://lccn.loc.gov/2023028287
LC ebook record available at https://lccn.loc.gov/2023028288

CONTENTS

INTRODUCTION

The Parliament-Funkadelic collective, spearheaded by the often-imitated-but-never-duplicated visionary mastermind George Clinton, is indeed an underappreciated musical entity, especially looking at it from a historical perspective. Coming from the seemingly unending creative spark that exploded out of the African diaspora in the Americas, P-Funk, even separate from all other "funk" music, became something far more representational of the storied artfulness of that diaspora, marrying music, artwork, production, business savvy, mythology, politics, social upheaval, science fiction, poetry, literature, concept, and even religion under the ever-expanding embodiment of the "Power of the One," as often quoted in the annals of this long-running movement. The "P-Funk" camp's production output, numbering well over 500 releases, represents the single largest discography of any one musical production family. In short, P-Funk and its satellites over the years have represented the longest-running popular musical group of all time. In addition, P-Funk's personnel and roster have been ever changing, often growing, shrinking, ebbing, and flowing through the decades, with some members being there only a brief period, a sizable subset of members coming and going and coming back again, and a smaller dedicated cadre of band members staying for long tenures with the musical institution. To complicate matters further, one's conscious effort in analyzing any single album from Clinton's P-Funk camp can reveal representations of different sessions sometimes spanning years or even decades, with altering combinations of players and rhythm, horn, string and vocal sections numbering sometimes several dozen people, even on a single song. If that were not enough to boggle the musicologist's mind, most albums have incomplete or vague liner notes, with no reference to personnel per song, and other albums have liner notes that have been completely mislabeled, with the wrong musicians erroneously listed on the song credits (according to some reports, sometimes "on purpose," whether it be due to infighting, jealousy, or legalistic procedures of the day).

All of this confusion also lends itself to the often-repeated phrase of "organized chaos" with reference to Clinton's funk machine. Indeed, anyone who has worked for George Clinton knows that there is actually a tightly woven patchwork of threads that keeps this organization running, and its vast 68-year history is attestation of that fact. However, the previously mentioned misunderstandings and misinformation with regard to "who played on what" is among the most notable defined qualifications of the "chaos" portion of the above statement. It has fueled debates, controversies, and mysteries revolving around the "P-Funk Thang," cultivating a cultish if not wholly dedicated swath of fans worldwide, even among some of the band members themselves.

This topic segues into my involvement: Parliament-Funkadelic had been my favorite band since I was at least 11 years old. A classically trained pianist since age four, I am the son of concert pianists and music educators, and from a family firmly entrenched in the arts; music was in my veins. I dreamed from a very young age of being the keyboardist for P-Funk. And after a decade spent studying not only the technical and artistic aspects of the music of P-Funk itself but also the minutiae of the personnel from session to session to better understand the tones and styles of each cog in the machine, I eventually landed that very position that I had strived for all those years ago; the long-heralded keyboard chair in Parliament-Funkadelic. I have continued an unbroken 20-year tenure ever since, now proudly being the longest-tenured keyboardist in the live band's history.

All along the way, I was making not only lists of musical charts and chords for each song for multiple instrumental parts but also lists of who played on each particular song or album. I spent years not only carefully studying the vocal phrasing and "character voices" that grace the very framework of this unique music but also figuring out and differentiating the different yet oddly well-blended coterie of singers who were a part of this groundbreaking singular genre in its own right. In a parallel vein, I knew from a very young age that P-Funk was something so special, almost a separate universe of musical thought from the other popular music forms, obviously indebted to the culture, history, and events happening around it yet extremely influential on all those said forms that came after it. It should not be forgotten that P-Funk is essentially the most sampled band on the planet, and it is not just hip-hop that owes a debt of gratitude to P-Funk's several important musical innovations, deserving of a book all its own to properly describe. Indeed, rhythm and blues, rock, metal, electronica, techno, house, rap, modern gospel, world music, and other subgenres, going seemingly ad infinitum, owe a serious debt to Clinton's world of still-expanding musical genius.

As a historian (a BA degree in history from the University of New Hampshire), my dedication to the spreading of knowledge about P-Funk's understated influence on music the world over has been one of my longtime passion projects, and that said dedication has earned me the moniker from George Clinton himself as the "band musicologist." Almost every day, as a result of publicizing the vastness of this music and the misinformation regarding personnel, I have received questions from fans all over the world about "who played on this song?," "is it true that so-and-so didn't actually play on this song?," and so on. Fully understanding the near impossibility of this undertaking, something in me finally decided (possibly because no one other person would) to take it on myself to finally compile everything I had learned in terms of personnel listing for the hundreds of releases in the P-Funk camp's history and put it to paper, so to speak. For the most debated and hardest-to-ascertain information, I began filling in the gaps with more than two dozen important interviews with key players—musicians, vocalists, and music business professionals—through each of the eight decades that span this music, including George Clinton himself, to most soundly obtain all the truth about the liner notes, often unlabeled or mislabeled, throughout this massive, organic, still-growing body of work.

After being in the band a few years, I felt a strong affinity with my bandmates, who had been mislabeled or left unmentioned multiple times in song listings by compilers, record labels, or others during their tenures with this legendary group. Some of these situations happened dozens of times over a period of up to 40 years or more. My understanding of these matters personalized when I too became one of the victims of this occurrence on several live albums released by a company in Europe in the early 2000s. On closer inspection, the albums in question not only mislabeled me as someone else but also had a completely incorrect band roster for the whole group on the recordings in question, with the compiler of the live album erroneously copying and pasting one of George's rosters from not only a different year but also a different decade altogether. It is hard enough for the fans of this music to ascertain the realities of who was on which record or, even more specifically, which song, but these musicological mistakes were furthering the oddly compiled stack of misinformation plaguing this enormous group of musical innovators. Although being a victim of this situation was still not enough for me to finally plunge into the abyss of this undertaking, the one thing that finally persuaded me to do this was much more simple: the concept of time.

As the geniuses who graced the early records get older (indeed, we have lost far too many of them already to mention here), we are threatened with the loss of this information forever. The historian in me could not bear witness to the tragic nature of such a situation. I feel that "duty" is a far more apropos term to use with reference to this book. And although I know that somewhere there may be one or two mistaken pieces of errata in this publication, far greater will be the benefit of there being one singular volume, regardless of band name, record label, artist focus, or year of focus in this long-running musical empire, for fans to relish and band members to cherish and for future generations to study in its entirety. People 1,000 years from now will see that there was a musical project simply called "P-Funk" and that its quality and quantity alike changed the arts and society forever.

SOME NOTES ON PROCESS

The encyclopedia was compiled with three processes. The primary process, which takes up the bulk of the work, is compiled historical information gathered from a combination of correct and/or incomplete liner notes, decades of conversations with primary sources on the works in question, and other literature and articles gathered over almost 30 years. Some of the conversations therein are also with valuable primary sources who are, sadly, no longer with us.

The secondary process was achieved through poring over acquired liner notes on lesser-known and rarer albums, numbering in the hundreds of releases. These include but are not limited to newer albums released since the 1990s and limited releases from earlier periods. The secondary process also included using the internet as a research device for secondary and tertiary sources.

The tertiary—but likely the most important—process has been through filling in the gaps via extensive interviews with primary sources. These are some of the most pivotal people involved in the recordings themselves, including lengthy interviews with George Clinton himself and various collaborators in virtually every era of P-Funk's illustrious and continuing existence. These interviews have exceeded 66 hours and represent a variety of extremely important primary sources. The information pertaining to the tertiary step is included in the following section.

SPECIAL THANKS

Special thanks to the individuals who agreed to be interviewed to help fill in the gaps on unknown, controversial, and often debated pieces of the puzzle: Mr. George Clinton, first and foremost for his impeccable memory and incredible attention to detail. Thanks to the following individuals for firsthand information and liner notes not previously acquired: Richard Boyce, Sidney Barnes, Gary "Mudbone" Cooper, Michael "Kidd Funkadelic" Hampton, Rick Gardner, Taka Boom, Dewayne "Blackbyrd" McKnight, Michael "Clip" Payne, Dawn Silva, Jim "Jay Double-You" Wright, Linda Shider, Rodney "Skeet" Curtis, Bennie Cowan, Greg Thomas, Greg Boyer, Lige Curry, Kevin Oliver, Satori Shakoor, Sheila "Amuka" Kelly, Ronald "Stozo" Edwards, Carl "Butch" Small, David Lee Spradley, Lonnie Greene, Andre "Foxxe" Williams, Tracey "Treylewd" Lewis, Muruga Booker, Joseph "Amp" Fiddler, Steve Boyd, Debra Barsha, Gabe Gonzalez, Gregg Fitz, Keith Thomas, Noel Haskins, Tim Shider, Lenny Holmes, Erik "Bone" Boon, E1 Ten, Juan Nelson, Sean "PapaSean" Franklin, Chuck Fishman, RonKat Spearman, Kendra Foster, Kim Manning, Toby Donahue, Gene "Poo Poo Man" Anderson, Shaunna Hall, Garrett Shider, Marshall Shider, Trazae Lewis-Clinton, Tonysha Nelson, Eli and Charlie from Soul Clap, and Shawn "Poppi" Clinton.

This book also contains vital information from conversations over the years with musicians, vocalists, and creatives in the P-Funk camp who have sadly passed away. They have imparted much information to the author in conversations and interviews over the past 20-plus years. Special thanks to Bernie "Woo" Worrell, Garry "Starchild" Shider, Cordell "Boogie" Mosson, Richard "Kush" Griffith, Robert "Peanut" Johnson, Joel "Razor Sharp" Johnson, Mallia "Queen of Funk" Franklin, Ron "Prophet" Ford, Ron Dunbar, Belita Woods, George E. Clinton III, and Dwayne "Sa'D Ali" Maultsby. Rest in beloved memory to all mentioned and not mentioned from this group of angels.

Additional special thanks to the band members who have imparted necessary information and details pertaining to specific songs over the years more casually in conversations during various tours: Billy "Bass" Nelson, Frankie "Kash" Waddy, Fred Wesley, Jeff "Cherokee" Bunn, Jerome Rodgers, Paul Hill, Foley, Shonda "Sativa" Clinton-Drennen, Ron Wright, Rico "Smoov" Lewis, and many more. Many apologies for those left out.

Additional thanks to the hardcore P-Funk fans over the years who have imparted information online or in person: Paul Felis, Melissa Weber, Marcel Visser, Chifumi Ui, Aris Wilson, Father Thyme, the Konings brothers, the Grau brothers, Peter Wetherbee, Tim Kinley, Chuck Haber, Rickey Vincent, Chris "Citrus" Sauthoff, Larry "Funkster" Jones, Chuck Fishman, Dan Wooridge, Tommy Barvick, Anthony D. Bryant, and others. These include the purveyors of the original Motherpage and the One Nation boardroom despite the occasional combination of bad information with good. This statement is especially true in the lifelong journey to obtain the truth. Luckily and hopefully, much of the previously erroneous information on the internet will be remedied with the existence of this volume.

A big thank-you goes out to the contributors to photographs used for this edition: Diem Jones, Mike Chiodo, William Thoren, Tim Kinley, and Rodney "Skeet" Curtis.

Contemporaneously, the author has conducted interviews with many of the still-living legends and contributors, mostly band members, and also family members of key contributors to form the bulk of the primary source material. However, due to collecting information over the many years of documenting the canon of P-Funk, the first 450 pages of the initial 725-page manuscript were outlined before starting the formal interview process. When the interviews were complete, the breakdown of newly interviewed primary sources was included in the accompanying interview list.

Special thanks to my wonderful, supportive wife Patavian and my three talented, amazing kids Nairi, Ani, and Lyric.

Extra special thanks to my parents Peter and Jeanne Bedrosian, pianists and educators both. I'm still awed by their talent and their knowledge, precious bits of which they passed down to me.

To my friend Nick Groff for sage advice and support when I was first shopping the book. To Mr. Christopher Horton and Jeff Paige from Funkatopia for introducing me to the great author Duane Tudahl. And thank you to Duane Tudahl for introducing me to my publishers at Rowman & Littlefield. To everyone at R&L who worked on the book, especially Michael Tan and Della Vache. Your help has been steadfast and invaluable.

INTERVIEW LIST

George Clinton: Interview 1: 5 hours. Interview 2: 3 hours. Interview 3: 45 minutes. Interview 4: 20 minutes. Interview 5: 20 minutes. Interview 6: 30 minutes. Interview 7: 30 minutes

Richard Boyce: Interview 1: 25 minutes. Interview 2: 1 hour

Sidney Barnes: Interview: 45 minutes

Gary "Mudbone" Cooper: Interview: 1 hour

Michael "Kidd Funkadelic" Hampton: Interview: 1 hour, 15 minutes

Archie Ivy: Interview: 1 hour, 15 minutes

Rick Gardner: Interview: 1 hour

Jim Wright: Interview: 30 minutes

Dawn Silva: Interview: 1 hour, 15 minutes

Linda Shider: Interview: 40 minutes

Rodney "Skeet" Curtis: Interview 1: 1 hour, 15 minutes. Interview 2: 15 minutes

Dewayne "Blackbyrd" McKnight: Interview: 2 hours, 45 minutes

Michael "Clip" Payne: Interview 1: 2 hours, 30 minutes. Interview 2: 2 hours, 45 minutes

Gregg "Daffy" Fitz: Interview 1: 1 hour. Interview 2: 30 minutes

Lenny Holmes: Interview: 45 minutes

Greg Thomas: Interview: 1 hour, 20 minutes

Greg Boyer: Interview: 40 minutes

Bennie Cowan: Interview: 1 hour

Lige Curry: Interview: 3 hours, 30 minutes

Kevin Oliver: Interview: 45 minutes

Carl "Butch" Small: Interview 1: 30 minutes. Interview 2: 2 hours, 50 minutes. Interview 3: 20 minutes

Sheila "Amuka" Kelly: Interview: 2 hours, 40 minutes

Satori Shakoor: Interview: 1 hour

David Spradley: Interview: 1 hour, 15 minutes

Tracey "Treylewd" Lewis: Interview 1: 1 hour, 45 minutes. Interview 2: 25 minutes

Andre "Foxxe" Williams: Interview: 2 hours, 30 minutes

Lonnie Greene: Interview: 45 minutes

Muruga Booker: Interview: 1 hour

LuShawn Clinton: Interview: 25 minutes

Seth Neblett: Interview: 35 minutes

Joseph "Amp" Fiddler: Interview 1: 10 minutes. Interview 2: 10 minutes. Interview 3: 20 minutes

Steve Boyd: Interview 1: 45 minutes. Interview 2: 20 minutes

Debra Barsha: Interview: 45 minutes

Gabe Gonzalez: Interview 1:– 3 hours, 30 minutes. Interview 2: 45 minutes

Keith Thomas: Interview: 40 minutes

Nowell Haskins: Interview: 40 minutes

Juan Nelson: Interview: 20 minutes

Sean "Papa Sean" Franklin: Interview: 10 minutes

Garrett Shider: Interview: 20 minutes

Marshall Shider: Interview: 25 minutes

RonKat Spearman: Interview: 20 minutes

Kendra Foster: Interview: 30 minutes

Toby Donahue: Interview: 1 hour

Gene "Poo Poo Man" Anderson: Interview: 20 minutes

Trazae Lewis-Clinton: Interview: 20 minutes

LuShawn "Young Poppi" Clinton: Interview: 20 minutes

67 hours pertaining to 63 formal interviews total.

INFORMATION ON THE LIST

The song list is broken down by band in chronological order. This follows each group through their discography in order of release before continuing with the next band to appear in the time line and so on. Rather than listing acts in alphabetical order, which I felt did not give the true scope of P-Funk's canonical age, I wanted to list each group as they first appeared "on wax." Each group will have a small introductory description of its inception and a brief overview of its history. In addition, each record label is listed with the exception of more postmodern independent or non-label albums that were left blank for obvious reasons. Most of the important albums are listed accordingly and chronologically with the accompanying songs contained therein.

Each song contains as much information as could be ascertained for said song, with noted exceptions. All the personnel (vocalists, musicians, and sometimes arrangers) are listed, but the writer credits and producer credits have been purposefully omitted. This is for several reasons.

First, with regard to writers, often this information has been quite well documented (as opposed to personnel credits) and therefore seemed redundant when such information can be garnered from the albums themselves as well as innumerable sites online. Also, many of these writing credits have been both the source of heated debate and the scourge of those who felt they were left off this or that writing credit due to the nature of the moment and the largesse of the collection of players and contributors. Indeed, the most often repeated comment I got from interviewees in the process was the line "I wrote that." As true as that may be, remedying this according to everyone's wishes would be an impossible task and also would take away from the accuracy of the writers' credits as they contemporaneously appear. For those reasons, as well as the wave of legal red tape surrounding this issue, writers were omitted from the book's contents.

Second, with regard to production, it is also a source of some debate across the various acts, as there are often coproducers who may or may not have gotten credit. To make things more confusing, in the case of the more modern era, the definition of a producer has changed, and the producer today often tangibly creates much of the track in question itself. In this way, the given producer(s) would have been credited therein as a big part of the personnel, giving them credit on the song regardless. It is no secret that the main producer of at least the bulk of the core material is George Clinton; only in specific spin-offs (and most of the additional solo acts) is the production more on a case-by-case basis, although even this facet has exceptions. Much like writers, the majority of production information has been provided in albums, whereas the specific musical and vocal personnel were not, and for that reason and all the previously mentioned ones, production was also (mostly) omitted from the list.

Additionally, engineers were for the most part left off the list. This is because in many cases, multiple engineers worked on the same tracks in different phases of said tracks' inception. This causes chaos and controversy as to who may or may not have engineered the recording of the various sessions that make up any one song, with few ways of remedying the problem. Special mention needs to be made to engineers Jim Vitti, Jim Callon, Greg Reily, Greg Ward, Mike Iacapelli, Pete Bishop, John Jascz, Bob Dennis, Larry Alexander, Mike Hutchinson, Allen Zentz, Dave Baker, Richard Akor, John Bauer, Mike Davis, Mark and Jeff Bass, Michael Wilder, Chris Baker, Alvin Speights, Carl Robinson, Neal Pogue, Bob Bishop, Larry Ferguson, Sue Brooks, Gary Wright, Dwayne Dungey, Toby Donahue, Barry Epperson, Tyler Pelt, Ricky Tan, and numerous others who engineered the songs in question over the years. Given the vastness of the catalog, however, this is not the case universally. There are thousands of cases where a single engineer may have worked on only one song, adding to the mystery and ease with which errors would be created. For these reasons, engineers have been left off the list.

Finally, two other groups were included when it was deemed necessary or gave additional credence to the songs at hand within P-Funk canon and/or were omitted when it was too difficult to truly ascertain the correct credits. This is with regards to arrangers and hand clappers. In some cases, when the arranger is vital to the song but said arranger did not play or sing on it or if the arranger is involved only in that one song, they are usually included. The reasons they have been left off are mostly because of space issues (this book would be thousands of pages instead of hundreds with the addition of arrangers, producers, and all writers) and the controversy of possible miscredits, as this credit is second only to writers in its tendentious turbulence. Much like the previously mentioned categories, arrangers are very often listed in the album credits (although not always, certainly more often than the overall musical and vocal personnel on a song-by-song basis).

As many people are well aware, handclaps are a big part of the P-Funk sound. In many cases, there were so many hand clappers and so many sessions involving a rotating cast of hand clappers, numbering in the hundreds of individuals, that it seemed impossible to correctly list all of them. In some cases, however, when those credits were clearly defined and corroborated by many or if the inclusion of handclaps made the session stylistically definable as "P-Funk," they were included. Special cases are made with reference to Carl "Butch" Small and his "handclap device," which was sometimes used in tandem with human handclaps and sometimes as a replacement for them. These cases are also noted in the book.

CRITERIA FOR CANON

The list is meant to be an authorized canon on P-Funk. What that means can be different things for different people. Essentially, all of the "core" P-Funk albums, along with all of the essential side projects and spin-off albums, were a certainty. Notably, almost all of the band member's solo albums are included, as are key side projects of said band members, as long as the release in question had some key connection to the P-Funk stylistically or in terms of personnel. Some albums that feature members of the band past and present were omitted; the reasons for this are as follows.

First, some albums were nearly impossible to find information on other than the fact that they existed at one point. Even the music itself was a mystery in a couple of these circumstances. In addition, when delving into discussions on the releases in question in interviews, the primary sources often wrote them off as "informally released." This has occurred in this process on half a dozen occasions and has compounded the investigative process and hampered the criteria for inclusion in the list. Perhaps with more time in the future, newer editions of this volume can contain some of these albums. Keep in mind, however, that this was the case with only about half a dozen very obscure albums.

Second, some band members' side projects have so many branches that are so far away from the P-Funk tree at large that they belong to another group's satellite or even another band's genre or sound. Indeed, the wormhole has been explored deeply in this regard, but at some point, a cutoff had to be made as to what could be and could not be considered officially in canon. Indeed, if every relatable album to P-Funk in every conceivable way was included, this book would be another couple of volumes, lending itself to the notion that there are truly only a couple degrees of separation at the most between all pop music throughout modern history and P-Funk.

Third, there are thousands of songs that have sampled and interpolated P-Funk. As vast as *that* list is on its own, meritable of a book in its own right, the use of sampling

P-Funk developed inside the hip-hop satellite. It is certainly containing the same DNA, but it is also maintaining something distinctly separate, again meritable of its own volume. Lists have been assembled in the past of songs sampling P-Funk, but much like the P-Funk canon itself prior to this volume, nothing really formative has been wholly compiled in that regard. Several important hip-hop songs interpolated P-Funk, some to the point where it seriously became part of the canon; many of those songs were included in this list.

Fourth, in regard to the multitude of remixes out there, most of them have been left out, unless the personnel on said remixes was so vastly different from the original that it needed its own listing in the book or if the remix was more famous than the original and deemed its inclusion important.

Fifth, live bootlegs have been left off for obvious reasons. If every single bootleg of every single show by every related P-Funk band was to be listed, this book would be 10 volumes or more. However, all the major live releases have been included and are at the end of book, immediately following the list of all the studio releases. Unlike the list of studio releases, which is listed chronologically by the act's debut release, the live list at the end of the book is listed alphabetically.

Finally, there have been a few releases that were left out because they were made on a "shoestring budget" and were never potentially released with any marketing. Some of these are very minor releases, put out by friends of members of P-Funk and/or people who might have recorded with someone in P-Funk. Many of these not-included releases are available only on a burned CD-R with either handwritten liner notes or no liner notes at all. These "bootleg studio releases" are so common that another wormhole situation can easily happen, so they were wisely left off of the list.

The importance of the complete canon in one single volume was very important in order to showcase P-Funk's seemingly never-ending vastness. Fitting everything into one large volume lends the canon a fitting posterior for its epic history. In doing so, much like all canon, criteria had to be created to help draw on conclusions of canonization. But as already iterated, P-Funk is seemingly never ending. It grows and changes with each successive release, further proving its ever-regenerating quality, constantly in flux. This is only a part of the majesty that is the P-Funk canon.

ERRATA

It is vital to note that this list is not absolutely perfect. It embodies a structural representation of what can be described as akin to a living, breathing, organism, subject to scrutiny, discovery, and change. Furthermore, although intense attention to detail has been at the forefront of this project, due to the grandiose goals and largesse associated with doing such a demanding task as this book, there are bound to be mistakes. Given the passion involved in this work and the personal closeness to the subject matter, it is this author's mission to right those particular wrongs. When primary sources could not be attained via direct contact (interview), some album information was collected from secondary sources, such as liner notes that have been deemed more accurate by primary sources, and from sites that publish those liner notes. Some of these sources contained notes pertaining to the personnel on an album as a whole and not on a song-by-song basis. In those rare cases, the word "or" is employed to denote when multiple players are listed for specific tasks on the album or for situations when information is not disseminated regarding the specifics with the songs. This happens only on certain occasions in the book, but it needs to be pointed out on albums where the song-by-song information via secondary sources was tendentious, missing, or incomplete. In cases of the latter, the "?" is also employed; it is important to note that this happened only on certain occasions but is notable when there is no one alive to speak to about said lack of information or if subjects who know said information have been unable or unwilling to take an interview. There were also, surprisingly, only a few cases where primary sources disagreed on certain personnel information. In those times, decisions had to be made on the basis of majority rules and individuals' cognition regarding memory of said sessions. These decisions are very difficult to make when dealing with opposing facts. This being the first edition, there will doubtlessly be corrections to be made, but for the overwhelming majority of the material, the information is valid, triple-checked, and legitimized.

ARTISTS STARTING IN 1956-1966

THE PARLIAMENTS: 1955–1969

When one begins to search for the origins of P-Funk, one needs to look no further than the Parliaments; George Clinton's original singing group started around 1955–1956 and, much like many of the later groups, had personnel changes throughout its 14-year run but solidified in the early 1960s with the lineup of George Clinton, Gene "Grady" Thomas, Calvin Simon, Ray Davis, and Clarence "Fuzzy" Haskins. "(I Wanna) Testify" was their biggest hit. This group went through drastic stylistic changes from the doo-wop days through the Motown era and into the psychedelic period.

"Sunday Kind of Love"

Vocals: George Clinton, Robert Lambert, Glen Carlos, Charles Davis, Gene Boykins

"The Wind"

Vocals: George Clinton, Robert Lambert, Glen Carlos, Charles Davis, Gene Boykins

"Sunday Kind of Love" and "The Wind" were recorded as acetates and featured an original (maybe not the original, though, for some personnel changes had already been made by even this early date in 1956) version of the Parliaments singing entirely a cappella.

APT Records

"Poor Willie"

Vocals: George Clinton, Grady Thomas, Charles Davis, Danny Mitchell, Robert Lambert
Arranger: TJo Wilshire

"Party Boys"

Lead Vocals: George Clinton
Backup Vocals: Robert Lambert, Grady Thomas, Charles Davis, Danny Mitchell
Arranger: TJo Wilshire

Flipp Records

"Lonely Island"

Lead Vocals: Johnny Murray
Backup Vocals: George Clinton, Grady Thomas, Calvin Simon, Charles Davis, Larry Fischer

"You Make Me Wanna Cry"

Lead Vocals: George Clinton
Backup Vocals: Grady Thomas, Calvin Simon, Charles Davis, Larry Fischer, Johnny Murray

Jobete Music Co.

"You're Not Hurting Him, You're Hurting Me"

Lead Vocals: George Clinton
Backup Vocals: Calvin Simon, Grady Thomas, Ray Davis, Fuzzy Haskins
Drums: Bernard Purdie
Guitar: Eric Gales
Bass: Winston
Piano: Richard Tee

Golden World Records

"Heart Trouble"

Lead Vocals: George Clinton
Backup Vocals: Calvin Simon, Grady Thomas, Ray Davis, Fuzzy Haskins, Pat Lewis, Diane Lewis, Rose Williams
Baritone Sax: Mike Terry
Drums: Uriel Jones
Bass: Bob Babbitt
Guitar: Bobby White, Eddie Willis
Strings: Detroit Symphony Orchestra
Trumpet: Herbie Williams
Trombone: McKinley Jackson
Sax: Hank Cosby
Organ: Ivy Joe Hunter

"That Was My Girl"

Lead Vocals: George Clinton
Backup Vocals: Fuzzy Haskins, Calvin Simon, Grady Thomas, Ray Davis, Pat Lewis, Diane Lewis, Rose Williams
Baritone Sax: Mike Terry
Strings: Detroit Symphony Orchestra

Drums: Uriel Jones
Bass: Bob Babbitt
Guitar: Eddie Willis, Robert White
Trumpet: Herbie Williams
Trombone: McKinley Jackson
Sax: Hank Cosby
Organ: Ivy Joe Hunter

Revilot Records

"(I Wanna) Testify"

Lead Vocals: George Clinton
Backup Vocals: Jack Holland, Jimmy Holland, Jay Reid, Tony Hestor
Drums: Uriel Jones
Bass: Bob Babbit
Guitar: Eddie Willis, Robert White
Organ: Ivy Joe Hunter
Trumpet: Herbie Williams
Sax: Hank Cosby
Trombone: McKinley Jackson
Baritone Sax: Mike Terry
Congas: Eddie Bongo

"I Wanna Testify" was the first major single for the then fledgling P-Funk empire. This was at a time when George Clinton was traveling back and forth from New Jersey to Detroit to make records and promote his groups. As on much of the early material, the great Funk Brothers, Motown's beloved house band, was the personnel on this hit song. In addition, the only one of the Parliaments to appear on the record was Clinton himself, as it was too costly to bring the other four members back and forth for every trip.

"I Can Feel the Ice Melting"

Lead Vocals: George Clinton
Backup Vocals: Calvin Simon, Pat Lewis
Vibraphone: Jack Ashford
Bass: James Jamerson
Piano: Johnny Griffith
Drums: Uriel Jones
Guitar: Eddie Willis, Robert White

"All Your Goodies Are Gone"

Lead Vocals: George Clinton
Backup Vocals: Grady Thomas, Calvin Simon, Ray Davis, Fuzzy Haskins
Baritone Sax: Mike Terry
Bass: Billy Nelson
Guitar: Eddie Willis Robert White
Organ: Ivy Joe Hunter
Congas: Eddie Bongo
Drums: Uriel Jones
Trumpet: Herbie Williams
Trombone: McKinley Jackson
Sax: Hank Cosby

"All Your Goodies Are Gone" would be the second single to chart fairly highly from the Parliaments, although it would not reach as high as "(I Wanna) Testify" did. And much like "(I Wanna) Testify," it too would be remade six or seven years later for the *Up for the Downstroke* album. This version, unlike "(I Wanna) Testify," features all the Parliaments, with George Clinton still taking the lead. This is one of the first songs to feature later Funkadelic bassist Billy Nelson but this time on guitar. Despite those mentioned here, most of the personnel on this song are from the Funk Brothers (Motown house band).

"Baby I Owe You Something Good" (instrumental)

Guitar: Eddie Willis, Robert White
Congas: Eddie Bongo
Tambourine: Jack Ashford
Organ: Ivy Joe Hunter
Drums: George McGregor
Bass: Bob Babbitt
Trumpet: Herbie Williams
Trombone: McKinley Jackson
Sax: Hank Cosby
Baritone Sax: Mike Terry

"Don't Be Sore at Me"

Lead Vocals: George Clinton, Calvin Simon
Backup Vocals: Pat Lewis, Grady Thomas, Ray Davis, Fuzzy Haskins
Baritone Sax: Mike Terry
Vibraphone: Jack Ashford
Trumpet: Herbie Williams
Sax: Hank Cosby
Trombone: McKinley Jackson
Drums: Uriel Jones
Bass: Bob Babbitt
Guitar: Eddie Willis Robert White
Piano: Johnny Griffith
Congas: Eddie Bongo

"Little Man"

Lead Vocals: George Clinton, Billy Nelson
Backup Vocals: Diane Lewis, Pat Lewis, Rose Williams
Baritone Sax: Mike Terry
Guitar: Billy Nelson
Trumpet: Herbie Williams
Trombone: McKinley Jackson
Bass: Bob Babbitt
Drums: Uriel Jones
Congas: Eddie Bongo

"The Goose (That Laid the Golden Egg)"

Lead Vocals: George Clinton
Backup Vocals: Calvin Simon, Fuzzy Haskins, Grady Thomas, Ray Davis
Guitar: Eddie Willis, Robert White
Drums: Uriel Jones
Bass: Bob Babbitt
Baritone Sax: Mike Terry
Trumpet: Herbie Williams
Trombone: McKinley Jackson
Sax: Hank Cosby
Congas: Eddie Bongo

"Look at What I Almost Missed"

Lead Vocals: George Clinton
Backup Vocals: Pat Lewis, Calvin Simon, Fuzzy Haskins, Grady Thomas, Ray Davis
Baritone Sax: Mike Terry
Drums: George McGregor
Trumpet: Herbie Williams
Trombone: McKinley Jackson
Guitar: Eddie Willis, Robert White
Congas: Eddie Bongo
Bass: Bob Babbitt
Organ: Ivy Joe Hunter

"What You Been Growing"

Lead Vocals: Calvin Simon, Ernie Harris, Fuzzy Haskins, Ray Davis
Backup Vocals: Pat Lewis, Grady Thomas, George Clinton, Diane Lewis, Rose Williams
Baritone Sax: Mike Terry
Drums: Uriel Jones
Bass: Bob Babbitt
Guitar: Eddie Hazel
Organ: Ivy Joe Hunter
Trombone: McKinley Jackson
Sax: Hank Cosby
Trumpet: Herbie Williams
Congas: Eddie Bongo

"Sgt. Pepper's Lonely Hearts Club Band"

Lead Vocals: George Clinton
Backup Vocals: Calvin Simon, Grady Thomas, Fuzzy Haskins, Ray Davis
Guitar: Eddie Hazel
Organ: Mickey Atkins
Bass: Billy Nelson
Congas: Eddie Bongo
Drums: Tiki Fulwood
Baritone Sax: Mike Terry
Trumpet: Herbie Williams
Sax: Hank Cosby
Trombone: McKinley Jackson

"Good Old Music"

Lead Vocals: George Clinton
Backup Vocals: Calvin Simon, Fuzzy Haskins, Grady Thomas, Ray Davis, Pat Lewis, Diane Lewis, Rose Williams
Drums: Tiki Fulwood
Bass: Billy Nelson
Guitar: Eddie Hazel
Organ: Billy Coorish

"Time"

Lead Vocals: George Clinton
Backup Vocals: Grady Thomas, Fuzzy Haskins, Calvin Simon, Ray Davis, Pat Lewis
Baritone Sax: Mike Terry
Sax: Hank Cosby
Drums: George McGregor
Trumpet: Herbie Williams
Trombone: McKinley Jackson
Guitar: Eddie Willis, Robert White
Congas: Eddie Bongo
Bass: Bob Babbitt

"A New Day Begins" (on Revilot and later Atco Records)

Lead Vocals: George Clinton
Backup Vocals: Calvin Simon, Pat Lewis, Grady Thomas, Fuzzy Haskins
Piano: Johnny Griffith
Guitar: Eddie Willis, Robert White
Bass: Bob Babbitt
Drums: Uriel Jones

"I'll Wait"

Lead Vocals: George Clinton
Backup Vocals: Calvin Simon, Pat Lewis, Rose Williams, Diane Lewis, Grady Thomas
Guitar: Eddie Willis, Robert White
Bass: Bob Babbitt
Drums: Uriel Jones
Piano: Ivy Joe Hunter
Congas: Eddie Bongo

— ☆ —

The Parliaments in one of their early incarnations. L–R: George Clinton, Charles "Butch" Davis, Herbie Jenkins, and Eugene Boykins around 1956. Kinley-McCoy / GROOVE MANEUVERS ARCHIVES

The Parliaments with an early lineup of Funkadelic. L–R (top): Brad Innis, Herb Sparkman, George Clinton, Eddie Hazel, and Grady Thomas. L–R (bottom): Clarence "Fuzzy" Haskins, Ray Davis, Billy "Bass" Nelson, and Calvin Simon. 1969. Kinley-McCoy / GROOVE MANEUVERS ARCHIVES

ERNIE HARRIS: 1964

Ernie Harris was described by George Clinton as a brilliant songwriter who worked in and had a share of ownership in the barbershop. He was also described as a big influence on Eddie Hazel, vocally speaking. He cowrote several important early Funkadelic songs, such as "I Wanna Know if It's Good to You," "Biological Speculation," and others.

Okeh Records

"Hold On" (George Clinton, Ernie Harris, Rosemarie McCoy)

Lead Vocals: Ernie Harris
Arranger, Conductor: Ed Bland
Production: Bobby Gregg
Drums: Bobby Gregg?
Backup Vocals: ?, Rosemarie McCoy?
Bass: Winston?
Guitar: Eric Gales?
Piano: Ed Bland?
Organ: Ed Bland?

ROY HANDY: 1965–1966

Detroit vocalist Roy Handy was often paired with the George Clinton girl group the Parlettes on early recordings and is one of the many northern soul artists with songs written by Clinton and company.

Marton Records

"Accidental Love"

Lead Vocals: Roy Handy, George Clinton, Calvin Simon
Backup Vocals: Vivian Lewis, George Clinton, Calvin Simon
Guitar: Frankie Boyce
Organ: Richard Tee
Drums: Brad Innis
Bass: Richard Boyce

"What Did He Do?"

Lead Vocals: Roy Handy
Drums: Brad Innis
Organ: Richard Tee
Guitar: Frankie Boyce
Bass: Richard Boyce

Stephanye Records

"Baby That's a Groove"

Lead Vocals: Roy Handy
Backup Vocals: George Clinton, Calvin Simon
Drums: Benny Benjamin
Vibraphone, Tambourine: Jack Ashford
Baritone Sax: Mike Terry
Trumpet: Herbie Williams
Trombone: McKinley Jackson
Sax: Hank Cosby
Bass: James Jamerson
Guitar: Robert White, Eddie Willis, Joe Messina
Keyboards: Gene Redd

— ☆ —

TAMALA LEWIS: 1965

Tamala Lewis was another early George Clinton collaborator and is the mother of Clinton's son Tracey "Treylewd" Lewis. She was also described by Clinton as a brilliant songwriter, with clever wordplay and reference to lyrical content of varying forms.

Marton Records

"You Won't Say Nothing"

Lead Vocals: Vivian Lewis, George Clinton
Backup Vocals: Calvin Simon, Grady Thomas
Drums: Brad Innis
Guitar: Frankie Boyce
Bass: Richard Boyce
Baritone Sax: Session horns from New York City
Trombone: Session horns from New York City
Trumpet: Session horns from New York City

"If You Can Stand Me"

Lead Vocals: Vivian Lewis
Backup Vocals: George Clinton, Calvin Simon
Drums: Brad Innis
Guitar: Frankie Boyce
Bass: Richard Boyce
Baritone Sax: Session horns from New York City
Trombone: Session horns from New York City
Trumpet: Session horns from New York City

— ☆ —

THE PETS: 1965

The Pets were a George Clinton vehicle for a girl group in the early years. The sessions had a mixture of New York City and Detroit players/singers.

Carnival Records

"I Say Yeah"

Lead Vocals: Vivian Lewis
Backup Vocals: George Clinton, Diane (last name unknown), the Pets
Producer: Parlar Productions
Drums: Bernard Purdie?
Organ: Richard Tee
Bass: Winston or Chuck Rainey
Guitar: Eric Gales?

"West Side Party"

Lead Vocals: Pat Lewis, Vivian Lewis, Diane Lewis
Producer: Joe Evans
Drums: Pete
Guitar: Joe Evans' guitar player
Horns: Joe Evans Band (from the Manhattans)
Piano: Richard Tee
Bass: Winston
Backup Vocals: Diane, the Pets

— ☆ —

PERIGENTS: 1965

This is an early recording/composition for the Geo-Si-Mik writing group.

Maltese Records

"One Girl Too Many"

Lead Vocals: Jackie Montre El (Minnie Lee Curry)
Backup Vocals: Perigents
Producer: Mr. Lucky
Horns: New York session musicians
Drums: Bernard Purdie
Guitar: Eric Gale?
Bass: Chuck Rainey?
Tambourine: Sidney Barnes
Keyboards: Richard Tee

TONY MICHAELS: 1966

This is another early recording/composition for the Geo-Si-Mik writing group.

Golden World Records

"Picture Me and You"

Lead Vocals: Anthony Michaels
Backup Vocals: George Clinton, Sidney Barnes
Drums: George McGregor
Bass: Bob Babbitt
Guitar: Robert White, Eddie Willis
Piano: Ivy Joe Hunter
Vibraphone: Jack Ashford
Trumpet: Herbie Williams
Trombone: McKinley Jackson
Sax: Hank Cosby
Baritone Sax: Mike Terry

PAT LEWIS: 1966–1967

Pat Lewis has the longest discography with George Clinton of any of the female vocalists in the P-Funk pantheon. Her work with Clinton goes back to the early 1960s and continues through the present day on a vast swathe of the overall P-Funk recording output. This is a vastly important piece of the P-Funk puzzle.

Golden World Records

"Can't Shake It Loose"

Lead Vocals: Pat Lewis
Backup Vocals: Calvin Simon, George Clinton, Diane Lewis, Rose Williams
Bass: Bob Babbitt
Guitar: Eddie Willis, Robert White
Drums: Uriel Jones
Trumpet: Herbie Williams
Sax: Hank Cosby
Trombone: McKinley Jackson
Baritone Sax: Mike Terry
Piano: Ivy Joe Hunter

Solid Hit Records

"Look at What I Almost Missed"

Lead Vocals: Pat Lewis
Backup Vocals: Diane Lewis, Rose Williams, George Clinton, Sidney Barnes
Guitar: Eddie Willis, Robert White
Piano: Ivy Joe Hunter
Bass: Bob Babbitt
Drums: Uriel Jones
Trumpet: Herbie Williams
Sax: Hank Cosby
Baritone Sax: Mike Terry
Trombone: McKinley Jackson
Vibraphone: Jack Ashford

"I'll Wait"

Lead Vocals: Pat Lewis
Backup Vocals: Calvin Simon, Pat Lewis, Grady Thomas, Fuzzy Haskins, Ray Davis
Drums: Uriel Jones
Bass: Bob Babbitt
Piano: Ivy Joe Hunter
Guitar: Eddie Willis
Congas: Eddie Bongo

"No One to Love"

Lead Vocals: Pat Lewis
Backup Vocals: Calvin Simon, George Clinton, Grady Thomas, Diane Lewis, Ray Davis
Drums: George McGregor
Strings: Detroit Symphony Orchestra
Guitar: Eddie Willis, Robert White
Bass: Bob Babbitt
Trumpet: Herbie Williams
Trombone: McKinley Jackson
Sax: Hank Cosby
Piano: Ivy Joe Hunter
Baritone Sax: Mike Terry
Congas: Eddie Bongo

"(I Owe You) Something"

Lead Vocals: Pat Lewis
Backup Vocals: Diane Lewis, Rose Williams, George Clinton, Sidney Barnes
Guitar: Eddie Willis, Robert White
Congas: Eddie Bongo
Tambourine: Jack Ashford
Organ: Ivy Joe Hunter
Drums: George McGregor
Bass: Bob Babbitt
Trumpet: Herbie Williams
Trombone: McKinley Jackson
Sax: Hank Cosby
Baritone Sax: Mike Terry

— ☆ —

DARRELL BANKS: 1966

Darrell Banks was also on Revilot Records (the label the Parliaments were on during that singing group's heyday) and, like many of George Clinton's early Detroit recordings, features the Funk Brothers: Motown's renowned house band.

Revilot Records

"Our Love (Is in the Pocket)"

Lead Vocals: Darrell Banks
Drums: George McGregor
Guitar: Eddie Willis, Robert White
Bass: Bob Babbitt
Organ: Johnny Griffith
Trumpet: Herbie Williams
Sax: Hank Cosby
Trombone: McKinley Jackson
Vibraphone: Jack Ashford
Baritone Sax: Mikey Terry
Backup Vocals: The Holidays, George Clinton, Pat Lewis

— ☆ —

THERESA LINDSAY: 1966

This was an early vehicle for the Geo-Si-Mik writing team. The original "I Bet You" was written for this artist.

Golden World Records

"I'll Bet You"

Lead Vocals: Theresa Lindsay
Bass: Bob Babbitt
Drums: Uriel Jones
Guitar: Eddie Willis, Robert White
Baritone Sax: Mike Terry
Organ: Ivy Joe Hunter
Trumpet: Herbie Williams
Sax: Hank Cosby
Trombone: McKinley Jackson

J. J. BARNES: 1966–1968

J. J. Barnes had several "hard soul" numbers written and/or produced by George Clinton in the mid-1960s, hinting at things to come in later psychedelic works by Funkadelic.

Ric-Tic Records

"Day Tripper"

Lead Vocals: J. J. Barnes
Drums: Uriel Jones
Bass: Bob Babbitt
Guitar: Eddie Willis, Robert White
Tambourine: Jack Ashford
Organ: Ivy Joe Hunter
Trumpet: Herbie Williams
Trombone: McKinley Jackson
Sax: Hank Cosby
Baritone Sax: Mike Terry

Revilot

"Our Love Is in the Pocket"

Lead Vocals: J. J. Barnes
Drums: George McGregor
Guitar: Eddie Willis, Robert White
Bass: Bob Babbitt
Organ: Johnny Griffith
Trumpet: Herbie Williams
Sax: Hank Cosby
Trombone: McKinley Jackson
Vibraphone: Jack Ashford
Baritone Sax: Mike Terry
Backup Vocals: The Holidays, George Clinton, Pat Lewis

"So Called Friends"

Lead Vocals: J. J. Barnes
Drums: Tiki Fulwood
Bass: Billy Nelson
Sax: ?
Guitar: Eddie Hazel
Organ: Mickey Atkins

— ☆ —

THE FANTASTIC FOUR: 1966

George Clinton wrote a couple songs for the singing group the Fantastic Four, including the early version of "Live Up."

Ric-Tic Records

"Girl Have Pity"

Vocals: James Epps, Ralph Pruitt, Joseph Pruitt, Wallace Childs
Drums: Uriel Jones
Piano: Gene Redd
Bass: Bob Babbitt
Guitar: Eddie Willis, Robert White
Strings, Woodwinds: Detroit Symphony Orchestra
Vibraphone: Jack Ashford

"Live Up to What She Thinks"

Vocals: James Epps, Ralph Pruitt, Joseph Pruitt, Wallace Childs
Drums: Uriel Jones
Piano: Gene Redd
Organ: Ivy Joe Hunter
Bass: Bob Babbitt
Guitar: Eddie Willis, Robert White
Trumpet: Herbie Williams
Sax: Hank Cosby
Trombone: McKinley Jackson
Baritone Sax: Mike Terry

DETROIT SYMPHONY ORCHESTRA

The Detroit Symphony Orchestra on the early Detroit recordings in the 1960s includes (but is not limited to) the following musicians:

Concertmaster: David Staples
Violins: Zinovi Bistritzky, Beatriz Budinsky, Lillian Downs, Virginia Halfmann, Richard Margitza, Felix Resnick, Alvin Score, Linda Sneeded Smith, James Waring
Violas: Nathan Gordon, David Ireland, Eduard Kesner, Anne Mischakoff, Meyer Shapiro
Cellos: Italo Babini, Edward Korkigian, Thaddeus Markiewicz, Marcy Scwheickhardt
Piccolo: Dayna Hartwick
Flute: Dayna Hartwick, Thomas Bowles
Conductors, Arrangers: Paul Riser, David Van DePitte, Wade Marcus, Willie Shorter, Johnny Allen

— ☆ —

ARTISTS STARTING IN 1967-1977

DEBONAIRS: 1967

This is another early girl group that worked with George Clinton. The Funk Brothers are, as usual in this period, present on these sessions.

Solid Hit Records

"Loving You Takes All My Time"

Vocals: Telma Hopkins, Joyce Vincent, Diane Hogans, Elsie Baker
Drums: George McGregor
Bass: Bob Babbitt
Guitar: Eddie Willis, Robert White
Vibraphone: Jack Ashford
Trumpet: Herbie Williams
Sax: Hank Cosby
Trombone: McKinley Jackson
Baritone Sax: Mike Terry

"Headache in My Heart"

Vocals: Telma Hopkins, Joyce Vincent, Diane Hogans, Elsie Baker
Drums: George McGregor
Vibraphone: Jack Ashford
Guitar: Eddie Willis, Robert White

Bass: Bob Babbitt
Trumpet: Herbie Williams
Trombone: McKinley Jackson
Sax: Hank Cosby
Baritone Sax: Mike Terry
Congas: Eddie Bongo

— ☆ —

FLAMING EMBERS: 1967

The Flaming Embers was a white rock group that worked with George Clinton in the mid-1960s during a shift in the climate of American music toward more psychedelic tendencies, albeit in a still more couched fashion here.

Ric-Tic Records

"Hey, Mama (What'cha Got Good for Daddy)"

Lead Vocals, Drums: Jerry Plunk
Backup Vocals, Keyboards: John Goins
Guitar: Joe Sladich
Bass: Jim Bugnel

— ☆ —

THE FELLOWS: 1967

The Fellows is essentially the Parliaments on another record label at the same time that the Parliaments were on Revilot records. George Clinton would use this tactic many times more than a decade later.

Solid Hit Records

"Let's Make It Last"

Lead Vocals: Fuzzy Haskins, Calvin Simon, George Clinton
Backup Vocals: Grady Thomas, Ray Davis, Pat Lewis
Organ: Ivy Joe Hunter
Drums: Uriel Jones
Bass: Bob Babbitt
Guitar: Eddie Willis, Robert White
Trumpet: Herbie Williams
Trombone: McKinley Jackson
Sax: Hank Cosby
Baritone Sax: Mike Terry

HOLIDAYS: 1968

This was a long-running Detroit singing group made up of several famous personalities from the Motown banner.

Revilot Records

"All That Is Required (Is You)"

Vocals: Edwin Starr, Eddie Anderson, Robert Earl Johnson, James Holland, Jack Holland, Maurice Wise
Guitar: Eddie Willis, Robert White
Drums: Uriel Jones
Bass: Bob Babbitt
Organ: Ivy Joe Hunter

ROSE WILLIAMS, GEORGE CLINTON, AND THE FUNKEDELICS: 1968

This was the first attempt to do a Funkadelic record. It features the original Funkadelics.

Funkedelic Records

"Whatever Makes My Baby Feel Good"

Lead Vocals: Rose Williams, George Clinton
Backup Vocals: Pat and Diane Lewis, Eddie Hazel
Drums: Tiki Fulwood
Bass: Billy Nelson
Guitar: Eddie Hazel, Tawl Ross
Organ: Mickey Atkins

MAGICTONES: 1969

This song features the same track that was featured on "Good Ole Music" from the first Funkadelic album, with added lead vocals.

Westbound Records

"Good Old Music"

Lead Vocals: Calvin Stephenson
Backup (Almost Lead) Vocals: Billy Nelson, Fuzzy Haskins, Pat Lewis, Calvin Simon, Diane Lewis, George Clinton, Grady Thomas, Eddie Hazel
Drums: Tiki Fulwood
Bass: Billy Nelson
Organ: Mickey Atkins
Guitars: Dennis Coffey, Eddie Hazel

FUNKADELIC: 1969–1981, 1989, 2014–

With a mix of loud guitar-dominated funk rock, heavily politicized lyrics, spooky LSD-laden concepts, and dark, experimental production, Funkadelic was a movement in itself. Much like all George Clinton bands, the personnel would shift dramatically throughout its history, but the most famous lineup (deemed "original," although even that has some slight deviations in origins) included bassist Billy "Bass" Nelson, lead guitarist Eddie Hazel, drummer Tiki Fulwood, keyboardist Bernie Worrell, and rhythm guitarist Tawl Ross. Although Parliament was presented as the more polished "hit machine" in contrast to the more underground Funkadelic, those lines would eventually blur and fade with such massive Funkadelic hits as "One Nation Under a Groove" (the longest-lasting #1 rhythm-and-blues hit in P-Funk history) and the dance floor smash and uber-sampled "(Not Just) Knee Deep," among others.

Westbound Records

Funkadelic

"Mommy, What's a Funkadelic?"

Lead Vocals: George Clinton
Backup Vocals: Eddie Hazel, Pat Lewis, Diane Lewis, Rose Williams, Calvin Simon, Billy Nelson, Fuzzy Haskins, Grady Thomas, Ray Davis
Drums: Tiki Fulwood
Bass: Billy Nelson
Guitars: Eddie Hazel, Dennis Coffey
Organ: Ivy Joe Hunter
Harmonica: Aaron "Little Sonny" Willis

"I Bet You"

Lead Vocals: Calvin Simon, Eddie Hazel, Ray Davis, Fuzzy Haskins, George Clinton
Backup Vocals: Grady Thomas, Pat Lewis, Rose Williams, Diane Lewis
Drums: Andrew Smith
Bass: Bob Babbitt
Guitar: Eddie Hazel, Tawl Ross
Organ: Ivy Joe Hunter

"I Bet You" would be a remake of a prior recorded Theresa Lindsay song, albeit with a more psychedelic edge, thanks in part to guitarist Eddie Hazel's guitar solo and in part due to George Clinton's penchant for very progressive production at this time. Not long after, the Jackson 5 would record this very song on their debut ABC album for Motown.

"Music for My Mother"

Lead Vocals: Herb Sparkman
Backup Vocals: George Clinton, Calvin Simon, Fuzzy Haskins, Grady Thomas, Ray Davis, Eddie Hazel
Drums: Brad Innis
Bass: Billy Nelson
Guitar: Eddie Hazel, Tawl Ross

"I Got a Thing, You Got a Thing, Everybody's Got a Thing"

Vocals: Billy Nelson, Eddie Hazel, Fuzzy Haskins, George Clinton, Calvin Simon, Pat Lewis, Ray Davis, Grady Thomas
Drums: Tiki Fulwood
Bass: Billy Nelson
Guitars: Tawl Ross (wah), Dennis Coffey (distorted), Eddie Hazel (clean)
Organ: Mickey Atkins

"I Got a Thing, You Got a Thing, Everybody's Got a Thing" was an early Funkadelic chant featuring the infectious wah guitar of Funkadelic rhythm guitarist Tawl Ross. The first Funkadelic album had a personnel mixture featuring the Parliafunkadelicment Thang (the five post-1960s Parliaments and the five original Funkadelics) as well as P-Funk mainstay vocalist Pat Lewis and members of the Motown house band. This record ingeniously combines the previously mentioned lineup.

"Good Old Music"

Lead Vocals: Billy Nelson, Fuzzy Haskins
Backup Vocals: Pat Lewis, Calvin Simon, Diane Lewis, George Clinton, Grady Thomas, Eddie Hazel, Rose Williams
Drums: Tiki Fulwood
Bass: Billy Nelson
Organ: Mickey Atkins
Guitars: Dennis Coffey, Eddie Hazel

"Qualify and Satisfy"

Lead Vocals: Calvin Simon
Voices: George Clinton, Grady Thomas
Drums: Tiki Fulwood
Bass: Billy Nelson
Guitars: Eddie Hazel, Tawl Ross
Organ: Mickey Atkins

"What Is Soul"

Lead Vocals: George Clinton
Backup Vocals: Fuzzy Haskins, Grady Thomas, Calvin Simon, Ray Davis, Grady Thomas, Billy Nelson
Drums: Zachary Frazier
Bass: Billy Nelson
Guitar: Eddie Hazel, Tawl Ross
Organ: Mickey Atkins

"Can't Shake It Loose"

Lead Vocals: George Clinton, Calvin Simon, Eddie Hazel
Backup Vocals: Pat Lewis, Diane Lewis, Rose Williams, Grady Thomas
Drums: Tiki Fulwood
Bass: Billy Nelson
Guitar: Eddie Hazel, Tawl Ross
Organ: Mickey Atkins

"Open Our Eyes"

Lead Vocals: Eddie Hazel
Backup Vocals: Pat Lewis, Diane Lewis, Rose Williams
Piano: Bernie Worrell
Guitars: Eddie Hazel

"As Good As I Can Feel"

Drums: Tiki Fulwood
Bass: Billy Nelson
Guitar: Eddie Hazel
Organ: Billy Coorish

"Fish, Chips, and Sweat"

Lead Vocals: Fuzzy Haskins, Eddie Hazel
Backup Vocals: Pat Lewis, Diane Lewis, Rose Williams
Drums: Tiki Fulwood
Bass: Billy Nelson
Organ: Bernie Worrell
Guitar: Eddie Hazel, Tawl Ross

Free Your Mind and Your Ass Will Follow

"Free Your Mind and Your Ass Will Follow"

Lead Vocals: George Clinton, Tawl Ross, Tiki Fulwood, Martha Reeves, Ernie Harris, Eddie Hazel
Drums: Tiki Fulwood
Bass: Billy Nelson
Keyboards: Bernie Worrell
Guitars: Eddie Hazel, Tawl Ross
Percussion: Tiki Fulwood

"Friday Night, August the 14th"

Lead Vocals: Eddie Hazel, Billy Nelson
Backup Vocals: Rose Williams, Diane Lewis, Pat Lewis
Drums: Tiki Fulwood
Bass: Billy Nelson
Guitars: Eddie Hazel
Organ: Bernie Worrell

"Funky Dollar Bill"

Vocals: Tawl Ross, George Clinton, Billy Nelson
Drums: Tiki Fulwood
Bass: Billy Nelson
Guitars: Eddie Hazel, Tawl Ross
Piano: Bernie Worrell

"Funky Dollar Bill" was an early sociopolitical song for Funkadelic, touching on the evils of capitalism in postmodern society. It features the five original Funkadelics at their height along with vocals that would later be described by pundits as "wooly booly."

"I Wanna Know if It's Good to You"

Lead Vocals: Eddie Hazel, Billy Nelson
Drums: Tiki Fulwood
Bass: Billy Nelson
Keyboards: Bernie Worrell
Guitars: Eddie Hazel, Tawl Ross

"I Wanna Know if It's Good to You" features classic vocals by Eddie Hazel and Billy Nelson. It is notable as well for some of the thickest rhythm guitar ever heard (Tawl Ross), the undisputable lead tones of Eddie Hazel, and one of the most captivating keyboard solos by Bernie Worrell, matched by the rhythmic bedrock of drummer Tiki Fulwood and bassist Billy Bass Nelson. This is prime Funkadelic.

"Some More"

Lead Vocals: George Clinton, Tawl Ross
Drums: Tiki Fulwood
Bass: Billy Nelson
Guitar: Tawl Ross
Organ: Bernie Worrell

"Eulogy and Light"

Lead Vocals: George Clinton, Ernie Harris
Backup Vocals: Eddie Hazel, Pat Lewis, Diane Lewis, Rose Williams
Piano: Bernie Worrell
Guitars: Eddie Hazel

Maggot Brain

"Maggot Brain"

Lead Vocals: George Clinton
Drums: Tiki Fulwood
Lead Guitar: Eddie Hazel
Rhythm Guitar: Tawl Ross

"Can You Get to That"

Vocals: Garry Shider, Pat Lewis, Diane Lewis
Rose Williams, Bernie Worrell, George
Clinton, Ray Davis
Drums: Fuzzy Haskins
Bass: Billy Nelson
Guitar: Tawl Ross
Piano: Bernie Worrell

"Can You Get to That" evoked a folksy side of
Funkadelic also seen on the Parliament Osmium
album released earlier. The lyrics use financial
terms as hyperbole, something George Clinton
would continue later with "Wizard of Finance"
as well as Bernie Worrell's "Hold On to You."
The original version of this song was by the
Parliaments and was called "What You Been
Growing?"

"Hit It and Quit It"

Lead Vocals: Bernie Worrell
Backup Vocals, Bass: Billy Nelson
Drums: Tiki Fulwood
Guitars: Eddie Hazel, Garry Shider
Organ: Bernie Worrell

"You and Your Folks, Me and My Folks"

Lead Vocals, Bass: Billy Nelson
Backup Vocals: Pat Lewis, Diane Lewis, Rose
Williams, Grady Thomas
Drums: Tiki Fulwood
Guitars: Eddie Hazel
Piano: Bernie Worrell

"You and Your Folks, Me and My Folks" is
another sociopolitical treatise by George Clinton
and company (this time with lead vocals by Funkadelic bassist Billy Nelson), dealing with racial
and cultural divides. It continues the tradition of
"I Got a Thing" from two albums earlier.

"Super Stupid"

Lead Vocals: Eddie Hazel
Drums, Percussion: Tiki Fulwood
Bass: Billy Nelson
Guitar: Eddie Hazel, Tawl Ross
Organ: Bernie Worrell

"Back in Our Minds"

Vocals: George Clinton, Tawl Ross
Drums: Tiki Fulwood
Bass: Billy Nelson
Guitar: Tawl Ross
Piano: Bernie Worrell
Juice Harp: James Wesley Jackson
Trombone: McKinley Jackson

"Wars of Armageddon"

Vocals: George Clinton, Tawl Ross, Tiki
Fulwood, Fuzzy Haskins, Grady Thomas
Drums: Tiki Fulwood
Bass: Billy Nelson
Guitars: Eddie Hazel, Tawl Ross
Organ: Bernie Worrell
Percussion: Tiki Fulwood, Fuzzy Haskins

Toys (unfinished, released later)

"Heart Trouble"

Lead Vocals: Billy Nelson, Eddie Hazel
Backup Vocals: Pat Lewis, Diane Lewis, Rose
Williams, Telma Hopkins
Drums: Tiki Fulwood
Bass: Billy Nelson
Guitar: Eddie Hazel
Organ: Bernie Worrell

"The Goose That Laid the Golden Egg"

Vocals: George Clinton, Calvin Simon, Fuzzy Haskins, Grady Thomas, Ray Davis
Drums: Tiki Fulwood
Bass: Billy Nelson
Guitars: Eddie Hazel, Tawl Ross
Organ: Bernie Worrell

"Funky Vampy Bernie"

Drums: Tiki Fulwood
Bass: Billy Nelson
Guitar: Eddie Hazel, Tawl Ross
Organ: Bernie Worrell
Percussion: Grady Thomas and/or Calvin Simon

"Talk about Jesus"

Vocals: Pat Lewis, Diane Lewis, Rose Williams
Drums: Ennis Bradley
Bass, Guitar: Billy Nelson
Piano: Bernie Worrell

"Slide On In"

Vocals: George Clinton, Fuzzy Haskins, Grady Thomas, Calvin Simon
Drums: Tiki Fulwood
Bass: Billy Nelson
Guitars: Eddie Hazel, Tawl Ross
Organ: Bernie Worrell

"Magnififunk"

Drums: Tiki Fulwood
Organ, Piano: Bernie Worrell

"Wars of Armageddon" (alternate version)

Drums: Tiki Fulwood
Bass: Billy Nelson
Guitars: Eddie Hazel, Tawl Ross
Organ: Bernie Worrell
Percussion: Tiki Fulwood, Fuzzy Haskins

"2 Dollars & 2 Dimes"

Vocals: George Clinton
Drums: Fuzzy Haskins
Bass: Billy Nelson
Guitar: Tawl Ross
Piano: Bernie Worrell

"Stinkfinger"

Vocals: George Clinton, Garry Shider, Ray Davis, Fuzzy Haskins, Grady Thomas, Calvin Simon
Drums: Tyrone Lampkin
Bass: Cordell Mosson
Guitar: Garry Shider
Keyboards: Bernie Worrell

B-Side Single

"A Whole Lot of BS"

Lead Vocals: George Clinton
Drums: Tyrone Lampkin
Bass: Cordell Mosson
Piano: Bernie Worrell
Guitar: Garry Shider

America Eats Its Young

"You Hit the Nail on the Head"

Vocals: George Clinton, Calvin Simon, Diane Brooks, Steve Kennedy, Garry Shider, Fuzzy Haskins
Drums: Tyrone Lampkin
Bass: Cordell Mosson
Guitar: Garry Shider, Harold Beane
Organ, Melodica: Bernie Worrell

FUNKADELIC

This is the first time that the Funkadelic have been in Detroit in over a year. This group must be good, for no matter where they appear, it's always before a capacity filled house. The people, both young and old alike, clamor to see and hear them.

Funkadelic was one of the first psychedelic bands in the midwest. They were ultra-different in both their sound and style of music and personal appearance. The music was extremely loud and relatively unknown. The group's attire was unlike that of any other, for they wore whatever they pleased.

Some of the hits of Funkadelic include "Music For My Mother," "Can You Get To That?" and their latest release, "Hit It And Quit It!". They also have five albums to their recording credit, "Funkadelic," "Free Your Mind," "Maggot Brain," and the very latest, "America Eats Its Young" and "Cosmic Slop".

Sepia magazine, 1970

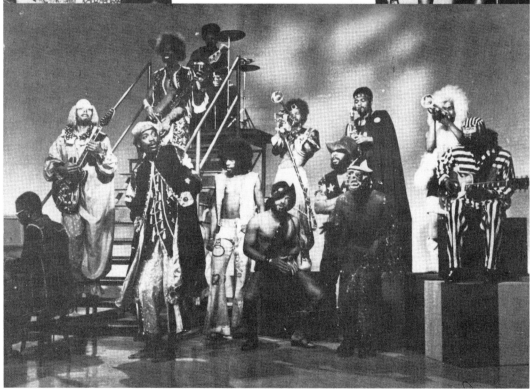

Top: Early images of George Clinton from the first Funkadelic *album era, 1970. Bottom: Funkadelic in the* America Eats Its Young *era (L-R): Bernie Worrell (keyboard) Phelps "Catfish" Collins (guitar), William "Bootsy" Collins (bass), Frankie "Kash" Waddy or Tyrone Lampkin (drums) Calvin Simon (vocals), Ray Davis (vocals) Clarence "Fuzzy" Haskins (vocals), Ronnie Greenway (trumpet), Grady Thomas (vocals), Robert McCullough (sax), George Clinton (vocals), "Chicken" Gunnells (trumpet), and Harold Beane (guitar), 1972.* Kinley-McCoy / GROOVE MANEUVERS ARCHIVES

"If You Don't Like the Effects, Don't Produce the Cause"

Vocals: George Clinton, Calvin Simon, Diane Brooks, Steve Kennedy, Garry Shider, Bernie Worrell
Drums: Tyrone Lampkin
Bass: Prkash John, Cordell Mosson
Guitar: Garry Shider
Keyboards: Bernie Worrell
Strings: Victoria Polley, Albert Pratz, Bill Richards, Joe Sera, Walter Babiuk, Stanley Solomon, Ronald Laurie, Peter Shenkman

"Everybody's Going to Make It This Time"

Lead Vocals: George Clinton
Backup Vocals: Diane Brooks, Steve Kennedy, Garry Shider, Calvin Simon, Bernie Worrell
Drums: Tiki Fulwood
Bass: Billy Nelson
Guitar: Eddie Hazel, Garry Shider
Organ: Bernie Worrell
Strings: Victoria Polley, Albert Pratz, Bill Richards, Joe Sera, Walter Babiuk, Stanley Solomon, Ronald Laurie, Peter Shenkman

"A Joyful Process"

Keyboards: Bernie Worrell
Guitar: Harold Beane
Bass: Cordell Mosson
Drums: Tyrone Lampkin
Strings: Victoria Polley, Albert Pratz, Bill Richards, Joe Sera, Walter Babiuk, Stanley Solomon, Ronald Laurie, Peter Shenkman
Trumpet: Bruce Cassidy, Arnie Chycoski, Al Stanwyck
Sax: Randy Wallace

"We Hurt Too"

Lead Vocals: George Clinton, Ray Davis, Calvin Simon
Backup Vocals: Grady Thomas, Fuzzy Haskins

Drums: Tyrone Lampkin
Bass: Cordell Mosson
Keyboards: Bernie Worrell
Strings: Victoria Polley, Albert Pratz, Bill Richards, Joe Sera, Walter Babiuk, Stanley Solomon, Ronald Laurie, Peter Shenkman

"Loose Booty"

Lead Vocals: George Clinton
Backup Vocals: Eddie Hazel, Pat Lewis, Diane Lewis, Rose Williams
Drums: Tiki Fulwood
Bass: Cordell Mosson
Guitar: Harold Beane
Keyboards: Bernie Worrell
Juice Harp: James Wesley Jackson

"Loose Booty" was first recorded in the Osmium period, though this is considered the pivotal version. Funkadelic comedian (enviromedian) James Wesley Jackson is heavy in the mix on juice harp. George Clinton delivers a very early rap though not even his first, as several songs predate this ("A Whole Lot of BS" is a notable one, and many could also argue for "Mommy What's a Funkadelic" and "What Is Soul," although arguably both are more spoken word than "Loose Booty" or "A Whole Lot of BS," which are more rapped). The lyrics deal with junkies and other street themes, predating hip-hop's style as well as its usage of a common subject matter therein.

"Philmore"

Lead Vocals: Bootsy Collins
Backup Vocals: Catfish Collins, Ronnie Greenway, Clayton Gunnels, Frank Waddy, Randy Wallace
Drums: Frank Waddy
Bass: Bootsy Collins
Guitar: Catfish Collins, Harold Beane
Piano: Bernie Worrell
Trumpet: Ronnie Greenway, Chicken Gunnels
Sax: Robert McCullough

"Pussy"

Lead Vocals: George Clinton
Backup Vocals: Eddie Hazel, Diane Brooks, Steve Kennedy, Garry Shider
Drums: Tyrone Lampkin
Bass: Cordell Mosson
Guitars: Garry Shider, Harold Beane
Organ: Bernie Worrell
Trumpet: Ronnie Greenway, Chicken Gunnels
Sax: Robert McCullough

"America Eats Its Young"

Lead Vocals: George Clinton
Backup Vocals: Diane Brooks, Garry Shider, Calvin Simon
Drums: Tyrone Lampkin
Percussion: Someone from Toronto
Bass: Cordell Mosson
Organ: Bernie Worrell
Guitars: Garry Shider
Strings: Victoria Polley, Albert Pratz, Bill Richards, Joe Sera, Walter Babiuk, Stanley Solomon, Ronald Laurie, Peter Shenkman

"Biological Speculation"

Lead Vocals: George Clinton, Calvin Simon
Backup Vocals: Fuzzy Haskins
Drums: Tiki Fulwood
Percussion: Someone from Toronto
Bass: Cordell Mosson
Organ: Bernie Worrell
Guitar: Garry Shider
Steel Guitar: Ollie Strong

"Biological Speculation" shows off more of Funkadelic's country music side and evinces some of George Clinton's most clever and recited lyrics ever. The *America Eats Its Young* album that it comes from would be P-Funk's most political at this point and lists among Clinton's most political albums along with *Some of My Best Jokes Are Friends*, *Dope Dogs*, and *Medicaid Fraud Dogg*.

"That Was My Girl"

Lead Vocals: George Clinton, Calvin Simon
Backup Vocals: Pat Lewis, Joyce Vincent, Telma Hopkins
Drums: Tyrone Lampkin
Bass: Cordell Mosson
Guitar: Garry Shider
Keyboards: Bernie Worrell

"Miss Lucifer's Love"

Lead Vocals: George Clinton, Fuzzy Haskins
Backup Vocals: Calvin Simon, Grady Thomas
Drums: Tyrone Lampkin
Bass: Cordell Mosson
Guitar: Garry Shider
Piano: Bernie Worrell
Strings: Victoria Polley, Albert Pratz, Bill Richards, Joe Sera, Walter Babiuk, Stanley Solomon, Ronald Laurie, Peter Shenkman

"Balance"

Lead Vocals: Bootsy Collins
Backup Vocals: Diane Brooks, Steve Kennedy, George Clinton, Joe Harris
Drums: Tyrone Lampkin
Bass: Cordell Mosson
Guitar: Garry Shider, Harold Beane
Piano, Organ: Bernie Worrell

"Wake Up"

Vocals: Calvin Simon, George Clinton, Garry Shider, Fuzzy Haskins, Diane Brooks, Steve Kennedy, Bernie Worrell, Eddie Hazel
Drums: Tyrone Lampkin
Bass: Cordell Mosson
Guitar: Garry Shider
Keyboards: Bernie Worrell
Trumpet: Chicken Gunnels, Ronnie Greenaway
Sax: Robert McCullough

Parliament-Funkadelic drummer Tyrone Lampkin. © Diem Jones

Unreleased

"Every Little Bit Hurts"

Vocals: George Clinton, Diane Brooks
Drums: Tyrone Lampkin
Bass: Cordell Mosson
Guitar: Garry Shider
Piano: Bernie Worrell
Strings: Victoria Polley, Albert Pratz, Bill Richards, Joe Sera, Walter Babiuk, Stanley Solomon, Ronald Laurie, Peter Shenkman

Cosmic Slop

"Nappy Dugout"

Vocals: George Clinton, Garry Shider, Calvin Simon, Fuzzy Haskins, Grady Thomas, Ray Davis, Mudbone Cooper
Drums: Tiki Fulwood
Congas, Tambourine: Eddie Bongo
Wood Block: Aaron Willis
Bass: Cordell Mosson
Clavinet, Melodica: Bernie Worrell
Guitar: Garry Shider

"You Can't Miss What You Can't Measure"

Lead Vocals: Garry Shider, Ray Davis, George Clinton
Backup Vocals: Pat Lewis, Diane Lewis, Rose Williams
Drums, Percussion: Tyrone Lampkin
Bass: Cordell Mosson
Guitar: Garry Shider
Organ, Melodica: Bernie Worrell

"March to the Witches Castle"

Lead Vocals: George Clinton
Backup Vocals: Garry Shider, Calvin Simon, Pat Lewis, George Clinton, Fuzzy Haskins, Grady Thomas
Drums: Tyrone Lampkin
Bass: Cordell Mosson
Guitar: Garry Shider, Ron Bykowski
Keyboards: Bernie Worrell

"Let's Make It Last"

Lead Vocals: Garry Shider
Backup Vocals: George Clinton, Calvin Simon, Fuzzy Haskins, Pat Lewis, Mudbone Cooper
Drums, Percussion: Tyrone Lampkin
Bass: Cordell Mosson
Guitar: Garry Shider, Ron Bykowski
Keyboards: Bernie Worrell

"Cosmic Slop"

Lead Vocals: Garry Shider
Backup Vocals: Ray Davis, George Clinton, Calvin Simon, Grady Thomas, Fuzzy Haskins, Pat Lewis
Drums, Percussion: Tyrone Lampkin
Bass: Cordell Mosson
Guitars: Garry Shider, Ron Bykowski
Keyboards: Bernie Worrell

"Cosmic Slop" was eloquently sung by P-Funk powerhouse Garry Shider. It also features Shider and guitarist Ron Bykowski trading both lead and rhythm guitars (something that both of them would do on the entire *Cosmic Slop* album). This is another song that was subject to controversy among primary and secondary sources, some saying that the bass was Boogie Mosson and some still claiming that it was Bootsy. The debate had been somewhat laid to rest with George Clinton stating that Bootsy probably played the original groove when they were performing it live, a year before it was recorded or released, but Mosson played on the record (indeed, Mosson is the sole bassist on the whole *Cosmic Slop* album).

"No Compute"

Lead Vocals: George Clinton
Drums, Percussion: Tyrone Lampkin
Bass: Cordell Mosson
Guitars: Garry Shider, Ron Bykowski
Organ: Bernie Worrell

"This Broken Heart"

Lead Vocals: Ben Edwards
Backup Vocals: Calvin Simon, Garry Shider, Mudbone Cooper, Pat Lewis?
Drums: Tyrone Lampkin
Bass: Cordell Mosson
Guitar: Garry Shider
Organ, Piano: Bernie Worrell
Strings: Victoria Polley, Albert Pratz, Bill Richards, Joe Sera, Walter Babiuk, Stanley Solomon, Ronald Laurie, Peter Shenkman

"Trash A-Go-Go"

Lead Vocals: George Clinton
Drums, Percussion: Tyrone Lampkin
Bass: Cordell Mosson
Guitar: Garry Shider, Ron Bykowski
Keyboards: Bernie Worrell

"Can't Stand the Strain"

Lead Vocals: Garry Shider, Calvin Simon, Ray Davis, George Clinton
Backup Vocals: Pat Lewis, Grady Thomas, Fuzzy Haskins
Drums, Percussion: Tyrone Lampkin
Bass: Cordell Mosson
Guitar: Garry Shider, Ron Bykowski
Clavinet: Bernie Worrell

Standing on the Verge of Getting It On

"Red Hot Mama"

Lead Vocals: George Clinton, Eddie Hazel
Backup Vocals: Calvin Simon?
Drums: Gary Bronson
Congas: Calvin Simon
Bass: Reggie McBride
Guitars: Eddie Hazel, Ron Bykowski
Clavinet: Bernie Worrell

"Vital Juices"

Drums: Gary Bronson
Bass: Reggie McBride
Guitars: Eddie Hazel, Ron Bykowski
Clavinet: Bernie Worrell
Congas: Calvin Simon

"Red Hot Mama" is a classic Funkadelic rocker. Like other songs, it was culled from a grungier, more experimental version on Parliament's *Osmium* and rehashed for a slightly more polished classic rock sound on the *Standing on the Verge of Getting It On* album. Eddie Hazel's guitar solo is a major standout.

"Alice in My Fantasies"

Lead Vocals: George Clinton
Drums: Tiki Fulwood
Bass: Cordell Mosson
Guitars: Eddie Hazel, Ron Bykowski, Garry Shider
Keyboards: Bernie Worrell

"I'll Stay"

Lead Vocals: George Clinton, Garry Shider, Eddie Hazel, Calvin Simon,
Drums: Gary Bronson
Bass: Cordell Mosson
Guitars: Ron Bykowski, Eddie Hazel, Garry Shider
Clavinet, Piano: Bernie Worrell

"Sexy Ways"

Lead Vocals: Garry Shider
Backup Vocals: George Clinton, Fuzzy Haskins, Calvin Simon, Grady Thomas, Ray Davis, Pat Lewis
Drums: Tiki Fulwood?
Tambourine: Eddie Bongo
Congas: Eddie Bongo
Bass: Cordell Mosson
Guitar: Eddie Hazel, Garry Shider
Keyboards: Bernie Worrell

"Standing on the Verge of Getting It On"

Vocals: George Clinton, Fuzzy Haskins, Ray Davis, Calvin Simon, Eddie Hazel, Garry Shider, Grady Thomas
Drums: Gary Bronson
Bass: Cordell Mosson
Guitars: Eddie Hazel, Garry Shider, Ron Bykowski
Keyboards: Bernie Worrell

"Standing on the Verge of Getting It on" was an anthem of anthems. Its chants are heard on P-Funk stages to this day. George Clinton and Eddie Hazel were largely responsible for most of the writing on the album (special credit, of course, to Bernie Worrell in an arranging capacity as well, which cannot be overlooked), and Hazel's guitar dominance is present here, although one can almost hear the hint of the dance floor creeping into Funkadelic's music, albeit in a subdued tone at this point. The trademark licks and lyrics of this song are now legendary among the cult following of die-hard fans.

"Jimmy's Got a Little Bit of Bitch in Him"

Lead Vocals: George Clinton
Backup Vocals: Ray Davis, Garry Shider, Fuzzy Haskins, Calvin Simon, Grady Thomas
Drums: Tiki Fulwood
Bass: Cordell Mosson
Guitar: Eddie Hazel, Garry Shider
Piano: Bernie Worrell

"Good Thoughts, Bad Thoughts"

Lead Vocals: George Clinton
Drums: Tyrone Lampkin
Guitars: Eddie Hazel, Ron Bykowski

Let's Take It to the Stage

"Good to Your Earhole"

Lead Vocals: George Clinton, Garry Shider
Backup Vocals: Eddie Hazel, Ray Davis, Fuzzy Haskins, Calvin Simon, Grady Thomas
Drums: Frosty
Bass: Cordell Mosson
Keyboards: Bernie Worrell
Guitar: Eddie Hazel

"Better by the Pound"

Lead Vocals: Garry Shider
Backup Vocals: Eddie Hazel, Pat Lewis, Telma Hopkins, Joyce Vincent, George Clinton, Calvin Simon
Drums: Frosty
Percussion: Eddie Guzman
Bass: Cordell Mosson
Keyboards: Bernie Worrell
Guitar: Eddie Hazel, Garry Shider

"Better by the Pound" was but one of the stellar songs that made up the masterpiece that is Funkadelic's *Let's Take It to the Stage*. The lyrics are transcendent and the music rollicking, and this song, like many other Funkadelic songs, features a mix of P-Funk mainstays and members of the Detroit funk rock band Rare Earth.

"Be My Beach"

Lead Vocals: Bootsy Collins, Ray Davis George Clinton, Calvin Simon
Backup Vocals: Fuzzy Haskins, Grady Thomas
Drums: Cordell Mosson
Bass: Bootsy Collins
Guitar: Garry Shider, Bootsy Collins, Michael Hampton
Organ: Bernie Worrell

"No Head, No Backstage Pass"

Lead Vocals: George Clinton
Backup Vocals: Pat Lewis, Diane Lewis, Rose Williams
Drums: Tyrone Lampkin
Bass: Cordell Mosson
Guitars: Ron Bykowski
Clavinet: Bernie Worrell

"Let's Take It to the Stage"

Lead Vocals: George Clinton
Backup Vocals: George Clinton, Pat Lewis, Bootsy Collins, Fuzzy Haskins, Calvin Simon, Grady Thomas, Ray Davis
Drums: Cordell Mosson
Bass: Bootsy Collins
Guitar: Garry Shider
Clavinet, Synthesizers: Bernie Worrell

"Let's Take It to the Stage" could be considered one of the first (if not the first) legitimate diss records. George Clinton jokingly wanted to poke fun at the competing funk bands of the time (James Brown, Sly and the Family Stone, Kool and the Gang, Rufus, and Earth, Wind & Fire) hoping it would spark a friendly competition of sorts. It also features a classic Clinton–Collins–Worrell combo that would be among the first of many with the soon-to-be-famous writing trio.

"Get Off Your Ass and Jam"

Vocals: George Clinton, Telma Hopkins, Joyce Vincent, Ray Davis, Mudbone Cooper, Garry Shider, Fuzzy Haskins, Calvin Simon, Grady Thomas, Pat Lewis, Diane Lewis, Rose Williams
Drums: Tiki Fulwood
Bass: Cordell Mosson
Guitars: Paul Warren, Garry Shider, Mike Hampton
Keyboards: Bernie Worrell

"Baby I Owe You Something Good"

Lead Vocals: Calvin Simon, Garry Shider
Backup Vocals: Pat Lewis, George Clinton, Mudbone Cooper, Ray Davis, Grady Thomas, Fuzzy Haskins
Drums: Tyrone Lampkin
Bass: Cordell Mosson
Guitars: Garry Shider, Ron Bykowski
Clavinet: Bernie Worrell

"Stuffs and Things"

Lead Vocals: Garry Shider, George Clinton
Backup Vocals: Eddie Hazel
Drums: Frosty
Percussion: Eddie Guzman
Bass: Cordell Mosson
Guitar: Michael Hampton, Eddie Hazel
Synthesizer: Bernie Worrell

"The Song Is Familiar"

Lead Vocals: Garry Shider, George Clinton
Backup Vocals: Telma Hopkins, Joyce Vincent, Pat Lewis
Drums, Bass: Bootsy Collins
Guitar: Garry Shider, Catfish Collins
Piano: Bernie Worrell

"Atmosphere"

Vocals: George Clinton
Organ, Synthesizers: Bernie Worrell
Guitar: Garry Shider

Tales of Kidd Funkadelic

"Butt-to-Butt Resuscitation"

Vocals: George Clinton, Glenn Goins, Mudbone Cooper, Garry Shider, Cordell Mosson
Drums: Cordell Mosson
Bass: Garry Shider
Guitar: Michael Hampton, Eddie Hazel
Organ, Synthesizers: Bernie Worrell

"Let's Take It to the People"

Lead Vocals, Clavinet: George Clinton
Backup Vocals: Glenn Goins, Garry Shider, Pat Lewis, Joyce Vincent, Telma Hopkins
Drums: Cordell Mosson
Bass: Bootsy Collins
Guitar: Ron Bykowski, Garry Shider, Michael Hampton

"Undisco Kidd"

Lead Vocals: George Clinton
Backup Vocals: George Clinton, Mudbone Cooper, Glenn Goins, Garry Shider
Drums, Bass: Bootsy Collins
Percussion, Laughing Box: Mudbone Cooper, Bootsy Collins
Synthesizers, Piano: Bernie Worrell
Guitar: Garry Shider

Up to this point, "Undisco Kidd" was the most (for lack of a better word) "rappadelic" songs to come out of the P-Funk camp, but it should behoove the reader to be aware that this is still three years before "Rappers Delight" and far from Clinton's first mingling with the not-yet-defined genre that would later take cues from P-Funk and become the dominant genre in the world. Again, the Clinton–Collins–Worrell writing and performing combination is extremely important, one may say vital, to the very creation and progressions of hip-hop itself in several instances of its history.

"Take Your Dead Ass Home"

Lead Vocals: George Clinton
Backup Vocals: Glenn Goins, Joyce Vincent, Telma Hopkins, Cordell Mosson, Garry Shider, Mudbone Cooper, Bootsy Collins
Drums: Jerome Brailey
Bass: Bootsy Collins and/or Cordell Mosson
Guitar: Garry Shider, Glenn Goins
Synthesizers, Keyboards: Bernie Worrell

"I'm Never Gonna Tell It"

Lead Vocals: Garry Shider
Backup Vocals: George Clinton, Mudbone Cooper, Glenn Goins, Cordell Mosson
Drums: Tyrone Lampkin
Percussion: Eddie Bongo
Bass: Cordell Mosson
Synthesizers: Bernie Worrell
Guitars: Garry Shider, Glenn Goins

"Tales of Kidd Funkadelic"

Vocals: George Clinton, Glenn Goins, Mudbone Cooper, Jessica Cleaves, Garry Shider, Ray Davis
Synthesizers: Bernie Worrell
Bongos: Eddie Bongo

"How Do You View Yeaw?"

Lead Vocals: George Clinton
Backup Vocals: Mudbone Cooper, Garry Shider, Telma Hopkins, Joyce Vincent
Drums, Bass: Bootsy Collins
Guitar: Garry Shider
Keyboards: Bernie Worrell

"How Do You View Yeaw" is a self-reflection on self-reflection, dealing with the topics of philautia, specifically narcissism. It is also a good example of how much the Beatles and Dylan had an influence on George Clinton's lyrical brain. Both this and "The Song Is Familiar" from the *Let's Take It to the Stage* album represent early versions of the silly-serious "love song" from the Clinton–Collins–Worrell team.

Warner Bros. Records

Hardcore Jollies

"Comin' Round the Mountain"

Vocals: Ray Davis, George Clinton, Glenn Goins, Mudbone Cooper, Garry Shider
Drums: Buddy Miles
Bass: Jimmy Calhoun
Guitar: Eddie Hazel

"Comin' Round the Mountain" was a Hendrix-inspired take on the classic nursery rhyme, replete with the Band of Gypsy's drummer himself: Buddy Miles. The lineup on this song would be found throughout Eddie Hazel's *Game, Dames and Guitar Thangs* album.

"Smokey"

Lead Vocals: Glenn Goins
Backup Vocals: George Clinton, Mudbone Cooper, Garry Shider
Drums: Tyrone Lampkin
Synth Bass, Synthesizers, Keyboards: Bernie Worrell
Guitars: Garry Shider, Glenn Goins

"Smokey" was the second A-side single to be released on the *Hardcore Jollies* album. It features a Glenn Goins lead vocal, a trademark Melodica solo from Bernie Worrell, and a fantastic keyboard outro leading directly into the cult favorite "If You Got Funk You Got Style." Although dedicated to the guitarists of the world, this single on *Hardcore Jollies* was slightly less rock oriented than the rest of the album.

"If You Got Fun, You Got Style"

Lead Vocals: George Clinton, Ray Davis
Drums: Jerome Brailey
Bass: Bootsy Collins
Guitar: Eddie Hazel
Clavinet: Bernie Worrell

"Hardcore Jollies"

Drums: Jerome Brailey
Bass: Cordell Mosson
Guitars: Eddie Hazel, Garry Shider, Glenn
Goins
Keyboards: Bernie Worrell

"Soul Mate"

Lead Vocals: George Clinton
Backup Vocals: George Clinton, Glenn Goins,
Telma Hopkins, Joyce Vincent, Garry Shider
Drums: Tyrone Lampkin
Bass, Guitars: Eddie Hazel
Organ: Bernie Worrell

"Cosmic Slop" (HJ Live version)

Lead Vocals: Fuzzy Haskins, Garry Shider,
Ray Davis
Backup Vocals: George Clinton, Grady
Thomas, Jeanette Washington, Debbie
Wright
Drums: Jerome Brailey
Bass: Cordell Mosson
Guitar: Michael Hampton, Garry Shider, Glenn
Goins

"You Scared the Lovin Outta Me"

Lead Vocals: Glenn Goins, George Clinton,
Mudbone Cooper
Backup Vocals: Telma Hopkins, Joyce
Vincent, Garry Shider
Drums: Jerome Brailey
Bass: Cordell Mosson
Guitar: Garry Shider, Eddie Hazel

"Adolescent Funk"

Vocals: Ray Davis, Grady Thomas, Calvin
Simon, George Clinton, Fuzzy Haskins,
Mudbone Cooper?
Drums: Jerome Brailey
Synth Bass, Synthesizers: Bernie Worrell
Guitars: Michael Hampton

Unreleased

"Clone Communicado"

Lead Vocals: Archie Ivy
Drums: Jerome Brailey
Guitar: Eddie Hazel, Michael Hampton
Synth Bass, Clavinet: Bernie Worrell

One Nation Under a Groove

"One Nation Under a Groove"

Lead Vocals: George Clinton, Junie Morrisson,
Garry Shider
Backup Vocals: Lynn Mabry, Junie Morrisson,
Jeanette Washington, Sheila Horne, Dawn
Silva, Robert Peanut Johnson, Ray Davis,
Garry Shider, Michael Clip Payne, Greg
Thomas, Shirley Hayden, Cheryl James,
Mallia Franklin, Linda Shider
Drums: Bootsy Collins
Percussion: Larry Fratangelo
Synth Bass, Synthesizer: Bernie Worrell
Guitar: Garry Shider
Banjo: Bobby Lewis
Synthesizer: Junie Morrison, Doug Duffy

"One Nation Under a Groove" was the longest-running #1 hit single in the P-Funk canon. It lasted at the top of the rhythm-and-blues charts for a whopping nine weeks in 1979, making it the longest-running #1 rhythm-and-blues hit that year. It is also the first record to have both Bernie Worrell and Walter "Junie" Morrison on keyboards together, two titans of the musical world at that time. This single truly marked a new phase for Funkadelic; the group had already had a somewhat cleaner rock sound since 1973's *Cosmic Slop* album, but now, for the first time, the group had chart-topping singles like its sister band Parliament, the traditional hit-making machine. Funkadelic would find itself more on the dance floor and less so idealizing sociopolitical treatises, as it had been doing prior to the release of this massive hit.

"Grooveallegience"

Lead Vocals: Junie Morrison, Garry Shider, George Clinton
Backup Vocals: Ray Davis, Robert Peanut Johnson, Dawn Silva, Lynn Mabry, Mallia Franklin, Shirley Hayden, Gary Mudbone Cooper, Greg Thomas
Drums: Tyrone Lampkin
Bass: Rodney Curtis
Guitar: Michael Hampton, Garry Shider, Junie Morisson
Keyboards: Bernie Worrell

"Who Says a Funk Band Can't Play Rock?"

Lead Vocals: Junie Morrison
Backup Vocals: Michael Clip Payne, Lynn Mabry, Dawn Silva, Sheila Horne, Jessica Cleaves, Jim Wright, Debbie Wright, Jeanette Washington, Linda Shider
Drums: Jim Wright
Bass: Rodney Curtis
Guitars: Michael Hampton, Junie Morrison

"Promentalshitbackwashpsychosis Enema Squad (the Doo-Doo Chasers)"

Lead Vocals: George Clinton, Garry Shider
Backup Vocals: Junie Morisson, Linda Shider, Michael Clip Payne, Shirley Hayden, Jeanette Washington, Patty Walker, Ron Ford
Drums: Jerome Brailey
Bass: Cordell Mosson
Guitars: Garry Shider

"Into You"

Lead Vocals: Ray Davis, Ron Ford, Garry Shider, Junie Morrisson
Backup Vocals: Dawn Silva, Lynn Mabry, Mallia Franklin, Sheila Horne, Babs Stewart, Michael Clip Payne, Robert Peanut Johnson, Greg Thomas, Linda Shider
Banjo: Cordell Mosson
Drums, Bass, Keyboards: Junie Morrison
Guitars: Michael Hampton, Junie Morrison

"Cholly (Funk Getting Ready to Roll)"

Lead Vocals: Garry Shider
Backup Vocals: Ray Davis, Junie Morrison, George Clinton, Dawn Silva, Lynn Mabry, Sheila Horne, Shirley Hayden, Mallia Franklin, Jeanette Washington, Debbie Wright, Mallia Franklin, Michael Clip Payne, Ron Ford, Robert Peanut Johnson, Jim Wright, Greg Thomas, Linda Shider
Drums: Tyrone Lampkin
Percussion: Larry Fratangelo
Bass: Rodney Curtis
Guitars: Garry Shider, Michael Hampton
Clavinet: Bernie Worrell

"Cholly" was one of guitarist Garry Shider's tours de force, especially becoming a live favorite. It also features standout bass lines from a rising star in the P-Funk camp at this time: Rodney "Skeet" Curtis.

"Lunchmeataphobia (Think . . . It Ain't Illegal Yet)"

Lead Vocals: George Clinton
Drums: Jerome Brailey
Bass: Cordell Mosson
Guitars: Michael Hampton
Clavinet: Bernie Worrell

"P.E. Squad/Doo-Doo Chasers" (Groovestrumental)

Drums: Jerome Brailey
Bass: Cordell Mosson
Guitars: Garry Shider
Organ: Bernie Worrell

"Maggot Brain (Live)"

Lead Vocals: George Clinton
Drums: Tyrone Lampkin
Bass: Rodney Curtis
Guitars: Michael Hampton, Garry Shider
Keyboards: Bernie Worrell

This live version of "Maggot Brain," from a show in Monroe, Louisiana, became more well known than even the original, with guitarist Michael Hampton playing Eddie Hazel's signature song note for note as well as bringing some original energy and phrasing to the ending. Hazel himself never played the song the same way twice, but Hampton's mastery of the song from a very young age made his name synonymous with the Funkadelic cult classic song, arguably as often as Hazel's.

Uncle Jam Wants You

"Freak of the Week"

Lead Vocals: George Clinton
Backup Vocals: Dawn Silva, Michael Clip Payne, Lige Curry, Sheila Horne, Jeanette MacGruder, Mallia Franklin
Drums: Dennis Chambers
Bass: Cherokee Bunn
Guitar: Dewayne Blackbyrd McKnight
Keyboards: Gary Hudgins
Percussion: Larry Fratangelo

"Freak of the Week" was originally intended for the Brides of Funkenstein. It features much of the Bride's band at that time.

"(Not Just) Knee Deep"

Lead Vocals: Garry Shider, George Clinton, Junie Morrison, Philippe Wynne
Backup Vocals: Jessica Cleaves, Ray Davis, Blackbyrd McKnight, Robert Peanut Johnson, Dawn Silva, Lynn Mabry, Greg Thomas, Sheila Horne, Jeanette MacGruder, Junie Morrison, Patty Walker, Michael Clip Payne, Gary Mudbone Cooper, Ron Ford, Mallia Franklin, Debbie Wright, Jeanette Washington, Linda Shider
Drums: Junie Morrison and/or Bootsy Collins
Synth Bass, Synthesizers, Rhodes: Junie Morrison
Piano: Bernie Worrell

Guitar: Michael Hampton, Junie Morrison
Cuica: Larry Fratangelo
Handclap Boards: Carl "Butch" Small

"(Not Just) Knee Deep" was the second really big charting single from Funkadelic. George originally wrote the song in 3/4 time signature and handed it over to former Ohio Players visionary Walter "Junie" Morrisson to arrange the tune. Also notable is the standout guitar solo from Michael "Kidd Funkadelic" Hampton. It stands as the longest-running (at a whopping 15 minutes) P-Funk hit song and, as many know, was sampled and interpolated heavily by De La Soul, Dr. Dre, Snoop Dogg, Ice Cube, and so many more rappers from the late 1980s on, revitalizing the song in new eras. Indeed, the base of much of what is considered within the subgenre of "G-Funk" comes from the bass line in the B section of this anthem. "Knee Deep" is also notable for the massive amount of vocals included therein, and fans would see many more vocal anthems of this type in the next few years of P-funk releases, though likely none would be as successful as this chart-topping favorite.

"Uncle Jam"

Lead Vocals: Philippe Wynne, George Clinton
Backup Vocals: Greg Thomas, Robert Peanut Johnson, Ron Ford, Eddie Hazel, Garry Shider, Greg Thomas, Patty Walker, Sheila Horne, Jessica Cleaves, Brandye, Tracey Lewis, Jeanette MacGruder, Lige Curry, Dawn Silva, Linda Shider
Drums: Tyrone Lampkin
Bass: Bootsy Collins
Synthesizers: Bernie Worrell
Guitar: Garry Shider

Uncle Jam Wants You brings the military theme into the forever-expanding elements of P-Funk theatrics—in the albums, the comic books, the imagery, and the stage show. Philippe Wynne of the Spinners is also famously sharing lead vocal duties with George Clinton (as he also did on "Knee Deep"), extolling the listener to be ready for "Uncle Jam."

"Field Maneuvers"

Drums: Jerome Brailey
Bass: Cordell Mosson
Guitars: Eddie Hazel, Michael Hampton
Clavinet: Bernie Worrell

"Holly Wants to Go to California"

Lead Vocals: George Clinton
Backup **Voices:** Michael Clip Payne, Vanessa (Miss Alabama), Robert Peanut Johnson, Jerome Rodgers, Garry Shider, another girl, Andre Williams
Piano: Bernie Worrell

"Foot Soldiers (Star Spangled Funky)"

Lead Vocals: George Clinton
Backup Vocals: Ron Ford, Ray Davis, Michael Clip Payne, Steve Pannell, Darryl Clinton, Jerome Rodgers, Dawn Silva, Sheila Horne, Jeanette MacGruder, Mallia Franklin, Shirley Hayden, Andre Williams, Tracey Lewis, Lige Curry, Robert Peanut Johnson, Garry Shider, Greg Thomas
Drums: Tyrone Lampkin
Synthesizer: Jerome Rodgers
Synth Bass, Keyboards: Bernie Worrell
Guitars: Michael Hampton, Garry Shider

Unreleased (slated for the *Uncle Jam Wants You* album)

"In the Cabin of My Uncle Jam"

Lead Vocals: Ron Ford
Backup Vocals: Michael Clip Payne, Archie Ivy, Ron Brembry, Bruce Peterson, Lige Curry, Patty Walker, Mallia Franklin, Dawn Silva, Nene Montes
Drums: Michael Clip Payne
Bass: Jeff Cherokee Bunn
Guitar: Kevin Oliver

Clavinet: Gary Hudgins

The Electric Spanking of War Babies

"The Electric Spanking of War Babies"

Lead Vocals: George Clinton, Junie Morrison, Garry Shider
Backup Vocals: Robert Peanut Johnson, Michael Clip Payne, Lige Curry, Ray Davis, Shirley Hayden, Tyrone Lampkin, Jeanette Washington, Mallia Franklin, Lynn Mabry, Dawn Silva, Ron Ford, Jeanette MacGruder, Sheila Horne, Linda Shider
Drums, Bass, Synthesizers, Keyboards: Junie Morrison
Guitars: Michael Hampton, Junie Morrison

"The Electric Spanking of War Babies" is one of many "children" of "One Nation Under a Groove" and "Knee Deep." Indeed, it seamlessly weaved important elements of both past hit records into the formula of the song. The inclusion of George Clinton, Junie, Michael Hampton, and many of the singers made the trend consistent and authentic. "May Day" is another version of this formula combination.

"Electro-Cuties"

Lead Vocals: George Clinton
Backup Vocals: Mallia Franklin, Garry Shider, Shirley Hayden, Jeanette MacGruder, Sheila Horne, Jeanette Washington, Ron Ford, Donnie Sterling, Michael Clip Payne, Robert Peanut Johnson, Andre Williams, Stevie Pannell, Patty Walker, Lige Curry, Dawn Silva
Drums: Kenny Colton
Bass: Jimmy Ali
Guitars: Michael Hampton, Jerome Ali, Gordon Carlton
Synthesizers: David Spradley

"Funk Gets Stronger" (Part 1)

Lead Vocals: George Clinton, Bootsy Collins, Sly Stone, Mallia Franklin, Jerome Rodgers, Robert Peanut Johnson
Backup Vocals: Michael Clip Payne, Robert Peanut Johnson, Mallia Franklin, Ron Ford, Patty Walker, Lige Curry
Drums: Tyrone Lampkin
Percussion: Larry Fratangelo, Muruga Booker
Bass: Lige Curry, Roger Troutman
Guitar: Michael Hampton, Roger Troutman
Electric Piano: Sly Stone
Synthesizer: Roger Troutman
Trumpet: Cynthia Robinson
Sax: Pat Rizzo

"Brettino's Bounce"

Percussion: Larry Fratangelo

"Funk Gets Stronger" (Killer Millameter Longer Version)

Lead Vocals: Sly Stone, George Clinton
Backup Vocals: Michael Clip Payne, Tamah, Guitar Sally
Drums: Sly Stone, Frankie Kash Waddy
Bass, Synthesizer: Sly Stone
Guitar: Eddie Hazel, Sly Stone
Trumpet: Cynthia Robinson
Sax: Pat Rizzo

"Funk Gets Stronger" featured important contributions from Funk legend Sly Stone. Stone and George Clinton would work together several more times in this way on later albums, such as *Urban Dancefloor Guerillas* by the P-Funk All Stars, *Gangsters of Love* by Clinton, and *First Ya Gotta Shake the Gate* by Funkadelic

"She Loves You"

Lead Vocals: Sly Stone, George Clinton, Ron Ford
Drums, Bass: Sly Stone
Guitar: Eddie Hazel, Sly Stone

"Shockwaves"

Lead Vocals: Donnie Sterling, Ron Dunbar, Garry Shider
Backup Vocals: Michael Clip Payne, Lige Curry, Andre Williams, Patty Walker, Linda Shider, Jeanette MacGruder, Shirley Hayden
Drums: Kenny Colton
Bass: Lige Curry
Guitar: Blackbyrd McKnight

"Oh, I"

Lead Vocals: Garry Shider, George Clinton
Backup Vocals: Ray Davis, Robert Peanut Johnson, Dawn Silva, Sheila Horne, Jeanette MacGruder, Shiley Hayden, Jeanette Washington, Mallia Franklin, Linda Shider, Patty Walker, Michael Clip Payne, Lige Curry, Ron Ford, Kenny Colton, Donnie Sterling
Drums: Kenny Colton
Bass: Rodney Curtis
Guitars: Michael Hampton, Jerome Ali, Garry Shider, Gordon Carlton
Piano: Manon Saulsby
Sax: Michael Brecker

"Icka Prick"

Lead Vocals: George Clinton
Backup Vocals: Ron Ford, Garry Shider, Lige Curry, Michael Clip Payne, Shirley Hayden, Linda Shider, Patty Walker, Jeanette MacGruder, Sheila Horne, Robert Peanut Johnson
Drums: Man in the Box
Bass: Lige Curry
Guitar: Michael Hampton
Synthesizer: David Spradley

Unreleased (slated for the *Electric Spanking of War Babies* album)

"May Day"

Lead Vocals: Garry Shider
Backup Vocals: Robert Peanut Johnson, George Clinton, Ron Ford, Dawn Silva, Shirley Hayden, Mallia Franklin, Jeanette McGruder, Sheila Horne, Andre Williams, Michael Clip Payne, Garry Shider, Patty Walker, Linda Shider, Jeanette Washington, Ray Davis, Lige Curry
Drums: Kenny Colton
Bass: Lige Curry
Guitar: Michael Hampton, Ron Bykowski, Garry Shider
Keyboards: David Spradley

"I Angle"

Lead Vocals: Ron Ford
Backup Vocals: Lige Curry, Jeanette MacGruder, Sheila Horne, Michael Clip Payne, Tony Thomas
Drums: Kenny Colton
Bass: Lige Curry
Guitar: Tony Thomas, Andre Williams
Synthesizers: David Spradley

"Too Tight for Light"

Lead Vocals: Junie Morrison, George Clinton
Backup Vocals: Robert Peanut Johnson
Drums, Synth Bass, Synthesizers, Keyboards: Junie Morrison

MCA Records

By Way of the Drum

"Nose Bleed"

Lead Vocals: George Clinton, Garry Shider
Backup Vocals: Belita Woods, Lige Curry, Robert Peanut Johnson, Michael Clip Payne, Shirley Hayden, Mallia Franklin, Pat Lewis, Sandra Feva

Drums, Bass, Guitars: Blackbyrd McKnight

"Sunshine of Your Love"

Vocals: George Clinton, Robert Peanut Johnson, Garry Shider, Paul Hill, Pat Lewis, Debra Barsha, Sandra Feva, Jessica Cleaves, Andre Williams
Drums, Percussion, Bass, Guitars: Blackbyrd McKnight

"Freaks Bearing Gifts"

Lead Vocals: Steve Boyd, Garry Shider, George Clinton, Paul Hill
Drums, Bass, Guitars: Steve Washington
Keyboards: David Spradley

"Yadadadda"

Lead Vocals: Tracey Lewis
Drum Programming: Mark Davis?
Synth Bass: Tracey Lewis
Guitars: Blackbyrd McKnight
Synthesizers: Tracey Lewis, David Spradley

"By Way of the Drum"

Lead Vocals: Keith Washington, Sandra Feva, George Clinton
Backup Vocals: George Clinton, Garry Shider, Pat Lewis, Paul Hill, Robert Peanut Johnson, Andre Williams, Lige Curry
Drums, Synth Bass, Synthesizers: David Spradley
Guitars: Garry Shider

The title track of the *By Way of the Drum* album was the only song to actually be released after George Clinton had announced the release of the first Funkadelic album in eight years; unfortunately, at that point, the title track, and its many remixes were the only thing to be released from said album until many years later when it was officially released, decades after the fact.

"Jugular"

Lead Vocals, Drums, Bass, Guitars: Blackbyrd McKnight
Backup Vocals: Blackbyrd McKnight, Gary Moody

"Some Fresh Delic"

Lead Vocals: George Clinton
Backup Vocals, Drums, Percussion: Blackbyrd McKnight
Guitars: Blackbyrd McKnight, Eddie Hazel

"Primal Instinct"

Vocals: Pat Lewis, Debra Barsha, Lynn Mabry, George Clinton, Sandra Feva, Jessica Cleaves, Diem Jones
Drums, Bass, Guitars, Synthesizers: Loic Gambas

C-Kunspyruhzy Records

First Ya Gotta Shake the Gate

"Baby Like Fonkin' It Up"

Vocals: Sly Stone, George Clinton, Tracey Lewis, Trazae Lewis-Clinton, Sidney Barnes, Gilberto Fuentes, Ebony Houston, Garrett Shider, Tonysha Nelson, Sa'D Ali, Bouvier Richardson, Brandi Scott, Barrence Dupree, Rey Joven, Miranda Mimms
Man in the Box, Keyboards, Synth Bass: Sly Stone
Trombone: Fred Wesley
Trumpets: Whitney Russell
Additional Drum Programming: Ricky Tan

"Get Low"

Vocals: George Clinton 13teen, LaShonda Clinton, Tracey Lewis
Synth Bass, Synthesizers: Danny Bedrosian
Music Programming: 13teen

"If I Didn't Love You"

Vocals: Sly Stone, George Clinton, Mary Griffin
All Instruments: Sly Stone

"Fucked Up"

Vocals: George Clinton, Robert Peanut Johnson, Bouvier Richardson, Barrence Dupree
Drums: Nestor Mumm-Altuve
Bass: Hunter Daws
Keyboards: Kennedy Jacobs

"Ain't That Funkin Kinda Hard on You?"

Vocals: George Clinton, Tonysha Nelson, Rey Joven, Robert Peanut Johnson, Sidney Barneys, G-Koop, 13teen, Ebony Houston, Brandi Scott, Ricky Tan
Bass: Lige Curry
Guitars: Blackbyrd McKnight, Garry Shider, Michael Hampton
Strings, Synthesizers: Danny Bedrosian
Music Programming: G-Koop

"Ain't That Funkin Kinda Hard on You?" (Remix)

Vocals: George Clinton, Tonysha Nelson, Kendrick Lamar, Ice Cube, others
Music: Marlon Barrow

"Ain't That Funkin Kinda Hard on You" saw Funkadelic returning, after 33 years, on an album, *Shake the Gate*, featuring 33 songs. This was the album's most popular song, with appearances and versions featuring Ice Cube, Kendrick Lamar, DJ Louie Vega, Fred Wesley, Pee Wee Ellis, and more. The Vega version was included in a Grammy nomination for best electronic album (Vega's album, which featured multiple versions of the song), and the music video for the version featuring Ice Cube and Kendrick Lamar was P-Funk's first music video in 18 years.

"I Mo B Yodog Fo Eva"

Vocals: George Clinton, 13teen, Rey Joven, Ebony Houston, Sa'D Ali, Larry Grams, LuShawn Clinton, Barrence Dupree
Guitars: Blackbyrd McKnight
Piano, Keyboards, Synthesizers: Danny Bedrosian

"In Da Kar"

Vocals: George Clinton, Tonysha Nelson, Robert Peanut Johnson
Drums: Max MacVeety
Synth Bass, Synthesizers: Sly Stone
Guitar, Keyboards: G-Koop
Music Programming: Charles Levine, Eli Goldstein
Handclaps: Will Thoren, Eli Goldstein, G-Koop

"Radio Friendly"

Vocals: George Clinton, El DeBarge, Chico DeBarge, Tracey Lewis,
All Music: Quaze, Josef Leimberg

"Mathematics of Love"

Vocals: Sly Stone, George Clinton, Kim Burrell, Garry Shider, Mary Griffin
Piano, Keyboards, Strings, Synthesizers: Corey Stoops
Synth Bass, Additional Keyboards, Synthesizers: Sly Stone
Additional Keyboards: Chris Davis

"Creases"

Vocals: Del tha Funkee Homosapien
All Music: Del tha Funkee Homosapien

"Not Your Average Rapper"

Vocals: Trazae Lewis-Clinton, George Clinton, Brandi Scott
Synthesizers: Danny Bedrosian
Music Programming: G-Koop

"First Ya Gotta Shake the Gate"

Vocals: George Clinton, Tonysha Nelson
Music Programming: Soul Clap, Barrence Dupree
Didjeridoo: William Thoren
Keyboards: Danny Bedrosian

"Roller Rink"

Vocals: Belita Woods, George Clinton, Steve Boyd, Kendra Foster, Robert Peanut Johnson, Tracey Lewis, Paul Hill, Jessica Cleaves, Michael Patterson, Kim Manning
Music Programming: K-OS Mixmaster, George Clinton, Ricky Tan, Dwayne Dungey
Bass Guitar: Lige Curry
Piano: Danny Bedrosian
Guitar: Blackbyrd McKnight
Organ: Jerome Rodgers

"Jolene"

Vocals: George Clinton, Garry Shider, Sidney Barnes, Scarface, Kathryn Griffin, Mary Griffin, Dayonne Rollins, 13teen, Sa'D Ali, Barrence Dupree, Bouvier Richardson
Drums: Savar Martin
Bass: Anthony Nickels
Guitars: Blackbyrd McKnight, Garry Shider, Scarface, Corey Stoops
Trumpet: O.J.
Trombone: Andre Grant
Additional Drum Programming: Barrence Dupree

"Nuclear Dog"

Vocals: Trazae Lewis-Clinton, Tracey Lewis, Howard Mann, Navid Movistavi
Drums, Synth Bass, Synthesizers: David Spradley
Guitars: Blackbyrd McKnight, Trafael Lewis
Didjeridoo: William Thoren

"Nuclear Dog Part II"

(Same personnel minus vocals)

"Dirty Queen"

Vocals: Trafael Lewis, Adam Maloney, Ali Schlick
Drums: Trafael Lewis, Rudge Ravinewood
Bass: Trafael Lewis, Bora Karaca
Guitar: Trafael Lewis, Cliff Miles
Violin: Jay Golden

"You Can't Unring the Bell"

Vocals: George Clinton, Robert Peanut Johnson, Rey Joven, 13teen, Tonysha Nelson
Bass: Cherokee Bunn
Guitar: Blackbyrd McKnight, G-Koop
Trombone: Fred Wesley
Sax: Maceo Parker
Additional Horns: Lincoln Adler
Trumpets: Richard Griffith, Rick Gardner
Keyboards, Synthesizers: Danny Bedrosian
Music Programming: G-Koop

"Old Fool"

Vocals: George Clinton, Sidney Barnes, Ebony Houston, Brandi Scott, 13teen, G Koop, Ricky Tan, Garrett Shider, Robert Peanut Johnson
Music Programming: G-Koop, Ricky Tan
Synth Bass, Synthesizers: Danny Bedrosian

"Pole Power"

Vocals: George Clinton, Tracey Lewis, Ebony Houston, Rey Joven, 13teen, Sa'D Ali, Sidney Barnes, Paul Hill, Patavian Lewis, Dayonne Rollins, Tonysha Nelson
Music Programming: G Koop
Synthesizers, Piano, Synth Bass: Danny Bedrosian
Guitars: Tracey Lewis, Trafael Lewis, Anthony Caruso
Horns, Additional Keyboards: Anthony Caruso

"Boom There We Go Again"

Vocals: George Clinton, Tonysha Nelson, Danny Bedrosian, Ray Davis, Robert Peanut Johnson, Dayonne Rollins, Rey Joven, G Koop, 13teen, Brandi Scott, Ricky Tan
Bass: Bootsy Collins
Percussion: Bootsy Collins, Larry Fratangelo, Mudbone Cooper
Piano, Synthesizer: Bernie Worrell
Keyboard, Synthesizer: Danny Bedrosian
Music Programming: G Koop

"As in"

Vocals: Jessica Cleaves, George Clinton, Robert Peanut Johnson, Dayonne Rollins, Rey Joven
Drums: Tyrone Lampkin
Bass: Cordell Mosson
Guitar: Michael Hampton
Piano, Keyboards, String Arrangement: Bernie Worrell
Violins: Lili Haydn
Orchestra: Detroit Symphony Orchestra

"Bernadette"

Vocals: Jamie Kaposta Pat Lewis, George Clinton
Drum Programming, Synth Bass, Keyboards: David Spradley
Keyboards, Synthesizer, Melodica: Danny Bedrosian
Orchestra: Detroit Symphony Orchestra
Arranger: Mike Terry

"Meow Meow"

Vocals: Brandi Scott, 13teen, Trazae Lewis-Clinton, Tonysha Nelson, George Clinton, Robert Peanut Johnson, G Koop, Buster the Cat
Bass, Guitar: Bootsy Collins
Synthesizers, Keyboards: Danny Bedrosian
Music Programming: G Koop

"Catchin Boogie Fever"

Vocals: Tracey Lewis
Trombone: Fred Wesley, Dave Richards
Sax: Maceo Parker
Trumpet: Dave Richards
Sound Effects: David Spradley
Guitars: G Koop
Percussion: Larry Fratangelo
Electric Piano, Synthesizers: Danny Bedrosian
Drums: DJ Toure
Additional Keyboards: Graham Richards

"Talking to the Wall"

Vocals: Garrett Shider, Dayonne Rollins
Drum Programming: Sa'D Ali
Bass: Rodney Curtis
Guitar: Garrett Shider
Piano, Strings: Danny Bedrosian

"The Naz"

Vocals: Sly Stone, Rob Manzoli
All Instruments: Rob Manzoli

"Where Would I Go?"

Vocals: George Clinton, Garrett Shider, Sidney Barnes, Robert Peanut Johnson
Guitars: Michael Hampton, Blackbyrd McKnight Garrett Shider
Synthesizer, Piano, Clavinet, Strings: Danny Bedrosian
Bass: Rodney Curtis
Drums: Nestor Mumm Altuve

"Yesterdejavu"

Vocals: George Clinton, Tracey Lewis, Jerome Rogers, Kendra Foster, Rob Manzoli
Guitar: Tracey Lewis, Rob Manzoli
Bass: Rob Manzoli
Piano: Sue Brooks, Bernie Worrell?
Drums: Law

"Zip It"

Vocals: Tracey Lewis, Beobe Jones
Bass Guitar: Jimmy Ali
Guitars: Jerome Ali
Piano: David Spradley
Music Programming, Synthesizers: G Koop
Additional Drum Programming: Barrence Dupree

"The Wall"

Vocals: George Clinton, Sidney Barnes, Trazae Lewis-Clinton, Rey Joven
Guitars: Jerome Rodgers
Music Programming, Keyboards: Ricky Tan

"Snot n' Booger"

Vocals: George Clinton, Trazae Lewis-Clinton, Sidney Barnes, Robert Peanut Johnson, Ron Ford, Sa'D Ali, 13teen, Dayonne Rollins
Samples, Drum Programming: George Clinton, Sa'D Ali, Ricky Tan
Synthesizers: Jerome Rodgers

"Yellow Light"

Vocals, Keyboards, Man in the Box: Sly Stone
Synth Bass: Sly Stone, Danny Bedrosian
Synthesizers, Sound Effects: Danny Bedrosian
Additional Drum Programming: William Tyler Pelt

"Dipety Dipety Doo Stop the Violence"

Vocals: George Clinton, Garry Shider, Robert Peanut Johnson, Sidney Barnes, Tonysha Nelson, Trazae Lewis-Clinton, Brandi Scott
Keyboards, Synth Bass: David Spradley
Music Programming: G Koop
Guitars: Eddie Hazel
Synthesizers: Danny Bedrosian

"First Ya Gotta Shake the Gate (Samplecopydupeitandloopittostupid Mix)"

Featuring: Soul Clap

Parliafunkadelicment thang in Detroit. Kinley-McCoy / GROOVE MANEUVERS ARCHIVES

Parliament-Funkadelic around 1980 L–R (top): Larry Fratangelo, Jerome Rodgers, Cordell "Boogie" Mosson, Ray Davis, Rodney "Skeet" Curtis, Dewayne "Blackbyrd" McKnight, Greg Boyer, Bennie Cowan, Dennis Chambers, Greg Thomas, Robert "Peanut" Johnson, Larry Hatcher, and David Spradley. L–R (bottom): Michael "Kidd Funkadelic" Hampton, Lige Curry, and Garry "Starchild" Shider. Kinley-McCoy / GROOVE MANEUVERS ARCHIVES

"Peep This"

Featuring: G Koop, Greg Paulus, Nick Monaco

— ☆ —

PARLIAMENT: 1970, 1974–1980, 2018–

Parliament evolved out of the vocal group the Parliaments during the late 1960s and early 1970s. Parliament started out with a Beatles-esque penchant for genre bending, something George Clinton would return to again and again in his career. By the mid-1970s, however, Parliament became a massive hit-making machine, showing off more the rhythm-and-blues and dance floor side of P-Funk, drawing a contrast with the more heady Funkadelic. The Clinton–Collins–Worrell writing team penned hit after hit in the heyday of P-Funk, which is evinced most consistently with the Parliament discography. Parliament's success is a key reason for P-Funk's continued existence to the present day.

Invictus Records

Osmium

"I Call My Baby Pussycat"

Vocals: Calvin Simon, Fuzzy Haskins, Ray Davis, George Clinton, Grady Thomas
Drums: Tiki Fulwood
Bass: Billy Nelson
Guitars: Eddie Hazel, Tawl Ross
Keyboards: Bernie Worrell

"I Call My Baby Pussycat" featured classic Parliament vocal swapping along with the original Funkadelic rhythm section. Osmium would be the first of many Parliament albums and is by far the most genre bending. The sound of this single was already indicative of what most would consider the Parliafunkadelicment sound.

"Put Love in Your Life"

Lead Vocals: George Clinton, Ray Davis, Fuzzy Haskins
Backup Vocals: Calvin Simon, Grady Thomas, Ruth Copeland, Pat Lewis, Diane Lewis, Rose Williams
Drums: Tiki Fulwood
Bass: Billy Nelson
Guitars: Eddie Hazel, Ray Monette
Organ: Bernie Worrell

"Put Love in Your Life" would be the first of several songs George Clinton would write that would have extremely varied stylistic genre and time changes (another notable one would be "Mixmaster Suite" some 16 years later). The song features some of the Parliaments' most beautiful vocal swaps and some more psychedelia from the Funkadelics.

"Little Ole Country Boy"

Lead Vocals: Fuzzy Haskins
Backup Vocals: George Clinton, Grady Thomas, Calvin Simon, Ruth Copeland
Drums: Tiki Fulwood
Acoustic Guitar: Tawl Ross
Steel Guitar: Paul Franklin
Juice Harp: James Wesley Jackson
Keyboards: Bernie Worrell
Fiddle: Unknown

"Little Old Country Boy" is considered by many P-Funk fans to be among the strangest songs in the P-Funk canon. A straight country-and-western tune with hilarious lyrics recited by Fuzzy Haskins (with the Parliaments backing him up), "Little Old Country Boy" is one of several songs from both *Osmium* and other P-Funk albums that showcase P-Funk's "yokel" side.

"Moonshine Heather (Takin Care of Business)"

Lead Vocals: George Clinton
Backup Vocals: Grady Thomas, Calvin Simon, Fuzzy Haskins, Tawl Ross
Drums: Tiki Fulwood
Organ: Bernie Worrell
Bass: Billy Nelson
Guitars: Eddie Hazel, Tawl Ross

"Oh Lord, Why Lord/Prayer"

Lead Vocals: Calvin Simon
Backup Vocals: Tommy Whitfield Singers
Harpsichord, Organ, Piano: Bernie Worrell
Harp: Detroit Symphony Orchestra
Acoustic Guitar: Eddie Hazel
Timpani: Detroit Symphony Orchestra

"My Automobile"

Lead Vocals: George Clinton, Fuzzy Haskins
Backup Vocals: Calvin Simon, Grady Thomas
Drums: Tiki Fulwood
Bass: Billy Nelson
Guitars: Eddie Hazel, Tawl Ross
Piano, Keyboards: Bernie Worrell

"There Is Nothing before Me but Thang"

Lead Vocals: George Clinton, Calvin Simon, Fuzzy Haskins, Ray Davis, Billy Nelson
Backup Vocals: George Clinton, Grady Thomas, Billy Nelson, Calvin Simon, Ray Davis, Fuzzy Haskins
Drums: Tiki Fulwood
Bass: Billy Nelson
Guitars: Eddie Hazel, Tawl Ross
Keyboards: Bernie Worrell

"Funky Woman"

Lead Vocals: George Clinton
Backup Vocals: Fuzzy Haskins, Grady Thomas, Calvin Simon, Ray Davis
Drums: Tiki Fulwood
Organ: Bernie Worrell

Guitar: Eddie Hazel
Bass: Billy Nelson

"Livin' the Life"

Lead Vocals: Calvin Simon
Backup Vocals: Ruth Copeland, Grady Thomas, George Clinton, Fuzzy Haskins, Ray Davis, Billy Nelson
Piano: Bernie Worrell
Guitar: Ray Monette
Drums: Tiki Fulwood
Acoustic Guitar: Eddie Hazel
Bass: Billy Nelson

"The Silent Boatman"

Lead Vocals: Jeffery Bowen
Backup Vocals: Calvin Simon, George Clinton, Grady Thomas, Fuzzy Haskins, Ray Davis, Ruth Copeland, Tommy Whitfield Singers
Acoustic Guitar: Ray Monette
Organ: Bernie Worrell
Drums: Tiki Fulwood
Bass: Billy Nelson
Harp: Detroit Symphony Orchestra
Bagpipes: Detroit Symphony Orchestra

"Red Hot Mama"

Lead Vocals: George Clinton
Backup Vocals: Pat Lewis, Diane Lewis, Rose Williams
Guitars: Eddie Hazel
Keyboards: Bernie Worrell
Drums, Percussion: Tiki Fulwood
Bass: Billy Nelson

"Come in Out of the Rain"

Lead Vocals: Clyde Wilson
Backup Vocals: Pat Lewis, Diane Lewis, Rose Williams, Ruth Copeland?
Drums: Tiki Fulwood
Bass: Billy Nelson
Piano: Bernie Worrell
Guitar: Eddie Hazel, Tawl Ross

"Breakdown"

Lead Vocals: Clyde Wilson
Backup Vocals: George Clinton, Calvin Simon, Grady Thomas, Fuzzy Haskins, Ray Davis
Drums: Tiki Fulwood
Bass: Billy Nelson
Guitar: Eddie Hazel, Tawl Ross
Piano: Bernie Worrell

"Fantasy Is Reality"

Lead Vocals: Fuzzy Haskins, Ernie Harris
Backup Vocals: Pat Lewis, Diane Lewis, Rose Williams
Drums: Tiki Fulwood
Bass: Billy Nelson
Guitars: Eddie Hazel, Tawl Ross
Keyboards: Bernie Worrell

"Loose Booty"

Lead Vocals: George Clinton
Drums: Tiki Fulwood
Bass: Billy Nelson
Guitar: Eddie Hazel, Tawl Ross
Organ, Piano, Keyboards, Xylophone: Bernie Worrell

"Unfinished Instrumental"

Drums: Tiki Fulwood
Bass: Billy Nelson
Guitar: Eddie Hazel
Piano: Bernie Worrell

Unreleased
(recorded the same time as *Osmium*)

"Eddie's Home: There's a Chariot Coming"

Drums: Tiki Fulwood
Bass: Billy Nelson
Guitars: Eddie Hazel, Tawl Ross
Organ: Bernie Worrell

"I Ain't Got Nobody"

Drums: Tiki Fulwood
Bass, Lead Vocals: Billy Nelson
Guitars: Eddie Hazel, Tawl Ross
Keyboards: Bernie Worrell
Backup Vocals: Eddie Hazel, Tawl Ross

"As Good As I Think I Can Feel"

Lead Vocals: Billy Nelson
Backup Vocals: Pat Lewis, Diane Lewis, Rose Williams
Drums: Tiki Fulwood
Bass: Billy Nelson
Guitars: Eddie Hazel, Tawl Ross
Piano: Bernie Worrell

"Common Law Wife"

Lead Vocals: George Clinton
Backup Vocals: Grady Thomas, Calvin Simon, Fuzzy Haskins, George Clinton
Drums: Tyrone Lampkin
Bass: Cordell Mosson
Guitar: Garry Shider, Harold Beane
Trumpet: Ronnie Greenaway, Chicken Gunnells
Sax: Randy Wallace
Keyboards: Bernie Worrell

Casablanca Records

Up for the Downstroke

"Up for the Downstroke"

Lead Vocals: George Clinton, Fuzzy Haskins, Eddie Hazel
Backup Vocals: Bootsy Collins, Garry Shider, Mallia Franklin, Ray Davis, Pat Lewis, Sidney Barnes
Drums: Tiki Fulwood
Party Whistle: ?
Bass: Bootsy Collins
Guitar: Eddie Hazel
Clavinet: Bernie Worrell
Trumpet: Detroit Musicians
Sax, Trombone: Detroit Musicians

"Up for the Downstroke" would be the first P-Funk song to chart since "I Wanna Testify." It firmly places Parliament on the dance floor as a more horn-dominated sound than the grungy rock and thematic, sometimes chaotic sounds of typical Funkadelic of the preceding period.

"Testify"

Lead Vocals: George Clinton
Backup Vocals: Garry Shider, Eddie Hazel, Calvin Simon, Grady Thomas, Ray Davis, Fuzzy Haskins
Clavinet: Bernie Worrell
Guitar: Eddie Hazel
Drums: Tiki Fulwood
Bass: Cordell Mosson
Trumpet, Sax, Trombone: Detroit Musicians

"Testify," without the "(I Wanna)," was a remake of the Parliaments' classic single. George Clinton had stated in an interview that he wanted to redo it because so many of the Parliaments' songs of the Revilot period featured them using a Dylanesque style of vocals, mostly on the endings of vocal phrases, as the idea was in vogue in Detroit at the time. Motown Classics like "Bernadette" by the Four Tops cemented the idea of approaching rhythm and blues with a Dylan vocal inflection added on top. However, it was now seven years later (1974), and musical landscapes had changed; Clinton's music world itself had changed even more so than the previously mentioned ones, and he wanted to do these songs with possibly more original intentions or evolved ones. The result is a transcendent combination of both; it is part of what makes the remakes of previously existing songs in the canon just as authentic and historically important as the originals themselves.

"The Goose"

Lead Vocals: George Clinton
Backup Vocals: Fuzzy Haskins, Calvin Simon, Grady Thomas, Ray Davis
Drums, Percussion: George Clinton, Bernie Worrell, Man in the Box
Bass: Cordell Mosson
Guitar: Eddie Hazel
Organ: Bernie Worrell

"I Can Move You (If You Let Me)"

Lead Vocals: Garry Shider
Backup Vocals: Calvin Simon, George Clinton, Pat Lewis
Drums: Tiki Fulwood
Bass: Bootsy Collins, Cordell Mosson
Guitar: Garry Shider, Bootsy Collins
Electric Piano: Bernie Worrell
Trumpet, Sax, Trombone: Detroit Musicians

"I Just Got Back"

Lead Vocals: George Clinton
Whistling: Peter Chase
Drums: Frosty
Bass: Jimmy Calhoun
Acoustic Guitar: Peter Chase
Piano: Leon Patillo

"All Your Goodies Are Gone"

Lead Vocals: George Clinton
Backup Vocals: Calvin Simon, Grady Thomas, Fuzzy Haskins
Drums: Tiki Fulwood
Bass: Cordell Mosson
Piano, Electric Piano: Bernie Worrell
Guitar: Garry Shider

"All Your Goodies Are Gone" is a remake that possibly outranks the original, with George Clinton extolling a singular character in wispy falsetto that outshined others on an album replete with the style. Bernie Worrell's piano work is among his best, and Cordell Mosson's bass line in the intro is extremely infectious. The trademark pocket and feel is none other than original Funkadelic drummer Tiki Fulwood.

"Whatever Makes Baby Feel Good"

Lead Vocals: George Clinton
Backup Vocals: Eddie Hazel, Garry Shider
Drums: Man in the Box, Tyrone Lampkin
Piano: Bernie Worrell
Bass: Cordell Mosson
Guitar: Eddie Hazel

"Presence of a Brain"

Lead Vocals: Garry Shider
Backup Vocals: Calvin Simon
Drums: Man in the Box
Bass: Calvin Simon
Clavinet, Organ: Bernie Worrell

Chocolate City

"Chocolate City"

Lead Vocals: George Clinton
Backup Vocals: Garry Shider, Mudbone Cooper, Mallia Franklin, Bootsy Collins
Drums: Man in the Box
Bass, Guitar: Bootsy Collins
Piano: Bernie Worrell
Sax: John Brumbach

"Chocolate City" was one of the most socially conscious of Parliament's singles, touching on the accession of African Americans to the highest ranks of American governmental offices and the like, including the presidency itself, something that George Clinton would touch on 33 years before it saw actual fruition. The song was ahead of its time thematically, musically, and, most of all, lyrically.

"Ride On"

Lead Vocals: George Clinton
Backup Vocals: Garry Shider, Mallia Franklin, Mudbone Cooper, Bootsy Collins
Drums, Bass: Bootsy Collins
Guitar: Garry Shider, Bootsy Collins
Clavinet: Bernie Worrell
Trumpet, Sax: Detroit Horn Section

"Ride On" was in the same vein as "Downstroke," but it had a slightly more "fuzzed-up" feel. Indeed, the song began a dance funk craze within the P-Funk canon that is all over the *Chocolate City* album. Bootsy is a big part of the rhythm section on this cut.

"Together"

Lead Vocals: Mudbone Cooper, Garry Shider
Backup Vocals: George Clinton, Bootsy Collins, Mallia Franklin
Drums, Bass: Bootsy Collins
Guitar: Catfish Collins
Clavinet: Bernie Worrell
Trumpet, Sax: Detroit Horn Section

"Side Effects"

Lead Vocals: George Clinton, Ray Davis
Backup Vocals: Pat Lewis, Diane Lewis, Rose Williams
Drums: Cordell Mosson
Bass: Bootsy Collins
Guitar: Garry Shider, Bootsy Collins
Clavinet: Bernie Worrell
Trumpet, Sax: Detroit Horn Section

"What Comes Funky"

Lead Vocals: George Clinton
Backup Vocals: Pat Lewis, Diane Lewis, Rose Williams, George Clinton
Drums: Gary Mudbone Cooper
Bass: Bootsy Collins
Piano: Bernie Worrell
Guitar: Bootsy Collins, Garry Shider
Trumpet, Sax: Detroit Horn Section

"Let Me Be"

Lead Vocals: Eddie Hazel
Backup Vocals: Ray Davis
All Keyboards, Piano, Strings: Bernie Worrell

"If It Don't Fit (Don't Force It)"

Lead Vocals: Eddie Hazel, Garry Shider
Backup Vocals: Eddie Hazel, George Clinton, Garry Shider
Drums: Tyrone Lampkin
Bass: Cordell Mosson
Guitar: Eddie Hazel, Garry Shider
Clavinet: Bernie Worrell

"I Misjudged You"

Lead Vocals: George Clinton, Calvin Simon
Backup Vocals: Fuzzy Haskins, Grady Thomas, Ray Davis
Drums: Tyrone Lampkin
Piano, Keyboards: Bernie Worrell
Strings, Woodwinds: Toronto Strings
Bass: Prkash John
Guitar: Garry Shider

"Big Footin'"

Lead Vocals: Glenn Goins
Backup Vocals: Ray Davis, Mallia Franklin, Debbie Wright, George Clinton, Garry Shider
Drums: Tyrone Lampkin or Fuzzy Haskins
Bass: Cordell Mosson
Guitar: Garry Shider
Keyboards: Bernie Worrell

Mothership Connection

"P.Funk (Wants to Get Funked Up)"

Lead Vocals: George Clinton
Backup Vocals: Mudbone Cooper, Glenn Goins, Garry Shider, Sidney Barnes, Taka Boom
Drums: Mudbone Cooper
Bass: Bootsy Collins
Piano, Strings: Bernie Worrell
Guitar: Garry Shider
Trombone: Fred Wesley
Sax: Michael Brecker, Maceo Parker, Joe Farrell
Trumpet: Randy Brecker

"P.Funk (Wants to Get Funked Up)," often surnamed "Make My Funk the P-Funk," is possibly the most important anthem of purpose—or at least the most significant treatise on the genre we know today as P-Funk. It solidified the intentions through George Clinton's wicked early DJ-style rap; Bootsy Collins's liquid space bass; Bernie Worrell's classically dipped phrases and chords; Garry Shider's consistent, rhythmic guitar strokes; the Horny Horns (fresh from the James Brown camp); and the Brecker Brothers' jazzy horn swells and the classic adage used therein: "Make my funk the P-Funk. I wants to get funked up."

"Mothership Connection (Star Child)"

Lead Vocals: George Clinton, Glenn Goins
Backup Vocals: George Clinton, Glenn Goins, Garry Shider, Mudbone Cooper, Bootsy Collins, Taka Boom, Rasputin Boutte, Bryna Chimenti, and Archie Ivy
Drums: Mudbone Cooper
Bass: Bootsy Collins
Keyboards, Synthesizers: Bernie Worrell
Guitar: Garry Shider, Glenn Goins
Trombone: Fred Wesley
Sax: Maceo Parker, Michael Brecker
Trumpet: Randy Brecker

"Mothership Connection (Star Child)" is the beginning of the phase of science fiction madness coming from the innovative brain of George Clinton. This song is another great example from the Clinton-Collins-Worrell writing team, and the "Swing Down Sweet Chariot" section is among P-Funk's most well-known moments and the most sampled. Dr. Dre won a Grammy using this section to create a new song called "Let Me Ride."

"Unfunky U.F.O."

Lead Vocals: Glenn Goins, George Clinton
Backup Vocals: Garry Shider, Glenn Goins, George Clinton, Mudbone Cooper
Drums: Jerome Brailey
Bass: Bootsy Collins
Guitar: Garry Shider
Synthesizers: Bernie Worrell
Trombone: Fred Wesley
Sax: Maceo Parker, Michael Brecker
Trumpet: Randy Brecker

"Supergroovalisticprosifunkstication (The Thumps Bump)"

Lead Vocals: Ray Davis, George Clinton, Glenn Goins

Backup Vocals: Glenn Goins, Garry Shider, Mudbone Cooper, Mallia Franklin, Debbie Wright

Drums: Gary Mudbone Cooper

Percussion: Gary Mudbone Cooper, Bootsy Collins

Bass: Bootsy Collins

Synthesizers, Piano: Bernie Worrell

Guitar: Glenn Goins, Garry Shider

"Handcuffs"

Lead Vocals: Glenn Goins, George Clinton

Backup Vocals: Garry Shider, Mudbone Cooper, Taka Boom, Glenn Goins, George Clinton, Mallia Franklin

Drums: Tiki Fulwood

Bass: Cordell Mosson

Guitar: Michael Hampton, Garry Shider, Glenn Goins

Keyboards: Bernie Worrell

Trombone: Fred Wesley

Sax: Michael Brecker, Maceo Parker

Trumpets: Randy Brecker

"Give Up the Funk (Tear the Roof Off the Sucker)"

Vocals: Ray Davis, George Clinton, Garry Shider, Glenn Goins, Mudbone Cooper, Jeannette Washington, Debbie Wright, Sidney Barnes, Taka Boom

Drums: Jerome Brailey

Bass: Bootsy Collins

Synth Strings: Bernie Worrell

Guitar: Garry Shider, Bootsy Collins

Trombone: Fred Wesley

Sax: Maceo Parker, Michael Brecker

Trumpet: Randy Brecker

"Give Up the Funk (Tear the Roof Off the Sucker)" did not hit the top of the rhythm-and-blues charts, but it was among the first (if not the first) P-Funk song to hit the pop charts. Indeed, many casual music listeners who are unindoctrinated with the subject matter still know the classic "We want the funk" chant in the main section of this song.

"Night of the Thumpasaurus Peoples"

Vocals: Ray Davis, George Clinton, Mudbone Cooper, Garry Shider, Sidney Barnes, Debbie Wright, Jeannette Washington, Grady Thomas, Fuzzy Haskins, Calvin Simon, Glenn Goins

Drums: Mudbone Cooper

Bass: Bootsy Collins

Guitar: Garry Shider

Synthesizers, Keyboards: Bernie Worrell

Trombone: Fred Wesley

Sax: Maceo Parker, Michael Brecker

Trumpet: Randy Brecker

Unreleased (slated for the *Mothership Connection* album)

"Live Up"

Lead Vocals: Glenn Goins

Backup Vocals: Garry Shider, Calvin Simon, Grady Thomas, Fuzzy Haskins, George Clinton, Pat Lewis, Telma Hopkins, Joyce Vincent

Drums: Jerome Brailey

Bass: Cordell Mosson

Guitar: Garry Shider

Keyboards, Strings: Bernie Worrell

Trombone: Fred Wesley

Sax: Maceo Parker

Trumpet: Richard Griffith, Rick Gardner

The Clones of Dr. Funkenstein

"Prelude"

Lead Vocals: George Clinton

Backup Vocals: Mudbone Cooper

Keyboards, Strings: Bernie Worrell

Percussion: Mudbone Cooper, George Clinton

"Gamin' on Ya"

Vocals: Glenn Goins, Garry Shider, Mudbone Cooper, Cordell Mosson, George Clinton, Taka Boom
Drums: Jerome Brailey
Bass: Bootsy Collins
Guitar: Garry Shider, Bootsy Collins
Keyboards: Bernie Worrell
Trombone: Fred Wesley
Sax: Maceo Parker, Michael Brecker
Trumpet: Richard Griffith, Rick Gardner, Randy Brecker

"Dr. Funkenstein"

Lead Vocals: George Clinton
Backup Vocals: Mudbone Cooper, Bootsy Collins, Debbie Wright, Jeannette Washington, Garry Shider, Glenn Goins, Taka Boom
Drums: Mudbone Cooper
Bass: Bootsy Collins
Guitar: Garry Shider, Glenn Goins
Synthesizers, Piano: Bernie Worrell
Trombone: Fred Wesley
Sax: Maceo Parker
Trumpet: Richard Griffith, Rick Gardner

"Dr. Funkenstein" adds a bit of "monster movie" lore into the already fantastical sci-fi trappings of Parliament, shifting the focus even more on character development and storylines. *The Clones of Dr. Funkenstein* would see the beginning of character-driven tunes that would soon feature "Bootzilla," "Sir Nose D'VoidofFunk," "Mr. Wiggles," "Uncle Jam," and many others.

"Children of Production"

Lead Vocals: George Clinton, Glenn Goins
Backup Vocals: Garry Shider, Mudbone Cooper, Jeannette Washington, Debbie Wright, Ray Davis, Grady Thomas, Calvin Simon, George Clinton, Glenn Goins, Taka Boom
Drums: Jerome Brailey

Bass: Bootsy Collins
Guitar: Bootsy Collins, Garry Shider
Synth Strings: Bernie Worrell
Trombone: Fred Wesley
Sax: Maceo Parker
Trumpet: Richard Griffith, Rick Gardner

"Children of Production" features Parliament closely within the grasp of a dizzying height of creative input from all. Vastly appealing sounds were spinning over the edifices of this song. The vocal section is delightful to recite and became a heralded a cappella chant when the song was done live. The album version has really intricate rhythm and horn work with special mention to Bootsy, Garry Shider, Bernie Worrell, and the Horny Horns (Fred Wesley, Maceo Parker, Richard "Kush" Griffith, and Rick Gardner), especially on the outro section.

"Getten' to Know You"

Lead Vocals: Garry Shider
Backup Vocals: Cordell Mosson, Glenn Goins, George Clinton, Mudbone Cooper, Taka Boom
Drums: Cordell Mosson
Bass, Guitar: Garry Shider
Piano, Strings: Bernie Worrell
Trombone: Fred Wesley
Sax: Michael Brecker, Maceo Parker
Trumpet: Richard Griffith, Rick Gardner

"Do That Stuff"

Lead Vocals: George Clinton, Glenn Goins, Garry Shider
Backup Vocals: Taka Boom, Mudbone Cooper, Ray Davis
Drums: Jerome Brailey
Bass: Cordell Mosson
Electric Piano: Bernie Worrell
Guitar: Garry Shider, Michael Hampton
Trombone: Fred Wesley
Sax: Maceo Parker
Trumpet: Rick Gardner, Richard Griffith

"Do That Stuff" was the biggest hit on the *Clones of Dr. Funkenstein* album and features classic Parliament lead vocal swapping by George Clinton and guitarists Garry Shider and Glenn Goins. It also features a classic riff that had already been used in "You Can't Miss What You Can't Measure" by Funkadelic. This process of recycling riffs and lyrics and altering the arrangements would be employed by P-Funk many times in its history.

"Everything Is on the One"

Vocals: George Clinton, Garry Shider, Glenn Goins, Cordell Mosson, Mudbone Cooper, Taka Boom
Drums: Bootsy Collins
Bass: Cordell Mosson
Guitars: Bootsy Collins, Garry Shider
Synthesizers, Strings: Bernie Worrell
Trombone: Fred Wesley
Sax: Michael Brecker, Maceo Parker
Trumpets: Randy Brecker, Richard Griffith, Rick Gardner

"I've Been Watching You (Move Your Sexy Body)"

Lead Vocals: Glenn Goins
Backup Vocals: George Clinton, Garry Shider, Mudbone Cooper, Cordell Mosson, Taka Boom
Drums, Bass: Cordell Mosson
Guitars: Garry Shider, Glenn Goins
Electric Piano: Bernie Worrell
Sax: Michael Brecker
Trumpet: Randy Brecker, Richard Griffith, Rick Gardner
Trombone: Fred Wesley

"Funkin' for Fun"

Lead Vocals: Glenn Goins
Backup Vocals: Garry Shider, George Clinton, Mudbone Cooper, Cordell Mosson, Taka Boom
Drums: Jerome Brailey
Bass: Cordell Mosson
Guitar: Michael Hampton, Garry Shider

Electric Piano: Bernie Worrell
Trombone: Fred Wesley
Sax: Michael Brecker, Maceo Parker
Trumpet: Randy Brecker, Richard Griffith, Rick Gardner

"Funkin' for Fun" was one of vocalist Glenn Goin's most well-known offerings to the P-Funk camp. In the heyday of the Mothership Tour, this would be the encore at many shows.

Studio tracks from *Parliament Live: P-Funk Earth Tour*

"This Is the Way We Funk with You"

Lead Vocals: Glenn Goins
Backup Vocals: Lynn Mabry, Dawn Silva, George Clinton, Garry Shider, Ray Davis
Snore: Michael Hampton
Drums: Gary Mudbone Cooper
Bass: Bootsy Collins
Guitar: Eddie Hazel
Keyboards, Synthesizer: Bernie Worrell

"Fantasy Is Reality"

Lead Vocals: Glenn Goins
Backup Vocals: Bernie Worrell, Dawn Silva, Lynn Mabry
Drums, Bass: Cordell Mosson
Guitar: Eddie Hazel
Piano: Bernie Worrell

Funkentelechy Vs. The Placebo Syndrome

"Bop Gun"

Lead Vocals: Glenn Goins
Backup Vocals: Jeannette Washington, Debbie Wright, Mallia Franklin, Lynn Mabry, Dawn Silva, Garry Shider, Glenn Goins, Gary Mudbone Cooper, George Clinton
Drums, Bass: Bootsy Collins
Guitar: Garry Shider, Glenn Goins

Parliament-Funkadelic's Glenn Goins and Garry Shider. © Diem Jones

Piano, Strings: Bernie Worrell
Clavinet: Joel Johnson
Trombone: Fred Wesley
Sax: Maceo Parker
Trumpet: Richard Griffith, Rick Gardner

"Bop Gun" has a classic guitar harmony intro, Glenn Goins lead vocal gospel gymnastics, and raw energy. It begins the concept of the massively successful *Funkentelechy Vs. The Placebo Syndrome* album. Of all the songs on the list, this one had the most debate between primary sources and secondary sources as to personnel. According to an interview with another musicologist, Bootsy Collins had allegedly stated that "Bop Gun" and "Sir Nose D'VoidofFunk" featured Frankie "Kash" Waddy on drums. However, both George Clinton and Gary Mudbone Cooper attest to Bootsy himself being the drummer (as he was on many records on this album) and Mudbone being the drummer on "Sir Nose." Garry Shider and Glenn Goins have been universally accepted as the guitarists on this album, but there had also been attestations in secondhand sources of

Cordell "Boogie" Mosson and Ricky Rouse being on guitar on this record, though there is no tangible primary source information to attest to this.

"Sir Nose D'VoidofFunk (Pay Attention-B3M)"

Lead Vocals: George Clinton
Backup Vocals: Glenn Goins, Cordell Mosson, Ray Davis, Debbie Wright, Jeannette Washington, Mallia Franklin, Garry Shider, Lynn Mabry, Dawn Silva, Linda Shider
Drums: Gary Mudbone Cooper
Bass: Bootsy Collins
Guitar: Garry Shider, Glenn Goins
Clavinet, Synthesizers, Strings: Bernie Worrell
Trombone: Clayton Lawrey
Sax: Darryl Dixon
Trumpet: Danny Cortez, Valerie Drayton

"Wizard of Finance"

Lead Vocals: George Clinton
Backup Vocals: Glenn Goins, Mudbone Cooper, Garry Shider
Drums, Bass: Cordell Mosson
Guitar: Garry Shider
Synthesizers: Bernie Worrell
Sax: Maceo Parker
Trombone: Fred Wesley
Trumpet: Richard Griffith, Rick Gardner

"Funkentelechy"

Lead Vocals: George Clinton
Backup Vocals: Glenn Goins, Ray Davis, Garry Shider, Cordell Mosson, Mudbone Cooper, Mallia Franklin, Dawn Silva, Lynn Mabry, Linda Shider
Drums, Bass: Bootsy Collins
Piano, Clavinet: Bernie Worrell
Guitar: Bootsy Collins, Catfish Collins, Garry Shider
Trombone: Fred Wesley
Sax: Maceo Parker
Trumpet: Richard Griffith, Rick Gardner

"Funkentelechy" is considered by most to be right in the "high-water mark" area of classic P-Funk. It features all the elements that made Parliament so popular. Before "Knee Deep," this was one of the longest-running cuts in the P-Funk canon up to this point. Later, songs like the previously mentioned ones, as well as "Never Buy Texas from a Cowboy" and several others, would surpass "Funkentelechy"'s 10-minute mark, though it remains one of the most important anthems in the band's history.

"Placebo Syndrome"

Lead Vocals: Glenn Goins
Backup Vocals: Dawn Silva, Lynn Mabry, Gary Mudbone Cooper, Linda Shider, Mallia Franklin
Drums: Gary Mudbone Cooper
Bass: Cordell Mosson
Guitar: Garry Shider
Synthesizers: Bernie Worrell
Sax: Michael Brecker, Maceo Parker
Trumpet: Randy Brecker, Richard Griffith, Rick Gardner

"Flash Light"

Lead Vocals: George Clinton
Backup Vocals: Garry Shider, Glenn Goins, Ray Davis, Gary Mudbone Cooper, Mallia Franklin, Dawn Silva, Lynn Mabry, Linda Shider
Drums: Bootsy Collins
Synth Bass, Synthesizers, Strings: Bernie Worrell
Guitar: Catfish Collins, Garry Shider, Bootsy Collins
Sax: Darryl Dixon
Handclap Boards: Carl "Butch" Small

"Flash Light" is the first #1 rhythm-and-blues hit in the Parliament-Funkadelic pantheon. The brand-new sound of Bernie Worrell's Moog synth bass, George Clinton's classic character depictions, and the loud, dense handclap sound, as well as the rhythms of the Collins brothers on guitars and drums, would make "Flash Light" an unbeatable hit in its time. Nothing sounded like it before, and although heavily copied, nothing has truly sounded quite like it since. To this day, it sounds unique on radio—a singular stand-alone in a band full of stand-alones. Incidentally, it was beaten by a week to the #1 spot by Bootsy's Rubber Band's "Bootzilla," written by Clinton and Collins, produced by Clinton, and featuring many P-Funk members. Indeed, by this period, it seems that the beginning of a "P-Funk Interregnum" was occurring on the rhythm-and-blues charts.

"Mr. Wiggles"

Lead Vocals: George Clinton
Backup Vocals: Clip Payne, Lynn Mabry, Dawn Silva, Sheila Horne, Ramon Spruell, Overton Lloyd
Drums: Tyrone Lampkin
Bass: Cordell Mosson
Guitar: Michael Hampton
Piano, Synthesizer: Bernie Worrell
Trombone: Fred Wesley
Sax: Maceo Parker
Trumpet: Richard Griffith, Rick Gardner

"Mr. Wiggles" begins the Atlantis element in the ever-expanding Parliament storyscape. The band took cues from Clinton's past success with songs like "P.Funk (Wants to Get Funked Up)." The DJ-style rap theme is again taken up, where character conceptualizations continue amid the walking bass of Cordell "Boogie" Mosson, the slick chords of Michael Hampton, and the gooey keyboards of Bernie Worrell along with the always classy Horny Horns.

"Rumpofsteelskin"

Lead Vocals: George Clinton, Garry Shider, Ray Davis
Backup Vocals: Ron Ford, Lynn Mabry, Dawn Silva, Jeannette McGruder, Sheila Horne, Mudbone Cooper, Linda Shider
Drums, Bass: Bootsy Collins
Clavinet, Synthesizers: Bernie Worrell
Guitar: Garry Shider, Bootsy Collins
Trombone: Fred Wesley
Sax: Maceo Parker
Trumpet: Richard Griffith, Rick Gardner

"Rumpofsteelskin" is to "Mr. Wiggles" as "Mothership Connection" is to "Make My Funk the P-Funk." It accompanies the DJ-infused jazz and ethereal presence of "Mr. Wiggles" with its character-based funk anthem. It features more Clinton-Collins-Worrell writing and is a continuation of the water theme.

"(You're a Fish and I'm a) Water Sign"

Lead Vocals: Junie Morrisson, George Clinton, Richard Griffith
Backup Vocals: Dawn Silva, Lynn Mabry, Ray Davis, Garry Shider, Sheila Horne, Jeanette McGruder, Greg Thomas, Ron Dunbar, Linda Shider
Drums, Bass, Keyboards, Guitar: Junie Morrison
Trumpet: Richard Griffith, Rick Gardner
Trombone: Fred Wesley
Sax: Maceo Parker

"Aqua Boogie (A Psychoalphadiscobetabioaquadoloop)"

Lead Vocals: George Clinton, Garry Shider, Junie Morrison, Ray Davis, Ron Ford
Backup Vocals: Dawn Silva, Lynn Mabry, Sheila Horne, Jeanette McGruder, Ron Brembry, Greg Thomas, Linda Shider
Drums: Mudbone Cooper
Synth Bass, Piano, Synthesizers: Bernie Worrell
Guitar: Catfish Collins, Bootsy Collins
Handclap Boards: Carl "Butch" Small

"Aqua Boogie" would be Parliament's last #1 rhythm-and-blues hit and their biggest song since "Flash Light." Bernie Worrell really goes all out here, employing the sounds of no fewer than seven synthesizers and keyboards throughout. It would be the last #1 rhythm-and-blues hit to feature the now-classic Clinton-Collins-Worrell writing team.

"One of Those Funky Thangs"

Vocals: George Clinton, Ray Davis, Lynn Mabry, Dawn Silva, Sheila Horne, Jeanette McGruder, Linda Shider
Drums: Jerry Jones
Bass: Tony Green
Percussion: Larry Fratangelo
Synth Bass, Strings, Keyboards: Bernie Worrell
Trumpet: Richard Griffith, Rick Gardner
Sax: Maceo Parker
Trombone: Fred Wesley

"Liquid Sunshine"

Lead Vocals: Garry Shider
Backup Vocals: Mudbone Cooper, Linda Shider, George Clinton, Bernie Worrell, Dawn Silva, Lynn Mabry, Mallia Franklin, Jeanette Washington
Drums: Mudbone Cooper
Synth Bass, Synthesizers: Bernie Worrell
Percussion: Larry Fratangelo
Guitar: Garry Shider

"The Motor Booty Affair"

Lead Vocals, Electric Piano: Junie Morisson
Backup Vocals: George Clinton, Dawn Silva, Lynn Mabry, Jeanette McGruder, Sheila Horne, Linda Shider, Garry Shider
Drums: Tyrone Lampkin
Bass: Rodney Curtis
Guitar: Garry Shider
Keyboards: Bernie Worrell

"Deep"

Lead Vocals: Junie Morisson
Backup Vocals: Jeannette McGruder, Mallia Franklin, Sheila Horne, Dawn Silva, Lynn Mabry, Shirley Hayden, Michael Clip Payne, Cheryl James, Greg Thomas
Drums: Junie Morrison
Synth Bass, Clavinet: Junie Morrisson
Bass: Bootsy Collins

Guitar: Junie Morrison, Bootsy Collins
Trombone: Fred Wesley
Sax: Maceo Parker
Trumpet: Richard Griffith, Rick Gardner

Unreleased

"Every Booty (Get on Down)"

Vocals: Bootsy Collins, Mudbone Cooper, Maceo Parker
Drums: Frank Waddy
Bass: Bootsy Collins
Guitar: Bootsy Collins, Michael Hampton
Trombone: Fred Wesley
Keyboards, Synthesizers: Bernie Worrell
Clavinet, Organ, Sax: Maceo Parker
Trumpets: Richard Griffith, Rick Gardner
Handclap Boards, Percussion: Carl "Butch" Small

Gloryhallastoopid

"Prologue"

Vocals: George Clinton
Synthesizers: Bernie Worrell

"Gloryhallastoopid (or Pin the Tail on the Funky)"

Lead Vocals: George Clinton
Backup Vocals: Dawn Silva, Shirley Hayden, Sheila Horne, Jeanette McGruder, Lynn Mabry, Jeanette Washington, Janice Evans, Robert Peanut Johnson, Garry Shider, Richard Griffith, Ray Davis, Lige Curry, Michael Clip Payne, Linda Shider, Mallia Franklin
Drums, Guitar: Bootsy Collins
Synth Bass, Piano: Bernie Worrell
Sax: Maceo Parker
Trumpet: Larry Hatcher
Trombone: Fred Wesley

"Party People"

Vocals: George Clinton, Garry Shider, Jerome Rodgers, Ron Ford, Lige Curry, Greg Thomas, Ron Dunbar, Jeanette MacGruder, Shirley Hayden, Jeanette Washington, Ray Davis, Jessica Cleaves, Lynn Mabry, Dawn Silva, Michael Clip Payne, Sheila Horne, Andre Williams, Linda Shider
Drums: Gary Mudbone Cooper
Bass: Bootsy Collins
Guitar: Bootsy Collins, Garry Shider
Keyboards: Bernie Worrell
Sax: Greg Thomas
Handclap Boards: Carl "Butch" Small

"Party People" was the first single selected to promote on the *Gloryhallastoopid* album. It also hints at P-Funk's few and rare attempts at a more disco-type sound, something P-Funk generally felt averse to conceptually and culturally. Most notable on this song are the extremely large and very well arranged vocal section.

"The Big Bang Theory"

Lead Vocals: George Clinton, Jessica Cleaves
Drums: Kenny Colton
Percussion: Larry Fratangelo
Synthesizers: David Spradley
Synthesizers: Bernie Worrell
Guitar: Tony Thomas
Trumpet: Bennie Cowan
Sax: Greg Thomas, Sam Peakes
Trombone: Greg Boyer

"The Big Bang Theory" is almost instrumental if not for the elegant soprano melodies of Jessica Cleaves and George Clinton's (possibly) cue mic take urging the band on. It also features Larry Fratangelo's classic percussion element and a new horn section that would remain with Clinton for the next 40+ years through today.

"The Freeze (Sizzleanmean)"

Lead Vocals: George Clinton
Backup Vocals: Jeanette McGruder, Sheila Horne, Dawn Silva, Lynn Mabry, Tony LaFoot, Darryl Clinton, Andre Williams, Cuz, Stevie Pannell, Tracey Lewis, Patty Walker
Drums, Bass, Guitar: Blackbyrd McKnight
Percussion: Larry Fratangelo
Sax: Maceo Parker

"Colour Me Funky"

Lead Vocals: George Clinton, Junie Morrison, Garry Shider
Backup Vocals: Lynn Mabry, Jeanette Washington, Mallia Franklin, Shirley Hayden, Jeanette MacGruder
Drums, Synth Bass, Keyboards, Guitar: Junie Morrison

"Theme from the Black Hole"

Lead Vocals: Garry Shider, George Clinton, Ray Davis
Backup Vocals: Jessica Cleaves, Shirley Hayden, Janice Evans, Jeanette Washington, Robert Peanut Johnson, Mallia Franklin, Ron Ford, Lige Curry, Greg Thomas, Jeanette MacGruder, Sheila Horne, Dawn Silva
Drums: Bootsy Collins
Synth Bass, Strings, Keyboards: Bernie Worrell
Guitar: Junie Morrison, Gordon Carlton
Trombone: Greg Boyer
Sax: Greg Thomas
Trumpet: Bennie Cowan
Handclap Boards, Percussion: Carl "Butch" Small

The highest-charting single from the *Gloryhallastoopid* album features classic Parliament elements of vocal swapping, synth bass, heavy handclaps, and dance floor bias. It features a classic Sir Nose appearance (the traditional enemy of the Funk in Parliament storylines) right before the Big Bang at the end.

"May We Bang You?"

Lead Vocals: Robert Peanut Johnson, George Clinton, Junie Morrisson
Backup Vocals: Ron Ford, Shirley Hayden, Janice Evans, Jessica Cleaves, Mallia Franklin, Jeanette MacGruder, Sheila Horne, Jerome Rodgers, Lige Curry, Greg Thomas, Dawn Silva, Lynn Mabry, Linda Shider
Drums, Bass, Guitar, Piano, Keyboards: Junie Morrisson

Unreleased (slated for *Gloryhallastoopid*)

"Flatman & Bobin"

Lead Vocals: George Clinton
Drums: Tyrone Lampkin
Bass: Bootsy Collins
Keyboards: Bernie Worrell
Guitar: Garry Shider
Trombone: Fred Wesley
Sax: Maceo Parker
Trumpet: Richard Griffith, Rick Gardner

Trombipulation

"Crush It"

Lead Vocals: George Clinton, Bootsy Collins
Backup Vocals: Shirley Hayden, Sheila Horne, Gary Mudbone Cooper, Mallia Franklin, Donnie Sterling, Lonnie Greene, Ron Ford, Gwen Dozier, Janice Evans, Jeanette MacGruder Lige Curry, Dawn Silva
Drums, Bass, Guitar: Bootsy Collins
Piano, Synthesizers: David Spradley
Trombone: Fred Wesley
Sax: Maceo Parker
Trumpet: Larry Hatcher

"Trombipulation"

Lead Vocals: George Clinton, Garry Shider, Michael Clip Payne, Jerome Rodgers
Backup Vocals: Sidney Barnes, Ray Davis, Shirley Hayden, Robert Peanut Johnson, Andre Williams, Ron Ford, Sheila Horne, Bootsy Collins, Dawn Silva, Jeanette MacGruder, Lige Curry, Linda Shider, Mallia Franklin
Drums, Bass: Bootsy Collins
Piano, Keyboards: David Spradley
Trumpet: Larry Hatcher
Sax: Maceo Parker
Trombone: Fred Wesley

"Long Way Around"

Lead Vocals: George Clinton, Junie Morrisson, Jerome Rodgers, Garry Shider
Backup Vocals: Robert Peanut Johnson, Mallia Franklin, Jessica Cleaves, Shirley Hayden, Ron Ford, Ray Davis, Jeanette MacGruder, Sheila Horne, Janice Evans, Jeanette Washington, Dawn Silva
Piano, Synth Bass: Bernie Worrell
Drums: Bootsy Collins
Orchestra: Detroit Symphony Orchestra
Horn and String Arrangement: Tony Camillo
Horns: Michael Brecker, Randy Brecker, Detroit Symphony Orchestra Horns

"Agony of DeFeet"

Lead Vocals: Donnie Sterling, Ron Dunbar
Backup Vocals: Donnie Sterling, Ron Dunbar, Sidney Barnes, Michael Clip Payne, Lige Curry, Stevie Pannell, Patty Walker, Robert Peanut Johnson, Mallia Franklin, Andre Williams, Dawn Silva, Jeanette MacGruder, Sheila Horne, Shirley Hayden
Drums: Lonnie Greene
Percussion: Larry Fratangelo
Handclap Boards: Carl "Butch" Small
Bass: Donnie Sterling
Guitar: Tony Thomas
Synthesizers: David Spradley

"Agony of DeFeet" would be the highest-charting song on the *Trombipulation* album. It is mostly the work of Ron Dunbar, Grammy-winning Detroit songwriter, along with his usual team—bassist Donnie Sterling, drummer Lonnie Greene, and guitarist Tony Thomas—as well as new P-Funk mainstays, such as Larry Fratangelo, Carl "Butch" Small, and David Spradley. The concept deals with a very silly "Foot" theme, which would be a repeated Dunbar writing strategy, specifically with his writing tenure for P-Funk.

"New Doo Review"

Lead Vocals: George Clinton, Ron Ford, Jerome Rodgers, Mallia Franklin

Backup Vocals: Robert Peanut Johnson, Shirley Hayden, Janice Evans, Jeanette Washington, Sheila Horne, Jeanette McGruder, Dawn Silva, Gary Mudbone Cooper, Lige Curry, Greg Thomas, Linda Shider, Lee Rosenbloom

Drums: Bootsy Collins

Bass: Lige Curry

Guitar: Michael Hampton

Orchestra: Detroit Symphony Orchestra

Horns: David Taylor, Barry Taylor, Barry Rogers, Danny Cahn, David Tofani, John Mical, David Majal Li (Detroit Symphony Orchestra Horns)

Horn and String Arrangement: Tony Camillo

"Let's Play House"

Lead Vocals: Junie Morrisson, Garry Shider, Jerome Rodgers, Bootsy Collins, George Clinton

Backup Vocals: Lonnie Greene, Jeanette Washington, Shirley Hayden, Mallia Franklin, Jessica Cleaves, Pat Lewis, Jeanette MacGruder, Sheila Horne, Lige Curry, Michael Clip Payne, Robert Peanut Johnson, LuShawn Clinton

Drums: Bootsy Collins

Percussion, Electronic Drums: Carl "Butch" Small

Synth Bass, Clavinet: Bernie Worrell

Sax: Maceo Parker

Trombone: Fred Wesley

Trumpet: Richard Griffith, Larry Hatcher

Harmonica: Aaron "Little Sonny" Willis

"Let's Play House" has the classic vocals and trademark P-Funk sound that would be sampled by Digital Underground for their #1 hit "The Humpty Dance." This song is also notable for a hefty lineup of, for lack of a better word, "P-Funk All Stars," about three years before that name would ever be alluded to.

"Body Language"

Lead Vocals: George Clinton

Backup Vocals: Garry Shider, Jeanette Washington, Shirley Hayden, Jeanette McGruder, Sheila Horne, Dawn Silva, Janice Evans, Donnie Sterling, Ron Ford, Andre Williams, Lige Curry, Michael Clip Payne, Robert Peanut Johnson, Mallia Franklin

Drums: Tyrone Lampkin

Percussion: Larry Fratangelo

Synth Bass, Synthesizers: David Spradley

Guitar: Gordon Carlton

Horns: David Taylor, Barry Taylor, Barry Rogers, Danny Cahn, David Tofani, John Mical, David Majal Li

Orchestra: Detroit Symphony Orchestra

String Arrangement: Tony Camillo

"Peek-A-Groove"

Lead Vocals: Garry Shider, Lige Curry, Ron Ford, George Clinton, Mallia Franklin,
Backup Vocals: Mallia Franklin, Debbie Wright, Sheila Horne, Jeanette McGruder, Dawn Silva, Michael Clip Payne, Robert Peanut Johnson, Jerome Rodgers, Kenny Colton, Lige Curry
Drums: Kenny Colton
Bass: Jimmy Ali
Guitar: Gordon Carlton, Jerome Ali
Trumpet: Bennie Cowan, Larry Hatcher
Sax: Darryl Dixon, Greg Thomas, Maceo Parker
Keyboards: Manon Saulsby, Ernestro Wilson
Synthesizers: David Spradley
Orchestra: Detroit Symphony Orchestra
String Arrangement: Bernie Worrell

Unreleased

"Go for Yer Funk"

Lead Vocals: George Clinton, Bootsy Collins, James Brown
Drums, Bass, Guitar: Bootsy Collins
Keyboards, Strings: Bernie Worrell
Trombone: Fred Wesley
Sax: Maceo Parker
Trumpet: Richard Griffith, Rick Gardner

"Does Disc Go with D.A.T. (Simon Says)"

Lead Vocals: Lonnie Greene, Donnie Sterling, Ron Dunbar
Backup Vocals: Shirley Hayden, Sheila Horne, Jeanette McGruder, Jeanette Washington
Drums: Dennis Chambers
Bass: Donnie Sterling
Guitar: Tony Thomas
Clavinet: Ernestro Wilson, Manon Saulsby
Trombone: Fred Wesley
Trumpet: Richard Griffith, Larry Hatcher
Sax: Maceo Parker

C-Kuspyruhzy Records

Medicaid Fraud Dogg

"Medicated Creep"

Vocals: Trazae Lewis-Clinton, Mahogany Kendrick
Synth Bass, Pads, Keyboards: Trazae Lewis-Clinton
Drum Programming, Percussion, Synth Bass, Synthesizers: Junie Morrisson
Trombone: Fred Wesley
Trumpet: Gary Winters, Kirk Gavin II
Sax: Jason Mitchell, Henry White, Nyan Feder

"Psychotropic"

Vocals: Tonysha Nelson, Patavian Lewis
Drums, Bass, Organ: Rob Poole
Guitar: Rob Poole, Blackbyrd McKnight
Piano: Danny Bedrosian

"69"

Vocals: George Clinton, Mudbone Cooper, Rey Joven, Ebony Houston, Robert Peanut Johnson, Thurteen, Brandi Scott, Tonysha Nelson, Patavian Lewis, Danny Bedrosian
Keyboards, Synthesizers: Danny Bedrosian
Drum Programming: Ricky Tan
Sax: Greg Thomas
Trumpet: Bennie Cowan

"Backwoods"

Vocals: Trazae Lewis-Clinton, Mahogany Kendrick, George Clinton
Music Programming: D'Artizt
Percussion: Michael Bakan

"Oil Jones"

Vocals: George Clinton, Tracey Lewis, Tonysha Nelson, Patavian Lewis, Evangeline Young, Kathy Griffin, Brandi Scott
Drum Programming: Ricky Tan
Piano: Danny Bedrosian
Guitars, Bass: Blackbyrd McKnight

"Proof Is in the Pudding"

Vocals: Tonysha Nelson, George Clinton, Trazae Lewis-Clinton
Synthesizer: Danny Bedrosian
Guitar: Brad Foutch
Trumpet: Whitney Russell
Drum Programming: Ricky Tan

"I'm Gon Make U Sick O' Me"

Vocals: George Clinton, Mudbone Cooper, Scarface, Brandi Scott, Tonysha Nelson, Mahogany Kendrick
Drums, Synth Bass, Piano, Strings, Keyboards: Junie Morrisson
Drums, Keyboards: Michael Clip Payne
Synthesizer: Danny Bedrosian
Trumpet: Bennie Cowan
Sax: Greg Thomas
Percussion: Juan Carlos

The single from the *Medicaid Fraud Dogg* album featured George Clinton, the band, and rapper Scarface for a cameo appearance. The song is also notable for being one of Junie's last contributions on a song by the P-Funk Mob.

"Antisocial Media"

Vocals: George Clinton, Mudbone Cooper, Brandi Scott, Thaddeus Streater, Robert Peanut Johnson, Tonysha Nelson, Mahogany Kendrick
Piano: Danny Bedrosian
Trumpets: Whitney Russell
Guitars: Brad Foutch
Drum Programming: Ricky Tan

"All In"

Vocals: George Clinton, Tonysha Nelson, Rey Joven, Mahogany Kendrick, Mudbone Cooper, Robert Peanut Johnson, Brandi Scott, Ebony Houston
Electric Piano, Synth Bass, Synthesizer: Danny Bedrosian
Bass Guitar: Logan McKnight
Drum Programming: Ricky Tan

"On Fire"

Vocals: George Clinton, Tonysha Nelson, Rey Joven, Mahogany Kendrick
Instrumental Programming: Gentry Gallmon
Drum Programming: Ricky Tan
Trumpets: Whitney Russell

"Loodie Poo Da Pimp"

Vocals: Tracey Lewis, Mahogany Kendrick, George Clinton, Thurteen, Mudbone Cooper, Tonysha Nelson, Brandi Scott
Synth Bass, Sound Effects, Synthesizers: David Spradley
Drum Programming: Ricky Tan
Trumpets: Whitney Russell

"Mama Told Me"

Vocals: Bouvier Richardson, George Clinton, Thurteen
Drum and Music Programming: Kendrick Harmon
Strings, Synthesizers: Danny Bedrosian
Drums: Benzel Cowan
Bass: Lige Curry
Guitar: Blackbyrd McKnight

"Set Trip"

Vocals: Tracey Lewis, George Clinton, Mahogany Kendrick, Mudbone Cooper, Gentry Gallmon, Tonysha Nelson, Brandi Scott
Trombone: Fred Wesley
Trumpet: Gary Winters, Kirk Gavin II
Sax: Jason Mitchell, Henry White, Nyan Feder
Drums: Chris Dave
Guitar, Bass, Drums: Blackbyrd McKnight
Keyboards: Danny Bedrosian, Amp Fiddler

"Kool Aid"

Vocals: Trazae Lewis-Clinton, George Clinton, Brandi Scott, Chris Revere, Bouvier Richardson, Robert Peanut Johnson, Mahogany Kendrick
Music Programming: Tmix
Trumpet: Jamelle Adisa
Sax: Reginald Paul
Trombone: J. P. Floyd

"Dada"

Vocals: George Clinton, Mudbone Cooper, Brandi Scott, Trazae Lewis-Clinton, Robert Peanut Johnson, Danny Bedrosian
Piano, Synthesizer: Danny Bedrosian
Trombone: Fred Wesley
Trumpet: Gary Winters, Kirk Gavin II
Sax: Jason Mitchell, Henry White, Nyan Feder
Guitar: Corey Stoot
Bass: Kendrick Thomas
Drum Programming: Ricky Tan
Drums: Savar Martin, Chris Dave

"Pain Management"

Vocals: George Clinton, Tracey Lewis, Mudbone Cooper, Tonysha Nelson, Patavian Lewis, Brandi Scott, Carlon Clinton, Mahogany Kendrick
Keyboards, Synthesizers: Danny Bedrosian
Trombone: Fred Wesley
Sax: Pee Wee Ellis
Trumpet: Whitney Russell
Music Programming: G Koop

"Riddle Me This"

Vocals: Tracey Lewis, Trazae Lewis-Clinton, George Clinton, Garry Shider, Tonysha Nelson, Patavian Lewis, Ricky Tan, Brandi Scott, Rob Manzoli, Sue Brooks, Jerome Rodgers
Instrumentation: Rob Manzoli and Sue Brooks
Trumpet: Bennie Cowan
Sax: Greg Thomas

Trombone: Lloyd Jones
Keyboards: Danny Bedrosian

"No Mos"

Vocals: George Clinton, Bouvier Richardson, Brandi Scott, Steve Arrington
Guitar, Bass, Drums: Blackbyrd McKnight
Synthesizer: Danny Bedrosian
Sound Effects: Ricky Tan

"Ya Habit"

Vocals: Tracey Lewis, George Clinton, Mudbone Cooper, Brandi Scott, Mahogany Kendrick, Tonysha Nelson
Trumpet: Bennie Cowan
Sax: Greg Thomas
Trombone: Lloyd Jones

"Higher"

Vocals: Kendra Foster, Mudbone Cooper, George Clinton, Brandi Scott, Robert Peanut Johnson, Rey Joven, Mahogany Kendrick
Electric Piano, Synthesizer: Danny Bedrosian
Trombone: Fred Wesley
Trumpet: Gary Winters, Kirk Gavin II
Sax: Jason Mitchell, Henry White, Nyan Feder
Guitar: Brad Foutch
Snare Drum: Quaze
Bass Guitar: Logan McKnight
Drum Programming: Ricky Tan

"Medicaid Fraud Dogg"

Vocals: George Clinton, Ebony Houston, Tonysha Nelson, Patavian Lewis, Robert Peanut Johnson, Tracey Lewis, Mudbone Cooper, Brandi Scott, Thurteen, Big T
Piano, Electric Piano, Strings: Danny Bedrosian
Trombone: Fred Wesley
Sax: Pee Wee Ellis
Trumpet: Whitney Russell
Percussion: Michael Bakan
Drum Programming, Guitar, Synthesizer, Bass: G Koop

"Insurance Man"

Vocals: George Clinton, Trazae Lewis-Clinton, Bethany Schmitt, Mahogany Kendrick
Electric Piano: Anthony Brice
Synthesizer, Strings: Danny Bedrosian
Guitar: Brad Foutch
Drum Programming: Ricky Tan

"Type Two"

Vocals: George Clinton, Michael Clip Payne, Brandi Scott, Mudbone Cooper, Robert Peanut Johnson, Tonysha Nelson, Trazae Lewis-Clinton, Garrett Shider
Synth Bass, Synthesizers, Keyboards: Danny Bedrosian
Bass: Hunter Daws
Drum Programming: Ricky Tan
Guitar: Brad Foutch
Trombone: Fred Wesley
Trumpet: Gary Winters, Kirk Gavin II
Sax: Jason Mitchell, Henry White, Nyan Feder
Percussion: Michael Bakan

"First Ya Gotta Shake the Gate"
Medley Live

Vocals: George Clinton, Trazae Lewis-Clinton, Tracey Lewis, Patavian Lewis, Tonysha Nelson, Brandi Scott, Thurteen, Michael Clip Payne, Bouvier Richardson, Garrett Shider
Clavinet, Piano, Strings, Electric Piano, Synthesizers, Synth Bass, Pads: Danny Bedrosian
Drums: Benzel Cowan
Bass: Lige Curry
Guitar: Blackbyrd McKnight, Trafael Lewis, Garrett Shider

— ☆ —

RUTH COPELAND: 1970–1972

Invictus Records

Self Portrait

"Prologue/Child of the North"

Vocals, Acoustic Guitar: Ruth Copeland
Orchestra: Detroit Symphony Orchestra
Bass: Billy Nelson
Piano: Bernie Worrell

"Thanks for the Birthday Card"

Vocals, Acoustic Guitar: Ruth Copeland
Orchestra: Detroit Symphony Orchestra
Bass: Bob Babbitt
Guitar: Dennis Coffey, Ray Monette
Drums: Andrew Smith
Keyboards: Bernie Worrell

"Your Love Been So Good to Me"

Vocals: Ruth Copeland
Drums: Tiki Fulwood
Guitar: Eddie Hazel, Tawl Ross
Keyboards: Bernie Worrell
Bass: Billy Nelson

"The Music Box"

Lead Vocals, Acoustic Guitar: Ruth Copeland
Orchestra: Detroit Symphony Orchestra
Backup Vocals: Ruth Copeland, the Choraliers
Drums: Tiki Fulwood
Guitar: Ray Monette, Dennis Coffey
Piano: Bernie Worrell
Bass: Bob Babbitt

"The Silent Boatman"

Lead Vocals: Ruth Copeland
Backup Vocals: Ruth Copeland, the Choraliers
Acoustic Guitar: Tawl Ross, Ruth Copeland
Organ: Bernie Worrell
Drums: Tiki Fulwood
Bass: Billy Nelson
Orchestra: Detroit Symphony Orchestra

"To William in the Night"

Lead Vocals: Ruth Copeland
Drums: Andrew Smith
Bass: Bob Babbitt
Guitar: Dennis Coffey, Ray Monette
Orchestra: Detroit Symphony Orchestra
Piano: Bernie Worrell

"No Commitment"

Lead and Backup Vocals, Acoustic Guitar:
  Ruth Copeland
Backup Vocals: The Choraliers
Guitar: Eddie Hazel, Tawl Ross
Piano: Bernie Worrell
Drums: Tiki Fulwood
Bass: Billy Nelson

"I Got a Thing for You Daddy"

Lead Vocals: Ruth Copeland
Guitar: Tawl Ross, Eddie Hazel
Drums: Tiki Fulwood
Keyboards: Bernie Worrell
Bass: Billy Nelson
Orchestra: Detroit Symphony Orchestra

"A Gift of Me"

Lead and Backup Vocals: Ruth Copeland
Backup Vocals: The Choraliers

"Un Bel Di (One Fine Day)"

Lead Vocals: Ruth Copeland
Guitar: Eddie Hazel
Orchestra: Detroit Symphony Orchestra
Bass: Bob Babbitt and/or Billy Nelson
Drums: Tiki Fulwood
Organ: Bernie Worrell

I Am What I Am

"The Medal"

Lead Vocals: Ruth Copeland
Piano: Bernie Worrell

Bass: Billy Nelson
Drums: Tiki Fulwood
Guitars: Eddie Hazel, Ron Bykowski, Ray
  Monette

"Cryin Has Made Me Stronger"

Lead Vocals: Ruth Copeland
Backup Vocals: Ruth Copeland, the Choraliers
Piano: Bernie Worrell
Bass: Billy Nelson
Drums: Tiki Fulwood
Guitar: Ray Monette, Ron Bykowski, Eddie
  Hazel

"Hare Krishna"

Lead and Backup Vocals: Ruth Copeland
Piano, Organ: Bernie Worrell
Bass: Billy Nelson
Drums: Tiki Fulwood
Guitar: Eddie Hazel

"Suburban Family Lament"

Lead Vocals: Ruth Copeland
Drums: Tiki Fulwood
Organ: Bernie Worrell
Guitar: Eddie Hazel

"Play with Fire"

Lead Vocals: Ruth Copeland
Piano: Bernie Worrell
Drums: Tiki Fulwood
Guitar: Eddie Hazel, Ray Monette, Ron
  Bykowski
Bass: Billy Nelson

"Don't You Wish You Had (What You Had When You Had It)"

Vocals: Ruth Copeland
Drums: Tiki Fulwood
Bass: Billy Nelson
Guitar: Eddie Hazel
Keyboards: Bernie Worrell

"Gimme Shelter"

Lead and Backup Vocals: Ruth Copeland
Drums: Tiki Fulwood
Organ: Bernie Worrell
Guitar: Eddie Hazel, Ron Bykowski, Ray Monette
Bass: Billy Nelson

On Ruth Copeland's first album, *Self Portrait*, and the follow-up, *I Am What I Am*, Funkadelic was essentially the band along with Motown heavyweights like Dennis Coffey, Bob Babbitt, Ray Monette, and "I Bet You" drummer Andrew Smith. George Clinton handled some of the songwriting and arrangements, guitarist Tom Neme (of Bob Seeger fame) provided some musical consulting on the first album, and Tony Camillo handled the string, harp, and horn arrangements. Jeffrey Bowen has been considered as ghost producer of Copeland's albums even though Copeland herself is credited on the albums themselves as producer. Ron Dunbar, Edith Wayne, Gwen Alexander, Clinton, Tal Ross, and Donald Charles Baldwin contributed as songwriters. Another interesting aspect of at least the first album is that it can be conspicuously paired with Parliament's *Osmium* album, also part of the Holland-Dozier-Holland output from the beginning of the 1970s. Also credited on one song at least on the second album is David Case on piano and Dawn Hatcher on bass, though it has not been ascertained which song that is at this time.

HOUSE GUESTS: 1971

This is the name that the Pacesetters/JBs (featuring the Collins brothers [William "Bootsy" and Phelps "Catfish"] as well as Frank "Kash" Waddy) took after leaving James Brown and before joining Funkadelic.

House Guest Records

"My Mind Set Me Free"

Lead Vocals: Rufus Allen
Drums: Frank Waddy
Bass: Bootsy Collins
Guitar: Catfish Collins
Trumpet: Ronnie Greenway, Chicken Gunnels
Sax: Robert McCullough

"What So Never the Dance"

Drums: Frank Waddy
Bass: Bootsy Collins
Guitar: Catfish Collins
Trumpet: Ronnie Greenway, Chicken Gunnels
Sax: Robert McCullough
Vocals: Bootsy Collins, Ronnie Greenway, Chicken Gunnels, Robert McCullough, Catfish Collins, Frank Waddy

JAMES WESLEY JACKSON: 1972

This is the self-proclaimed "enviromedian," who opened for Funkadelic in the early days and also did routines in between the acts on the later, more lavish P-Funk arena tours of the late 1970s. Much of his humor was intangibly connected to both George Clinton's lyrical ideas and concepts and the iconic art and liner notes of Pedro Bell, Overton Lloyd, and Ron "Stozo" Edwards.

Plum Records

"Part 1"

Lead Vocals: James Wesley Jackson
Guitar: Harold Beane
Drums: Frankie Kash Waddy
Organ: Bernie Worrell

"Part 2"

Lead Vocals: James Wesley Jackson
Guitar: Harold Beane
Drums: Frankie Kash Waddy
Organ: Bernie Worrell

"I Got a Thing" (album outro)

Guitar: Harold Beane
Drums: Frankie Kash Waddy
Organ: Bernie Worrell

— ☆ —

FLO: 1972

Two versions of this song exist; one is sung by Flo (one of the Ikettes), as seen here; the other, a reputed B-side from the *Chocolate City* album, features George Clinton singing the lead.

"Common Law Wife"

Lead Vocals: Flo
Backup Vocals: Grady Thomas, Calvin Simon, Fuzzy Haskins, George Clinton
Drums: Tyrone Lampkin
Bass: Cordell Mosson
Guitar: Garry Shider, Bootsy Collins
Trumpet: Ronnie Greenaway, Chicken Gunnells
Sax: Robert McCullough
Keyboards: Bernie Worrell

— ☆ —

UNITED SOUL: 1972

United Soul was a group featuring, among others, what would become two major future legacy P-Funkers: Garry "Starchild" Shider and Cordell "Boogie" Mosson.

Westbound Records

"I Miss My Baby"

Lead Vocals, Guitar: Garry Shider
Backup Vocals: Larry Mosson, Ben Edwards, Cordell Mosson
Drums: Tyrone Lampkin
Bass: Cordell Mosson
Piano, Keyboards: Bernie Worrell

"Baby I Owe You Something Good"

Lead Vocals, Guitar: Garry Shider
Backup Vocals: Larry Mosson, Ben Edwards, Cordell Mosson
Drums: Tyrone Lampkin
Bass: Cordell Mosson
Piano, Keyboards: Bernie Worrell

"This Broken Heart"

Lead Vocals: Ben Edwards
Backup Vocals: Calvin Simon, Garry Shider, Mudbone Cooper, Pat Lewis?
Drums: Tyrone Lampkin
Bass: Cordell Mosson
Guitar: Garry Shider
Organ, Piano: Bernie Worrell
Strings: Victoria Polley, Albert Pratz, Bill Richards, Joe Sera, Walter Babiuk, Stanley Solomon, Ronald Laurie, Peter Shenkman

"Be What You Is"

Vocals: Larry Mosson, Cordell Mosson, Garry Shider, Ben Edwards
Drums: Harvey McGhee
Bass: Cordell Mosson
Guitar: Garry Shider

"Rat Kissed the Cat on the Naval"

Vocals: Garry Shider, Ben Edwards, Larry Mosson, George Clinton
Drums: Harvey McGhee
Bass: Cordell Mosson
Guitar: Garry Shider

— ☆ —

THE COMPLETE STRANGERS: 1972-1974

This is another moniker for the House Guests/JBs/Pacesetters, featuring Bootsy and company. The group now also featured the vocal talents of Gary Mudbone Cooper, who would go on to be a major contributor in the P-Funk canon for the decades to follow. If the House Guests represent Bootsy and company between their tenure with James Brown and their tenure with Funkadelic, the Complete Strangers represent Bootsy and company between their tenure with Funkadelic on *America Eats Its Young* and their tenure with Parliament on *Up for the Downstroke*.

Philmore Sound and General American Records

"Fun in Your Thang"

Lead Vocals: Bootsy Collins
Drums: Frank Waddy
Bass: Bootsy Collins
Guitar: Catfish Collins
Trumpet: Ronnie Greenway, Chicken Gunnels
Sax: Robert McCullough

"Together in Heaven"

Lead Vocals: Mudbone Cooper, Bootsy
   Collins, Catfish Collins
Drums: Frank Waddy
Bass: Bootsy Collins
Guitar: Catfish Collins
Clavinet, Piano: Sonny Talbert

THE TEMPTATIONS: 1975-1976

Although not necessarily part of the P-Funk canon, the P-Funk connection with the Motown singing group sensation is palatable. Producers Norman Whitfield and Jefferey Bowen were heavily influenced by the sounds and clothes of early Funkadelic in the late 1960s, and it informed the Temptations' style through the mid-1970s, even to the point of employing Funkadelic founding members Billy "Bass" Nelson and Eddie Hazel some on their albums. Note: From among Norman Whitfield's Temptations productions in the late 1960s, it has been said that musical parts of "Can't Get Next to You" and "Psychedelic Shack" were ripped directly from Funkadelic's early shows at the Twenty Grand in Detroit. The sections in question are easily deciphered as Funkadelic licks that were "borrowed" long before the advent of sampling.

Motown Records

A Song for You

"Happy People"

"Glasshouse"

"Shakey Ground"

"The Prophet"

"Happy People" (instrumental)

"A Song for You"

"Memories"

"I'm a Bachelor"

"Firefly"

The Temptations, with producer Jeffrey Bowen, had a huge hit with "Shakey Ground." Part of the success of this hit song was the employing of Funkadelic bedrock players Billy "Bass" Nelson on bass and Eddie Hazel on guitar.

Horns: James Carmichael
Clavinet, Piano, Sax: Donald Baldwin
Drums: James Gadson, Ollie Brown, Zachary
  Frazier
Guitar: Eddie Hazel, Melvin Ragin
Bass: Billy Bass Nelson

Wings of Love

"Sweet Gypsy Lane"

"Sweetness in the Dark"

"Up the Creek (Without a Paddle)"

"China Doll"

"Mary Ann"

"Dream Word (Wings of Love)"

"Paradise"

Bass: Billy Bass Nelson, Rustee Allenn, Freddie
  Stewart
Keyboards: Truman Thomas
Drums, Percussion: Ollie Brown
Guitar: Billy Bass Nelson, Freddie Stewart
Trumpet: Pat Rizzo, Steve Madaio

— ☆ —

BOBBY WOMACK
(SELECT TRACKS): 1975

The iconic soul singer Bobby Womack had a few cuts that featured P-Funk's Glenn Goins on guitar.

"Interlude #1/I Don't Know"
Drums: Robert Robertie, Ron Selico
Electric Piano, Organ, Clavinet: Truman
  Thomas
Electric Violin: Jonathan Blair
Guitar: Glenn Goins
Harp: Catherine Gotthoffer
Piano: Roger Dollarhide
Steel Guitar: Sneaky Pete Kleinow
Strings: Rene Hall
Vocals, Bass, Guitar, Strings: Bobby Womack

"Git It"
Bass: Paul Stallworth
Drums: Jim Keltner, Robert Robertie
Lead Guitar: Glenn Goins
Organ: William Smith
Vocals, Bass, Tambourine, Guitar: Bobby
  Womack

"What's Your World"
Bass: Paul Stallworth
Congas: Joe Lala
Drums: Bill Lordan
Electric Piano, Piano: Leon Ware, Truman
  Thomas
Fuzz Guitar: Glenn Goins
Horns: Peace
Lead Vocals, Bass, Guitar: Bobby Womack
Steel Guitar: Sneaky Pete Kleinow
Violin: Jonathan Blair
Vocals: Sunday

— ☆ —

BOOTSY'S RUBBER BAND: 1976–1979

Along with Parliament and Funkadelic, Bootsy's Rubber Band forms the triumvirate of platinum-selling acts within P-Funk's core groups. Operating chiefly during the post–*Mothership Connection* "heyday" era of P-Funk, Bootsy's Rubber Band served as a vehicle for bassist Bootsy Collins to "stretch out" (pun intended or not) on his own records and tours, featuring albums and songs coproduced and cowritten by George Clinton. The hit song "Bootzilla," which beat "Flash Light" to the top of the charts, can be considered the first #1 rhythm-and-blues hit in the P-Funk canon. The chief members of Bootsy's Rubber Band were the Collins brothers (Bootsy and Catfish), drummer Frankie "Kash" Waddy, vocalists Gary "Mudbone" Cooper and Robert "Peanut" Johnson, keyboardist Joel "Razor Sharp" Johnson, and the Horny Horns (Fred Wesley, Maceo Parker, Richard "Kush" Griffith, and Rick Gardner). It is important to note, however, that much like most of P-Funk's albums, the Rubber Band albums also are conspicuously filled with Parliament-Funkadelic mainstays like Bernie Worrell, Jerome Brailey, Garry Shider, Glenn Goins, Michael Hampton, Clinton himself, and many others. It is no doubt, however, that the star of this party is Collins himself, who created a sonic landscape of new sounds with his already famous "Space Bass." The Bootsy persona also is continually developed here with Clinton's help, with the inception of the character arguably since the 1975 Funkadelic song "Be My Beach." The Rubber Band had several gold- and platinum-selling albums.

Warner Bros. Records

Stretchin' Out in Bootsy's Rubber Band

"Stretchin' Out (In a Rubber Band)"
Lead Vocals, Drums, Bass: Bootsy Collins
Backup Vocals: Mudbone Cooper, Robert Peanut Johnson, Leslyn Bailey
Percussion: Mudbone Cooper, Robert Peanut Johnson
Guitar: Michael Hampton, Garry Shider
Synth Strings: Bernie Worrell
Trombone: Fred Wesley
Sax: Maceo Parker, Michael Brecker
Trumpet: Richard Griffith, Randy Brecker

"Stretchin Out," as a song and as an album, introduced the world to Bootsy's persona (beyond the first appearance of the character in Funkadelic's "Be My Beach." It also stands as both important and little known that this was one of Michael Hampton's first sessions for P-Funk (if not the very first). It features an incredible mix of talent from the then new Rubber Band itself and Parliament-Funkadelic mainstays as well as both the Horny Horns and the Brecker Brothers. It would set up the style for later Bootsy work much as "More Bounce to the Ounce" later did for fellow Ohioans Zapp in their sound to come. In so many words, it is notable to credit "Stretchin' Out" as a formula starter.

"Psychotic Bump School"
Lead Vocals, Bass: Bootsy Collins
Backup Vocals: Mudbone Cooper, Leslyn Bailey, Catfish Collins, Frank Waddy, Rick Gardner, Maceo Parker
Drums: Frank Waddy
Guitar: Catfish Collins
Trombone: Fred Wesley
Sax: Maceo Parker
Trumpet: Richard Griffith, Rick Gardner

"Another Point of View"
Lead Vocals: Mudbone Cooper, Bootsy Collins, Leslyn Bailey
Drums, Percussion: Mudbone Cooper
Bass: Bootsy Collins
Synthesizers: Bernie Worrell
Organ: Sonny Talpert
Guitar: Michael Hampton, Garry Shider
Trombone: Fred Wesley
Sax: Maceo Parker, Michael Brecker
Trumpet: Rick Gardner, Richard Griffith, Randy Brecker

Frankie "Kash" Waddy and William "Bootsy" Collins performing live. © Diem Jones

"I'd Rather Be with You"

Lead Vocals: Bootsy Collins, Mudbone Cooper
Drums: Cordell Mosson
Bass: Bootsy Collins
Guitar: Catfish Collins, Garry Shider
Melodica, Celeste: Bernie Worrell

"Love Vibes"

Lead Vocals: Mudbone Cooper, Leslyn Bailey
Drums: Mudbone Cooper
Bass: Bootsy Collins
Piano: Bernie Worrell
Organ: Sonny Talpert
Trombone: Fred Wesley
Sax: Maceo Parker, Michael Brecker
Trumpet: Rick Gardner, Randy Brecker

"Physical Love"

Lead Vocals: Mudbone Cooper, Bootsy Collins, Leslyn Bailey

Drums: Cordell Mosson
Bass: Bootsy Collins
Guitar: Eddie Hazel
Synthesizers: Bernie Worrell

"Vanish in Our Sleep"

Lead Vocals: Bootsy Collins, Mudbone Cooper, Robert Peanut Johnson
Drums: Cordell Mosson
Bass: Bootsy Collins
Electric Piano, Piano: Frederick Allen
Guitar: Garry Shider

"Vanish in Our Sleep" is one of the early "Silly Serious" love songs from the Clinton–Collins team and features some really sticky sweet playing and singing. This song would later be a part of the Brides of Funkenstein live show (interestingly, at that time, the Brides band would feature Bootsy's Rubber Band members Richard Kush Griffith, Frankie Kash Waddy, Joel Razor Sharp Johnson, and others, so this would be apropos).

Ahh . . . The Name Is Bootsy, Baby!

"Ahh . . . the Name Is Bootsy, Baby!"

Lead Vocals: Maceo Parker, Bootsy Collins, Mudbone Cooper, Robert Peanut Johnson, George Clinton
Drums, Bass: Bootsy Collins
Guitar: Bootsy Collins, Catfish Collins
Trombone: Fred Wesley
Sax: Maceo Parker
Trumpet: Richard Griffith, Rick Gardner
Synthesizers: Joel Johnson

"Ahh . . . the Name Is Bootsy, Baby!" would further the mythology of the Bootsy character. It also features some amazing Space Bass from Collins and inspired lines from the Horny Horns, including a rare Mu-tronned sax solo from Funk pioneer Maceo Parker, whose presence on the P-Funk releases in this period is extremely important. Of equal import is the magnitude of vocalists Gary Mudbone Cooper and Robert Peanut Johnson, who, aside from being the vocal backbone of the Rubber Band, also went on to be among some of the most recorded people mentioned in this book.

"The Pinocchio Theory"

Lead Vocals: Bootsy Collins, Mudbone Cooper, Robert Peanut Johnson
Drums, Bass: Bootsy Collins
Clavinet: Joel Johnson
Synthesizers, Strings: Bernie Worrell
Guitar: Catfish Collins
Trombone: Fred Wesley
Sax: Maceo Parker
Trumpet: Richard Griffith, Rick Gardner

"The Pinocchio Theory" was a precursor to the Sir Nose concept exerted by George Clinton. It features a standout Razor Sharp keyboard line underneath Bernie's synth wizardry and a common theme: Bootsy on drums and bass. The horn arrangements are standout.

"Rubber Duckie"

Lead Vocals: Bootsy Collins, Mudbone Cooper, Robert Peanut Johnson
Drums: Mudbone Cooper
Bass: Bootsy Collins
Guitar: Catfish Collins
Synthesizers: Bernie Worrell
Trombone: Fred Wesley
Sax: Maceo Parker, Michael Brecker
Trumpet: Randy Brecker, Richard Griffith, Rick Gardner

"Preview Side Too"

Drums: Cordell Mosson
Bass: Bootsy Collins
Guitar: Garry Shider, Glenn Goins
Keyboards: Bernie Worrell

"What's a Telephone Bill?"

Lead Vocals: Bootsy Collins, Mudbone Cooper, Robert Peanut Johnson
Organ, Keyboards, Melodica: Bernie Worrell
Flute: Maceo Parker
Bass: Bootsy Collins
Guitar: Catfish Collins, Garry Shider
Percussion: Larry Fratangelo?
Drums: Mudbone Cooper

"Munchies for Your Love"

Lead Vocals: Mudbone Cooper, Bootsy Collins, Robert Peanut Johnson
Drums: Cordell Mosson
Guitar: Garry Shider, Glenn Goins
Keyboards, Synthesizer: Bernie Worrell
Bass: Bootsy Collins

"Can't Stay Away"

Lead Vocals: Mudbone Cooper, Robert Peanut Johnson, Bootsy Collins
Drums: Mudbone Cooper
Bass: Bootsy Collins
Guitar: Catfish Collins
Strings: Bernie Worrell
Trombone: Fred Wesley
Sax: Michael Brecker, Maceo Parker
Trumpet: Randy Brecker, Rick Gardner, Richard Griffith

"Can't Stay Away" features some really strong vocal chops from Gary Mudbone Cooper (as well as Robert Peanut Johnson and Bootsy himself) and some memorable melodies. It follows the "Silly Serious" love song dynamic.

"Reprise: We Want Bootsy"

Vocals: Bootsy Collins, Maceo Parker, Mudbone Cooper, Robert Peanut Johnson
Bass: Bootsy Collins

Bootsy? Player of the Year

"Bootsy? (What's the Name of This Town?")

Lead Vocals: Bootsy Collins, Mudbone Cooper, Maceo Parker, Robert Peanut Johnson
Drums, Bass: Bootsy Collins
Flute: Maceo Parker
Guitar: Catfish Collins
Sax: Maceo Parker
Trombone: Fred Wesley
Trumpet: Richard Griffith, Rick Gardner

"May the Force Be with You"

Lead Vocals: Bootsy Collins, Mudbone Cooper, Robert Peanut Johnson
Drums: Cordell Mosson
Bass: Bootsy Collins
Guitar: Garry Shider, Catfish Collins
Keyboards: Joel Johnson

"Very Yes"

Lead Vocals: Mudbone Cooper, Robert Peanut Johnson, Bootsy Collins
Drums: Cordell Mosson
Bass: Bootsy Collins
Guitar: Catfish Collins, Bootsy Collins
Strings: Bernie Worrell
Organ: Joel Johnson
Trombone: Fred Wesley
Sax: Maceo Parker
Trumpet: Richard Griffith, Rick Gardner
Flute: Maceo Parker

"Bootzilla"

Lead Vocals: Bootsy Collins, Mudbone Cooper, Robert Peanut Johnson
Drums, Bass: Bootsy Collins
Guitar: Bootsy Collins, Catfish Collins
Strings: Bernie Worrell
Piano: Joel Johnson
Trombone: Fred Wesley
Sax: Maceo Parker
Trumpet: Richard Griffith, Rick Gardner

"Bootzilla" is technically the first P-Funk canon song to make it to #1 on the rhythm-and-blues charts (being itself bumped off the charts by "Flash Light" by Parliament). At this time, Bootsy's Rubber Band had become a force all its own but still within the P-Funk Universe. This hit single solidified Bootsy's career as a star (no pun intended) from that point forward, and trends continued thereafter with a series of #1 hits on the charts from Parliament and Funkadelic alike.

"Hollywood Squares"

Lead Vocals: Bootsy Collins, Mudbone Cooper, Robert Peanut Johnson
Drums: Frank Waddy
Bass: Bootsy Collins
Guitar: Catfish Collins
Harpsichord: Bernie Worrell
Trombone: Fred Wesley
Sax: Maceo Parker
Trumpet: Richard Griffith, Rick Gardner

"Hollywood Squares" exhibits a fiery orchestral introduction, a funky harpsichord groove, and more signature vocal parts from the Mudbone/Peanut/Bootsy combination of character voices. It also features someone who may be the true unsung hero of the Rubber Band: Bootsy's older brother, guitarist Phelps "Catfish" Collins.

"Roto-Rooter"

Lead Vocals: Gary Mudbone Cooper, Bootsy Collins, Robert Peanut Johnson
Drums: Mudbone Cooper
Bass: Bootsy Collins
Synthesizers: Bernie Worrell
Clavinet: Joel Johnson
Guitar: Catfish Collins
Trombone: Fred Wesley
Sax: Maceo Parker
Trumpet: Richard Griffith, Rick Gardner

"As in "I Love You""

Lead Vocals: Bootsy Collins, Mudbone Cooper, Robert Peanut Johnson
Electric Piano: Bernie Worrell
Percussion, Drums: Bootsy Collins
Sax: Eli Fontaine

This Boot Is Made for Fonk-N

"Under the Influence of a Groove"

Lead Vocals: Bootsy Collins, Mudbone Cooper, George Clinton, Robert Peanut Johnson
Drums, Bass: Bootsy Collins
Percussion: Mudbone Cooper, Robert Peanut Johnson
Strings, Synth Bass: Bernie Worrell
Synthesizers: Bernie Worrell
Guitar: Catfish Collins
Trombone: Fred Wesley
Sax: Maceo Parker
Trumpet: Richard Griffith, Rick Gardner
Percussion: Carl "Butch" Small

"Bootsy Get Live"

Lead Vocals: Bootsy Collins, Mudbone Cooper, Robert Peanut Johnson, George Clinton, Greg Thomas, Seth Neblett
Drums, Bass: Bootsy Collins
Percussion: Carl Butch Small
Synthesizers: Joel Johnson
Trombone: Fred Wesley
Sax: Maceo Parker
Trumpet: Richard Griffith, Rick Gardner
Percussion: Carl "Butch" Small

"Oh Boy Gorl"

Lead Vocals: Robert Peanut Johnson, Bootsy Collins, Mudbone Cooper, Greg Thomas,
Drums, Bass: Bootsy Collins
Guitar: Catfish Collins
Keyboards, Synthesizers: Joel Johnson
Trombone: Fred Wesley
Sax: Maceo Parker
Trumpet: Richard Griffith, Rick Gardner
Percussion: Carl "Butch" Small

"Jam Fan (Hot)"

Lead Vocals, Drums, Bass: Bootsy Collins
Backup Vocals: Parlet, Dawn Silva, Sheila Horne, Jeanette McGruder, Mudbone Cooper, George Clinton, Robert Peanut Johnson, Greg Thomas
Guitar: Catfish Collins
Synthesizers: Joel Johnson
Handclap Boards: Carl Butch Small
Percussion: Larry Fratangelo
Trombone: Fred Wesley
Sax: Maceo Parker
Trumpet: Richard Griffith, Rick Gardner

"Chug-A-Lug (The Bun Patrol)"

Lead Vocals: Bootsy Collins, Mudbone Cooper, George Clinton, Robert Peanut Johnson
Drums, Bass, Guitar: Bootsy Collins
Percussion: Carl Butch Small
Organ: Joel Johnson
Trombone: Fred Wesley
Sax: Maceo Parker
Trumpet: Richard Griffith, Rick Gardner

"Shejam (Almost Bootsy Show)"

Lead Vocals: Maceo Parker, Mudbone Cooper, Bootsy Collins, George Clinton, Robert Peanut Johnson, Greg Thomas
Drums, Bass, Guitar: Bootsy Collins
Synthesizers: Joel Johnson, Bernie Worrell
Percussion, Handclap Boards: Carl Butch Small
Trombone: Fred Wesley
Sax: Maceo Parker
Trumpet: Richard Griffith, Rick Gardner

"Reprise (Get Live)"

Lead Vocals: Bootsy Collins, Mudbone Cooper, Robert Peanut Johnson, George Clinton, Greg Thomas
Drums, Bass: Bootsy Collins
Percussion: Carl Butch Small
Synthesizers: Joel Johnson
Trombone: Fred Wesley
Sax: Maceo Parker
Trumpet: Richard Griffith, Rick Gardner
Percussion: Carl "Butch" Small

Single

"Body Slam"

Lead Vocals: Bootsy Collins, Joel Johnson
Synth Strings: Joel Johnson, Bootsy Collins
Drums, Bass, Guitar: Bootsy Collins
Percussion: Bootsy Collins, Wes Boatman, Joel Johnson

Grand Piano: Kae Williams Jr.
Organ: Bruce Weeden

"Body Slam" became a well-known post–Rubber Band single from Bootsy and features some electronic elements although still retaining authenticity with Razor's keyboards and excellent musicianship from all.

4th & Broadway

Jungle Bass

"Jungle Bass"

Lead Vocals: Mudbone Cooper, Bootsy Collins
Drums, Guitar: Bootsy Collins
Bass: Bootsy Collins, Bill Laswell
Synthesizers: Bernie Worrell, Joel Johnson, Jeff Bova
Trombone: Fred Wesley
Sax: Maceo Parker
Trumpet: Richard Griffith, Rick Gardner

"Disciples of Funk"

Lead Vocals: Mudbone Cooper, Bootsy Collins
Drums, Guitar: Bootsy Collins
Bass: Bootsy Collins, Bill Laswell
Synthesizers: Bernie Worrell, Joel Johnson, Jeff Bova
Trombone: Fred Wesley
Sax: Maceo Parker
Trumpet: Richard Griffith, Rick Gardner

"Interzone"

Lead Vocals: Mudbone Cooper, Bootsy Collins
Drums, Guitar: Bootsy Collins
Bass: Bootsy Collins, Bill Laswell
Synthesizers: Bernie Worrell, Joel Johnson, Jeff Bova
Trombone: Fred Wesley
Sax: Maceo Parker
Trumpet: Richard Griffith, Rick Gardner

— ★ —

FUZZY HASKINS: 1976–1978

These are solo albums by co–lead vocalist of the Parliaments, Mr. Clarence "Fuzzy" Haskins.

Westbound Records

A Whole Nother Thang

"Tangerine Green"

Lead Vocals: Fuzzy Haskins
Drums: Tiki Fulwood
Bass: Cordell Mosson
Guitar: Donald Austin, Ron Bykowski
Keyboards: Bernie Worrell
Trumpet: ?
Sax: ?
Trombone: ?

"Cookie Jar"

Lead Vocals: Fuzzy Haskins
Drums: Tiki Fulwood
Bass: Cordell Mosson
Guitar: Donald Austin, Ron Bykowski
Keyboards: Bernie Worrell
Strings: Detroit Symphony Orchestra?
Trumpet: ?
Sax: ?
Trombone: ?

"Mr. Junk Man"

Lead Vocals, Drums: Fuzzy Haskins
Bass: Cordell Mosson
Guitar: Donald Austin, Ron Bykowski
Keyboards: Bernie Worrell
Strings: Detroit Symphony Orchestra
Trumpet: ?
Sax: ?
Trombone: ?

"I Can See Myself in You"

Lead Vocals, Drums: Fuzzy Haskins
Bass: Cordell Mosson
Guitar: Donald Austin, Ron Bykowski
Keyboards: Bernie Worrell
Trumpet: ?
Sax: ?
Trombone: ?

"The Fuzz and Da Boog"

Drums: Fuzzy Haskins
Bass: Cordell Mosson
Guitar: Donald Austin, Ron Bykowski
Keyboards: Bernie Worrell
Trumpet: ?
Sax: ?
Trombone: ?

"Which Way Do I Disco?"

Lead Vocals, Drums: Fuzzy Haskins
Bass: Bootsy Collins
Guitar: Donald Austin, Ron Bykowski
Keyboards: Bernie Worrell
Trumpet: ?
Sax: ?
Trombone: ?

"Love's Now Is Forever"

Lead Vocals: Fuzzy Haskins
Drums, Bass: Cordell Mosson
Guitar: Donald Austin, Ron Bykowski
Keyboards: Bernie Worrell
Strings: Detroit Symphony Orchestra
Trumpet: ?
Sax: ?
Trombone: ?

"Sometimes I Rock and Roll"

Lead Vocals, Drums: Fuzzy Haskins
Bass: Cordell Mosson
Guitar: Donald Austin, Ron Bykowski
Keyboards: Bernie Worrell
Trumpet: ?
Sax: ?
Trombone: ?

"I'll Be Loving You"

Lead Vocals: Fuzzy Haskins
Drums, Bass: Cordell Mosson
Guitar: Donald Austin, Ron Bykowski
Keyboards: Bernie Worrell
Trumpet: ?
Sax: ?
Trombone: ?

Later released B-side from
A Whole Nother Thang

"Right Back Where I Started From"

Lead Vocals: Fuzzy Haskins
Drums: Tiki Fulwood
Bass: Cordell Mosson
Guitar: Donald Austin, Ron Bykowski
Keyboards: Bernie Worrell

Radio-Active

"Not Yet"

Lead Vocals, Drums: Fuzzy Haskins
Bass: Cordell Mosson
Guitar: Garry Shider
Keyboards: Bernie Worrell
Trumpet: ?
Sax: ?
Trombone: ?

"I Think I Got My Thang Together"

Lead Vocals, Drums: Fuzzy Haskins
Percussion: Jerome Podjajski
Bass: Cordell Mosson
Guitar: Michael Hampton
Keyboards: Bernie Worrell
Trumpet: ?
Sax: ?
Trombone: ?
Orchestra: Detroit Symphony Orchestra

"This Situation Called Love"

Lead Vocals: Fuzzy Haskins
Backup Vocals: ?
Drums: Jerome Brailey
Bass: Cordell Mosson
Guitar, Keyboards: Glenn Goins
Trumpet: ?
Sax: ?
Trombone: ?

"Gimme Back (Some of the Love You Got from Me)"

Lead Vocals: Fuzzy Haskins
Backup Vocals: ?
Drums: Jerome Brailey
Bass: Cordell Mosson
Guitar: Glenn Goins
Keyboards: Garry Schunk?
Trumpet: ?
Sax: ?
Trombone: ?
Orchestra: Detroit Symphony Orchestra

"Thangs We Used to Do"

Lead Vocals, Drums: Fuzzy Haskins
Bass: Bruce Nazarian
Guitar: Garry Shider, Michael Hampton
Keyboards: Bruce Nazarian
Orchestra: Detroit Symphony Orchestra
Trumpet: ?
Sax: ?
Trombone: ?

"Woman"

Lead Vocals, Drums: Fuzzy Haskins
Percussion: Jerome Podjajski
Bass: Bruce Nazarian
Guitar: Michael Hampton
Keyboards: Bruce Nazarian
Orchestra: Detroit Symphony Orchestra
Trumpet: ?
Sax: ?
Trombone: ?

"Sinderella"

Lead Vocals: Fuzzy Haskins
Drums: Jerome Brailey
Bass: Bruce Nazarian
Guitar: Glenn Goins, Fuzzy Haskins
Keyboards: Glenn Goins
Orchestra: Detroit Symphony Orchestra
Trumpet: ?
Sax: ?
Trombone: ?

"Silent Day"

Lead Vocals: Fuzzy Haskins
Drums: Jerome Brailey?, Tyrone Lampkin?
Percussion: Jerome Podjajski
Bass: Cordell Mosson
Guitar: Garry Shider, Michael Hampton
Keyboards: Bernie Worrell
Trumpet: ?
Sax: ?
Trombone: ?

Note: It still has not been ascertained who the horn section is on both of Fuzzy Haskins's solo albums. Hopefully with future editions, this mystery will be solved.

THE BRECKER BROTHERS (SELECT TRACKS): 1976–1994

The Brecker Brothers are truly a musical force of their own. Much like Chops Horns, the Brecker Brothers' full discography cannot be truly contained within this volume. They were featured, along with the Horny Horns, on most of the major Parliament and Horny Horns albums. Their albums are listed here, but there is so much material and so many different session players that their discography could be given its own book in terms of discographic appearances. There were not many P-Funk bandmates on their albums, but artists such as David Sanborn and Luther Vandross had early appearances in their career on the Brecker Bros. albums.

Saxophone: Michael Brecker
Trumpet: Randy Brecker

Arista Records

The Brecker Bros.

"Some Skunk Funk"
"Sponge"
"A Creature of Many Faces"
"Twilight"
"Sneakin' Up behind You"
"Rocks"
"Levitate"
"Oh My Stars"
"D.B.B."

Back to Back

"Keep It Steady (Brecker Bump)"
"It You Wanna Boogie . . . Forget It"
"Lovely Lady"
"Night Flight"

"Slick Stuff"

"Dig a Little Deeper"

"Grease Piece"

"What Can a Miracle Do"

"I Love Wastin' Time with You"

Don't Stop the Music

"Finger Lickin' Good"

"Funky Sea, Funky Dew"

"As Long As I've Got Your Love"

"Squids"

"Don't Stop the Music"

"Petals"

"Tabula Rasa"

Heavy Metal Be-Bop

"East River"

"Inside Out"

"Some Skunk Funk"

"Sponge"

"Funky Sea, Funky Dew"

"Squids"

Detente

"You Ga (Ta Give It)"

"Not Tonight"

"Dont' Get Funny with My Money"

"Tee'd Off"

"You Left Something Behind"

"Squish"

"Dream Theme"

"Baffled"

"I Don't Know Either"

Straphangin'

"Straphangin'"

"Threesome"

"Bathsheba"

"Jacknife"

"Why Can't I Be There"

"Not Ethiopia"

"Spreadeagle"

GRP Records

Return of the Brecker Bros.

"Song for Barry"

"King of the Lobby"

"Big Idea"

"Above & Below"

"That's All There Is to Do"

"Wakaria (What's Up?)"

"On the Backside"

"Sozinho (Alone)"

"Spherical"

"Good Gracious"

"Roppongi"

Out of the Loop

"Slang"

"Evocations"

"Scrunch"

"Secret Heart"

"African Skies"

"When It Was"

"Harpoon"

"The Nightwalker"

"And Then She Wept"

— ☆ —

JOHNNIE TAYLOR (SELECT): 1976

Soul singer Johnnie Taylor (who recorded at United Sound, the famous Detroit studio where much of P-Funk's heyday music was produced) had much of Parliament play on his #1 hit single Disco Lady, which came right behind the smash Parliament hit "Give Up the Funk (Tear the Roof Off the Sucker)." Indeed, both songs featured many conspicuously relative melodies and rhythms.

"Disco Lady"

Lead Vocals: Johnnie Taylor
Drums: Zachary Slater (Frazier)
Tambourine, Percussion: Carl "Butch" Small
Bass: Bootsy Collins
Guitar: Garry Shider, Glenn Goins
Keyboards: Rudi Robinson, Bernie Worrell
Horns: Johnny Trudell Horns

— ☆ —

EDDIE HAZEL: 1977, 1993–1994

These are solo albums by the heralded lead guitarist for Parliament-Funkadelic, Mr. Eddie Hazel. His *Game, Dames and Guitar Thangs*, produced by George Clinton, is (along with albums like Bernie Worrell's *All the Woo in the World*) considered "height era" P-Funk canon.

Warner Bros. Records

"California Dreamin'"

Guitar, Lead Vocals: Eddie Hazel
Piano: Bernie Worrell
Bass: Bootsy Collins
Drums: Tiki Fulwood
Backup Vocals: Lynn Mabry, Dawn Silva

"Frantic Moment"

Guitar: Eddie Hazel
Bass, Drums: Bootsy Collins
Clavinet: Bernie Worrell
Vocals: Lynn Mabry, Dawn Silva

"So Goes the Story"

Drums: Jerome Brailey
Guitar: Eddie Hazel, Michael Hampton, Gary Shider
Bass: Bootsy Collins
Keyboards: Bernie Worrell
Vocals: Lynn Mabry, Dawn Silva

"I Want You (She's So Heavy)"

Drums: Tiki Fulwood
Guitar: Eddie Hazel, Garry Shider
Bass: Billy Nelson
Piano: Doug Duffy
Vocals: Lynn Mabry, Dawn Silva

"Physical Love"

Drums: Cordell Mosson
Bass: Bootsy Collins
Guitar: Eddie Hazel
Synthesizers: Bernie Worrell

"What About It?"

Drums: Jerome Brailey
Guitar: Eddie Hazel, Michael Hampton
Synth Bass: Bernie Worrell

"California Dreamin' (Reprise)"

Guitar, Lead Vocals: Eddie Hazel
Piano: Bernie Worrell
Bass: Bootsy Collins
Drums: Tiki Fulwood
Backup Vocals: Lynn Mabry, Dawn Silva

P-Vine Records

Rest in P

"Until It Rains"
Guitar: Eddie Hazel
Drums: Buddy Miles
Bass: Jimmy Calhoun

"Beyond Word and Measure"
Guitar, Bass: Eddie Hazel
Drums: Jerome Brailey
Vocals: Dawn Silva, Lynn Mabry

"Relic 'Delic (Purple Hazel)"
Guitar: Eddie Hazel
Drums: Jerome Brailey
Bass: Bootsy Collins

"Straighten Up"
Guitar, Bass, Vocals: Eddie Hazel
Drums: Tyrone Lampkin
Piano: Bernie Worrell

"Juicy Fingers"
Guitar: Eddie Hazel
Drums: Buddy Miles
Bass: Jimmy Calhoun

"We Three"
Guitar, Vocal: Eddie Hazel
Drums: Buddy Miles
Piano: Bernie Worrell
Bass: Jimmy Calhoun

"Why Cry"
Guitar, Bass: Eddie Hazel
Drums: Buddy Miles

"We Are One"
Guitar: Eddie Hazel
Drums: Tyrone Lampkin?, Tiki Fulwood?
Bass: Jimmy Calhoun

"No, It's Not!"
Guitar: Eddie Hazel
Drums: Buddy Miles
Bass: Jimmy Calhoun

"Until It Rains (Reprise)"
Guitar: Eddie Hazel
Drums: Buddy Miles
Bass: Jimmy Calhoun

JDC Records

(Posthumously)

Jams from the Heart

"Smedley Smorganoff"
Guitar: Eddie Hazel
Drums: Buddy Miles
Bass: Jimmy Calhoun

"Lampoc Boogie"
Guitar: Eddie Hazel
Bass: Jimmy Calhoun
Drums: Tyrone Lampkin

"From the Bottom of My Soul"
Guitar: Eddie Hazel
Bass: Jimmy Calhoun
Drums: Buddy Miles

"Uncut Funk"
Guitar: Eddie Hazel
Bass: Reggie McBride, Jimmy Calhoun
Drums: Buddy Miles

— ★ —

FRED WESLEY & THE HORNY HORNS: 1977–1979, 1994

These albums focus on the horn side of P-Funk and feature the Horny Horns, who are considered by most to be among the chief architects of Funk composition and arranging as we know it. This is due largely to both their long tenure with P-Funk and, prior to working with George Clinton, their long association with James Brown, when the previously mentioned section was known as the JB's.

Atlantic Records

A Blow for Me, a Toot for You

"Up for the Downstroke"

Trombone: Fred Wesley
Sax: Maceo Parker, Michael Brecker
Trumpet: Richard Griffith, Rick Gardner, Randy Brecker
Drums: Frank Waddy
Bass: Bootsy Collins
Piano: Bernie Worrell
Guitar: Catfish Collins
Vocals: Lynn Mabry, Dawn Silva, George Clinton, Bootsy Collins, Mudbone Cooper, Taka Khan, Robert Peanut Johnson, Randy Crawford

"A Blow for Me, a Toot for You"

Trombone: Fred Wesley
Sax: Maceo Parker, Michael Brecker
Trumpet: Richard Griffith, Rick Gardner, Randy Brecker
Vocals: George Clinton, Maceo Parker, Mudbone Cooper, Richard Griffith, Fred Wesley, Rick Gardner, Robert Peanut Johnson, Randy Crawford
Drums: Jerome Brailey
Bass: Bootsy Collins
Guitar: Glenn Goins, Garry Shider
Piano, Strings, Synth Bass: Bernie Worrell

"When in Doubt, Vamp"

Trombone: Fred Wesley
Sax: Maceo Parker, Michael Brecker
Trumpet: Richard Griffith, Rick Gardner, Randy Brecker
Synthesizers, Synth Bass: Bernie Worrell
Drums: Tyrone Lampkin?
Guitar: Michael Hampton, Garry Shider, Catfish Collins
Bass: Bootsy Collins

"Between Two Sheets"

Trombone: Fred Wesley
Sax: Maceo Parker,
Trumpet: Richard Griffith, Rick Gardner
Bass: Bootsy Collins
Guitar: Glenn Goins, Garry Shider
Vocals: Bootsy Collins, Robert Peanut Johnson, Mudbone Cooper, Maceo Parker, Fred Wesley, Richard Griffith, Rick Gardner, Dawn Silva, Lynn Mabry
Drums: Mudbone Cooper

"Four Play"

Trombone: Fred Wesley
Sax: Maceo Parker
Trumpet: Richard Griffith, Rick Gardner
Drums: Jerome Brailey
Bass: Bootsy Collins
Piano: Bernie Worrell
Guitar: Michael Hampton, Glenn Goins

"Peace Fugue"

Bass Trumpet: Fred Wesley
Sax: Maceo Parker
Trumpet: Rick Gardner
Electric Piano, Clavinet: Peabody Conservatory Pianist (Richard Ocean?)
Orchestra: New York Symphony Orchestra
Drums: Frankie Kash Waddy
Bass: Bootsy Collins

The Horny Horns. L–R: Fred Wesley, Maceo Parker, Richard "Kush" Griffith, and Rick Gardner. © Diem Jones

Say Blow by Blow Backwards

"We Came to Funk Ya"

Trombone: Fred Wesley
Sax: Maceo Parker
Trumpet: Richard Griffith, Rick Gardner
Flute: Maceo Parker
Drums: Mudbone Cooper
Bass: Bootsy Collins
Synth Strings: Bernie Worrell
Guitar: Catfish Collins, Garry Shider
Vocals: Maceo Parker, Bootsy Collins,
    Mudbone Cooper, Robert Peanut Johnson,
    George Clinton

"Half a Man"

Trombone: Fred Wesley
Sax: Maceo Parker
Trumpet: Richard Griffith, Rick Gardner
Bass: Billy Nelson
Drums: Tyrone Lampkin
Guitar: Michael Hampton, Garry Shider
Vocals: Maceo Parker, Robert Peanut Johnson,
    Mudbone Cooper, Jessica Cleaves

"Say Blow by Blow Backwards"

Trombone: Fred Wesley
Sax: Maceo Parker
Trumpet: Richard Griffith, Rick Gardner
Drums: Frank Waddy
Bass: Bootsy Collins
Keyboards: Joel Johnson
Guitar: Catfish Collins, Bootsy Collins
Vocals: Maceo Parker, Mudbone Cooper,
    Robert Peanut Johnson, Bootsy Collins
Percussion: Larry Fratangelo

"Mr. Melody Man"

Sax: Maceo Parker
Orchestra: Detroit Symphony Orchestra
Keyboards: Bernie Worrell
Bass: Bootsy Collins
Drums: Gary Mudbone Cooper

"Just Like You"

Sax: Maceo Parker
Bass, Drums: Bootsy Collins
Percussion: Carl Butch Small
Guitar: Garry Shider, Catfish Collins
Keyboards: Bernie Worrell
Organ: Jerome Rodgers?

"Circular Motion"

Trombone: Fred Wesley
Sax: Maceo Parker
Trumpet: Richard Griffith, Rick Gardner,
Drums: Frank Waddy
Cowbell: Carl "Butch" Small
Bass, Guitars: Bootsy Collins
Keyboards: Joel Johnson

P-Vine Records

The Final Blow

"Bells"

Trombone: Fred Wesley
Sax: Maceo Parker
Trumpet: Richard Griffith, Rick Gardner
Percussion: Fred Wesley, Maceo Parker,
    Richard Griffith, Rick Gardner

"Fallen Off the Edge"

Trombone: Fred Wesley
Sax: Maceo Parker
Trumpet: Richard Griffith, Rick Gardner
Drums: Frank Waddy
Bass: Rodney Curtis
Guitar: Michael Hampton, Garry Shider

"The Cookie Monster"

Trombone: Fred Wesley
Sax: Maceo Parker
Trumpet: Richard Griffith, Rick Gardner
Drums: Tyrone Lampkin
Bass: Bootsy Collins
Percussion: Carl Butch Small
Synth Strings, Synth Bass: Bernie Worrell
Guitar: Garry Shider, Glenn Goins

"West Ward Ho"

Trombone: Fred Wesley
Sax: Maceo Parker
Trumpet: Richard Griffith, Rick Gardner
Voice: ?, George Clinton
Drums: Jesse Williams
Percussion: Larry Fratangelo
Bass: Donnie Sterling?
Synthesizer: Bernie Worrell?, Amp Fiddler?
Piano, Pad: Joel Johnson?, Amp Fiddler?

"Oh I Don't Think Sew"

Trombone: Fred Wesley
Sax: Maceo Parker, Michael Brecker
Trumpet: Richard Griffith, Rick Gardner, Randy Brecker
Drums: Tyrone Lampkin
Bass: Rodney Curtis
Guitar: Rodney Crutcher, Garry Shider, Jerome Ali
Piano: Manon Saulsby
Orchestra: Detroit Symphony Orchestra

"Lickity Split"

Trombone: Fred Wesley
Sax: Maceo Parker
Trumpet: Richard Griffith, Rick Gardner
Drums: Tyrone Lampkin
Percussion: Larry Fratangelo
Bass: Bootsy Collins
Guitar: Michael Hampton
Clavinet: Bernie Worrell
Electric Piano: Maceo Parker

"Discositdown"

Trombone: Fred Wesley
Sax: Maceo Parker
Trumpet: Richard Griffith, Rick Gardner
Drums: Jesse Williams
Bass: Rodney Curtis
Guitar: Michael Hampton, Garry Shider
Vocals: George Clinton, ?
DJ: ?
Synth Bass: ?

ARTISTS STARTING IN 1978-1988

THE DELLS (SELECT TRACKS): 1978

Famous rhythm-and-blues singing group the Dells recorded their own versions of the Parliaments' two biggest hits. Although containing new vocals, the music was snatched literally from the instrumental tracks of the later remade versions featured on Parliament's *Up for the Downstroke* album. United Sound Studios' Don Davis is most likely to credit for this practice.

ABC Records

New Beginnings

"Testify"

Vocals: Marvin Junior, Johnny Funches, Johnny Carter, Verne Allison, Mickey McGill
All Musicians: Same personnel as "Testify" from the Parliament *Up for the Downstroke* album

"All Your Goodies Are Gone"

Vocals: Marvin Junior, Johnny Funches, Johnny Carter, Verne Allison, Mickey McGill

All Musicians: Same personnel as "Testify" from the Parliament *Up for the Downstroke* album

— ☆ —

BONNIE POINTER (SELECT TRACKS): 1978

P-Funk guitar master Eddie Hazel turned up during his brief Motown stint in the mid-1970s on Bonnie Pointer's self-named album, which features the mentor of Hazel's bandmate Billy Nelson: the late great James Jamerson.

Motown Records

Bonnie Pointer

"When I'm Gone"

Vocals: Bonnie Pointer
String Arrangement: Paul Riser
Bass: James Jamerson
Drums, Percussion: Ollie Brown
Guitar: Eddie Hazel
Keyboards: Truman Thomas

"Free Me from My Freedom"

Banjo, Bass, Guitar: Eddie Hazel
Drums: Ollie Brown
Vocals: Bonnie Pointer

"Heaven Must Have Sent You"

Vocals: Bonnie Pointer
String Arrangement: Paul Riser
Bass: James Jamerson
Drums: Ollie Brown
Guitar: Eddie Hazel
Keyboards: Truman Thomas
Percussion: Jack Ashford

"Ah Shoot"

Vocals: Bonnie Pointer
Arp: Truman Thomas
Bass, Guitar: Eddie Hazel
Drums: Ollie Brown

"More and More"

Acoustic Guitar, Bass, Electric Guitar: Donald Baldwin
String Arrangement: Lee Holdridge
Drums: Ollie Brown
Vocals: Bonnie Pointer

"I Love to Sing to You"

Acoustic Guitar: Donald Baldwin
String Arrangement: Lee Holdridge
Bass, Electric Guitar: Eddie Hazel
Drums: Ollie Brown

"I Wanna Make It (In Your World)"

Acoustic Guitar, Marimba: Donald Baldwin
Bass: Eddie Hazel
Drums: Ollie Brown
Piano: Truman Thomas

"My Everything"

String Arrangement: Lee Holdridge
Bass, Piano, Moog: Donald Baldwin
Drums: Nigel Olsson

— ☆ —

QUAZAR: 1978

This group featured the Goins brothers (Parliament co–lead singer Glenn Goins and his brother Kevin) as well as future Woo Warriors and 420 Funk Mob Keyboardist Gregg Fitz, P-Funk/Mutiny drummer Jerome Brailey, and many others. It features some of Glenn Goins's last work before his untimely death at a very young age.

Arista Records

"Funk with a Big Foot"

Vocals: Glenn Goins, Kevin Goins, Gregg Fitz
Drums: Jerome Brailey
Bass: Glenn Goins
Keyboards: Gregg Fitz, Garry Schunk
Guitar: Kevin Goins
Horns: Darryl Dixon, Monica Peters

"Funk with a Capital "G""

Vocals: Kevin Goins, Gregg Fitz, Harvey Banks, Peachena, Jeff Adams, Eugene Jackson
Drums: Jeff Adams
Bass: Eugene Jackson
Keyboards: Gregg Fitz, Richard Banks, Garry Schunk
Guitar: Kevin Goins
Horns: Darryl Dixon, Monica Peters

"Funk 'n' Roll (Dancin in the "Funkshine")"

Vocals: Glenn Goins
Drums: Jerome Brailey
Bass: Glenn Goins
Keyboards: Gregg Fitz, Glenn Goins, Garry Schunk
Guitar: Kevin Goins, Glenn Goins, Harry and Butch Watson, Johnny Guitar Watson
Horns: Darryl Dixon, Monica Peters

"Workin' on the Buildin'"

Vocals: Glenn Goins, Kevin Goins
Drums: Jeff Adams
Bass: Glenn Goins, Donald Payne
Keyboards: Gregg Fitz, Glenn Goins, Richard Banks, Garry Schunk
Guitar: Harry and Butch Watson
Horns: Daryl Dixon, Monica Peters

"Your Lovin' Is Easy"

Vocals: Glenn Goins, Kevin Goins, Jeff Adams, Eugene Jackson, Peachena, Gregg Fitz
Drums: Glenn Goins, Man in the Box
Bass: Glenn Goins
Keyboards: Gregg Fitz, Glenn Goins, Garry Schunk
Guitar: Glenn Goins, Kevin Goins
Horns: Daryl Dixon, Monica Peters

"Love Me Baby"

Vocals: Peachena, Gregg Fitz
Drums: Jeff Adams
Bass: Eugene Jackson
Keyboards: Gregg Fitz, Garry Schunk
Guitar: Glen or Kevin Goins, Harvey Banks or Harry or Butch Watson
Horns: Daryl Dixon, Monica Peters

"Savin' My Love for a Rainy Day"

Vocals: Glenn Goins, Richard Banks, Kevin Goins, Jeff Adams, Eugene Jackson, Gregg Fitz, Peachena, Harvey Banks
Drums: Glenn Goins
Bass: Glenn Goins
Keyboards: Glenn Goins, Richard Banks, Garry Schunk
Guitar: Glenn Goins
Horns: Daryl Dixon, Monica Peters

"Starlight Circus"

Vocals: Eugene Jackson, Gregg Fitz, Jeff Adams, Kevin Goins, Peachena
Drums: Jeff Adams
Bass: Eugene Jackson
Keyboards: Gregg Fitz
Guitar: Glenn Goins?
Horns: Daryl Dixon, Monica Peters

"Shades of Quaze"

Drums: Jeff Adams
Bass: Eugene Jackson, Glenn Goins
Keyboards: Richard Banks
Guitar: Kevin Goins, Glenn Goins
Horns: Daryl Dixon, Monica Peters

— ☆ —

PARLET: 1978–1980

This important George Clinton–produced female singing group featured the P-Funk female backup vocalists now up front on their own records. Several women were in the group during Parlet's existence, but the most prominent have to include Jeanette Washington, Debbie Wright, Mallia Franklin, Shirley Hayden, and Janice Evans.

Casablanca Records

Pleasure Principle

"Pleasure Principle"

Vocals: Mallia Franklin, Debbie Wright, Jeanette Washington, Dawn Silva, Lynn Mabry
Orchestra: Detroit Symphony Orchestra
Drums: Jim Wright
Bass: Rodney Curtis
Keyboards: Bernie Worrell
Sax: Eli Fountaine
Clarinet: Eli Fountaine
Guitar: Garry Shider

"Love Amnesia"

Vocals: Mallia Franklin, Debbie Wright, Jeanette Washington
Drums: Mudbone Cooper
Bass: Billy Nelson
Guitar: Billy Nelson
Clavinet, Strings: Bernie Worrell
Trombone: Fred Wesley
Trumpet: Richard Griffith, Rick Gardner
Sax: Maceo Parker

"Cookie Jar"

Vocals: Mallia Franklin, Debbie Wright, Jeanette Washington, George Clinton, Ron Ford, Garry Shider, Glenn Goins
Drums: Jim Wright
Piano: Bernie Worrell
Bass: Bootsy Collins
Guitar: Garry Shider, Glenn Goins

"Misunderstanding"

Vocals: Mallia Franklin, Debbie Wright, Jeanette Washington, Mudbone Cooper, Robert Peanut Johnson, Ron Ford, Bernie Worrell
Piano: Bernie Worrell
Sax: Eli Fontaine
Bass: Rick Gilmore
Drums: Mudbone Cooper or Tyrone Lampkin

"Are You Dreaming?"

Vocals: Mallia Franklin, Debbie Wright, Jeanette Washington
Drums: Jim Wright
Bass: Rodney Curtis or Rick Gilmore
Guitar: Garry Shider
Piano, Synthesizer: Bernie Worrell
Sax: Eli Fontaine

"Mr. Melody Man"

Vocals: Debbie Wright, Jeanette Washington, Brandye, Mudbone Cooper, Mallia Franklin
Drums: Mudbone Cooper
Bass: Rodney Curtis
Keyboards: Bernie Worrell
Orchestra: Detroit Symphony Orchestra
Sax: Eli Fountaine

Invasion of the Booty Snatchers

"Ridin' High"

Vocals: Mallia Franklin, Jeanette Washington, Shirley Hayden, Lige Curry, Michael Clip Payne, Garry Shider, George Clinton
Drums: Gary Mudbone Cooper
Bass: Donnie Sterling
Keyboards, Synthesizers: Ernestro Wilson, Manon Saulsby
Guitar: Gordon Carlton
Trumpet: Bennie Cowan
Sax: Greg Thomas
Trombone: Greg Boyer
Handclap Boards: Carl Butch Small
Percussion: Larry Fratangelo

"Ridin' High" was the highest-charting song by Parlet. It featured a heavy hand from coproducer Ron Dunbar. It is marked by an increasingly disco-influenced sound, something not common to most P-Funk music, even in this era. The disco sound was arguably most heard on the second and third Parlet albums. What set them apart from regular disco was that the music was played by stellar jazz musicians, such as keyboardists Ernestro Wilson and Manon Saulsby, guitarist Gordon Carlton, the Ali Brothers, the Baltimore Connection, and many more. Parlet had one of the most talented bands at the time, hailing mostly from Detroit.

"No Rump to Bump"

Vocals: Jeanette Washington, Shirley Hayden, Cheryl James, Lige Curry, Michael Clip Payne
Drums: Bootsy Collins
Percussion: Carl Butch Small
Bass: Jimmy Ali
Keyboards: Manon Saulsby, Ernestro Wilson
Guitar: Kevin Oliver, Bootsy Collins
Trumpet: Bennie Cowan
Sax: Greg Thomas
Trombone: Greg Boyer

"Don't Ever Stop (Lovin' Me, Needing' Me)"

Vocals: Jeanette Washington, Shirley Hayden, Cheryl James, Mudbone Cooper
Drums: Bootsy Collins
Percussion: Carl Butch Small
Bass: Bootsy Collins
Keyboards, Synthesizers: Manon Saulsby, Ernestro Wilson
Guitar: Bootsy Collins, Catfish Collins, Glenn Goins
Horns: David Majal Ti, Ernie Fields Jr., Nolan A. Smith Jr., Raymond Lee Brown

"Booty Snatchers"

Vocals: Jeanette Washington, Shirley Hayden, Ron Dunbar, George Clinton, Ray Davis, Cheryl James, Jeanette MacGruder, Mallia Franklin
Drums: Kenny Colton
Percussion: Larry Fratangelo
Bass: Donnie Sterling
Keyboards, Synthesizers: Manon Saulsby, Ernestro Wilson
Guitar: Gordon Carlton
Trumpet: Bennie Cowan
Sax: Greg Thomas
Trombone: Greg Boyer

"You're Leaving"

Vocals: Jeanette Washington, Janice Evans, Cheryl James, Mudbone Cooper, Robert Peanut Johnson
Drums: Mudbone Cooper
Bass: Jeff Bunn
Clavinet: Joel Johnson
Guitar: Kevin Oliver, Timmy Moore
Horns: David Majal Ti, Ernie Fields Jr., Nolan A. Smith Jr., Raymond Lee Brown

Jeanette Washington, Jerome "Bigfoot" Brailey, and Robert "Peanut" Johnson. © Diem Jones

"Huff-N-Puff"

Vocals: Jeanette Washington, Shirley Hayden, Lige Curry, Ron Ford, Robert Peanut Johnson, Mudbone Cooper, Jeanette MacGruder, Michael Clip Payne, Mallia Franklin
Drums: Kenny Colton
Percussion: Carl Butch Small
Bass: Jimmy Ali
Keyboards, Synthesizers: Ernestro Wilson, Manon Saulsby
Guitar: Michael Hampton

Play Me or Trade Me

"Help from My Friends"

Vocals: Jeanette Washington, Shirley Hayden, Janice Evans
Drums: Kenny Colton

Percussion: Larry Fratangelo, Janice Carlton
Bass: Donnie Sterling
Piano, Synthesizer, Synth Bass: David Spradley
Guitar: Gordon Carlton, Kevin Oliver
Horns: David Majal Ti, Ernie Fields Jr., Nolan A. Smith Jr., Raymond Lee Brown

"Watch Me Do My Thang"

Vocals: Jeanette Washington, Janice Evans, Shirley Hayden, George Clinton, Cheryl James, Gwen Dozier, Ron Dunbar
Drums: Tyrone Lampkin
Percussion: Carl Butch Small
Bass: Bootsy Collins
Keyboards, Synthesizers: David Spradley
Guitar: Bootsy Collins, Catfish Collins
Trumpet: Bennie Cowan
Sax: Greg Thomas
Trombone: Greg Boyer

"Wolf Tickets"

Vocals: George Clinton, Jeanette Washington, Janice Evans, Shirley Hayden, Robert Peanut Johnson, Jimmie Ali, Jerome Ali, Gwen Dozier
Drums: Kenny Colton
Percussion: Carl Butch Small
Bass: Jimmy Ali
Keyboards, Synthesizers: Manon Saulsby, Ernestro Wilson
Guitar: Jerome Ali, Gordon Carlton
Trumpet: Bennie Cowan, Larry Hatcher
Sax: Greg Thomas, Maceo Parker
Trombone: Greg Boyer

"Wolf Tickets" was the other Parlet song to chart. It benefited from having George Clinton on the record as well. It features the Ali Brothers, the already mentioned Parlet band, the Baltimore Connection (also known as the P-Funk Horns), and the last iteration of the Parlet vocal lineup.

"Play Me or Trade Me"

Vocals: Jeanette Washington, Janice Evans, Shirley Hayden, Ron Ford, Robert Peanut Johnson, Tony Davis, Andre Williams, Lige Curry
Drums: Kenny Colton
Bass: Donnie Sterling
Keyboards, Synthesizers: David Spradley, Manon Saulsby, Ernestro Wilson
Guitar: Gordon Carlton
Trumpet: Bennie Cowan
Sax: Greg Thomas
Trombone: Greg Boyer

"I'm Mo Be Hittin' It"

Vocals: Jeanette Washington, Janice Evans, Shirley Hayden, Ron Dunbar
Drums: Tyrone Lampkin
Percussion: Carl Butch Small
Bass: Lige Curry
Keyboards, Synthesizers: Manon Saulsby, Ernestro Wilson
Guitar: Garry Shider, Michael Hampton
Trumpet: Bennie Cowan

Sax: Greg Thomas
Trombone: Greg Boyer

"Funk until the Edge of Time"

Vocals: Jeanette Washington, Janice Evans, Shirley Hayden, Steve Pannell, Andre Williams
Drums: Kenny Colton
Percussion: Carl "Butch" Small
Bass: Steve Pannell
Keyboards, Synthesizers: David Spradley
Guitar: Gordon Carlton
Trumpet: Bennie Cowan
Sax: Greg Thomas
Trombone: Greg Boyer

"Wonderful One"

Vocals: Jeanette Washington, Janice Evans, Shirley Hayden
Drums: Tyrone Lampkin
Percussion: Carl "Butch" Small
Bass: Cordell Mosson
Keyboards, Synthesizers: Bernie Worrell
Guitar: Garry Shider
Horns: David Majal Ti, Ernie Fields Jr., Nolan A. Smith Jr., Raymond Lee Brown

— ☆ —

BRIDES OF FUNKENSTEIN: 1978–1980

Having perhaps slightly more success (or promotion) than Parlet, the Brides of Funkenstein had two George Clinton–produced albums that are considered the prime P-Funk canon. The main female vocalists from P-Funk who had been slated for the Brides included Dawn Silva, Lynn Mabry, Sheila Horne, Jeanette MacGruder, and others. "Disco to Go" and "Never Buy Texas from a Cowboy" are as important to the P-Funk canon as almost any Parliament-Funkadelic songs you would wish to name, with obvious exceptions.

Atlantic Records

Funk or Walk

"Disco to Go"

Vocals: Dawn Silva, Lynn Mabry
Drums: Bootsy Collins
Bass: Bootsy Collins
Keyboards, Synthesizers: Bernie Worrell
Guitar: Bootsy Collins, Garry Shider
Trumpet: Richard Griffith, Rick Gardner
Sax: Maceo Parker
Trombone: Fred Wesley

"Disco to Go" is an important piece of the P-Funk canon, recorded with Bootsy, Bernie, Shider, and the Horny Horns. Dawn Silva and Lynn Mabry, the original Brides of Funkenstein, are introduced here, although they were a mainstay of the P-Funk vocal section (much like Parlet) already by this point. It has an important intro/outro that would be used in P-Funk shows thereafter.

"War Ship Touchante"

Vocals: Lynn Mabry, Dawn Silva
Drums: Jim Wright
Bass: Rodney Curtis
Piano, Synthesizers, Synth Bass: Bernie Worrell

"Nappy"

Vocals: Lynn Mabry, Dawn Silva, Jeanette Washington
Drums: Jerome Brailey
Bass: Bootsy Collins
Piano: Bernie Worrell
Guitar: Garry Shider, Michael Hampton

"Birdie"

Vocals: Dawn Silva, Lynn Mabry, George Clinton
Drums: Jerome Brailey
Bass: Rodney Curtis
Clavinet, Strings: Bernie Worrell
Guitar: Garry Shider, Mike Hampton
Trumpet: Richard Griffith, Rick Gardner
Sax: Maceo Parker
Trombone: Fred Wesley

"Just Like You"

Vocals: Lynn Mabry, Dawn Silva
Drums: Tyrone Lampkin
Bass: Rodney Curtis
Electric Piano, Strings: Bernie Worrell
Guitar: Garry Shider

"When You're Gone"

Vocals: Dawn Silva, Lynn Mabry, Mudbone Cooper
Drums: Mudbone Cooper
Bass: Rick Gilmore
String Synthesizer: Bernie Worrell
Orchestra: Detroit Symphony Orchestra
Guitar: Catfish Collins, Garry Shider
Trumpet: Waymond Reed
Sax: Maceo Parker
Trombone: Fred Wesley

"Amorous"

Vocals: Lynn Mabry, Dawn Silva
Drums: Jim Wright
Bass: Rodney Curtis
Keyboards, Synthesizers: Bernie Worrell
Guitar: Garry Shider
Trumpet: Richard Griffith, Rick Gardner
Sax: Maceo Parker
Trombone: Fred Wesley
Orchestra: Detroit Symphony Orchestra

Never Buy Texas from a Cowboy

"Never Buy Texas from A Cowboy"

Vocals: Sheila Horne, Dawn Silva, Jeanette McGruder

Backup Vocals: George Clinton, Lige Curry, Mallia Franklin, Pat Lewis, Michael Clip Payne, Garry Shider, Robert Peanut Johnson, Joe Pep Harris

Drums: Jerry Jones

Bass: Bruce Nazarian

Keyboards, Synthesizers: Bernie Worrell, Rudi Robinson

Guitar: Bruce Nazarian, Michael Hampton, Gordon Carlton

Handclap Boards: Carl "Butch" Small

"Never Buy Texas from a Cowboy" was the Brides of Funkenstein's highest-charting single. Much like "Knee Deep," it is a whopping 15 minutes long and features lots of backup singers, and this time, the second iteration of the Brides is featured (Silva staying on, with the addition of Sheila Horne and Jeannette McGruder). In addition to Bernie Worrell and Michael Hampton, much of the band on this record is the same group of session players that recorded much of the Philippe Wynne album *Wynne Jammin* a year later.

"I'm Holding You Responsible"

Vocals: Dawn Silva, Jeanette McGruder, Sheila Horne, Lige Curry, Michael Clip Payne, Garry Shider, Robert Peanut Johnson, Mallia Franklin

Drums: Dennis Chambers

Bass: Jeff Bunn

Keyboards, Synthesizers: Jerome Rodgers

Guitar: Eddie Hazel

Orchestra: Detroit Symphony Orchestra

"Smoke Signals"

Vocals: Dawn Silva, Jeanette McGruder, Sheila Horne, George Clinton, Lige Curry, Eddie Hazel, Michael Clip Payne, Garry Shider, Robert Peanut Johnson, Mallia Franklin, Jessica Celaves

Drums: Bootsy Collins

Bass: Bootsy Collins

Keyboards, Synthesizers: David Spradley

Guitar: Catfish Collins, Bootsy Collins

Trumpet: Richard Griffith, Rick Gardner

Sax: Maceo Parker

Trombone: Fred Wesley

"Mother May I?"

Vocals: Dawn Silva, Jeanette McGruder, Sheila Horne, Tracey Lewis, Jessica Cleaves, Lige Curry, George Clinton, Garry Shider, Michael Clip Payne, Robert Peanut Johnson

Drums: Dennis Chambers

Percussion: Larry Fratangelo

Bass: Jeff Bunn

Keyboards, Synthesizers: Bernie Worrell

Guitar: Dewayne Blackbyrd McKnight, Garry Shider

Trumpet: Bennie Cowan

Sax: Greg Thomas

Trombone: Fred Wesley

"Party Up in Here"

Vocals: Dawn Silva, Jeanette McGruder, Sheila Horne, Lige Curry, Robert Peanut Johnson, Michael Clip Payne, George Clinton, Garry Shider, Mallia Franklin

Drums: Dennis Chambers

Bass: Rodney Curtis

Handclap Boards, Synth Drums: Carl Butch Small

Percussion: Larry Fratangelo

Keyboards, Synthesizers: Ernestro Wilson

Guitar: Dewayne McKnight

Trumpet: Bennie Cowan

Sax: Greg Thomas

Trombone: Greg Boyer

The Brides of Funkenstein. Front to back—Lynn Mabry & Dawn Silva. © Diem Jones

"Didn't Mean to Fall in Love"

Vocals: Dawn Silva, Jeanette McGruder, Sheila Horne,
Drums: Jerry Jones
Bass: Donnie Sterling
Percussion: Carl "Butch" Small
Keyboards, Synthesizers: Rudy Robinson
Guitar: Bruce Nazarian, Rodney Crutcher
Orchestra: Detroit Symphony Orchestra

Released Later

"Love Is Something"

Vocals: Dawn Silva, Lynn Mabry, Eddie Hazel, Jim Callon
Drums: Tiki Fulwood or Jon Gerlach
Bass: Billy Nelson
Keyboards, Synthesizers: Bernie Worrell
Guitar: Eddie Hazel, Jim Callon
Sax: Eli Fontaine

"Take My Love"

Vocals: Lynn Mabry, Dawn Silva, Mudbone Cooper
Drums: Mudbone Cooper
Percussion: Mudbone Cooper
Bass: Cordell Mosson
Guitar: Garry Shider
Piano: Bernie Worrell

"Ice Melting in Your Heart"

Vocals: Lynn Mabry, Dawn Silva
Drums: Tyrone Lampkin
Bass: Junie Morrison
Guitar: Garry Shider, Junie Morrison
Electric Piano: Bernie Worrell
Orchestra: Detroit Symphony Orchestra

"Love Don't Come Easy"

Vocals: Dawn Silva, Sheila Horne, Jeanette MacGruder
Drums: Donnie Sterling
Bass: Donnie Sterling
Keyboards, Synthesizers: David Spradley
Guitar: Gordon Carlton, Tony Thomas
Orchestra: Detroit Symphony Orchestra

"Twenty Bucks"

Vocals: Dawn Silva, Jeanette McGruder, Sheila Horne
Drums: Jerry Jones
Percussion: Carl "Butch" Small
Bass: Donnie Sterling
Piano: Rudy Robinson
Guitar: Bruce Nazarian, Rodney Crutcher
Strings, Horns: Wade Marcus

"Just for Play"

Vocals: Dawn Silva, Jeanette McGruder, Sheila Horne, Janice Evans, Shirley Hayden, Jeanette Washington, Ron Ford, Lige Curry, Michael Clip Payne
Drums: Kenny Colton
Bass: Lige Curry
Piano, Synthesizers: David Spradley
Guitar: Tony Thomas

"Up Up Up and Away"

Vocals: Dawn Silva, Jeanette McGruder, Sheila Horne
Drums: Jerry Jones
Percussion: Carl "Butch" Small
Bass: Rodrick Chandler
Keyboards, Synthesizers: Rudy Robinson, Bernie Worrell
Guitar: Eddie Willis
Orchestra: Detroit Symphony Orchestra

— ☆ —

The Brides of Funkenstein and Dr. Funkenstein. L–R: Dawn Silva, George Clinton, and Lynn Mabry. © Diem Jones

DR. FUNKENSTEIN AND BRIDES OF FUNKENSTEIN: 1978

Originally Unreleased

"Rat Kissed the Cat"

Vocals: Lynn Mabry, Dawn Silva, George Clinton
Drums: Tyrone Lampkin
Bass: Billy Nelson
Guitar: Garry Shider
Piano: Bernie Worrell
Trumpet: Richard Griffith, Rick Gardner
Sax: Maceo Parker
Trombone: Fred Wesley

— ☆ —

BERNIE WORRELL: 1978, 1990–2016

The albums released by the massively influential keyboardist Bernie Worrell, featuring his musical intuition and taste, arranging abilities, and classical training, are a keystone of the P-Funk sound. Any conversation about the genius of P-Funk's music could not hold weight if Bernie's name was not involved. He was an extremely important composer, string and horn arranger, and contributor to most of the albums in the heyday of the canon, and almost all of the hits had his trademark keyboards, piano, synth bass, synth leads, clavinet, and organ. He was a key contributor to the Parliament-Funkadelic sound and to popular music as it is known today. Likewise, his solo albums prove his sterling musical reputation as well as his extremely gifted versatility. He was comfortable in all genres.

Arista Records

All the Woo in the World

"Woo Together"

Vocals: Bernie Worrell, Junie Morrisson, Dawn Silva, Sheila Horne, Jeanette MacGruder, Linda Shider
Drums: Tyrone Lampkin
Bass: Rodney Curtis
Keyboards, Synthesizers: Bernie Worrell
Guitar: Garry Shider
Trumpet: Richard Griffth, Rick Gardner
Sax: Maceo Parker
Trombone: Fred Wesley

"I'll Be with You"

Vocals: Junie Morrison, Garry Shider, Dawn Silva, Sheila Horne, and Jeanette MacGruder

Drums: Tyrone Lampkin
Bass: Rodney Curtis
Keyboards, Synthesizers: Junie Morrison, Bernie Worrell
Guitar: Garry Shider

"Hold On"

Vocals: Bernie Worrell, Dawn Silva, Sheila Horne, and Jeanette MacGruder

Drums: Tyrone Lampkin
Bass: Rodney Curtis
Keyboards, Synthesizers: Bernie Worrell, Junie Morrison
Guitar: Garry Shider
Trombone: Fred Wesley

"Much Thrust"

Vocals: Bernie Worrell, Sheila Horne
Drums: Gary Mudbone Cooper
Bass: Bootsy Collins
Keyboards, Synthesizers: Bernie Worrell
Guitar: Bootsy Collins

"Happy to Have (Happiness on Our Side)"

Vocals: Bernie Worrell
Drums: Tyrone Lampkin
Bass: Rodney Curtis
Keyboards, Synthesizers: Bernie Worrell
Guitar: Garry Shider, Michael Hampton

"Insurance Man for the Funk"

Vocals: George Clinton, Bernie Worrell, Mudbone Cooper, Robert Peanut Johnson, Dawn Silva, Sheila Horne, Jeanette MacGruder
Drums: Gary Mudbone Cooper
Bass: Bootsy Collins
Keyboards, Synthesizers: Bernie Worrell
Guitar: Garry Shider, Bootsy Collins
Trumpet: Rick Gardner, Richard Kush Griffith
Sax: Maceo Parker
Trombone: Fred Wesley

"Insurance Man for the Funk" was the single from Bernie Worrell's first album, *All the Woo in the World*, produced by George Clinton. Indeed, George sings the lead on this cut. The whole album showcased the Parliament-Funkadelic machine itself at the time (Bernie's input was always massively important), as this album could almost as easily be a Parliament, Funkadelic, or Bootsy record from the time.

"Reprise (Much Thrust)"

Vocals: Bernie Worrell
Drums: Gary Mudbone Cooper
Bass: Bootsy Collins
Keyboards, Synthesizers: Bernie Worrell
Guitar: Bootsy Collins

Originally Unreleased

"Who Do You Love?"

Vocals: Bernie Worrell
Drums: Tyrone Lampkin

Bass: Rodney Curtis
Keyboards, Synthesizers: Bernie Worrell
Orchestra: Detroit Symphony Orchestra
Guitar: Garry Shider
Sax: Eli Fontaine?

Gramavision Records

Funk of Ages

"Y-Spy"

Clavinet, Synthesizer, Organ, Lead Vocals: Bernie Worrell
Drums, Guitar, Percussion, Vocal: Steve Jordan
Bass, Snare, Lap Steel Guitar: Charlie Drayton
Guitar: Keith Richards
Backup Vocals: Mudbone Cooper, Loren Qualls

"B.W. Jam"

Clavinet, Synthesizer, Synth Bass, Percussion: Bernie Worrell
Drum Programming, Synth Horns, Samples, Sequencing: Joe Polanco, Mudbone Cooper
Sax: Crispin Cioe, Arno Hecht
Trumpet: Paul Litteral
Trombone: Robert Fund
Backup Vocals: Bernie Worrell, Mudbone Cooper, Sheila Washington, Steve Washington, Jenny Douglas-McRae

"Funk-A-Hall-Licks"

Clavinet, Synthesizer, Organ, Lead Vocals: Bernie Worrell
Drums: Steve Jordan
Guitar: Keith Richards, Jimmy Ripp
Sax: Maceo Parker
Backup Vocals: Mudbone Cooper, Sheila Washington, Jody Bell, Doug Duffy

"Ain't She Sweet"

Piano, Synthesizer, Synth Bass, Vocals:
Bernie Worrell

Bass, Drum Programming, Vocals: Bootsy
Collins

Synthesizer: Herbie Hancock

Percussion: Larry Fratangelo

Banjo: Jimmy Ripp

Vocals: Mudbone Cooper

"Straight Ahead"

**Clavinet, Synthesizer, Synth Bass, Lead
Vocals:** Bernie Worrell

Drums: Steve Ferrone

Guitar: Jimmy Ripp

Bass: Warren McRae

Backup Vocals: Mudbone Cooper, Sheila
Washington, Patty Maloney, John DeNicola,
Michael Camacho, Doug Duffy

"Real Life Dreams"

Organ, Clavinet, Synthesizer, Lead Vocals:
Bernie Worrell

Drums: Sly Dunbar

Bass: Robbie Shakespeare

Guitar: Jimmy Ripp, Steve Jordan

Percussion: Larry Fratangelo, Mudbone
Cooper

Backup Vocals: Sheila Washington, Jody Bell

"Sing"

Synthesizer, Organ, Synth Bass, Lead Vocals:
Bernie Worrell

Drums: Steve Ferrone

Guitar, Electric Sitar: Jimmy Ripp

Guitar: Michael Hampton

Percussion: Larry Fratangelo

Backup Vocals: David Byrne, Mudbone
Cooper, Sheila Washington

"Don't Piss Me Off"

Synthesizer, Synth Bass, Samples: Bernie
Worrell

Lead Vocals: Phoebe Snow, Mudbone Cooper

Organ: Jerry Harrison

Drums: Dennis Chambers

Slide Guitar: Chris Spedding

Guitar: Keith Richards, Jimmy Ripp

Turntable: Davy D

Percussion: Jerome Brailey

Backup Vocals: Bernie Worrell, Sheila
Washington, Butch Alexander, Mudbone
Cooper, Rosemary Camera, Jody Bell

"Beware of Dog"

Clavinet, Organ, Synthesizer: Bernie Worrell

Guitar: Vernon Reid

Drums: Doug Bowne

Bass: Jimmy Hawkes

Sax: Maceo Parker

"Volunteered Slavery/Bern's Blues/Outer
Spaceways"

Hammond B-3 Organ, Electric Piano, Vocals:
Bernie Worrell

Vocals: Mudbone Cooper

Chatan, Conga, Tambourine, Bells: Aiyb
Dieng

"At Mos' Pheres"

Hammond B-3, DX-7: Bernie Worrell

"Real Life Dreams On"

Organ, Clavinet, Synthesizer, Lead Vocals:
Bernie Worrell

Drums: Sly Dunbar

Bass: Robbie Shakespeare

Guitar: Jimmy Ripp, Steve Jordan

Percussion: Larry Fratangelo, Mudbone
Cooper

Blackatronic Science

"Revelation in Black Light"

Harpsichord: Bernie Worrell
Strings: Material strings arranged by Bernie Worrell, conducted by Karl Berger

"Flex"

Hammond B-3 Organ, Minimoog: Bernie Worrell
Vocals: James Sumbi, Mike G., George Clinton, Bootsy Collins, Mudbone Cooper
Guitar: Bootsy Collins
Sax: Maceo Parker
Trombone: Fred Wesley
Loops, Beats: Bill Laswell, Darryl Mack

"Time Was (Events in the Elsewhere)"

Hammond B-3 Organ, Minimoog, Melodica, Vocals: Bernie Worrell
Vocals: George Clinton, Bootsy Collins, Mudbone Cooper, Debra Barsha
Cowbells: Aiyb Dieng
Samples: Bill Laswell

"Blood Secrets"

Hammond B-3 Organ: Bernie Worrell
Sax: Maceo Parker
Drums: Tony Williams

"Dissinfordollars"

Synthesizer, Clavinet, Minimoog: Bernie Worrell
Vocals: George Clinton, Bootsy Collins, Mudbone Cooper
Sax: Maceo Parker
Trombone: Fred Wesley
Guitar: Bootsy Collins
Drum Loop: Sly Dunbar
Chatan: Aiyb Dieng
Sound Effects: Bill Laswell

"The Vision"

Clavinet, Synthesizer, Electric Piano: Bernie Worrell
Vocals: James Sumbi, Mike G.
Acoustic Bass Guitar: Bootsy Collins
Sax: Maceo Parker
Trombone: Fred Wesley
Drum Loop: Sly Dunbar
Talking Drums, Chatan, Cowbells: Aiyb Dieng

"Won't Go Away"

Synthesizer, Clavinet, Minimoog: Bernie Worrell
Strings: Material strings arranged by Bernie Worrell, conducted by Karl Berger
Vocals: Mike G, George Clinton, Mudbone Cooper
Guitar: Bootsy Collins
Loops: Bill Laswell

"X-Factor"

Hammond B-3 Organ: Bernie Worrell
Sax, Flute: Maceo Parker
Drums: Tony Williams

"Disappearance"

Strings: Material strings arranged by Bernie Worrell, conducted by Karl Berger

CMP Records

Pieces of Woo: The Other Side

"Witness for the Defense"

Organ, Synthesizer: Bernie Worrell
Trombone: Fred Wesley
French Horn: Vincent Chancey
Bass Clarinet: Marty Ehrlich
Bassoon: Janet Grice
Clarinet: Patience Higgins
Woodwind Arrangement: Bernie Worrell

"Set the Tone/Victory"

Minimoog, Clavinet: Bernie Worrell
Organ: Bernie Worrell, Amina Claudine Myers
Vocals: Umar Bin Hassan

"The Mask"

Organ: Bernie Worrell
Guitar, Effects: Buckethead

"Gladiator Skull"

Organ, Synthesizer: Bernie Worrell
Beats, Loops, Samples: Bill Laswell

"Moon over Brixton"

Organ, Synthesizer: Bernie Worrell
Trombone: Fred Wesley
French Horn: Vincent Chancey
Bass Clarinet: Marty Ehrlich
Bassoon: Janet Grice
Clarinet: Patience Higgins
Woodwind Arrangement: Bernie Worrell
Noise: Bill Laswell

"Judie's Passion Purple"

Electric Piano, Organ: Bernie Worrell
Organ: Amina Claudine Myers
Noise: Bill Laswell

"Fields of Play"

Synthesizer: Bernie Worrell
Samples, Effects: Bill Laswell
Sounds: Oz Fritz

Polystar Records

Free Agent: A Spaced Odyssey

"Hope Is Here"

Keyboards, Synthesizers, Vocals: Bernie
Worrell

"Afrofuturism (Phazedone)"

Keyboards, Synthesizers, Vocals: Bernie
Worrell
Drums, Tabla Percussion: Hamid Drake
Bass: Bill Laswell
Chatan, Congas, Percussion, Bells: Aiyb
Dieng

"In Pursuit"

All Keyboards and Synthesizers: Bernie
Worrell
Drums, Tabla, Percussion: Hamid Drake
Chatan, Congas, Percussion, Bells: Aiyb
Dieng
Guitar: Dominic Kanza
Bass, Bells: Bill Laswell

"Woo Awakens, the Wizard Cometh"

All Keyboards and Synthesizers: Bernie
Worrell
Guitar: Buckethead

"Re-enter Black Light (Entersection)"

All Keyboards and Synthesizers: Bernie
Worrell
Bass, Guitar, Beats, Sound Effects: Jean Pierre
Sluys

"Warriors Off to Woo"

All Keyboards and Synthesizers: Bernie
Worrell
Guitar: Buckethead

Improvisczario

"New Boss"

Drums: Will Calhoun
Bass: Brett Bass
Baby Grand Piano: Bernie Worrell

"Up in the Hills"

Baby Grand Piano: Bernie Worrell
Banjo: Mike Gordon
Bass: Brett Bass
Drums: Will Calhoun

"Bass on the Line"

Bass: Brett Bass
Drums: Will Calhoun
Electric Piano: Bernie Worrell
Sax, Flute: Darryl Dixon

"Dirty"

Bass: Brett Bass
Clavinet: Bernie Worrell
Drums: Will Calhoun
Guitar: Warren Haynes

"Killer Mosquito"

Bass: Brett Bass
Drums: Will Calhoun
Guitar: Warren Haynes
Organ: Bernie Worrell

"OK, You Can Leave Now"

Drums: Will Calhoun
Bass: Brett Bass
Electric Piano: Bernie Worrell
Sax: Darryl Dixon

"Celeste"

Bass: Brett Bass
Drums: Will Calhoun
Celeste Piano: Bernie Worrell

Independent Releases

Christmas Woo

"Little Drummer Boy"

All Keyboards and Synthesizers: Bernie
 Worrel

"Hark the Herald Angels Sing"

All Keyboards: Bernie Worrell

"Deck the Halls"

All Keyboards: Bernie Worrell

"Oh Holy Night"

All Keyboards: Bernie Worrell

"We Three Kings"

All Keyboards: Bernie Worrell

"Silent Night"

All Keyboards and Synthesizers: Bernie
 Worrell

"Oh Come All Ye Faithful"

All Keyboards and Synthesizers: Bernie
 Worrell

I Don't Even Know

"First Things First"

Piano, Keyboards: Bernie Worrell

"Tribal Up"

Keyboards, Synthesizers: Bernie Worrell

"Shades of the Kid"

Synthesizers, Keyboards: Bernie Worrell

"Next"

Vocoder, Synthesizers, Keyboards: Bernie
 Worrell
Drums: Evan Taylor?, JT Lewis?

"Thug"

All Keyboards, Synthesizers, Vocals: Bernie
 Worrell
Drum Programming: Evan Taylor?, JT Lewis?

"Refurbish"

Vocals, Keyboards: Bernie Worrell
Drum Programming: Evan Taylor?, JT Lewis?

"Tribale"

Drums: Evan Taylor?, JT Lewis?
Vocoder, Keyboards: Bernie Worrell

"Tree-Fore"

Melodicas: Bernie Worrell

"One Rabbit"

Keyboards: Bernie Worrell
Guitar: Kyle Cadena?
Drums: Evan Taylor?, JT Lewis?
Bass: Tim Luntzell?

"Judicious"

Piano, Keyboards: Bernie Worrell
Drums: Evan Taylor?, JT Lewis?
Bass: Tim Luntzell?

"Hearin' Dis, Playin' Dat"

Drum Programming: Evan Taylor?, JT Lewis?
Organ, Clavinet, Vocoder, Synthesizer:
   Bernie Worrell

"Sunrise"

Keyboards: Bernie Worrell
Drum Programming: Evan Taylor?, JT Lewis?

"Beef"

Vocals, Melodica, Synthesizer: Bernie Worrell
Drum Programming: Evan Taylor?, JT Lewis?

"Once Again (First Things First Reprise)"

Piano, Keyboards: Bernie Worrell

"Take the A Train"

Piano: Bernie Worrell

Standards

"Take Five"

Synthesizer, Keyboards: Bernie Worrell
Drums: Evan Taylor or JT Lewis
Bass: Tim Luntzel or Melvin Gibbs
Guitar: Ronny Drayton, Smokey Hormel,
   Andrew Kimball, or Kyle Cadena

"Aqua De Beber"

Piano: Bernie Worrell
Drums: Evan Taylor or JT Lewis
Bass: Tim Luntzel or Melvin Gibbs
Guitar: Ronny Drayton, Smokey Hormel,
   Andrew Kimball, or Kyle Cadena

"All the Things You Are"

Synthesizer, Keyboards, Synth Bass: Bernie
   Worrell
Drums: Evan Taylor or JT Lewis
Percussion, Vibraphone: Glen Fittin
Bass: Tim Luntzel or Melvin Gibbs
Guitar: Ronny Drayton, Smokey Hormel,
   Andrew Kimball, or Kyle Cadena
Alto Sax: Darryl Dixon
Tenor, Baritone Sax, Flute: David Watson
Trombone: Jonathan Arons
Trumpet, Flugelhorn: Freddie Hendrix

"You're My Thrill"

Organ: Bernie Worrell
Drums: Evan Taylor or JT Lewis
Percussion, Vibraphone: Glen Fittin
Bass: Tim Luntzel or Melvin Gibbs
Guitar: Ronny Drayton, Smokey Hormel,
   Andrew Kimball, or Kyle Cadena

"Bye Blackbyrd"

Synthesizer, Keyboards: Bernie Worrell
Drums: Evan Taylor or JT Lewis
Percussion: Glen Fittin
Bass: Tim Luntzel or Melvin Gibbs
Guitar: Ronny Drayton, Smokey Hormel,
  Andrew Kimball, or Kyle Cadena
Alto Sax: Darryl Dixon
Tenor, Baritone Sax, Flute: David Watson
Trombone: Jonathan Arons
Trumpet, Flugelhorn: Freddie Hendrix

"Watermelon Man"

Clavinet, Synthesizer: Bernie Worrell
Drums: Evan Taylor or JT Lewis
Bass: Tim Luntzel or Melvin Gibbs
Guitar: Ronny Drayton, Smokey Hormel,
  Andrew Kimball, or Kyle Cadena

"Killer Joe"

Electric Piano, Keyboards: Bernie Worrell
Drums: Evan Taylor or JT Lewis
Percussion, Vibraphone: Glen Fittin
Bass: Tim Luntzel or Melvin Gibbs
Guitar: Ronny Drayton, Smokey Hormel,
  Andrew Kimball, or Kyle Cadena
Alto Sax: Darryl Dixon
Tenor, Baritone Sax, Flute: David Watson
Trombone: Jonathan Arons
Trumpet, Flugelhorn: Freddie Hendrix

"Moon River"

Melodica: Bernie Worrell
Vibraphone: Glen Fittin
Drums: Evan Taylor or JT Lewis
Bass: Tim Luntzel or Melvin Gibbs
Guitar: Ronny Drayton, Smokey Hormel,
  Andrew Kimball, or Kyle Cadena

BWO Is Landing—Bernie Worrell Orchestra

"So Uptight"

Drums, Percussion: Evan Taylor
Bass: Scott Hogan
Guitar: Andrew Kimball, Kyle Cadena
Keyboards: Bernie Worrell
Alto Sax: Shlomi Cohen
Tenor Sax: Ofer Assaf
Trumpet: Justin Mullens
Violin: Nicole Scorsone

"BWO Is Landing"

Drums, Percussion: Evan Taylor
Bass: Scott Hogan
Guitar: Andrew Kimball, Kyle Cadena
Keyboards: Bernie Worrell
Alto Sax: Shlomi Cohen
Tenor Sax: Ofer Assaf
Trumpet: Justin Mullens
Violin: Nicole Scorsone

"Spread the WOO in the World"

Drums, Percussion: Evan Taylor
Bass: Scott Hogan
Guitar: Andrew Kimball, Kyle Cadena
Keyboards: Bernie Worrell
Alto Sax: Shlomi Cohen
Tenor Sax: Ofer Assaf
Trumpet: Justin Mullens
Violin: Nicole Scorsone

"Moneypenny"

Drums, Percussion: Evan Taylor
Bass: Scott Hogan
Guitar: Andrew Kimball, Kyle Cadena
Keyboards: Bernie Worrell
Alto Sax: Shlomi Cohen
Tenor Sax: Ofer Assaf
Trumpet: Justin Mullens
Violin: Nicole Scorsone

"Double W"

Drums, Percussion: Evan Taylor
Bass: Mike Watt
Guitar: Andrew Kimball, Kyle Cadena
Keyboards: Bernie Worrell
Alto Sax: Shlomi Cohen
Tenor Sax: Ofer Assaf
Trumpet: Justin Mullens
Violin: Nicole Scorsone

"Piri"

Drums, Percussion: Evan Taylor
Bass: Scott Hogan
Guitar: Andrew Kimball, Kyle Cadena
Keyboards: Bernie Worrell
Alto Sax: Shlomi Cohen
Tenor Sax: Ofer Assaf
Trumpet: Justin Mullens
Violin: Nicole Scorsone

"Get Your Hands Off"

Drums, Percussion: Evan Taylor
Bass: Scott Hogan
Guitar: Andrew Kimball, Kyle Cadena
Keyboards: Bernie Worrell
Alto Sax: Shlomi Cohen
Tenor Sax: Ofer Assaf
Trumpet: Justin Mullens
Violin: Nicole Scorsone

"Thug (Live)"

Drums, Percussion: Evan Taylor
Bass: Scott Hogan
Guitar: Andrew Kimball, Kyle Cadena
Keyboards: Bernie Worrell
Alto Sax: Shlomi Cohen
Tenor Sax: Ofer Assaf
Trumpet: Justin Mullens
Violin: Nicole Scorsone

Single

"Gnawing Jaws of the Jack O'Lantern"

Bass: Scott Hogan
Drums: Evan Taylor
Guitar: Andrew Kimball, Kyle Cadena
Keyboards: Bernie Worrell
Percussion: Glen Fittin

Elecation (The Upper Air)

"In a Silent Way"

Piano: Bernie Worrell

"I'd Rather Be with You"

Piano: Bernie Worrell

"Alabama"

Piano: Bernie Worrell

"Goodbye Pork Pie Hat"

Piano: Bernie Worrell

"Light on Water"

Piano: Bernie Worrell

"Ooh Child"

Piano: Bernie Worrell

"Samba Pa Ti"

Piano: Bernie Worrell

"Realm of Sight"

Piano: Bernie Worrell

"I Wanna Go Outside in the Rain"

Piano: Bernie Worrell

"Wings"

Piano: Bernie Worrell

"Redemption Song"

Piano: Bernie Worrell

Retrospective

"A Joyful Process"

Clavinet, Organ, Synth Bass: Bernie Worrell
Drums: Evan Taylor

"If You Got Funk You Style"

Synthesizer, Keyboards, Synth Bass, Piano:
  Bernie Worrell
Drums: Evan Taylor

"Grooveallegience"

Drums: Evan Taylor
Synthesizers, Keyboards, Synth Bass: Bernie
  Worrell

"Sir Nose D'VoidofFunk"

Drums: Evan Taylor
Synthesizer, Piano, Keyboards, Synth Bass:
  Bernie Worrell

"Wake Up"

Synthesizers, Organ, Clavinet, Synth Bass:
  Bernie Worrell

"Flashlight"

Drums: Evan Taylor
Keyboards, Synth Bass, Synthesizer: Bernie
  Worrell

"You Hit the Nail on the Head"

Organ, Melodica, Synth Bass, Keyboards:
  Bernie Worrell
Drums: Evan Taylor

"Adolescent Funk"

Drums: Evan Taylor

Synth Bass, Organ, Synthesizer: Bernie
  Worrell

"Aqua Boogie"

Drums: Evan Taylor
Synthesizers, Keyboards, Synth Bass, Piano:
  Bernie Worrell

"Balance"

Drums: Evan Taylor
Synth Bass, Keyboard, Organ, Piano: Bernie
  Worrell

"The Moment"

Synth Bass, Synthesizers, Keyboard: Bernie
  Worrell
Drums: Evan Taylor

"With Bill Laswell: By a River (For Peter)"

Electric Piano: Bernie Worrell
Fretless Bass, Electronics: Bill Laswell

— ☆ —

JUNIE: 1978–2017

Originally the keyboardist (and one of the strongest vocal personalities) for the Ohio Players, Junie Morrison would go on to join George Clinton and P-Funk on some of the most commercially successful P-Funk outings to date, including "One Nation Under a Groove," "Aqua Boogie," "Knee Deep," and several others. A multi-instrumentalist and master arranger, most of Junie's best work is mostly or completely performed by Junie on all instruments and vocals, with notable exceptions, including the previously mentioned songs. His solo career is no different, with Junie handling almost all the chores from record to record (special mention to contributor Lynn Mabry on many of Junie's most famous post–P-Funk solo albums).

"Super Spirit"
All Vocals and Instruments: Junie Morrison

"Triune"
All Vocals and Instruments: Junie Morrison

"Can't Get Over Losing You"
All Vocals and Instruments: Junie Morrison

Columbia Records

Bread Alone

"Love Has Taken Me Over"
All Vocals and Instruments: Junie Morrison
Additional Vocals: Lynn Mabry

"Why"
All Vocals and Instruments: Junie Morrison
Additional Vocals: Lynn Mabry

"Bread Alone"
All Vocals and Instruments: Junie Morrison

"Naguals Theme"
All Vocals and Instruments: Junie Morrison

"Funky Parts"
All Vocals and Instruments: Junie Morrison
Additional Vocals: Lynn Mabry

"Seaman First Class"
All Vocals and Instruments: Junie Morrison

"Apple Song"
All Vocals and Instruments: Junie Morrison

5

"Rappin' about Rappin'"
All Vocals and Instruments: Junie Morrison
Additional Vocals: Lynn Mabry

"I Love You Madly"
All Vocals and Instruments: Junie Morrison
Additional Vocals: Lynn Mabry

"Cry Me a River"
All Vocals and Instruments: Junie Morrison

"Victim of Love"
All Vocals and Instruments: Junie Morrison
Additional Vocals: Lynn Mabry

"5"
All Vocals and Instruments: Junie Morrison
Additional Vocals: Lynn Mabry

"Last One to Know"
All Vocals and Instruments: Junie Morrison
Additional Vocals: Lynn Mabry

"Jarr the Ground"
All Vocals and Instruments: Junie Morrison

"Taste of Love"
All Vocals and Instruments: Junie Morrison
Additional Vocals: Lynn Mabry

Independent Releases

Evacuate Your Seats

"Tease Me"
All Vocals and Instruments: Junie Morrison

"Show Me Yours"
All Vocals and Instruments: Junie Morrison

"Stick It In"
All Vocals and Instruments: Junie Morrison

"Gyrate"
All Vocals and Instruments: Junie Morrison

"Break 6"
All Vocals and Instruments: Junie Morrison

"Driving in a Porsche"
All Vocals and Instruments: Junie Morrison

"Techno Freqs"
All Vocals and Instruments: Junie Morrison

"Here with You Tonight"
All Vocals and Instruments: Junie Morrison

When the City

"When the City"
All Vocals and Instruments: Junie Morrison

"Booty 4-2"
All Vocals and Instruments: Junie Morrison

"Friends"
All Vocals and Instruments: Junie Morrison

"Now and Evermore"
All Vocals and Instruments: Junie Morrison

"L.A. Stories"
All Vocals and Instruments: Junie Morrison

"Robot Love"
All Vocals and Instruments: Junie Morrison

"I'm Lying"
All Vocals and Instruments: Junie Morrison

"Discreet"
All Vocals and Instruments: Junie Morrison

"That Dress"
All Vocals and Instruments: Junie Morrison

"When the City (Ride Mix)"
All Vocals and Instruments: Junie Morrison

"Cloud Sorcerer's Lament"
All Vocals and Instruments: Junie Morrison

Late-Period Singles

"Pieces"
All Vocals and Instruments: Junie Morrison

"Bobblehead"
All Vocals and Instruments: Junie Morrison

"West 4th Street"
All Vocals and Instruments: Junie Morrison

"Sunday Morning"
All Vocals and Instruments: Junie Morrison

"Freckles"
All Vocals and Instruments: Junie Morrison

"Sneaky"
All Vocals and Instruments: Junie Morrison

"Rain"
All Vocals and Instruments: Junie Morrison

"Those Days"
All Vocals and Instruments: Junie Morrison

"Back Tu Da Funk"
All Vocals and Instruments: Junie Morrison

"Techno Freqs"

All Vocals and Instruments: Junie Morrison

"Pretend I Don't Love You"

All Vocals and Instruments: Junie Morrison

"Stick It In"

All Vocals and Instruments: Junie Morrison

"The Algorithm Tacheon Flow"

All Vocals and Instruments: Junie Morrison

"Contemplating Sound for Mind and Body"

All Vocals and Instruments: Junie Morrison

"Copying Atlantis (BoyInSea)"

All Vocals and Instruments: Junie Morrison

"Abstractia (BoyInSea)"

All Vocals and Instruments: Junie Morrison

"Tekadelic Good for You"

All Vocals and Instruments: Junie Morrison

"MicroNagual: Space Wars on the Dance Floor"

All Vocals and Instruments: Junie Morrison

"Love Has Taken Me Over Reloaded"

All Vocals and Instruments: Junie Morrison

"The Algorithm: The Daydreamers"

All Vocals and Instruments: Junie Morrison

"MicroNagual: Vibrate You"

All Vocals and Instruments: Junie Morrison

— ☆ —

TREYLEWD'S FLASTIC BRAIN FLAM: 1978–1981

This was the band of George Clinton's son, vocalist/guitarist/songwriter Tracey "Treylewd" Lewis, which also featured guitarist/vocalist/songwriter Andre "Foxxe" Williams, drummer Tony LaFoot, bassist Stevie Parnell, and others. These songs were unreleased at the time and later released on the George Clinton Family Series albums in 1993.

"Personal Problems"

Vocals: Tracey Lewis, Andre Williams
Drums: Dean Ragland
Bass: Ken Williams
Guitar: Andre Williams, Tracey Lewis

"I Can't Stand It"

Vocals: Tracey Lewis, Garry Shider, Linda Shider, Ray Davis, Andre Williams, Patty Walker, Tony Davis, Stevie Pannell, Dawn Silva, Jeanette McGruder, Sheila Horne
Drums: Tony LaFoot
Bass: Stevie Pannell
Guitar: Andre Williams, Garry Shider
Keyboards, Synthesizers: David Spradley

"She Never Do's Things"

Vocals: Tracey Lewis, Garry Shider, Linda Shider, Kevin Shider, Andre Williams, Patty Walker, Sheila Horne, Jeanette McGruder, Dawn Silva, Janice Evans, Shirley Hayden, Jeanette Washington, Ray Davis
Drums: Tony LaFoot
Bass: Garry Shider
Guitar: Garry Shider
Keyboards, Synthesizers: David Spradley

"Clone Ranger"

Vocals: Tracey Lewis, Andre Williams, George Clinton, Patty Walker, Darryl Clinton
Drums: Darryl Clinton
Bass: Tracey Lewis
Guitar: Tracey Lewis, Andre Williams
Keyboards, Synthesizers: Andre Williams

"Michelle"

Lead Vocals: Tracey Lewis
Backup Vocals: Kevin Shider, Andre Williams, Tracey Lewis, Patty Walker, Garry Shider, Linda Shider, Dawn Silva, Jeanette McGruder, Sheila Horne, Shirley Hayden, Jeanette Washington, Ray Davis, Robert Peanut Johnson, Jessica Cleaves, Pat Lewis, Stevie Pannell
Drums: Dennis Chambers
Bass: Jeff Bunn
Synthesizers: Gary Hudgins
Guitar: Garry Shider

MUTINY (SELECT TRACKS): 1979–

> This was Jerome Brailey's band and project after leaving Parliament-Funkadelic around 1978. It features concepts and albums critical of George Clinton and P-Funk.

Columbia Records

Mutiny on the Mamaship

"Go Away from Here"

Vocals: Raymond Carter, Jerome Brailey, Wayne Cooper, Lenny Holmes, Skitch Lovett
Drums: Jerome Brailey
Bass: Raymond Carter
Keyboards: Nat Lee

Guitar: Lenny Holmes, Skitch Lovett
Horns: Darryl Dixon, Danny Cortez, Valerie Drayton

"What More Can I Say"

Vocals: Skitch Lovett, Jerome Brailey, Lenny Holmes, Raymond Carter
Drums: Jerome Brailey
Bass: Raymond Carter
Keyboards: Nat Lee
Guitar: Lenny Holmes, Skitch Lovett
Horns: Darryl Dixon, Danny Cortez, Valerie Drayton

"Lump"

Vocals: Raymond Carter, Jerome Brailey, Lenny Holmes, Skitch Lovett
Drums: Jerome Brailey
Bass: Raymond Carter
Keyboards: Nat Lee
Guitar: Lenny Holmes, Skitch Lovett
Horns: Darryl Dixon, Danny Cortez, Valerie Drayton

"Funk N' Bop"

Vocals: Raymond Carter, Jerome Brailey, Lenny Holmes, Skitch Lovett
Drums: Jerome Brailey
Bass: Raymond Carter
Keyboards: Nat Lee
Guitar: Lenny Holmes, Skitch Lovett
Horns: Darryl Dixon, Danny Cortez, Valerie Drayton

"Burning Up"

Vocals: Raymond Carter, Jerome Brailey, Lenny Holmes, Skitch Lovett
Drums: Jerome Brailey
Bass: Raymond Carter
Keyboards: Nat Lee
Guitar: Lenny Holmes, Skitch Lovett
Horns: Darryl Dixon, Danny Cortez, Valerie Drayton

"Voyage to the Bottom of the P"

Vocals: Jerome Brailey, Lenny Holmes, Skitch Lovett, Raymond Carter
Drums: Jerome Brailey
Bass: Raymond Carter
Keyboards: Nat Lee
Guitar: Lenny Holmes, Skitch Lovett
Horns: Darryl Dixon, Danny Cortez, Valerie Drayton

"Every Time You Come Around"

Vocals: Raymond Carter, Jerome Brailey, Lenny Holmes, Skitch Lovett
Drums: Jerome Brailey
Bass: Raymond Carter
Keyboards: Nat Lee
Guitar: Lenny Holmes, Skitch Lovett
Horns: Darryl Dixon, Danny Cortez, Valerie Drayton

"Romeo (Hope You're Feeling Better)"

Vocals: Jerome Brailey, Lenny Holmes, Skitch Lovett, Raymond Carter
Drums: Jerome Brailey
Bass: Raymond Carter
Keyboards: Nat Lee
Guitar: Lenny Holmes, Skitch Lovett
Horns: Darryl Dixon, Danny Cortez, Valerie Drayton

Funk Plus the One

"Will It Be Tomorrow"

Vocals: Jerome Brailey, Lenny Holmes, Skitch Lovett, Raymond Carter
Drums: Jerome Brailey
Bass: Raymond Carter
Keyboards: Nat Lee
Guitar: Lenny Holmes, Skitch Lovett
Horns: Darryl Dixon, Danny Cortez, Valerie Drayton

"Anti-Disco"

Vocals: Raymond Carter Jerome Brailey, Lenny Holmes, Skitch Lovett
Drums: Jerome Brailey
Bass: Raymond Carter
Keyboards: Nat Lee
Guitar: Lenny Holmes, Skitch Lovett
Horns: Darryl Dixon, Danny Cortez, Valerie Drayton

"Don't Bust the Groove"

Vocals: Hockaday, Jerome Brailey, Lenny Holmes, Skitch Lovett, Raymond Carter
Drums: Jerome Brailey
Bass: Hockaday
Keyboards: Nat Lee
Guitar: Lenny Holmes, Skitch Lovett
Horns: Darryl Dixon, Danny Cortez, Valerie Drayton

"Reality"

Vocals: Jerome Brailey, Lenny Holmes, Skitch Lovett, Raymond Carter
Drums: Jerome Brailey
Bass: Raymond Carter
Keyboards: Nat Lee
Guitar: Lenny Holmes, Skitch Lovett
Horns: Darryl Dixon, Danny Cortez, Valerie Drayton

"Semi-First Class Seat"

Vocals: Jerome Brailey, Skitch Lovett
Drums: Jerome Brailey
Bass: Raymond Carter
Keyboards: Nat Lee
Guitar: Lenny Holmes, Skitch Lovett
Horns: Darryl Dixon, Danny Cortez, Valerie Drayton

"One on One"
Drums: Jerome Brailey
Bass: Raymond Carter
Keyboards: Nat Lee
Guitar: Lenny Holmes, Skitch Lovett
Horns: Darryl Dixon, Danny Cortez, Valerie Drayton

Independent Releases

How's Your Loose Booty?

"Funk N Roll"
Vocals: Jerome Brailey, Lenny Holmes, Skitch Lovett, Raymond Carter
Drums: Jerome Brailey
Bass: Raymond Carter
Keyboards: Nat Lee
Guitar: Lenny Holmes, Skitch Lovett
Horns: Darryl Dixon, Danny Cortez, Valerie Drayton

"Just Want to Know"
Vocals: Jerome Brailey, Lenny Holmes, Skitch Lovett, Raymond Carter
Drums: Jerome Brailey
Bass: Raymond Carter
Keyboards: Nat Lee
Guitar: Lenny Holmes, Skitch Lovett
Horns: Darryl Dixon, Danny Cortez, Valerie Drayton

"How's Your Loose Booty?"
Vocals: Jerome Brailey, Lenny Holmes, Skitch Lovett, Raymond Carter
Drums: Jerome Brailey
Bass: Raymond Carter
Keyboards: Nat Lee
Guitar: Lenny Holmes, Skitch Lovett
Horns: Darryl Dixon, Danny Cortez, Valerie Drayton

"Electric Hot Dog"
Vocals: Skitch Lovett
Drums: Jerome Brailey
Bass: Raymond Carter
Keyboards: Nat Lee
Guitar: Lenny Holmes, Skitch Lovett
Horns: Darryl Dixon, Danny Cortez, Valerie Drayton

A Night Out with the Boys

"In the Pocket"
Vocals: Jerome Brailey
Drums: Jerome Brailey
Keyboards: Kenni Hairston or Maceo Bond
Guitar: Lenny Holmes, Skitch Lovett

"And You Know That"
Vocals: Jerome Brailey
Drums: Jerome Brailey
Bass: Rodney Curtis
Keyboards: Kenni Hairston or Maceo Bond
Guitar: Lenny Holmes, Skitch Lovett
Horns: Darryl Dixon, Marvin Daniels, Melvin El

"Hand Maid (Old Lady Mine)"
Vocals: Jerome Brailey
Drums: Jerome Brailey
Bass: Hockaday
Keyboards: Kenni Hairston or Maceo Bond
Guitar: Lenny Holmes, Skitch Lovett

"Don't Bust a Groove"
Vocals: Hockaday
Drums: Jerome Brailey
Bass: Hockaday
Guitar: Lenny Holmes, Skitch Lovett

"Peanut Butter and Jam"

Vocals: Jerome Brailey
Drums: Jerome Brailey
Bass: Rodney Curtis
Keyboards: Kenni Hairston or Maceo Bond
Guitar: Lenny Holmes

"A Night Out with the Boys"

Drums: Jerome Brailey
Bass: Rodney Curtis
Keyboards: Kenni Hairston or Maceo Bond
Guitar: Michael Hampton, Lenny Holmes, Skitch Lovett

"Child Support"

Vocals: Jerome Brailey
Drums: Jerome Brailey
Bass: Rodney Curtis
Keyboards: Nat Lee
Guitar: Michael Hampton, Skitch Lovett

"Raise"

Vocals: Jerome Brailey, Kenni Hairston, Lenny Holmes, Skitch Lovett
Drums: Jerome Brailey
Bass: Rodney Curtis
Keyboards: Kenni Hairston or Maceo Bond
Guitar: Lenny Holmes, Skitch Lovett

"Just Want to Know"

Vocals: Jerome Brailey
Drums: Jerome Brailey
Bass: Raymond Carter, Hockaday, or Rodney Curtis
Keyboards: Kenni Hairston or Maceo Bond
Guitar: Lenny Holmes, Skitch Lovett

"P.Moe"

Drums: Jerome Brailey
Bass: Raymond Carter, Hockaday, or Rodney Curtis
Guitar: Dave Roeder, Ricky Hitchcock
Keyboards: Kenni Hairston or Maceo Bond
Vocals: Jerome Brailey, Kenni Hairston, Lenny Holmes, Skitch Lovett

*The following Mutiny/Jerome Brailey albums have large amounts of unknown/dubious personnel information; out of the entire canon, these albums were the hardest to find any information on, be it from primary or secondary sources. Hopefully, a future interview with Jerome Brailey can clear up the confusion with regard to three or four of his albums from the 1995 period.

Funk in a Latin Groove*

"Funkin' in Rio"

Drums: Jerome Brailey
Bass: Juan Nelson?
Guitar: Wilbur Harri?
Keyboards: ?
Vocals: ?

"Freedom"

Drums: Jerome Brailey
Bass: Juan Nelson?
Guitar: Wilbur Harris?
Keyboards: ?
Vocals: ?

"Interlude (See You Wanna)"

Drums: Jerome Brailey
Bass: Juan Nelson?
Guitar: Wilbur Harris?
Keyboards: ?
Vocals: ?

"Someday This Pain"

Drums: Jerome Brailey
Bass: Juan Nelson
Guitar: Wilbur Harris
Keyboards: ?
Vocals: ?

"Tequilla Sunrise"

Drums: Jerome Brailey
Bass: Juan Nelson?
Guitar: Wilbur Harris?
Keyboards: ?
Vocals: ?

"Celebrate"

Drums: Jerome Brailey
Bass: Juan Nelson?
Guitar: Wilbur Harris?
Keyboards: ?
Vocals: ?

"Spicy"

Drums: Jerome Brailey
Bass: Juan Nelson?
Guitar: Wilbur Harris?
Keyboards: ?
Vocals: ?

"Donkey Ha Cha"

Drums: Jerome Brailey
Bass: Juan Nelson?
Guitar: Wilbur Harris?
Keyboards: ?
Vocals: ?

"P-Funk in a Latin Groove"

Drums: Jerome Brailey
Bass: Juan Nelson?
Guitar: Wilbur Harris?
Keyboards: ?
Vocals: ?

Rome-Dog Vol. 1

"Rock the Boat"

Drums: Jerome Brailey
Bass: Juan Nelson?
Guitar: Wilbur Harris?
Keyboards: ?
Vocals: ?

"Assault with Intent"

Drums: Jerome Brailey
Bass: Juan Nelson?
Guitar: Wilbur Harris?
Keyboards: ?
Vocals: ?

"Mary"

Drums: Jerome Brailey
Bass: Juan Nelson?
Guitar: Wilbur Harris?
Keyboards: ?
Vocals: ?

"Desireless"

Drums: Jerome Brailey
Bass: Juan Nelson?
Guitar: Wilbur Harris?
Keyboards: ?
Vocals: ?

"Tickin' Like a Time Bomb"

Programming: D-Tech, Jerome Brailey
Vocals: Derrick Ross, Sean Sally

"Bad News"

Drums: Jerome Brailey
Bass: Juan Nelson?
Guitar: Wilbur Harris?
Keyboards: ?
Vocals: ?

*The Funky Mad Men**

"No Choice"

Drums: Jerome Brailey
Bass: Juan Nelson?
Guitar: Wilbur Harris?
Keyboards: ?
Vocals: ?

"Back It Up"

Drums: Jerome Brailey
Bass: Juan Nelson?
Guitar: Wilbur Harris?
Keyboards: ?
Vocals: ?

"Right Stuff"

Drums: Jerome Brailey
Bass: Juan Nelson?
Guitar: Wilbur Harris?
Keyboards: ?
Vocals: ?

"They Coming for Me"

Drums: Jerome Brailey
Bass: Juan Nelson?
Guitar: Wilbur Harris?
Keyboards: ?
Vocals: ?

"Feeling So High"

Drums: Jerome Brailey
Bass: Juan Nelson ?
Guitar: Wilbur Harris?
Keyboards: ?
Vocals: ?

"Put Em Up"

Drums: Jerome Brailey
Bass: Juan Nelson?
Guitar: Wilbur Harris?
Keyboards: ?
Vocals: ?

*Southern Sway**

"Southern Sway"

Drums: Jerome Brailey
Bass: Juan Nelson?
Guitar: Wilbur Harris?
Keyboards: ?
Vocals: ?

"Prayer for the Livin' (On & On)"

Drums: Jerome Brailey
Bass: Juan Nelson?
Guitar: Wilbur Harris?
Keyboards: ?
Vocals: ?

"Is It for Real"

Drums: Jerome Brailey
Bass: Juan Nelson?
Guitar: Wilbur Harris?
Keyboards: ?
Vocals: ?

"True Represent"

Drums: Jerome Brailey
Bass: Juan Nelson?
Guitar: Wilbur Harris?
Keyboards: ?
Vocals: ?

"That Kinda Woman"

Drums: Jerome Brailey
Bass: Juan Nelson?
Guitar: Wilbur Harris?
Keyboards: ?
Vocals: ?

"You Make Me Happy"

Drums: Jerome Brailey
Bass: Juan Nelson
Guitar: Wilbur Harris
Keyboards: ?
Vocals: ?

"Something Better to Do"

Drums: Jerome Brailey
Bass: Juan Nelson?
Guitar: Wilbur Harris?
Keyboards: ?
Vocals: ?

"Put Em-Up"

Drums: Jerome Brailey
Bass: Juan Nelson?
Guitar: Wilbur Harris?
Keyboards: ?
Vocals: ?

Rykodisc Records

Aftershock 2005

"The Growl"

Drums: Jerome Brailey
Bass: Linn Washington
Guitar: Chris Beasley, Kevan Wilkins, Skitch Lovett
Keyboards: Juan Nelson
Turntables: DXT

"It's All Good"

Drums: Jerome Brailey
Bass: Jeff Cherokee Bunn
Guitar: Nicky Skopelitis, Chris Beasley, Kevan Wilkins, Skitch Lovett
Vocals: Fashe Forde

"No Choice"

Drum Programming: D-Tech, Jerome Brailey
Guitar: Michael Hampton
Keyboards: Bernie Worrell
Vocals: Clarence Allen, Derrick Ross, John Burnett
Turntables: DXT

"Passion"

Drums: Jerome Brailey
Bass: Jeff Cherokee Bunn
Guitar: Michael Hampton, Chris Beasley, Kevan Wilkins
Keyboards: Bernie Worrell, Juan Nelson
Vocals: Fashe Ford

"Tickin' Like a Time Bomb"

Programming: D-Tech, Jerome Brailey
Vocals: Derrick Ross, Sean Sally

"Rock the Boat"

Drums: Jerome Brailey
Bass: Alan Quick Flowers
Guitar: Jim Prideaux, Wilbur Harris
Sampler: B. C. Seville, Jerome Brailey
Vocals: Brian Champion

"2005"

Drums: Jerome Brailey
Bass: Jeff Cherokee Bunn
Guitar: Chris Beasley, Kevan Wilkins
Vocals: Fashe Ford
Turntables: DXT

"Desires"

Drums: Jerome Brailey
Bass: Alan "Quick" Flowers
Guitar: Jim Prideaux, Wilbur Harris
Keyboards: Craig Day
Vocals: Wilbur Harris, Jerome Brailey

"Moments"

Keyboards: Craig Day
Vocals: Fashe Ford, Jerome Brailey

"The Growl Reprise"

Drums: Jerome Brailey
Bass: Linn Washington
Guitar: Chris Beasley, Kevan Wilkins, Skitch Lovett
Keyboards: Juan Nelson
Turntables: DXT

Funk Road*

"Thought Patterns"

"Something Better to Do"

"Delta Dog"

"What? YEAH!"

"Ninety Nine and One Half"

"Thee Funky Prez"

"Ouch"

"Promanade (Git'er Done)"

"We Keep Doing Our Thang"

"Lump"

"Sweet Blessing"

"Lights, Camera, Action"

"Diggy Don Dotta"

"Rome Dog Roaming"

*The personnel information on these albums has not been discovered yet, but hopefully with further editions, this will be remedied.

OSIRIS: 1979

This project features the Horny Horns, drummer Jerome Brailey, and others.

"Fantality"

Lead Vocals: Osiris Marsh
Backup Vocals: Jill Wells, Osiris Marsh
Drums: Jerome Brailey

Bass: Ty Brunson
Guitar: Brett Mingle, Stewart Smith
Keyboard: Maceo Bond
Percussion: Jimmy "Sha Sha" Stapleton
Sax: Maceo Parker
Trombone: Fred Wesley
Trumpet: Kush Griffith, Rick Gardner

"Prelude (Is It Clear)"

Lead Vocals: Osiris Marsh
Backup Vocals: Jill Wells, Osiris Marsh
Drums: Jerome Brailey
Bass: Tony Jones
Guitar: Brett Mingle, Stewart Smith
Keyboard: Maceo Bond
Percussion: Jimmy "Sha Sha" Stapleton
Sax: Maceo Parker
Trombone: Fred Wesley
Trumpet: Kush Griffith, Rick Gardner

"Say You Will"

Lead Vocals: Osiris Marsh
Backup Vocals: Jill Wells, Osiris Marsh
Drums: Kenny Jones
Bass: Tony Jones
Guitar: Brett Mingle, Stewart Smith
Keyboard: Maceo Bond
Percussion: Jimmy "Sha Sha" Stapleton
Sax: Maceo Parker
Trombone: Fred Wesley
Trumpet: Kush Griffith, Rick Gardner

"You and I"

Lead Vocals: Osiris Marsh
Backup Vocals: Jill Wells, Osiris Marsh
Drums: Jerome Brailey
Bass: Ty Brunson
Guitar: Brett Mingle, Stewart Smith
Keyboard: Maceo Bond
Percussion: Jimmy "Sha Sha" Stapleton
Sax: Maceo Parker
Trombone: Fred Wesley
Trumpet: Kush Griffith, Rick Gardner

"Travellin' Salesman"

Lead Vocals: Osiris Marsh
Backup Vocals: Jill Wells, Osiris Marsh
Drums: Jerome Brailey
Bass: Ty Brunson
Guitar: Brett Mingle, Stewart Smith
Keyboard: Maceo Bond
Percussion: Jimmy "Sha Sha" Stapleton
Sax: Maceo Parker
Trombone: Fred Wesley
Trumpet: Kush Griffith, Rick Gardner

"Love in Your Heart"

Lead Vocals: Osiris Marsh
Backup Vocals: Jill Wells, Osiris Marsh
Drums: Jerome Brailey
Bass: Tony Jones or Ty Brunson
Guitar: Brett Mingle, Stewart Smith
Keyboard: Maceo Bond
Percussion: Jimmy "Sha Sha" Stapleton
Sax: Maceo Parker
Trombone: Fred Wesley
Trumpet: Kush Griffith, Rick Gardner

"I'll Never Let You Go" Lead Vocals: Osiris Marsh

Backup Vocals: Jill Wells, Osiris Marsh
Drums: Jerome Brailey or Kenny Jones
Bass: Ty Brunson
Guitar: Brett Mingle, Stewart Smith
Keyboard: Maceo Bond
Percussion: Jimmy "Sha Sha" Stapleton
Sax: Maceo Parker
Trombone: Fred Wesley
Trumpet: Kush Griffith, Rick Gardner

— ☆ —

THE GLASS FAMILY (SELECT TRACKS): 1979

This group features P-Funk members.

"Dancin' round the World"

Saxophone Solo: Michael Morera
Synthesizer: Bernie Worrell
Vocals: Debbie Wright, Jeanette Washington
Bass, Vocals: Gary Itri
Drums, Timbales, Percussion: Jon Gerlach
Guitar, Vocals: David Storrs
Percussion, Vocals: Steve St. Clair
Other Keyboards: Dexter De Los Angeles
Producer, Arranger, Vocals, Guitar: Jim Callon

"Only in Spring"

Piano: Bernie Worrell
Saxophone Solo: Boom
Bass, Vocals: Gary Itri
Drums, Timbales, Percussion: Jon Gerlach
Guitar, Vocals: David Storrs
Percussion, Vocals: Steve St. Clair
Other Keyboards: Dexter De Los Angeles
Producer, Arranger, Vocals, Guitar: Jim Callon

— ☆ —

FIVE SPECIAL (SELECT TRACKS): 1980, 1981

This Detroit singing group featured standout vocals from future P-Funk vocalist Steve Boyd. Five Special had albums that featured Fred Wesley and Bernie Worrell, among others.

"Why Leave Us Alone?"

Vocals: Greg Fendely, Steve Harris, Steve Boyd, Bryan Banks, Mike Patillo
Drums: Jerry Jones
Bass: Tony Green
Keyboards: Raymond Johnson
Guitar: Darnell Johnson, Ricky Rouse
Horns: Detroit Symphony Orchestra
Handclaps: George Clinton, Robert Peanut Johnson, Michael Clip Payne, Brides of Funkenstein

"It's a Wonderful Day"

Vocals: Greg Fendely, Steve Harris, Steve Boyd, Bryan Banks, Mike Patillo
Drums: Jerry Jones
Bass: Tony Green
Keyboards: Raymond Johnson
Guitar: Darnell Johnson
Horns: Detroit Symphony Orchestra

"Do It Baby"

Vocals: Greg Fendely, Steve Harris, Steve Boyd, Bryan Banks, Mike Patillo
Drums: Jerry Jones
Bass: Tony Green
Keyboards: Raymond Johnson
Guitar: Darnell Johnson
Horns: Detroit Symphony Orchestra

"It's Such a Groove (Pt. II—Whatcha Got for Music!)"

Vocals: Greg Fendely, Steve Harris, Steve Boyd, Bryan Banks, Mike Patillo
Drums: Jerry Jones
Bass: Tony Green
Keyboards: Raymond Johnson
Guitar: Darnell Johnson
Horns: Detroit Symphony Orchestra

"Baby"

Vocals: Greg Fendely, Steve Harris, Steve Boyd, Bryan Banks, Mike Patillo
Drums: Jerry Jones
Bass: Tony Green
Keyboards: Raymond Johnson
Guitar: Darnell Johnson
Horns: Detroit Symphony Orchestra

"Rock Dancin'"

Vocals: Greg Fendely, Steve Harris, Steve Boyd, Bryan Banks, Mike Patillo
Drums: Jerry Jones
Bass: Tony Green
Keyboards: Raymond Johnson
Guitar: Darnell Johnson
Horns: Detroit Symphony Orchestra

"You're Something Special"

Vocals: Greg Fendely, Steve Harris, Steve Boyd, Bryan Banks, Mike Patillo
Drums: Jerry Jones
Bass: Tony Green
Keyboards: Raymond Johnson
Guitar: Darnell Johnson
Horns: Detroit Symphony Orchestra

"Jam"

Vocals: Greg Fendely, Steve Harris, Steve Boyd, Bryan Banks, Mike Patillo
Drums: Jerry Jones
Bass: Tony Green
Keyboards: Bernie Worrell, Raymond Johnson
Guitar: Darnell Johnson
Horns: Fred Wesley, Maceo Parker, Richard Kush Griffith

"Heaven"

Vocals: Greg Fendely, Steve Harris, Steve Boyd, Bryan Banks, Mike Patillo
Drums: Jerry Jones
Bass: Tony Green
Keyboards: Raymond Johnson
Guitar: Darnell Johnson
Horns: Detroit Symphony Orchestra

"Who You Been Lovin'"

Vocals: Greg Fendely, Steve Harris, Steve Boyd, Bryan Banks, Mike Patillo
Drums: Jerry Jones
Bass: Tony Green
Keyboards: Raymond Johnson
Guitar: Darnell Johnson
Horns: Detroit Symphony Orchestra

"Choosin' for Me"

Vocals: Greg Fendely, Steve Harris, Steve Boyd, Bryan Banks, Mike Patillo
Drums: Jerry Jones
Bass: Tony Green
Keyboards: Raymond Johnson
Guitar: Darnell Johnson
Horns: Maceo Parker, Fred Wesley, Richard Kush Griffith

"Do Something Special"

Vocals: Greg Fendely, Steve Harris, Steve Boyd, Bryan Banks, Mike Patillo
Drums: Jerry Jones
Bass: Tony Green
Keyboards: Raymond Johnson
Guitar: Darnell Johnson
Horns: Detroit Symphony Orchestra

"Why Not Be Mine"

Vocals: Greg Fendely, Steve Harris, Steve Boyd, Bryan Banks, Mike Patillo
Drums: Jerry Jones
Bass: Tony Green
Keyboards: Raymond Johnson
Guitar: Darnell Johnson
Horns: Detroit Symphony Orchestra

"Had You a Lover"

Vocals: Greg Fendely, Steve Harris, Steve Boyd, Bryan Banks, Mike Patillo
Drums: Jerry Jones
Bass: Tony Green
Keyboards: Raymond Johnson
Guitar: Darnell Johnson
Horns: Detroit Symphony Orchestra

— ☆ —

JEROME AND JIMMY ALI (SELECT TRACKS): 1980

These guitarist/bassist brothers were best known for working with Parlet and having several offerings with Parliament-Funkadelic in 1980–1981.

"She's Crazy"

Drums: Drummer from Ali Bros. Band
Bass: Jimmy Ali
Guitar: Jerome Ali

— ☆ —

RON DUNBAR (SELECT TRACKS): 1980

A Grammy Award–winning songwriter/producer, Dunbar was a big part of the late 1970s and early 1980s studio administration of P-Funk. He was famous in the P-Funk world for being one of the lead vocalists and writers on "Agony of DeFeet" by Parliament. He wrote and produced songs within the P-Funk realm for Parliament, the Brides of Funkenstein, Parlet, and many others.

"These Feets Are Made for Dancing (Foot Stranger)"

Lead Vocals: Ron Dunbar
Backup Vocals: Mallia Franklin, Jeanette Washington, Shirley Hayden, Janice Evans, Sheila Horne, Jeanette McGruder
Drums: Donnie Sterling
Percussion: Carl "Butch" Small
Bass: Donnie Sterling
Guitar: Tony Thomas, Rodney Crutcher
Keyboards, Synthesizers: David Spradley
Trombone: Fred Wesley
Sax: Maceo Parker
Trumpet: Richard Griffith, Rick Gardner

THE FOUR TOPS (SELECT TRACKS): 1980

"To Care," a Ron Dunbar/George Clinton–produced Four Tops song, was eventually released on the George Clinton Family Series, 13 years after it was recorded. It also features many of the same session players who graced Philippe Wynne's album.

"To Care"

Drums: Jerry Jones
Percussion: Carl "Butch" Small
Bass: Rodrick Chandler

Guitar: Eddie Willis
Keyboards: Rudi Robinson
Strings, Horns: Detroit Symphony Orchestra
Vocals: The Four Tops

PHILIPPE WYNNE: 1980

Wynne was a former lead singer of the Spinners (of "Rubber Band Man" fame) who went on to work with Funkadelic in time for the *Uncle Jam Wants You* album in 1979. He did the original scat solo on "(Not Just) Knee Deep" and lead vocals on "Uncle Jam Wants You." His album *Wynne Jammin'* was one of the first to be released by the fledgling Uncle Jam label in 1980. One little-known fact about Wynne is that he was in one of Bootsy's groups before joining the Spinners. Shortly after working on the P-Funk All Stars' first album, Wynne passed away. He is prominent on the P-Funk All Stars' cult classic "Hydraulic Pump."

Uncle Jam Records

Wynne Jammin'

"Never Gonna Tell It"

Vocals: Philippe Wynne
Backup Vocals: Garry Shider, Ray Davis, Robert Peanut Johnson, George Clinton, Jessica Cleaves, Ron Ford, Michael Clip Payne, Dawn Silva, Sheila Horne, Jeanette MacGruder, Andre Williams, Stevie Pannell, Patty Walker, Lige Curry, Sidney Barnes
Drums: Jerry Jones
Bass: Bruce Nazarian
Keyboards, Synthesizers: Bernie Worrell
Guitar: Michael Hampton
Strings: Detroit Symphony Orchestra

Four pivotal P-Funk artists at the inception of the Uncle Jam record label in 1980: Philippe Wynne, William "Bootsy" Collins, George Clinton, and Maceo Parker. Kinley-McCoy / GROOVE MANEUVERS ARCHIVES

"Put Your Own Puzzle Together"

Lead Vocals: Philippe Wynne
Drums: Jerry Jones
Percussion, Synth Drums: Carl Butch Small
Bass: Rodrick Chandler
Keyboards, Synthesizers: Rudi Robinson
Guitar: Bruce Nazarian
Strings: Detroit Symphony Orchestra

"You Make Me Happy (You Got the Love I Need)"

Vocals: Philippe Wynne
Backup Vocals: Philippe Wynne, Jerome Rodgers, others
Drums: Jerry Jones
Percussion: Carl Butch Small
Bass: Rodrick Chandler
Keyboards, Synthesizers: Rudi Robinson
Guitar: Bruce Nazarian

"We Dance So Good Together"

Vocals: Philippe Wynne
Backup Vocals: Brandye
Drums: Jerry Jones
Percussion: Carl Butch Small
Bass: Bruce Nazarian
Keyboards, Synthesizers: Rudi Robinson
Guitar: Bruce Nazarian

"Hotel Eternity"

Vocals: Philippe Wynne
Backup Vocals: Sidney Barnes, Andre Williams, George Clinton, Tracey Lewis, Chante Payne
Drums: Tyrone Lampkin
Bass: Dewayne Blackbyrd McKnight
Keyboards, Synthesizers: Gary Hudgins?, Bernie Worrell?

"Breakout"

Vocals: Philippe Wynne
Drums: Jerry Jones
Percussion: Carl Butch Small
Bass: Rodrick Chandler
Keyboards, Synthesizers: Rudi Robinson
Guitar: Bruce Nazarian
Strings: Detroit Symphony Orchestra

"You Gotta Take Chances"

Vocals: Philippe Wynne
Backup Vocals: Brandye
Drums: Jerry Jones
Percussion: Carl Butch Small
Bass: Rodrick Chandler
Keyboards, Synthesizers: Rudi Robinson
Guitar: Bruce Nazarian

Unreleased

"I Found You"

Vocals: Philippe Wynne
Backup Vocals: Jerome Rodgers, Jessica Cleaves, Telma Hopkins, Joyce Vincent, Greg Thomas

Drums: Jerry Jones
Bass: Rodrick Chandler
Piano: Bernie Worrell
Guitar: Bruce Nazarian

— ☆ —

FRED WESLEY: 1980–

The highly influential and massively important trombonist/arranger Fred Wesley would go on to have a storied solo career after long tenures with James Brown and P-Funk. His input and arranging abilities and their impact on the funk world cannot be overstated. One needs to look no further than "Pass the Peas" to understand Fred's massive influence on funk music, but his contributions to the JB's, Parliament, Bootsy's Rubber Band, the Horny Horns, and so many others continually solidify his incredibly important role in the progression of funk music. It is no surprise and no secret that he, like saxophonist and longtime collaborator Maceo Parker, is equally adept at jazz and other forms.

Curtom Records

House Party

"House Party"

Trombone: Fred Wesley
Vocals: Fred Wesley, Alton McClain, D'Marie Warren, Fannie Dees, Lyn Collins, Robyrda Stiger, Melvin Webb, Rudy Copeland
Sax: David Li
Trumpet: Delbert Taylor
Drums: Melvin Webb
Bass: Lewis Du Priest
Keyboards: Gary Bell, Rudy Copeland
Guitar: Butch Bonner, Spencer Bean

Not only would "House Party" go on to be Fred Wesley's premiere song and single from his solo career, but it would easily be considered his most important. It now stands alongside songs like "FourPlay" by the Horny Horns and "Pass the Peas" by the JB's as one of his true standards. Wesley stands almost unrivaled as one of the chief arrangers of funk music as we know it.

"Bop to the Boogie"

Trombone: Fred Wesley
Vocals: Fred Wesley, Alton McClain, D'Marie Warren, Fannie Dees, Lyn Collins, Robyrda Stiger, Melvin Webb, Rudy Copeland
Sax: David Li
Trumpet: Delbert Taylor
Drums: Melvin Webb
Bass: Lewis Du Priest
Keyboards: Gary Bell, Rudy Copeland
Guitar: Butch Bonner, Spencer Bean

"Still on the Loose"

Trombone: Fred Wesley
Vocals: Fred Wesley, Alton McClain, D'Marie Warren, Fannie Dees, Lyn Collins, Robyrda Stiger, Melvin Webb, Rudy Copeland
Sax: David Li
Trumpet: Delbert Taylor
Drums: Melvin Webb
Bass: Lewis Du Priest
Keyboards: Gary Bell, Rudy Copeland
Guitar: Butch Bonner, Spencer Bean

"I Make Music"

Trombone: Fred Wesley
Vocals: Fred Wesley, Alton McClain, D'Marie Warren, Fannie Dees, Lyn Collins, Robyrda Stiger, Melvin Webb, Rudy Copeland
Sax: David Li
Trumpet: Delbert Taylor
Drums: Melvin Webb
Bass: Lewis Du Priest
Keyboards: Gary Bell, Rudy Copeland
Guitar: Butch Bonner, Spencer Bean

"If This Be a Dream"

Trombone: Fred Wesley
Vocals: Fred Wesley, Alton McClain, D'Marie Warren, Fannie Dees, Lyn Collins, Robyrda Stiger, Melvin Webb, Rudy Copeland
Sax: David Li
Trumpet: Delbert Taylor
Drums: Melvin Webb
Bass: Lewis Du Priest
Keyboards: Gary Bell, Rudy Copeland
Guitar: Butch Bonner, Spencer Bean

"Let's Go Dancing"

Trombone: Fred Wesley
Vocals: Fred Wesley, Alton McClain, D'Marie Warren, Fannie Dees, Lyn Collins, Robyrda Stiger, Melvin Webb, Rudy Copeland
Sax: David Li
Trumpet: Delbert Taylor
Drums: Melvin Webb
Bass: Lewis Du Priest
Keyboards: Gary Bell, Rudy Copeland
Guitar: Butch Bonner, Spencer Bean

"Are You Guilty"

Trombone: Fred Wesley
Vocals: Fred Wesley, Alton McClain, D'Marie Warren, Fannie Dees, Lyn Collins, Robyrda Stiger, Melvin Webb, Rudy Copeland
Sax: David Li
Trumpet: Delbert Taylor
Drums: Melvin Webb
Bass: Lewis Du Priest
Keyboards: Gary Bell, Rudy Copeland
Guitar: Butch Bonner, Spencer Bean

"Life Is Wonderful"

Trombone: Fred Wesley
Vocals: Fred Wesley, Alton McClain, D'Marie Warren, Fannie Dees, Lyn Collins, Robyrda Stiger, Melvin Webb, Rudy Copeland
Sax: David Li
Trumpet: Delbert Taylor
Drums: Melvin Webb
Bass: Lewis Du Priest
Keyboards: Gary Bell, Rudy Copeland
Guitar: Butch Bonner, Spencer Bean

Urban Records

Single

"Blow Your Head (With the JB's)"

Alto Sax: St. Clair Pinckney
Bass: Fred Thomas
Drums: John Jabo Starks
Sax: Maceo Parker
Synthesizer: Bobby Byrd
Trombone: Fred Wesley

Hi Note Records (later on Solar Records and P-Vine Records)

As the Fred Wesley Quartet: To Someone

"Sandu"

Bass: Ken Walker
Drums: Bruno Carr
Piano: Joe Bonner
Trombone: Fred Wesley

"La Bossa"

Bass: Ken Walker
Drums: Bruno Carr
Piano: Joe Bonner
Trombone: Fred Wesley

"To Someone"

Bass: Ken Walker
Drums: Bruno Carr
Piano: Joe Bonner
Trombone: Fred Wesley

"Work Song"

Bass: Ken Walker
Drums: Bruno Carr
Piano: Joe Bonner
Trombone: Fred Wesley

"Autumn Leaves"

Bass: Ken Walker
Drums: Bruno Carr
Piano: Joe Bonner
Trombone: Fred Wesley

"Tippin'"

Bass: Ken Walker
Drums: Bruno Carr
Piano: Joe Bonner
Trombone: Fred Wesley

Gramavision Records

New Friends

"Rockin' in Rhythm"

Alto Sax, Percussion: Maceo Parker
Bass: Anthony Cox
Drums: Bill Stewart
Keyboards: Geri Allen
Tenor Sax, Soprano Sax, Percussion: Tim Green
Trombone: Fred Wesley
Trumpet, Flugelhorn: Stanton Davis

"Honey Love"

Alto Sax, Percussion: Maceo Parker
Bass: Anthony Cox
Drums: Bill Stewart
Keyboards: Geri Allen
Tenor Sax, Soprano Sax, Percussion: Tim Green
Trombone: Fred Wesley
Trumpet, Flugelhorn: Stanton Davis

"Bright Mississippi"

Alto Sax, Percussion: Maceo Parker
Bass: Anthony Cox
Drums: Bill Stewart
Keyboards: Geri Allen
Tenor Sax, Soprano Sax, Percussion: Tim Green
Trombone: Fred Wesley
Trumpet, Flugelhorn: Stanton Davis

"The Love We Had"

Vocals: Carmen Lundy
Alto Sax, Percussion: Maceo Parker
Bass: Anthony Cox
Drums: Bill Stewart
Keyboards: Geri Allen
Tenor Sax, Soprano Sax, Percussion: Tim Green
Trombone: Fred Wesley
Trumpet, Flugelhorn: Stanton Davis

"For the Elders"

Alto Sax, Percussion: Maceo Parker
Bass: Anthony Cox
Drums: Bill Stewart
Keyboards: Geri Allen
Tenor Sax, Soprano Sax, Percussion: Tim Green
Trombone: Fred Wesley, Robin Eubanks, Steve Turre
Trumpet, Flugelhorn: Stanton Davis

"Plenty, Plenty Soul"

Alto Sax, Percussion: Maceo Parker
Bass: Anthony Cox
Drums: Bill Stewart
Keyboards: Geri Allen
Tenor Sax, Soprano Sax, Percussion: Tim Green
Trombone: Fred Wesley
Trumpet, Flugelhorn: Stanton Davis

"Blue Monk"

Alto Sax, Percussion: Maceo Parker
Bass: Anthony Cox
Drums: Bill Stewart
Keyboards: Geri Allen
Tenor Sax, Soprano Sax, Percussion: Tim Green
Trombone: Fred Wesley
Trumpet, Flugelhorn: Stanton Davis

"Peace Fugue"

Alto Sax, Percussion: Maceo Parker
Bass: Anthony Cox
Drums: Bill Stewart
Keyboards: Geri Allen
Tenor Sax, Soprano Sax, Percussion: Tim Green
Trombone: Fred Wesley, Robin Eubanks, Steve Turre
Trumpet, Flugelhorn: Stanton Davis

"Eyes So Beautiful As Yours"

Vocals: Carmen Lundy
Alto Sax, Percussion: Maceo Parker
Bass: Anthony Cox
Drums: Bill Stewart
Keyboards: Geri Allen
Tenor Sax, Soprano Sax, Percussion: Tim Green
Trombone: Fred Wesley
Trumpet, Flugelhorn: Stanton Davis

Minor Music

Comme Ci Comme Ca

"Smiley Stacey"

Alto Sax: Maceo Parker
Bass: Anthony Cox
Drums: Bill Stewart
Guitar: Rodney Jones
Piano: Peter Madsen
Trombone: Fred Wesley
Tenor Sax, Soprano Sax, Flute: Karl Denson
Trumpet, Flugelhorn: Hugh Ragin
Vocals: Teresa Carroll

"Love in L.A."

Alto Sax: Maceo Parker
Bass: Anthony Cox
Drums: Bill Stewart
Guitar: Rodney Jones
Piano: Peter Madsen
Trombone: Fred Wesley
Tenor Sax, Soprano Sax, Flute: Karl Denson
Trumpet, Flugelhorn: Hugh Ragin
Vocals: Teresa Carroll

"On Green Dolphin Street"

Alto Sax: Maceo Parker
Bass: Anthony Cox
Drums: Bill Stewart
Guitar: Rodney Jones
Piano: Peter Madsen
Trombone: Fred Wesley
Tenor Sax, Soprano Sax, Flute: Karl Denson
Trumpet, Flugelhorn: Hugh Ragin
Vocals: Teresa Carroll

"Comme Ci Comme Ca"

Alto Sax: Maceo Parker
Bass: Anthony Cox
Drums: Bill Stewart
Guitar: Rodney Jones
Piano: Peter Madsen
Trombone: Fred Wesley
Tenor Sax, Soprano Sax, Flute: Karl Denson
Trumpet, Flugelhorn: Hugh Ragin
Vocals: Teresa Carroll

"Love Child"

Alto Sax: Maceo Parker
Bass: Anthony Cox
Drums: Bill Stewart
Guitar: Rodney Jones
Piano: Peter Madsen
Trombone: Fred Wesley
Tenor Sax, Soprano Sax, Flute: Karl Denson
Trumpet, Flugelhorn: Hugh Ragin
Vocals: Teresa Carroll

"Just Like That"

Alto Sax: Maceo Parker
Bass: Anthony Cox
Drums: Bill Stewart
Guitar: Rodney Jones
Piano: Peter Madsen
Trombone: Fred Wesley
Tenor Sax, Soprano Sax, Flute: Karl Denson
Trumpet, Flugelhorn: Hugh Ragin
Vocals: Teresa Carroll

"This One Is for You"

Alto Sax: Maceo Parker
Bass: Anthony Cox
Drums: Bill Stewart
Guitar: Rodney Jones
Piano: Peter Madsen
Trombone: Fred Wesley
Tenor Sax, Soprano Sax, Flute: Karl Denson
Trumpet, Flugelhorn: Hugh Ragin
Vocals: Teresa Carroll

"Moose the Mooch"

Alto Sax: Maceo Parker
Bass: Anthony Cox
Drums: Bill Stewart
Guitar: Rodney Jones
Piano: Peter Madsen
Trombone: Fred Wesley
Tenor Sax, Soprano Sax, Flute: Karl Denson
Trumpet, Flugelhorn: Hugh Ragin
Vocals: Teresa Carroll

"Prayer"

Alto Sax: Maceo Parker
Bass: Anthony Cox
Drums: Bill Stewart
Guitar: Rodney Jones
Piano: Peter Madsen
Trombone: Fred Wesley
Tenor Sax, Soprano Sax, Flute: Karl Denson
Trumpet, Flugelhorn: Hugh Ragin
Vocals: Teresa Carroll

Sing and Be Funky

"For the Elders"

Bass, Vocals: Dwayne Dolphin
Drums, Vocals: Bruce Cox
Piano, Keyboards, Vocals: Peter Madsen
Tenor Sax, Soprano Sax, Alto Sax, Vocals: Karl Denson
Trombone, Vocals: Fred Wesley
Trumpet, Flugelhorn, Vocals: Hugh Ragin

"Just Like That"

Bass, Vocals: Dwayne Dolphin
Drums, Vocals: Bruce Cox
Piano, Keyboards, Vocals: Peter Madsen
Tenor Sax, Soprano Sax, Alto Sax, Vocals: Karl Denson
Trombone, Vocals: Fred Wesley
Trumpet, Flugelhorn, Vocals: Hugh Ragin

"On Green Dolphin Street"

Bass, Vocals: Dwayne Dolphin
Drums, Vocals: Bruce Cox
Piano, Keyboards, Vocals: Peter Madsen
Tenor Sax, Soprano Sax, Alto Sax, Vocals: Karl Denson
Trombone, Vocals: Fred Wesley
Trumpet, Flugelhorn, Vocals: Hugh Ragin

"In Love in L.A."

Bass, Vocals: Dwayne Dolphin
Drums, Vocals: Bruce Cox
Piano, Keyboards, Vocals: Peter Madsen
Tenor Sax, Soprano Sax, Alto Sax, Vocals: Karl Denson
Trombone, Vocals: Fred Wesley
Trumpet, Flugelhorn, Vocals: Hugh Ragin

"Swing & Be Funky"

Bass, Vocals: Dwayne Dolphin
Drums, Vocals: Bruce Cox
Piano, Keyboards, Vocals: Peter Madsen
Tenor Sax, Soprano Sax, Alto Sax, Vocals: Karl Denson
Trombone, Vocals: Fred Wesley
Trumpet, Flugelhorn, Vocals: Hugh Ragin

"Bop to the Boogie"

Bass, Vocals: Dwayne Dolphin
Drums, Vocals: Bruce Cox
Piano, Keyboards, Vocals: Peter Madsen
Tenor Sax, Soprano Sax, Alto Sax, Vocals: Karl Denson
Trombone, Vocals: Fred Wesley
Trumpet, Flugelhorn, Vocals: Hugh Ragin

Amalgamation

"No One"

Bass: Dwayne Dolphin
Saxes, Vocals: Karl Denson
Drums: Bruce Cox
Flugelhorn, Trumpet, Vocals: Hugh Ragin
Organ, Piano, Keyboards: Peter Madsen
Trombone, Vocals: Fred Wesley

"Peace Power"

Bass: Dwayne Dolphin
Saxes, Vocals: Karl Denson
Drums: Bruce Cox
Flugelhorn, Trumpet, Vocals: Hugh Ragin
Organ, Piano, Keyboards: Peter Madsen
Trombone, Vocals: Fred Wesley

"My Neighbourhood"

Bass: Dwayne Dolphin
Saxes, Vocals: Karl Denson
Drums: Bruce Cox
Flugelhorn, Trumpet, Vocals: Hugh Ragin
Organ, Piano, Keyboards: Peter Madsen
Trombone, Vocals: Fred Wesley

"Careless Whisper"

Bass: Dwayne Dolphin
Saxes, Vocals: Karl Denson
Drums: Bruce Cox
Flugelhorn, Trumpet, Vocals: Hugh Ragin
Organ, Piano, Keyboards: Peter Madsen
Trombone, Vocals: Fred Wesley

"Herbal Turkey Breast"

Bass: Dwayne Dolphin
Saxes, Vocals: Karl Denson
Drums: Bruce Cox
Flugelhorn, Trumpet, Vocals: Hugh Ragin
Organ, Piano, Keyboards: Peter Madsen
Trombone, Vocals: Fred Wesley

"The Next Thing I Knew"

Bass: Dwayne Dolphin
Saxes, Vocals: Karl Denson
Drums: Bruce Cox
Flugelhorn, Trumpet, Vocals: Hugh Ragin
Organ, Piano, Keyboards: Peter Madsen
Trombone, Vocals: Fred Wesley

"Trick-Bag"

Bass: Dwayne Dolphin
Saxes, Vocals: Karl Denson
Drums: Bruce Cox
Flugelhorn, Trumpet, Vocals: Hugh Ragin
Organ, Piano, Keyboards: Peter Madsen
Trombone, Vocals: Fred Wesley

"Soft Soul and All That Jazz"

Bass: Dwayne Dolphin
Saxes, Vocals: Karl Denson
Drums: Bruce Cox
Flugelhorn, Trumpet, Vocals: Hugh Ragin
Organ, Piano, Keyboards: Peter Madsen
Trombone, Vocals: Fred Wesley

Eagle Records

Full Circle (From Be-Bop to Hip Hop)

"Rehab"

Bass: Dwayne Dolphin
Clavinet: Bernie Worrell
Drums: Bruce Cox, Bootsy Collins
Guitar: Bruno Speight
Electric Piano: Fred Wesley
Piano: Peter Madsen
Tenor Sax, Flute: Allan Barnes
Trumpet: Dwight Adams
Vocals: Bobby Byrd, Fred Wesley, Vicki Anderson

"Chocolate Scoop"

Bass: Dwayne Dolphin
Drums: Bruce Cox, Bootsy Collins
Electric Piano: Fred Wesley
Guitar: Bruno Speight
Organ: Johnny Davis
Programming: Bootsy Collins
Tenor Sax, Flute: Allan Barnes
Trombone, Euphonium: Fred Wesley
Vocals: Bobby Byrd, Fred Wesley, Vicki Anderson

"Funk School Hymn"

Bass: Donald Segar
Guitar: Bootsy Collins
Drums: Bruce Cox, Bootsy Collins
Electric Piano: Fred Wesley
Piano: Peter Madsen
Programming: Johnny Davis
Tenor Sax, Flute, Alto Sax: Karl Denson
Trombone, Euphonium: Fred Wesley
Trumpet: Dwight Adams
Vocals: Bobby Byrd, Fred Wesley, Vicki Anderson

"Funk School"

Bass: Donald Segar
Guitar: Bootsy Collins
Drums: Bruce Cox, Bootsy Collins
Electric Piano: Fred Wesley
Piano: Peter Madsen
Programming: Johnny Davis
Tenor Sax, Flute, Alto Sax: Karl Denson
Trombone, Euphonium: Fred Wesley
Trumpet: Hugh Ragin
Vocals: Bobby Byrd, Fred Wesley, Vicki Anderson

"Like This, Like That"

Bass: Dwayne Dolphin
Drums: Bruce Cox, Bootsy Collins

Electric Piano: Fred Wesley
Guitar: Bruno Speight
Piano: Peter Madsen
Programming: Frederic Wesley III
Rap: Brian McKinney
Tenor Sax, Flute, Alto Sax: Karl Denson
Trombone, Euphonium: Fred Wesley
Trumpet: Hugh Ragin
Vocals: Gary Mudbone Cooper

"Mo'Money"

Bass: Dwayne Dolphin
Drums: Tony Byrd
Electric Piano: Fred Wesley
Guitar: Bruno Speight
Piano: Peter Madsen
Tenor Sax, Flute, Alto Sax: Karl Denson
Trombone, Euphonium: Fred Wesley
Trumpet: Hugh Ragin
Vocals: Bobby Byrd, Fred Wesley, Vicki Anderson

"Wanna Be"

Bass: Dwayne Dolphin
Electric Piano: Fred Wesley
Guitar: Bruno Speight
Piano: Peter Madsen
Trombone, Euphonium: Fred Wesley
Vocals: Bobby Byrd, Fred Wesley, Vicki Anderson

"Time for US"

Bass: Dwayne Dolphin
Drums: Bruce Cox, Bootsy Collins
Electric Piano: Fred Wesley
Guitar: Bruno Speight
Vocals: Leon Ware
Piano: Peter Madsen
Trombone, Euphonium: Fred Wesley
Vocals: Bobby Byrd, Fred Wesley, Vicki Anderson

"Beautiful Temptress"

Bass: Dwayne Dolphin
Drums: Bruce Cox, Bootsy Collins
Electric Piano: Fred Wesley
Guitar: Bruno Speight
Piano: Peter Madsen
Programming: David Cochran
Trombone, Euphonium: Fred Wesley
Vocals: Bobby Byrd, Fred Wesley, Vicki Anderson

"Hey You in the Neighborhood"

Bass: Dwayne Dolphin
Drums: Bruce Cox, Bootsy Collins
Electric Piano: Fred Wesley
Guitar: Bruno Speight
Piano: Peter Madsen
Programming: David Cochran
Trombone, Euphonium: Fred Wesley
Vocals: Bobby Byrd, Fred Wesley, Vicki Anderson

"Slide Man"

Bass: Dwayne Dolphin
Drums: Bruce Cox, Bootsy Collins
Electric Piano: Fred Wesley
Guitar: Bruno Speight
Piano: Peter Madsen
Tenor Sax, Flute: Allan Barnes
Tenor Sax, Flute, Alto Sax: Karl Denson
Trombone, Euphonium: Fred Wesley
Trumpet: Dwight Adams, Hugh Ragin
Vocals: Bobby Byrd, Fred Wesley, Vicki Anderson

"Keep a Thang Happ'ning"

Bass: Dwayne Dolphin
Drums: Bruce Cox, Bootsy Collins
Electric Piano: Fred Wesley
Guitar: Bruno Speight
Piano: Peter Madsen

Trombone, Euphonium: Fred Wesley
Vocals: Bobby Byrd, Fred Wesley, Vicki Anderson

"Offering"

Bass: Dwayne Dolphin
Drums: Bruce Cox, Bootsy Collins
Electric Piano: Fred Wesley
Guitar: Bruno Speight
Piano: Peter Madsen
Synthesizer: Bernie Worrell
Tenor Sax, Flute, Alto Sax: Karl Denson
Trombone, Euphonium: Fred Wesley
Trumpet: Hugh Ragin
Vocals: Bobby Byrd, Fred Wesley, Vicki Anderson

Hip Bop Essence Records

Wuda Cuda Shuda

"Getcho Money Ready"

Alto Sax, Tenor Sax, Flute, Bagpipes: Ernie Fields Jr.
Bass: Michael Mondesir
Drums, Vocals: Bruce Cox
Guitar, Voice: Reggie Ward
Keyboards: Barney McAll
Trombone, Vocals: Fred Wesley
Trumpet, Flugelhorn: Gary Winters

"Geek Goom"

Alto Sax, Tenor Sax, Flute, Bagpipes: Ernie Fields Jr.
Bass: Michael Mondesir
Drums, Vocals: Bruce Cox
Guitar, Voice: Reggie Ward
Keyboards: Barney McAll
Trombone, Vocals: Fred Wesley
Trumpet, Flugelhorn: Gary Winters

"The Ballad of Beulah Baptist"

Alto Sax, Tenor Sax, Flute, Bagpipes: Ernie
  Fields Jr.
Bass: Michael Mondesir
Drums, Vocals: Bruce Cox
Guitar, Voice: Reggie Ward
Keyboards: Barney McAll
Trombone, Vocals: Fred Wesley
Trumpet, Flugelhorn: Gary Winters

"Wuda Cuda Shuda"

Alto Sax, Tenor Sax, Flute, Bagpipes: Ernie
  Fields Jr.
Bass: Michael Mondesir
Drums, Vocals: Bruce Cox
Guitar, Voice: Reggie Ward
Keyboards: Barney McAll
Trombone, Vocals: Fred Wesley
Trumpet, Flugelhorn: Gary Winters

"I Love You Like a Brother"

Alto Sax, Tenor Sax, Flute, Bagpipes: Ernie
  Fields Jr.
Bass: Michael Mondesir
Drums, Vocals: Bruce Cox
Guitar, Voice: Reggie Ward
Keyboards: Barney McAll
Trombone, Vocals: Fred Wesley
Trumpet, Flugelhorn: Gary Winters

"Can't Leave It Alone"

Alto Sax, Tenor Sax, Flute, Bagpipes: Ernie
  Fields Jr.
Bass: Michael Mondesir
Drums, Vocals: Bruce Cox
Guitar, Voice: Reggie Ward
Keyboards: Barney McAll
Trombone, Vocals: Fred Wesley
Trumpet, Flugelhorn: Gary Winters

"El Paso"

Alto Sax, Tenor Sax, Flute, Bagpipes: Ernie
  Fields Jr.
Bass: Michael Mondesir
Drums, Vocals: Bruce Cox
Guitar, Voice: Reggie Ward
Keyboards: Barney McAll
Trombone, Vocals: Fred Wesley
Trumpet, Flugelhorn: Gary Winters

"Andrea"

Alto Sax, Tenor Sax, Flute, Bagpipes: Ernie
  Fields Jr.
Bass: Michael Mondesir
Drums, Vocals: Bruce Cox
Guitar, Voice: Reggie Ward
Keyboards: Barney McAll
Trombone, Vocals: Fred Wesley
Trumpet, Flugelhorn: Gary Winters

"Get Down Widcho Baad Self"

Alto Sax, Tenor Sax, Flute, Bagpipes: Ernie
  Fields Jr.
Bass: Michael Mondesir
Drums, Vocals: Bruce Cox
Guitar, Voice: Reggie Ward
Keyboards: Barney McAll
Trombone, Vocals: Fred Wesley
Trumpet, Flugelhorn: Gary Winters

"Ernie's Bag"

Alto Sax, Tenor Sax, Flute, Bagpipes: Ernie
  Fields Jr.
Bass: Michael Mondesir
Drums, Vocals: Bruce Cox
Guitar, Voice: Reggie Ward
Keyboards: Barney McAll
Trombone, Vocals: Fred Wesley
Trumpet, Flugelhorn: Gary Winters

"E-Mail for Dad"

Alto Sax, Tenor Sax, Flute, Bagpipes: Ernie Fields Jr.
Bass: Michael Mondesir
Drums, Vocals: Bruce Cox
Guitar, Voice: Reggie Ward
Keyboards: Barney McAll
Trombone, Vocals: Fred Wesley
Trumpet, Flugelhorn: Gary Winters

"Smooth Move"

Alto Sax, Tenor Sax, Flute, Bagpipes: Ernie Fields Jr.
Bass: Michael Mondesir
Drums, Vocals: Bruce Cox
Guitar, Voice: Reggie Ward
Keyboards: Barney McAll
Trombone, Vocals: Fred Wesley
Trumpet, Flugelhorn: Gary Winters

Sons of Sound Recorded Music

Fred Wesley and the Swing'n Jazz All-Stars—It Don't Mean a Thing if It Ain't Got That Swing

"Wicked Walk"

Alto Sax, Baritone Sax: Carl Atkins
Bass: Keter Betts
Bass, Vocals: Jay Leonhart
Drums: Akira Tana, Rich Thompson
Guitar: Bob Sneider
Piano: Mike Holober
Trombone: Fred Wesley
Trumpet, Flugelhorn: Marvin Stamm

"Dream Catcher"

Alto Sax, Baritone Sax: Carl Atkins
Bass: Keter Betts
Bass, Vocals: Jay Leonhart
Drums: Akira Tana, Rich Thompson
Guitar: Bob Sneider
Piano: Mike Holober

Trombone: Fred Wesley
Trumpet, Flugelhorn: Marvin Stamm

"Eventually"Alto Sax, Baritone Sax: Carl Atkins

Bass: Keter Betts
Bass, Vocals: Jay Leonhart
Drums: Akira Tana, Rich Thompson
Guitar: Bob Sneider
Piano: Mike Holober
Trombone: Fred Wesley
Trumpet, Flugelhorn: Marvin Stamm

"Body & Soul"

Alto Sax, Baritone Sax: Carl Atkins
Bass: Keter Betts
Bass, Vocals: Jay Leonhart
Drums: Akira Tana, Rich Thompson
Guitar: Bob Sneider
Piano: Mike Holober
Trombone: Fred Wesley
Trumpet, Flugelhorn: Marvin Stamm

"Missin' RB Blues"

Alto Sax, Baritone Sax: Carl Atkins
Bass: Keter Betts
Bass, Vocals: Jay Leonhart
Drums: Akira Tana, Rich Thompson
Guitar: Bob Sneider
Piano: Mike Holober
Trombone: Fred Wesley
Trumpet, Flugelhorn: Marvin Stamm

"Emily"

Alto Sax, Baritone Sax: Carl Atkins
Bass: Keter Betts
Bass, Vocals: Jay Leonhart
Drums: Akira Tana, Rich Thompson
Guitar: Bob Sneider
Piano: Mike Holober
Trombone: Fred Wesley
Trumpet, Flugelhorn: Marvin Stamm

"It Don't Mean a Thing (If It Ain't Got That Swing)"

Alto Sax, Baritone Sax: Carl Atkins
Bass: Keter Betts
Bass, Vocals: Jay Leonhart
Drums: Akira Tana, Rich Thompson
Guitar: Bob Sneider
Piano: Mike Holober
Trombone: Fred Wesley
Trumpet, Flugelhorn: Marvin Stamm

"Just Squeeze Me"

Alto Sax, Baritone Sax: Carl Atkins
Bass: Keter Betts
Bass, Vocals: Jay Leonhart
Drums: Akira Tana, Rich Thompson
Guitar: Bob Sneider
Piano: Mike Holober
Trombone: Fred Wesley
Trumpet, Flugelhorn: Marvin Stamm

"Par Three"

Alto Sax, Baritone Sax: Carl Atkins
Bass: Keter Betts
Bass, Vocals: Jay Leonhart
Drums: Akira Tana, Rich Thompson
Guitar: Bob Sneider
Piano: Mike Holober
Trombone: Fred Wesley
Trumpet, Flugelhorn: Marvin Stamm

"Acirfa"

Alto Sax, Baritone Sax: Carl Atkins
Bass: Keter Betts
Bass, Vocals: Jay Leonhart
Drums: Akira Tana, Rich Thompson
Guitar: Bob Sneider
Piano: Mike Holober
Trombone: Fred Wesley
Trumpet, Flugelhorn: Marvin Stamm

"Head Start"

Alto Sax, Baritone Sax: Carl Atkins
Bass: Keter Betts
Bass, Vocals: Jay Leonhart
Drums: Akira Tana, Rich Thompson
Guitar: Bob Sneider
Piano: Mike Holober
Trombone: Fred Wesley
Trumpet, Flugelhorn: Marvin Stamm

Fujipacific Music Ent.

Funk for Your Ass (A Tribute to the Godfather of Soul)

"Funk for Your Ass"

Backup Vocals: Bootsy Collins, Keisha Byrd, Vicky Anderson Byrd
Bass: Bootsy Collins
Drums: Bootsy Collins
Horns: Brian Hogg, Fred Wesley, Gary Winters, Michael Wade, Randy Villars

"Livin' in America"

Vocals: iCandi
Backup Vocals: Bootsy Collins, Keisha Byrd, Vicky Anderson Byrd
Bass: Bootsy Collins
Drums: Bootsy Collins
Horns: Brian Hogg, Fred Wesley, Gary Winters, Michael Wade, Randy Villars

"Get on the Good Foot"

Backup Vocals: Bootsy Collins, Keisha Byrd, Vicky Anderson Byrd
Bass: Bootsy Collins
Drums: Bootsy Collins
Horns: Brian Hogg, Frcd Wcslcy, Gary Winters, Michael Wade, Randy Villars

"I'm Gonna Getcha"

Backup Vocals: Bootsy Collins, Keisha Byrd, Vicky Anderson Byrd
Bass: Bootsy Collins
Drums: Bootsy Collins
Horns: Brian Hogg, Fred Wesley, Gary Winters, Michael Wade, Randy Villars

"Mans' World"

Vocals: Candice
Backup Vocals: Bootsy Collins, Keisha Byrd, Vicky Anderson Byrd
Bass: Bootsy Collins
Drums: Bootsy Collins
Horns: Brian Hogg, Fred Wesley, Gary Winters, Michael Wade, Randy Villars

"Hippy Hobbit"

Backup Vocals: Bootsy Collins, Keisha Byrd, Vicky Anderson Byrd
Bass: Bootsy Collins
Drums: Bootsy Collins
Horns: Brian Hogg, Fred Wesley, Gary Winters, Michael Wade, Randy Villars

"Crazy"

Backup Vocals: Bootsy Collins, Keisha Byrd, Vicky Anderson Byrd
Bass: Bootsy Collins
Drums: Bootsy Collins
Horns: Brian Hogg, Fred Wesley, Gary Winters, Michael Wade, Randy Villars

"I Got the Feelin'"

Backup Vocals: Bootsy Collins, Keisha Byrd, Vicky Anderson Byrd
Bass: Bootsy Collins
Drums: Bootsy Collins
Horns: Brian Hogg, Fred Wesley, Gary Winters, Michael Wade, Randy Villars

"Lap Dancer"

Vocals: Leroy "Sugarfoot" Bonner
Backup Vocals: Bootsy Collins, Keisha Byrd, Vicky Anderson Byrd
Bass: Bootsy Collins
Guitar: Leroy "Sugarfoot" Bonner
Drums: Bootsy Collins
Horns: Brian Hogg, Fred Wesley, Gary Winters, Michael Wade, Randy Villars

"Sex Machine"

Backup Vocals: Bootsy Collins, Keisha Byrd, Vicky Anderson Byrd
Bass: Bootsy Collins
Drums: Bootsy Collins
Horns: Brian Hogg, Fred Wesley, Gary Winters, Michael Wade, Randy Villars

"Scoot Your Bootie"

Backup Vocals: Bootsy Collins, Keisha Byrd, Vicky Anderson Byrd
Bass: Bootsy Collins
Drums: Bootsy Collins
Horns: Brian Hogg, Fred Wesley, Gary Winters, Michael Wade, Randy Villars

"Out of Sight"

Rap: DJizzle
Backup Vocals: Bootsy Collins, Keisha Byrd, Vicky Anderson Byrd
Bass: Bootsy Collins
Drums: Bootsy Collins
Horns: Brian Hogg, Fred Wesley, Gary Winters, Michael Wade, Randy Villars

"The Big Payback"

Backup Vocals: Bootsy Collins, Keisha Byrd, Vicky Anderson Byrd
Bass: Bootsy Collins
Drums: Bootsy Collins
Horns: Brian Hogg, Fred Wesley, Gary Winters, Michael Wade, Randy Villars

"Love for Sale"

Backup Vocals: Bootsy Collins, Keisha Byrd, Vicky Anderson Byrd
Bass: Bootsy Collins
Drums: Bootsy Collins
Horns: Brian Hogg, Fred Wesley, Gary Winters, Michael Wade, Randy Villars

"Making It Up"

Backup Vocals: Bootsy Collins, Keisha Byrd, Vicky Anderson Byrd
Bass: Bootsy Collins
Drums: Bootsy Collins
Horns: Brian Hogg, Fred Wesley, Gary Winters, Michael Wade, Randy Villars

"Let It Flow"

Vocals: Bobby Byrd
Backup Vocals: Bootsy Collins, Keisha Byrd, Vicky Anderson Byrd
Bass: Bootsy Collins
Drums: Bootsy Collins
Horns: Brian Hogg, Fred Wesley, Gary Winters, Michael Wade, Randy Villars

BHM Records

With a Little Help from My Friends

"Spring Like"

Baritone Sax: Sal Oliveri
Bass: Dwayne Dolphin
Drums, Vocals: Bruce Cox
Guitar: Reggie Ward
Keyboards: Peter Madsen
Percussion: Roland Peil
Tenor Sax: Phillip Whack
Trombone: Fred Wesley, Victor Wesley
Trumpet: Paul Henderson

"Swedish Funkballs"

Baritone Sax: Sal Oliveri
Bass: Dwayne Dolphin
Drums, Vocals: Bruce Cox
Guitar: Reggie Ward
Keyboards: Peter Madsen
Percussion: Roland Peil
Tenor Sax: Phillip Whack
Trombone: Fred Wesley, Victor Wesley, Nils Landgren
Trumpet: Paul Henderson

"Beautiful"

Baritone Sax: Sal Oliveri
Bass: Dwayne Dolphin
Drums, Vocals: Bruce Cox
Guitar: Reggie Ward
Keyboards: Peter Madsen
Percussion: Roland Peil
Tenor Sax: Phillip Whack
Trombone: Fred Wesley, Victor Wesley
Trumpet: Paul Henderson

"Ashes to Ashes"

Baritone Sax: Sal Oliveri
Bass: Dwayne Dolphin
Drums, Vocals: Bruce Cox
Guitar: Reggie Ward
Keyboards: Peter Madsen
Percussion: Roland Peil
Tenor Sax: Phillip Whack
Trombone: Fred Wesley, Victor Wesley
Trumpet: Paul Henderson

"Palms Up"

Baritone Sax: Sal Oliveri
Bass: Dwayne Dolphin
Drums, Vocals: Bruce Cox
Guitar: Reggie Ward
Keyboards: Peter Madsen
Percussion: Roland Peil
Tenor Sax: Phillip Whack
Trombone: Fred Wesley, Victor Wesley
Trumpet: Paul Henderson

"Homeboy"

Baritone Sax: Sal Oliveri
Bass: Dwayne Dolphin
Drums, Vocals: Bruce Cox
Guitar: Reggie Ward
Keyboards: Peter Madsen
Percussion: Roland Peil
Tenor Sax: Phillip Whack
Trombone: Fred Wesley, Victor Wesley
Trumpet: Paul Henderson

"Obamaloo"

Baritone Sax: Sal Oliveri
Bass: Dwayne Dolphin
Drums, Vocals: Bruce Cox
Guitar: Reggie Ward
Keyboards: Peter Madsen
Percussion: Roland Peil
Tenor Sax: Phillip Whack
Trombone: Fred Wesley, Victor Wesley
Trumpet: Paul Henderson

"Everywhere Is Out of Town"

Baritone Sax: Sal Oliveri
Vocals: Will Amrod
Drums, Vocals: Don Stroffolino
Guitar, Bass: Daniel "Bat" Sheehan
Keyboards: Peter Madsen
Percussion: Roland Peil
Tenor Sax: Peter Bittner
Trombone: Fred Wesley, Victor Wesley
Trumpet: Paul Henderson

"Peace Fugue"

Baritone Sax: Sal Oliveri
Bass: Dwayne Dolphin
Drums, Vocals: Bruce Cox
Guitar: Reggie Ward
Keyboards: Peter Madsen
Percussion: Roland Peil
Tenor Sax: Phillip Whack
Trombone: Fred Wesley, Victor Wesley
Trumpet: Paul Henderson

Lo End Records

Studio Live Session

"Breaking Bread"

Bass: Dwayne Dolphin
Drums: Bruce Cox
Guitar: Reggie Ward
Keyboards: Peter Madsen
Sax, Vocals: Phillip Whack
Trombone, Vocals: Fred Wesley
Trumpet, Vocals: Gary Winters

"Pass the Peas"

Bass: Dwayne Dolphin
Drums: Bruce Cox
Guitar: Reggie Ward
Keyboards: Peter Madsen
Sax, Vocals: Phillip Whack
Trombone, Vocals: Fred Wesley
Trumpet, Vocals: Gary Winters

"Doin' It to Death (Funky Good Time)"

Bass: Dwayne Dolphin
Drums: Bruce Cox
Guitar: Reggie Ward
Keyboards: Peter Madsen
Sax, Vocals: Phillip Whack
Trombone, Vocals: Fred Wesley
Trumpet, Vocals: Gary Winters

"House Party"

Bass: Dwayne Dolphin
Drums: Bruce Cox
Guitar: Reggie Ward
Keyboards: Peter Madsen
Sax, Vocals: Phillip Whack
Trombone, Vocals: Fred Wesley
Trumpet, Vocals: Gary Winters

"Get on the Good Foot"

Bass: Dwayne Dolphin
Drums: Bruce Cox
Guitar: Reggie Ward
Keyboards: Peter Madsen
Sax, Vocals: Phillip Whack
Trombone, Vocals: Fred Wesley
Trumpet, Vocals: Gary Winters

PARLET AND BRIDES OF FUNKENSTEIN: 1980

Originally Unreleased

"Think Right"

Vocals: Dawn Silva, Jeanette McGruder, Sheila Horne, Lige Curry, Ron Ford, Patty Walker
Drums: Kenny Colton
Bass: Lige Curry
Guitar: Tony Thomas
Piano: Ernestro Wilson, Manon Saulsby

"Think Right" was one of the few songs to have some divide from primary sources on who exactly all the singers were on this record. However, given the penchant for P-Funk's process of recording different sections of vocals at different times in the studio, the previously mentioned personnel are likely correct.

BUSTA JONES: 1980

Jones, a bassist from Memphis, Tennessee, featured some P-Funk members on his solo debut.

Impulse Reaction

"Superstar"

"I Put a Rush on You"

"Loose Change"

"(Everybody's) Dancing All Over the World"

"Just a Little Misunderstanding"

"(You) Keep Making Me Hot"

"Take Me Back Now"

Backup Vocals: Cheryl Carriere, Dolette McDonald, The Energetic, Loni Clark, Margo Thunder, Pat Thomson, Rich Forlenza, Busta Jones
Drums: Terry Martell, Tyrone Lampkin, Paul Duskin
Guitar: Barry Cohen, Bobby Eli, Nairobi Sailcat, Piers Lawrence, Walter Rossi, Busta Jones
Bass: Busta Jones
Lead Vocals: Busta Jones
Keyboards, Synthesizer: Allen Wentz, Bernie Worrell, Danielle Barb, Maurice Starr
Percussion: Russ Presto

ROGER/ZAPP/HUMAN BODY: 1980–

All the important early Roger/Zapp/Human Body songs that have notable connections to P-Funk are listed here.

Warner Bros./Records

Zapp

"More Bounce to the Ounce"

Vocals/Talkbox: Roger Troutman
Drums: Lester Troutman
Handclap Boards with Tambourine: Carl Butch Small
Guitar: Roger Troutman, Bootsy Collins
Keyboards: Roger Troutman, Greg Jackson
Bass: Zapp Troutman

"More Bounce to the Ounce" was the most important single in the Zapp/Roger story. It solidified their sound and brought them onto the charts. George Clinton actually made the song as it is known today by looping what was originally a more complex song that had many sections that made the song not work as well, as Clinton stated. There are several testimonies to Clinton's idea to loop the tape, thus creating the pulse that would end up being the entire backbone of the sound of Zapp. This is a story that both has not been told often and also ties Zapp to P-Funk inextricably.

"Freedom"

Vocals: Bobby Glover, Roger Troutman, Janetta Boyce, Marchelle Smith, Delores Smith, Greg Jackson
Talkbox: Roger Troutman
Drums: Lester Troutman
Percussion: Larry and Lester Troutman
Guitar: Roger Troutman
Keyboards: Greg Jackson
Bass: Zapp Troutman

"Brand New Player"

Vocals: Bobby Glover, Roger Troutman, Janetta Boyce, Marchelle Smith, Delores Smith, Greg Jackson
Talkbox: Roger Troutman
Drums: Lester Troutman
Percussion: Larry and Lester Troutman
Guitar: Roger Troutman
Keyboards: Greg Jackson
Bass: Zapp Troutman
Sax: Carl Cowen

"Funky Bounce"

Bobby Glover, Roger Troutman, Janetta Boyce, Marchelle Smith, Delores Smith, Greg Jackson, Ray Davis
Talkbox: Roger Troutman
Drums: Lester Troutman
Guitar: Roger Troutman, Bootsy Collins
Keyboards: Greg Jackson
Bass: Zapp Troutman

"Be Alright"

Vocals: Bobby Glover, Roger Troutman, Janetta Boyce, Marchelle Smith, Delores Smith, Greg Jackson
Drums: Lester Troutman
Guitar: Roger Troutman
Keyboards: Greg Jackson, Roger Troutman
Vibraphone: Roger Troutman
Bass: Zapp Troutman
Sax: Carl Cowen

"Coming Home"

Vocals: Bobby Glover, Roger Troutman, Janetta Boyce, Marchelle Smith, Delores Smith, Greg Jackson
Drums: Lester Troutman
Guitar: Roger Troutman
Keyboards: Roger Troutman
Bass: Zapp Troutman
Harmonica: Roger Troutman

The Many Facets of Roger

"I Heard It through the Grapevine"

Vocals: Roger Troutman, Bobby Glover, Roger Troutman, Janetta Boyce, Marchelle Smith, Delores Smith, Greg Jackson, Dick Smith, Zapp Troutman, Jeanette MacGruder
Talkbox: Roger Troutman
Drums: Lester Troutman
Percussion: Larry Troutman
Guitar: Roger Troutman
Keyboards: Roger Troutman
Bass: Zapp Troutman
Horns: Carl Cowen

"So Ruff, So Tuff"

Vocals: Roger Troutman, Bobby Glover, Roger Troutman, Janetta Boyce, Marchelle Smith, Delores Smith, Greg Jackson, Dick Smith, Zapp Troutman, Jeanette MacGruder
Talkbox: Roger Troutman
Drums: Lester Troutman
Percussion: Larry Troutman
Guitar: Roger Troutman
Keyboards: Roger Troutman
Bass: Zapp Troutman
Horns: Carl Cowen

"A Chunk of Sugar"

Vocals: Roger Troutman, Bobby Glover, Roger Troutman, Janetta Boyce, Marchelle Smith, Delores Smith, Greg Jackson, Dick Smith, Zapp Troutman, Jeanette MacGruder
Talkbox: Roger Troutman
Drums: Lester Troutman
Percussion: Larry Troutman
Guitar: Roger Troutman
Keyboards: Roger Troutman
Bass: Zapp Troutman
Horns: Carl Cowen

"Do It Roger"

Vocals: Roger Troutman, Bobby Glover, Roger Troutman, Janetta Boyce, Marchelle Smith, Delores Smith, Greg Jackson, Dick Smith, Zapp Troutman, Jeanette MacGruder
Talkbox: Roger Troutman
Drums: Lester Troutman
Percussion: Larry Troutman
Guitar: Roger Troutman
Keyboards: Roger Troutman
Bass: Zapp Troutman
Horns: Carl Cowen

"Maxx Axe"

Vocals: Roger Troutman, Bobby Glover, Roger Troutman, Janetta Boyce, Marchelle Smith, Delores Smith, Greg Jackson, Dick Smith, Zapp Troutman, Jeanette MacGruder
Talkbox: Roger Troutman
Drums: Lester Troutman
Percussion: Larry Troutman
Guitar: Roger Troutman
Keyboards: Roger Troutman
Bass: Zapp Troutman
Horns: Carl Cowen

"Blue (A Tribute to the Blues)"

Vocals: Roger Troutman, Bobby Glover, Roger Troutman, Janetta Boyce, Marchelle Smith, Delores Smith, Greg Jackson, Dick Smith, Zapp Troutman, Jeanette MacGruder
Talkbox: Roger Troutman
Drums: Lester Troutman
Percussion: Larry Troutman
Guitar: Roger Troutman
Keyboards: Roger Troutman
Bass: Zapp Troutman
Horns: Carl Cowen

Bearsville Records

The Human Body, Make You Shake It

"Make You Shake It"

Vocals: Ray Davis, Roger Troutman, Zapp Troutman, Larry Hatcher, Billy Beck, Bobby Glover, Greg Jackson, Jannetta Boyce, Linda McDougal, Mallia Franklin, Oliver Dollar, Shelley Smith,
Talkbox: Roger Troutman
Drums: Lester Troutman
Percussion: Roger and Larry Troutman
Guitar: Roger Troutman
Keyboards: Billy Beck
Bass: Roger Troutman
Horns: Michael Warren, Eddie Barber, Randy Wallace

"Tomorrow"

Vocals: Ray Davis, Roger Troutman, Zapp Troutman, Larry Hatcher, Billy Beck, Bobby Glover, Greg Jackson, Jannetta Boyce, Linda McDougal, Mallia Franklin, Oliver Dollar, Shelley Smith,
Drums: Lester Troutman
Percussion: Roger and Larry Troutman
Guitar: Roger Troutman
Keyboards: Billy Beck
Bass: Zapp Troutman
Horns: Carl Cowen

"Keep Your Head Up"

Vocals: Ray Davis, Roger Troutman, Zapp Troutman, Larry Hatcher, Billy Beck, Bobby Glover, Greg Jackson, Jannetta Boyce, Linda McDougal, Mallia Franklin, Oliver Dollar, Shelley Smith,
Drums: Lester Troutman
Percussion: Roger and Larry Troutman
Guitar: Roger Troutman
Keyboards: Billy Beck, Roger Troutman
Bass: Roger Troutman

"Hit Me"

Vocals: Ray Davis, Roger Troutman, Zapp Troutman, Larry Hatcher, Billy Beck, Bobby Glover, Greg Jackson, Jannetta Boyce, Linda McDougal, Mallia Franklin, Oliver Dollar, Shelley Smith,
Drums: Lester Troutman
Percussion: Roger and Larry Troutman
Guitar: Roger Troutman
Keyboards: Billy Beck
Bass: Zapp and Roger Troutman
Horns: Michael Warren, Eddie Barber, Randy Wallace

"As We Lay"

Vocals: Ray Davis, Roger Troutman, Larry Hatcher, Billy Beck, Bobby Glover,
Drums: Lester Troutman
Guitar: Roger Troutman
Keyboards: Billy Beck
Bass: Zapp Troutman
Horns/Winds: Carl Cowen

"Please Help Me Find Her"

Vocals: Ray Davis, Roger Troutman, Larry Hatcher, Billy Beck, Bobby Glover, Jannetta Boyce, Linda McDougal, Mallia Franklin, Oliver Dollar, Shelley Smith
Drums: Lester Troutman
Guitar: Roger Troutman
Keyboards: Billy Beck, Roger Troutman
Bass: Roger Troutman

"There Is Nobody"

Vocals: Ray Davis, Roger Troutman, Larry Hatcher, Billy Beck, Bobby Glover, Jannetta Boyce, Linda McDougal, Mallia Franklin, Oliver Dollar, Shelley Smith
Drums: Lester Troutman
Guitar: Roger Troutman
Keyboards: Billy Beck, Roger Troutman
Bass: Roger Troutman
Saxes: Carl Cowen

"I Believe We Can"

Vocals: Ray Davis, Roger Troutman, Zapp Troutman, Larry Hatcher, Billy Beck, Bobby Glover, Greg Jackson, Jannetta Boyce, Linda McDougal, Mallia Franklin, Oliver Dollar, Shelley Smith,
Drums: Lester Troutman
Percussion: Roger and Larry Troutman
Guitar: Roger Troutman
Keyboards: Billy Beck
Bass: Zapp and Roger Troutman
Horns: Michael Warren, Eddie Barber, Randy Wallace

JIMMY G: 1980–1981

Jimmy G was the bass-playing brother of George Clinton and had a group called the Tackheads, produced by Clinton half a decade after these songs were recorded.

"Shove On"

Keyboards: David Spradley
Bass: Jimmy Giles
Lead Vocals: Jimmy Giles
Backup Vocals: Jeanette Washington, Janice Evans, Shirley Hayden, Ron Ford, Lige Curry, Sheila Horne, Jeanette MacGruder
Guitar: Ron Ford
Drums: Dean Ragland

"Get It On"

Keyboards: David Spradley
Bass: Jimmy Giles
Vocals: Jimmy Giles, Ron Ford, Lige Curry,
Guitar: Ron Ford
Drums: Dean Ragland

RON FORD: 1980–1981

Vocalist/songwriter Ron Ford was an integral part of P-Funk from the latter half of the 1970s on but originally hailed from Plainfield, New Jersey, like the core of the original P-Funkers. He also wrote songs for Parlet and the Brides of Funkenstein, among others.

"Rock Jam"

Vocals: Ron Ford, Shirley Hayden, Jeanette Washington, Janice Evans, Lige Curry, Michael Clip Payne, Mallia Franklin, Seth Neblett
Drums: Dean Ragland
Bass: Lige Curry
Synthesizers: David Spradley
Guitar: Ron Ford

"Monster Dance"

Vocals: Ron Ford, Shirley Hayden, Jeanette Washington, Janice Evans, Lige Curry
Drums: Kenny Colton
Synthesizers: David Spradley
Bass: Jimmy Ali
Horns: Bennie Cowan, Greg Thomas, Greg Boyer
Guitar: Jerome Ali

"Thumparella"

Vocals: Ron Ford, Shirley Hayden, Jeanette Washington, Janice Evans, Lige Curry
Drums: Kenny Colton
Synthesizers: David Spradley
Guitar: Ron Ford, Gordon Carlton

— ☆ —

STERLING SILVER STARSHIP: 1980–1981

This group was fronted by bassist and vocalist Donnie Sterling, who was featured on "Agony of DeFeet" and other later Parliament and Parlet songs.

"Funk It Up"

Lead Vocals: Donnie Sterling
Backup Vocals: Mallia Franklin, Jeanette Washington, Janice Evans, Shirley Hayden, Cheryl James, Jeanette McGruder
Drums: Lonnie Greene
Bass: Donnie Sterling
Keyboards: Jerome Rodgers, Donnie Sterling
Guitar: Tony Thomas, Rodney Crutcher

"Booty Body Ready for the Plush Funk"

Vocals: Donnie Sterling, Mallia Franklin, Lonnie Greene, Shirley Hayden, Jeanette Washington, Ray Davis
Drums: Lonnie Greene
Bass: Donnie Sterling
Keyboards, Synthesizers: David Spradley
Guitar: Tony Thomas

— ☆ —

JESSICA CLEAVES: 1980–1981

Cleaves was a notable soprano from the Friends of Distinction and Earth, Wind & Fire before joining P-Funk in 1976. Her soprano parts on "(Not Just) Knee Deep" are trademark.

"Send a Gram"

Lead Vocals: George Clinton, Jessica Cleaves
Backup Vocals: Sidney Barnes, Andre Williams, Tracey Lewis, Robert Peanut Johnson

Drums: Tyrone Lampkin
Bass: Danan Potts
Guitar: Ron Brembry
Keyboards: Bernie Worrell
Orchestra: Detroit Symphony Orchestra

"My Love"

Vocals: Jessica Cleaves
Drums: Tyrone Lampkin?
Bass: Rodney Curtis?
Electric Piano: Manon Saulsby, Ernestro Wilson
Guitar: Bruce Nazarian

"I Envy the Sunshine"

Vocals: Jessica Cleaves, Telma Hopkins, Joyce Vincent
Drums: Tyrone Lampkin
Bass: Cordell Mosson
Guitar: Ron Brembry, Blackbyrd McKnight
Piano: David Spradley
Trombone: Fred Wesley
Sax: Maceo Parker, Michael Brecker
Trumpet: Richard Griffith, Rick Gardner, Randy Brecker

"Off the Wall"

Vocals: Jessica Cleaves
All Instruments: Junie Morrison

The Eyes of a Dreamer

Vocals: Jessica Cleaves
Drums: Tyrone Lampkin
Percussion:
Bass: Rodney Curtis?
Guitar: Bruce Nazarian
Electric Piano: Manon Saulsby, Ernestro Wilson
String and Horn Arrangement: Wade Marcus

— ☆ —

P-Funk's Michael "Kidd Funkadelic" Hampton. © Diem Jones

MICHAEL HAMPTON: 1980, 1995, 1998

Listed here are outings from seminal Funkadelic lead guitarist Michael Hampton, a P-Funk mainstay who joined the group in 1974.

"We're Just Funkers"

Lead Guitar: Michael Hampton
Drums: Lonnie Greene
Bass: Donnie Sterling
Rhythm Guitar: Tony Thomas
Keyboards: David Spradley
Orchestra: Detroit Symphony Orchestra

Heavy Metal Funkason

"Acapella Unsung Love Song"

Vocals: George Clinton
Guitar: Michael Hampton

"Sloppy Metal"

Vocals: George Clinton
Guitar: Michael Hampton
Drums: Roger Parker
Bass: Lige Curry

"Me Anti?"

Guitar: Michael Hampton
Drums: Roger Parker
Bass: Lige Curry

"Tryin' to Get Dis World Alive"

Guitar: Michael Hampton
Drums: Roger Parker
Bass: Lige Curry

"Heavy Metal Funkadelic"

Guitar: Michael Hampton
Drums: Roger Parker
Bass: Lige Curry

"ComebackSly"

Keyboards: Charlie Wilson
Bass: Lige Curry
Vocals: Belita Woods, George Clinton, Charlie Wilson, Lige Curry
Guitar: Michael Hampton
Drums: Roger Parker

"Club Metalfunkadelamack"

Guitar: Michael Hampton
Drums: Roger Parker
Bass: Michael Hampton

"Cracked Up Soldier"

Bass: Lige Curry
Guitar: Michael Hampton
Drums: Roger Parker

"Wrongsididus"

Guitar: Michael Hampton
Drums: Roger Parker
Bass: Lige Curry

"Chronic Reggae"

Guitar: Michael Hampton
Drums: Roger Parker
Bass: Lige Curry

"Time to Get Up"

Guitar: Michael Hampton
Drums: Roger Parker
Bass: Lige Curry

"Dub Kidd Funkadelic Anthem"

Guitar: Michael Hampton
Drums: Roger Parker
Bass: Lige Curry

"Backinadaze"

Guitar: Michael Hampton
Drums: Roger Parker
Bass: Lige Curry

"Girls of Duh World"

Vocals: Michael Hampton, Lige Curry, Louie Kababbie
Guitar: Michael Hampton
Drums: Roger Parker
Bass: Lige Curry

— ☆ —

SIDNEY BARNES
(SELECT TRACKS): 1980

Sidney Barnes was a very important early writing partner with George Clinton and Motown baritone saxophonist Mike Terry (part of the Geo-Si-Mik writing team). He had several successes with the Rotary Connection and his prior work in the northern soul subgenre.

"Secrets"

Vocals: Sidney Barnes
Backup Vocals: Sidney Barnes, Robert Peanut Johnson, Lige Curry
Drums: Kenny Colton
Bass: Lige Curry
Keyboards, Synthesizers: Ernestro Wilson
Guitar: Michael Hampton, Tony Thomas

— ☆ —

LONNIE GREENE
(SELECT TRACKS): 1980

Greene was an early 1980s P-Funk contributor, erstwhile drummer for Sly Stone, and drummer for Sterling Silver Starship and also featured on "Agony of DeFeet."

"I Didn't Know That Funk Was Loaded"

Vocals: Lonnie Greene, Kenny Cromer, Craig Lane, Gregory Nicks
Drums: Lonnie Greene
Bass: Avery Davis

Keyboards, Synthesizers: Craig Lane
Guitar: Kenny Cromer

— ☆ —

SWEAT BAND: 1980

Sweat Band was essentially Bootsy's Rubber Band with a new emphasis on players like percussionist Carl "Butch" Small, keyboardist Joel "Razor Sharp" Johnson, saxophonist Maceo Parker, and others. It is one of the few Uncle Jam Records releases.

Uncle Jam Records

Sweat Band

"Hyper Space"

Drums: Jerry Jones
Percussion: Carl "Butch" Small
Synth Bass: Joel Johnson
Piano, Clavinet, Synthesizers: Joel Johnson
Guitar: Michael Hampton

"Freak to Freak"

Vocals: Bootsy Collins, Dawn Silva, Shirley Hayden, Janice Evans, Jeanette Washington, Jeanette MacGruder, Sheila Horne, Mallia Franklin, Tracey Lewis, Andre Williams, Lloyd Bradley
Drums: Jerry Jones
Percussion, Synth Drums, Handclap Boards: Carl "Butch" Small
Bass: Bootsy Collins
Melodica: Bernie Worrell
Keyboards: David Spradley
Piano, Keyboards, Synthesizers: Bernie Worrell
Guitar: Michael Hampton, Garry Shider
Trumpet: Richard Griffith, Larry Hatcher
Sax: Maceo Parker
Trombone: Fred Wesley

"Love Much"

Drums: Jerry Jones
Percussion: Carl "Butch" Small
Bass: Bootsy Collins
Guitar: Garry Shider
Sax: Maceo Parker
Keyboards: Joel Johnson
Strings: Detroit Symphony Orchestra

"We Do It All Day Long"

Vocals: Shirley Hayden, Janice Evans, Dawn Silva, Jeanette Washington, Tracey Lewis, Andre Williams
Drums: Jerry Jones
Percussion, Synth Drums: Carl "Butch" Small
Bass: Bootsy Collins
Organ, Keyboards, Synthesizers: Bernie Worrell
Guitar: Garry Shider
Sax: Maceo Parker
Strings: Detroit Symphony Orchestra

"Jamaica"

Vocals: Bootsy Collins, Carl "Butch" Small, Cheryl James, Lloyd Bradley, Robert Peanut Johnson
Drums: Andy Combs
Percussion: Carl "Butch" Small
Bass: Bootsy Collins
Organ, Clavinet, Synthesizers: Joel Johnson, Maceo Parker
Guitar: Bootsy Collins
Trumpet: Richard Griffith, Larry Hatcher
Sax: Maceo Parker
Trombone: Fred Wesley

"Body Shop"

Vocals: Jeanette Washington, Janice Evans, Shirley Hayden, Gwen Dozier, Robert Peanut Johnson, Michael Clip Payne, Bootsy Collins, Ray Davis, Dawn Silva, Jeanette MacGruder, Sheila Horne, Mallia Franklin, Carolyn Miles, Arneta Walker, Linda Shider

Drums: Bootsy Collins
Percussion: Carl "Butch" Small
Bass: Bootsy Collins
Keyboards, Synthesizers: Joel Johnson
Guitar: Bootsy Collins, Gary Shider
Trumpet: Richard Griffith, Larry Hatcher
Sax: Maceo Parker
Trombone: Fred Wesley

"We Do It All Day Long (Reprise)"

Vocals: Shirley Hayden, Janice Evans, Dawn Silva, Jeanette Washington, Tracey Lewis, Andre Williams
Drums: Jerry Jones
Percussion, Synth Drums: Carl "Butch" Small
Bass: Bootsy Collins
Organ, Keyboards, Synthesizers: Bernie Worrell
Guitar: Garry Shider
Sax: Maceo Parker
Strings: Detroit Symphony Orchestra

— ☆ —

BOOTSY: 1980–1982, 1988–

This section focuses on the post–Rubber Band albums, the continuation of bassist Bootsy Collins's long, storied career into the modern era. Bootsy's image and iconography have become legendary, and his subsequent solo releases feature a laundry list of famous "who's who's" in popular music, indeed from throughout popular culture itself.

Originally Unreleased

"The Chong Show"

Lead Vocals: Bootsy Collins, David Spradley
Backup Vocals: Bootsy Collins, David Spradley
Keyboards: David Spradley, Bootsy Collins
Guitar: Bootsy Collins
Percussion: Carl "Butch" Small

William "Bootsy" Collins and members of his fan club. © Diem Jones

Warner Bros.

Ultra Wave

"Mug Push"

Lead Vocals: Bootsy Collins, George Clinton
Backup Vocals: Robert Peanut Johnson,
 Cynthia Girty, Tony Walker, Carolyn Miles
Drums: Bootsy Collins
Percussion: Carl Butch Small
Bass: Bootsy Collins
Keyboards, Synthesizers: David Spradley
Guitar: Bootsy Collins, Catfish Collins

"Mug Push" was the lead-off single from the *Ultra Wave* album. It features the new addition of the singers known as Godmoma, percussionist Butch Small, and keyboardist David Spradley.

"F-Encounter"

Lead Vocals: Bootsy Collins, George Clinton
Backup Vocals: Shirley Hayden, Janice Evans,
 Jeanette Washington, Robert Peanut Johnson
Drums: Jerry Jones
Bass: Bootsy Collins
Keyboards, Synthesizers: Mark Johnson
Guitar: Rick Evans
Percussion: Carl "Butch" Small
Trumpet: Richard Griffith, Larry Hatcher
Sax, Flute: Maceo Parker
Trombone: Fred Wesley

"Is That My Song"

Vocals: Bootsy Collins
Backup Vocals: Telma Hopkins, Joyce Vincent
Drums: Bootsy Collins
Handclap Boards: Carl "Butch" Small
Bass: Bootsy Collins
Keyboards, Synthesizers: David Spradley
Guitar: Bootsy Collins

"It's a Musical"

Lead Vocals: Bootsy Collins, George Clinton
Backup Vocals: Dawn Silva, Jeanette McGruder, Sheila Horne
Drums: Bootsy Collins
Percussion: Carl "Butch" Small
Bass: Bootsy Collins
Keyboards, Synthesizers: Joel Johnson
Guitar: Catfish Collins, Bootsy Collins
Trumpet: Richard Grifith, Larry Hatcher
Sax: Maceo Parker
Trombone: Fred Wesley

"Fat Cat"

Lead Vocals: Bootsy Collins
Drums: Bootsy Collins
Bass: Carolyn Miles, Cynthia Girty, Tony Walker, Robert Peanut Johnson, Dawn Silva, Sheila Horne, Jeanette MacGruder
Keyboards, Synthesizers: David Spradley
Guitar: Catfish Collins

"Sacred Flower"

Lead Vocals: Bootsy Collins
Backup Vocals: Robert Peanut Johnson, Cynthia Girty, Tony Walker, Carolyn Miles
Drums: Bootsy Collins
Bass: Bootsy Collins
Lyricon: David McMurray
Keyboards, Synthesizers: David Spradley
Guitar: Bootsy Collins, Catfish Collins

"Sound Crack"

Vocals: Bootsy Collins
Backup Vocals: Carolyn Miles, Tony Walker, Cynthia Girty, Robert Peanut Johnson
Drums: Bootsy Collins
Percussion, Synth Drums: Carl "Butch" Small
Cowbell: Bootsy Collins
Bass: Bootsy Collins
Keyboards, Synthesizers: Bootsy Collins
Guitar: Bootsy Collins

Originally Unreleased

"Scenery"

Lead Vocals: Bootsy Collins
Bass, Guitar, Drums: Bootsy Collins
Mandolin: Tony Ray
Keyboards: Bernie Worrell
Backup Vocals: Cynthia Girty, Tony Walker, Carolyn Miles

The One Giveth, the Count Taketh Away

"Shine-O-Myte (Rag Popping)"

Lead Vocals: Bootsy Collins, George Clinton
Backup Vocals: Robert Peanut Johnson, Ron Ford, Garry Shider, Jeanette McGruder, Mallia Franklin
Drums: Bootsy Collins
Bass: Bootsy Collins
Keyboards, Synthesizers: David Spradley, Bootsy Collins
Guitar: Bootsy Collins, Kevin Oliver

"Landshark (Just When You Thought It Was Safe)"

Vocals: Maceo Parker, Bootsy Collins, H. Bissantz
Backup Vocals: Bootsy Collins, Carolyn Miles, Arneneta Walker, Cynthia Girty
Drums: Bootsy Collins
Bass: Bootsy Collins
Keyboards, Synthesizers: Joel Johnson, Bootsy Collins, Rahni Harris
Guitar: Bootsy Collins, Catfish Collins
Trumpet: Richard Griffith, Larry Hatcher
Sax: Maceo Parker
Trombone: Fred Wesley

William "Bootsy" Collins with his "Space Bass" © Diem Jones

"Countracula (This One's for You)"

Lead Vocals: Bootsy Collins
Backup Vocals: Jeanette McGruder, Mallia Franklin
Drums: Bootsy Collins
Bass: Bootsy Collins
Keyboards, Synthesizers: Joel Johnson, Bootsy Collins, Wes Boatman
Guitar: Bootsy Collins, Catfish Collins

"#1 Funkateer"

Lead Vocals: Bootsy Collins
Drums: Bootsy Collins
Bass: Bootsy Collins
Keyboards, Synthesizers: Bootsy Collins, Joel Johnson
Guitar: Kevin Oliver, Catfish Collins
Trumpet: Larry Hatcher, Richard Griffith
Sax: Maceo Parker
Trombone: Fred Wesley

"Excon (of Love)"

Lead Vocals: Bootsy Collins
Backup Vocals: Robert Peanut Johnson
Drums: Frank Waddy
Bass: Bootsy Collins
Keyboards, Synthesizers: Joel Johnson
Guitar: Bootsy Collins, Catfish Collins

"So Nice You Name Him Twice"

Lead Vocals: Maceo Parker, Bootsy Collins
Backup Vocals: Carolyn Miles, Cynthia Girty, Tony Walker
Piano: Bernie Worrell
Bass, Drums: Bootsy Collins
Guitar: Catfish Collins, Kevin Oliver
Trombone: Fred Wesley
Sax: Maceo Parker
Trumpet: Richard Griffith, Larry Hatcher

"What's W-R-O-N-G Radio"

Lead Vocals: Bootsy Collins
Backup Vocals: Cynthia Girty, Tony Walker, Carolyn Miles, Robert Peanut Johnson
Drums: Bootsy Collins
Bass: Bootsy Collins
Keyboards, Synthesizers: Joel Johnson, Bootsy Collins
Guitar: Bootsy Collins, Catfish Collins

"Music to Smile By"

Lead Vocals: Bootsy Collins
Backup Vocals: Robert Peanut Johnson, Carolyn Miles, Cynthia Girty, Tony Walker
Drums: Frank Waddy
Bass: Bootsy Collins
Keyboards, Synthesizers: Joel Johnson, Bootsy Collins
Guitar: Catfish Collins, Bootsy Collins

"Play on Playboy"

Lead Vocals: Bootsy Collins
Backup Vocals: Cynthia Girty, Tony Walker, Carolyn Miles, H. Bissantz
Drums: Bootsy Collins
Bass: Bootsy Collins
Keyboards, Synthesizers: Joel Johnson, Bootsy Collins
Guitar: Catfish Collins, Bootsy Collins

"Take a Lickin' and Keep On Kickin'"

Lead Vocals: Bootsy Collins
Backup Vocals: Robert Peanut Johnson
Drums: Bootsy Collins
Bass: Bootsy Collins
Keyboards, Synthesizers: Joel Johnson, Bernie Worrell
Guitar: Catfish Collins, Kevin Oliver

"The Funky Funktioneer"

Lead Vocals: Bootsy Collins
Backup Vocals: Robert Peanut Johnson
Drums: Bootsy Collins
Bass: Bootsy Collins
Keyboards, Synthesizers: Joel Johnson, Bernie Worrell
Guitar: Catfish Collins, Bootsy Collins

Columbia Records

What's Bootsy Doin?

"Party on Plastic (What's Bootsy Doin'?)"

Lead Vocals: Bootsy Collins,
Backup Vocals: Vicky Vea, Pretty Fat, Yraizer, Billy Johnson, Mico Wave
Drum Machine: Bootsy Collins, Mico Wave
Bass: Bootsy Collins
Guitar: Catfish Collins, Ron Jennings
Keyboards: Bootsy Collins

"Subliminal Seduction (Funk-Me-Dirty)"

Lead Vocals: Bootsy Collins
Backup Vocals: Pretty Fatt, Yolanda Fraizer, Vicky Vea, George Clinton, Mico Wave, Mudbone Cooper, Robert Peanut Johnson
Drums: Bootsy, Mico Wave
Bass: Bootsy Collins
Guitar: Stevie Salas
Keyboards: Wes Boatman, Bootsy Collins
Trumpet: Richard Griffith, Rick Gardner
Sax: Maceo Parker
Trombone: Fred Wesley

"Leakin"

Lead Vocals: Bootsy Collins, George Clinton
Backup Vocals: Uncle Tom and Uncle Al, Sharir Forman, Mudbone Cooper, Robert Peanut Johnson, Taka Boom, Mallia Franklin
Drums: Bootsy Collins, Mico Wave
Bass: Bootsy Collins, Trey Stone
Guitar: Stevie Salas, Bootsy Collins

Keyboards: Trey Stone
Trombone: Fred Wesley
Sax: Maceo Parker
Trumpet: Richard Griffith, Rick Gardner

"Shock It to Me"

Lead Vocals: Maceo Parker, Bootsy Collins
Backup Vocals: Cynthia Girty, Anita Walker, Carolyn Stanford, Mudbone Cooper, George Clinton, Robert Peanut Johnson
Drums: Bootsy Collins
Bass: Bootsy Collins
Guitar: Nicky Skopelitis, Stevie Salas
Keyboards: Wes Boatman, Bootsy Collins, Bernie Worrell
Sound Effects: Bill Laswell
Violin: Billy Bang
Trombone: Fred Wesley
Sax: Maceo Parker
Trumpet: Richard Griffith, Rick Gardner

"1st One 2 the Egg Wins"

Lead Vocals: Bootsy Collins
Backup Vocals: Mudbone Cooper, Robert Peanut Johnson
Drums: Bootsy Collins, Mico Wave
Bass: Bootsy Collins
Guitar: Ron Jennings
Keyboards: Wes Boatman, Bootsy Collins
Trumpet: Richard Griffith, Rick Gardner
Sax: Maceo Parker
Trombone: Fred Wesley

"Love Song"

Lead Vocals: Bootsy Collins
Backup Vocals: Mudbone Cooper, Tony Feldman, Carolyn Stanford, Anita Walker, Cynthia Girty, Mico Wave, Joe Harris, George Clinton
Drums: Bootsy Collins, Mico Wave
Bass: Bootsy Collins
Guitar: Bernard Fowler
Keyboards: Trey Stone, Bootsy Collins

"I Wannabee Kissin' U"

Lead Vocals: Bootsy Collins
Backup Vocals: Mudbone Cooper, Vicky Vea
Drums: Mico Wave
Bass: Bootsy Collins
Guitar: Eddie Martinez
Keyboards: Mico Wave, Bootsy Collins

"#-ing the Love Gun"

Lead Vocals: Bootsy Collins
Backup Vocals: Mudbone Cooper, Cynthia Girty, Anita Walker, Carolyn Stanford
Drums: Bootsy Collins
Bass: Bootsy Collins
Guitar: Ron Jennings
Keyboards: Wes Boatman

"Yo Moma Loves Ya"

Lead Vocals: Mama Collins, Bootsy Collins
Backup Vocals: Mudbone Cooper
Drums: Bootsy Collins, Mico Wave
Bass: Bootsy Collins
Guitar: Ron Jennings, Bootsy Collins
Keyboards: Mico Wave

"Save What's Mine for Me"

Lead Vocals: Bootsy Collins
Backup Vocals: Mudbone Cooper
Drums: Bootsy Collins, Mico Wave
Bass: Bootsy Collins
Guitar: Catfish Collins, Bootsy Collins
Keyboards: Mico Wave, Bootsy Collins

Independent

Fresh Outta P University

"Off Da Hook"

Lead Vocals: Mrs. D of K.C., BRIXX, Bootsy Collins
Backup Vocals: Mudbone Cooper, Henry Benefield, Michael Gaitheright, Inaya Davis, Kristen Gray, Melanie Eiland

Drums: Boogieman, Tabularasa
Bass: Bootsy Collins
Guitar: Bootsy Collins, Boogieman
Keyboards: Boogieman
Trombone: Fred Wesley
Sax: Allan Barnes, Ed Jones
Trumpet: Dwight Adams

"I'm Leaving U (Gotta Go, Gotta Go)"

Lead Vocals: MC Lyte, Bootsy Collins
Backup Vocals: Inaya Davis, Kristen Gray, Melanie Eiland, Henry Benefield, Michael Gaitheright
Drums: Joe Belmaati
Bass: Bootsy Collins
Guitar: Wilbur Longmire
Keyboards: Joe Belmaati
Electric Piano: Tue Rob

"Funk Ain't Broke"

Lead Vocals: Rodney O, Bootsy Collins
Drums: Bootsy Collins
Bass: Bootsy Collins
Guitar: Ron Jennings, Bootsy Collins
Keyboards: Joel Johnson, Bootsy Collins
Trumpet: Dwight Adams

"Party Lick-A-Ble's"

Lead Vocals: Bootsy Collins
Backup Vocals: April Woods, Mudbone Cooper
Drums: Bootsy Collins
Bass: Bootsy Collins
Guitar: Bootsy Collins
Keyboards: Bootsy Collins

"Ever Lost Your Lover"

Lead Vocals: Bootsy Collins
Backup Vocals: Inaya Davis, Kristen Gray, Melanie Eiland, Mudbone Cooper
Drums: Tony Byrd
Bass: Bootsy Collins
Guitar: Fan Fan La Tulipe
Keyboards: Johnny Davis, Mousse T
Trombone: Avi Leibovich
Sax, Flute: Chris de'Margary
Trumpet, Flugelhorn: Duncan MacKay
Vibraharp: Vincent Monatana

"Pearl Drops"

Lead Vocals: Bootsy Collins
Backup Vocals: Mudbone Cooper, Henry Benefield, Michael Gaitheright
Drums: Bootsy Collins
Bass: Bootsy Collins
Guitar: Bootsy Collins, Ron Jennings
Keyboards: Anthony Cole

"Do the Freak"

Lead Vocals: Bootsy Collins, A.J., Gizmo, Teray
Backup Vocals: Herbert, Cash, Nathalie, Eugen, Caspar, Terry
Drums: Boogieman
Bass: Bootsy Collins
Guitar: Boogieman
Keyboards: Ralph Petter, Boogieman

"Fragile (So Sensitive)"

Lead Vocals: Bootsy Collins Inaya Davis, Dmeka Sykes
Backup Vocals: Inaya Davis, Kristen Gray, Melanie Eiland, Mike Marshall
Drums: Boogieman, Tabularasa
Bass: Bootsy Collins
Guitar: Bootsy Collins, Boogieman
Keyboards: Ralph Petter, Boogieman

"Holly-Wood-If-She-Could"

Lead Vocals: Bootsy Collins, D.O.C.
Backup Vocals: Mudbone Cooper, Robert Peanut Johnson, April Woods, Kyle Jason
Drums: Bootsy Collins
Bass: Bootsy Collins
Guitar: Ron Jennings
Keyboards: Mousse T

"Wind Me Up"

Lead Vocals: Bootsy Collins, Ono
Backup Vocals: Mudbone Cooper, Henry Benefield, Michael Gaitheright, Rico, Greg Holloway, Brenda, Sweet Lipps, Sunflower, Alan Cann, Flipp Cornett, Alton Hood, Kevin Harvey, Michael Brown
Drums: Boogieman
Bass: Bootsy Collins
Guitar: Boogieman, Bootsy Collins
Keyboards: Ralph Petter, Boogieman
Trombone: Fred Wesley
Sax: Allan Barnes, Ed Jones
Trumpet: Dwight Adams

"Good-N-Nasty (Personal Stash)"

Vocals: Mudbone Cooper, Henry Benefield, Michael Gaitheright, Bootsy Collins
Drums: Bootsy Collins
Bass: Bootsy Collins
Guitar: Ron Jennings
Keyboards: Greg Fitz, Joel Johnson

"Penetration (In Funk We Trust)"

Lead Vocals: Bootsy Collins
Backup Vocals: Garry Shider, Linda Shider, Michael Anthony, April Woods, Kyle Jason
Drums: Bootsy Collins
Bass: Bootsy Collins
Guitar: Garry Shider
Keyboards: Bernie Worrell
Trombone: Fred Wesley
Sax: Allan Barnes, Ed Jones
Trumpet: Dwight Adams

"Home-Of-Da-Freaks"

Lead Vocals: Bootsy Collins, Thomas D, SMUDO
Backup Vocals: Rico, Greg Holloway, Brenda, Sweet Lipps, Sunflower, Alan Cann, Flip Cornett, Alton Hood, Kevin Harvey, Michael Brown
Drums: Boogieman, Tabularasa
Bass: Bootsy Collins
Guitar: Bootsy Collins, Boogieman
Keyboards: Ralph Petter, Boogieman

"Fresh Outta P-University"

Lead Vocals: Bootsy Collins, Robert Harding, Moma Collins
Backup Vocals: Garry Shider, Linda Shider, Mudbone Cooper, April Woods, Michael Anthony
Drums: Bootsy Collins
Bass: Bootsy Collins
Guitar: Garry Shider
Keyboards: Bernie Worrell
Trombone: Fred Wesley
Sax: Alan Barnes, Ed Jones

Play with Bootsy

"Inner-Planetary Funksmanship"

Lead Vocals: Bootsy Collins
Keyboards: Mousse T
Samples found throughout the album.

"Play with Bootsy"

Lead Vocals: Bootsy Collins, Kelli Ali
Backup Vocals: Johnny Douglas
Drums: Johnny Douglas
Bass: Bootsy Collins
Guitar: Ron Jennings
Keyboards: Johnny Douglas

"Love Gangsta"

Lead Vocals: Bootsy Collins, Snoop Dogg, Daz
Backup Vocals: Kokane
Drums: Mousse T
Bass: Bootsy Collins
Guitar: Michael Hampton
Keyboards: Mousse T

"Soul Sista"

Lead Vocals: Joe, Bootsy Collins
Backup Vocals: Cherine Anderson
Drums: Sly Dunbar
Bass: Robbie Shakespeare
Guitar: William Guice?
Keyboards: Handel Tucker

"Don't Let Em"

Lead Vocals: Rosie Gaines, Bootsy Collins, Snoop Dogg
Backup Vocals: Adrian Hall, One, Kokane
Drums: B.La
Bass: Bootsy Collins
Talkbox: Bart Thomas
Guitar: Ingo Schroder
Keyboards: Lutz Krajenski
Horns: Till Brohner

"A Life for Da Sweet Ting"

Lead Vocals: Eased, Bootsy Collins
Backup Vocals: Eased
DJ: DJ Illvibe
Horns: Champ, Mo Delgado
Bass: Bootsy Collins

"Groove Eternal"

Lead Vocals: Bootsy Collins, One, Bobby Womack
Backup Vocals/Claps: D'Maub, Harp D, Second Chance, Catfish Collins
Drums: Royal Garden
Bass: Royal Garden, Bootsy Collins
Guitar: Ingo Schroder
Keyboards: Bootsy Collins

"Dance to the Music"

Lead Vocals: Bootsy Collins, One
Backup Vocals: One
Drums: Royal Garden
Bass: Bootsy Collins
Guitar: One, Bootsy Collins
Keyboards: Bootsy

"Funky and You Know It"

Lead Vocals: Macy Gray, George Clinton, Bootsy Collins
Backup Vocals: Giz Driver, Cordell Mosson, Garry Shider, Wanda Sloan, Catfish Collins
Drums: Mandrax and Seb K
Bass: Marcello Guilliani
Guitar: Catfish Collins
Trombone: Fred Wesley
Keyboards: Mandrax and Seb K

"I'm Tired of Good, I'm Trying Bad"

Lead Vocals: Bootsy Collins, Lady Miss Kier
Guitar: Catfish Collins, Bootsy Collins
Bass: Bootsy Collins
Production: Martin Buttrich, Martin Bettinghaus

A"ll Star Funk"

Lead Vocals: Lady Miss Kier, Bootsy Collins
Backup Vocals: Raz Hirschey, Inisha Clark, William Hagan, Ouiwey Collins, Giz Driver, Rapps Kool-Aydd, Cubbie Bear
Trombone: Fred Wesley
Trumpet: Patrick Anthony
Production: Levent Can 7 and Guido Craveiro
Bass: Bootsy Collins
Guitar: Catfish Collins, Bootsy Collins
Keyboards: Levent Can 7 and Guido Caveiro

"The Bomb"

Lead Vocals: Bootsy Collins
Backup Vocals: Fatboy Slim
Samples, Cuts: Fatboy Slim
Guitar: Bootsy Collins

"Funkship"

Lead Vocals: George Clinton, Garry Shider, Belita Woods, Bootsy Collins, Ray Davis, Giz Driver, Snoop Dogg, Raz Hirshey, Inisha Clark, Kendra Foster
Drums: Bootsy Collins
Bass: Bootsy Collins
Guitar: Garry Shider, Bootsy Collins
Keyboards: Bernie Worrell
Horns: Fred Wesley, Randy Valares, Michael Wade, Michael Winters

Fear Da Tiger

"Fear Da Tiger"

Lead Vocals: Bootsy Collins, Battle Cries & Bengal Bites
Backup Vocals: Bootsy Collins, Battle Cries & Bengal Bites
Drums: Bootsy Collins
Drum Programming: Ouiwey Collins, Tobe
Bass: Bootsy Collins, Battle Cries & Bengal Bites
Guitar: Sean
DJ: Tobe
Violin: Paul Patterson
Keyboards: Morris Mingo

"Big Kats"

Lead Vocals: Bootsy Collins, Battle Cries & Bengal Bites
Backup Vocals: Bootsy Collins, Battle Cries & Bengal Bites
Drum Programming: Ouiwey Collins
Bass: Bootsy Collins
Guitar: Bootsy Collins
Keyboards: Morris Mingo

"Make-It-Shake"

Lead Vocals: Bootsy Collins, Battle Cries & Bengal Bites
Backup Vocals: Bootsy Collins, Battle Cries & Bengal Bites
Drums: Bootsy Collins
Drum Programming: Ouiwey Collins
Bass: Bootsy Collins, Battle Cries & Bengal Bites
Guitar: Bootsy Collins
DJ: Tobe
Violin: Paul Patterson
Keyboards: Morris Mingo

The Official Bootsy Collins Boot-Legged CD

"You Ain't No Accident (You R on Purpose)"

Lead Vocals: James Brown, Danny Ray, Bootsy Collins
Backup Vocals: Bootsy Collins
Drums: Bootsy Collins
Synth Bass: Bernie Worrell
Keyboards: Bernie Worrell, Joel Johnson

"That's Right! James Brown Tight!"

Lead Vocals: Bobby Byrd, DJizzle, Bootsy Collins
Backup Vocals: Bootsy Collins
DJ: DJizzle
Drums: Bootsy Collins
Bass: Bootsy Collins
Guitar: Bootsy Collins, Kevin Oliver
Keyboards: David Spradley

"Buckethead Meets Bootsy N Da Slammer!"

Lead Vocals: Dave Stewart, Bootsy Collins
Drums: Bootsy Collins, Bucket Bots
Bass: Bootsy Collins

Guitar: Buckethead
Keyboards: Bootsy Collins

"The Groovement Has Begun!"

Lead Vocals: Moma Collins, O & U, Bootsy Collins
Drums: Bootsy Collins
Bass: Bootsy Collins
Guitar: Ron Jennings, Bootsy Collins
Keyboards: Joel Johnson, Bootsy Collins,
Trumpet: Dwight Adams

"Mom's Love 4 Ever"

Lead Vocals: Bootsy Collins
Samples: Bootsy Collins
Backup Vocals: Bootsy Collins, Gary Mudbone Cooper
Drums: Bootsy Collins, Mico Wave
Bass: Bootsy Collins
Guitar: Ron Jennings, Bootsy Collins
Keyboards: Mico Wave

"Thee Ram Da Grand Slam (U Cain't Funk D)"

Lead Vocals: Bootsy Collins
Samples: Bootsy Collins
Drum Programming: Bootsy Collins
Percussion: Bootsy Collins
Bass: Bootsy Collins
Keyboards: Bootsy Collins

"Red White and Bleached Git a Brother Off Da Streets"

Lead Vocals: Young Wild Life, Bootsy
Backup Vocals: Bootsy Collins
Samples: Bootsy Collins
Drums: Bootsy Collins
Track: Fatboy Slim
Bass: B Ram The Grand Slam, Bootsy Collins
Guitar: Bootsy Collins
Keyboards: Bootsy Collins

"Strugglin' N Da Tulips"

Lead Vocals: PumpkinPie, SweetLipps, Bootsy Collins
Backup Vocals: Mudbone Cooper, Henry Benefield, Michael Gaitheright
Drums: Bootsy Collins
Bass: Bootsy Collins
Guitar: Bootsy Collins, Ron Jennings
Keyboards: Anthony Cole

"Matt Mauphin & the Soldiers"

Lead Vocals: Bootsy Collins, the Youngest Soldier Boy and the Vets, iCandi
Backup Vocals: Bootsy Collins
Drums: Bootsy Collins
Track: DJizzle
Bass: Bootsy Collins
Guitar: Dee Dee James
Keyboards: Gregg Fitz

"Kool Silly Hands"

Lead Vocals: Bootsy Collins, Baby K, SugarBear, Swedish Lipps
Backup Vocals: Mudbone Cooper,
Drums: Bootsy Collins, Mico Wave
Bass: Bootsy Collins
Guitar: Catfish Collins, Bootsy Collins
Keyboards: Mico Wave, Bootsy Collins
DJ: Tobotius-The-Master-Wax-Manipulator

"She Deep & Juicy!"

Lead Vocals: Bootsy Collins, Jiffona, Poppin' Fresh Doe
Backup Vocals: Bootsy Collins, Gary Mudbone Cooper
Drums: Bootsy Collins
Samples: Bootsy Collins
Bass: Bootsy Collins
Guitar: Catfish Collins, Bootsy Collins
Keyboards: Bernie Worrell

"Da Devil's Playground?" Lead Vocals:

Bootsy Collins, Crazy Guy From NY, The Math-O-Logical Liar
Samples: Bootsy Collins
Backup Vocals: Bootsy Collins
Drums: Bootsy Collins
Bass: Bootsy Collins
Guitar: Dee James
Keyboards: Bernie Worrell
DJ: Tobotius-The-Master-Wax-Manipulator

"I Can Pee N Da Dark & Not Git Wet"

Lead Vocals: Battered Biscuits, JellyCream, Bootsy Collins, Henry Benefield, Michael Gatheright
Backup Vocals: Bootsy Collins, Gary Mudbone Cooper, Henry Benefield, Michael Gatheright
Drums: Bootsy Collins
Bass: Bootsy Collins
Guitar: Catfish Collins
Keyboards: Greg Fitz

Christmas Is 4 Ever

"N-Yo-City"

Lead Vocals: MC Danny Ray
Backup Vocals: Bobby Byrd
Samples: Bootsy Collins
Bass: Bootsy Collins
Horns: Austin Vickrey, Gary Winters, Marc Fields, Michael Wade, Randy Villars, William Hogg
Keyboards, Drums: Morris Mingo
Guitar: Keith Cheatham

"Merry Christmas Baby"

Lead Vocals, Backup Vocals, Bass, Percussion: Bootsy Collins
Keyboards, Drums: Morris Mingo
Drums: Teddy Wilburn
Horns: Austin Vickrey, Gary Winters, Marc Fields, Michael Wade, Randy Villars, William Hogg
Guitar: Keith Cheatham, Bootsy Collins

"Jingle Belz"

Lead Vocals, Guitar, Bass, Drums: Bootsy Collins
Backup Vocals: Tyesha Grissom, Tyreka Grissom
Beatbox: Ian Haiku Herzog
Voice: Bishop Don Magic Juan
Trombone: Fred Wesley
Horns: Austin Vickrey, Gary Winters, Marc Fields, Michael Wade, Randy Villars, William Hogg
Keyboards, Drums: Morris Mingo

"Happy Holidaze"

Lead Vocals, Backup Vocals, Guitar, Bass, Percussion: Bootsy Collins
Lead Vocals: Snoop Dogg, DJizzle
Lead Vocals, Backup Vocals: Danielle Withers
Voice: Bishop Don Magic Juan
Keyboards, Drums: Morris Mingo
Drums: Teddy Wilburn
Guitar: Keith Cheatham
Turntables: Tobe Casual T

"Chestnutz "

Lead Vocals, Backup Vocals: Danielle Withers
Lead Vocals, Backup Vocals, Guitar, Percussion: Bootsy Collins
Horns: Austin Vickrey, Gary Winters, Marc Fields, Michael Wade, Randy Villars, William Hogg
Keyboards, Drums: Morris Mingo
Drums: Teddy Wilburn
Guitar: Keith Cheatham

"WinterFunkyLand"

Lead Vocals, Guitar, Percussion: Bootsy Collins
Backup Vocals: Kendra Foster, Kim Manning
Drums: Frank Kash Waddy
Lead Vocals: Garry Shider
Guitar: Dewayne Blackbyrd McKnight, Michael Hampton
Keyboards: Joel Johnson
Percussion: Tobe Donohue
Strings: Paul Patterson
Lead Vocals, Backup Vocals: Belita Woods, RonKat Spearman

"Santa's Coming"

Guitar: Keith Cheatham
Beats, Rap: Keith Cheatham Jr., Miguel Cheatham
Lead Vocals, Beats: Candis Cheatham
Lead Vocals, Percussion: Bootsy Collins
Horns: Austin Vickrey, Gary Winters, Marc Fields, Michael Wade, Randy Villars, William Hogg

"Boot Off"

Drums: Tobe Donohue
Guitar: Catfish Collins
Lead Vocals, Backup Vocals, Guitar, Bass, Drums, Percussion: Bootsy Collins
Sax: Donn Bynum
Voice: George Clinton

"Silent Night"

Lead Vocals, Backup Vocals: Candis Cheatham
Lead Vocals, Backup Vocals, Guitar, Keyboards, Drums, Percussion: Bootsy Collins
Horns: Austin Vickrey, Gary Winters, Marc Fields, Michael Wade, Randy Villars, William Hogg
Keyboards, Drums: Morris Mingo

"Sleigh Ride"

Backup Vocals: SugarFoot
Clavinet, Piano: Bernie Worrell
Drums: Melvin Parker
Fiddle, Backup Vocals: Charlie Daniels
Lead Vocals: Razzberry
Lead Vocals, Guitar, Bass: Bootsy Collins
Keyboards, Drums: Morris Mingo
Drums: Teddy Wilburn
Mandolin, Violin: Paul Patterson
Sax: Randy Villars

"Dis-Christmas"

Lead Vocals, Backup Vocals: Matt Dawson
Lead Vocals, Backup Vocals, Drums: Bootsy Collins
Backup Vocals: Jerome Johnson
Keyboards, Drums: Morris Mingo
Guitar: Keith Cheatham

"Be-With-You"

Guitar: Keith Cheatham
Backup Vocals: Greg Jackson
Keyboards, Talkbox, Percussion: Zapp Troutman
Vocals, Guitar, Bass, Drums: Bootsy Collins
Voice: Roger Troutman

"Christmas Is 4-Ever"

Backup Vocals: Cherine Anderson
Keyboards: Bernie Worrell
Lead Vocals: Belita Woods, Bobby Womack
Lead Vocals, Backup Vocals, Guitar, Bass, Drums, Percussion: Bootsy Collins
Horns: Austin Vickrey, Gary Winters, Marc Fields, Michael Wade, Randy Villars, William Hogg

Funk Capital of the World

"Spreading Hope Like Dope"

Vocals: Cornel West, Bootsy Collins
Keyboards: Joel Johnson
Programming, Bass: Bootsy Collins

"Hip Hop @ Funk U"

Lead Vocals: Ice Cube, Snoop Dogg, Chuck D
Backup Vocals: Bootsy Collins, Lil Diamond, Candice Cheatham, Faith Daniels
Drums: Bootsy Collins
Bass: Bootsy Collins
Guitar: Catfish Collins, Bootsy Collins, Ron Jennings
Keyboards: Bernie Worrell
Horns: Andrew Olson, Farnell Newton, Kyle Molitor, Michael Phillip

"Mirrors Tell Lies"

Lead Vocals: Bootsy Collins
Backup Vocals: Bootsy Collins, Penny Ford
Voice: Jimmi Hendrix
Drums: Steve Jordan
Bass: Bootsy Collins
Guitar: Ron Jennings

"JB Still the Man"

Lead Vocals: Rev. Al Sharpton
Backup Vocals: Penny Ford
Drums: Frankie Kash Waddy
Bass: Bootsy Collins
Guitar: Catfish Collins, Guitar Sallye
Horns: Fred Wesley, Marc Fields

"Freedumb (Wheel Love Becomes a Threat)"

Lead Vocals: Bootsy Collins
Backup Vocals: Cornel West
Drums: Steve Jordan
Bass: Bootsy Collins
Guitar: Bootsy Collins, Catfish Collins
Keyboards: Morris Mingo
Horns: Andrew Olson, Farnell Newton, Kyle Molitor, Michael Phillip
Strings: Casey Driessen, Jerald Daemyon, Paul Patterson and the Bootzilla Orchestra

"After These Messages"

Lead Vocals: Bootsy Collins, Samuel L. Jackson
Backup Vocals: Adrian Hall, Candice Cheatham
Drums: Frankie Kash Waddy
Bass: Bootsy Collins
Guitar: Bootsy Collins
Keyboards: Joel Johnson
Horns: Andrew Olson, Farnell Newton, Kyle Molitor, Michael Phillip

"Kool Whip"

Lead Vocals: Candi Sweetz, Phil Ade
Backup Vocals: Adrian Hall, Candice Cheatham
Drums: Frankie Kash Waddy, Bootsy Collins
Bass: Bootsy Collins
Guitar: Catfish Collins, Bootsy Collins
Keyboards: Morris Mingo
Strings: Casey Driessen, Jerald Daemyon, Paul Patterson and the Bootzilla Orchestra
Horns: Andrew Olson, Farnell Newton, Kyle Molitor, Michael Phillip

"The Real Deal"

Lead Vocals: CandiSweetz, Mike Phillips
Backup Vocals: Candice Cheatham, Danny Ray
Drums: Bootsy Collins
Percussion: Sheila E
Bass: Bootsy Collins
Guitar: Catfish Collins, Bootsy Collins
Keyboards: Joel Johnson
Sax: Maceo Parker

"Don't Take My Funk"

Lead Vocals: Bobby Womack
Backup Vocals: Catfish Collins
Drums: Steve Jordan
Bass: Bootsy Collins
Guitar: Catfish Collins
Keyboards: Morris Mingo
Horns: Andrew Olson, Farnell Newton, Kyle Molitor, Michael Phillip

"If Looks Could Kill"

Lead Vocals: Bootsy Collins, Zion Planet 10
Backup Vocals: Bootsy Collins, Zion Planet 10
Drums: Dennis Chambers
Bass: Bootsy Collins
Guitar: Bootsy Collins
Banjo: Bela Fleck
Violin: Paul Patterson
Keyboards: Morris Mingo

"Minds under Construction"

Lead Vocals: Bootsy Collins
Drum Programming: Ouiwey Collins
Bass: Bootsy Collins
Guitar: Buckethead

"Siento Bombo"

Lead Vocals: Bootsy Collins, Olvido Ruiz, Ouiwey
Drum Programming: Ouiwey Collins
Bass: Bootsy Colins
Guitar: Tamah
Keyboards: Morris Mingo

"The Jazz Greats (A Tribute to Jazz)"

Lead Vocals: Bootsy Collins
Drums: Steve Jordan
Drum Programming: Claude Von Stroke
Bass: Ron Carter
Guitar: Shawn Steele
Keyboards: George Duke, Johnny Davis

"Garry Shider Tribute"

Lead Vocals: George Clinton
Lead Vocals: Linda Shider
Drum Programming: Bootsy Collins
Guitar: Garry Shider

"Stars Have No Names (They Just Shine)"

Lead Vocals: Bootsy Collins, Chrissy Dunn, Nick Arnold
Drums: Bootsy Collins
Bass: Bootsy Collins
Guitar: Shawn Steele
Banjo: Bela Fleck

"Chocolate Caramel Angel"

Lead Vocals: Faith Daniels, Bootsy Collins, Ronni Rackett
Backup Vocals: Bootsy Collins
Drums, Percussion: Bootsy Collins
Bass: Bootsy Collins
Guitar: Ron Jennings, Bootsy Collins

"Yummy, I Got the Munchies"

Lead Vocals: Tom Joyner, Musiq Soulchild, Bootsy Collins, Razberry White
Backup Vocals: Razberry White
Drums: Jerome Brailey
Bass: Bootsy Collins
Guitar: Garry Shider, Glenn Goins
Keyboards: Bernie Worrell
Horns: Andrew Olson, Farnell Newton, Kyle Molitor, Michael Phillip
Violin: Paul Patterson

World Wide Funk

"World Wide Funk"

Lead Vocals: Doug E. Fresh, Bootsy Collins, Mama Rose, Tyshawn Colquitt, Zachary Adams
Backup Vocals: Bootsy Collins
Beatbox: Doug E. Fresh
Drums: A. Spears, Senri Kwaguchi
Bass: Bootsy Collins, Alissia Beneveniste
Guitar: Buckethead, Bootsy Collins, Alissia Beneveniste
Keyboards: Alissia Benveniste, Nicholas Semrad
Horns: A. Crutchfield, S. Onyejiaka, B. Rayfield, L. Grisset

"Bass Rigged System"

Lead Vocals: Bootsy Collins
Backup Vocals: Candice Cheatham, K. Cheatham
Drums: E. Moore
Bass: Alissia Benveniste, Stanley Clarke, Victor Wooten, Manou Gallo, Bootsy Collins
Guitar: Bootsy Collins, K. Cheatham
Samples: Bootsy Collins
Keyboards: Bootsy Collins, K. Cheatham

"Pusherman"

Lead Vocals: Dru Down, Blvckseeds, Mr. Talkbox, Bootsy Collins, A. Thompson, J. Reinhold, J. Lofton, S. Imani, W. Hagan, Ouiwey Collins
Drums: E. Moore, J. Blackwell
Percussion: Bootsy Collins
Bass: Bootsy Collins
Turntables: Tobotius
Guitar: Bootsy Collins, Keith Cheatham
Keyboards: NoFace

"Thera P"

Lead Vocals: Tyshawn Colquitt, Zach Adams, Bootsy Collins
Backup Vocals: Tyshawn Colquit, Alissia Benveniste, Bootsy Collins
Drum Programming: Alissia Beneveniste
Drums: A. Spears, Bootsy Collins
Bass: Bootsy Collins, Alissia Beneveniste
Guitar: Bootsy Collins, M. Rice
Keyboards: Alissia Beneveniste, Bootsy Collins

"Hot Saucer"

Lead Vocals: Musiq Soulchild, Big Daddy Kane, Bootsy Collins
Backup Vocals: Musiq Soulchild, Big Daddy Kane, Bootsy Collins
Drums: Bootsy Collins
Drum Programming: Ouiwey Collins
Bass: Bootsy Collins
Guitar: K. Cheatham, M. Rice, J. Mass
Keyboards, Strings, Bass, Drum Programming: Alissia Beneveniste

"Heaven Yes"

Lead Vocals: Bootsy Collins, April Showers, Gary Mudbone Cooper, Henry Benefield, Michael Gatheright, K. Gray, M. Eiland
Backup Vocals: Gary Mudbone Cooper, Alissia Benveniste
Drums: Bootsy Collins, Tobotius
Bass: Bootsy Collins
Guitar: J. Mass
Keyboards: Alissia Beneveniste, J. Davis, N. Semrad

The Power of the One

"Ladies Night"

Lead Vocals: MC Eiht, Blvckseeds, Bootsy Collins, A. Thompson, B. Graham, C. Houston, J. Jumanji, S. Ivy

Drum Programming: DJ Quik
Bass: Bootsy Collins
Guitar: Bootsy Collins, DJ Quik
Keyboards: DJ Quik, Morris Mingo

"Candy Coated Lover"

Lead Vocals: X-Zact, Kali Uchis, Bootsy Collins, Razzberry White, Z. Adams
Samples: Bootsy Collins
Drums: E. Moore
Percussion: Bootsy Collins
Bass: Bootsy Collins
Guitar: K. Cheatham
Keyboards: Chew Fu, Morris Mingo
Sax: B. Thompson, Chew Fu

"Snowbunny"

Lead Vocals: Tyshawn Colquitt, Snowbunny, Bootsy Collins, J. Reinhold, Z. Adams
Drums: Bootsy Collins, K Bamn Dmith
Bass: M. Cobb
Guitar: K. Cheatham
Keyboards: Morris Mingo
Sax: R. Villars

"Hi on Heels"

Lead Vocals: October London, Bootsy Collins, Ouiwey Collins
Drums: J. D. Blair
Drum Programming: Bootsy Collins
Synth Bass: Ouiwey Collins
Guitar: Bootsy Collins
Keyboards: Ouiwey Collins

"Salute to Bernie"

Lead Vocals: C. Walker, Bootsy Collins
Drum Programming: Bootsy Collins
Drums: J. D. Blair
Bass: Bootsy Collins
Guitar: Bootsy Collins
Keyboards: Bernie Worrell

"Boomerang"

Lead Vocals: Bootsy Collins, Z. Adams
Backup Vocals: Bootsy Collins, Justin Johnson
Drums: Bootsy Collins
Bass: Bootsy Collins, Manou Gallo
Guitar: Justin Johnson
Slide Guitar: Justin Johnson

"Worth My While"

Lead Vocals: Bootsy Collins, Kali Uchis
Drums: W. White Jr.
Bass: Bootsy Collins
Guitar: J. Ellison
Keyboards: F. Ray Jr.

"Come Back Bootsy"

Lead Vocals: Bootsy Collins
Backup Vocals: G. Driver, J. Reinhold, Soul by the Pound, Z. Adams, Clyde Stubblefield
Drums: Frankie Kash Waddy, Dennis Chambers
Bass: Bootsy Collins
Horns: K. Molitor
Guitar: Eric Gales, Bootsy Collins, Flip Cornett
Keyboards: Justin Johnson

"Illusions"

Vocals: Chuck D, Blvckseeds, Bootsy Collins, Danny Ray, A. Thompson, J. Reinhold, J. Lofton, J. Jackson, L. Thompson, S. Imani, Z. Adams, Tyshawn Colquitt
Drums: Bootsy Collins, Dennis Chambers
Bass: Bootsy Collins
Guitar: Buckethead, Eric Gales, Bootsy Collins
DJ: Toe Donohue
Keyboards: Morris Mingo

"Funk Formula"

Lead Vocals: Bootsy Collins
Backup Vocals: Bootsy Collins
Drums: Bootsy Collins
Bass: Bootsy Collins
Guitar: Bootsy Collins

"The Power of the One"

Lead Vocals: Bootsy Collins, The Williams Singers, Ouiwey Collins
Backup Vocals: The Williams Singers
Drums, Percussion: Bootsy Collins
Bass: Bootsy Collins
Guitar: George Benson, Bootsy Collins
Keyboards: Brian Culbertson
Horns: Brennan Johns

"Slide Eazy"

Lead Vocals: Ellis Hall, Bootsy Collins
Backup Vocals: Bootsy Collins
Drums, Percussion: Bootsy Collins
Bass: Bootsy Collins
Guitar: Rod Castro, Bootsy Collins
Keyboards: Brennan Johns, Ellis Hall, JSkillz, Johnny Davis
Horns: Brennan Johns

"Bootsy Creepin'"

Lead Vocals: Christone Kingfish Ingram, Bootsy Collins
Backup Vocals: Patti Sweet Lips, Bootsy Collins
Drums, Percussion: Bootsy Collins
Bass: Bootsy Collins
Guitar: Christone Kingfish Ingram, Bootsy Collins, Alex Goldblatt
Horns: Brennan Johns

"Jam On"

Lead Vocals: Snoop Dogg, Bootsy Collins
Backup Vocals: Belinda Lipscomb
Drums, Percussion: Bootsy Collins
Bass: Bootsy Collins
Guitar: Brandon Taz Niederauer, Bootsy Collins
Keyboards: Morris Mingo

"Lips Turn Blue"

Lead Vocals: Bootsy Collins, Emmaline
Backup Vocals: Bootsy Collins, Emmaline, Danielle Withers
Drum Programming: Ouiwey Collins
Percussion: Bootsy Collins
Bass: Bootsy Collins
Guitar: Adam Delmonte
Keyboards: Greg Fitz
Horns: Brennan Johns

"Funkship-Area-51"

Lead Vocals: Bootsy Collins, Brother Nature
Backup Vocals: Bootsy Collins
Drums: Bootsy Collins
Bass: Christian McBride
Guitar: Bootsy Collins
Keyboards: Morris Mingo
Horns: Brennan Johns

"Bewise"

Lead Vocals: Bootsy Collins, Robert Bewise Harding
Backup Vocals: Bootsy Collins
Drums, Percussion: Bootsy Collins
Bass: Bootsy Collins
Guitar: Bootsy Collins
Keyboards: Bootsy Collins, Bewise

"Soul Not 4-Sale"

Lead Vocals: Bootsy Collins, Hollywood Anderson
Backup Vocals: Bootsy Collins
Drums: Bootsy Collins
Bass: Bootsy Collins
Guitar: Bootsy Collins
Keyboards: Morris Mingo

"Club Funkateers"

Lead Vocals: Bootsy Collins, Danielle Rene Withers
Backup Vocals: Bootsy Collins
Drums, Percussion: Bootsy Collins

Bass: Bootsy Collins, Victor Wooten
Guitar: Bootsy Collins
Sax: Branford Marsalis
Keyboards: Brennan Johns
Horns: Brennan Johns

"Want Me 2 Stay"

Lead Vocals: Uche
Backup Vocals: Bootsy Collins
Drums, Percussion: Bootsy Collins
Bass: Larry Graham, Bootsy Collins
Sax: Branford Marsalis
Horns: Brennan Johns
Guitar: Bootsy Collins
Keyboards: Brennan Johns

"Funktropolis"

Lead Vocals: Bootsy Collins, Brother Nature
Backup Vocals: Bootsy Collins
Drums, Percussion: Bootsy Collins
Bass: Bootsy Collins
Guitar: Bootsy Collins
Horns: Brennan Johns
Keyboards: Johnny Davis

"Wishing Well"

Lead Vocals: Ellis Hall, Bootsy Collins
Backup Vocals: Bootsy Collins
Drums: Bootsy Collins
Bass: Bootsy Collins
Guitar: Bootsy Collins
Keyboards: Greg Fitz

"Bootsy Off Broadway"

Lead Vocals: Emmaline, Bootsy Collins, Frankie Kash Waddy
Backup Vocals: Emmaline, Bootsy Collins, Frankie Kash Waddy
Drums: Frankie Kash Waddy
Bass: Bootsy Collins, Christian McBride
Guitar: Bootsy Collins
Keyboards: Johnny Davis

"Stargate"

Lead Vocals: Dr. Cornel West, Ellis Hall, EmiSunshine, Bootsy Collins
Samples: Bootsy Collins
Backup Vocals: Ellis hall, EmiSunshine, Bootsy Collins
Drums: Bootsy Collins
Basses: Victor Wooten, Bootsy Collins
Guitar: Bootsy Collins
Keyboards: Morris Mingo

"Stolen Dreams"

Lead Vocals: Bootsy Collins, Brother Nature
Backup Vocals: Bootsy Collins, Brother Nature
Drum Programming, Percussion: Henry Invisible
Drums, Percussion: Bootsy Collins
Bass: Bootsy Collins
Guitar: Rod Castro, Henry Invisible
Keyboards: Henry Invisible

— ☆ —

GODMOMA 1981

This was an outing by late-era Bootsy singing group Godmoma. Godmoma is Cynthia Girty, Anita Walker, and Carolyn Miles.

Elektra Records

Godmoma Here

"Taste of Magic"

Drums: Bootsy Collins
Keyboards: David Spradley
Bass: Bootsy Collins
Guitar: Bootsy Collins
Vocals: Cynthia Girty, Anita Walker, Carolyn Myles

"Godmoma Here"

Drums: Bootsy Collins
Keyboards: Joel Johnson
Bass: Bootsy Collins
Guitar: Catfish Collins
Vocals: Cynthia Girty, Anita Walker, Carolyn Myles
Backup Vocals: Sheila Horne, Jeanette MacGruder

"Hands Up (Punk Funk)"

Drums: Bootsy Collins
Keyboards: David Spradley
Percussion: Carl "Butch" Small
Bass: Bootsy Collins
Guitar: Bootsy Collins
Vocals: Cynthia Girty, Anita Walker, Carolyn Myles
Backup Vocals: Sheila Horne, Jeanette MacGruder

"I Like It"

Drums: Jerry Jones
Keyboards: Joel Johnson
Bass: Bootsy Collins
Guitar: Bootsy Collins
Vocals: Cynthia Girty, Anita Walker, Carolyn Myles

"Spice (Too Nice)"

Drums: Bootsy Collins
Keyboards: David Spradley, Joel Johnson
Bass: Bootsy Collins
Guitar: Catfish Collins
Vocals: Cynthia Girty, Anita Walker, Carolyn Myles
Backup Vocals: Sheila Horne, Jeanettte MacGruder

"Be All You Can Be"

Drums: Bootsy Collins
Keyboards: Sly Stone
Bass: Bootsy Collins
Guitar: Bootsy Collins
Vocals: Cynthia Girty, Anita Walker, Carolyn Myles

"Godmoma of Love"

Drums: Bootsy Collins
Keyboards: Joel Johnson
Percussion: Carl "Butch" Small
Bass: Bootsy Collins
Sax: Maceo Parker
Guitar: Bootsy Collins
Vocals: Cynthia Girty, Anita Walker, Carolyn Myles, Bootsy Collins

— ☆ —

TOM TOM CLUB (SELECT TRACK): 1981

Both Tina Weymouth and Chris Frantz of Talking Heads were members of this group. The band's name was coined by none other than George Clinton.

Island Records

Tom Tom Club

"Genius of Love"

Keyboards: Bernie Worrell

The Tom Tom Club is Tina Weymouth, Chris Frantz, Steven Stanley, Lani Weymouth, Laura Weymouth, Loric Weymouth, Adrian Belew, Benjamin Armbrister, James Rizzi, Kendall Stubbs, Monte Browne, and Tyrone Downie (though it is dubious that all the names listed here are featured on this track).

— ☆ —

FUNKADELIC (ORIGINAL P): 1981

The Parliaments members Fuzzy Haskins, Calvin Simon, and Grady Thomas (60 percent of the singing group) struck out on their own in 1981 with a one-off album. Much like Jerome Brailey's Mutiny work, it would be highly critical of Clinton and company. They would come back a decade later using the name "Original P" on another album and a slew of touring.

LAX Records

Connections and Disconnections

"Phunk Lords"

Vocals: Calvin Simon, Fuzzy Haskins, Grady Thomas, Dede Dickerson, Ngoh Spencer, Vicky Randal, Betty Jo Drake, Billy Mims, Ben Powers
Drums: Ben Powers Jr.
Guitar: Michael Williams, Billy Mims
Keyboards: Billy Mims
Bass: Ben Powers Jr.
Percussion: Calvin Simon, Grady Thomas, Fuzzy Haskins

"You'll Like It Too"

Vocals: Calvin Simon, Fuzzy Haskins, Grady Thomas, Dede Dickerson, Ngoh Spencer, Vicky Randal, Betty Jo Drake, Michael Williams
Drums: Ben Powers Jr.
Guitar: Michael Williams, Billy Mims
Keyboards: Michael Williams
Bass: Ken Blackmon

"The Witch"

Vocals: Calvin Simon, Fuzzy Haskins, Grady Thomas, Dede Dickerson, Ngoh Spencer, Vicky Randal, Betty Jo Drake, Ben Powers Jr., Billy Mims, Johnny Wiley
Drums: Ben Powers Jr.
Guitar: Michael Williams, Billy Mims
Keyboards: Johnny Wiley, Stan Thorn
Bass: Ken Blackmon

"Connections and Disconnections"

Vocals: Calvin Simon, Fuzzy Haskins, Grady Thomas, Dede Dickerson, Ngoh Spencer, Vicky Randal, Betty Jo Drake, Billy Mims
Drums: Ben Powers Jr.
Guitar: Michael Williams, Billy Mims
Keyboards: Billy Mims
Bass: Ken Blackmon

"Come Back"

Vocals: Calvin Simon, Fuzzy Haskins, Grady Thomas, Dede Dickerson, Ngoh Spencer, Vicky Randal, Betty Jo Drake, Billy Mims, Ben Powers Jr.
Drums: Ben Powers Jr.
Guitar: Michael Williams, Billy Mims
Keyboards: Billy Mims
Bass: Ben Powers Jr.

"Call the Doctor"

Vocals: Calvin Simon, Fuzzy Haskins, Grady Thomas, Dede Dickerson, Ngoh Spencer, Vicky Randal, Betty Jo Drake, Billy Mims
Drums: Ben Powers Jr.
Guitar: Michael Williams, Billy Mims
Keyboards: Billy Mims
Bass: Ken Blackmon

"Who's a Funkadelic"

Vocals: Calvin Simon, Fuzzy Haskins, Grady Thomas, Dede Dickerson, Ngoh Spencer, Vicky Randal, Betty Jo Drake, Billy Mims, Johnny Wiley, Ben Powers Jr., Michael Williams

Drums: Ben Powers Jr.
Guitar: Michael Williams, Billy Mims
Keyboards: Billy Mims, Johnny Wiley, Stan Thorn
Bass: Ken Blackmon

— ☆ —

MURUGA AND THE SODA JERKS: 1981

Muruga Booker is a percussionist that joined the P-Funk ranks in the early 1980s. He had a "New Wave"–style punk rock band called the Soda Jerks. Muruga's solo material in later decades is included here as well.

"Superstar Madness"

Vocals: Muruga Booker, Shock T
Drums: Muruga Booker
Percussion: Muruga Booker
Bass: Sly Stone
Guitar: Pat LaRose, Muruga Booker
Keyboards: Muruga Booker
Bell Tree: Louie Babblin Kabbabie

"Boogy with You"

Guitar: Muruga Booker
Drums: Shock T
Vocals: Muruga Booker, Shock T
Keyboards: Jim David
Bass: Hube Crawford

"Ju Ju Man (Rock the Planet)"

Drums: Muruga Booker
Percussion: Muruga Booker
Bass: Hubie Crawford
Keyboards, Violin: Elia Reisman
Guitar: James Gurley, Vince DaLuiso
Vocals: George Clinton, Pamela Hawkins, Shock T

"Thought of You"

Drums: Muruga Booker
Percussion: Muruga Booker
Bass, Harmonica: Hubie Crawford
Keyboards: Elia Reisman
Guitar: James Gurley
Guitar: Vince DaLuiso
Effects: Muruga Booker
Vocals: Shock T

"Love of Your Life"

Drum Machine: Muruga Booker
Percussion: Muruga Booker
Vocals: Muruga Boooker, Shock T
Bass: Hubie Crawford
Keyboards: Elia Reisman
Guitar: James Gurley
Guitar: Vince DaLuiso
Effects: Muruga Booker

"Tired of Livin'"

Drums: Muruga Booker
Percussion: Muruga Booker
Vocals: Muruga Boooker
Bass: Hubie Crawford
Keyboards: Elia Reisman
Guitar: James Gurley, Vince DaLuiso

"Dysfunktion"

Drums: Muruga Booker
Percussion: Muruga Booker
Vocals: Muruga Boooker, Shock T
Bass: Hubie Crawford
Keyboards: Elia Reisman
Guitar: James Gurley, Vince DaLuiso

"Sleazy"

Drum Machine: Muruga Booker
Percussion: Muruga Booker
Vocals: Muruga Boooker, Shock T
Bass: Hubie Crawford
Keyboards: Elia Reisman
Guitar: James Gurley, Vince DaLuiso

"Air Head"

Drum Machine: Muruga Booker
Percussion: Muruga Booker
Vocals: Muruga Boooker, Shock T
Bass: Hubie Crawford
Keyboards: Elia Reisman
Guitar: James Gurley, Vince DaLuiso

"Anna's Island Song"

Nada Drums, Drum Machine: Muruga Booker
Percussion: Muruga Booker
Vocals: Muruga Boooker, Shock T
Bass: Hubie Crawford
Keyboards: Elia Reisman
Guitar: James Gurley, Vince DaLuiso

"Nectar of the Silence"

Drums: Muruga Booker
Percussion: Muruga Booker
Vocals: Muruga Boooker, Shock T
Bass: Hubie Crawford
Keyboards: Elia Reisman
Guitar: James Gurley
Guitar: Vince DaLuiso
Accordion: Al Rapone

"Freedom of Speech"

Drum Loop: Aaron Bookvitch
Percussion: Muruga Booker
Vocals: Aaron Bookvitch, Muruga Booker,
    Bob Dennis, Shock T, Hubie Crawford, Elia
    Reisman, James Gurley, Vince DaLuiso
Bass: Hubie Crawford
Keyboards: Elia Reisman
Guitar: James Gurley, Vince DaLuiso

"Gum Improvisation"

Drums: Muruga Booker
Percussion: Muruga Booker
Bass: Hubie Crawford
Keyboards: Elia Reisman
Guitar: James Gurley, Vince DaLuiso

— ★ —

GARY FABULOUS AND BLACK SLACK: 1981

Gary Fabulous and Black Slack was an early funk rap group from Detroit featuring artist Gary Fabulous. Several P-Funkers were involved in his music at the time.

"Funkin' for My Mama's Rent"

Lead Vocals: Gary Fabulous
Backup Vocals: Clip Payne, Lige Curry, Ron Ford, Ron Dunbar, George Clinton, Andre Williams, Patty Walker
Drums: Clip Payne
Percussion: Muruga Booker
Bass: Lige Curry
Guitar: Michael Hampton, Andre Williams
Keyboards: David Spradley

RON FORD AND PARLET: 1981

P-Funk vocalist Ron Ford wrote several songs for Parlet. "Bubblegum Gangster" came out much later on the George Clinton Family Series.

"Bubblegum Gangster"

Vocals: Ron Ford, Shirley Hayden, Jeanette Washington, Janice Evans, Lige Curry, Jeanette MacGruder
Drums: Man in the Box
Synthesizers, Piano, Synth Bass: David Spradley
Guitar: Ron Ford

SLY STONE (SELECT TRACK): 1981

Sly Stone worked with Clinton and company several times in the 1970s, 1980s, and 2010s. Clinton and Stone are good longtime friends.

"Who in the Funk Do You Think You Are"

Piano, Bass, Guitar, Vocals: Sly Stone

NICK SAVANNAH AND DWARF: 1981

This was a project in more of a folk rock vein, coproduced by Garry Shider and featuring the Brides of Funkenstein.

"Comin' Down from Your Love"

Lead Vocals: Nick Savannah
Drums: Merle
Bass: Peter Madary
Guitar: Nick Savannah, Mike Finn
Backup Vocals: Dawn Silva, Lynn Mabry, Dwarf

ANDRE FOXXE WILLIAMS: 1981, 1991, 1998, 2001

This longtime P-Funk contributor connected mostly in the 1980s and 1990s. Visually, he was known for wearing a nun's habit and bride's gown onstage.

Previously Unreleased "Better Days"

Keyboards: Marvin Williams
Bass: Marvin Williams
Lead Vocals: Andre Williams
Backup Vocals: Garry Shider
Guitar: Marvin Williams
Drums: Ron Wright

Sly Stone and George Clinton. William Thoren

A Dossier on Sex and Animals

"Loves Party"

Lead Vocals: Andre Williams
Backup Vocals: Andre Williams, Matt Guarnere, Erik Williams, Robert Evans
Guitar: Andre Williams
Keyboards: Amp Fiddler
Drum Programming: Andre Williams, Amp Fiddler

"Fox Hunt"

Keyboards: Robert Garrett, Patrick Drummond
Bass: Ken Wiliams
Vocals: Andre Williams
Backup Vocals: George Clinton, Lige Curry, Patty Walker
Guitar: Andre Williams, Billy Parker
Drums: Dean Ragland

"Toyota Corolla"

Keyboards: Patrick Drummond, Robert Garrett
Bass: Lige Curry
Vocals: Andre Williams
Guitar: Andre Williams
Drum Programming: Michael Clip Payne

"Love Deeper"

Keyboards: Andre Williams
Bass: Andre Williams
Vocals: Andre Williams, George Clinton
Guitar: Blackbyrd McKnight
Drum Programming: Andre Williams

"Pizzaz"

Bass: Bootsy Collins
Vocals: Andre Williams
Backup Vocals: George Clinton, Gary Mudbone Cooper, Bootsy Collins
Guitar: Bootsy Collins
Drums: Bootsy Collins

"Reputation"

Bass: Flea
Vocals: Andre Williams, Anthony Kiedis, Michael Clip Payne
Guitar: Hillel Slovak, Billy Parker, Andre Williams
Drums: Cliff Martinez

"Mature Freak"

Keyboards: Patrick Drummond, Robert Garrett
Bass: Ken Williams
Vocals: Andre Williams, Steve Boyd, Shirley Hayden, Michael Clip Payne, Ken Williams
Guitar: Andre Williams, Billy Parker
Drums: Dean Ragland

"Puppy Love"

Vocals: Andre Williams , Anita Hill, George Clinton, Joe Harris
Guitar: Jessie Talbert, Clip Payne
Keyboards: Andre Williams
Piano: Amp Fiddler
Drums: Man in the Box

"Squirrel Looking for a Nut"

Keyboards: Patrick Drummond, Robert Garrett
Bass: Ken Williams
Vocals: Andre Williams, Erik Williams, Clip Payne, Patti Curry, Steve Boyd, Pat Lewis, Garry Shider, Ken Williams, Patrick Drummond, Robert Evans, Lige Curry, Robert Peanut Johnson, George Clinton
Guitar: Billy Parker
Drums: Dean Ragland

"Open House"

Keyboards: Patrick Drummond, Robert Garrett
Bass: Chris Bruce
Vocals: Andre Williams, Patrick Drummond, Joe Harris, Pat Lewis, Clip Payne, Steve Boyd, Robert Garrett, Lloyd Williams
Guitar: Chris Bruce, Carl Robinson
Drums: Chris Bruce

"When Ends Meet"

Keyboards: Amp Fiddler, Andre William
Vocals: Paul Hill, Andre Williams, Steve Boyd, Kim Crowley, Lige Curry, Starr Cullars, Clip Payne, Louie Kabbabie
Guitar: Andre Williams, Jessie Talbert, Michael Hampton
Drums: Man in the Box

"Black Beach"

Keyboards: Patrick Drummond, Robert Garrett
Bass: Ken Williams
Vocals: Andre Williams, Belita Woods, Clip Payne, Garry Shider
Guitar: Andre Williams, Billy Parker
Drums: Andre Williams

"In My Mind"

Vocals: Andre Williams, Clip Payne, Amp Fiddler, Ron Ford, Jessie Talbert
Bass: Ken Williams
Guitar: Jessie Talbert
Keyboards: Andre Williams, Clip Payne, Amp Fiddler
Percussion: Sundiata O.M.
Drums: Man in the Box

Myllenium

"Closer"

Bass: Andre Williams
Vocals: Andre Williams
Guitar: Andre Williams
Drums: Andre Williams

"Summer Girl"

Bass: Matt Schiedt
Vocals: Andre Williams
Guitar: Andre Williams
Drums: Doug Walls

"Sunshine"

Keyboards: Andre Williams
Bass: Matt Schiedt
Vocals: Andre Williams, Matt Schiedt, Matt Guanari
Guitar: Andre Willims
Drums: Matt Guanari

"Into the Sun"

Bass: Matt Schiedt
Vocals: Andre Williams
Guitar: Andre Williams
Samples: Andre Williams
Drums: Warren "Hand"

"Laughin'"

Keyboards: Andre Williams
Bass: Matt Scheidt
Vocals: Andre Williams , Belita Woods, Garry Shider, Tracey Lewis, George Clinton Jr.
Guitar: Andre Williams
Drums: Doug Walls

"Moonjelly"

Bass: Matt Schiedt
Guitar: Herb Hines, Andre Williams
Drums: Sample

"Shame"

Keyboards: Shaw
Bass: Adam Pitcher
Vocals: Andre Williams
Guitar: Vinny Pastoria, Ted Pitcher, Andre Williams
Drums: Doug Walls

"Good for Yourself"

Keyboards: Michael Hampton, Bass Man
Bass: Michael Hampton
Vocals: Andre Williams
Guitar: Michael Hampton
Drums: Gabe Gonzalez

"Home"

Bass: Matt Schiedt
Vocals: Andre Williams
Guitar: Andre Williams, Herb Hines
Drums: Matt Guanari

"Alone"

Bass: Adam Pitcher
Vocals: Andre Williams
Guitar: Kenny Pitcher, Andre Williams, Vinny Pastoria
Drums: Doug Walls

"Anymore"

Bass: Adam Pitcher
Vocals: Andre Williams
Guitar: Kenny Pitcher, Andre Williams, Vinny Pastoria
Drums: Doug Walls

"Myllenium"

Producer: Keith Henderson
(contains samples of all the songs on the album)

— ☆ —

SPACE CADETS: 1981

The early 1980s group Space Cadets would feature P-Funk keyboardist Bernie Worrell and P-Funk drummer Tyrone Lampkin.

Vanguard Records

Space Cadets

"Let's Pump It Up"

Drums: Tyrone Lampkin
Keyboards: Bernie Worrell, Nairobi Sailcat
Bass: T. M. Stevens or Tinker Barfield
Guitar: Larry Campbell, Nairobi Sailcat
Vocals: Connie Harvey, Gail Freeman, Janice Pendarvis, Nairobi Sailcat, Zephryn Conte

"You Make Me Wanna Do It"

Drums: Tyrone Lampkin
Keyboards: Bernie Worrell, Nairobi Sailcat
Bass: T. M. Stevens or Tinker Barfield
Guitar: Larry Campbell, Nairobi Sailcat
Vocals: Connie Harvey, Gail Freeman, Janice
    Pendarvis, Nairobi Sailcat, Zephryn Conte

"I Love What You're Doing to Me"

Drums: Tyrone Lampkin
Keyboards: Bernie Worrell, Nairobi Sailcat
Bass: T. M. Stevens or Tinker Barfield
Guitar: Larry Campbell, Nairobi Sailcat
Vocals: Connie Harvey, Gail Freeman, Janice
    Pendarvis, Nairobi Sailcat, Zephryn Conte

"Loveslave (Nosejob)"

Drums: Tyrone Lampkin
Keyboards: Bernie Worrell, Nairobi Sailcat
Bass: T. M. Stevens or Tinker Barfield
Guitar: Larry Campbell, Nairobi Sailcat
Vocals: Connie Harvey, Gail Freeman, Janice
    Pendarvis, Nairobi Sailcat, Zephryn Conte

"Make Me Funk (Fonkin' Straight Ahead)"

Drums: Tyrone Lampkin
Keyboards: Bernie Worrell, Nairobi Sailcat
Bass: T. M. Stevens or Tinker Barfield
Guitar: Larry Campbell, Nairobi Sailcat
Vocals: Connie Harvey, Gail Freeman, Janice
    Pendarvis, Nairobi Sailcat, Zephryn Conte

"I Might Be Crazy (But I Ain't No Fool)"

Drums: Tyrone Lampkin
Keyboards: Bernie Worrell, Nairobi Sailcat
Bass: T. M. Stevens, Tinker Barfield
Guitar: Larry Campbell, Nairobi Sailcat
Vocals: Connie Harvey, Gail Freeman, Janice
    Pendarvis, Nairobi Sailcat, Zephryn Conte

"Your Mother"

Drums: Tyrone Lampkin
Keyboards: Bernie Worrell, Nairobi Sailcat
Bass: T. M. Stevens, Tinker Barfield
Guitar: Larry Campbell, Nairobi Sailcat
Vocals: Connie Harvey, Gail Freeman, Janice
    Pendarvis, Nairobi Sailcat, Zephryn Conte

— ☆ —

GEORGE CLINTON: 1982–

This section focuses on Clinton's solo career post-Parliament and Funkadelic. The hit song "Atomic Dog" from his massively popular first solo album, *Computer Games*, should be known to everyone reading this book, as it represents one of the biggest and indeed one of the last major hits in the P-Funk canon to date (if we do not include sampling). Speaking of which, Clinton is one of the most sampled artists on the planet (if not the most sampled) with "Atomic Dog" garnering some thousands of samples and interpolations alone. Clinton's solo career enjoyed a big resurgence during the sampling era, which brought him in touch with a new generation of fans two or three more times in the coming decades.

Capitol Records

Computer Games

"Get Dressed"

Lead Vocals: George Clinton
Backup Vocals: Ray Davis, Mudbone Cooper,
    Garry Shider, Greg Thomas, Mallia Franklin
Drums: Bootsy Collins
Bass: Bootsy Collins
Piano: Bernie Worrell
Guitar: Bootsy Collins
Trumpet: Richard Griffith, Larry Hatcher
Sax: Maceo Parker
Trombone: Fred Wesley

P-Funk ringleader George Clinton. © Diem Jones

"Man's Best Friend"

Lead Vocals: George Clinton
Backup Vocals: Garry Shider, Linda Shider, Mudbone Cooper, Robert Peanut Johnson, Andre Williams, Greg Thomas, Jessica Cleaves, Mallia Franklin
Drums: Dennis Chambers
Synth Bass: David Spradley
Percussion: Larry Fratangelo
Keyboards, Synthesizers: David Spradley, Garry Shider
Guitar: Eddie Hazel

"Loopzilla"

Lead Vocals: George Clinton
Backup Vocals: Mudbone Cooper, Ray Davis, Robert Peanut Johnson, Garry Shider, Sheila Horne
Drums: Dennis Chambers
Percussion: Larry Fratangelo

Synth Bass: David Spradley
Keyboards, Synthesizers: David Spradley
Guitar: Eddie Hazel

"Loopzilla" was the first single from George Clinton's *Computer Games* album. It predates the "mash-up" by some three decades, but that is essentially what it is: a series of chants from many rhythm-and-blues favorites are medleyed here over an infectious rhythm track.

"Pot Sharing Tots"

Lead Vocals: George Clinton
Backup Vocals: Sheila Horne, Jeanette MacGruder
Drums: Junie Morrison
Bass: Junie Morrison
Electric Piano: Junie Morrison
Guitar: Junie Morrison
Sax: Maceo Parker

"Computer Games"

Lead Vocals: George Clinton
Backup Vocals: George Clinton, Mama Funkenstein
Drums: Junie Morrison
Bass: Junie Morrison
Piano, Synthesizers: Junie Morrison
Guitar: Junie Morrison
Sax: Maceo Parker

"Atomic Dog"

Lead Vocals: George Clinton
Backup Vocals: Garry Shider, Shirley Hayden, Mudbone Cooper, Mallia Franklin, Sheila Horne, Jeanette MacGruder, Vanessa (last name unknown), Ray Davis, Eddie Hazel, Robert Peanut Johnson, Clip Payne, David Spradley, Ron Ford, Greg Thomas
Drums: Mudbone Cooper, Dennis Chambers, Zachary Frazier
Synth Bass: David Spradley
Keyboards, Synthesizers: David Spradley, Bernie Worrell

"Atomic Dog" would be George Clinton's highest-charting song in his solo career and would catapult him to a world of dogs and dog mythology prevalent in later albums and his multifaceted artwork as well. This song was constructed in pieces (containing three distinct drum parts), with several sessions of vocal parts recorded over time. The popularity of "Dog" would send the P-Funk All Stars on scores of tours after the success of the song that would arguably continue to this day. It would also be the inspiration for much of Snoop Dogg's original creative output.

The African American fraternity Omega Psi Phi, (whose members identify under the name of "Que Dogs") helped further solidify "Atomic Dog"'s staying power by making it their theme song. The song is, for members of this fraternity, deeply associated with the Que Dogs' trademark dance. Additionally, a Que Dogs version of "Atomic Dog" is set for release in the near future.

"Free Alterations"

Lead Vocals: George Clinton
Backup Vocals: George Clinton, Mudbone Cooper, Robert Peanut Johnson, Darryl Clinton, Andre Williams, Tracey Lewis
Drums: Terry Jones
Bass: Darryl Clinton
Keyboards, Synthesizers: David Spradley
Keyboards: Rahni P. Harris

"One Fun at a Time"

Lead Vocals: George Clinton
Backup Vocals: Junie Morrison, George Clinton
Drums: Junie Morrison
Bass: Junie Morrison
Keyboards, Synthesizers: Junie Morrison
Guitar: Junie Morrison
Trumpet: Junie Morrison

You Shouldn't Nuf Bit Fish

"Nubian Nut"

Lead Vocals: George Clinton, Lane Strickland
Backup Vocals: Eddie Hazel, Garry Shider, Lane Strickland, Mallia Franklin, Mudbone Cooper, Greg Thomas, Linda Shider
Drums: LinnDrums
Synth Bass, Keyboards: David Spradley
Keyboards, Synthesizers: Ron Cronovich
Guitar: Eddie Hazel

"Nubian Nut" does something that previous Clinton raps had not. It truly nods to the style of rapping that already existed, that is, the rapping style of early New York hip-hop. It also is influenced by a Fela Kuti song and is one the first P-Funk singles (if not the first) to feature the LinnDrum machine.

George Clinton—funk innovator. William Thoren

"Quickie"

Lead Vocals: George Clinton, Andre Williams

Backup Vocals: Andre Williams, Robert Peanut Johnson, Ron Ford, Mallia Franklin, Shirley Hayden, Blackbyrd McKnight, Greg Thomas, Lige Curry, Sheila Horne, Kim Seay

Drums: Junie Morrison, LinnDrums

Synth Bass: Junie Morrison

Piano, Synthesizers: Junie Morrison

Guitar: Andre Williams (rhythm, solo 1), Blackbyrd McKnight (solo 2), Junie Morrison (intro, melody)

"Quickie" has slick vocals and a 1980s style of Funkadelic that would become synonymous with P-Funk's album style in that decade.

"Last Dance"

Lead Vocals: George Clinton

Backup Vocals: Garry Shider, Robert Peanut Johnson, Eddie Hazel, Clip Payne, Shirley Hayden, Kim Seay, Greg Thomas, Sheila Horne, Linda Shider

Drums: Bootsy Collins, LinnDrums

Bass: Bootsy Collins

Keyboards, Synthesizers: David Spradley

Guitar: Garry Shider, Bootsy Collins

"Last Dance" harkens back to earlier Parliament vocal and rhythm parts. It featured a music video as well.

"Silly Millameter"

Lead Vocals: George Clinton, Mudbone Cooper, Garry Shider

Backup Vocals: Ron Ford, Eddie Hazel, Robert Peanut Johnson, Lige Curry, Darryl Clinton, Tracey Lewis, Clip Payne, Patty Curry, Kim Seay, Sheila Horne

Drums: Bootsy Collins

Percussion: Larry Fratangelo

Bass: Bootsy Collins

Keyboards, Synthesizers: Doug Duffy

Lead Guitar: Eddie Hazel

Rhythm Guitar: Dewayne Blackbyrd McKnight

Trumpet: Richard Griffith, Larry Hatcher

Sax: Maceo Parker

Trombone: Fred Wesley

"Stingy"

Lead Vocals: George Clinton, Mudbone Cooper, Garry Shider

Drums: Michael Hampton

Percussion: Larry Fratangelo

Bass: Lige Curry

Keyboards, Synthesizers: Ron Cronovich

Guitar: Michael Hampton

Avatar: Michael Hampton

"You Shouldn't Nuf-Bit Fish"

Lead Vocals: George Clinton

Backup Vocals: Clip Payne, Robert Peanut Johnson

Drums: Clip Payne, LinnDrums

Synth Bass: Clip Payne

Keyboards, Synthesizers: Clip Payne, Ron Cron

Percussion: Larry Fratangelo

Guitar: Blackbyrd McKnight

Some of My Best Jokes Are Friends

"Double Oh-Oh"

Lead Vocals: George Clinton

Backup Vocals: Pat Lewis, Garry Shider, Sandra Feva, Belita Woods, Jimmy Giles, Steve Washington, Andre Williams, Sheila Washington, Linda Shider, Mallia Franklin

LinnDrums: David Spradley

Bass: Steve Washington

Keyboards: David Spradley

Drum Chips: David Spradley

"Double Oh-Oh" features one of the most political themes since "Electric Spanking of War Babies." Dealing with the threat of nuclear apocalypse during flare-ups of the Cold War (mid-1980s), it also features standout vocals from Pat Lewis.

George Clinton signing copies of his autobiography. William Thoren

"Bullet Proof"

Lead Vocals: Garry Shider
Backup Vocals: Sandra Feva, George Clinton, Archie Ivy, Linda Shider, Steve Washington, Andre Foxxe Williams, Tracey Lewis, Jeanette McGruder, Sheila Washington, Mallia Franklin, LuShawn Clinton
Drums: David Spradley
Synth Bass: David Spradley
Guitar: Garry Shider
Keyboards, Synthesizer: David Spradley

"Bullet Proof" was another one of George Clinton's Capitol Records singles (like "Atomic Dog," "Last Dance," and others) that would have a music video. Videos were a relatively new convention at the time, and Clinton was ahead of the curve with the medium.

"Pleasures of Exhaustion"

Lead Vocals: George Clinton
Backup Vocals: Andre Williams, Shirley Hayden, Robert Peanut Johnson, Clip Payne, Lige Curry, Patty Curry, Sheila Washington, Ray Davis, Debbie Wright, Jim Wright, Mike Flemming
LinnDrums: Steve Washington
Bass: Stevie Washington
Guitar: Steve Washington
Keyboards: Steve Washington
Flute: Mike Flemming

"Bodyguard"

Lead Vocals: George Clinton, Garry Shider, Lige Curry

Backup Vocals: Garry Shider, Lige Curry, Bootsy Collins, Junie Morrison, Robert Peanut Johnson, Clip Payne, Mudbone Cooper, Ron Ford, Ray Davis, Shirley Hayden, Mallia Franklin, Jeanette McGruder, Sheila Horne, Andre Williams, Cuz, Linda Shider, LuShawn Clinton

Drums: Bootsy Collins

Drum Chips: Bootsy Collins

Percussion: Bootsy Collins

Bass: Bootsy Collins, Junie Morrison

Guitar: Bootsy Collins, Dewayne Blackbyrd McKnight

Piano, Synthesizers: Junie Morrison

"Bangladesh"

Lead Vocals: George Clinton, Tracey Lewis

Drum Chips: Tracey Lewis

Bass: (an engineer from Florida)

Guitar: (an engineer from Florida)

Piano: Tracey Lewis

Horns: Eric White, Ken Faulk, Ed Calle

Sax Solo: Ed Calle

Strings: Bob Basso, David Everheart Manny Capote, Lorraine Basso, Bodgen Chrusey, Gary Wedder, Stu McDonald

"Thrashin'"

Lead Vocals: George Clinton, Thomas Dolby

Backup Vocals: Garry Shider, James Wilkerson, Beverly Wilson, Jerome Rodgers, Clip Payne, Lige Curry, Shirley Hayden, Jeanette McGruder, Sheila Horne, Louie Kababbie

Drums: Dennis Chambers

Bass: Rodney Curtis

Guitar: Blackbyrd McKnight

Keyboards: Thomas Dolby

Trumpet: Bennie Cowan

Sax: Greg Thomas, Maceo Parker

Trombone: Greg Boyer

"Some of My Best Jokes Are Friends"

Lead Vocals: George Clinton, Thomas Dolby

Backup Vocals: Garry Shider, James Wilkerson, Beverly Wilson, Linda Shider

Drum Chips: Bernard Alexander

Bass: Doug Wimbush, Eric White

Guitar: Bernard Alexander, Skip McDonald

Keyboards: Doug Wimbush,

Percussion: Muruga Booker

R&B Skeletons in the Closet

"Hey Good Lookin'"

Lead Vocals: George Clinton, Debra Barsha, Vanessa Williams, Steve Washington, Bootsy Collins, Andre Williams

Backup Vocals: Debra Barsha, Sheila Washington, Garry Shider, Lige Curry

Drums: Steve Washington

Bass: Steve Washington

Guitar: Steve Washington

Keyboards: Steve Washington

"Hey Good Lookin'" was a single to feature former Miss America and rising star Vanessa Williams. This song was among her first forays into music.

"Do Fries Go with That Shake?"

Lead Vocals: George Clinton

Backup Vocals: Robert Peanut Johnson, Sheila Washington, Steve Washington, Debra Barsha, Vanessa Williams, Stephanie Clinton, Greg Thomas, Linda Shider

Drums: Steve Washington

Bass: Steve Washington

Guitar: Steve Washington

Keyboards: Amp Fiddler

Trumpet: Steve Washington

"Do Fries Go with That Shake" would be the last major single for Clinton's Capitol Records run. It also featured maybe one of the best Clinton Music videos, featuring very young members of Fishbone, Norwood Fischer among them.

"Mix Master Suite"

Lead Vocals: George Clinton
Backup Vocals: George Clinton
Percussion: Rick Marotta
Horns: Jerry Hay, the SeaWind Horns
Synclavier: George Clinton
Piano: Ed Johnson
Arrangers: Debra Barsha, Ed Johnson

"Electric Pygmies"

Lead Vocals: George Clinton, Sandra Feva
Drum Programming: David Spradley
Synthesizers, Synth Bass: David Spradley

"Intense"

Lead Vocals: George Clinton, Debra Barsha,
  Sandra Feva, male singer
Backup Vocals: Debra Barsha
Synclavier: George Clinton, David Spradley
Keyboards: David Spradley
Sax: Maceo Parker

"Cool Joe"

Lead Vocals: George Clinton, Andre Jackson
Drums: Andre Jackson
Bass: Andre Jackson
Guitar: Andre Jackson
Keyboards: Bernie Worrell
Sax: Maceo Parker
Trombone: Fred Wesley

"R&B Skeletons in the Closet"

Lead Vocals: George Clinton
Backup Vocals: Andre Williams, Michael Clip
  Payne, Garry Shider, Sheila Washington,
  Jenny Peters
Synclavier: George Clinton
Synth Bass: David Spradley
Keyboards: David Spradley
Sax: Maceo Parker

Paisley Park Records

The Cinderella Theory

"Airbound"

Lead Vocals: George Clinton
Backup Vocals: Tracey Lewis, Andre
  Williams, Sandra Feva, Jimmy Giles, Sheila
  Washington, Garry Shider, Clip Payne, Pat
  Lewis, Robert Peanut Johnson, Lige Curry
Drums: Clip Payne
Bass: Tracey Lewis
Synth Bass: Amp Fiddler
Guitar: Tracey Lewis, Andre Williams
Keyboards: Amp Fiddler, Boogie Drummond

"Tweakin'"

Lead Vocals: George Clinton, Clip Payne, Belita
  Woods, Tracey Lewis, Flavor Flav, Chuck D
Backup Vocals: Belita Woods, Angela
  Workman, Tambra Makowsky?, Pennye Ford
DJ: Anthony Jones, Darrin
Drums: David Spradley
Synth Bass: David Spradley
Keyboards: David Spradley

"Tweakin" dealt with social issues similar to those
being talked about in hip-hop at this time, dealing
with street violence and its effects on the family.
The song features notable appearances from Public Enemy as well.

"The Cinderella Theory"

Lead Vocals: George Clinton, Tracey Lewis
Backup Vocals: Lige Curry, Patty Curry, Jennie
  Peters, Sheila Washington, Joe Harris, Garry
  Shider, Clip Payne, Andre Williams
Drums: Amp Fiddler
Bass: Amp Fiddler
Keyboards: Amp Fiddler
Guitar: Blackbyrd McKnight

"Why Should I Dog U Out?"

Lead Vocals: George Clinton
Backup Vocals: Lige Curry, Angela Workman, Robert Peanut Johnson, Andre Williams, Clip Payne, Shirley Hayden, Sheila Washington, Mallia Franklin, Greg Thomas
DJs: Anthony Jones, Darrin
Drum Programming: Amp Fiddler
Spoons: A.J.
Bass: Blackbyrd McKnight
Guitar: Blackbyrd McKnight, Andre Williams
Keyboards: Amp Fiddler
Sax: Eric Leeds
Trumpet: Atlanta Bliss

"Why Should I Dog U Out" features vocals about being ahead of one's time and never selling the funk out. It features the trademark guitar chords and style of Blackbyrd McKnight. It also featured a music video.

"Serious Slammin'"

Lead Vocals: George Clinton
Backup Vocals: Jessica Cleaves, Karen Foster, Anita Johnson, Louie Kabbabie, Mike Harris, Andre Williams, Dean Ragland
Drums: Leland Zales
Bass: Greg Crockett
Keyboards, Synthesizers: Greg Crockett

"There I Go Again"

Lead Vocals: George Clinton
Backup Vocals: Joe Harris, Garry Shider, Andre Williams
Drum Machine: Michael Clip Payne
Bass: Danan Potts?
Keyboards: Bill Brown

"She Got It Goin' On"

Lead Vocals: George Clinton
Backup Vocals: Pennye Ford, Sheila Horne, Clip Payne
Drums: Amp Fiddler

Synth Bass: Amp Fiddler
Keyboards: Amp Fiddler
Sax: Eric Leeds
Trumpet: Atlanta Bliss

"The Banana Boat Song"

Lead Vocals: George Clinton
Backup Vocals: Mike Harris, Joe Harris, Darryl Clinton, Garry Shider?
Drums: Ritchie Stevens?
Bass: Steve Washington
Keyboards: Bill Brown

"French Kiss"

Lead Vocals: George Clinton
Backup Vocals: Shirley Hayden, Steve Boyd, Angela Workman, Doc Holliday, Andre Williams, Sheila Washington, Lige Curry, Joe Pep Harris
Drums: Clip Payne
Bass: Steve Washington
Guitar: Blackbyrd McKnight, Andre Williams
Keyboards: David Spradley, Steve Washington

"Rita Bewitched"

Lead Vocals: George Clinton, Tracey Lewis
Backup Vocals: Pat Lewis, Jessica Cleaves, Lige Curry, Pennye Ford, Patty Curry, Navarro Berman
Drums: Clip Payne
Bass: Andre Williams
Guitar: Tracey Lewis, Andre Williams
Keyboards: Amp Fiddler

"Kredit Kard"

Lead Vocals: George Clinton
Backup Vocals: Clip Payne, Garry Shider, Shirley Hayden, Lige Curry, Patty Curry, Sandra Feva, Pat Lewis
Drums: Clip Payne
Bass: Clip Payne
Keyboards: Clip Payne, Amp Fiddler

"Airbound (Reprise)"

Lead Vocals: George Clinton
Backup Vocals: Tracey Lewis, Andre Williams, Sandra Feva, Jimmy Giles, Sheila Washington, Garry Shider, Clip Payne, Pat Lewis, Robert Peanut Johnson, Lige Curry
Drums: Clip Payne
Bass: Tracey Lewis
Synth Bass: Amp Fiddler
Guitar: Tracey Lewis
Keyboards: Amp Fiddler, Boogie Drummond

Hey Man, Smell My Finger

"Martial Law"

Lead Vocals: Louie Kabbabie, George Clinton, Anthony Kiedis
Backup Vocals: Mudbone Cooper, Robert Peanut Johnson, Belita Woods, Garry Shider, Clip Payne, Ray Davis, Kerry Gordy, Joe Harris, Lloyd Williams, Shirley Hayden, Sheila Horne, Andre Williams, Lige Curry, Linda Shider
Drums: Dennis Chambers, Mudbone Cooper, Zachary Frazier
Bass: Flea
Guitar: Garry Shider
Keyboards: David Spradley, Amp Fiddler

"Martial Law" was one of two songs coproduced by Berry Gordy's son Kerry Gordy. This song also featured another music video.

"Paint the White House Black"

Lead Vocals: Ice Cube, Dr. Dre, George Clinton, Kam, X-Clan, Yo-Yo, MC Breed, Daddy Freddy?
Backup Vocals: Mudbone Cooper, Robert Peanut Johnson, Belita Woods, Garry Shider, Clip Payne, Greg Thomas, Ray Davis, Kerry Gordy, Joe Harris, Lloyd Williams, Shirley Hayden, N'Dea Davenport
(sample from *Undisputed Truth*)

"Paint the White House Black" was considered at a time to be the "We Are the World" of rappers. It brought a previously unprecedented amount of hip-hop talent to one record.

"Way Up"

Lead Vocals: Foley, George Clinton, Jerome Rodgers, Pat Lewis, Sandra Feva, Clip Payne, Garry Shider, Robert Peanut Johnson, J. D. Steele, Jearlyn Steele, Jeveeta Steele, Fred Steele, the Steele Singers, Andre Williams, Sheila Horne
Drums: Foley
Bass: Foley
Guitar: Foley
Keyboards: Bernie Worrell
Sax: Eric Leeds
Trumpet: Atlanta Bliss

"Dis Beat Disrupts"

Lead Vocals: George Clinton, Tracey Lewis
Backup Vocals: Glenn Goins, Steele Singers
Drums: Blackbyrd McKnight
Bass: Blackbyrd McKnight
Guitar: Blackbyrd McKnight
Keyboard: Blackbyrd McKnight
Sax: Eric Leeds
Trumpet: Atlanta Bliss

"Get Satisfied"

Lead Vocals: Clip Payne, George Clinton
Backup Vocals: Prince, Robert Peanut Johnson, Garry Shider, Linda Shider, The Steele Singers, Steve Boyd
Drums: Foley
Bass: Foley
Guitar: Foley
Keyboards: Prince
Sax: Maceo Parker
Trombone: Fred Wesley

"Hollywood"

Lead Vocals: George Clinton, Belita Woods, Ray Davis
Backup Vocals: Dallas Austin, Tracey Lewis, Debra Barsha, Pat Lewis, Andre Williams
Drums: Dallas Austin
Bass: Dallas Austin
Guitar: Dallas Austin
Keyboards: Dallas Austin

"Rhythm & Rhyme"

Lead Vocals: Shock G, George Clinton
Backup Vocals: Pat Lewis, Sandra Feva, Belita Woods
Drums: Engineer at The Disc (Mark Davis?, Bootsy?)
Bass: Bootsy Collins
Keyboards: Bernie Worrell
Guitar: Catfish Collins

"The Big Pump"

Lead Vocals: George Clinton, rapper (T. C. Ellis?)
Backup Vocals: Sandra Feva, others
Drums: Prince
Bass: Prince
Guitar: Prince
Keyboards: Prince

"If True Love"

Lead Vocals: George Clinton, Belita Woods
Backup Vocals: Mudbone Cooper, Robert Peanut Johnson, Chrissy Sepolen
Drums: Dewayne Blackbyrd McKnight
Synth Bass: David Spradley
Guitar: Tracey Lewis
Keyboards: Tracey Lewis, David Spradley

"High in My Hello"

Lead Vocals: George Clinton
Backup Vocals: Garry Shider, Ray Davis, Clip Payne, Shirley Hayden, Robert Peanut Johnson, The Steele Singers, Sheila Washington, Sharon Chism
Drums: Steve Washington
Bass: Steve Washington
Guitar: Steve Washington
Keyboards: Bernie Worrell
Trumpet: Atlanta Bliss
Sax: Eric Leeds, Maceo Parker
Trombone: Fred Wesley

"Maximumisness"

Lead Vocals: George Clinton
Backup Vocals: George Clinton, Mudbone Cooper, Bootsy Collins, Mallia Franklin
Drums: Anton Fier
Bass: Bill Laswell
Guitar: Bootsy Collins
Piano: Herbie Hancock
Congas: Daniel Ponce
Cowbells, Percussion: Aiyb Deng
Tuba: Edwin Rodriguez
Baritone Horn, Euphonium: Joe Daly
Trumpet, Flugelhorn: Ted Daniel
Bassoon: Janet Grice
Tenor Sax, Flute: J. D. Parron

"Kickback"

Lead Vocals: George Clinton
Backup Vocals: Garry Shider, Pat Lewis, Sandra Feva, Belita Woods
Drums: Foley
Bass: Foley
Guitar: Foley
Keyboards: Bernie Worrell
Trombone: Fred Wesley
Sax: Maceo Parker, Eric Leeds
Trumpet: Atlanta Bliss

"The Flag Was Still There"

Lead Vocals: George Clinton, Clip Payne, Nicole Tindall
Backup Vocals: Ray Davis, Clip Payne, Steve Boyd, Robert Peanut Johnson, Garry Shider, Crystal Gaynor, Shirley Hayden, Linda Shider, Lige Curry, Sheila Horne, Tracey Lewis, Andre Williams
Drums: Mudbone Cooper
Percussion: Larry Fratangelo
Bass: Amp Fiddler
Guitar: Catfish Collins, Blackbyrd McKnight
Keyboards: Amp Fiddler, Bernie Worrell

Capitol Records

Greatest Funkin Hits

"Atomic Dog (Dogs of the World Unite Remix)"

Lead Vocals: George Clinton, Coolio
Backup Vocals: Garry Shider, Eddie Hazel, Mudbone Cooper, Robert Peanut Johnson, Mallia Franklin, Jessica Cleaves, Michael Clip Payne
Drums: Mudbone Cooper, Dennis Chambers, Zachary Frazier
Bass: David Spradley
Keyboards: David Spradley

"Flashlight (The Groovemaster's Mix)"

Lead Vocals: Garry Shider, Belita Woods, Q-Tip, Tracey Lewis, Busta Rhymes, Ol Dirty Bastard
Drums: Amp Fiddler
Guitar: Dewayne Blackbyrd McKnight, Tracey Lewis
Synth Bass, Keyboards: Amp Fiddler

"Mothership Connection (Fully Equipped Mix)"

Lead Vocals: George Clinton, Glenn Goins
Backup Vocals: Glenn Goins, Garry Shider

Drums: Jerome Brailey
Drum Programming: Mike E. Clark
Bass: Cordell Mosson
Guitar: Garry Shider
Keyboards: Bernie Worrell

"Knee Deep (Deep as a Mutha Funker Remix)"

Lead Vocals: Garry Shider, George Clinton, Junie Morrison, Shock G, Money B, Philippe Wynne
Backup Vocals: Jessica Cleaves, Ray Davis, Sheila Horne
Drums: Bootsy Collins
Synth Bass: Junie Morrison
Guitar: Junie Morrison, Michael Hampton
Keyboards: Junie Morrison, Bernie Worrell
Independent Releases

Single

"Get Yo Ass in the Water and Swim Like Me!"

Lead Vocals: George Clinton
Backup Vocals: George Clinton
All Music: Bill Laswell

Gangsters of Love

"Ain't That Peculiar"

Vocals: El Debarge, Sly Stone, George Clinton, RonKat Spearman
Drums: Foley
Bass: Ronkat Spearman
Guitar: Rickey Rouse, BJ
Keyboards: Wizard, Sly Stone

"Never Gonna Give You Up"

Vocals: El DeBarge, George Clinton
Guitar: Bobby Eli, Rickey Rouse
Drums: Foley
Keyboards: Chris Davis

"Mathematics of Love"

Vocals: George Clinton, Kim Burrell
Keyboards: Chris Davis
Drums: Foley

"Let the Good Times Roll"

Vocals: Kim Manning, George Clinton, El DeBarge, John Frusciante
Keyboards: El DeBarge
Bass: Flea
Drums: Chad Smith
Guitar: John Frusciante

"Pledging My Love"

Vocals: George Clinton
Programming: Bobby Eli
Guitar: Rickey Rouse, Bobby Eli
Keyboards: Chris Davis

"Gypsy Woman"

Vocals: George Clinton, El DeBarge
Guitar: Carlos Santana, Rickey Rouse, Bobby Eli
Keyboards: Chris Davis
Bass: Foley
Drums: Foley

"It's All in the Game"

Vocals: Belita Woods, George Clinton, Chiquita Green, Janice McClain
Keyboards: Chris Davis
Drum Programming: Bobby Eli
Guitar: Bobby Eli, Rickey Rouse

"Heart Trouble"

Vocals: George Clinton, Paul Hill, Eban Kelly, Chiquita Green, Janice McClain
Keyboards: Chris Davis
Guitar: Bobby Eli, Rickey Rouse
Bass: Foley
Drums: Foley

"Our Day Will Come"

Vocals: Kendra Foster, George Clinton, Chiquita Green, Janice McClain
Keyboards: Chris Davis, David Spradley
Guitar: Rickey Rouse, Bobby Eli
Programming: Mark Bass
Percussion: Larry Fratangelo

"Sway"

Vocals: Belita Woods, George Clinton, Chiquita Green, Janice McClain
Keyboards: Chris Davis
Guitar: Rickey Rouse, Bobby Eli
Programming: Mark Bass
Percussion: Larry Fratangelo

"A Thousand Miles Away"

Vocals: George Clinton, Darryl Scott, Robert Peanut Johnson, Garry Shider
Keyboards: Chris Davis
Guitar: Rickey Rouse, Bobby Eli
Programming: Bobby Eli

"Stillness in Motion"

Lead Vocals: George Clinton, Kendra Foster
Backup Vocals: Shavo Odadjian, Garry Shider
Drum Programming: Shavo Odadjian
Bass: Shavo Odadjian
Guitar: Shavo Odadjian
Keyboards: Danny Bedrosian

GRANDMASTER FLASH AND THE FURIOUS FIVE (SELECT TRACK): 1982

Old-school hip-hop pioneers, their biggest hit contains P-Funk drummer Dennis Chambers.

Sugarhill Records

"The Message"

Lead Vocals: Melle Mel
DJ: Grandmaster Flash
Drums: Dennis Chambers
Bass: Doug Wimbush
Guitar: Skip McDonald
Keyboards: Dwain Mitchell, Gary Henry, Jiggs, or Reggie Griffin
Percussion: Ed Fletcher

— ☆ —

XAVIER FTG. GEORGE CLINTON AND BOOTSY: 1983

This 1980s P-Funk record has prominent Clinton and Bootsy involvement.

"Work That Sucker to Death"

Lead Vocals: George Clinton, Bootsy Collins, Xavier*
Drums, Bass, Guitar: Bootsy Collins
Percussion: Carl "Butch" Small
Synthesizers: Rahni Harris
Horns: Xavier

*Xavier is Ayanna Little, Chuck Hughes, Emonie Branch, Ernest Smith, Jeffrey Mitchell, Lyburn Downing, Ralph Hunt and Timothy Williams

— ☆ —

P-FUNK ALL STARS: 1983

The P-Funk All Stars would be the unbroken continuation of Parliament and Funkadelic after the shake-up in 1981 that would only temporarily sideline the group. The P-Funk All Stars' debut in 1983, after the massive success of George Clinton's #1 hit "Atomic Dog," would solidify their continued presence in the music world, along with important P-Funk All Stars albums in the 1980s, 1990s, and 2000s.

CBS Records

Urban Dancefloor Guerillas

"Generator Pop"

Vocals: George Clinton
Backup Vocals: Garry Shider, Eddie Hazel, Robert Peanut Johnson, Mallia Franklin, Jeannette McGruder, Lynn Mabry, Clip Payne, Andre Williams, Greg Thomas, Lige Curry, Linda Shider
Drums: Jerry Jones
Keyboards, Synthesizers: David Spradley
Guitar: Garry Shider

"Acupuncture"

Vocals: George Clinton
Drums: Blackbyrd McKnight
Bass: Blackbyrd McKnight
Guitar: Blackbyrd McKnight
Sax: Norma Jean Bell

"One of Those Summers"

Vocals: George Clinton, Junie Morisson, Rev Uriah Hughboyington

Backup Vocals: Janice Evans, Shirley Hayden, Sheila Horne, Mallia Franklin, Jeanette McGruder

Drums: Junie Morrison

Synth Bass: Junie Morrison

Piano, Strings: Junie Morrison

Guitar: Junie Morrison

Trumpet: Richard Griffith, Larry Hatcher

Trombone: Fred Wesley

Sax: Maceo Parker

"Catch a Keeper"

Vocals: Dawn Silva, Sheila Horne, Mallia Franklin, Jeannette McGruder, Clip Payne, Sly Stone, George Clinton

Drums: Dean Ragland

Electric Drums: Muruga Booker

Bass: Donnie Sterling

Keyboards, Synthesizers: David Spradley

Guitar: Tony Thomas

"Pumpin It Up"

Vocals: Sly Stone, Robert Peanut Johnson, Garry Shider, Mudbone Cooper, Ron Ford, George Clinton, Clip Payne, Andre Williams, Greg Thomas, Lige Curry, Linda Shider

Drums: Kenny Colton

Bass: Eddie Hazel

Keyboards, Synth Bass, Synthesizers: David Spradley

Guitar: Eddie Hazel, Garry Shider

"Pumpin It Up" was a big hit in the United States and also in the United Kingdom. It features the stylistic bedrock of many P-Funk classics: rollicking polyrhythms, massive vocal sections, and a standout Eddie Hazel guitar solo.

"Copy Cat"

Vocals: George Clinton, Bootsy Collins, Robert Peanut Johnson, Mallia Franklin, Debbie Wright, Darryl Clinton, Rev Uriah Hughboyington, Garry Shider, Linda Shider, Mudbone Cooper, Greg Thomas, Clip Payne

Drums: Mudbone Cooper

Keyboards, Synth Bass, Synthesizers: David Spradley

Guitar: Michael Hampton, Eddie Hazel, Garry Shider, Bootsy Collins

Trumpet: Bennie Cowan

Sax: Greg Thomas, Maceo Parker

Trombone: Greg Boyer, Fred Wesley

"Hydraulic Pump"

Vocals: Philippe Wynne, George Clinton, Sly Stone, Jimmy Giles, Norma Jean Jenkins, Bobby Womack, Ron Ford, Mallia Franklin, Lige Curry

Drums: Dean Ragland

Bass: Jimmy Giles

Keyboards, Synthesizers: Sly Stone, David Spradley, Roger Dollarhide

Guitar: Tony Thomas

Trumpet: Cynthia Robinson

"Pumpin It Up (Reprise)"

Vocals: George Clinton

Drums: Dean Ragland

Keyboards, Synthesizers: David Spradley, Sly Stone, Roger Dollarhide

"It's Too Funky in Here"

Lead Vocals: Garry Shider

Backup Vocals: Dawn Silva, Sheila Horne, Shirley Hayden, Jeanette Washington

Bass: Avery Davis, Bootsy Collins

Drums: Lonnie Greene

Sax: Maceo Parker

Trombone: Fred Wesley

Organ: Craig Lane

Guitar: Kenny Cromer

Percussion: Larry Fratangelo

— ★ —

TALKING HEADS (SELECT TRACKS): 1983–

The Talking Heads' music, hard to categorize but extremely popular in its heyday, benefited from the inclusion of Bernie Worrell in their roster starting in 1983 after he left the P-Funk All Stars. Former Brides of Funkenstein singer Lynn Mabry would also sing with this supergroup. A mighty force all their own, only some of the band's output is listed here for obvious reasons of it falling more inside its own orbit. For the importance of Worrell's input into this band, the following must be included within the canon. The Talking Heads consisted of David Byrne, Tina Weymouth, Jerry Harrison, and Chris Frantz.

Sire Records

Speaking in Tongues

"Girlfriend Is Better"
Synthesizer: Bernie Worrell

Stop Making Sense

"On All Tracks:"

Lead Vocals: David Byrne
Backup Vocals: Lynn Mabry, Ednah Holt, Alex Weir, Jerry Harrison, Chris Frantz, Tina Weymouth
Bass: Tina Weymouth
Drums: Chris Frantz
Keyboards: Bernie Worrell, Jerry Harrison
Guitar: David Byrne, Alex Weir, Jerry Harrison
Percussion: Steve Scales
Songs:

"Psycho Killer"

"Swamp"

"Slippery People"

"Burning Down the House"

"Girlfriend Is Better"

"Once in a Lifetime"
"What a Day That Way"
"Life during Wartime"
"Take Me to the River"

— ☆ —

KIDDO: 1983–1984

This is another Donnie Sterling band that also featured Michael Hampton briefly.

A&M Records

Kiddo

"Tired of Looking"

Drums: Rock Goodin
Percussion: Leon Ndugu Chancler
Guitar: Donnie Sterling
Keyboards: Reggie Andrews, Rory Kaplan
Lead Vocals: Donnie Sterling
Vocoder: Reggie Andrews, Leon Ndugu Chancler
Backup Vocals: Rock Goodin, Carl Caldwell, Jim Gilstrap, Marlena Jeter, Maxi Anderson, Oren Waters
Bass: Nathan East or Juice Johnson

"What I See, I Like"

Drums: Rock Goodin
Percussion: Willie Jenkins, Leon Ndugu Chancler
Guitar: Tony Thomas, Donnie Sterling
Keyboards: Reggie Andrews, Rory Kaplan
Sax: Leroy Davis
Vocals: Donnie Sterling
Backup Vocals: Rock Goodin, Carl Caldwell, Jim Gilstrap, Marlena Jeter, Maxi Anderson, Oren Waters, Leroy Davis, Willie Jenkins
Concertmaster: William Henderson

"Try My Loving"

Drums: Rock Goodin
Guitar: Donnie Sterling, Charles Fearing
Keyboards: Reggie Andrews, Rory Kaplan
Vocals: Donnie Sterling
Backup Vocals: Backup Vocals: Rock Goodin, Carl Caldwell, Jim Gilstrap, Marlena Jeter, Maxi Anderson, Oren Waters
Vocoder: Reggie Andrews, Leon Ndugu Chancler

"Thinking about Your Charm"

Drums: Rock Goodin
Guitar: Donnie Sterling, Charles Fearing
Acoustic Guitar: Greg Poree
Keyboards: Arthur Brown
Vocals: Donnie Sterling, Arthur Brown,
Backup Vocals: Rock Goodin, Carl Caldwell, Jim Gilstrap, Marlena Jeter, Maxi Anderson, Oren Waters
Bass: Juice Johnson or Nathan East
Harp: Dorothy Ashby
Orchestra: Detroit Symphony Orchestra

"Give It Up"

Drums: Rock Goodin
Guitar: Donnie Sterling, Charles Fearing
Keyboards: Reggie Andrews, Rory Kaplan
Vocals: Donnie Sterling
Backup Vocals: Rock Goodin, Carl Caldwell, Jim Gilstrap, Marlena Jeter, Maxi Anderson, Oren Waters
Bass: Nathan East or Juice Johnson

"Strangers"

Drums: Rock Goodin
Percussion: Leon Ndugu Chancler
Vocoder: Reggie Andrews, Leon Ndugu Chancler
Guitar: Donnie Sterling
Keyboards: Reggie Andrews, Steve Cox
Vocals: Donnie Sterling
Backup Vocals: Rock Goodin, Carl Caldwell, Jim Gilstrap, Marlena Jeter, Maxi Anderson, Oren Waters

"Suzy's Gone"

Drums: Rock Goodin
Percussion: Leon Ndugu Chancler
Guitar: Donnie Sterling, Charles Fearing
Keyboards: Reggie Andrews
Vocals: Donnie Sterling
Backup Vocals: Rock Goodin, Carl Caldwell, Jim Gilstrap, Marlena Jeter, Maxi Anderson, Oren Waters
Bass: Nathan East or Juice Johnson

"Cheated, Mistreated"

Drums: Rock Goodin
Guitar: Donnie Sterling, Charles Fearing
Keyboards: Reggie Andrews
Vocals: Donnie Sterling
Backup Vocals: Rock Goodin, Carl Caldwell, Jim Gilstrap, Marlena Jeter, Maxi Anderson, Oren Waters
Bass: Nathan East or Juice Johnson
Sax: Leroy Davis

Action

"She's Got the Body"

Drums: Rock Goodin
Guitar: Donnie Sterling, Charles Fearing
Keyboards: Donnie Sterling, Bernie Worrell, Derek Nakamoto, John Barnes
Vocals: Donnie Sterling
Backup Vocals: Jim Gilstrap, Marva King, Rock Goodin

"Hyperactive"

Drums: Rock Goodin
Guitar: Donnie Sterling
Keyboards: Leroy Davis
Vocals: Donnie Sterling
Backup Vocals: Leroy Davis, Marva King, Jim Gilstrap
Bass: Juicy Johnson or Donnie Sterling
Sax: Leroy Davis

"This Live Will Last"

Drums: Rock Goodin
Percussion: Willie Jenkins
Guitar: Donnie Sterling, Steve Fox
Keyboards: Donnie Sterling, Eddie N. Watkins Jr.
Vocals: Donnie Sterling
Backup Vocals: Jim Gilstrap, Marva King, Rock Goodin
Bass: Donnie Sterling, Juicy Johnson, or Eddie N. Watkins Jr.

"Can't Explain"

Drums: Rock Goodin
Guitar: Donnie Sterling
Keyboards: Arthur Brown
Vocals: Donnie Sterling
Backup Vocals: Jim Gilstrap, Marva King, Arthur Brown
Bass: Donnie Sterling or Juicy Johnson

"Action Speaks Louder Than Words"

Drums: Rock Goodin
Guitar: Donnie Sterling, Charles Fearing
Keyboards: Donnie Sterling, Derek Nakamoto, John Barnes
Vocals: Donnie Sterling
Backup Vocals: Jim Gilstrap, Mava King, Rock Goodin

"Cool Me Off"

Drums: Rock Goodin
Guitar: Donnie Sterling
Keyboards: Derek Nakamato, John Barnes, Donnie Sterling
Vocals: Donnie Sterling
Backup Vocals: Jim Gilstrap, Marva King, Rock Goodin

"Young Love"

Drums: Rock Goodin
Guitar: Donnie Sterling
Keyboards: Donnie Sterling

Vocals: Donnie Sterling
Bass: Donnie Sterling

"Telephone Fantasy"

Drums: Rock Goodin
Guitar: Donnie Sterling, Charles Fearing
Keyboards: Donnie Sterling, Eddie Watkins Jr.
Vocals: Donnie Sterling
Backup Vocals: Marva King, Jim Gilstrap, Rock Goodin

— ☆ —

ERAMUS HALL: 1984

This 1980s-era Detroit P-Funk band was heavily influenced by synth and LinnDrums, as was much of the Capitol Records P-Funk output. It features several P-Funkers.

Capitol Records

Go Head

"I Can't Keep My Head (I Always Lose It to You)"

Drums: Bernard Provost
Percussion: Larry Fratangelo
Guitar: Garry Shider
Keyboards: Michael Gatheright
Vocals: James Wilkerson, Michael Gatheright, George Clinton, Mallia Franklin, Lige Curry, Mudbone Cooper, Clip Payne, Garry Shider, Robert Peanut Johnson

"Stuck in the Mud"

Drums: Bernard Provost
Guitar: Marvin Willaims
Keyboards: Michael Gatheright
Vocals: James Wilkerson, Michael Gateright, Grady Smith

"Freaky but Sneaky"

Drums: Bernard Provost
Percussion: James Wilkerson
Keyboards: Michael Gatheright
Vocals: James Wilkerson, Michael Gatheright, Grady Smith, Garry Shider, Mallia Franklin, Gary Mudbone Cooper, Michael Clip Payne, Lige Curry, Robert Peanut Johnson

"Stir It Up"

Drums: Bernard Provost
Guitar: Garry Shider,
Keyboards: Michael Gatheright
Vocals: James Wilkerson, Michael Gatheright, Gary Mudbone Cooper, Garry Shider, Mallia Franklin, Clip Payne, Lige Curry, Robert Peanut Johnson

"Keep Me Burnin'"

Drums: Bernard Provost
Guitar: Garry Shider, Dewayne Blackbyrd McKnight?
Keyboards: Michael Gatheright
Vocals: James Wilkerson, Michael Gatheright, George Clinton, Gary Mudbone Cooper, Garry Shider, Mallia Franklin, Clip Payne, Lige Curry, Robert Peanut Johnson
Trombone: Fred Wesley
Sax: Maceo Parker

"Checkin' You Checkin' Yourself Out"

Drums: Bernard Provost
Percussion: James Wilkerson
Guitar: Garry Shider, Dewayne Blackbyrd McKnight?
Keyboards: Michael Gatheright
Vocals: James Wilkerson, Michael Gatheright, Joe Anderson
Bass: Joe Anderson

"Will You Love Me (The Same Way Tomorrow)"

Drums: Jerry Jones
Percussion: James Wilkerson, Carl Butch Small?
Guitar: Bruce Nazarian
Keyboards: Rudi Robinson
Bass: Rodrick Chandler
Orchestra: Detroit Symphony Orchestra
Vocals: James Wilkerson, Michael Gatheright

CHOPS HORNS: 1984, 2009

This horn section was led by saxophonist Darryl Dixon (of "Flash Light" fame) and was P-Funk's horn section in between the tenures of the JBs/Horny Horns (1975–1977) and the Baltimore Connection/P-Funk Horns (1978–present). Chops was active in Parliament on stages mostly in 1977–1978 during the platinum-selling *Funkentelechy Vs. The Placebo Syndrome* album release. Chops would go on to be the horn sections for dozens of well-known artists, including Alicia Keys.

"Bust It Out"

Bass, Synthesizer, Backup Vocals: Doug Wimbush
Keyboards, Lead Vocals: Funki
Alto Sax, Backup Vocals: Darryl Dixon
Baritone Sax, Tenor Sax, Flute: David Watson
Tenor Sax: Michael Porter
Trombone, Backup Vocals: Clarence Lawry, Melvin El
Trumpet: Danny Collette, Joseph Smithers
Trumpet, Flugelhorn, Vocals: Marvin Daniels
Backup Vocals: Cindy Mizelle, Craig Derry, Fiona, La Juan Carter
Keyboards, Backup Vocals: Dwain Mitchell, Keith LeBlanc, or Chris Lord-Alge
Drums: Dennis Chambers, Darryl Burgee, or Keith LeBlanc
Percussion: Edward Fletcher
Guitar, Backup Vocals: Bernard Alexander

"Does Your Mama Know"

Bass: Doug Wimbush
Keyboards, Lead Vocals: Funki
Alto Sax, Backup Vocals: Darryl Dixon
Baritone Sax, Tenor Sax, Flute: David Watson
Tenor Sax: Michael Porter
Trombone, Backup Vocals: Clarence Lawry, Melvin El
Trumpet: Danny Collette, Joseph Smithers
Trumpet, Flugelhorn, Vocals: Marvin Daniels
Backup Vocals: Cindy Mizelle, Craig Derry, Fiona, La Juan Carter
Keyboards, Backup Vocals: Dwain Mitchell, Keith LeBlanc, or Chris Lord-Alge
Drums: Dennis Chambers, Darryl Burgee, or Keith LeBlanc
Percussion: Edward Fletcher
Guitar, Backup Vocals: Bernard Alexander

"Your Red Hot Love"

Bass: Doug Wimbush
Keyboards, Lead Vocals: Funki
Alto Sax, Backup Vocals: Darryl Dixon
Baritone Sax, Tenor Sax, Flute: David Watson
Tenor Sax: Michael Porter
Trombone, Backup Vocals: Clarence Lawry, Melvin El
Trumpet: Danny Collette, Joseph Smithers
Trumpet, Flugelhorn, Vocals: Marvin Daniels
Backup Vocals: Svengali, Cindy Mizelle, Craig Derry, Fiona, La Juan Carter
Keyboards, Backup Vocals: Dwain Mitchell, Keith LeBlanc, or Chris Lord-Alge
Drums: Dennis Chambers, Darryl Burgee, or Keith LeBlanc
Percussion: Edward Fletcher
Guitar, Backup Vocals: Bernard Alexander

"Still Breaking My Heart"

Bass: Doug Wimbush
Keyboards, Lead Vocals: Funki
Alto Sax, Backup Vocals: Darryl Dixon
Baritone Sax, Tenor Sax, Flute: David Watson
Tenor Sax: Michael Porter
Trombone, Backup Vocals: Clarence Lawry, Melvin El
Trumpet: Danny Collette, Joseph Smithers
Trumpet, Flugelhorn, Vocals: Marvin Daniels
Backup Vocals: Svengali, Cindy Mizelle, Craig Derry, Fiona, La Juan Carter
Keyboards, Backup Vocals: Dwain Mitchell, Keith LeBlanc, or Chris Lord-Alge
Drums: Dennis Chambers, Darryl Burgee, or Keith LeBlanc
Percussion: Edward Fletcher
Guitar, Backup Vocals: Bernard Alexander

"I Just Feel Like Dancing"

Bass: Doug Wimbush
Keyboards, Lead Vocals: Funki
Alto Sax, Backup Vocals: Darryl Dixon
Baritone Sax, Tenor Sax, Flute: David Watson
Tenor Sax: Michael Porter
Trombone, Backup Vocals: Clarence Lawry, Melvin El
Trumpet: Danny Collette, Joseph Smithers
Trumpet, Flugelhorn, Vocals: Marvin Daniels
Backup Vocals: Svengali, Cindy Mizelle, Craig Derry, Fiona, La Juan Carter
Keyboards, Backup Vocals: Dwain Mitchell, Keith LeBlanc, or Chris Lord-Alge
Drums: Dennis Chambers, Darryl Burgee, or Keith LeBlanc
Percussion: Edward Fletcher
Guitar, Backup Vocals: Bernard Alexander

"We're All in the Same Boat"

Bass: Doug Wimbush
Keyboards, Lead Vocals: Funki
Alto Sax, Backup Vocals: Darryl Dixon
Baritone Sax, Tenor Sax, Flute: David Watson
Tenor Sax: Michael Porter
Trombone, Backup Vocals: Clarence Lawry, Melvin El
Trumpet: Danny Collette, Joseph Smithers
Trumpet, Flugelhorn, Vocals: Marvin Daniels
Backup Vocals: Svengali, Cindy Mizelle, Craig Derry, Fiona, La Juan Carter
Keyboards, Backup Vocals: Dwain Mitchell, Keith LeBlanc, or Chris Lord-Alge
Drums: Dennis Chambers, Darryl Burgee, or Keith LeBlanc
Percussion: Edward Fletcher
Guitar, Backup Vocals: Bernard Alexander

"I Know You"

Bass: Doug Wimbush
Keyboards, Lead Vocals: Funki
Alto Sax, Backup Vocals: Darryl Dixon
Baritone Sax, Tenor Sax, Flute: David Watson
Tenor Sax: Michael Porter
Trombone, Backup Vocals: Clarence Lawry, Melvin El
Trumpet: Danny Collette, Joseph Smithers
Trumpet, Flugelhorn, Vocals: Marvin Daniels
Backup Vocals: Svengali, Cindy Mizelle, Craig Derry, Fiona, La Juan Carter
Keyboards, Backup Vocals: Dwain Mitchell, Keith LeBlanc, or Chris Lord-Alge
Drums: Dennis Chambers, Darryl Burgee, or Keith LeBlanc
Percussion: Edward Fletcher
Guitar, Backup Vocals: Bernard Alexander

"When the World Is Runnin' Down (You Make the Best of What's Still Around)"

Bass: Doug Wimbush
Alto Sax: Darryl Dixon

Baritone Sax, Tenor Sax, Flute: David Watson
Tenor Sax: Michael Porter
Trombone: Clarence Lawry, Melvin El
Trumpet: Danny Collette, Joseph Smithers
Trumpet, Flugelhorn: Marvin Daniels
Keyboards: Funki, Dwain Mitchell, Keith LeBlanc, or Chris Lord-Alge
Drums: Dennis Chambers, Darryl Burgee, or Keith LeBlanc
Percussion: Edward Fletcher
Guitar: Bernard Alexander

DOLBY'S CUBE (SELECT TRACK): 1985

This funk project by British New Waver Thomas Dolby, of "She Blinded Me with Science" fame, featured George Clinton and others.

"May the Cube Be with You"

Trumpet: Randy Brecker
Sax: Michael Brecker
Clarinet: Ed Johnson
Drums: Dennis Chambers
Bass: Rodney Curtis
Guitar: Thomas Dolby
Keyboards: Thomas Dolby
Clarinet: Ed Johnson
Lead Vocals: Thomas Dolby, George Clinton
Backup Vocals: Debra Barsha, George Clinton, Jessica Cleaves, Lene Lovich

"May the Cube Be with You" was recorded around the same time as George Clinton's "Thrashin'" from the *Some of My Best Jokes Are Friends* album, which features many of the same players as well.

JIMMY G AND THE TACKHEADS: 1985

George Clinton's brother Jimmy G's band, which is almost entirely populated by members of the P-Funk All Stars, was produced by Clinton himself.

Capitol Records

Federation of Tackheads

"Clockwork"

Lead Vocals: Robert Peanut Johnson
Backup Vocals: Andre Williams, Pat Lewis, Garry Shider, Michael Clip Payne, Sandra Feva, Robert Peanut Johnson, Lige Curry
Drums: Robert Peanut Johnson
Bass: Robert Peanut Johnson
Synthesizers: Robert Peanut Johnson
Guitar: Dewayne Blackbyrd McKnight

"Break My Heart"

Lead Vocals: George Clinton, Sheila Horne, Jimmy Giles,
Backup Vocals: Andre Williams, Garry Shider, Dean Ragland, Lige Curry
Drums: Steve Washington
Bass: Steve Washington
Synthesizers: David Spradley
Guitar: Dewayne Blackbyrd McKnight

"All or Nothin'"

Lead Vocals: Andre Williams, Sheila Horne George Clinton, Dewayne Blackbyrd McKnight, Jimmy Giles, Lige Curry
Backup Vocals: Andre Williams, Sheila Horne, George Clinton, Dewayne Blackbyrd McKnight, Jimmy Giles, Lige Curry
Drums: Steve Washington
Bass: Steve Washington
Synthesizers: Steve Washington
Guitar: Dewayne Blackbyrd McKnight

"Lies"

Lead Vocals: Jimmy Giles
Backup Vocals: Andre Williams, Dean Ragland, Jimmy Giles, George Clinton
Drums: Dean Ragland
Bass: Jimmy Giles
Synthesizers: Andre Williams
Guitar: Dewayne Blackbyrd McKnight, Andre Williams

"Slingshot"

Lead Vocals: Jimmy Giles
Backup Vocals: Sheila Horne, Belita Woods, George Clinton, Robert Peanut Johnson
Drums: David Spradley
Synth Bass: David Spradley
Synthesizers: David Spradley
Guitar: Dewayne Blackbyrd McKnight

"I Want Yo Daughter"

Lead Vocals: Andre Williams, Jimmy Giles
Backup Vocals: Garry Shider, George Clinton, Andre Williams, Pat Lewis, Robert Peanut Johnson, Sandra Feva, Jimmy Giles, Dean Ragland
Drums: Michael Clip Payne
Bass: Jimmy Giles
Synthesizers: David Spradley
Guitar: Garry Shider

"Family Funk"

Lead Vocals: Jimmy Giles
Backup Vocals: Pat Lewis, George Clinton, Sandra Feva, Andre Williams, Robert Peanut Johnson, Sheila Horne, George E. Clinton III
Drums: Steve Washington
Bass: Steve Washington
Synthesizers: Steve Washington
Guitar: Steve Washington

— ☆ —

SLY FOX: 1985

This group featured Gary Mudbone Cooper and David Spradley and scored a hit with their single "Let's Go All the Way," which borrowed some of the same concepts that made "Atomic Dog" a hit; both of the previously mentioned gentlemen were part of that record as well.

Capitol Records

"Let's Go All the Way"

Drums: Johnny Ventura, Steve Sprouse
Guitar: Binky Brice
Keyboards: David Spradley, Alec Shantzis
Vocals: Mudbone Cooper, Michael Camacho
Bass: Tony Bridges

"Let's Go All the Way" was a massive hit, playing on radio stations through the present day. It features Mudbone Cooper's trademark vocals and David Spradley's synthesizers, which propelled his work to similar heights with "Atomic Dog." Indeed, this song had some of the same elements in the rhythm track as "Atomic Dog" as well, albeit while touching on new elements as well.

"Don't Play with Fire"

Drums: Johnny Ventura, Steve Sprouse
Guitar: David Lavender
Keyboards: David Spradley, Alec Shantzis
Vocals: Mudbone Cooper, Michael Camacho
Backup Vocals: April Lang, Cindy Mizelle, David Sanchez, Evan Rogers
Bass: Tony Bridges

"I Still Remember"

Drums: Johnny Ventura, Steve Sprouse
Guitar: Frank Finley
Keyboards: David Spradley
Vocals: Mudbone Cooper, Michael Camacho
Backup Vocals: April Lang, Cindy Mizelle, David Sanchez, Evan Rogers
Bass: Tony Bridges

"Won't Let You Go"

Drums: Johnny Ventura, Steve Sprouse
Guitar: Kennan Keating
Keyboards: David Spradley, Alec Shantzis
Vocals: Mudbone Cooper, Michael Camacho
Bass: Tony Bridges

"Como Tu the Llama?"

Drums: Johnny Ventura, Steve Sprouse
Keyboards: David Spradley
Vocals: Mudbone Cooper, Michael Camacho

"Stay True"

Drums: Johnny Ventura, Steve Sprouse
Guitar: Frank Finley
Keyboards: David Spradley, Alec Shantzis
Vocals: Mudbone Cooper, Michael Camacho
Bass: Tony Bridges

"If Push Comes to a Shove"

Drums: Johnny Ventura, Steve Sprouse
Guitar: Frank Finley
Keyboards: David Spradley, Alec Shantzis
Vocals: Mudbone Cooper, Michael Camacho
Bass: Tony Bridges

"Merry-Go-Round"

Drums: Johnny Ventura, Steve Sprouse
Guitar: Frank Finley
Keyboards: David Spradley
Vocals: Mudbone Cooper, Michael Camacho
Bass: Tony Bridges

— ☆ —

THE RED HOT CHILI PEPPERS (SELECT TRACKS): 1985–

George Clinton produced the Red Hot Chili Peppers' second album, *Freakey Styley*, and it would feature several P-Funk alumni as well.

EMI Records

Freakey Styley

"Jungle Man"

Vocals: Anthony Kiedis, George Clinton
Drums: Cliff Martinez
Guitar: Hillel Slovak
Bass: Flea
Horns: Bennie Cowan, Maceo Parker, Fred Wesley

"Hollywood (Africa)"

Vocals: Anthony Kiedis, George Clinton
Drums: Cliff Martinez
Guitar: Hillel Slovak
Bass: Flea
Horns: Bennie Cowan, Maceo Parker, Fred Wesley

"American Ghost Dance"

Vocals: Anthony Kiedis
Drums: Cliff Martinez
Guitar: Hillel Slovak
Bass: Flea
Horns: Bennie Cowan, Maceo Parker, Fred Wesley

"If You Want Me to Stay"

Vocals: Anthony Kiedis, George Clinton
Backup Vocals: George Clinton, RHCP, P-Funk
Drums: Cliff Martinez
Guitar: Hillel Slovak
Bass: Flea
Horns: Bennie Cowan, Maceo Parker, Fred Wesley

"Nevermind"

Vocals: Anthony Kiedis
Drums: Cliff Martinez
Guitar: Hillel Slovak
Bass: Flea
Horns: Bennie Cowan, Maceo Parker, Fred Wesley

"Freaky Styley"

Vocals: Anthony Kiedis, George Clinton
Drums: Cliff Martinez
Guitar: Hillel Slovak
Bass: Flea
Horns: Bennie Cowan, Maceo Parker, Fred Wesley

"Blackeyed Blonde"

Vocals: Anthony Kiedis, George Clinton
Drums: Cliff Martinez
Guitar: Hillel Slovak
Bass: Flea
Horns: Bennie Cowan, Maceo Parker, Fred Wesley

"The Brother's Cup"

Vocals: Anthony Kiedis, George Clinton
Backup Vocals: Flea, Hillel Slovak, Garry Shider, Garrett Shider, others
Drums: Cliff Martinez
Guitar: Hillel Slovak
Bass: Flea
Horns: Bennie Cowan, Maceo Parker, Fred Wesley

"Battle Ship"

Vocals: Anthony Kiedis
Drums: Cliff Martinez
Guitar: Hillel Slovak
Bass: Flea
Horns: Bennie Cowan, Maceo Parker, Fred Wesley

"Lovin' and Touchin'"

Vocals: Anthony Kiedis
Drums: Cliff Martinez
Guitar: Hillel Slovak
Bass: Flea
Horns: Bennie Cowan, Maceo Parker, Fred Wesley

"Catholic School Girls Rule"

Vocals: Anthony Kiedis
Drums: Cliff Martinez
Guitar: Hillel Slovak
Bass: Flea
Horns: Bennie Cowan, Maceo Parker, Fred Wesley

"Sex Rap"

Vocals: Anthony Kiedis
Drums: Cliff Martinez
Guitar: Hillel Slovak
Bass: Flea
Horns: Bennie Cowan, Maceo Parker, Fred Wesley

"Thirty Dirty Birds"

Vocals: Anthony Kiedis

"Yertle the Turtle"

Vocals: Anthony Kiedis, Louie Kabbabie
Drums: Cliff Martinez
Guitar: Hillel Slovak
Bass: Flea
Horns: Bennie Cowan, Maceo Parker, Fred Wesley

JAY DOUBLE-YOU!: 1985–1986, 2001, 2003, 2016

Jim Wright was the original drummer for Parlet and brother of Parlet vocalist Debbie Wright.

Jazz Boo-Gay Records

Singles

"Talking to Myself"

Bass Guitar: Kern Brantley
Guitar: Ufuoma-D Wallace and Sparky Lawson
Guitar Solo: Ron Smith
LinnDrum Programming: Jim Wright
Simmons Drums: Jim Wright
Congas: Sundeada
Sax Solo: Dave McMurry
Keyboards: Jim Wright
Vocals: Jim Wright

"You Know What She Said?"

Bass Guitar: Walter "Leon" Callaway
Guitar: Ronnie "Fresh" Smith, Ufuma "D" Wallace, Sparky Lawson
Drum, LinnDrum, RX-11 Beat Box Programming: Jim Wright
Synclavier, Synth Programming: Eric Morgeson
Percussion: Sundiata O.M.
Lead Vocals: Jim Wright, Debbie Wright
Keyboards, Grand Piano, Hohner D6 Clavinet, Yamaha DX7: Jim Wright
Backup Vocals: Cynthia Girty, Mamie Brown, Debbie Wright, Robin "E" Lee
Horn, Synthesizer: Ernestro Wilson

— ☆ —

"Catch Me on the Turnaround" (both versions)

Drums: Jim Wright
Percussion: Jim Wright, Melvin Wells
Bass Guitar: Adam Hammonds or Melvin Wells
Bass Keyboards: Jim Wright
Lead and Rhythm Guitars: Jonathan J.B. Bonds, Bob Star, or Melvin Wells
Lead Vocals: Jim Wright
Backup Vocals: Jim Wright, Melvin Wells
Piano, Clavinet: Jim Wright
Piano, Organ: Melvin Wells

"If You Don't Believe, Who Will"

Drums: Jim Wright
Percussion: Jim Wright, Melvin Wells
Bass Guitar: Adam Hammonds or Melvin Wells
Bass Keyboards: Jim Wright
Lead and Rhythm Guitars: Jonathan J.B. Bonds, Bob Star, or Melvin Wells
Lead Vocals: Jim Wright
Backup Vocals: Jim Wright, Melvin Wells
Piano, Clavinet: Jim Wright
Piano, Organ: Melvin Wells

"Get All the Way Down" (both versions)

Drums: Jim Wright
Percussion: Jim Wright, Melvin Wells
Bass Guitar: Adam Hammonds or Melvin Wells
Bass Keyboards: Jim Wright
Lead and Rhythm Guitars: Jonathan J.B. Bonds, Bob Star, or Melvin Wells
Lead Vocals: Jim Wright
Backup Vocals: Jim Wright, Melvin Wells
Piano, Clavinet: Jim Wright
Piano, Organ: Melvin Wells

Talking Music Records

I'll See You Soon

"I'll See You Soon"

Lead Vocals: Jim Wright
Backup Vocals: Deidra Adams
Rhythm Guitar: Billy Parker
Bass Guitar: Torrance Scott
Drums: Jim Wright
Tenor Sax: Erik Armstrong
Keyboards: Jim Wright

"Ever Wonder Why"

Lead and Backup Vocals: Jim Wright
Vocals, Ad Libs: Deidra Adams
Backup Vocals: Ronnie Gizmo Clay
Lead and Rhythm Guitars: Billy Parker
Lead Guitar Solo: Keith Williams
Bass Guitar: Torrance Scott
Drums: Jim Wright
Keyboards: Jim Wright

"Handle Your Business"

Vocals: Jim Wright
Bass Guitar: Torrance Scott
Rhythm Guitar: Billy Parker
Keyboards: Jim Wright
Drums: Jim Wright

"I Hurt So Bad"

Lead and Backup Vocals: Jim Wright
Backup Vocals, Ad Libs: Deidra Adams
Guitar: Billy Parker
Bass Guitar: Torrance Scott
Drums: Jim Wright
Sax: Erik Armstrong
Clavinet: Jim Wright
Electric Piano: Rene'e Dabrowski Wright

"Ooooh—Yeah!"

Lead and Backup Vocals: Jim Wright
Lead Vocals, Ad Libs: Steve Boyd
Guitar: Cordell Mosson
Bass Guitar: Torrance Scott
Drums: Jim Wright
Tenor Sax: Erik Armstrong
Bass Keyboards: Jim Wright

"My Stuff"

Lead and Backup Vocals: Jim Wright
Backup Vocals, Ad Libs: Deidra Adams
Rhythm Guitar: Billy Parker
Bass Guitar: Torrance Scott
Drums: Reggie Vickers
Keyboards: Jim Wright

"Getcha Gotcha"

Lead Vocals: Jim Wright
Rhythm Guitar: Billy Parker, Cordell Mosson
Bass Guitar: Torrance Scott
Drums: Jim Wright
Keyboards: Jim Wright

"Funk & Roll"

Lead and Backup Vocals: Jim Wright
Backup Vocals: Deidra Adams
Lead and Rhythm Guitars: Billy Parker
Bass Guitar: Torrance Scott
Drums: Jim Wright
Keyboards: Jim Wright

Love Every Day

"Love Every Day"

Drums, Percussion, Vocals: Jim Wright
Bass: Rene'e Wright
Guitar: Billy Parker
Horns: Cecil P-Nut Daniels

"Wise Up Rise Up"

Drums, Percussion, Vocals: Jim Wright
Bass: Torrance Scott
Guitar: Kent Hill
Keyboards: Rene'e Wright

"I Feel Fantastic"

Drums, Keyboards, Vocals: Jim Wright
Bass: Torrance Scott
Guitar: Kent Hill
Percussion: Charles "Spike" Jones III

"I Don't Want This Night to Be Over"

Drums, Bass, Guitar, Keyboards, Thangs: Andre Williams
Keyboards, Thangs: Keith Henderson
Vocals: Jim Wright
MIDI Horn Xylophone: Cecil P-Nut Daniels

"Who Said Life Was Fair"

Drums, Percussion, Keyboards, Vocals: Jim Wright
Bass: Torrance Scott
Guitar: Jerome Romo Hill

"Who Are You Under"

Drums, Percussion, Bass, Vocals: Jim Wright
Rhythm Guitar: Kent HIll
Lead Guitar: Jerome Romo Hill

"Fun"

Drums, Keyboard: Jim Wright
Bass: Torrance Scott
Guitar: Kent Hill
Horns, Thangs: Rick Gardner

"It's About Time"

Drums, Percussion, Keyboards, Vocals: Jim Wright
Bass: Rene'e Wright

"A Thang on Me"

Drums, Percussion, Bass, Vocals: Jim Wright
Guitar: Kent Hill

I Want the White Boy Deal!!

"I Want the White Boy Deal!!"

Drums, Piano, Vocals: Jim Wright
Lead and Rhythm Guitars: Billy Parker
Bass: Torrance Scott

"Get the Money/Co Je El Dinero" (both mixes)

Drums, Bass, Vocals: Jim Wright
Lead and Rhythm Guitars: Bryan "Slappy" Goodman
Congas, Percussion: JefWah/Peace
Keyboards: Wizard

"Beautiful Ladies"

Drums, Bass, Keyboards: Jim Wright
Rhythm Guitar: Billy Parker
Congas, Percussion: JefWah/Peace
Trumpet: Randy Skinner

"Give to Live"

Drums, Bass, Keyboards, Vocals: Jim Wright
Lead and Rhythm Guitars: Billy Parker

"Hit Cha Like a Boom Boom"

Drums, Percussion, Bass, Keyboards, Vocals: Jim Wright
Lead and Rhythm Guitars: Marshell Delaney

"I Faced It Too!" Live

Piano, Vocals: Jim Wright
Bass: Nat Collins
Lead and Rhythm Guitars: Joe Arnold
Congas, Percussion: JefWah/Peace

"More & Moe"

Drums, Vocals: Jim Wright
Bass: Gregg Holsey
Lead and Rhythm Guitars: Billy Parker
Keyboards: Edwin Birdsong

"JTRP Presents Jay Double You! My Stuff (the K.C. mix with toppings)"

Keyboard Bass, Clavinet, Vocals: Jim Wright
Backup Vocals, Ad Libs: Deidra Adams
Drums: Reggie Vickers
Bass: Torrance Scott
Rhythm Guitar: Billy Parker
Synthesizer, Keyboards: Kevin Kazual Collins

"The Club"

Drums, Keyboards, Vocals: Jim Wright
Bass: Gregg Holsey
Guitar: Billy Parker

"U Know I Know"

Drums, Rhythm Guitar, Vocals: Jim Wright
Bass: Marshall Delaney
Lead Guitar: Jeremy L. Kendrick
Electric Trumpet: Randy Skinner

"What You Want What Did You Come Here 4 Live @ the Crib"

Piano, Vocals: Jim Wright
Bass: Nat Collins
Lead and Rhythm Guitars: Joe Arnold, Bob Starr
Congas, Percussion: JefWah/Peace

"You Make Me Smile"

Acoustic Guitar, Keyboards, Vocals: Jim Wright
Trumpet: Randy Skinner

"It Don't Matter"

Drums, Bass, Vocals: Jim Wright
Lead Guitar: Gregg Holsey
Keyboards, Rhythm Guitar: Ricky Lane

— ☆ —

KURTIS BLOW
(SELECT TRACK): 1986

Old-school rap pioneer Kurtis Blow was ahead of his time by incorporating George Clinton into his music; this appearance occurred a couple of years before the sampling era reached its zenith.

Mercury Records

Kingdom Blow

"Magilla Gorilla"

Lead Vocals: Kurtis Blow, George Clinton
Production: Eddison Electrik, Salaam Remi

— ☆ —

THE NIGHT BEFORE
SOUNDTRACK: 1987

George Clinton, Garry Shider, William "Bootsy" Collins, Dewayne "Blackbyrd" McKnight, Jessica Cleaves, Tracey "Treylewd" Lewis, Joe "Pep" Harris, Amp Fiddler, and Lynn Mabry appeared as a fictional band in the early Keanu Reeves movie *The Night Before.* Producer Mark Davis also was heavily involved in the soundtrack. Here are the songs that appeared in the film that had a P-Funk connection.

"Danny Boy" (M. Davis)
"Way Over There" (G. Clinton, G. Shider, W. Collins)

"Honk It" (G. Clinton, G. Shider, W. Collins)
"Baby Boy" (G. Clinton, W. Collins)
"Who'd Have Ever Thought We'd Be Friends" (G. Clinton, G. Shider)
"J.B." (M. Davis)
"Salsa Groove" (M. Davis)
"Betty's Working Late Tonight" (M. Davis)

— ☆ —

JESSE RAE (SELECT TRACKS):
1987–

Scottish funkateer Jesse Rae, clad in full regalia including a kilt, worked with P-Funkers Bernie Worrell and Michael Hampton and members of Zapp.

Luzuli Video Records

The Thistle

"Inside Out"

Backup Vocals: Jesse Rae, Roger Troutman, The Thistles
Drums: Lester Troutman
Lead and Rhythm Guitars: Roger Troutman
Percussion: Lester Troutman
Vocals: Jesse Rae

"That Kind O' Girl"

Backup Vocals: Jesse Rae, Roger Troutman, The Thistles
Bass: Onnie McIntyre, Roger Troutman
Drums: Lester Troutman
Keyboards: Roger Lynch
Lead and Rhythm Guitars: Onnie McIntyre, Roger Troutman
Percussion: Lester Troutman
Vocals: Jesse Rae

"Hou-Di-Ni"

Backup Vocals: Donna Sloss, Jesse Rae, Ray Davis, Sandy Turner, The Thistles, Toika Troutman-David
Drums: Steve Ferrone
Keyboards, Synth Bass, Guitar: Roger Troutman
Percussion: Lester Troutman
Vocals: Jesse Rae

"Don't Give Up"

Backup Vocals: Jesse Rae, Roger Troutman, The Thistles
Bass Guitar, Keyboards, Guitar: Roger Troutman
Drums, Percussion: Lester Troutman
Keyboards: Roger Lynch
Vocals: Jesse Rae

"Friend-Ship"

Backup Vocals: Jesse Rae, Roger Troutman
Bass: Roger Lynch
Drums, Percussion: Lester Troutman
Keyboards: Bernie Worrell, Roger Lynch
Lead and Rhythm Guitars: Michael Hampton, Roger Troutman
Vocals: Jesse Rae

"The Thistle"

Backup Vocals: Knox Academy Girls Choir, The Thistles
Synth Bass: Bernie Worrell
Drums: Steve Ferrone
Keyboards: Bernie Worrell, Roger Troutman
Lead Guitar: Michael Hampton
Percussion: Lester Troutman
Vocals: Jesse Rae

"Be Yer Sel"

Backup Vocals: Jesse Rae, Roger Troutman, The Thistles
Bass Guitar, Keyboards, Key Bass, Guitar: Roger Troutman
Drums, Percussion: Lester Troutman
Vocals: Jesse Rae

"Rusha"

All Vocals: Jesse Rae
Bass, Keyboards, Guitar: Roger Troutman
Drums: Steve Ferrone
Keyboards: Bernie Worrell
Percussion: Lester Troutman

"Over the Sea"

Backup Vocals: Connie Harvey, Jocelyn Brown, Mary Davis
Drums: Steve Jordan
Keyboards: Bernie Worrell
Keyboards, Guitar: Roger Troutman
Snare (Pipeband Snare Drums): Calum Kilgour, Michael Hunter
Vocals: Jesse Rae

"Scotland the Brave/Idio-Syn-Crazy"

Vocals: Jesse Rae
Backup Vocals: Jesse Rage, The Thistles
Bagpipes: Graham Niven
Drums: James Lock
Keyboards, Synth Bass: Bernie Worrell
Guitar: Michael Hampton
Percussion: Lester Troutman
Snare (Pipeband Snare Drums): Craig Blakie

Echo Beach Label

Compression

"Tam O'Shanter"

"Brave Heart"

"Virtual 'U'"

"Body Blast'n"

"Wha's Like Us"

"Umhlaba Jikelele"

"Almost Ma Sel Again"

"Slip and Slide - Shelela"

"Deil's Awa Wi Excisemen"

"Testing the Skins"

"Global Africa"

"The Cotter's Saturday Night"

"Iphupho (A Dream)"

"A.E.S. - New York City - Man Was
"made Tae Mourn - Mama Africa"

Backup Vocals: Akabu, Om Alec Khaoli,
Bernie Worrell, Jesse Rae, Kristen Gray,
Oupa Segwai, Patricia Gumede, Skip
McDonald, Thelma Segonah
Instruments: Om Alec Khaoli, Bernie Worrell,
David Harrow, Doug Wimbish, Gregg Fitz,
Jesse Rae, Keith Leblanc, Michael Hampton,
Onnie McIntyre, Skip McDonald, Steve
Washington, Tim Shider

Luzuli Music

WORAE (Bernie Worrell & Jesse Rae)

"I Want to Contribute More"
Interviewee: Bernie Worrell

"Flight Attendant"
Drums: Steve Jordan
Guitar: Hiram Bullock
Keyboards: Bernie Worrell

"(It's Just) the Dog in Me"
(video soundtrack mix)
Backup Vocals: Connie Harvey, Jocelyn
Brown, Mary Davis
Drums: Steve Ferrone
Guitar: Jesse Rae, Jimmy Ripp
Synth Bass: Bernie Worrell

"Together in Spirit, Mind and Soul"
Interviewee: Bernie Worrell

"The Thistle" (funk invasion mix)
Backup Vocals: Knox Academy Girls Choir,
The Thistles
Synth Bass: Bernie Worrell
Drums: Steve Ferrone
Keyboards: Bernie Worrell, Roger Troutman
Lead Guitar: Michael Hampton
Percussion: Lester Troutman
Vocals: Jesse Rae

"(O' We) Wish Ye Merry Disco"
Bass: T. M. Stevens
Drums: Steve Jordan
Keyboards: Bernie Worrell

"Later for the Haggis Baby!"
Interviewee: Bernie Worrell

"Pork the Pig" (video soundtrack mix)
Bass: Anthony Jackson, Jesse Rae
Drums: Steve Jordan
Guitar: Jimmy Ripp
Keyboards: Bernie Worrell

"Keep the Funk Alive"
Interviewee: Bernie Worrell

"Party Crackers" (filler)
(video soundtrack mix)

Bass: Jesse Rae, T. M. Stevens
Drums: Steve Jordan
Guitar: Hiram Bullock
Keyboards: Bernie Worrell

"Teach-er" (room sound mix)

Drums: Steve Jordan
Guitar: Hiram Bullock
Synth, Synth Bass: Bernie Worrell

"Rusha" (emptied-out mix)

Bass: Jesse Rae
Drums: Steve Ferrone
Keyboards: Bernie Worrell

"Together We Will Conquer . . . Thee"

Interviewee: Bernie Worrell

"Over the Sea" (video soundtrack mix, instrumental)

Drums: Steve Jordan
Keyboards: Bernie Worrell
Keyboards, Guitar: Roger Troutman
Snare (Pipeband Snare Drums): Calum
  Kilgour, Michael Hunter

"Watching the Whole Thing"

Interviewee: Bernie Worrell

"Worae" (telephone mix)

Bass, Sampler : Jesse Rae
Drums: Steve Jordan
Guitar: Hiram Bullick
Horns: The Brecker Brothers
Synth, Synth Bass: Bernie Worrell

"The Passage of Time"

Interviewee: Bernie Worrell

"Den-tist-Me
(Woo Wi' Me)/Milkmaid Me"

Bass: Anthony Jackson
Drums: Steve Jordan
Guitar: Jesse Rae, Jimmy Rip
Keyboards: Bernie Worrell

"Straight Oot O' Knowhere" (Version 2)

Drum Machine: Jesse Rae
Guitar: Michael Hampton
Keyboards: Bernie Worrell

"Hearts O' Steel/Friend-Ship"

Guitar: Michael Hampton
Keyboards: Bernie Worrell

"Piobaireachd Worae"

Keyboards: Bernie Worrell

Global '95

"Wha's Like Us?"

"Virtual 'U'"

"Treble Negative"

"Brave Heart"

"Homo-phonic Line"

"Swithc Tae U"

"Auld Lang Syne"

"Slip and Slide (Shelela)"

"Time and It Makes Me"

"Tam O'Shanter"

"Almost Ma Sel Again"

"Umhlaba Jikelele"

"Body Blast'n"

"Man Was Made Tae Mourn
('Indoda Izalelwi Kuzila')"

"Global '95"

Backup Vocals: Akabu, Om Alec Khaoli, Oupa
Segwai, Patricia Gumede, Thelma Segonah
Bass: Doug Wimbush, Onnie McIntyre
Drums: Keith LeBlanc
Guitar: Skip McDonald, Onnie McIntyre
Keyboards: Bernie Worrell, Gregg Fitz
Vocals: Jesse Rae, Nigel Tranter
Snare: Alex Duthart

Funk Warrior—A Collection

"Switch Tae U"
"Pump It Up" (video soundtrack mix)
"Homophonic Line"
"(It's Just) the Dog in Me"
"Be Yourself" (video soundtrack mix)
"Skydiver"
"All Souls"
"Worae"
"Jacob's Pillow"
"Victory Horn"
"Pride"
"Politics"

Performers: Akabu, Anthony Jackson, Basil
Clarke, Bernie Worrell, Connie Harvey,
David Harrow, Doug Wimbish, Gregg Fitz,
Hiram Bullock, Jesse Rae, Jimmy Douglass,
Jimmy Ripp, Jocelyn Brown, Keith LeBlanc,
Kevin Goins, Mary Davis, Michael Hampton,
Nairobi Sailcat, Nick Michaels, Paul Beckett,
Rod Houison, Skip McDonald, Steve
Ferrone, Steve Jordan, T. M. Stevens, Talvin
Singh, Tinker Barfield, Tyrone Lampkin,
Warren McRae

NONA HENDRYX (SELECT TRACKS): 1987

The former "LaBelle" vocalist embarked on a successful solo career with songs and albums that feature some P-Funk members and many others.

EMI Records

"Baby Go-Go"
Vocals: Nona Hendryx, George Clinton, Mavis
Staples, Dan Hartman
Handclaps: Glen Ellison
Horns: Uptown Horns
Keyboards: Robby Kilgore, Dan Hartman
Percussion: Steve Scales

"Winds of Change (Mandela to Mandela)"
Vocals: Nona Hendryx, Peter Gabriel, Dan
Hartman
Programming: Nona Hendryx, Gary Pozner
Piano: Bernie Worrell
Keyboards: Peter Gabriel, Dan Hartman

SLY AND ROBBIE (SELECT TRACKS): 1987

The Jamaican godfathers of drum and bass and dub featured many P-Funkers on their works with producer Bill Laswell.

Island Records

"Fire"
Bass: Robbie Shakespeare
Drums, Percussion: Sly Dunbar
Strings etc.: Karl Berger
Vocals: Gary Mudbone Cooper, Bernard
Fowler, Shinehead, Bootsy Collins
Guitar: Bootsy Collins, Pat Thrall
Percussion: Aiyb Deng

"Boops (Here to Go)"

Bass: Robbie Shakespeare
Drums, Percussion: Sly Dunbar
Strings etc.: Karl Berger
Vocals: Shinehead
Guitar: Bootsy Collins, Pat Thrall
Percussion: Aiyb Deng
Turntable: D.S.T.
Sax, Flute: Henry Threadgill

"Let's Rock"

Bass: Robbie Shakespeare
Drums, Percussion: Sly Dunbar
Strings etc.: Karl Berger
Vocals: Gary Mudbone Cooper, Bernard
Fowler, Bootsy Collins
Guitar: Bootsy Collins, Pat Thrall, Nicky
Skopelitis
Percussion: Aiyb Deng
Piano: Bernie Worrell

"Yes We Can Can"

Bass: Robbie Shakespeare
Drums, Percussion: Sly Dunbar
Strings etc.: Karl Berger
Vocals: Gary Mudbone Cooper, Bernard
Fowler, Rammellzee
Guitar: Bootsy Collins, Pat Thrall, Nicky
Skopelitis
Percussion: Aiyb Deng, Daniel Ponce
Turntable: D.S.T.

"Rhythm Killer"

Vocals: Shinehead, Rammellzee, Gary
Mudbone Cooper, Bernard Fowler, Bootsy
Collins
Bass: Robbie Shakespeare
Drums, Percussion: Sly Dunbar
Strings etc.: Karl Berger
Guitar: Pat Thrall, Bootsy Collins
Fairlight: Nicky Skopelitis
Percussion: Aiyb Deng, Daniel Ponce
Sax, Flute: Henry Threadgill
Material: Keyboards

"Bank Job"

Lead Vocals: Rammellzee, Shinehead
Bass: Robbie Shakespeare
Drums, Percussion: Sly Dunbar
Strings etc.: Karl Berger
Backup Vocals: Gary Mudbone Cooper,
Bernard Fowler, Bootsy Collins
Guitar: Bootsy Collins, Pat Thrall, Nicky
Skopelitis
Percussion: Aiyb Deng, Daniel Ponce
Turntable: D.S.T.
Sax, Flute: Henry Threadgill
Material: Keyboards

— ☆ —

WARREN ZEVON (SELECT TRACKS): 1987

This pop-rock icon's album features George Clinton and members of PFAS.

Virgin Records

Sentimental Hygiene

"Leave My Monkey Alone"

Drums: Craig Krampf
Bass: Flea
Keyboards: Amp Fiddler
Guitar: Dewayne Blackbyrd McKnight
Computer: Warren Zevon
Vocals: Warren Zevon
Arrangement: George Clinton

— ☆ —

STEVIE SALAS (SELECT TRACKS): 1987

These make up rock guitarist Stevie Salas's relevant solo outings. Salas would play in several bands with Bootsy, Bernie Worrell, and others.

"Stand Up"

Synth Bass: Bernie Worrell
Guitar, Lead and Backup Vocals: Stevie Salas
Bass, Sitar, Backup Vocals: C. J. DeVillar
Computer Manipulation: James Faulkner
Backup Vocals: Gary Mudbone Cooper

"Blind"

Guitar, Lead and Backup Vocals: Stevie Salas
Bass, Sitar, Backup Vocals: C. J. DeVillar
Computer Manipulation: James Faulkner
Backup Vocals: Gary Mudbone Cooper

"Caught in the Middle of It"

Keyboards: Jeff Bova
Guitar, Lead and Backup Vocals: Stevie Salas
Bass, Sitar, Backup Vocals: C. J. DeVillar
Computer Manipulation: James Faulkner
Backup Vocals: Gary Mudbone Cooper

"Just Like That"

Keyboards: Jeff Bova
Guitar, Lead and Backup Vocals: Stevie Salas
Bass, Sitar, Backup Vocals: C. J. DeVillar
Computer Manipulation: James Faulkner
Backup Vocals: Gary Mudbone Cooper

"Two Bullets and a Gun"

Drums, Percussion, Backup Vocals: Winston A. Watson Jr.
Vocals: Bootsy Collins
Guitar, Lead and Backup Vocals: Stevie Salas
Bass, Sitar, Backup Vocals: C. J. DeVillar
Computer Manipulation: James Faulkner
Backup Vocals: Gary Mudbone Cooper

"The Harder They Come"

Keyboards: Jeff Bova
Guitar, Lead and Backup Vocals: Stevie Salas
Bass, Sitar, Backup Vocals: C. J. DeVillar
Computer Manipulation: James Faulkner
Backup Vocals: Gary Mudbone Cooper

"Over and Over Again"

Guitar, Lead and Backup Vocals: Stevie Salas
Bass, Sitar, Backup Vocals: C. J. DeVillar
Computer Manipulation: James Faulkner
Backup Vocals: Gary Mudbone Cooper

"Baby Walk On"

Synth Bass: Bernie Worrell
Guitar, Lead and Backup Vocals: Stevie Salas
Bass, Sitar, Backup Vocals: C. J. DeVillar
Computer Manipulation: James Faulkner
Backup Vocals: Gary Mudbone Cooper

"Indian Chief"

Keyboards: Jeff Bova
Guitar, Lead and Backup Vocals: Stevie Salas
Bass, Sitar, Backup Vocals: C. J. DeVillar
Computer Manipulation: James Faulkner
Backup Vocals: Gary Mudbone Cooper

"Cover Me"

Guitar, Lead and Backup Vocals: Stevie Salas
Bass, Sitar, Backup Vocals: C. J. DeVillar
Computer Manipulation: James Faulkner
Backup Vocals: Gary Mudbone Cooper

— ☆ —

WELL RED (SELECT TRACKS): 1988

The British band Well Red did some work briefly with George Clinton in the late 1980s.

"Get Lucky"

Lead Vocals: Lorenzo Hall
Backup Vocals: Helen Terry, Marquis Birtch, Paget Kind, Robbie Ellington, Tunga
Drum Programming: Richie Stevens
Production/Remix: George Clinton
Bass: Dave Clarke, Graham Edwards
Flute: Marquis Birch
Guitar: Sean Lyons, Tunga
Percussion: Jeff Scantlebury
Tenor Sax: Roger

OTIS DAY AND THE KNIGHTS (SELECT TRACKS) 1988

This is the famous "Shout" vocal group from the movie *National Lampoon's Animal House*. This one outing was produced by George Clinton and features several P-Funk All Stars.

MCA Records

Otis! My Man!

"Something Dumb"

Lead Vocals: Dewayne Jesse, George Clinton
Drum Programming: Trey Stone
Synthesizers: Trey Stone
Guitar: Dewayne Blackbyrd McKnight

"I Knock the Bottom Outta Mine"

Lead Vocals: Dewayne Jesse, George Clinton
Backup Vocals: George Clinton, Robert Peanut Johnson, Andre Williams, Lige Curry, Patty Walker, Steve Boyd
Drum Programming: Amp Fiddler
Bass: Lige Curry
Synthesizers: Amp Fiddler
Guitar: Dewayne Blackbyrd McKnight

"Ice Melting"

Lead Vocals: Dewayne Jesse
Backup Vocals: Pat Lewis, Sandra Feva, Jessica Cleaves
Drum Programming: Mark Davis?
Synthesizers: Bernie Worrell

"You and Your Folks"

Lead Vocals: Dewayne Jesse
Backup Vocals: George Clinton, Robert Peanut Johnson, Pat Lewis, Jessica Cleaves, Sandra Feva
Drums: Amp Fiddler
Keyboards, Synthesizers: Bernie Worrell

"Shout"

Lead Vocals: Dewayne Jesse
Backup Vocals: George Clinton, Robert Peanut Johnson, Pat Lewis, Jessica Cleaves, Sandra Feva
Drum Programming: Mark Davis?
Piano, Organ, Synth Bass: Bernie Worrell

"Function at the Junction"

Lead Vocals: Dewayne Jesse

Backup Vocals: George Clinton, Robert Peanut Johnson, Andre Foxxe Williams, Pat Lewis, Jessica Cleaves, Sandra Feva

Sax: Maceo Parker

Guitar: Dewayne Blackbyrd McKnight?, Andre Foxxe Williams?

Drum Programming: Mark Davis?

Piano, Synths: David Spradley

"I Wanna Testify"

Lead Vocals: Dewayne Jesse

Backup Vocals: George Clinton, Pat Lewis, Jessica Cleaves, Sandra Feva, Robert Peanut Johnson, Andre Foxxe Williams

Drum Programming: Mark Davis?

Guitar: Andre Foxxe Williams?

Organ, Synthesizers: Bernie Worrell

"Who's Making Love"

Lead Vocals: Dewayne Jesse

Backup Vocals: George Clinton, Andre Foxxe Williams, Robert Peanut Johnson, Pat Lewis, Sandra Feva, Jessica Cleaves

Drum Programming: Mark Davis?

Piano, Synthesizers: Mark Davis?

"Shamalamma Ding Dong"

Lead Vocals: Dewayne Jesse

Backup Vocals: Pat Lewis, Sandra Feva, Jessica Cleaves, George Clinton, Robert Peanut Johnson, Andre Foxxe Williams

Drum Programming: Mark Davis?

Guitar: Andre Foxxe Williams?

Synthesizers: Mark Davis?

— —

INCORPORATED THANG BAND: 1988

This is another George Clinton side group, featuring several important 1980s contributors to P-Funk. The group included bassist Lige Curry, guitarist Andre "Foxxe" Williams, drummer Dean Ragland, and others.

Rhino/Warner Bros.

Lifestyles of the Roach and Famous

"Body Jackin"

Lead Vocals: Jimmy Giles,

Backup Vocals: Andre Williams, Lige Curry, George Clinton, Dean Ragland, Claudia White, Angel Keener, Crystal Gaynor, Michael Clip Payne, Joe Harris, Pat Lewis, Sandra Feva,

Drums: Amp Fiddler

Synth Bass: Amp Fiddler

Synthesizers: Amp Fiddler

Guitar: Chris Bruce

"Storyteller"

Lead Vocals: Lige Curry

Backup Vocals: Andre Williams, Robert Peanut Johnson, Garry Shider, Pat Lewis

Drums: Steve Washington

Bass: Steve Washington

Synthesizers: Steve Washington

Guitar: Steve Washington

"Still Tight"

Lead Vocals: Tracey Lewis, Andre Williams

Backup Vocals: Garry Shider, Jessica Cleaves

Drum Programming: Tracey Lewis

Synth Bass: David Spradley

Synthesizers: Archie Ivy, David Spradley

"Androgynous View"

Lead Vocals: Andre Williams, Lige Curry, George Clinton, Garry Shider
Backup Vocals: Pat Lewis, Sandra Feva, Michael Clip Payne, Garry Shider, Lige Curry
Drums: Steve Washington
Bass: Steve Washington
Synthesizers: Steve Washington
Guitar: Steve Washington

"Jack of All Trades"

Lead Vocals: Lige Curry, Andre Williams, George Clinton
Backup Vocals: Garry Shider, Pat Lewis
Drums: Andre Williams
Bass: Lige Curry
Synthesizers: Andre Williams
Sax: Greg Thomas

"I'd Do Anything"

Lead Vocals: Robert Peanut Johnson
Backup Vocals: Robert Peanut Johnson, Pat Lewis
Drums: Robert Peanut Johnson
Synth Bass: Robert Peanut Johnson
Synthesizers: Robert Peanut Johnson
Guitar: Dewayne Blackbyrd McKnight

"What If the Girl Says Yes"

Lead Vocals: George Clinton, Andre Williams, Lige Curry, Garry Shider
Backup Vocals: Dean Ragland, Andre Williams, George Clinton, Garry Shider, Lige Curry
Drum Programming: Amp Fiddler
Synth Bass: Amp Fiddler
Synthesizers: Amp Fiddler
Guitar: Blackbyrd McKnight

"44-22-38"

Lead Vocals: Andre Williams, Jimmy Giles
Backup Vocals: Dean Ragland, Pat Lewis, George Clinton, Robert Peanut Johnson, Garry Shider, Lige Curry
Drums: Amp Fiddler
Bass: Amp Fiddler
Synthesizers: Amp Fiddler
Guitar: Dewayne Blackbyrd McKnight

— ☆ —

GEORGE CLINTON PRESENTS OUR GANG FUNKY: 1988

This is another late 1980s George Clinton production, featuring Mico Wave, Garry Shider, Bootsy, Jessica Cleaves, and others.

MCA Records

"Beautiful"

Lead Vocals: Garry Shider, Mico Wave
Backup Vocals: Andre Williams, Belita Woods, Pat Lewis, Joe Harris
Bass: Bootsy Collins
Drum Programming: Mark Davis?
Keyboards, Synthesizers: Amp Fiddler, David Spradley
Guitar: Garry Shider, Bootsy Collins?

"Nice"

Lead Vocals: Stefan Frank
Backup Vocals: Sandra Feva, Clip Payne, Tracey Lewis, George Clinton, Andre Williams, Robert Peanut Johnson
Drum Programming: David Spradley
Synth Bass: David Spradley
Synthesizers: David Spradley
Guitar: Chris Bruce

"Manopener"

Lead Vocals: Yosefa Bari, Phaedra Harris, Michelle Hill, Tracy Roberson, Linda Williams
Backup Vocals: Joe Harris, George Clinton, Robert Peanut Johnson
Drums: Trey Stone
Bass: Bootsy Collins
Synthesizers: David Spradley
Guitar: Bootsy Collins

"Hooray"

Lead Vocals: Jessica Cleaves
Backup Vocals: George Clinton, Pennye Ford, Michael Lane, Stefan Frank, Andre Williams
Drum Programming: David Spradley
Bass: David Spradley
Synthesizers: David Spradley, Amp Fiddler
Guitar: Chris Bruce, Jerome Ali?

"He Dance Funny"

Lead Vocals: Garry Shider, Tracey Lewis
Backup Vocals: Pat Lewis, Sandra Feva, Jessica Cleaves, Peanut Johnson, Joe Harris, Lloyd Williams, Clip Payne
Drums: Wes Boatman
Bass: Bootsy Collins
Synthesizers: Wes Boatman
Guitar: Bootsy Collins

"I Want Your Car"

Lead Vocals: Maxine Sands
Backup Vocals: Maxine Sands, Garry Shider?, George Clinton?
Drums: Mark Davis
Bass: Blackbyrd McKnight
Synthesizers: Mark Davis
Guitar: Blackbyrd McKnight

— ☆ —

JERRY HARRISON (SELECT TRACK): 1988

This Talking Heads contributor's solo album features P-Funk/Talking Heads keyboardist Bernie Worrrell.

Sire Records

Casual Gods

"A Perfect Lie"

Guitar, Keyboards, Vocals: Jerry Harrison
Synth Bass: Bernie Worrell
Guitar: Robbie McIntosh
Sax: Dickie Landry
Vocals: Arthur Russell, Joyce Bowden

— ☆ —

KEITH RICHARDS (SELECT TRACKS): 1988

The Rolling Stones' famous axman went for his own with his debut solo album, which featured Bernie Worrell, Bootsy Collins, and Maceo Parker.

Virgin Records

Talk Is Cheap

"Big Enough"

Guitar, Vocals, Percussion: Keith Richards
Bass: Bootsy Collins
Organ: Bernie Worrell
Sax: Maceo Parker
Drums, Percussion, Vocals: Steve Jordan
Backup Vocals: Sarah Dash

"Make No Mistake"

Guitar: Keith Richards
Organ: Bernie Worrell
Bass: Charley Drayton
Drums: Steve Jordan
Vocals: Sarah Dash
Horns: Andrew Love, Ben Cauley, Gray E.
Topper, Jack Hale, James Mitchell, Jimmy
Kinnard

"You Don't Move Me"

Guitars, Vocals: Keith Richards
Organ: Bernie Worrell
Slide Guitar: Waddy Wachtel
Drums, Percussion, Backup Vocals: Steve
Jordan
Bass, Backup Vocals: Charley Drayton
Accordion: Stanley "Buckwheat" Dural

"Rockawhile"

Guitars, Vocals: Keith Richards
Clavinet: Bernie Worrell
Accordion: Stanley "Buckwheat" Dural
Backup Vocals: Charley Drayton, Sam Butler,
Sarah Dash
Bass: Joey Spampinato
Drums, Backup Vocals: Steve Jordan
Guitar: Waddy Wachtel

ARTISTS STARTING
IN 1989-1999

MICO WAVE (SELECT TRACKS): 1989

This is multi-instrumentalist/vocalist Mico Wave's solo outing. Mico Wave did a lot of work during this period with Bootsy and other P-Funk members.

Columbia Records

"Star Search"

Vocals, Synth Bass, Synthesizers: Mico Wave
Drum Programming: Mico Wave, Bootsy Collins
Guitar: Catfish Collins, Ron Jennings
Piano: Bernie Worrell

"Misunderstood"

Vocals: Mico Wave, Vicky Vee
Drum Programming: Mico Wave, Bootsy Collins
Synth Bass, Synthesizers: Mico Wave
Harmonica: Peter Ruth

"First Impression"

Vocals: Mico Wave, Gary Mudbone Cooper, Vicky Vee
Drum Programming: Mico Wave, Bootsy Collins
Synth Bass, Synthesizers: Mico Wave
Guitar: Ron Jennings, Catfish Collins
Strings: Karl Berger

"It Happens Everytime"

Vocals: Mico Wave, Vicky Vee
Drum Programming: Mico Wave, Bootsy Collins
Synth Bass, Synthesizers: Wes Boatman

"Instant Replay"

Vocals: Mico Wave, Vicky Vee, Gary Mudbone Cooper
Drum Programming: Mico Wave, Bootsy Collins
Bass: Bootsy Collins
Synthesizers: Mico Wave
Sax: Maceo Parker

"Sleeping Single"

Vocals: Mico Wave, Vicky Vee
Drum Programming: Mico Wave, Bootsy Collins
Synth Bass: Mico Wave
Synthesizers: Mico Wave, Bootsy Collins
Guitar: Catfish Collins, Ron Jennings

"Can We Love Again"

Vocals: Mico Wave, Vicky Vee
Drum Programming: Mico Wave, Bootsy Collins
Bass: Bootsy Collins
Synthesizers: Mico Wave
Guitar: Mark Woerpel

"American Dream"

Vocals, Synth Bass, Synthesizers: Mico Wave
Drum Programming: Mico Wave, Bootsy Collins
Guitar: Mark Woerpel

"Kiss"

Vocals: Mico Wave, Gary Mudbone Cooper, Vicky Vee
Drum Programming: Mico Wave, Bootsy Collins
Bass: Bootsy Collins
Synthesizers: Mico Wave
Strings: Karl Berger
Piano: Bernie Worrell

— ☆ —

MENACE 1990

This features several P-Funk members, including Gary Mudbone Cooper.

"Doghouse"

Keyboards: Bernie Worrell
Bass, Guitars: Bootsy Collins
Vocals: Menace, Gary Mudbone Cooper
Sax: Maceo Parker
Drum Programming, Keyboards: Keith LeBlanc

— ☆ —

PRINCE (SELECT TRACKS): 1990

Although Prince is certainly the head of his own world of music, he often cited George Clinton as a key inspiration and influence and even signed Clinton in 1988 to his Paisley Park Record label. Much like Sly Stone's collaborations with Clinton, Prince and Clinton had a long partnership across many great funk songs in the 1980s–2000s.

Paisley Park Records

"We Can Funk"

Lead Vocals: George Clinton, Prince
Backup Vocals: Garry Shider, Steve Boyd, Clip Payne, Belita Woods, Amp Fiddler, Tracey Lewis, Mike Harris, Pat Lewis, Sandra Feva
Sax: Eric Leeds
Trumpet: Atlanta Bliss
Keyboards: Amp Fiddler
All Other Instruments: Prince

— ☆ —

MACEO PARKER: 1990–

This is James Brown and George Clinton's most famous sax man. Maceo Parker basically wrote the book on funk saxophone and was a key soloist in the JB's, Parliament, and Bootsy's Rubber Band, to name but a few. His work with P-Funk and his subsequent solo work is now legendary, the latter largely due to his incessant touring in the past several decades. His solo work includes a vast output of funk, jazz, blues, and soul music. His influential tenures under two of funk's biggest personalities have helped earn Parker himself a mastery of bandleading. Indeed, all of Parker's bands were extremely tight and concise over his long career.

4th Island Records

For All the King's Men

"Sax Machine"

Sax: Maceo Parker
Trombone: Fred Wesley
Drums: T-Bone
Keyboards: Bernie Worrell
Bass: Bootsy Collins, Bill Laswell
Guitar: Bootsy Collins
Vocals: Maceo Parker, Bobby Byrd, Bootsy Collins

"Let 'em Out"

Sax: Maceo Parker
Trombone: Fred Wesley
Drum Programming, Guitar, Bass: Bootsy Collins
Keyboards: Jeff Bova, Joel Johnson
Fairlight: Nicky Skopelitis
Vocals: Maceo Parker, Bobby Byrd, Joel Johnson, Bootsy Collins

"Tell the World"

Drums, Guitar, Bass: Bootsy Collins
Keyboards: Sly Stone
Vocals: Maceo Parker, Bobby Byrd, Sly Stone, Godmoma

Verve Records

Roots Revisited

"Them That Got"

Sax: Maceo Parker, Pee Wee Ellis, Vince Henry
Trombone: Fred Wesley
Drums: Bill Stewart
Keyboards: Don Pullen
Guitar: Rodney Jones

"Children's World"

Sax: Maceo Parker, Pee Wee Ellis
Trombone: Fred Wesley
Drums: Bill Stewart
Keyboards: Don Pullen
Guitar: Rodney Jones

"Better Get Hit in Yo' Soul"

Sax: Maceo Parker, Pee Wee Ellis
Trombone: Fred Wesley
Drums: Bill Stewart
Keyboards: Don Pullen
Guitar: Rodney Jones

"People Get Ready"

Sax: Maceo Parker, Pee Wee Ellis
Trombone: Fred Wesley
Drums: Bill Stewart
Keyboards: Don Pullen
Guitar: Rodney Jones

"Up and Down East Street"
Sax: Maceo Parker, Pee Wee Ellis
Trombone: Fred Wesley
Drums: Bill Stewart
Keyboards: Don Pullen
Guitar: Rodney Jones

"Over the Rainbow"
Sax: Maceo Parker, Pee Wee Ellis
Trombone: Fred Wesley
Drums: Bill Stewart
Keyboards: Don Pullen
Guitar: Rodney Jones

"Jumpin' the Blues"
Sax: Maceo Parker, Pee Wee Ellis
Trombone: Fred Wesley
Drums: Bill Stewart
Keyboards: Don Pullen
Guitar: Rodney Jones

"In Time"
Sax: Maceo Parker, Pee Wee Ellis
Trombone: Fred Wesley
Drums: Bill Stewart
Keyboards: Maceo Parker
Bass, Guitar: Bootsy Collins

Minor Music

Mo Roots

"Funky Christmas"
Sax: Pee Wee Ellis, Maceo Parker
Trombone: Fred Wesley
Drums: Bill Stewart
Keyboards: Larry Goldings
Guitar: Rodney Jones
Vocals: Fred Wesley, Pee Wee Ellis, Maceo Parker

"Hallelujah I Love Her So"
Sax: Maceo Parker, Pee Wee Ellis
Trombone: Fred Wesley
Drums: Bill Stewart
Keyboards: Larry Goldings
Guitar: Rodney Jones

"Chicken"
Sax: Maceo Parker, Pee Wee Ellis
Trombone: Fred Wesley
Drums: Bill Stewart
Keyboards: Larry Goldings
Guitar: Rodney Jones

"Let's Get It On"
Sax: Maceo Parker, Pee Wee Ellis
Trombone: Fred Wesley
Drums: Bill Stewart
Keyboards: Larry Goldings
Guitar: Rodney Jones

"Hamp's Boogie Woogie"
Sax: Maceo Parker, Pee Wee Ellis
Trombone: Fred Wesley
Drums: Bill Stewart
Keyboards: Larry Goldings
Guitar: Rodney Jones

"Fa Fa Fa (The Sad Song)"
Sax: Maceo Parker, Pee Wee Ellis
Trombone: Fred Wesley
Drums: Jimmy Madison
Keyboards: Larry Goldings
Guitar: Rodney Jones
Vocals: Maceo Parker, Kym Mazelle

"Jack's Back"
Sax: Maceo Parker, Steve Williamson, Pee Wee Ellis
Trombone: Fred Wesley
Drums: Bill Stewart
Keyboards: Larry Goldings
Guitar: Rodney Jones

"Sister Sadie"

Sax: Maceo Parker, Pee Wee Ellis
Trombone: Fred Wesley
Drums: Bill Stewart
Keyboards: Larry Goldings
Guitar: Rodney Jones

"Daddy's Home"

Sax: Maceo Parker, Pee Wee Ellis
Trombone: Fred Wesley
Drums: Bill Stewart
Keyboards: Larry Goldings
Guitar: Rodney Jones

"Down by the Riverside"

Sax: Maceo Parker, Pee Wee Ellis
Trombone: Fred Wesley
Drums: Bill Stewart
Keyboards: Larry Goldings
Guitar: Rodney Jones

"Southwick"

Sax: Maceo Parker, Pee Wee Ellis
Trombone: Fred Wesley
Drums: Bill Stewart
Keyboards: Larry Goldings
Guitar: Rodney Jones

Southern Exposure

"Blues for Shorty Bill"

Sax: Maceo Parker
Drums: Herman Ernest III
Bass: George Porter Jr.
Keyboards: Will Boulware
Guitar: Leo Nocentelli

"Keep On Marching"

Sax: Maceo Parker
Bass: George Porter Jr.
Drums: Herman Ernest III
Keyboards: Will Boulware
Guitar: Leo Nocentelli

"Mercy, Mercy, Mercy"

Sax: Maceo Parker, Roderick Paulin
Trombone: Reginald Steward, Stafford Agee
Trumpet: Derrick Shezbie, Kermit Ruffins
Tuba: Phillip Frazier
Bass Drum: Keith Frazier
Snare: Ajay Mallory

"Every Saturday Night"

Sax: Maceo Parker
Trombone: Fred Wesley
Keyboards: Will Boulware

"The Way You Look Tonight"

Sax: Maceo Parker
Trombone: Fred Wesley
Keyboards: Will Boulware
Guitar: Leo Nocentelli

"Splashin"

Sax: Maceo Parker
Drums: Herman Ernest III
Bass: George Porter Jr.
Keyboards: Will Boulware

"Walking Home Together"

Sax: Maceo Parker, Roderick Paulin
Trombone: Reginald Steward, Stafford Agee
Trumpet: Derrick Shezbie, Kermit Ruffins
Tuba: Phillip Frazier
Bass Drum: Keith Frazier
Snare: Ajay Mallory

"Sister Sanctified"

Sax: Maceo Parker
Drums: Herman Ernest III
Percussion: Michael Ward
Bass: George Porter Jr.
Keyboards: Will Boulware
Guitar: Leo Nocentelli

"Fun in the Sun"

Sax: Maceo Parker
Drums: Herman Ernest III
Bass: George Porter Jr.
Keyboards: Will Boulware
Guitar: Leo Nocentelli

ESC Records

Funk Overload

"Uptown Up"

Sax, Percussion: Maceo Parker
Trombone: Fred Wesley
Trumpet: Ron Tooley
Drums: Jamal Thomas
Vocals: Maceo Parker, Corey Parker
Backup Vocals: Diann Sorrell, Kara Dio
  Guardi, Sweet Charles Sherrell, Jerry Preston
Bass: Jerry Preston
Keyboards: Will Boulware
Guitar: Bruno Speight

"Sing a Simple Song"

Sax, Percussion, Vocals: Maceo Parker
Trombone: Fred Wesley
Trumpet: Ron Toole
Drums: Jamal Thomas
Backup Vocals: Diann Sorrell, Kara Dio
  Guardi, Sweet Charles Sherrell, Jerry Preston
Bass: Jerry Preston
Keyboards: Will Boulware
Guitar: Bruno Speight

"Maceo's Groove"

Sax, Percussion: Maceo Parker
Trombone: Fred Wesley
Trumpet: Ron Tooley
Drums: Jamal Thomas
Vocals: Maceo Parker, Corey Parker
Backup Vocals: Diann Sorrell, Kara Dio
  Guardi, Sweet Charles Sherrell, Jerry Preston

Bass: Jerry Preston
Keyboards: Will Boulware
Guitar: Bruno Speight

"Elephant's Foot"

Sax, Vocals: Maceo Parker
Trombone: Fred Wesley
Trumpet: Ron Tooley
Drums: Jamal Thomas
Percussion: Maceo Parker
Backup Vocals: Diann Sorrell, Kara Dio
  Guardi, Sweet Charles Sherrell, Jerry Preston
Bass: Jerry Preston
Keyboards: Will Boulware
Guitar: Bruno Speight

"Let's Get It On"

Sax: Maceo Parker
Trombone: Fred Wesley
Trumpet: Ron Tooley
Drums: Jamal Thomas
Percussion: Maceo Parker
Vocals: Maceo Parker, Corey Parker
Backup Vocals: Diann Sorrell, Kara Dio
  Guardi, Sweet Charles Sherrell, Jerry Preston
Bass: Jerry Preston
Keyboards: Will Boulware
Guitar: Bruno Speight

"Tell Me Something Good"

Sax, Percussion, Vocals: Maceo Parker
Trombone: Fred Wesley
Trumpet: Ron Tooley
Drums: Jamal Thomas
Backup Vocals: Diann Sorrell, Kara Dio
  Guardi, Sweet Charles Sherrell, Jerry Preston
Bass: Jerry Preston
Keyboards: Will Boulware
Guitar: Steve Conte

"Youth of the World"

Sax: Maceo Parker
Trombone: Fred Wesley
Trumpet: Ron Tooley
Drums: Jamal Thomas
Percussion: Maceo Parker
Vocals: Maceo Parker
Backup Vocals: Diann Sorrell, Kara Dio Guardi, Sweet Charles Sherrell, Jerry Preston
Bass: Jerry Preston
Keyboards: Will Boulware
Guitar: Bruno Speight

"We're on the Move"

Sax, Percussion, Vocals: Maceo Parker
Trombone: Fred Wesley
Trumpet: Ron Tooley
Drums: Jamal Thomas
Backup Vocals: Diann Sorrell, Kara Dio Guardi, Sweet Charles Sherrell, Jerry Preston
Bass: Jerry Preston
Keyboards: Will Boulware
Guitar: Bruno Speight

"Inner City Blues"

Sax, Percussion, Vocals: Maceo Parker
Trombone: Fred Wesley
Trumpet: Ron Tooley
Drums: Jamal Thomas
Backup Vocals: Diann Sorrell, Kara Dio Guardi, Sweet Charles Sherrell, Jerry Preston
Bass: Jerry Preston
Keyboards: Will Boulware
Guitar: Bruno Speight

"Do You Love Me"

Sax, Percussion, Vocals: Maceo Parker
Trombone: Fred Wesley
Trumpet: Ron Tooley
Drums: Jamal Thomas
Backup Vocals: Diann Sorrell, Kara Dio Guardi, Sweet Charles Sherrell, Jerry Preston
Bass: Jerry Preston

Keyboards: Will Boulware
Guitar: Bruno Speight

"Going in Circles"

Sax, Percussion, Vocals: Maceo Parker
Trombone: Fred Wesley
Trumpet: Ron Tooley
Drums: Jamal Thomas
Backup Vocals: Diann Sorrell, Kara Dio Guardi, Sweet Charles Sherrell, Jerry Preston
Bass: Jerry Preston
Keyboards: Will Boulware
Guitar: Bruno Speight

What Are Records?

Dial M.A.C.E.O.

"Rabbits in the Pea Patch"

Sax: Maceo Parker
Bass: Rodney Curtis
Drums: Jamal Thomas
Keyboards: Will Boulware
Guitar: Bruno Speight
Vocals: Maceo Parker, Corey Parker, Charles Sherrell, Diann Sorrell, Audrey Martells

"My Baby Loves You"

Sax: Maceo Parker, Vincent Henry
Trumpet: Ron Tooley
Trombone: Greg Boyer
Bass: Rodney Curtis
Drums: Jamal Thomas
Keyboards: Will Boulware
Guitar: Bruno Speight
Vocals: Maceo Parker, James Taylor
Percussion: Kevin Hupp

"The Greatest Romance Ever Sold"

Sax, Flute: Maceo Parker
All Other Instruments: Prince

"Black Widow"

Flute: Maceo Parker
Vocals: Corey Parker, Diann Sorrell, Audrey Martells
Guitar: Bruno Speight
Keyboards: Will Boulware
Bass: Rodney Curtis
Drums, Percussion: Kevin Hupp

"I've Got Work to Do"

Sax: Maceo Parker
Trumpet: Ron Tooley
Trombone: Greg Boyer
Bass: Rodney Curtis
Drums, Percussion: Kevin Hupp
Keyboards: Will Boulware
Guitar: Bruno Speight
Vocals: Corey Parker, Diann Sorrell, Audrey Martells

"Coin Toss"

Vocals: Ani DiFranco, Maceo Parker
Guitar: Ani DiFranco, Bruno Speight
Sax: Maceo Parker, Vincent Henry
Trumpet: Ron Tooley
Trombone: Greg Boyer
Keyboards: Will Boulware
Bass: Rodney Curtis
Drums: Jamal Thomas

"Simply Tooley"

Sax, Flute: Maceo Parker
Trombone: Greg Boyer
Trumpet: Ron Tooley
Drums: Jamal Thomas
Keyboards: Will Boulware
Guitar: Bruno Speight
Vocals: Maceo Parker

"Latin Like"

Sax: Maceo Parker
Percussion: Maceo Parker, Kevin Hupp
Trombone: Greg Boyer
Trumpet: Ron Tooley
Drums: Jamal Thomas
Keyboards: Will Boulware
Guitar: Bruno Speight
Vocals: Maceo Parker

"The Closer I Get to You"

Sax: Maceo Parker, Vincent Henry
Trombone: Greg Boyer
Trumpet: Bennie Cowan, Ron Tooley
Flugelhorn: Ron Tooley
Drums: Jamal Thomas
Keyboards: Will Boulware
Guitar: Bruno Speight
Bass: Rodney Curtis
Vocals: Diann Sorrell, Audrey Martells

"My Love"

Sax, Flute, Vocals: Maceo Parker
Drums: Kevin Hupp
Keyboards: Will Boulware
Guitar: Bruno Speight
Bass: Rodney Curtis

"Homeboy"

Sax: Maceo Parker
Trombone: Greg Boyer
Trumpet: Ron Tooley
Drums: Jamal Thomas
Keyboards: Will Boulware
Bass: Rodney Curtis
Guitar: Bruno Speight
Percussion: Kevin Hupp

Made by Maceo

"Come By and See"

Sax: Maceo Parker, Candy Dulfer, Vincent Henry
Trombone: Greg Boyer
Trumpet: Ron Tooley
Drums: James Son Thomas
Bass: Rodney Curtis
Keyboards: Will Boulware
Guitar: Bruno Speight
Vocals: Maceo Parker, Corey Parker, Cynthia Johnson, Giorge Pettus, Carrie Harrington

"Off the Hook"

Sax: Maceo Parker, Candy Dulfer, Vincent Henry
Trombone: Greg Boyer
Trumpet: Ron Tooley
Drums: James Son Thomas
Bass: Rodney Curtis
Keyboards: Will Boulware
Guitar: Bruno Speight
Vocals: Maceo Parker, Corey Parker, Cynthia Johnson, Giorge Pettus, Carrie Harrington

"Hats Off to Harry"

Sax: Maceo Parker, Candy Dulfer, Vincent Henry
Trombone: Greg Boyer
Trumpet: Ron Tooley
Drums: James Son Thomas
Bass: Rodney Curtis
Keyboards: Will Boulware
Guitar: Bruno Speight
Vocals: Maceo Parker, Corey Parker, Cynthia Johnson, Giorge Pettus, Carrie Harrington

"Quick Step"

Sax: Maceo Parker, Candy Dulfer, Vincent Henry
Trombone: Greg Boyer
Trumpet: Ron Tooley

Drums: James Son Thomas
Bass: Rodney Skeet Curtis
Keyboards: Will Boulware
Guitar: Bruno Speight
Vocals: Maceo Parker, Corey Parker, Cynthia Johnson, Giorge Pettus, Carrie Harrington

"Those Girls"

Sax: Maceo Parker, Candy Dulfer, Vincent Henry
Trombone: Greg Boyer
Trumpet: Ron Tooley
Drums: James Son Thomas
Bass: Rodney Skeet Curtis
Keyboards: Will Boulware
Guitar: Bruno Speight
Vocals: Maceo Parker, Corey Parker, Cynthia Johnson, Giorge Pettus, Carrie Harrington

"Moonlight in Vermont"

Sax: Maceo Parker, Candy Dulfer, Vincent Henry
Trombone: Greg Boyer
Trumpet: Ron Tooley
Drums: James Son Thomas
Bass: Rodney Skeet Curtis
Keyboards: Will Boulware
Guitar: Bruno Speight
Vocals: Maceo Parker, Corey Parker, Cynthia Johnson, Giorge Pettus, Carrie Harrington

"Lady Luck"

Sax: Maceo Parker, Candy Dulfer, Vincent Henry
Trombone: Greg Boyer
Trumpet: Ron Tooley
Drums: James Son Thomas
Bass: Rodney Skeet Curtis
Keyboards: Will Boulware
Guitar: Bruno Speight
Vocals: Maceo Parker, Corey Parker, Cynthia Johnson, Giorge Pettus, Carrie Harrington

"Don't Say Goodnight"

Sax: Maceo Parker, Candy Dulfer, Vincent Henry
Trombone: Greg Boyer
Trumpet: Ron Tooley
Drums: James Son Thomas
Bass: Rodney Skeet Curtis
Keyboards: Will Boulware
Guitar: Bruno Speight
Vocals: Maceo Parker, Corey Parker, Cynthia Johnson, Giorge Pettus, Carrie Harrington

"Once You Get Started"

Sax: Maceo Parker, Candy Dulfer, Vincent Henry
Trombone: Greg Boyer
Trumpet: Ron Tooley
Drums: James Son Thomas
Bass: Rodney Skeet Curtis
Keyboards: Will Boulware
Guitar: Bruno Speight
Vocals: Maceo Parker, Corey Parker, Cynthia Johnson, Giorge Pettus, Carrie Harrington

"To Be or Not to Be"

Sax: Maceo Parker, Peter Weniger
Trombone: Greg Boyer
Trumpet: Ron Tooley
Vocals: Maceo Parker, Corey Parker, Cynthia Johnson, Kip Blackshire, Sadie Hayes
Bass: Rodney Curtis
Drums: Jamal Thomas
Guitar: Bruno Speight
Keyboards: Morris Hayes

BHM Productions

School's In

"Basic Funk: 101"

Sax: Maceo Parker, Peter Weniger
Trombone: Greg Boyer
Trumpet: Ron Tooley
Vocals: Maceo Parker, Corey Parker
Bass: Rodney Curtis
Drums: Jamal Thomas
Guitar: Bruno Speight
Keyboards: Morris Hayes

"What You Know about Funk?"

Sax: Maceo Parker, Peter Weniger
Trombone: Greg Boyer
Trumpet: Ron Tooley
Vocals: Maceo Parker, Corey Parker, Martha High
Bass: Rodney Curtis
Drums: Jamal Thomas
Guitar: Bruno Speight
Keyboards: Morris Hayes

"ABC"

Sax: Maceo Parker, Peter Weniger
Trombone: Greg Boyer
Trumpet: Ron Tooley
Vocals: Maceo Parker, Corey Parker, Cynthia Johnson, Kip Blackshire, Sadie Hayes
Bass: Rodney Curtis
Drums: Jamal Thomas
Guitar: Bruno Speight
Keyboards: Morris Hayes

"Song for My Teacher"

Sax: Maceo Parker, Peter Weniger
Trombone: Greg Boyer
Trumpet: Ron Tooley
Vocals: Maceo Parker, Corey Parker
Bass: Rodney Curtis
Drums: Jamal Thomas
Guitar: Bruno Speight
Keyboards: Morris Hayes

"Speed Reading (It-si-bi-ya)"

Sax: Maceo Parker, Peter Weniger
Trombone: Greg Boyer
Trumpet: Ron Tooley
Vocals: Maceo Parker, Corey Parker
Bass: Rodney Curtis
Drums: Jamal Thomas
Guitar: Bruno Speight
Keyboards: Morris Hayes

"What a Wonderful World"

Sax: Maceo Parker, Peter Weniger, Candy
  Dulfer
Trombone: Greg Boyer
Trumpet: Ron Tooley
Vocals: Maceo Parker, Corey Parker, Candy
  Dulfer, Kip Blackshire
Bass: Rodney Curtis
Drums: Jamal Thomas
Guitar: Bruno Speight
Keyboards: Morris Hayes

"Arts & Crafts"

Sax: Maceo Parker, Peter Weniger
Trombone: Greg Boyer
Trumpet: Ron Tooley
Vocals: Maceo Parker, Corey Parker
Bass: Rodney Curtis
Drums: Jamal Thomas
Guitar: Bruno Speight
Keyboards: Morris Hayes

"Advanced Funk"

Sax: Maceo Parker, Peter Weniger
Trombone: Greg Boyer
Trumpet: Ron Tooley
Vocals: Maceo Parker, Corey Parker
Bass: Rodney Curtis
Drums: Jamal Thomas
Guitar: Bruno Speight
Keyboards: Morris Hayes

"I'm Gonna Teach You"

Sax: Maceo Parker, Peter Weniger
Trombone: Greg Boyer
Trumpet: Ron Tooley
Vocals: Maceo Parker, Corey Parker, Cynthia
  Johnson, Kip Blackshire
Bass: Rodney Curtis
Drums: Jamal Thomas
Guitar: Bruno Speight
Keyboards: Morris Hayes

"Who's Making Love"

Sax: Maceo Parker
Vocals: Maceo Parker
Guitar: Paul Shigihara
Orchestra: WDR Big Band Cologne,
  conducted by Michael Abene

Leopard Label

It's All about Love

"I'm in Love"

Sax: Maceo Parker
Trombone: Andy Hunter
Orchestra: WDR Big Band Cologne,
  conducted by Michael Abene

"Gonna Put Your Lovin' in the Lay Away"

Sax: Maceo Parker, Paul Heller
Drums: Cora Coleman Dunham
Keyboards: Frank Chastenier
Vocals: Maceo Parker
Orchestra: WDR Big Band Cologne,
conducted by Michael Abene

"Love the One You're With"

Sax, Vocals: Maceo Parker
Keyboards: Frank Chastenier
Orchestra: WDR Big Band Cologne,
conducted by Michael Abene

"Love Won't Let Me Wait"

Trumpet: Andy Haderer
Vocals: Maceo Parker
Orchestra: WDR Big Band Cologne,
conducted by Michael Abene

"Isn't She Lovely"

Sax: Karolina Strassmayer, Maceo Parker
Orchestra: WDR Big Band Cologne,
conducted by Michael Abene

"I Love You a Bushel and a Peck"

Trombone: Shannon Barnett
Trumpet: Rud Breuls
Vocals: Maceo Parker
Orchestra: WDR Big Band Cologne,
conducted by Michael Abene

Intuition Records

Roots and Grooves

"Hallelujah I Love Her So"

Sax: Maceo Parker, Heiner, Wiberny, Karolina
Strassmayer, Macus Barthelt, Olivier Peters,
Paul Heller
Vocals: Maceo Parker
Acoustic Bass: John Goldsby
Drums: Hans Dekker

Guitar: Paul Shigihara
Trombone: Bernt Laukamp, Dave Horler,
Ludwig Nuss, Mattis Cederberg
Trumpet: Andy Haderer, John Marshall, Klaus
Osterloh, Rob Bruynen, Wim Both

"Busted"

Sax: Maceo Parker, Heiner, Wiberny, Karolina
Strassmayer, Macus Barthelt, Olivier Peters,
Paul Heller
Vocals: Maceo Parker
Acoustic Bass: John Goldsby
Drums: Hans Dekker
Guitar: Paul Shigihara
Trombone: Bernt Laukamp, Dave Horler,
Ludwig Nuss, Mattis Cederberg
Trumpet: Andy Haderer, John Marshall, Klaus
Osterloh, Rob Bruynen, Wim Both

"Them That's Got"

Sax: Maceo Parker, Heiner, Wiberny, Karolina
Strassmayer, Macus Barthelt, Olivier Peters,
Paul Heller
Vocals: Maceo Parker
Acoustic Bass: John Goldsby
Drums: Hans Dekker
Guitar: Paul Shigihara
Trombone: Bernt Laukamp, Dave Horler,
Ludwig Nuss, Mattis Cederberg
Trumpet: Andy Haderer, John Marshall, Klaus
Osterloh, Rob Bruynen, Wim Both

"You Don't Know Me"

Sax: Maceo Parker, Heiner, Wiberny, Karolina
Strassmayer, Macus Barthelt, Olivier Peters,
Paul Heller
Vocals: Maceo Parker
Acoustic Bass: John Goldsby
Drums: Hans Dekker
Guitar: Paul Shigihara
Trombone: Bernt Laukamp, Dave Horler,
Ludwig Nuss, Mattis Cederberg
Trumpet: Andy Haderer, John Marshall, Klaus
Osterloh, Rob Bruynen, Wim Both

"Hit the Road Jack"

Sax: Maceo Parker, Heiner, Wiberny, Karolina Strassmayer, Macus Barthelt, Olivier Peters, Paul Heller
Vocals: Maceo Parker
Acoustic Bass: John Goldsby
Drums: Hans Dekker
Guitar: Paul Shigihara
Trombone: Bernt Laukamp, Dave Horler, Ludwig Nuss, Mattis Cederberg
Trumpet: Andy Haderer, John Marshall, Klaus Osterloh, Rob Bruynen, Wim Both

"Margie"

Sax: Maceo Parker, Heiner, Wiberny, Karolina Strassmayer, Macus Barthelt, Olivier Peters, Paul Heller
Vocals: Maceo Parker
Acoustic Bass: John Goldsby
Drums: Hans Dekker
Guitar: Paul Shigihara
Trombone: Bernt Laukamp, Dave Horler, Ludwig Nuss, Mattis Cederberg
Trumpet: Andy Haderer, John Marshall, Klaus Osterloh, Rob Bruynen, Wim Both

"Georgia on My Mind"

Sax: Maceo Parker, Heiner, Wiberny, Karolina Strassmayer, Macus Barthelt, Olivier Peters, Paul Heller
Vocals: Maceo Parker
Acoustic Bass: John Goldsby
Drums: Hans Dekker
Guitar: Paul Shigihara
Trombone: Bernt Laukamp, Dave Horler, Ludwig Nuss, Mattis Cederberg
Trumpet: Andy Haderer, John Marshall, Klaus Osterloh, Rob Bruynen, Wim Both

"What I'd Say"

Sax: Maceo Parker, Heiner, Wiberny, Karolina Strassmayer, Macus Barthelt, Olivier Peters, Paul Heller
Vocals: Maceo Parker
Acoustic Bass: John Goldsby
Drums: Hans Dekker
Guitar: Paul Shigihara
Trombone: Bernt Laukamp, Dave Horler, Ludwig Nuss, Mattis Cederberg
Trumpet: Andy Haderer, John Marshall, Klaus Osterloh, Rob Bruynen, Wim Both

"Uptown Up"

Sax: Maceo Parker, Heiner, Wiberny, Karolina Strassmayer, Macus Barthelt, Olivier Peters, Paul Heller
Vocals: Maceo Parker
Bass: Rodney Curtis
Drums: Dennis Chambers
Guitar: Paul Shigihara
Trombone: Bernt Laukamp, Dave Horler, Ludwig Nuss, Mattis Cederberg
Trumpet: Andy Haderer, John Marshall, Klaus Osterloh, Rob Bruynen, Wim Both

"To Be or Not to Be"

Sax: Maceo Parker, Heiner, Wiberny, Karolina Strassmayer, Macus Barthelt, Olivier Peters, Paul Heller
Vocals: Maceo Parker
Bass: Rodney Curtis
Drums: Dennis Chambers
Guitar: Paul Shigihara
Trombone: Bernt Laukamp, Dave Horler, Ludwig Nuss, Mattis Cederberg
Trumpet: Andy Haderer, John Marshall, Klaus Osterloh, Rob Bruynen, Wim Both

"Off the Hook"

Sax: Maceo Parker, Heiner, Wiberny, Karolina Strassmayer, Macus Barthelt, Olivier Peters, Paul Heller
Vocals: Maceo Parker
Bass: Rodney Skeet Curtis
Drums: Dennis Chambers
Guitar: Paul Shigihara
Trombone: Bernt Laukamp, Dave Horler, Ludwig Nuss, Mattis Cederberg
Trumpet: Andy Haderer, John Marshall, Klaus Osterloh, Rob Bruynen, Wim Both

"Advanced Funk"

Sax: Maceo Parker, Heiner, Wiberny, Karolina Strassmayer, Macus Barthelt, Olivier Peters, Paul Heller
Vocals: Maceo Parker
Bass: Rodney Skeet Curtis
Drums: Dennis Chambers
Guitar: Paul Shigihara
Trombone: Bernt Laukamp, Dave Horler, Ludwig Nuss, Mattis Cederberg
Trumpet: Andy Haderer, John Marshall, Klaus Osterloh, Rob Bruynen, Wim Both

"Shake Everything You Got"

Sax: Maceo Parker, Heiner, Wiberny, Karolina Strassmayer, Macus Barthelt, Olivier Peters, Paul Heller
Vocals: Maceo Parker
Bass: Rodney Skeet Curtis
Drums: Dennis Chambers
Guitar: Paul Shigihara
Trombone: Bernt Laukamp, Dave Horler, Ludwig Nuss, Mattis Cederberg
Trumpet: Andy Haderer, John Marshall, Klaus Osterloh, Rob Bruynen, Wim Both

"Pass the Peas"

Sax: Maceo Parker, Heiner, Wiberny, Karolina Strassmayer, Macus Barthelt, Olivier Peters, Paul Heller
Vocals: Maceo Parker
Bass: Rodney Skeet Curtis
Drums: Dennis Chambers
Guitar: Paul Shigihara
Trombone: Bernt Laukamp, Dave Horler, Ludwig Nuss, Mattis Cederberg
Trumpet: Andy Haderer, John Marshall, Klaus Osterloh, Rob Bruynen, Wim Both

— ☆ —

HARRIET ROBERTS (SELECT TRACK): 1990

This British soul singer was produced by George Clinton and features some P-Funk All Stars members.

WEA EastWest Label

"Only the Lonely"

Vocals: Harriet Roberts
Vocal Rap: Tracey Lewis
Bass: Paul Snook
Guitar: Paul Gendler
Keyboards: Dave Klevatt
Additional Vocals: Mark Stent
Sax: Gary Plumbley
Trumpet: Laurence Parry
Producer: George Clinton
Guitar: Dewayne Blackbyrd McKnight

— ☆ —

DENNIS CHAMBERS: 1990, 2004

Chambers was a fusion Drummer for P-Funk in 1979–1981, 1982–1984, and 1986 and was also a drummer for the Brides of Funkenstein. He has since become synonymous in drummer circles as a master of the instrument, garnering international attention with his playing and endorsements. Much like the Brecker Brothers, Chambers's full discography, though it fits within the criteria of canon, would be too much to fit within this volume. But it is important to note his involvement with jazz and rock acts such as Santana, John Scofield, John McLaughlin, Mike Stern, Victor Wooten, Niacin, Steely Dan, Billy Sheehan, and many more.

Pioneer Records

Getting Even

"Fortune Dance"

Drums: Dennis Chambers
Guitar: Jimi Tunnell
Bass: Gary Grainger
Percussion: Victor Williams
Sax: Bob Berg
Synthesizer: Jim Beard

"The Opener"

Drums: Dennis Chambers
Guitar: Jimi Tunnell
Bass: Gary Grainger
Percussion: Victor Williams
Sax: Bob Berg
Synthesizer: Jim Beard

"Keep Walking"

Drums: Dennis Chambers
Guitar: John Scofield
Bass: Anthony Jackson
Percussion: Victor Williams
Sax: Bob Berg
Synthesizer: Jim Beard

"Red Eyes"

Drums: Dennis Chambers
Guitar: John Scofield
Bass: Anthony Jackson
Percussion: Victor Williams
Sax: Bob Berg
Synthesizer: Jim Beard

"Getting Even"

Drums: Dennis Chambers
Guitar: John Scofield
Bass: Anthony Jackson
Percussion: Victor Williams
Synthesizer: Jim Beard

"Widow's Peak"

Drums: Dennis Chambers
Guitar: Jimi Tunnell
Bass: Gary Grainger
Sax: Bob Berg
Synthesizer: Jim Beard

"Boo"

Drums: Dennis Chambers
Guitar: Jimi Tunnell
Bass: Gary Grainger
Percussion: Victor Williams
Sax: Bob Berg
Synthesizer: Jim Beard

"Until We Return"

Drums: Dennis Chambers
Guitar: John Scofield
Bass: Anthony Jackson
Percussion: Victor Williams
Sax: Bob Berg
Synthesizer: Jim Beard

Planet Earth

"Planet Earth"

Drums: Dennis Chambers
Guitar: Dean Brown
Keyboards: Jim Beard
Bass: Will Lee
Tenor Sax: Bob Malach

"Dance Music for Borneo Horns #13"

Drums: Dennis Chambers
Alto Sax: Stan Harrison
Tenor Sax: Lenny Pickett
Baritone Sax: Steve Elson
Horns: The Borneo Horns

"Amos Ignored"

Drums: Dennis Chambers
Guitar: Dean Brown
Keyboards: Jim Beard
Bass: Will Lee
Alto Sax: Kenny Garrett
Tenor Sax: Bob Malach
Trumpet: Jim Hynes
Trombone: Mike Davis

"Elroy"

Drums: Dennis Chambers
Guitar: Adam Rogers
Keyboards: Jim Beard
Bass: Anthony Jackson

"El Is the Sound of Joy"

Drums: Dennis Chambers
Guitar: Dean Brown
Keyboards: Jim Beard
Bass: Will Lee
Flute, Alto Sax, Bass Sax, Tenor Sax: Bob
   Malach
Trumpet: Jim Hynes
Trombone: Mike Davis

"Camel Hump"

Drums: Dennis Chambers
Guitar: Dean Brown
Keyboards: Jim Beard
Bass: Will Lee
Saxes: Bob Malach

"Dance Music for Borneo Horns #6"

Drums: Dennis Chambers
Alto Sax: Stan Harrison
Tenor Sax: Lenny Pickett
Baritone Sax: Steve Elson
Horns: The Borneo Horns

"Overtones of China"

Drums: Dennis Chambers
Guitar: Dean Brown
Keyboards: Jim Beard
Bass: Will Lee
Alto Sax: Kenny Garrett
Flute, Tenor, and Bass Saxes: Bob Malach

"Giphini's Song"

Drums: Dennis Chambers
Acoustic Guitar: Dean Brown
Keyboards: Jim Beard
Bass: Will Lee

"Ant"

Drums: Dennis Chambers
Guitar: Adam Rogers
Keyboards: Jim Beard
Bass: Anthony Jackson

"Loose Bloose"

Drums: Dennis Chambers
Guitar: Adam Rogers
Sax: Kenny Garrett
Bass: Anthony Jackson

"Dance Music for Borneo Horns #4"

Drums: Dennis Chambers
Alto Sax: Stan Harrison
Tenor Sax: Lenny Pickett
Baritone Sax: Steve Elson
Horns: The Borneo Horns

— ☆ —

STANLEY CLARKE AND GEORGE DUKE (SELECT TRACK): 1990

Jazz-fusion bassist Clarke and keyboardist Duke, after famous tenures with Chick Corea and Frank Zappa, respectively, as well as solo careers, began collaborating. The Clarke/Duke project began long before the date listed above. However, for the sake of this book, Clarke/Duke's cover of "Mothership Connection," replete with drums by Dennis Chambers, had to be included.

Epic Records

3

"Mothership Connection (Star Child)"

Keyboards: George Duke
Bass: Stanley Clarke
Alto Sax: Brandon Fields
Trumpet: Jerry Hey
Tenor Sax: Kirk Whalum
Trombone: George Bohanon
Drums: Dennis Chambers
Vocals: Carl Carwell, Darrell Cox, George Duke, Stanley Clarke, Ndugu Chancler, Phil Perry, Phillip Bailey

— ☆ —

DEEE-LITE: 1990–1992

This famous 1990s dance music group featured heavy involvement from Bootsy Collins, Maceo Parker, Fred Wesley, Bernie Worrell, Michael Hampton, and others.

Elektra Records

World Clique

"Deee-Lite Theme"

Lead and Backup Vocals: Lady Miss Kier
DJ, Keyboards, Drum Programming: DJ Dmitry
DJ, Keyboards, Drum Programming: DJ Towa

"Good Beat"

Lead and Backup Vocals: Lady Miss Kier
DJ, Keyboards, Drum Programming: DJ Dmitry
DJ, Keyboards, Drum Programming: DJ Towa Towa

"Power of Love"

Lead and Backup Vocals: Lady Miss Kier
DJ, Keyboards, Drum Programming: DJ Dmitry
DJ, Keyboards, Drum Programming: DJ Towa Towa

"Try Me On . . . I'm Very You"

Lead and Backup Vocals: Lady Miss Kier
DJ, Keyboards, Drum Programming: DJ Dmitry
DJ, Keyboards, Drum Programming: DJ Towa Towa
Guitar: Bootsy Collins
Trombone: Fred Wesley
Sax: Maceo Parker

"Smile On"

Lead and Backup Vocals: Lady Miss Kier
DJ, Keyboards, Drum Programming: DJ
    Dmitry
DJ, Keyboards, Drum Programming: DJ
    Towa Towa
Guitar: Bootsy Collins
Trombone: Fred Wesley
Sax: Maceo Parker

"What Is Love?"

Lead and Backup Vocals: Lady Miss Kier
DJ, Keyboards, Drum Programming: DJ
    Dmitry
DJ, Keyboards, Drum Programming: DJ
    Towa Towa

"World Clique"

Lead Vocals: Lady Miss Kier
DJ, Keyboards, Drum Programming: DJ
    Dmitry
DJ, Keyboards, Drum Programming: DJ
    Towa Towa
Backup Vocals: Sahira, Sheila Slappy

"E.S.P."

Lead and Backup Vocals: Lady Miss Kier
DJ, Keyboards, Drum Programming: DJ
    Dmitry
DJ, Keyboards, Drum Programming: DJ
    Towa Towa

"Groove Is in the Heart"

Lead and Backup Vocals: Lady Miss Kier
DJ, Keyboards, Drum Programming: DJ
    Dmitry
DJ, Keyboards, Drum Programming: DJ
    Towa Towa
Backup Vocals: Bootsy Collins
Rap: Q-Tip
Trombone: Fred Wesley
Sax: Maceo Parker

"Groove Is in the Heart" was a massive success. It features the heavy presence of P-Funk players, making it easily fit into the P-Funk canon as the same way Johnnie Taylor's "Disco Lady" is. The music video featured Bootsy Collins, and several P-Funkers would go on tour with the group following the success of the song and music video.

"Who Was That?"

Lead and Backup Vocals: Lady Miss Kier
DJ, Keyboards, Drum Programming: DJ
    Dmitry
DJ, Keyboards, Drum Programming: DJ
    Towa Towa
Bass: Bootsy Collins

"Deep Ending"

Lead and Backup Vocals: Lady Miss Kier
DJ, Keyboards, Drum Programming: DJ
    Dmitry
DJ, Keyboards, Drum Programming: DJ
    Towa Towa

"Build the Bridge"

Lead and Backup Vocals: Lady Miss Kier
DJ, Keyboards, Drum Programming: DJ
    Dmitry
DJ, Keyboards, Drum Programming: DJ
    Towa Towa
Vocals: Bill Coleman

Infinity Within

"I.F.O."Lead and Backup Vocals: Lady Miss
Kier
DJ, Keyboards, Drum Programming: DJ
    Dmitry
DJ, Keyboards, Drum Programming: DJ
    Towa Towa

"Runaway"

Lead and Backup Vocals: Lady Miss Kier

DJ, Keyboards, Drum Programming: DJ Dmitry

DJ, Keyboards, Drum Programming: DJ Towa Towa

Backup Vocals: Danny Madden, Sahirah Moore, Sheila Slappy

"Heart Be Still"

Lead and Backup Vocals: Lady Miss Kier

DJ, Keyboards, Drum Programming: DJ Dmitry

DJ, Keyboards, Drum Programming: DJ Towa Towa

Guitar, Bass: Bootsy Collins

Clavinet: Bernie Worrell

Trombone: Fred Wesley

Sax: Maceo Parker

Percussion: Robin Lobe

Backup Vocals: Mudbone Cooper

"I Won't Give Up"

Lead and Backup Vocals: Lady Miss Kier

DJ, Keyboards, Drum Programming: DJ Dmitry

DJ, Keyboards, Drum Programming: DJ Towa Towa

Guitar: Bootsy Collins

Trombone: Fred Wesley

Sax: Maceo Parker

Backup Vocals Mudbone Cooper

"Vote, Baby, Vote"

Lead and Backup Vocals: Lady Miss Kier

DJ, Keyboards, Drum Programming: DJ Dmitry

DJ, Keyboards, Drum Programming: DJ Towa Towa

"Two Clouds above Nine"

Lead and Backup Vocals: Lady Miss Kier

DJ, Keyboards, Drum Programming: DJ Dmitry

DJ, Keyboards, Drum Programming: DJ Towa Towa

Guitar: Bootsy Collins

Trombone: Fred Wesley

Sax: Maceo Parker

"Electric Shock"

Lead and Backup Vocals: Lady Miss Kier

DJ, Keyboards, Drum Programming: DJ Dmitry

DJ, Keyboards, Drum Programming: DJ Towa Towa

"I Had a Dream (I Was Falling through a Hole in the Ozone Layer)"

Lead and Backup Vocals: Lady Miss Kier

DJ, Keyboards, Drum Programming: DJ Dmitry

DJ, Keyboards, Drum Programming: DJ Towa Towa

Guitar: Bootsy Collins

Piano: Bernie Worrell

Trombone: Fred Wesley

Sax: Maceo Parker

Backup Vocals: Danny Madden, Mudbone Cooper, Sahirah Moore, Sheila Slappy

"Fuddy Duddy Judge"

Lead and Backup Vocals: Lady Miss Kier

DJ, Keyboards, Drum Programming: DJ Dmitry

DJ, Keyboards, Drum Programming: DJ Towa Towa

Guitar: Bootsy Collins

Minimoog: Bernie Worrell

Trombone: Fred Wesley

Sax: Maceo Parker

Backup Vocals: Zhana Saunders

"Pussycat Meow"

Lead and Backup Vocals: Lady Miss Kier
DJ, Keyboards, Drum Programming: DJ Dmitry
DJ, Keyboards, Drum Programming: DJ Towa Towa
Bass: Bootsy Collins

"Thank You Everyday"

Lead and Backup Vocals: Lady Miss Kier
DJ, Keyboards, Drum Programming: DJ Dmitry
DJ, Keyboards, Drum Programming: DJ Towa Towa
Guitar: Bootsy Collins
Keyboards, Programming: Satoshi Tomiie
Backup Vocals: Danny Madden, Sahirah Moore, Sheila Slappy

"Rubber Lover"

Lead and Backup Vocals: Lady Miss Kier
DJ, Keyboards, Drum Programming: DJ Dmitry
DJ, Keyboards, Drum Programming: DJ Towa Towa
Bass, Guitar: Bootsy Collins
Backup Vocals: Bootsy Collins

"Come On in, the Dreams Are Fine"

Lead and Backup Vocals: Lady Miss Kier
DJ, Keyboards, Drum Programming: DJ Dmitry
DJ, Keyboards, Drum Programming: DJ Towa Towa
Piano, Synthesizer: Satoshi Tomiie
Percussion: Robin Lobe

"Love Is Everything"

Lead and Backup Vocals: Lady Miss Kier
DJ, Keyboards, Drum Programming: DJ Dmitry
DJ, Keyboards, Drum Programming: DJ Towa Towa

Guitar: Bootsy Collins, Catfish Collins
Melodica: Bernie Worrell
Tablas: Misha Masud
Backup Vocals: Mudbone Cooper

— ☆ —

THE RICHARD SMALLWOOD SINGERS (SELECT TRACKS): 1990–1992

This gospel group features the Baltimore Connection/P-Funk Horns.

"He's Able"

Lead Vocals: Richard Smallwood
Backup Vocals: Carolene Evans, Darlene Simmons, Dottie Jones, Jackie Ruffin, Richard Smallwood, Rickie LaFontaine, the Smallwood Singers
Bass: Tim Linzy
Drums: Andre Webb
Guitar: Jonathan DuBose
Trumpet: Bennie Cowan
Sax: Greg Thomas
Trombone: Greg Boyer
Keyboards: Bryant Pugh, Richard Smallwood

"Without Holiness"

Lead Vocals: Jackie Ruffin
Backup Vocals: Carolene Evans, Darlene Simmons, Dottie Jones, Jackie Ruffin, Richard Smallwood, Rickie LaFontaine, the Smallwood Singers
Bass: Tim Linzy
Drums: Andre Webb
Guitar: Jonathan DuBose
Trumpet: Bennie Cowan
Sax: Greg Thomas
Trombone: Greg Boyer
Keyboards: Bryant Pugh, Richard Smallwood

"I Give You Praise"

Lead Vocals: Rickie LaFontaine
Backup Vocals: Carolene Evans, Darlene Simmons, Dottie Jones, Jackie Ruffin, Richard Smallwood, Rickie LaFontaine, the Smallwood Singers
Bass: Tim Linzy
Drums: Andre Webb
Guitar: Jonathan DuBose
Trumpet: Bennie Cowan
Sax: Greg Thomas
Trombone: Greg Boyer
Keyboards: Bryant Pugh, Richard Smallwood

"Someday"

Lead Vocals: Dottie Jones
Backup Vocals: Carolene Evans, Darlene Simmons, Dottie Jones, Jackie Ruffin, Richard Smallwood, Rickie LaFontaine, the Smallwood Singers
Bass: Tim Linzy
Drums: Andre Webb
Guitar: Jonathan DuBose
Trumpet: Bennie Cowan
Sax: Greg Thomas
Trombone: Greg Boyer
Keyboards: Bryant Pugh, Richard Smallwood

"Who Will Go"

Lead Vocals: Darlene Simmons, Richard Smallwood
Backup Vocals: Carolene Evans, Darlene Simmons, Dottie Jones, Jackie Ruffin, Richard Smallwood, Rickie LaFontaine, the Smallwood Singers
Bass: Tim Linzy
Drums: Andre Webb
Guitar: Jonathan DuBose
Trumpet: Bennie Cowan
Sax: Greg Thomas
Trombone: Greg Boyer
Keyboards: Bryant Pugh, Richard Smallwood

"Holy Spirit"

Lead Vocals: Richard Smallwood
Backing Vocals: The Metropolitan Young Adult Fellowship Ensemble, directed by David E. Warr
Backup Vocals: Carolene Evans, Darlene Simmons, Dottie Jones, Jackie Ruffin, Richard Smallwood, Rickie LaFontaine, the Smallwood Singers
Bass: Tim Linzy
Drums: Andre Webb
Guitar: Jonathan DuBose
Trumpet: Bennie Cowan
Sax: Greg Thomas
Trombone: Greg Boyer
Keyboards: Bryant Pugh, Richard Smallwood

"Blessed Assurance"

Piano, Soloist: Richard Smallwood

"I Will Pray"

Lead Vocals: Carolene Evans
Backup Vocals: Carolene Evans, Darlene Simmons, Dottie Jones, Jackie Ruffin, Richard Smallwood, Rickie LaFontaine, the Smallwood Singers
Bass: Tim Linzy
Drums: Andre Webb
Guitar: Jonathan DuBose
Trumpet: Bennie Cowan
Sax: Greg Thomas
Trombone: Greg Boyer
Keyboards: Bryant Pugh, Richard Smallwood

"Joy Will Come"

Lead Vocals: Darlene Simmons
Backup Vocals: Carolene Evans, Darlene Simmons, Dottie Jones, Jackie Ruffin, Richard Smallwood, Rickie LaFontaine, the Smallwood Singers
Bass: Tim Linzy
Drums: Andre Webb
Guitar: Jonathan DuBose
Trumpet: Bennie Cowan
Sax: Greg Thomas
Trombone: Greg Boyer
Keyboards: Bryant Pugh, Richard Smallwood

"Great Is the Lord"

Backup Vocals: Carolene Evans, Darlene Simmons, Dottie Jones, Jackie Ruffin, Richard Smallwood, Rickie LaFontaine, the Smallwood Singers
Bass: Tim Linzy
Drums: Andre Webb
Guitar: Jonathan DuBose
Trumpet: Bennie Cowan
Sax: Greg Thomas
Trombone: Greg Boyer
Keyboards: Bryant Pugh, Richard Smallwood

"What He's Done for Me"

Backup Vocals: Carolene Evans, Darlene Simmons, Dottie Jones, Jackie Ruffin, Richard Smallwood, Rickie LaFontaine, the Smallwood Singers
Bass: Tim Linzy
Drums: Andre Webb
Guitar: Jonathan DuBose
Trumpet: Bennie Cowan
Sax: Greg Thomas
Trombone: Greg Boyer
Keyboards: Bryant Pugh, Richard Smallwood

"His Mercy Endureth Forever"

Backup Vocals: Carolene Evans, Darlene Simmons, Dottie Jones, Jackie Ruffin, Richard Smallwood, Rickie LaFontaine, the Smallwood Singers
Bass: Tim Linzy
Drums: Andre Webb
Guitar: Jonathan DuBose
Trumpet: Bennie Cowan
Sax: Greg Thomas
Trombone: Greg Boyer
Keyboards: Bryant Pugh, Richard Smallwood

"The Light"

Backup Vocals: Carolene Evans, Darlene Simmons, Dottie Jones, Jackie Ruffin, Richard Smallwood, Rickie LaFontaine, the Smallwood Singers
Bass: Tim Linzy
Drums: Andre Webb
Guitar: Jonathan DuBose
Trumpet: Bennie Cowan
Sax: Greg Thomas
Trombone: Greg Boyer
Keyboards: Bryant Pugh, Richard Smallwood

"Jesus, Lover of My Soul"

Backup Vocals: Carolene Evans, Darlene Simmons, Dottie Jones, Jackie Ruffin, Richard Smallwood, Rickie LaFontaine, the Smallwood Singers
Bass: Tim Linzy
Drums: Andre Webb
Guitar: Jonathan DuBose
Trumpet: Bennie Cowan
Sax: Greg Thomas
Trombone: Greg Boyer
Keyboards: Bryant Pugh, Richard Smallwood

"Wonderful Counselor"

Backup Vocals: Carolene Evans, Darlene Simmons, Dottie Jones, Jackie Ruffin, Richard Smallwood, Rickie LaFontaine, the Smallwood Singers
Bass: Tim Linzy
Drums: Andre Webb
Guitar: Jonathan DuBose
Trumpet: Bennie Cowan
Sax: Greg Thomas
Trombone: Greg Boyer
Keyboards: Bryant Pugh, Richard Smallwood

"Great Is Thy Faithfulness"

Backup Vocals: Carolene Evans, Darlene Simmons, Dottie Jones, Jackie Ruffin, Richard Smallwood, Rickie LaFontaine, the Smallwood Singers
Bass: Tim Linzy
Drums: Andre Webb
Guitar: Jonathan DuBose
Trumpet: Bennie Cowan
Sax: Greg Thomas
Trombone: Greg Boyer
Keyboards: Bryant Pugh, Richard Smallwood

"I Won't Be Troubled"

Backup Vocals: Carolene Evans, Darlene Simmons, Dottie Jones, Jackie Ruffin, Richard Smallwood, Rickie LaFontaine, the Smallwood Singers
Bass: Tim Linzy
Drums: Andre Webb
Guitar: Jonathan DuBose
Trumpet: Bennie Cowan
Sax: Greg Thomas
Trombone: Greg Boyer
Keyboards: Bryant Pugh, Richard Smallwood

"Come Unto Me"

Backup Vocals: Carolene Evans, Darlene Simmons, Dottie Jones, Jackie Ruffin, Richard Smallwood, Rickie LaFontaine, the Smallwood Singers
Bass: Tim Linzy
Drums: Andre Webb
Guitar: Jonathan DuBose
Trumpet: Bennie Cowan
Sax: Greg Thomas
Trombone: Greg Boyer
Keyboards: Bryant Pugh, Richard Smallwood

"T'will Be Sweet"

Backup Vocals: Carolene Evans, Darlene Simmons, Dottie Jones, Jackie Ruffin, Richard Smallwood, Rickie LaFontaine, the Smallwood Singers
Bass: Tim Linzy
Drums: Andre Webb
Guitar: Jonathan DuBose
Trumpet: Bennie Cowan
Sax: Greg Thomas
Trombone: Greg Boyer
Keyboards: Bryant Pugh, Richard Smallwood

— ☆ —

MR. FIDDLER: 1990

This album was made by the Fiddler brothers, Thomas "Bubz" Fiddler (bass) and Joseph "Amp" Fiddler (keyboards), both of whom worked with P-Funk. Amp himself had been keyboardist for P-Funk from about 1986 to 1997.

Elektra Records

With Respect

"So You Wanna Be a Gangster"

Keyboards, Vocals: Amp Fiddler
Bass: Bubz Fiddler
Backup Vocals: Brian McKnight
Trumpet: Bennie Cowan
Sax: Greg Thomas
Trombone: Greg Boyer
Guitar: Dewayne Blackbyrd McKnight, Chris Bruce
Drums: Amp Fiddler, Carmen Rizzo Jr.

"Cool about It"

Keyboards: Amp Fiddler, Danny Faber
Bass: Bubz Fiddler
Vocals: Amp Fiddler, Bubz Fiddler
Backup Vocals: Andre Williams, Amp Fiddler, Lige Curry
Guitar: Andre Williams
Drums: Amp Fiddler, Danny Faber

"Blackout"

Keyboards: Amp Fiddler, Rodrick Buckingham
Bass: Bubz Fiddler
Lead Vocals: Amp Fiddler
Sax: Skip Pruitt
Backup Vocals: Bubz Fiddler, Andre Williams, Cordell Mosson, Stuart Nalley, Overton Lloyd, T. C. Ellis

Guitar: Dewayne Blackbyrd McKnight, Cordell Mosson, Chris Bruce
Drums: Rodrick Buckingham
Drum Programming: Carmen Rizzo Jr.

"Cat in the Hat"

Keyboards, Lead Vocals: Amp Fiddler
Backup Vocals: Bubz Fiddler, Steve Boyd, Clip Payne, Paul Hill, Amp Fiddler
Guitar: Ras Kente
Drum Programming: Amp Fiddler, Clip Payne

"Pay Party"

Keyboards, Vocals, Drums: Amp Fiddler
Backup Vocals: Amp Fiddler, Dewayne McKnight, George Clinton, Pamela Starks, Diem Jones, Overton Lloyd
Guitar: Dewayne Blackbyrd McKnight, Michael Hampton

"Henpecked"

Keyboards, Lead Vocals: Amp Fiddler
Trombone: Greg Boyer
Sax: Greg Thomas
Trumpet: Bennie Cowan
Backup Vocals: Amp Fiddler, Bubz Fiddler, Andre Williams, Leland Zales, Pamela Starks
Guitar: Dewayne Blackbyrd McKnight Stevie Salas, Chris Bruce
Drums: Steve Jordan

"Starvin' Like Marvin"

Keyboards, Lead Vocals, Drum Programming: Amp Fiddler
Bass: Bubz Fiddler
Backup Vocals: Bubz Fiddler, Paul Hill, Sandra Fiddler
Trumpet: Bennie Cowan
Sax: Greg Thomas
Trombone: Greg Boyer
Guitar: Dewayne Blackbyrd McKnight

"Cutie on Duty"

Keyboards: Amp Fiddler, Rodrick Buckingham
Lead Vocals: Amp Fiddler
Backup Vocals: Amp Fiddler Bubz Fiddler, Andre Williams
Guitar: Chris Bruce
Trumpet: Bennie Cowan
Sax: Greg Thomas
Trombone: Greg Boyer
Drum Programming: Rodrick Buckingham

"Me and My Girlfriend"

Keyboards, Lead Vocals: Amp Fiddler
Trumpet: Bennie Cowan
Sax: Greg Thomas
Trombone: Greg Boyer
Backup Vocals: Amp Fiddler, Bubz Fiddler, Andre Williams
Guitar: Dewayne Blackbyrd McKnight, Eddie Hazel
Drum Programming: Amp Fiddler, Michael Clip Payne

"I Wanna Hang Out with You"

Keyboards, Lead Vocals: Amp Fiddler
Backup Vocals: Amp Fiddler, Bubz Fiddler, Andre Williams, Lynette Sanford (monologue)
Guitar: Andre Williams, Dewayne Blackbyrd McKnight
Drum Programming: Michael Clip Payne

— ☆ —

GOTCHA (SELECT TRACKS): 1990–2014

This Dutch hip-hop/go-go group features cameos and contributions from several P-Funk members, most notably Michael "Clip" Payne.

Ariola Records

Words and Music from the Lowlands

"Funky Farm"

Sax, Trumpet, Backup Vocals: Yo EB On Da Funkphone
Bass, Backup Vocals: E-Bone
Congas, Percussion: Rudiment
Keyboards, Hammond, Piano: Pooperman
Drums, Bass, Percussion, Clavinet, Piano, Guitar, Claps, Backup Vocals: Vincent Smeenk
Programming, Sampling: W 30
Vocals, Tambourine, Boozeharp: Rockattack Ten
Vocals, Guitars, Drums, Percussion, Bass, Claps, Scratches, Samples: Robadope Ro
Vocals: Mark Dwiezels
Backup Vocals: Pieter 'Ootop

"Holybukowski"

Sax, Trumpet, Backup Vocals: Yo EB On Da Funkphone
Bass, Backup Vocals: E-Bone
Congas, Percussion: Rudiment
Keyboards, Hammond, Piano: Pooperman
Drums, Bass, Percussion, Clavinet, Piano, Guitar, Claps, Backup Vocals: Vincent Smeenk
Programming, Sampling: W 30
Vocals, Tambourine, Boozeharp: Rockattack Ten
Vocals, Guitars, Drums, Percussion, Bass, Claps, Scratches, Samples: Robadope Ro
Featuring: Marsman

"Mathilda Da Wicked Witch"

Sax, Trumpet, Backup Vocals: Yo EB On Da Funkphone
Bass, Backup Vocals: E-Bone
Congas, Percussion: Rudiment
Keyboards, Hammond, Piano: Pooperman
Drums, Bass, Percussion, Clavinet, Piano, Guitar, Claps, Backup Vocals: Vincent Smeenk
Programming, Sampling: W 30
Vocals, Tambourine, Boozeharp: Rockattack Ten
Vocals, Guitars, Drums, Percussion, Bass, Claps, Scratches, Samples: Robadope Ro
Vocals: Jeroen den Hengst
Guitar Solo: Paul Strootman
Backup Vocals: Pieter Ootop

"Kingdom Come"

Sax, Trumpet, Backup Vocals: Yo EB On Da Funkphone
Bass, Backup Vocals: E-Bone
Congas, Percussion: Rudiment
Keyboards, Hammond, Piano: Pooperman
Drums, Bass, Percussion, Clavinet, Piano, Guitar, Claps, Backup Vocals: Vincent Smeenk
Programming, Sampling: W 30
Vocals, Tambourine, Boozeharp: Rockattack Ten
Vocals, Guitars, Drums, Percussion, Bass, Claps, Scratches, Samples: Robadope Ro
Vocals: Wouter Smeenk
Backup Vocals: Iris

"Dance with EM"

All Guitars: Wouter Planteijdt
Sax, Trumpet, Backup Vocals: Yo EB On Da Funkphone
Bass, Backup Vocals: E-Bone
Congas, Percussion: Rudiment
Keyboards, Hammond, Piano: Pooperman

Drums, Bass, Percussion, Clavinet, Piano, Guitar, Claps, Backup Vocals: Vincent Smeenk
Programming, Sampling: W 30
Vocals, Tambourine, Boozeharp: Rockattack Ten
Vocals, Guitars, Drums, Percussion, Bass, Claps, Scratches, Samples: Robadope Ro

"Romancing on Da Sound That'll Make You Move"

Sax, Trumpet, Backup Vocals: Yo EB On Da Funkphone
Bass, Backup Vocals: E-Bone
Congas, Percussion: Rudiment
Keyboards, Hammond, Piano: Pooperman
Drums, Bass, Percussion, Clavinet, Piano, Guitar, Claps, Backup Vocals: Vincent Smeenk
Programming, Sampling: W 30
Vocals, Tambourine, Boozeharp: Rockattack Ten
Vocals, Guitars, Drums, Percussion, Bass, Claps, Scratches, Samples: Robadope Ro

"Words and Music from Da Lowlands"

Sax, Trumpet, Backup Vocals: Yo EB On Da Funkphone
Bass, Backup Vocals: E-Bone
Congas, Percussion: Rudiment
Keyboards, Hammond, Piano: Pooperman
Drums, Bass, Percussion, Clavinet, Piano, Guitar, Claps, Backup Vocals: Vincent Smeenk
Programming, Sampling: W 30
Vocals, Tambourine, Boozeharp: Rockattack Ten
Vocals, Guitars, Drums, Percussion, Bass, Claps, Scratches, Samples: Robadope Ro
Vocals: Wouter Smeenk

"(Funk)2"

Sax, Trumpet, Backup Vocals: Yo EB On Da Funkphone
Bass, Backup Vocals: E-Bone
Congas, Percussion: Rudiment
Keyboards, Hammond, Piano: Pooperman
Drums, Bass, Percussion, Clavinet, Piano, Guitar, Claps, Backup Vocals: Vincent Smeenk
Programming, Sampling: W 30
Vocals, Tambourine, Boozeharp: Rockattack Ten
Vocals, Guitars, Drums, Percussion, Bass, Claps, Scratches, Samples: Robadope Ro
Backup Vocals: Iris
Featuring: Marsman
Lead Guitar: Wouter Planteijdt

"D'Chase"

Guitar Solo: Piet van Steenis
Sax, Trumpet, Backup Vocals: Yo EB On Da Funkphone
Bass, Backup Vocals: E-Bone
Congas, Percussion: Rudiment
Keyboards, Hammond, Piano: Pooperman
Drums, Bass, Percussion, Clavinet, Piano, Guitar, Claps, Backup Vocals: Vincent Smeenk
Programming, Sampling: W 30
Vocals, Tambourine, Boozeharp: Rockattack Ten
Vocals, Guitars, Drums, Percussion, Bass, Claps, Scratches, Samples: Robadope Ro
Rhythm Guitar: Jeroen den Hengst

"Free to Feel Free"

Vocals: George Clinton
Sax, Trumpet, Backup Vocals: Yo EB On Da Funkphone
Bass, Backup Vocals: E-Bone
Congas, Percussion: Rudiment
Keyboards, Hammond, Piano: Pooperman

Drums, Bass, Percussion, Clavinet, Piano, Guitar, Claps, Backup Vocals: Vincent Smeenk
Programming, Sampling: W 30
Vocals, Tambourine, Boozeharp: Rockattack Ten
Vocals, Guitars, Drums, Percussion, Bass, Claps, Scratches, Samples: Robadope Ro
Backup Vocals: Iris

"Everybody Is a Superstar"

Sax, Trumpet, Backup Vocals: Yo EB On Da Funkphone
Bass, Backup Vocals: E-Bone
Congas, Percussion: Rudiment
Keyboards, Hammond, Piano: Pooperman
Drums, Bass, Percussion, Clavinet, Piano, Guitar, Claps, Backup Vocals: Vincent Smeenk
Programming, Sampling: W 30
Vocals, Tambourine, Boozeharp: Rockattack Ten
Vocals, Guitars, Drums, Percussion, Bass, Claps, Scratches, Samples: Robadope Ro

"Funk in Yo Ass"

Vocals: George Clinton
Sax, Trumpet, Backup Vocals: Yo EB On Da Funkphone
Bass, Backup Vocals: E-Bone
Congas, Percussion: Rudiment
Keyboards, Hammond, Piano: Pooperman
Drums, Bass, Percussion, Clavinet, Piano, Guitar, Claps, Backup Vocals: Vincent Smeenk
Programming, Sampling: W 30
Vocals, Tambourine, Boozeharp: Rockattack Ten
Vocals, Guitars, Drums, Percussion, Bass, Claps, Scratches, Samples: Robadope Ro

"Da 10 Is Mightier Than Da Sword"

Sax, Trumpet, Backup Vocals: Yo EB On Da Funkphone
Bass, Backup Vocals: E-Bone
Congas, Percussion: Rudiment
Keyboards, Hammond, Piano: Pooperman
Drums, Bass, Percussion, Clavinet, Piano, Guitar, Claps, Backup Vocals: Vincent Smeenk
Programming, Sampling: W 30
Vocals, Tambourine, Boozeharp: Rockattack Ten
Vocals, Guitars, Drums, Percussion, Bass, Claps, Scratches, Samples: Robadope Ro

"Higher Heaven"

Sax, Trumpet, Backup Vocals: Yo EB On Da Funkphone
Bass, Backup Vocals: E-Bone
Congas, Percussion: Rudiment
Keyboards, Hammond, Piano: Pooperman
Drums, Bass, Percussion, Clavinet, Piano, Guitar, Claps, Backup Vocals: Vincent Smeenk
Programming, Sampling: W 30
Vocals, Tambourine, Boozeharp: Rockattack Ten
Vocals, Guitars, Drums, Percussion, Bass, Claps, Scratches, Samples: Robadope Ro

"Put Yo Body into It"

Sax, Trumpet, Backup Vocals: Yo EB On Da Funkphone
Bass, Backup Vocals: E-Bone
Congas, Percussion: Rudiment
Keyboards, Hammond, Piano: Pooperman
Drums, Bass, Percussion, Clavinet, Piano, Guitar, Claps, Backup Vocals: Vincent Smeenk
Programming, Sampling: W 30
Vocals, Tambourine, Boozeharp: Rockattack Ten

Vocals, Guitars, Drums, Percussion, Bass, Claps, Scratches, Samples: Robadope Ro

"Bold As Love"

Sax, Trumpet, Backup Vocals: Yo EB On Da Funkphone
Bass, Backup Vocals: E-Bone
Congas, Percussion: Rudiment
Keyboards, Hammond, Piano: Pooperman
Drums, Bass, Percussion, Clavinet, Piano, Guitar, Claps, Backup Vocals: Vincent Smeenk
Programming, Sampling: W 30
Vocals, Tambourine, Boozeharp: Rockattack Ten
Vocals, Guitars, Drums, Percussion, Bass, Claps, Scratches, Samples: Robadope Ro

BlueFunk Records

Gotcha Gotcha Gotcha

"Tell It Like It Is"

All Guitars, DJ, Vocals, Drums, Percussion, Beats: Robadope Ro
Vocals, Percussion, Programming, Bass, Melodica, Hammond: Rockattack Ten
All Keyboards, Backup Vocals: Pooperman
Drums, Piano, Accordion, Backup Vocals, Percussion: Homie
Funkphone: Joep Da Dupe
Bass: Bone
Percussion: Rudiment Conga
Backup Vocals: Michael Clip Payne, Lige Curry, Mango Juice, Date Melle, Michael Parkinson, Wouter S, Adrian Borland, Pietere Ootop, Mark Uli
Djembe: Martin Werkman
Double Bass: Eric Timmermans
Guitar: Wouter P, Sander Janssen

"Naked"

All Guitars, DJ, Vocals, Drums, Percussion, Beats: Robadope Ro

Vocals, Percussion, Programming, Bass, Melodica, Hammond: Rockattack Ten

All Keyboards, Backup Vocals: Pooperman

Drums, Piano, Accordion, Backup Vocals, Percussion: Homie

Funkphone: Joep Da Dupe

Bass: Bone

Percussion: Rudiment Conga

Backup Vocals: Michael Clip Payne, Lige Curry, Mango Juice, Date Melle, Michael Parkinson, Wouter S, Adrian Borland, Pietere Ootop, Mark Uli

Djembe: Martin Werkman

Double Bass: Eric Timmermans

Guitar: Wouter P, Sander Janssen

"Stronger Than Ajax, Save Da Day"

All Guitars, DJ, Vocals, Drums, Percussion, Beats: Robadope Ro

Vocals, Percussion, Programming, Bass, Melodica, Hammond: Rockattack Ten

All Keyboards, Backup Vocals: Pooperman

Drums, Piano, Accordion, Backup Vocals, Percussion: Homie

Funkphone: Joep Da Dupe

Bass: Bone

Percussion: Rudiment Conga

Backup Vocals: Michael Clip Payne, Lige Curry, Mango Juice, Date Melle, Michael Parkinson, Wouter S, Adrian Borland, Pietere Ootop, Mark Uli

Djembe: Martin Werkman

Double Bass: Eric Timmermans

Guitar: Wouter P, Sander Janssen

"Bonesong"

All Guitars, DJ, Vocals, Drums, Percussion, Beats: Robadope Ro

Vocals, Percussion, Programming, Bass, Melodica, Hammond: Rockattack Ten

All Keyboards, Backup Vocals: Pooperman

Drums, Piano, Accordion, Backup Vocals, Percussion: Homie

Funkphone: Joep Da Dupe

Bass: Bone

Percussion: Rudiment Conga

Backup Vocals: Michael Clip Payne, Lige Curry, Mango Juice, Date Melle, Michael Parkinson, Wouter S, Adrian Borland, Pietere Ootop, Mark Uli

Djembe: Martin Werkman

Double Bass: Eric Timmermans

Guitar: Wouter P, Sander Janssen

"Red Hot Momma"

All Guitars, DJ, Vocals, Drums, Percussion, Beats: Robadope Ro

Vocals, Percussion, Programming, Bass, Melodica, Hammond: Rockattack Ten

All Keyboards, Backup Vocals: Pooperman

Drums, Piano, Accordion, Backup Vocals, Percussion: Homie

Funkphone: Joep Da Dupe

Bass: Bone

Percussion: Rudiment Conga

Backup Vocals: Michael Clip Payne, Lige Curry, Mango Juice, Date Melle, Michael Parkinson, Wouter S, Adrian Borland, Pietere Ootop, Mark Uli

Djembe: Martin Werkman

Double Bass: Eric Timmermans

Guitar: Wouter P, Sander Janssen

"Love O' My Life/Madame Butterfly"

All Guitars, DJ, Vocals, Drums, Percussion, Beats: Robadope Ro
Vocals, Percussion, Programming, Bass, Melodica, Hammond: Rockattack Ten
All Keyboards, Backup Vocals: Pooperman
Drums, Piano, Accordion, Backup Vocals, Percussion: Homie
Funkphone: Joep Da Dupe
Bass: Bone
Percussion: Rudiment Conga
Backup Vocals: Michael Clip Payne, Lige Curry, Mango Juice, Date Melle, Michael Parkinson, Wouter S, Adrian Borland, Pietere Ootop, Mark Uli
Djembe: Martin Werkman
Double Bass: Eric Timmermans
Guitar: Wouter P, Sander Janssen

"Where Have You Been So Long"

All Guitars, DJ, Vocals, Drums, Percussion, Beats: Robadope Ro
Vocals, Percussion, Programming, Bass, Melodica, Hammond: Rockattack Ten
All Keyboards, Backup Vocals: Pooperman
Drums, Piano, Accordion, Backup Vocals, Percussion: Homie
Funkphone: Joep Da Dupe
Bass: Bone
Percussion: Rudiment Conga
Backup Vocals: Michael Clip Payne, Lige Curry, Mango Juice, Date Melle, Michael Parkinson, Wouter S, Adrian Borland, Pietere Ootop, Mark Uli
Djembe: Martin Werkman
Double Bass: Eric Timmermans
Guitar: Wouter P, Sander Janssen

"Any Better Love"

All Guitars, DJ, Vocals, Drums, Percussion, Beats: Robadope Ro
Vocals, Percussion, Programming, Bass, Melodica, Hammond: Rockattack Ten
All Keyboards, Backup Vocals: Pooperman
Drums, Piano, Accordion, Backup Vocals, Percussion: Homie
Funkphone: Joep Da Dupe
Bass: Bone
Percussion: Rudiment Conga
Backup Vocals: Michael Clip Payne, Lige Curry, Mango Juice, Date Melle, Michael Parkinson, Wouter S, Adrian Borland, Pietere Ootop, Mark Uli
Djembe: Martin Werkman
Double Bass: Eric Timmermans
Guitar: Wouter P, Sander Janssen

"Funky Creature"

All Guitars, DJ, Vocals, Drums, Percussion, Beats: Robadope Ro
Vocals, Percussion, Programming, Bass, Melodica, Hammond: Rockattack Ten
All Keyboards, Backup Vocals: Pooperman
Drums, Piano, Accordion, Backup Vocals, Percussion: Homie
Funkphone: Joep Da Dupe
Bass: Bone
Percussion: Rudiment Conga
Backup Vocals: Michael Clip Payne, Lige Curry, Mango Juice, Date Melle, Michael Parkinson, Wouter S, Adrian Borland, Pietere Ootop, Mark Uli
Djembe: Martin Werkman
Double Bass: Eric Timmermans
Guitar: Wouter P, Sander Janssen

"Money"

All Guitars, DJ, Vocals, Drums, Percussion, Beats: Robadope Ro
Vocals, Percussion, Programming, Bass, Melodica, Hammond: Rockattack Ten
All Keyboards, Backup Vocals: Pooperman
Drums, Piano, Accordion, Backup Vocals, Percussion: Homie
Funkphone: Joep Da Dupe
Bass: Bone
Percussion: Rudiment Conga
Backup Vocals: Michael Clip Payne, Lige Curry, Mango Juice, Date Melle, Michael Parkinson, Wouter S, Adrian Borland, Pietere Ootop, Mark Uli
Djembe: Martin Werkman
Double Bass: Eric Timmermans
Guitar: Wouter P, Sander Janssen

"Higher"

All Guitars, DJ, Vocals, Drums, Percussion, Beats: Robadope Ro
Vocals, Percussion, Programming, Bass, Melodica, Hammond: Rockattack Ten
All Keyboards, Backup Vocals: Pooperman
Drums, Piano, Accordion, Backup Vocals, Percussion: Homie
Funkphone: Joep Da Dupe
Bass: Bone
Percussion: Rudiment Conga
Backup Vocals: Michael Clip Payne, Lige Curry, Mango Juice, Date Melle, Michael Parkinson, Wouter S, Adrian Borland, Pietere Ootop, Mark Uli
Djembe: Martin Werkman
Double Bass: Eric Timmermans
Guitar: Wouter P, Sander Janssen

"Heroine"

All Guitars, DJ, Vocals, Drums, Percussion, Beats: Robadope Ro
Vocals, Percussion, Programming, Bass, Melodica, Hammond: Rockattack Ten
All Keyboards, Backup Vocals: Pooperman
Drums, Piano, Accordion, Backup Vocals, Percussion: Homie
Funkphone: Joep Da Dupe
Bass: Bone
Percussion: Rudiment Conga
Backup Vocals: Michael Clip Payne, Lige Curry, Mango Juice, Date Melle, Michael Parkinson, Wouter S, Adrian Borland, Pietere Ootop, Mark Uli
Djembe: Martin Werkman
Double Bass: Eric Timmermans
Guitar: Wouter P, Sander Janssen

"MTV-ling"

All Guitars, DJ, Vocals, Drums, Percussion, Beats: Robadope Ro
Vocals, Percussion, Programming, Bass, Melodica, Hammond: Rockattack Ten
All Keyboards, Backup Vocals: Pooperman
Drums, Piano, Accordion, Backup Vocals, Percussion: Homie
Funkphone: Joep Da Dupe
Bass: Bone
Percussion: Rudiment Conga
Backup Vocals: Michael Clip Payne, Lige Curry, Mango Juice, Date Melle, Michael Parkinson, Wouter S, Adrian Borland, Pietere Ootop, Mark Uli
Djembe: Martin Werkman
Double Bass: Eric Timmermans
Guitar: Wouter P, Sander Janssen

Funkface Records

Four: It' the Terra P-Funk from Beyond Space

"Very "Long" Tale"

Guitar: Cordell Mosson
Bass, Guitar, Backup Vocals: Bone
Drums, Percussion, Samples, Guitar, Sub-Bass: Vincent Smeenk
Keyboards, Backup Vocals, Samples, Claps: Pooper
Guitars, Backup Vocals, Drum, Vocoder: Koen Fu
Rap Vocals, Scratching, DrumComputer, Guitar: Ten
Sax, Laughing Man, Clarinet: Joep
Additional Guitar: Peter N
Guest Vocals: Shy Rock

"Terra P-Funk"

Bass, Guitar, Backup Vocals: Bone
Drums, Percussion, Samples, Guitar, Sub-Bass: Vincent Smeenk
Keyboards, Backup Vocals, Samples, Claps: Pooper
Guitars, Backup Vocals, Drum, Vocoder: Koen Fu
Rap Vocals, Scratching, DrumComputer, Guitar: Ten
Sax, Laughing Man, Clarinet: Joep
Sax: Fred L
Trumpet: Jan W
Guest Vocals: Shy Rock

"Words Nothing but Words"

Guitar Solo: Cordell Mosson
Bass, Guitar, Backup Vocals: Bone
Drums, Percussion, Samples, Guitar, Sub-Bass: Vincent Smeenk
Keyboards, Backup Vocals, Samples, Claps: Pooper

Guitars, Backup Vocals, Drum, Vocoder: Koen Fu
Rap Vocals, Scratching, DrumComputer, Guitar: Ten
Sax, Laughing Man, Clarinet: Joep
Congas: Sherwin
Sax: Fred L
Trumpet: Jan W
Percussion: Rudiment Conga, Marc Hendrix, Serge
Vocals: Kid Crack

"Think about It"

Drums: Homie
Bass, Guitar, Backup Vocals: Bone
Percussion, Samples, Guitar, Sub-Bass: Vincent Smeenk
Keyboards, Backup Vocals, Samples, Claps: Pooper
Guitars, Backup Vocals, Drum, Vocoder: Koen Fu
Rap Vocals, Scratching, DrumComputer, Guitar: Ten
Sax, Laughing Man, Clarinet: Joep
Congas: Sherwin
Sax: Fred L
Trumpet: Jan W
Vocals: Count Crackula, Pieter B, Gerrit E

"The Wigger Gravediggers"

Drums: Homie
Bass, Guitar, Backup Vocals: Bone
Percussion, Samples, Guitar, Sub-Bass: Vincent Smeenk
Keyboards, Backup Vocals, Samples, Claps: Pooper
Guitars, Backup Vocals, Drum, Vocoder: Koen Fu
Rap Vocals, Scratching, DrumComputer, Guitar: Ten
Sax, Laughing Man, Clarinet: Joep
Vocals: Humble

"Asshole"

Bass: Cordell Mosson
Bass, Guitar, Backup Vocals: Bone
Drums, Percussion, Samples, Guitar, Sub-Bass: Vincent Smeenk
Keyboards, Backup Vocals, Samples, Claps: Pooper
Guitars, Backup Vocals, Drum, Vocoder: Koen Fu
Rap Vocals, Scratching, DrumComputer, Guitar: Ten
Sax, Laughing Man, Clarinet: Joep
Vocals: Sylvia O.E., Pieter B

"Mountain Top"

Drums: Homie
Vocals: Clip Payne
Bass, Guitar, Backup Vocals: Bone
Percussion, Samples, Guitar, Sub-Bass: Vincent Smeenk
Keyboards, Backup Vocals, Samples, Claps: Pooper
Guitars, Backup Vocals, Drum, Vocoder: Koen Fu
Rap Vocals, Scratching, DrumComputer, Guitar: Ten
Sax, Laughing Man, Clarinet: Joep
Vocals: Marc Hendrix, Monte C, Fridge

"Mirror on the Wall, Get on Your Back Let's Have a Ball"

Guitar: Cordell Mosson
Bass, Guitar, Backup Vocals: Bone
Drums, Percussion, Samples, Guitar, Sub-Bass: Vincent Smeenk
Keyboards, Backup Vocals, Samples, Claps: Pooper
Guitars, Backup Vocals, Drum, Vocoder: Koen Fu
Rap Vocals, Scratching, DrumComputer, Guitar: Ten
Sax, Laughing Man, Clarinet: Joep
Vocals: Marc Hendrix, Serge

"B Funk"

Drums: Homie
Bass, Guitar, Backup Vocals: Bone
Percussion, Samples, Guitar, Sub-Bass: Vincent Smeenk
Keyboards, Backup Vocals, Samples, Claps: Pooper
Guitars, Backup Vocals, Drum, Vocoder: Koen Fu
Rap Vocals, Scratching, DrumComputer, Guitar: Ten
Sax, Laughing Man, Clarinet: Joep
Congas: Sherwin
Piano Solo: Mauritz de L
Sax: Fred L
Trumpet: Jan W
Guest Vocals: Shy Rock
Vocals: Count Crackula

"Mistakes"

Vocals: Clip Payne
Bass, Guitar: Cordell Mosson
Bass, Guitar, Backup Vocals: Bone
Percussion, Samples, Guitar, Sub-Bass: Vincent Smeenk
Keyboards, Backup Vocals, Samples, Claps: Pooper
Guitars, Backup Vocals, Drum, Vocoder: Koen Fu
Rap Vocals, Scratching, DrumComputer, Guitar: Ten
Sax, Laughing Man, Clarinet: Joep
Vocals: Oliffe, Marc Hendrix

"Three (You, Me & the Baby)"

Drums: Homie
Bass, Guitar, Backup Vocals: Bone
Percussion, Samples, Guitar, Sub-Bass: Vincent Smeenk
Keyboards, Backup Vocals, Samples, Claps: Pooper
Guitars, Backup Vocals, Drum, Vocoder: Koen Fu
Rap Vocals, Scratching, DrumComputer, Guitar: Ten
Sax, Laughing Man, Clarinet: Joep
Vocals: Sylvia O.E.
Backup Vocals: Wouter, Kim, Boris and Lot
Vocals: Oliffe

"It! The Terra P-Funk from Beyond Space"

Vocals: Clip Payne
Bass, Guitar, Backup Vocals: Bone
Drums, Percussion, Samples, Guitar, Sub-Bass: Vincent Smeenk
Keyboards, Backup Vocals, Samples, Claps: Pooper
Guitars, Backup Vocals, Drum, Vocoder: Koen Fu
Rap Vocals, Scratching, DrumComputer, Guitar: Ten
Sax, Laughing Man, Clarinet: Joep

5.259551/2200

"Glory"

Bass: Bone
Drums, Programming, Percussion: Vince
Guitar: Ivar Leliveld
Keyboards, Programming: Pooper
Vocals, Programming: I Repeat
Rap: Kid Crash
Sax: Ube

"Thru with That"

Bass: Bone, Vince
Guitar: Ivar Leliveld
Keyboards, Programming: Pooper
Programming: Sander v.d. Reijken
Rap: Ked Crash, Senna
Whistle: Ube

"The Way We Roll (Part 1)"

Bass, Guitar: Bone
Guitar: Arnold Smits
Programming: Pooper, Vince
Sax: Ube
Vocals: Charles Sherrell, Graziella Hunsel, Kid Crash

"The Girl in the Front"

Bass, Guitar: Bone
Drums: Vince
Programming: Pooper, Sander v.d. Reijken
Rap: Kid Crash, Senna
Sax: Ube

"5259551/2200"

Acoustic Guitar, Keyboards: Pooper
Bass: Koen Fu
Bass, Percussion: Bone
Drums: Vince
Guitar: Arnold Smits

"When Our Love Walks By"

Bass: Bone
Clarinet: Ube
Drums, Melodica, Harmonica, Percussion: Vince
Guitar: Pooper
Vocals: I Repeat, Senna

"She Loves Me"

Bass: Bone
Drums: Vince
Guitar: Ivar Leliveld
Keyboards: Pooper
Sax: Ube
Vocals: Kid Crash, Pete Philly, Senna

"The Funk's in My Corner"

Drums, Guitar, Glockenspiel, Percussion:
   Vince
Percussion: Gijs Beusenberg
Programming: Pooper
Rap: Kid Crash
Sax: Ube
Sax: Arjan Van Tintelen
Trombone: Frank Molenaar
Trumpet: John Kijlstra, Marcel Klingeler
Vocals: I Repeat

"Damn"

Bass: Bone
Congas: Janco
Drums, Organ: Vince
Guitar: Ivar Leliveld
Lead Vocals, Rap: Rollarock
Organ, Clavinet, Electric Piano, Keyboards:
   Pooper
Rap: Kid Crash
Sax: Ube
Vocals: Charles Sherrell

"Please"

Drums, Bass: Vince
Guitar: Henk Schoorl
Organ, Guitar, Programming: Pooper
Vocals: I Repeat

Marista Records

Back to the Moon

"Free As a Bird"

Vocals: Chris T. Bradley, E1 Ten
Drums: Martijn Bosman
Percussion: Ruud de Graaff
Guitar: Arnold Smit, E1 Ten
Keyboards: Pieter Smeenk
Sax: Joep Smeenk

"Come Rain, Come Shine"

Vocals: Andy W, M.A. Parkinson, E1 Ten,
Udu: Janco van der Kaaden
Drums: Martijn Bosman
Percussion: Ruud de Graaff
Guitar: Arnold Smit, E1 Ten
Keyboards: Pieter Smeenk
Sax: Joep Smeenk

"Home (Back to the Moon)"

Vocals: E1 Ten
Drums: Martijn Bosman
Percussion: Ruud de Graaff
Guitar: Arnold Smit, E1 Ten
Keyboards: Pieter Smeenk
Sax: Joep Smeenk

"More Than Love"

Vocals: E1 Ten
Trumpet: Lourens van der Zwaag
Sax: Wiechert Warntjes
Drums: Martijn Bosman
Percussion: Ruud de Graaff
Guitar: Arnold Smit, E1 Ten
Keyboards: Pieter Smeenk
Sax: Joep Smeenk

"Heartbeat"

Vocals: E1 Ten
Synthesizer: Danny Bedrosian
Drums: Martijn Bosman
Percussion: Ruud de Graaff
Guitar: Arnold Smit, E1 Ten
Keyboards: Pieter Smeenk
Sax: Joep Smeenk

"Love Forever"

Vocals: E1 Ten
Drums: Martijn Bosman
Percussion: Ruud de Graaff
Guitar: Arnold Smit, E1 Ten
Keyboards: Pieter Smeenk
Sax: Joep Smeenk

"No Robot"

Vocals: M. A. Parkinson, Mary Griffin, Joshua Nolet, E1 Ten
Drums: Martijn Bosman
Percussion: Ruud de Graaff
Guitar: Arnold Smit, E1 Ten
Keyboards: Pieter Smeenk
Sax: Joep Smeenk

"Crystal Clear"

Vocals: E1 Ten
Drums: Martijn Bosman
Percussion: Ruud de Graaff
Guitar: Arnold Smit, E1 Ten
Keyboards: Pieter Smeenk
Sax: Joep Smeenk

"Re-Entry"

Vocals: M. A. Parkinson, E1 Ten
Drums: Martijn Bosman
Percussion: Ruud de Graaff
Guitar: Arnold Smit, E1 Ten
Keyboards: Pieter Smeenk
Sax: Joep Smeenk

"Peace"

Vocals: E1 Ten
Drums: Martijn Bosman
Percussion: Ruud de Graaff
Guitar: Arnold Smit, E1 Ten
Keyboards: Pieter Smeenk
Sax: Joep Smeenk

— ☆ —

DIGITAL UNDERGROUND (SELECT TRACKS): 1990–1991

This hip-hop group, led by the late Gregory Jacobs (Shock G/Humpty Hump), had an unmistakable P-Funk aesthetic both conceptually and stylistically.

Tommy Boy Music

Sex Packets (whole album)

George Clinton contributed ideas and production to much of the debut album by Digital Underground.

Sons of the P

"Sons of the P"

Lead Vocals: Shock G (Humpty Hump), George Clinton

"Sons of the P" is but one song in Digital Underground's vast P-Funk–inspired catalog. Indeed, the whole catalog could be considered part and parcel with the P-Funk canon.

— ☆ —

LIMBOMANIACS (SELECT TRACKS): 1991

The Limbomaniacs was a 1990s funk rock group that featured Bootsy, Bernie Worrell, and others. Drummer Brain from this group would go on to play with Collins and Worrell in the funk/metal/ambient fusion band Praxis.

In Effect Records

"Butt Funkin'"

Percussion: T-Bone
Vocals: Bootsy Collins
Drums: Brain
Guitar: Mirv
Lead Vocals, Bass: Butthouse
Keyboards: Pete

"Maniac"

Drums: Brain
Guitar: Mirv
Lead Vocals, Bass: Butthouse
Keyboards: Pete
Percussion: Adrien B. Isabell

"Freestyle"

Sax: Maceo Parker
Drums: Brain
Guitar: Mirv
Lead Vocals, Bass: Butthouse
Keyboards: Pete
Percussion: Adrien B. Isabell

"Porno"

Drums: Brain
Guitar: Mirv
Lead Vocals, Bass: Butthouse
Keyboards: Pete
Percussion: Adrien B. Isabell

"Shake It"

Percussion: T-Bone
Drums: Brain
Guitar: Mirv
Lead Vocals, Bass: Butthouse
Keyboards: Pete

"That's the Way"

Sax: Maceo Parker
Drums: Brain
Guitar: Mirv
Lead Vocals, Bass: Butthouse
Keyboards: Pete
Percussion: Adrien B. Isabell

"The Toilet's Flooded"

Drums: Brain
Guitar: Mirv
Lead Vocals, Bass: Butthouse
Keyboards: Pete
Percussion: Adrien B. Isabell

"Pavlov's Frothing Dogs"

Sax: Maceo Parker
Drums: Brain
Guitar: Mirv
Lead Vocals, Bass: Butthouse
Keyboards: Pete
Percussion: Adrien B. Isabell

— ☆ —

T. C. ELLIS (SELECT TRACKS): 1991

T. C. Ellis is a rapper and artist who worked with both Prince and George Clinton and, like Prince, hails from the Minneapolis area.

Paisley Park Records

"Pussycat"

Keyboards: Amp Fiddler, Levi Seacer Jr.
Vocals: George Clinton, Mallia Franklin, T. C. Ellis, Garry Shider

"Bustin'"

Vocals: T. C. Ellis, Candace Harrison, George Clinton, Michael Clip Payne, Tracey Lewis, Paul Hill, Belita Woods, Garry Shider
Drum Programming: Michael Clip Payne
Keyboards: Amp Fiddler

"True Confession"

Vocals: T. C. Ellis, Mallia Franklin, Rosie Gaines
Turntables: B-Quik
Programming: Gary Owens

— ☆ —

FFF (SELECT TRACKS): 1991

This French funk band worked with Clip Payne, Mudbone Cooper, and others.

"New Funk Generation"

Congas, Bongos: T-Bone
Vocals: Gary Mudbone Cooper, Michael Clip Payne
Bass: Niktus
Drums, Percussion: Krichou

Guitar: Yarol
Keyboards: Felix
Sax: Phillippe Herpin
Trombone, Vocals: Marco Prince

"Marco"

Congas, Bongos: T-Bone
Ghatam, Bells, Congas: Aiyb Dieng
Vocals: Gary Mudbone Cooper, Michael Clip Payne
Bass: Niktus
Drums, Percussion: Krichou
Guitar: Yarol
Keyboards: Felix
Sax: Phillippe Herpin
Trombone, Vocals: Marco Prince

"Doctor Love"

Congas, Bongos: T-Bone
Ghatam, Bells, Congas: Aiyb Dieng
Vocals: Gary Mudbone Cooper, Michael Clip Payne
Bass: Niktus
Drums, Percussion: Krichou
Guitar: Yarol
Keyboards: Felix
Sax: Phillippe Herpin
Trombone, Vocals: Marco Prince

— ☆ —

MATERIAL: 1991, 1994

This Funk/dub/fusion/world/hip-hop project was put together by producer Bill Laswell and features several members of Parliament-Funkadelic

Axiom Records

The Third Power

"Reality"

Vocals: Shabba Ranks
Drums, Drum Programming: Sly Dunbar
Bass: Robbie Shakespeare
Percussion: Aiyb Deng
Guitar, Fairlight: Nicky Skopelitis
Keyboards: Jeff Bova
Effects: Bill Laswell
Backup Vocals: Mudbone Cooper

"Playin' with Fire"

Vocals: Baby Bam, Mike G.
Effects: Bill Laswell
Vocals, Guitar: Bootsy Collins
Drums, Drum Programming: Sly Dunbar
Bass: Robbie Shakespeare
Percussion: Aiyb Deng
Guitar, Fairlight: Nicky Skopelitis
Vocals: Mudbone Cooper
Trombone: Fred Wesley
Sax: Maceo Parker, Pee Wee Ellis
Piano: Herbie Hancock

"Cosmic Slop"

Drums: Sly Dunbar
Percussion: Aiyb Deng
Bass: Robbie Shakespeare
Guitar: Garry Shider, Michael Hampton, Bootsy Collins
Fairlight: Nicky Skopelitis
Keyboards: Bernie Worrell
Vocals: Garry Shider, Mudbone Cooper

"E-Pluribus-Unum"

Vocals: Jalaluddin Mansur Nuriddin
Effects: Bill Laswell
Drums, Drum Programming: Sly Dunbar
Bass: Robbie Shakespeare
Guitar: Nicky Skopelitis
Synthesizer: Jeff Bova
Cornet, African Trumpet: Olu Dara
Baritone Horn: Joe Daly
Flute: Henry Threadgill
Euphonium: Richard Harper
Tuba: Marcus Rojas
Whistling: Joel Brandon

"Drive By"

Effects: Bill Laswell
Drums, Drum Programming: Sly Dunbar
Bass: Robbie Shakespeare
Fairlight: Nicky Skopelitis
Piano: Herbie Hancock
Percussion: Aiyb Deng
Strings: Material Strings, conducted by Karl Berger

"Power of Soul (Black Chant)"

Vocals: Jalal Mansur Nuriddin
Effects: Bill Laswell
Vocals, Guitar: Bootsy Collins
Drums, Drum Programming: Sly Dunbar
Bass: Robbie Shakespeare
Percussion: Aiyb Deng
Vocals: Mudbone Cooper
Cornet, African Trumpet: Olu Dara
Baritone Horn: Joe Daly
Flute: Henry Threadgill
Euphonium: Richard Harper
Tuba: Marcus Rojas
Whistling: Joel Brandon
Organ: Bernie Worrell

"Mellow Mood"

Effects: Bill Laswell
Strings: Material Strings, conducted by Karl Berger
Drums, Drum Programming: Sly Dunbar
Bass: Robbie Shakespeare
Vocals: Jenny Peters
Guitar, Fairlight: Nicky Skopelitis
Vocals: Mudbone Cooper
Vocals: Shabba Ranks

"Glory"

Effects: Bill Laswell
Vocals, Guitars: Bootsy Collins
Drums, Drum Programming: Sly Dunbar
Bass: Robbie Shakespeare
Strings: Material Strings, conducted by Karl Berger
Trombone: Fred Wesley
Sax: Maceo Parker, Pee Wee Ellis
Percussion: Aiyb Deng
Cornet, African Trumpet: Olu Dara
Baritone Horn: Joe Daly
Flute: Henry Threadgill
Euphonium: Richard Harper
Tuba: Marcus Rojas
Whistling: Joel Brandon

Hallucination Engine

"Black Light"

Bass, Beats, Loops, Samples: Bill Laswell
Sax: Wayne Shorter
Baglama, Fairlight, Guitars: Nicky Skopelitis
Tabla: Zakir Hussain
Percussion: Aiyb Deng

"Mantra"

Bass, Beats, Loops, Samples: Bill Laswell
Electric Violin: Shankar
Tablas: Zakir Hussain
Ney: Jihad Racy
Ghatam: Vikku Vinayakram

"Ruins (Submutation Dub)"

Bass, Beats, Loops, Samples: Bill Laswell
Drums: Sly Dunbar
Voice: Liu Sola
Violin: Simon Shaheen
Guitars: Nicky Skopelitis
Percussion: Aiyb Deng
Synthesizers: Jeff Bova

"Eternal Drift"

Bass, Beats, Loops, Samples: Bill Laswell
Guitars, Fairlight: Nicky Skopelitis
Voice: Liu Sola
Synthesizers: Jeff Bova
Sax: Wayne Shorter

"Words of Advice"

Bass, Beats, Loops, Samples: Bill Laswell
Voice: William S. Burroughs
Electric Piano: Bernie Worrell
Percussion: Michael Baklouk
Guitar: Nicky Skopelitis
Sax: Wayne Shorter

"Cucumber Slumber"

Effects, Beats, Loops, Samples: Bill Laswell
Tabla: Zakir Hussain
Synthesizer: Jeff Bova
Sitar, Guitars: Nicky Skopelitis
Basses: Jonas Hellborg
Electric Piano: Bernie Worrell
Sax: Wayne Shorter

"The Hidden Garden/Naima"

Bass, Beats, Loops, Samples: Bill Laswell
Violin, Oud: Simon Shaheen
Guitars, Fairlight, Sitar: Nicky Skopelitis
Percussion: Michael Baklouk
Voice: Fahim Dandan
Qanoun: George Basil
Bass: Bootsy Collins
Organ: Bernie Worrell
Tabla: Trilok Gurtu
Ney: Jihad Racy

"Shadows of Paradise"

Bass, Beats, Loops, Samples: Bill Laswell
Electric Violin: Shankar
Guitars, Fairlight, Sitar: Nicky Skopelitis
Tabla: Zakir Hussain
Ney: Jihad Racy
Ghatam: Vikku Vinayakram

— ☆ —

PRAXIS: 1992–2015

This funk metal group started out featuring Bootsy Collins, Bernie Worrell, guitarist Buckethead, drummer Brain, and mixmaster DST and was produced by Bill Laswell, who was doing a lot of P-Funk–related material at this time .

Axiom

Transmutation (Mutatis Mutandis)

"Blast/War Machine Dub"

Guitars: Buckethead
Bass: Bootsy Collins
Keyboards: Bernie Worrell
Turntables: AF Next Man Flip
Drums: Brain

"Interface/Stimulation Loop"

Guitars: Buckethead
Bass: Bootsy Collins
Keyboards: Bernie Worrell
Turntables: AF Next Man Flip
Drums: Brain

"Crash Victim/Black Science Navigator"

Guitars: Buckethead
Bass: Bootsy Collins, Vocals
Keyboards: Bernie Worrell
Turntables: AF Next Man Flip
Drums: Brain

"Animal Behavior"

Guitars: Buckethead
Bass: Bootsy Collins, Vocals
Keyboards: Bernie Worrell
Turntables: AF Next Man Flip
Drums: Brain

"Dead Man Walking"

Guitars: Buckethead
Bass: Bootsy Collins
Keyboards: Bernie Worrell
Turntables: AF Next Man Flip
Drums: Brain

"Seven Laws of Woo"

Guitars: Buckethead
Bass: Bootsy Collins
Keyboards: Bernie Worrell
Turntables: AF Next Man Flip
Drums: Brain

"The Interworld and the New Innocence"

Guitars: Buckethead
Bass: Bootsy Collins
Keyboards: Bernie Worrell
Turntables: AF Next Man Flip
Drums: Brain

"Giant Robot/Machines in the Modern City/Godzilla"

Guitars: Buckethead
Bass: Bootsy Collins
Keyboards: Bernie Worrell
Turntables: AF Next Man Flip
Drums: Brain

"After Shock (Chaos Never Died)"

Guitars: Buckethead
Bass: Bootsy Collins
Keyboards: Bernie Worrell
Turntables: AF Next Man Flip
Drums: Brain

"Stronghold"

Guitars: Buckethead
Bass: Bill Laswell
Drums: Brain
Vocals: Mick Harris
Sax: John Zorn

Sacrifist

"Cold Rolled/Iron Dub"

Guitars: Buckethead, Andy Hawkins
Bass: Gabriel Katz
Drums: Ted Epstein
Vocals: Mick Harris

"Suspension"

Guitars: Buckethead
Bass, Effects: Bill Laswell
Drums: Brain
Sax: John Zorn
Vocals: Yamatsuka Eye

"Rivet"

Guitars: Buckethead
Drums: Brain
Bass: Bill Laswell
Vocals: Mick Harris, Yamatsuka Eye

"Nine Secrets"

Guitars: Buckethead
Bass: Bill Laswell
Drums: Brain
Vocals: Mick Harris

"Deathstar"

Effects: Bill Laswell
Bass: Bootsy Collins

"The Hook"

Guitars: Buckethead
Bass: Bill Laswell
Drums: Brain

Vocals: Mick Harris
Sax: John Zorn
Turntables: AF Next Man Flip

"Nine Secrets"

Guitars: Buckethead
Bass: Bill Laswell
Drums: Brain
Vocals: Yamatsuka Eye, Mick Harris

Douglas Music

Praxis Collection

"Crossing"

Effects: Bill Laswell
Keyboards: Bernie Worrell

"Wake the Dead"

Guitars: Buckethead
Drums: Brain
Bass: Bill Laswell

"Cathedral Space (Soft Hail of Electrons)"

Guitars: Buckethead
Drums: Brain
Bass: Bill Laswell

"Triad (The Saw Is Family)"

Guitars: Buckethead
Drums: Brain
Bass: Bill Laswell

"Skull Crack (We Are Not Sick Men)"

Guitars: Buckethead
Drums: Brain
Bass: Bill Laswell

"Meta Matic"

Guitars: Buckethead
Drums: Brain
Bass: Bill Laswell

ARTISTS STARTING IN 1989-1999

"Vacuum-Mass"**Guitars:** Buckethead
Drums: Brain
Bass: Bill Laswell

"Cannibal (Heart Shape of the
Iron Blade)"
Guitars: Buckethead
Drums: Brain
Bass: Bill Laswell

"Inferno/Heatseeker/Exploded Heart"
Guitars: Buckethead
Drums: Brain
Bass: Bill Laswell

"Warm Time Machine/Low End
Transmission/Over the Foaming Deep"
Guitars: Buckethead
Drums: Brain
Bass: Bill Laswell

"Double Vision"
Guitars: Buckethead
Drums: Brain
Bass: Bill Laswell

"Maggot Dream"
Guitars: Buckethead

"Turbine"
Guitars: Buckethead
Drums: Brain
Bass: Bill Laswell

"Suspension"
Guitars: Buckethead
Drums: Brain
Bass: Bill Laswell

"Warcraft (Bruce Lee's Black Hour
of Chaos)"
Guitars: Buckethead
Drums: Brain
Bass, Effects: Bill Laswell

"Space After (The Consciousness That
Dances and Kills)"
Guitars: Buckethead
Drums: Brain
Bass: Bill Laswell

"Dark Hood"
Guitar: Buckethead
Effects: Bill Laswell

Yikes Records

Mold

"Meldt"
Bass, Cuts, Scratches, Scans: Bill Laswell
Treatments, Keyboards, Process: Alex Haas
**Drums, Guitars, Voice, Synthesis, Loops,
 Beats, Noise:** Peter Wetherbee
Dark Step Junglist: Julian Joyce
Guitars: Pat Thrall
Flutes: Anne Pollack
Voice: Charlotta Jansen

"Narcolepsy"
Bass, Cuts, Scratches, Scans: Bill Laswell
Treatments, Keyboards, Process: Alex Haas
**Drums, Guitars, Voice, Synthesis, Loops,
 Beats, Noise:** Peter Wetherbee
Dark Step Junglist: Julian Joyce
Guitars: Pat Thrall
Flutes: Anne Pollack
Voice: Charlotta Jansen

253

"Electric Soil"

Bass, Cuts, Scratches, Scans: Bill Laswell
Treatments, Keyboards, Process: Alex Haas
Drums, Guitars, Voice, Synthesis, Loops, Beats, Noise: Peter Wetherbee
Dark Step Junglist: Julian Joyce
Guitars: Pat Thrall
Flutes: Anne Pollack
Voice: Charlotta Jansen

"Sunshine"

Bass, Cuts, Scratches, Scans: Bill Laswell
Treatments, Keyboards, Process: Alex Haas
Drums, Guitars, Voice, Synthesis, Loops, Beats, Noise: Peter Wetherbee
Dark Step Junglist: Julian Joyce
Guitars: Pat Thrall
Flutes: Anne Pollack
Voice: Charlotta Jansen

"Bubble Stream"

Bass, Cuts, Scratches, Scans: Bill Laswell
Treatments, Keyboards, Process: Alex Haas
Drums, Guitars, Voice, Synthesis, Loops, Beats, Noise: Peter Wetherbee
Dark Step Junglist: Julian Joyce
Guitars: Pat Thrall
Flutes: Anne Pollack
Voice: Charlotta Jansen

"First Wish after Death"

Bass, Cuts, Scratches, Scans: Bill Laswell
Treatments, Keyboards, Process: Alex Haas
Drums, Guitars, Voice, Synthesis, Loops, Beats, Noise: Peter Wetherbee
Dark Step Junglist: Julian Joyce
Guitars: Pat Thrall
Flutes: Anne Pollack
Voice: Charlotta Jansen

"Lichenous Shock"

Bass, Cuts, Scratches, Scans: Bill Laswell
Treatments, Keyboards, Process: Alex Haas
Drums, Guitars, Voice, Synthesis, Loops, Beats, Noise: Peter Wetherbee
Dark Step Junglist: Julian Joyce
Guitars: Pat Thrall
Flutes: Anne Pollack
Voice: Charlotta Jansen

"Throes of Rasputin"

Bass, Cuts, Scratches, Scans: Bill Laswell
Treatments, Keyboards, Process: Alex Haas
Drums, Guitars, Voice, Synthesis, Loops, Beats, Noise: Peter Wetherbee
Dark Step Junglist: Julian Joyce
Guitars: Pat Thrall
Flutes: Anne Pollack
Voice: Charlotta Jansen

"Sqlxzm"

Bass, Cuts, Scratches, Scans: Bill Laswell
Treatments, Keyboards, Process: Alex Haas
Drums, Guitars, Voice, Synthesis, Loops, Beats, Noise: Peter Wetherbee
Dark Step Junglist: Julian Joyce
Guitars: Pat Thrall
Flutes: Anne Pollack
Voice: Charlotta Jansen

"Septic Plague"

Bass, Cuts, Scratches, Scans: Bill Laswell
Treatments, Keyboards, Process: Alex Haas
Drums, Guitars, Voice, Synthesis, Loops, Beats, Noise: Peter Wetherbee
Dark Step Junglist: Julian Joyce
Guitars: Pat Thrall
Flutes: Anne Pollack
Voice: Charlotta Jansen

"Viral Sonata #69"

Bass, Cuts, Scratches, Scans: Bill Laswell
Treatments, Keyboards, Process: Alex Haas
Drums, Guitars, Voice, Synthesis, Loops,
   Beats, Noise: Peter Wetherbee
Dark Step Junglist: Julian Joyce
Guitars: Pat Thrall
Flutes: Anne Pollack
Voice: Charlotta Jansen

Profanation

"Caution"

Vocals: Rammellzee
Guitars: Buckethead
Bass: Bill Laswell
Drums: Brain
Turntables: PhonosyncographDISK

"Worship"

Vocals: Hawkman, Maximum Bob
Guitar: Buckethead
Bass: Bill Laswell
Drums: Brain

"Ancient World"

Vocals: Dr. Israel
Guitars: Buckethead
Bass: Bill Laswell
Turntables: Grandmaster DXT
Beats: Monkey, Large

"Furies"

Vocals: Iggy Pop
Guitars: Buckethead
Bass: Bill Laswell
Drums: Brain

"Galaxies"

Vocals: Killah Priest
Guitars: Buckethead
Drums: Brain

Bass: Bill Laswell
Keyboards: Bernie Worrell
Turntables: PhonosycographDISK

"Sulfur and Cheese"

Vocals: Serj Tankian
Guitars: Buckethead
Bass: Bill Laswell
Drums: Brain

"Larynx"

Vocals: Mike Patton
Guitars: Buckethead
Bass: Bill Laswell
Turntables: PhonosycographDISK
Beats: Future Prophecies

"Revelations Part 2"

Vocals: Rammellzee
Guitar: Buckethead
Bass: Bill Laswell
Drums: Brain
Keyboards: Bernie Worrell
Turntables: PhonosycographDISK

"Ruined"

Bass: Bill Laswell
Drums: Tatsuya Yoshida

"Garbage God's"

Vocals: Rammellzee
Guitars: Buckethead
Bass: Bill Laswell
Turntables: Grandmixer DXT
Beats: Rawthang

"Babylon Blackout"

Guitars: Buckethead, Otomo Yoshihide
Bass: Bill Laswell
Drums: Brain
Keyboards: Bernie Worrell

"Endtime"

Guitars: Buckethead
Bass: Bill Laswell
Drums: Brain
Keyboards: Bernie Worrell

"Wedge"

Guitars: Buckethead
Bass: Bill Laswell
Drums: Brain

"Subgrid"

Guitars: Buckethead
Bass: Bill Laswell
Drums: Brain

— ☆ —

HARDWARE: 1992

This funk rock outing featured Band of Gypsies drummer Buddy Miles, Bootsy, and Stevie Salas as well as Mudbone Cooper, Bernard Fowler (of Rolling Stones fame), and George Clinton.

Rykodisc Records

Third Eye Open

"Got a Feelin'"

Guitar, Vocals: Stevie Salas
Bass, Vocals: Bootsy Collins
Drums, Vocals: Buddy Miles
Vocals: Mudbone Cooper, Bernard Fowler, George Clinton

"Waiting on You"

Guitar, Vocals: Stevie Salas
Bass, Vocals: Bootsy Collins
Drums, Vocals: Buddy Miles
Vocals: Mudbone Cooper, Bernard Fowler, George Clinton

"What's Goin' Down"

Guitar, Vocals: Stevie Salas
Bass: Bootsy Collins
Drums, Vocals: Buddy Miles
Vocals: Mudbone Cooper, Bernard Fowler, George Clinton

"Love Obsession (When the Eagle Flies)"

Guitar: Stevie Salas
Bass: Bootsy Collins
Drums, Bass, Vocals: Buddy Miles
Vocals: Mudbone Cooper, Bernard Fowler, George Clinton

"Hard Look"

Guitar: Stevie Salas
Bass: Bootsy Collins
Drums, Vocals: Buddy Miles
Vocals: Mudbone Cooper, Bernard Fowler, George Clinton

"Shake It"

Guitar, Vocals: Stevie Salas
Bass, Vocals: Bootsy Collins
Drums, Vocals: Buddy Miles
Digital Bollocks: David Friendly
Vocals: Mudbone Cooper, Bernard Fowler, George Clinton

"The Walls Came Down"

Guitar, Vocals: Stevie Salas
Bass: Bootsy Collins
Drums: Buddy Miles

"500 Years"

Guitar: Stevie Salas
Bass: Bootsy Collins
Drums, Vocals: Buddy Miles
Digital Bollocks: Vince MacLean

"Tell Me"

Guitar, Vocals: Stevie Salas
Bass: Bootsy Collins
Drums: Buddy Miles

"Leakin'"

Guitar: Stevie Salas
Bass, Vocals: Bootsy Collins
Drums: Buddy Miles
Vocals: Mudbone Cooper, Bernard Fowler,
    George Clinton

— ☆ —

DR. DRE (SELECT TRACKS): 1992

This West Coast gangsta rap pioneer and award-winning producer made many albums containing large amounts of interpolations and samples of P-Funk.

Death Row Records

"Let Me Ride"

Drum Programming, Lead Vocals: Dr. Dre
Drum Sample: Gary Mudbone Cooper
Guitar Sample: Garry Shider, Glenn Goins
Bass Sample: Bootsy Collins, Cordell Mosson
Backup Vocals: Snoop Dogg
Additional Vocals: Jewell, Ruben, Glenn Goins
    (sample)
Keyboards: Dr. Dre, Justin Reinhardt, Colin
    Wolfe, Bernie Worrell (sample)
Bass: Tony Green
Flute: Katisse Buckingham

"Let Me Ride," Dr. Dre's Grammy-winning rap song, has the advantage of containing some very addictive grooves and chants from Parliament's "Mothership Connection." Both studio versions and the live version (from the P-Funk *Earth Tour* album) were sampled as well as interpolated to make the song.

"The Roach (The Chronic Outro)"

**Drum Programming, Keyboards, Lead
    Vocals:** Dr. Dre
Drums: Cheron Moore
Sampled Drums: Gary Mudbone Cooper
Additional Vocals: Daz, Emmage, Jewell, RBX,
    Ruben, Rage
Sampled Bass: Bootsy Collins
Sampled Keyboards: Bernie Worrell
Sax: Katisse Buckingham

— ☆ —

TREY LEWD: 1992, 2003, 2018–

This is solo work by George Clinton's son Tracey Treylewd Lewis.

Warner Bros.

Drop the Line

"I'll Be Good to You"

Lead Vocals: Tracey Lewis
Backup Vocals: Pennye Ford, George Clinton
Rap: Dazzie Dee
Drums, Bass, Keyboards: Cecil Womack
Guitar: Binky Womack

"Hoodlums Who Ride"

Lead Vocals: Tracey Lewis
Backup Vocals: Pennye Ford, Andre Williams,
    Lloyd Williams, Joe Pep Harris, Amelia
    Jesse, Chris Hale, Claudia, Sidney Barnes
Drums, Bass, Guitar: Trey Stone
Keyboards: Trey Stone, Stewart Hanley

"Duck and Cover (Nuclearbuttbombbootybangbang)"

Lead Vocals: Tracey Lewis

Backup Vocals: Pennye Ford, Andre Williams,
Marcie Wilson, Joe Pep Harris, Amelia Jesse,
Chris Hale, Claudia, Sidney Barnes
Drums, Bass, Guitar: Trey Stone
Keyboards: Trey Stone, Andre Williams,
Stewart Hanley

"Yank My Doodle"

Lead Vocals: Tracey Lewis
Backup Vocals: Sheila Horne, Andre Williams
Drums, Keyboards: Amp Fiddler

"Rooster"

Lead Vocals: Tracey Lewis
Backup Vocals: Pennye Ford, Andre Williams
Drums: Michael Hampton
Bass, Guitar, Keyboards: Michael Hampton

"Nothing Comes to a Sleeper but Dream"

Lead Vocals: Tracey Lewis
Backup Vocals: George E. Clinton III, George
Clinton, Robert Peanut Johnson
Drums, Keyboards: Amp Fiddler
Sax: Greg Thomas
Trumpet: Bennie Cowan
Trombone: Greg Boyer

"Wipe of the Week"

Lead Vocals: Tracey Lewis
Backup Vocals: Pat Lewis, Sandra Feva, Jessica
Cleaves, Belita Woods, Michael Clip Payne
Drum Programming: Michael Clip Payne
Keyboards: David Spradley
Horns: Bennie Cowan, Greg Boyer, Greg
Thomas

"Drop the Line"

Lead Vocals: Tracey Lewis
Backup Vocals: Jessica Cleaves
Drums: Mark Bass
Bass: Lige Curry
Guitar: Tracey Lewis
Keyboards: Amp Fiddler

"Man of All Seasons"

Lead Vocals: Tracey Lewis
Backup Vocals: George Clinton
Drums, Synth Bass, Keyboards: Amp Fiddler
Horns: Gerald Albright, Mike Harris

"The Next Thing You'll Know (We'll Be)"

Lead Vocals: Tracey Lewis
Backup Vocals: Biti Straugn, Karen Jones, Sue
Ann Carwell
Rap: Klassy K
Drums: Mark Bass
Keyboards: Tracey Lewis

"Squeeze Toy"

Lead Vocals: Tracey Lewis,
Backup Vocals: Kevin Shider, Garry Shider,
Andre Williams, Patty Walker, George
Clinton
Drum Programming: Andre Williams
Bass: Tracey Lewis
Guitar: Tracey Lewis, Andre Williams, Kevin
Shider

RNB Boy: Return of the Clone Ranger

"Techno Pimp Part 1 & 2"
Lead Vocals: Tracey Lewis

"Let's Play Hooky"
Lead Vocals: Tracey Lewis

"Girlie Poo"

Lead Vocals: Tracey Lewis

"Victory Vaseline"

Lead Vocals: Tracey Lewis

"Party Me Up"

Lead Vocals: Tracey Lewis

"Hey Baybee"

Lead Vocals: Tracey Lewis

Independent Releases

Single

"Sex on the Beach"

Lead Vocals: Tracey Lewis
Backup Vocals: Curtis Womack, Sheila Horne
Drums, Bass, Guitar, Keyboards: Binky
   Womack

Do the Potty

"Do the Potty"

Lead Vocals: Tracey Lewis, Cribble Creo Sybil
All Instruments: Cory Jacobs

"Ya Mommy"

Lead Vocals: Tracey Lewis
All Instruments: Binky Womack

"I Should Not Be Doing This"

Lead Vocals: Tracey Lewis, George Clinton,
   Robert Peanut Johnson
Keyboards: Danny Bedrosian
Other Instruments: Rob Mandell

"Cluckwheat"

Lead Vocals: Tracey Lewis, Sheila Amuka
   Kelly
All Instruments: Binky Womack

"Manufactured Crackheads"

Lead Vocals: Tracey Lewis
All Instruments: Binky Womack

"So Much Fun"

Lead Vocals: Tracey Lewis
All Instruments: Binky Womack

— ☆ —

UMAR BIN HASSAN (SELECT TRACKS): 1992

This is the Last Poets cofounder's solo album, produced by Bill Laswell and featuring Bernie Worrell and others.

Axiom Label

Be Bop or Be Dead

"Niggers Are Scared of Revolution"

Vocals: Umar Bin Hassan
Backup Vocals: Abiodun Oyewole, Foday
   Musa Suso, Asante
Congas: Aiyb Dieng, Guilherme Franco
Drums: Buddy Miles
Guitar: Bootsy Collins
Kora Other: Foday Musa Suso
Drum Loops: Anton Fier
Organ: Amina Claudine Myers, Bernie Worrell

"Am"

Vocals: Umar Bin Hassan
Backup Vocals: Abiodun Oyewole, Foday Musa Suso, Asante
Congas: Aiyb Dieng, Guilherme Franco
Drums: Buddy Miles
Guitar: Bootsy Collins
Kora Other: Foday Musa Suso
Drum Loops: Anton Fier
Organ: Amina Claudine Myers, Bernie Worrell

"Bum Rush"

Vocals: Umar Bin Hassan
Backup Vocals: Abiodun Oyewole, Foday Musa Suso, Asante
Congas: Aiyb Dieng, Guilherme Franco
Drums: Buddy Miles
Guitar: Bootsy Collins
Kora Other: Foday Musa Suso
Drum Loops: Anton Fier
Organ: Amina Claudine Myers, Bernie Worrell

"This Is Madness"

Vocals: Umar Bin Hassan
Backup Vocals: Abiodun Oyewole, Foday Musa Suso, Asante
Congas: Aiyb Dieng, Guilherme Franco
Drums: Buddy Miles
Guitar: Bootsy Collins
Kora Other: Foday Musa Suso
Drum Loops: Anton Fier
Organ: Amina Claudine Myers, Bernie Worrell

"Malcolm"

Vocals: Umar Bin Hassan
Backup Vocals: Abiodun Oyewole, Foday Musa Suso, Asante
Congas: Aiyb Dieng, Guilherme Franco
Drums: Buddy Miles
Guitar: Bootsy Collins
Kora Other: Foday Musa Suso
Drum Loops: Anton Fier
Organ: Amina Claudine Myers, Bernie Worrell

"Pop"

Vocals: Umar Bin Hassan
Backup Vocals: Abiodun Oyewole, Foday Musa Suso, Asante
Congas: Aiyb Dieng, Guilherme Franco
Drums: Buddy Miles
Guitar: Bootsy Collins
Kora Other: Foday Musa Suso
Drum Loops: Anton Fier
Organ: Amina Claudine Myers, Bernie Worrell

"Love"

Vocals: Umar Bin Hassan
Backup Vocals: Abiodun Oyewole, Foday Musa Suso, Asante
Congas: Aiyb Dieng, Guilherme Franco
Drums: Buddy Miles
Guitar: Bootsy Collins
Kora Other: Foday Musa Suso
Drum Loops: Anton Fier
Organ: Amina Claudine Myers, Bernie Worrell

"40 Deuce Street"

Vocals: Umar Bin Hassan
Backup Vocals: Abiodun Oyewole, Foday Musa Suso, Asante
Congas: Aiyb Dieng, Guilherme Franco
Drums: Buddy Miles
Guitar: Bootsy Collins
Kora Other: Foday Musa Suso
Drum Loops: Anton Fier
Organ: Amina Claudine Myers, Bernie Worrell

"Personal Things"

Vocals: Umar Bin Hassan
Backup Vocals: Abiodun Oyewole, Foday Musa Suso, Asante
Congas: Aiyb Dieng, Guilherme Franco
Drums: Buddy Miles
Guitar: Bootsy Collins
Kora Other: Foday Musa Suso
Drum Loops: Anton Fier
Organ: Amina Claudine Myers, Bernie Worrell

— ☆ —

GEORGE CLINTON AND THE P-FUNK ALL STARS: 1993–1998, 2005–

This is a continuation of Parliament-Funkadelic's output into the 1990s and beyond. Much like Maceo Parker, Clinton and the All Star's longevity was boosted with incessant domestic and international live work. Many of the songs listed below have become cult classics due to the live shows that continue to the present day.

Independent Release

Dope Dogs

"Dog Star (Fly On)"

Lead Vocals: George Clinton
Backup Vocals: George Clinton, Michael Clip Payne, Louie Kabbabie, Andre Williams, Gabe Gonzalez
Drums: Gabe Gonzalez
Bass: Lige Curry
Guitar: Blackbyrd McKnight
Organ: Bernie Worrell

"U.S. Custom Coast Guard Dope Dog (slow P-Dope version)"

Lead Vocals: George Clinton
Backup Vocals: George Clinton Patavian Lewis, Greg Thompson, Robert Peanut Johnson, Andre Williams, Steve Boyd
Keyboards, Guitar: Jeff Bass
Drums: Mark Bass

"U.S. Custom Coast Guard Dope Dog (hyper P-Dope version)"

Lead Vocals: George Clinton
Backup Vocals: Andre Williams, Robert Peanut Johnson, George Clinton, Louie Kabbabie, Belita Woods, Paul Hill, Patavian Lewis, Steve Boyd
Keyboards: Andre Williams

Sax: Greg Thomas
Guitar: Andre Williams, Eddie Hazel

"Fifi"

Lead Vocals: Belita Woods, Robert Peanut Johnson
Backup Vocals: Lige Curry, George Clinton, Robert Peanut Johnson
Drums: Tiki Fulwood
Guitar, Synth Guitar: Dewayne Blackbyrd McKnight

"Some Next Shit"

Lead Vocals: George Clinton, Lige Curry, Clip Payne
Backup Vocals: George Clinton, Clip Payne, Lige Curry, Gabe Gonzalez, Fuzzy Haskins, Calvin Simon, Ray Davis, Grady Thomas, Starr Cullars, Shawn Clinton, Barbarella Bishop, Louie Kababbie, Linda Shider
Drums: Frankie Kash Waddy
Percussion: Larry Fratangelo
Bass: Bootsy Collins, Bruce Nazarian
Guitar: Blackbyrd McKnight, Michael Hampton
Keyboards: Bernie Worrell, Amp Fiddler
Sax: Greg Thomas
Trumpet: Bennie Cowan
Trombone: Greg Boyer

"Follow the Leader"

Lead Vocals: George Clinton, Derek Rossen,
Drum Programming, Guitar: Dewayne Blackbyrd McKnight
Bass: Bootsy Collins
Keyboards: Bernie Worrell, Amp Fiddler
Sax: Maceo Parker

"Just Say Ding (Data Boy)"

Lead Vocals: George Clinton, Tracey Lewis
Backup Vocals: Trafael Lewis
Drums, Bass, Guitar: Blackbyrd McKnight

**"Help Scottie, Help,
(I'm Tweakin' and I Can't Beam Up)"**

Lead Vocals: Tracey Lewis
Backup Vocals: George Clinton
Drums: Tiki Fulwood
Synth Bass, Keyboards: Tracey Lewis

"Police Doggy"

Lead Vocals: George Clinton, Derrick Rossen
Guitar: Blackbyrd McKnight
Keyboards: Amp Fiddler

"Lost Dog"

Lead Vocals: George Clinton
Backup Vocals: George Clinton, Denise
  Johnson, Bobby Gillespie, Jerome Rodgers,
  Charlie Wilson, Louie Kababbie
Drums: Steve
Bass: Henry Olsen
Guitar: Andrew Innes, Dennis White
Keyboards: Martin Duffy

"All Sons of Bitches"

Lead Vocals: Belita Woods, George Clinton,
  Derrek Rossen
Backup Vocals: Sa'D Ali, Belita Woods, Derrek
  Rossen, George Clinton
Drums: Mark Bass
Synth Bass, Keyboards: Amp Fiddler
Guitar: Blackbyrd McKnight, Michael
  Hampton

"Dopey Dope Dog"

Lead Vocals: Daddy Freddy, George Clinton
Backup Vocals: Lige Curry, Garry Shider,
  Sandra Feva, Pat Lewis, Joe Harris, Lloyd
  Williams, Andre Williams, George Clinton,
  Shirley Hayden, Janet Evans, Michael Clip
  Payne
Drum Programming: Amp Fiddler, Michael
  Clip Payne
Bass: Lige Curry

Guitar: Andre Foxxe Williams, Dewayne
  Blackbyrd McKnight
Keyboards: Amp Fiddler

"Sick Em"

Samples: George Clinton
Drums: Bootsy Collins
808: Mike E. Clark
Percussion: Michael Clip Payne
Lead Guitar: Eddie Hazel
Rhythm Guitar: Catfish Collins
Synthesizer: Bernie Worrell

"Pepe"

Lead Vocals: Patavian Lewis, Trafael Lewis,
  Belita Woods, Kevin Johnson, Tonysha
  Nelson
Keyboards: Amp Fiddler, Charlie Wilson
Drums: George Clinton, Michael Clip Payne
Clarinet: Perry Robinson
Percussion, Brushes: Muruga Booker
Guitar: Michael Hampton, Blackbyrd
  McKnight

"Pack of Wild Dogs"

Lead Vocals: George Clinton
Backup Vocals: Andre Williams, Robert Peanut
  Johnson, George Clinton, Louie Kabbabie,
  Belita Woods, Paul Hill, Patavian Lewis,
  Starr Cullars, Barbarella Bishop, Shawn
  Clinton, Clip Payne, Lige Curry, Ray Davis
Keyboards: Andre Williams
Guitar: Andre Williams, Eddie Hazel
Sax: Greg Thomas
Drums: Mike Clark

"I Ain't the Lady (He Ain't the Tramp)"

Lead Vocals: Jessica Cleaves, Amelia Jesse
Backup Vocals: George Clinton
Drums: Loic Gambas
Bass: Lonnie Motley
Guitar: Blackbyrd McKnight, Loic Gambas
Keyboards: Amp Fiddler
Trombone: Fred Wesley
Sax: Maceo Parker
Trumpet: Richard Griffith, Rick Gardner

"Tales That Wag the Dog Part 1 & 2"

Lead Vocals: George Clinton, Tracey Lewis, Derek Rossen
Backup Vocals: Steve Boyd, Garry Shider
Drums: Guy Curtis
Bass: Cordell Mosson
Guitar: Garry Shider
Keyboards: Bernie Worrell
Trumpet: Richard Griffith, Rick Gardner
Sax: Maceo Parker
Trombone: Fred Wesley

"Kibbles & Bits"

Lead Vocals: Patavian Lewis
All Samples: George Clinton
Backup Vocals: George Clinton, Louie Kababbie

"G-Man Dawg"

Lead Vocals: Greg Thompson
Backup Vocals: Greg Thompson, George Clinton, Keith Christian, Andre Robinson
Keyboards, Guitar: Jeff Bass
Drums: Mark Bass

"Jazz Stash"

Lead Vocals: George Clinton
Backup Vocals: Louie Kababbie, Patavian Lewis, Greg Thompson, Robert Peanut Johnson, Andre Williams, George Clinton
Keyboards: Amp Fiddler

"Hoe's Prairie Dog"

Lead Vocals: Louie Kababbie
Backup Vocals: Patavian Lewis
Drums: Mark Bass, Jeff Bass
Keyboards: Amp Fiddler

"My Dog"

Lead Vocals: George Clinton
Backup Vocals: Crop Holyfield, Belita Woods
Drums, Keyboards: Crop Holyfield

Sony 550 Music

The Awesome Power of a Fully Operational Mothership (T.A.P.O.A.F.O.M.)

"If Anybody Gets Funked Up (It's Gonna Be You)"

Vocals: George Clinton, Belita Woods, Mudbone Cooper, MC Breed, Erik Sermon, Michael Clip Payne, Andre Williams, Sheila Horne, Garry Shider, Linda Shider
Drums, Bass, Keyboards: Amp Fiddler

"Summer Swim"

Lead Vocals: George Clinton
Backup Vocals: Junie Morrison, Rob Manzoli, Michael Clip Payne, Andre Williams, Sheila Horne
Drums, Bass, Guitar, Keyboards, Trumpet: Junie Morrison

"Funky Kind (Gonna Knock It Down)"

Lead Vocals: George Clinton, Tracey Lewis
Backup Vocals: Tracey Lewis, Sa'D Ali, Pat Lewis, Junie Morrison, Sheila Horne
Drums: Sa'D Ali
Bass: Rodney Curtis
Guitar: Garry Shider
Keyboards: Amp Fiddler
Organ: Eddie Harsch

"Mathematics"

Lead Vocals: George Clinton, Belita Woods
Drums: Blackbyrd McKnight
Bass: Jeff Cherokee Bunn
Guitar, Synth Guitar: Blackbyrd McKnight

"Hard as Steel"

Lead Vocals: George Clinton
Backup Vocals: Sa'D Ali, Andre Williams
Drums: Sa'D Ali
Bass: A producer
Guitar: Dewayne Blackbyrd McKnight
Keyboards: A producer

"New Spaceship"

Lead Vocals: George Clinton, Charlie Wilson
Backup Vocals: Mudbone Cooper, Robert Peanut Johnson
Drums: Mudbone Cooper?, Bootsy Collins?
Bass, Guitar: Bootsy Collins
Keyboards: Charlie Wilson

"Underground Angel"

Lead Vocals: George Clinton, Nicole Tindall, Sheila Horne
Backup Vocals, Bass: Steve Boyd
Drums: Michael Clip Payne, Mark Bass
Guitar: Blackbyrd McKnight
Keyboards: Amp Fiddler, Steve Boyd

"Let's Get Funky"

Lead Vocals: George Clinton
Backup Vocals: Garry Shider, Andre Williams
Drum Programming, Keyboards: Amp Fiddler
Bass: Bubz Fiddler

"Flatman & Bobin"

Lead Vocals: Derrick Rossen, Clip Payne, George Clinton
Backup Vocals: Pat Lewis, Olivia Ewing, Sheila Horne, Nita Jason, Angela Workman
Drums: Tyrone Lampkin

Bass: Rodney Curtis
Guitar: Garry Shider
Keyboards: Bernie Worrell

"Sloppy Seconds"

Lead Vocals: George Clinton
Backup Vocals: Mudbone Cooper, Belita Woods, Pat Lewis, Robert Peanut Johnson, Sheila Horne
Drums: Mudbone Cooper
Bass: Bootsy Collins
Guitar: Blackbyrd McKnight
Keyboards: Bernie Worrell

"Rock the Party"

Lead Vocals: George Clinton
Backup Vocals: Olivia Ewing
Drums, Keyboards: Amp Fiddler
Bass: Bubz Fiddler
Strings: Detroit Symphony Orchestra

"Get Your Funk On"

Lead Vocals: George Clinton
Backup Vocals: Pat Lewis, Mudbone Cooper, Robert Peanut Johnson, Andre Williams
Drums: Ken Scott
Bass: Rodney Curtis
Keyboards: David Spradley
Sax: Eli Fountaine

"T.A.P.O.A.F.O.M (Fly Away)"

Lead Vocals: George Clinton
Backup Vocals: Glenn Goins, Mudbone Cooper, Robert Peanut Johnson, Clip Payne, Stephanie Clinton, Andre Williams, Sheila Horne, Charlie Wilson
Samples: Sa'D Ali
Drums: ?
Bass: ?
Guitar: Michael Hampton, Eddie Hazel

"If Anybody Gets Funked Up (It's Gonna Be You)" (Colin Wolfe mix)

Lead Vocals: George Clinton, Belita Woods, Mudbone Cooper
Backup Vocals: Michael Clip Payne, Andre Williams, Sheila Horne, Garry Shider, Linda Shider
Track: Colin Wolfe
Trumpet: Bennie Cowan
Sax: Greg Thomas
Trombone: Greg Boyer

Intersound Records

Live & Kickin

"Good Love"

Drums, Guitar: Blackbyrd McKnight
Bass: Lonnie Motley

"Aint Nuthin but A Jam Y'All"

Lead Vocals: George Clinton, the Dazz Band
Backup Vocals: The Dazz Band
Guitars: Garry Shider

"State of the Nation"

Lead Vocals: George Clinton
Backup Vocals: Garry Shider, Robert Peanut Johnson, Gary Mudbone Cooper
Drums: Frankie Kash Waddy
Bass: Lige Curry
Guitar: Garry Shider
Keyboards: Kelly

C-Kunspyruhzy Records

How Late Do U Have 2BB4UR Absent?

"Bounce to This"

Vocals: Kendra Foster, George Clinton, Garry Shider, Paul Hill, Mudbone Cooper, Belita Woods, Sheila Brody, Pat Lewis, Sandra Feva, Kim Manning
Drums: Blackbyrd McKnight
Bass: Shock G, Blackbyrd McKnight
Guitar: Blackbyrd McKnight, Rickey Rouse
Keyboards: Bernie Worrell

"Su, Su, Su"

Vocals: Tracey Lewis, George Clinton
Drum Programming: Gary Wright
Keyboards: Bernie Worrell

"Paradigm"

Vocals: George Clinton, Prince
Programming: Kool Ace
Bass, Guitar, Keyboards: Prince

"U Can Depend on Me"

Vocals: George Clinton, Kendra Foster, Rob Manzoli
Drums: Rob Manzoli, Sue Brooks
Bass, Guitar: Rob Manzoli
Keyboards: Sue Brooks

"U Ain't Runnin Shit"

Vocals: George Clinton, Que Bo Gold, Kool Ace, Jazze Pha, Little Blunt
All Instruments: Blackbyrd McKnight

"Inhale Slow"

Lead Vocals: Paul Hill
Man in the Box, Synthesizer, Vocals: Clip Payne
Organs, Synthesizer: Amp Fiddler
Guitar Solo: The Flash
Guitar: Chris Bittner

"Because/Last Time Zone"

Vocals: Clip Payne, Garry Shider, Elizabeth Withers,
Guitar: Felicia Collins, Garry Shider, and unknown classical guitarist

"Never Ending Love"

Vocals: George Clinton, Garry Shider, Robert Peanut Johnson, Mudbone Cooper, Lige Curry, Pat Lewis, Sandra Feva, Paul Hill, Steve Boyd, Belita Woods, Sheila Brody, Clip Payne
Drums: Frankie Kash Waddy
Bass: Rodney Curtis
Guitar: Blackbyrd McKnight, Dallas Austin, Colin Wolfe
Keyboards: Amp Fiddler, Bernie Worrell

"Sexy Side of You"

Vocals: George Clinton, Steve Boyd, Kevin Shider, Noel Haskins, Nate Shider
Drums: Noel Scott
Bass, Guitar: Nate Shider
Keyboards: Tim Shider, Jerome Rodgers

"Saddest Day"

Vocals: Belita Woods, Kendra Foster
Guitar: Cordell Mosson, Tracey Lewis
Keyboards: Jerome Rodgers

"I Can Dance"

Vocals: George Clinton, Raquel Brussolo, Sue Dog
Drums: Tiki Fulwood
Bass: Cordell Mosson
Guitar: Garry Shider
Keyboards: Bernie Worrell
Violin: Lili Haydn

"I'll Be Sittin Here"

Vocals: George Clinton, Joi Gilliam, Kenny Brazil
All Instruments: Kenny Brazil

"Don't Dance Too Close"

Vocals: Belita Woods, Jim Wright
All Instruments: Vaughn Wilson

"More Than Words Can Say"

Vocals: Belita Woods, Mudbone Cooper
Instruments: Parliament-Funkadelic

"Butt-a-Butt"

Vocals: George Clinton, Poo Poo Man, RonKat Spearman, Kendra Foster, J. T. Money, J. T. Bigger Figger, Kim Manning, Robert Peanut Johnson, Vaughn Wilson, Belita Woods
Programming, Keyboards: Leslee at DARP, Bigger Figger
Guitar: Rob Manzoli

"Something Stank"

Vocals: Shonda Clinton, Tracey Lewis
Drums: Dennis Chambers
Bass: Donnie Sterling
Guitar: Gordon Carlton, Tony Thomas
Keyboards: Manon Saulsby, Ernestro Wilson

"Our Secret"

Vocals: Tracey Lewis, Belita Woods, Mudbone Cooper, Pat Lewis, Robert Peanut Johnson, George Clinton
Drums: Mudbone Cooper
Bass: Tracey Lewis
Guitar: Blackbyrd McKnight, Michael Hampton, Eddie Hazel
Keyboards: Tracey Lewis

"Viagra"

Vocals: George Clinton, Del tha Funky Homosapien
Drums: Ron Wright
Bass: Lige Curry
Guitar: Blackbyrd McKnight, Michael Hampton, Eric McFadden

"Gypsy Woman"

Vocals: George Clinton
Drums, Percussion: Ron Wright
Bass: Lige Curry
Guitar: Blackbyrd McKnight
Mandolin: Eric McFadden

"Whole Lotta Shakin'"

Vocals: George Clinton, Bobby Womack, RonKat Spearman, Belita Woods
Drums: DCat Cornelius
Samples: Jasper Bunk
Bass: RonKat Spearman
Guitar: Rickey Rouse, Blackbyrd McKnight, Martin Jepsen Anderson
Keyboards: Jerome Rodgers, Billy Preston

"Goodnight, Sweetheart, Goodnight"

Vocals: George Clinton, Ray Davis, Fuzzy Haskins, Calvin Simon, Grady Thomas
All Music: George Clinton, Gary Wright

"Whatchamacallit"

Vocals: George Clinton, Belita Woods
Drums: Tiki Fulwood
Bass: Billy Nelson, Eddie Hazel
Keyboards, Synthesizers: Bernie Worrell
Guitar: Eddie Hazel, Jim Callon
Sax: Eli Fontaine

"Trust in Yourself"

Vocals: George Cinton, Kendra Foster, Kenny Brazil
All Instruments: Kenny Brazil

"Booty"

Vocals: Louie Kababbie, George Cinton
Drums: Vaughn Wilson
Bass: Steve Boyd
Guitar: Vaughn Wilson
Keyboards: George Clinton, Vaughn Wilson

"Get the Fuck Out"

Vocals: Shonda Clinton, Rico Lewis, Tracey Lewis, Clip Payne
Drums: Frankie Kash Waddy
Bass: Lige Curry
Guitar: Blackbyrd McKnight, Shaunna Hall
Keyboards: Jerome Rodgers, Danny Bedrosian

GEORGE CLINTON SAMPLE SOME OF DISC . . . SAMPLE SOME OF D.A.T.: 1993

George Clinton put out a series of sample albums for producers, DJs, and rappers in the 1990s. It would be nearly impossible to find a way to acquire all the personnel info on these compilations of thousands of samples. Instead, the author has listed all the samples included and what is exactly on each sample both instrumentally and vocally. This series, released by P-Vine, represents a massive collection in itself.

P-Vine Records

First Collection

Blackbird or Michael: full live band samples
Partys over Horns: full live band samples
Partys over Horns: full live band samples
Here comes Dad: full live band sample (break)
Lift Off: full band
Were unlisted: full band
No zip code: full band and vocals
Fake ID: full band vocals too
I like it: full band vocals too multiple samples
Its LAI to me: breaks full band (pickups only)
Too Hungry: full band
For Weed: full band
Blopity Blopity: full band with piano
Blip Blip Tik: full band with piano and solos
Now Time: full band with piano and changes

We Funk U2: drums, guitar, bass, all changes, full song

Come on one mar . . . : drums, guitar, bass, all changes, full song

Sly one: full band all changes

Time was: Vox only

I Spy Vocals: piano

Vocals from somewhere: Vox only

Oatmeal cookies: full band, synthesizer, changes

Oatmeal Guitars: guitars, drums

Oatmeal Horns: horns, guitar

Holy Smoke Full: horns, guitar

Holy Fuzz: bass, drums, guitar, bass, keyboards

Holy Guitar & 1: bass, drums

Holy Piano: bass, drums

Holy Horn Solo: bass, drums

Holy Bass Pops: guitar, drums

Holy Drums . . . : piano, bass, drums

All Night Full Mix: horns only

All Night Bass & D: horns only

Cap it Full: horns only

Cap it Bass and . . . : bass only

I didn't come up: drums only

I didn't come bass . . . : full song with changes and keyboards

I didn't come Horns . . . : drums and bass, all changes

I didn't come rhythm . . . : drums, all changes

I didn't come Boo . . . : guitars and keyboards, all changes

I didn't come clap: bass, all changes

I didn't come percussion: full band with keyboards and changes

I didn't come horns: bass and drums and changes

Live and Love Full: guitar, bass, drums, keyboards, change

Im Pretty Sure Bass: count off, bass, drums (break)

Im Pretty Sure Guitar: full band with horns, changes, keyboards, etc.

Untitled Full: drums, bass, claps, changes

Can you name Da . . . : drums, claps

Can you name Da . . . : drums, claps, horns

Can you name Da . . . : horns only

Can you name Da . . . : horns only

Your place . . . : horn hit (one), guitar, keyboards, drums (changes)

1 Mo Time: bass, clap

Secrets Part 1: percussion, claps

Sexy Thing: breaks and full band with changes and synthesizer

Mickey Mouse: drums and bass, changes

Ricky Rank: drums, bass, guitars

Get up with . . . : drums, bass, guitars, changes

Fannyland: drums, bass, guitars, changes

Not Tonite: bass, drums, pickup

Not Tonite pickup: drums, a little guitar, pickup

Not Tonite G, CL: drums, bass, guitar

Not Tonite Drum: drums, bass, guitar

Not Tonite Drum: drums, bass, guitar

Not Tonite G & CL: full song, synthesizer included, changes, etc.

Open All night: full song change, piano included

Open all Night B &: full song change, piano included

Open all Night G &: full song change, synthesizer included

Open all Night Drums: bass and claps and piano, Vox, guitar

Open all Night Guitar: bass, claps, drums, vocals, piano

Open all night Bass: bass, claps, piano solo, Vox, guitar, drums

Where is the Party: drums and bass

Party Drums, Bass..: drums, bass, guitar, keyboards

Party Bass & Claps: drums, claps, synthesizers

Party Bass: synthesizers, claps, percussion

Party Drums: full band, drums, guitars, bass

Party here Full: drums, guitar, keyboards

Party here D, B &: full band, changes

Partys Here Drum . . . : drums, bass, guitar, keyboards

Partys here B&D: drums, bass

Partys over B&D: drums, guitar, keyboards
Partys over horns: drums
Partys over Horns: drums
Here Comes Dad: guitar, keyboards
Here comes Dad: bass, drums, guitar, full part
Here Comes Dad: bass, drums
Here Comes Dad: guitar, drums
Here Comes Dad: drums only
Here Comes Dad: guitars only
Can you get some: bass only
Can you get Some: full band, including keyboards, drums, horns, guitar, bass
Can you get some: full band minus horns
Can you get some: keyboards, bass
+ 1 Full: bass only
+1 no piano: drums, voice
+1 Drum: full song with horns, bass, drums, keyboards, guitar
+ 1 Bass: drums, bass, keyboards
+ 1 2: bass, drums
+1 PART 2: 7 minutes long, bass, drums, other full songs, horns, drums, organ, bass, multiple full songs and parts

Second Collection

Make Me Smile Full: full song with all instruments, horns, keyboards
Make Me Smile: full song change, synthesizer
Make Me Smile: drums, guitar, piano
Make Me Smile: horns only
Make Me Smile: piano only
Make me Smile: full change with piano, horns, etc.
Make Me Smile: change, horns, drums
Make Me Smile: drums change
Fannyland: drums, guitar, keyboards
Fannyland Fanny . . . : drums
Fannyland Bass &: bass, drums
Fannyland Drums &: drums, keyboards
Fannyland (Bass): bass only
Closed 4 inventory: bass, drums, keyboards, guitar
Closed 4 inventory: bass, drums
Closed 4 Inventory: drums only

Closed 4 inventory: guitars and keyboards
Injuns get Funky: full song with horns and synthesizer
Indians get Funky: change full band
Injuns: bass, guitar
Injuns: drums, percussion
Injuns: change guitar, bass
Just Because: drums, bass, guitar, keyboards
Just Because, Full Change: drums, bass, guitar, keyboards
Just Because, another change: drums, bass, guitar, keyboards
Just Because: drums, guitar, keyboards
Just Because 2: bass, drums, keyboards, guitar
Just Because 2: bass, drums, keyboards, guitar
Lets keep it upstr . . . : drums, bass, guitar (changes)
Lets keep it upstr . . . : drums, bass, guitar (changes)
Can I play: drums, man in the box, guitar, bass
Can I play #2: drums, man in the box, guitar
Apple BRN Betty: full song with horns, synthesizer, etc.
Apple BRN Betty: full song with sax solo
Apple BRN Betty: drums, percussion, bass, horns
Apple BRN Betty: drums, percussion
Apple BRN Betty: guitar, keyboards, drums
Apple BRN Betty: horns, guitars, keyboards
Betty Piece: horns only
Betty Piece 3: horns only
Betty's Piece 4: horns only
Betty Biggest hit: horn hits
Betty's Biggest hit: horn hits
Betty's Biggest Hit: horn hits
Stick It: bass, keyboards, drums, guitar, full song
Stick It: drums, horns
Stick it: drums, bass
Slam it: drums, guitar, keyboards, horns, bass, full song
Slam it 2: drums, guitar, keyboards, bass
Slam it: drums, guitar, keyboards, bass
Speed Stick: bass, keyboards, guitars, horns

Top Hat: drums, guitar, bass
Top Hat: drums, bass
Top Hat: drums, bass
Top Hat: drums, guitar, bass
She's with the Band: drums, guitar, bass, semi-full band
She's with the band: drums, bass
She's with the Band: drums, guitar
Funk Attack: drums, percussion, bass, synthesizer, guitar
Funk Attack: drums, bass, guitar
Funk Attack: percussion, guitar
Funk Attack: guitar
Funk Attack: bass
Funk Attack: synthesizer, guitar
Funk Attack: bass, synthesizer
Funk Attack: synthesizer, guitar
Funk Attack: change, bass, guitar, drums
Batty Batty Batty: drums, bass, keyboards, guitar, full song
Wild Westley: drums, bass
Wild Westley: bass
Wild Westley: bass, keyboards
Wild Westley: keyboards
Wild Westley: drums, guitars, keyboards, bass
Wild Westley: drums, guitars, keyboards, bass
Wild Westley: full band with horns
Wild Westley: full band with horns change and pickup
Wild Westley: full band with horns
Wild Westley: full band with horns
Wild Westley: horns, guitar, bass
Wild Westley: horns, guitar, bass
Wild Westley: horns
Wild Westely: horns
Wild Westley: horns
Wild Westley: horns
Wild Westley: horns
Wild Westley: horns
Wild Westley: sax
Wild Westley: sax
Skip to a Gruv: count in, full song
Skip to a Gruv: full change

Skip to a Gruv: full change with bass and drums only
Funky Skips: full change, third part
More Skippy: full change, fourth part
Atomic Rooster: Red Hot Mama take, with drums, bass, keyboards, guitars
Rippin Rooster: Red Hot Mama take with keyboard section
Rooster Organs: keyboard
Rooster: guitar only
Rooster: full band

Third Collection

We Need Full: full band with count in
We Need . . . : bass, drums
We Need . . . : bass, drums, guitar
We Need: change, bass, drums, guitar
We Need: change, full band
We Need: guitar
Elevator: keyboard, guitar
Elevator: change, keyboard, guitar, bass
Elevator: change, keyboard, guitar, bass
Elevator: piano, guitar, bass
Disco, *Cosmic Slop*: bass, keyboards, drums
Disco: bass, drums, keyboards, cosmic slop
Disco, "Undisco Kidd": drums, bass, keyboards
Disco, "Do That Stuff": drums, bass, keyboards
Disco, "Do That Stuff": drums, bass, key keyboards change
Disco, "I Can Move You (If You Let Me)": drums, bass, keyboards
Disco, "I Can Move You (If You Let Me)": drums, bass, keyboards
Disco, "Groove": bass, drums, keyboards
Disco, more *Cosmic Slop* pickups: bass, drums, keyboards
Disco, more *Cosmic Slop* pickups: drums, bass, keyboards
Disco, "Groove": bass, drums, keyboards
Close: drums, bass, guitars
Close: change, drums, bass, guitars

Close: bass, guitars
Close: change, bass, guitars
Close: guitar 1
Tease: bass, guitars
Teasin Turn: bass, guitars
Teasing more . . . : bass, guitars
Teasin Changey: bass, guitars, break
Teasin Chicka: bass, guitars
Gimme that mouth: full band
Gimme Mouth: change full band
Gimme Mouth band: full band change
Gimme Mouth G&: drums, guitar
Gimme Mouth G&: drums, guitar, keyboards
Mouf: bass, drums
Mouf: drums
Half and Half: full band with pickups
Half turn: full band with guitar solo
Left Turn: full band with guitar solo
Half Time: full band with guitar solo
Full Time Out: full band, one part with guitar solo
Half Clap: drums, clap, bass, guitar
The Encounter: drums, piano
Encounter da . . . : drums, string section
Encounter: piano, drums
Staccato encounter: drums, piano, strings
Encounter the Bernie: drums, piano, strings
Encounter Group: change, drums, piano, strings
Solo String Encounter: strings only
Drum da String: strings, piano, drums
You'll Never Work: piano, drums
Diggin on a Gruv: drums, guitars, bass
D.I.G.: change drums, guitar, bass
Phunck: full band
PU2: full band
Master Blastr: drums, guitar, bass, keyboards
Dance your Full: full band with guitar solo
Dance: synthesizer, guitar, drums
Window Pane: count off, synth bass, piano, guitars,
Nu Wave: drums, percussion, breaks, guitars, bass, keyboards, multiple takes

Keep it Solid: GC vocal takes
Ugh Anytime: GC vocal takes
Aint it funky: GC vocal takes
Hang Loose: GC vocal takes (piano in background)
Lay right there: GC vocal takes
Aww . . . : GC vocal takes
Solid: GC vocal takes
Piff it: GC vocal takes
Bass Du Jour: Dope Dogs synth bass
Dogs on Dope: vocal, cello sample, Dope Dog breaks, voices
Moog over Miami: synthesizer
Rocky Mt guitar: guitar, samples, bass, sax
CIA chants: vocal parts, bass, guitar, keyboards, samples, vocal chants, drum programming
Dog Poop: vocal chants
Dumper notes: bass or synth bass
Pfunk Sampler: samples, drums, bass, horn, piano, guitar
Echo Valley Dog: GC vocal takes with echo
Bass Drools: synth bass
Guitars and Bongos: guitars, synthesizer
Waroc Guitars: lead guitar
Dogs with the Clap: drums, vocal samples, percussion
keys in my hand: keyboard, samples, synthesizer
Mutations: guitar
Clears . . . : guitar
Living Funk: Dr. Funkenstein live sample, keyboards, vocal chants
Blow Me: Horn solo samples separated (multiple)

— ☆ —

THE GOOMBAS FTG. GEORGE CLINTON: 1993

Capitol Records

Super Mario Bros. Soundtrack

"Walk the Dinosaur"

Lead and Backup Vocals: George Clinton
Instrumentation, Production: Don Was
Production: Peter Afterman, Tim Devine
Programming: Tom Daugherty
Additional Parts: Keith Cohen

"Walk the Dinosaur" was a remake of the "Was (Not Was)" song and was used as one of the main songs in the ill-fated *Super Mario Bros.* movie from the same year.

— ☆ —

PAUL SHAFFER AND THE PARTY BOYS OF ROCK N' ROLL: 1993

Paul Shaffer was the influential keyboardist for *Late Night with David Letterman* for decades. His 1993 album features several P-Funkers. Bernie Worrell was briefly in Shaffer's Late Night Band.

SBK Records

"Black Dog"

Vocals: Dana Carvey, Jon Lovitz, Mike Myers, George Clinton
Drums: Anton Fig
Keyboards: Paul Shaffer
Guitar: Sid McGinns
Bass: Will Lee

"1999"

Vocals: Bootsy Collins, Leonard Cohen
Drums: Anton Fig
Keyboards: Paul Shaffer
Guitar: Sid McGinnis
Bass: Bootsy Collins, Will Lee

"Jamp"

Vocals: Bootsy Collins, Carles Koppelman, Dana Carvey, David Sanborn, Derek Smalls & Cindy, Eartha Kitt, Irving Cohen, Jennifer Finch, Joan Jett, Jon Lovitz, Mike Myers
Guitar: Todd Rundgren, Sid McGinnis
Bass: Will Lee
Drums: Anton Fig
Keyboards: Paul Shaffer

— ☆ —

FOLEY: 1993

Foley was the bassist for Miles Davis in the 1990s, known for his "lead bass" playing on those shows, as well as a key musical contributor to *Arrested Development*. He joined George Clinton and crew for the 1993 *Hey Man Smell My Finger* album on bass, vocals, and songwriting. His solo album *7 Years*, produced around the same time, has a heavy P-Funk presence in personnel and output. Foley would later go on to be one of the drummers for Clinton and Parliament-Funkadelic from 2008 to 2014.

Blue Note

7 Years

"Preface"

Voice: George Clinton

"Cum Round"

Bass Solo: Byron Miller
Vocals: Belita Woods
Guitar: Andre Foxxe Williams
Keyboard Solo: Larry Dunn
Performer, Additional Hoot Nanny: Foley

"Ain't No Class (In the Middle)"

Horns: Bennie Cowan, Greg Boyer, Greg
 Thomas
Rap: Foley, George Clinton, Speech, May May
Voice: Aerle Taree
Other Instruments: Foley

"R U Gonna B"

Alto Sax: Kenny Garrett
Backup Vocals: Foley, Garry Shider, Ligge
 Curry, Stokley Williams, The Steele Singers
Lead Vocals: Belita Woods
Other Instruments: Foley

"Better Not Die (N Amerikka Being Black)"

Rap: J.L. MC
All Instruments: Foley

"If It's Positive"

Backup Vocals: Steele Singers
Rap: Speech
Synthesizers: Larry Dunn
Voice: Aerle Taree

"September 28th, 1991"

String Arrangement: Larry Dunn
Lead Bass: Foley
Conductor: Eddie Del Barrio
Piano: Deron Johnson

"Love Is . . . Strange"

Alto Sax: Kenny Garrett
Backup Vocals: Belita Woods, Garry Shider,
 Lynn Davis, Lynn Mabry, Steele Singers
Other Instruments: Foley

"Tell Miss Thang"

Alto Sax: Kenny Garrett
Backup Vocals: Belita Woods, Garry Shider,
 Lige Curry, Lynn Davis, Lynn Mabry, the
 Steele Singers
Lead Vocals: Belita Woods
Other Instruments: Foley
Performer: Foley, May May

"Little Davis"

Piano: Deron Johnson
Tenor Sax: Gary Thomas

"Black Dog"

Bass, Electric Piano, Vocals: Foley
Drums: Michael Bland
Guitar Solo 1: Dewayne Blackbyrd McKnight
Guitar Solo 2: Michael Hampton
Guitar Solo 3: Keith Staten

"Date Rape (Remix) 40 Solos and a Mule"

Alto Sax: Kenny Garrett
Lead Bass Solo: Foley
Drums: Blaine Emerson
Keyboard Solo 1: Deron Johnson
Keyboard Solo 2: Larry Dunn
Keyboards, Piano: Jim Maneri

"The Godfather"

Lead Bass, Bass: Foley
Drums: Blaine Emerson
Keyboards, Piano: Jim Maneri

"Dreams on Da Floor"

Alto Sax: Kenny Garrett
Backup Vocals: Lynn Davis, Selandra Wright
Voice: Sister Souljah

"Closing"

Voice: George Clinton

"The Senate"

Drums, Bass, Keyboards, Piano, Bass: Foley

— ☆ —

ZILLATRON: 1993

This metal/funk project by Bootsy and company was produced by Bill Laswell. Features several P-Funk and Praxis members.

Rykodisc

Lord of the Harvest

"C.B.I. Files"

Bass, Voices, Samples, Beats: Bootsy Collins
Synthesizers: Bernie Worrell
Guitar: Buckethead
Ambient Sounds, Noises: Bill Laswell

"Buggg Lite"

Bass, Voices, Samples, Beats: Bootsy Collins
Electric Piano, Synthesizer: Bernie Worrell
Guitar: Buckethead
Ambient Sounds, Noises: Bill Laswell
Chant: Grandmaster Melle Mel

"Fuzz Face"

Bass, Voices, Samples, Beats: Bootsy Collins
Hammond Organ, Synthesizers: Bernie
    Worrell
Guitar: Buckethead
Ambient Sounds, Noises: Bill Laswell
Backup Vocals: Moma Collins

"Exterminate"

Bass, Voices, Samples, Beats: Bootsy Collins
Hammond Organ, Synthesizers: Bernie
    Worrell
Guitar: Buckethead
Ambient Sounds, Noises: Bill Laswell

"Smell the Secrets"

Bass, Voices, Samples, Beats: Bootsy Collins
Hammond Organ, Synthesizers: Bernie
    Worrell
Guitar: Buckethead
Ambient Sounds, Noises: Bill Laswell
Chant: Grandmaster Melle Mel, Umar bin
    Hassan

"Count Zero"

Bass, Voices, Samples, Beats: Bootsy Collins
Ambient Sounds, Noises: Bill Laswell

"Bootsy and the Beast"

Bass, Voices, Samples, Beats: Bootsy Collins
Hammond Organ, Synthesizers: Bernie
    Worrell
Guitar: Buckethead
Ambient Sounds, Noises: Bill Laswell
Chant: Umar bin Hassan

"No Fly Zone (The Devil's Playground)"

Bass, Voices, Samples, Beats: Bootsy Collins
Hammond Organ, Synthesizers: Bernie
    Worrell
Guitar: Buckethead
Ambient Sounds, Noises: Bill Laswell

"The Passion Continues"

Lead Vocals, Voices, Samples: Bootsy Collins
Hammond Organ: Bernie Worrell
Acoustic and Electric Guitars: Buckethead
Ambient Sounds, Noises: Bill Laswell
Backup Vocals: Debra Barsha, Kristen Gray,
    Momma Collins, Brenda Holloway, Patti
    Willis

— ☆ —

SNOOP DOGG (SELECT TRACK): 1993

Snoop Dogg's career has a lot thematically to do with the music of P-Funk. It is no wonder that the featured track features both an interpolation of "(Not Just) Knee Deep" and George Clinton himself. Truly, the entire *Doggystyle* album is chock-full of P-Funk interpolations, largely thanks to producer Dr. Dre.

Death Row Records

"G-Funk Intro"

Vocals: George Clinton, The Lady of Rage, Snoop Dogg, Dr. Dre
Production: Dr. Dre

— ☆ —

ICE CUBE (SELECT TRACK): 1993

This West Coast gangsta rap pioneer made several albums featuring a bevy of samples of P-Funk and a well-known performance with George Clinton that became a massive hit.

Priority Records

"Bop Gun (One Nation)"

Lead Vocals: Ice Cube
Lead Vocals: George Clinton
Backup Vocals: George Clinton, Bootsy Collins
Production: Ice Cube, QDIII

"Bop Gun" by Ice Cube is essentially a "One Nation Under a Groove" interpolated remake, featuring George Clinton and Bootsy in the music video, and features Ice Cube using almost all P-Funk song titles or lyrics to make up the lyrics of the song. It also was a big part of P-Funk's comeback in the 1990s (other key reasons for Clinton's comeback at this time include the debut albums by Dr. Dre and Snoop Dogg, the Lollapalooza Tour, and the movie *PCU*).

O.G. FUNK 1994

This solo album is by original Funkadelic bassist Billy Nelson and features several P-Funk mainstays and old school rap pioneers. it was coproduced by Bill Laswell.

Rykodisc

Out of the Dark

"Yeah Yeah Yeah"

Lead Vocals: Prince Whipper Whip, Billy Nelson, Melle Mel
Backup Vocals: Billy Nelson, Bernard Fowler, Mudbone Cooper, Bernie Worrell, C-Dog, Billy Spruill, Marque Gilmore, Peter Wetherbee, J. Maximina Juson, Latasha Natasha Diggs, Chris Ashley, Sekenya Nelson, Archie Ford
Drums: Jerome Brailey
Bass: Billy Nelson
Guitar: Spacey T. Singleton, Billy Nelson, Blake Smith, Billy Spruill
Keyboards: Bernie Worrell

"Funk Is in the House"

Lead Vocals: Prince Whipper Whip, Billy Nelson
Backup Vocals: Billy Nelson, Mudbone Cooper, Bernard Fowler, Bernie Worrell, C-Dog, Billy Spruill, Marque Gilmore, Peter Wetherbee, J. Maximina Juson, Latasha Natasha Diggs, Chris Ashley, Sekenya Nelson, Archie Ford
Drums: Jerome Brailey
Bass: Billy Nelson
Guitar: Spacey T. Singleton, Billy Nelson, Blake Smith, Billy Spruill
Keyboards: Bernie Worrell

"Funkadelic Groupie"

Lead Vocals, Bass: Billy Nelson
Backup Vocals: Billy Nelson, Mudbone Cooper, Bernard Fowler, Bernie Worrell
Drums: Jerome Brailey
Guitar: Spacey T. Singleton
Keyboards: Bernie Worrell

"Music for My Brother"

Drums: Jerome Brailey
Bass: Billy Nelson
Guitar: Spacey T. Singleton, Billy Nelson, Blake Smith, Billy Spruill
Keyboards: Bernie Worrell

"I've Been Alone"

Lead Vocals: Billy Nelson, Prince Whipper Whip, Melle Mel
Backup Vocals: Billy Nelson, Mudbone Cooper, Bernard Fowler
Drums: Jerome Brailey
Bass: Billy Nelson
Guitar: Spacey T. Singleton, Billy Nelson, Blake Smith, Billy Spruill
Keyboards: Bernie Worrell

"I Wanna Know"

Lead Vocals: Billy Nelson, Prince Whipper Whip, Melle Mel
Backup Vocals: Billy Nelson, Mudbone Cooper, Bernard Fowler, Bernie Worrell, C-Dog, Billy Spruill, Marque Gilmore, Peter Wetherbee, J. Maximina Juson, Latasha Natasha Diggs, Chris Ashley, Sekenya Nelson, Archie Ford
Drums: Jerome Brailey
Bass: Billy Nelson
Guitar: Spacey T. Singleton, Billy Nelson, Blake Smith, Billy Spruill
Keyboards: Bernie Worrell

"Don't Take Your Love from Me"

Lead Vocals, Bass: Billy Nelson
Backup Vocals: Billy Nelson, Mudbone Cooper, Bernard Fowler
Drums: Jerome Brailey
Guitar: Spacey T. Singleton, Billy Nelson, Blake Smith, Billy Spruill
Keyboards: Bernie Worrell

"Out of the Dark"

Lead Vocals, Bass: Billy Nelson
Backup Vocals: Billy Nelson, Mudbone Cooper, Bernard Fowler
Drums: Jerome Brailey
Guitar: Spacey T. Singleton, Billy Nelson, Blake Smith, Billy Spruill
Keyboards: Bernie Worrell

"Angie"

Lead Vocals: Billy Nelson, Prince Whipper Whip
Backup Vocals: Billy Nelson, Mudbone Cooper, Bernard Fowler
Drums: Jerome Brailey
Bass: Billy Nelson
Guitar: Spacey T. Singleton, Blake Smith, Billy Spruill
Keyboards: Bernie Worrell

— ☆ —

GEORGE CLINTON AND PARLIAMENT-FUNKADELIC: 1994

"Erotic City"

Lead Vocals: George Clinton
Backup Vocals: Garry Shider, Ray Davis, Belita Woods, Mudbone Cooper, Tracey Lewis, Clip Payne
Drums: Keith LeBlanc
Bass: Doug Wimbush
Guitar: Blackbyrd McKnight, Andre Williams
Keyboards: Amp Fiddler

"Tear the Roof Off the Sucker '94"

Lead Vocals: Ray Davis, George Clinton, Garry Shider, Mudbone Cooper
Backup Vocals: Belita Woods, Tracey Lewis
Drums: Frankie Kash Waddy
Bass: Cordell Mosson
Guitar: Dewayne Blackbyrd McKnight, Garry Shider
Keyboards: Amp Fiddler
Trumpet: Bennie Cowan
Sax: Greg Thomas
Trombone: Greg Boyer

"Stomp"

Lead Vocals: George Clinton
Backup Vocals: Garry Shider, Ray Davis, Gary Mudbone Cooper, Belita Woods
Drums: Keith LeBlanc
Bass: Doug Wimbush
Guitar: Blackbyrd McKnight, Skip McDonald, Andre Williams
Keyboards: Amp Fiddler
Trumpet: Bennie Cowan
Sax: Greg Thomas
Trombone: Greg Boyer

The songs listed above are part of the *PCU* movie soundtrack.

— ☆ —

P-FUNK GUITAR ARMY: 1994, 1997

This two-volume tribute to Jimi Hendrix features many of P-Funk's most well-known six-string axmen.

P-Vine Records

Tributes to Jimi Hendrix Vols. 1 and 2

"Scuse Me while I Kiss the Sky"

Guitar: Ras Kente
Vocals: John Sinclair

"Purple Hazel"

Drums: Jerome Brailey?
Guitar: Eddie Hazel
Bass: Bootsy Collins

"Pleasure with the Dirt Devil"

Drums: Gabe Gonzalez
Guitar: Dewayne Blackbyrd McKnight
Bass: Lige Curry
Keyboards: Amp Fiddler
Lead Vocals: Dewayne McKnight, Michael Clip Payne
Backup Vocals: Larry Heckstall, Andre Williams

"Positivity"

Drums, Guitar, Bass, Vocals: Michael Hampton

"Look Now Baby"

Guitar: James Glass

Billy "Bass" Nelson, Garry Shider, Cordell "Boogie" Mosson and Dewayne "Blackbyrd" McKnight, part of the P-Funk Guitar Army around 1995. Kinley-McCoy / GROOVE MANEUVERS ARCHIVES

"Fly On"
Drums: Gabe Gonzalez
Guitar: Dewayne Blackbyrd McKnight
Bass: Lige Curry
Organ: Bernie Worrell
Vocals: George Clinton, Michael Clip Payne, Louie Kabbabie, Andre Williams, Gabe Gonzalez

"Reflections on Jimi Part 1"
Voice: George Clinton

"Funky Kazoo"
Drum Programming, Guitar, Bass: Michael Hampton

"The Wind Cries Colors"
Guitar: Ras Kente

"Get to the Gettin'"
Guitar: James Glass

"Future Past"
Drums, Percussion, Backup Vocals: Allen Lynch
Guitar, Bass, Lead Vocals: Randall Lynch

"Shoulda' Known"
Drums, Percussion, Backup Vocals: Allen Lynch
Guitar, Bass, Lead Vocals: Randall Lynch

"Reflections on Jimi Part 2"
Voice: George Clinton

"Debbie Does the Voodoo Child"
Guitar: Ras Kente
Vocals: Point Blank

"Thanks Jimi"

Drums: Ron Wright
Guitar: Andre Williams
Bass: Lonnie Motley
Keyboards: Amp Fiddler
Vocals: Andre Williams
Intro Voice: Louie Kabbabie

"Return of the Gypsy"

Vocals, Lead and Rhythm Guitars, Drum Programming, Percussion: Johnny Graham

"Oh Say Can You See, The Red, The White, and the Blues"

Vocals, Lead and Rhythm Guitars, Synthesizers, Synth Bass, Piano, Drum Programming, Effects: Johnny Graham

"Father Forgive Um"

Drums: Gary Mudbone Cooper
Guitar: Michael Hampton
Bass: Chris Sherman

"Jimi Why D-U Hav Ta Go"

Drums: Frankie Kash Waddy
Guitar: Dirty Mugg
Keyboards: Bernie Worrell
Bass, Effects, Samples: Bootsy Collins
Vocals: Bootsy Collins, Mudbone Cooper

"Revolutions of Jimi"

Voice: Bootsy Collins

"Future Equations"

Drums: Keith Root
Guitar: Darryl Plummer
Bass: Randy Barnett

"What You Gonna Do?"

Drums: Ron Wright
Guitar: Blackbyrd McKnight, Ras Kente
Bass: Lonnie Motley

"Fishin' Da Sea"

Drums, Loops: Mykel Love
Guitar, Keyboards, Bass Lead Vocals: Menace

"I Need a Man"

Drums, Loops: Dizzy Black
Guitar, Keyboards, Bass Lead Vocals: Menace
Backup Vocals: Elsa Cornish

"Last Days"

Drums, Loops: Dizzy Black
Guitar, Keyboards, Bass Lead Vocals: Menace

"Crash & Burn"

Drums: Charlie Grover
Guitar: Andre Williams, Steve King, Carl Robinson
Bass: Lonnie Motley
Keyboards: Amp Fiddler
Vocals: Andre Williams

— ☆ —

SLAVEMASTER: 1994

This funk rock album features Gary "Mudbone" Cooper and Michael "Kidd Funkadelic" Hampton. It is part of Rykodisc's "Black Arc" series along with Zillatron, Out of the Dark, and others.

Rykodisc

"Godless"

Vocals, Bass: Islam Shabazz
Guitar, Backup Vocals: Bill McKinney
Guitar: Michael Hampton
Vocals: Gary Mudbone Cooper

"Heal"

Vocals, Bass: Islam Shabazz
Guitar, Backup Vocals: Bill McKinney
Guitar: Michael Hampton
Vocals: Gary Mudbone Cooper

"Damnation"

Vocals, Bass: Islam Shabazz
Guitar, Backup Vocals: Bill McKinney
Guitar: Michael Hampton
Vocals: Gary Mudbone Cooper

"Come Out"

Vocals, Bass: Islam Shabazz
Guitar, Backup Vocals: Bill McKinney
Guitar: Michael Hampton
Vocals: Gary Mudbone Cooper

"Day of Requital"

Vocals, Bass: Islam Shabazz
Guitar, Backup Vocals: Bill McKinney
Guitar: Michael Hampton
Vocals: Gary Mudbone Cooper

"Final Call"

Vocals, Bass: Islam Shabazz
Guitar, Backup Vocals: Bill McKinney
Guitar: Michael Hampton
Vocals: Gary Mudbone Cooper

"Walk the Water"

Vocals, Bass: Islam Shabazz
Guitar, Backup Vocals: Bill McKinney
Guitar: Michael Hampton
Vocals: Gary Mudbone Cooper

"Down"

Vocals, Bass: Islam Shabazz
Guitar, Backup Vocals: Bill McKinney
Guitar: Michael Hampton
Vocals: Gary Mudbone Cooper

"Each One, Teach One"

Vocals, Bass: Islam Shabazz
Guitar, Backup Vocals: Bill McKinney
Guitar: Michael Hampton
Vocals: Gary Mudbone Cooper

"Freedom"

Vocals, Bass: Islam Shabazz
Guitar, Backup Vocals: Bill McKinney
Guitar: Michael Hampton
Vocals: Gary Mudbone Cooper

— ☆ —

DAVE STEWART (SELECT TRACKS): 1994

This Eurythmics cofounder's album features several P-Funk members.

EastWest Records

Heart of Stone

"Heart of Stone"

Vocals, Guitar: Dave Stewart
Bass: Bootsy Collins
Keyboards: Bernie Worrell, Terry Disley
Drums: Jerome Brailey
Programming: Olle Romo
Backup Vocals: Barbara Tucker, Kristen Gray, Lady Miss Kier, Zhana Sanders, Shara Nelson, Antony Cole, Bootsy Collins, Carolyn Sanford, Debra Barsha, Gary Mudbeon Cooper, Henry Benefield, John Winfield, Mick Jagger, Nona Hendryx, Siobhan Fahey, Sleepy Stone, Sue Shattock (not all backup singers are on all songs)

"Greetings from the Gutter"

Vocals, Guitar: Dave Stewart
Percussion: Larry Fratangelo
Drums: Jerome Brailey
Bass: Bootsy Collins
Keyboards: Bernie Worrell
Programming: Olle Romo
Backup Vocals: Barbara Tucker, Kristen Gray, Lady Miss Kier, Zhana Sanders, Shara Nelson, Antony Cole, Bootsy Collins, Carrolyn Sanford, Debra Barsha, Gary Mudbeon Cooper, Henry Benefield, John Winfield, Mick Jagger, Nona Hendryx, Siobhan Fahey, Sleepy Stone, Sue Shattock (not all backup singers are on all songs)

"Crazy Sister"

Vocals, Guitar: Dave Stewart
Bass: Bootsy Collins
Drums: Jerome Brailey
Keyboards: Bernie Worrell
Programming: Ollie Romo
Backup Vocals: Barbara Tucker, Kristen Gray, Lady Miss Kier, Zhana Sanders, Shara Nelson, Antony Cole, Bootsy Collins, Carrolyn Sanford, Debra Barsha, Gary Mudbeon Cooper, Henry Benefield, John Winfield, Mick Jagger, Nona Hendryx, Siobhan Fahey, Sleepy Stone, Sue Shattock (not all backup singers are on all songs)

"Chelsea Lovers"

Vocals, Guitar: Dave Stewart
Bass: Bootsy Collins
Keyboards: Bernie Worrell
Drums: Ollie Romo
Flute, Piccolo, Recorder: Peter Thomas
Backup Vocals: Barbara Tucker, Kristen Gray, Lady Miss Kier, Zhana Sanders, Shara Nelson, Antony Cole, Bootsy Collins, Carrolyn Sanford, Debra Barsha, Gary Mudbeon Cooper, Henry Benefield, John Winfield, Mick Jagger, Nona Hendryx, Siobhan Fahey, Sleepy Stone, Sue Shattock (not all backup singers are on all songs)

"Jealousy"

Vocals, Guitar: Dave Stewart
Acoustic Guitar, Drums: Bootsy Collins
Percussion, Vocals: Gary Mudbone Cooper, Henry Benefield
Drums: Jerome Brailey
Keyboards: Bernie Worrell
Backup Vocals: Barbara Tucker, Kristen Gray, Lady Miss Kier, Zhana Sanders, Shara Nelson, Antony Cole, Bootsy Collins, Carrolyn Sanford, Debra Barsha, Gary Mudbeon Cooper, Henry Benefield, John Winfield, Mick Jagger, Nona Hendryx, Siobhan Fahey, Sleepy Stone, Sue Shattock (not all backup singers are on all songs)

"St. Valentine's Day"

Vocals, Guitar: Dave Stewart
Bass: Bootsy Collins
Keyboards: Bernie Worrell
Drums: Jerome Brailey
Backup Vocals: Barbara Tucker, Kristen Gray, Lady Miss Kier, Zhana Sanders, Shara Nelson, Antony Cole, Bootsy Collins, Carrolyn Sanford, Debra Barsha, Gary Mudbeon Cooper, Henry Benefield, John Winfield, Mick Jagger, Nona Hendryx, Siobhan Fahey, Sleepy Stone, Sue Shattock (not all backup singers are on all songs)

"Kinky Sweetheart"

Bass: Chucho Merchan
Violin, Vocals: Laurie Anderson
Vocals, Guitar: Dave Stewart
Keyboards: Bernie Worrell
Drums: Jerome Brailey
Programming: Olle Romo
Backup Vocals: Barbara Tucker, Kristen Gray, Lady Miss Kier, Zhana Sanders, Shara Nelson, Antony Cole, Bootsy Collins, Carrolyn Sanford, Debra Barsha, Gary Mudbeon Cooper, Henry Benefield, John Winfield, Mick Jagger, Nona Hendryx, Siobhan Fahey, Sleepy Stone, Sue Shattock (not all backup singers are on all songs)

"Damien Save Me"

Vocals, Guitar: Dave Stewart
Bass: Bootsy Collins
Keyboards: Bernie Worrell, Terry Disley
Drums: Jerome Brailey
Programming: Olle Romo
Sax: Lenny Pickett
Backup Vocals: Barbara Tucker, Kristen Gray, Lady Miss Kier, Zhana Sanders, Shara Nelson, Antony Cole, Bootsy Collins, Carrolyn Sanford, Debra Barsha, Gary Mudbeon Cooper, Henry Benefield, John Winfield, Mick Jagger, Nona Hendryx, Siobhan Fahey, Sleepy Stone, Sue Shattock (not all backup singers are on all songs)

"Tragedy Street"

Vocals, Guitar: Dave Stewart
Drums: Bootsy Collins
Keyboards: Bernie Worrell, Terry Disley
Backup Vocals: Barbara Tucker, Kristen Gray, Lady Miss Kier, Zhana Sanders, Shara Nelson, Antony Cole, Bootsy Collins, Carrolyn Sanford, Debra Barsha, Gary Mudbeon Cooper, Henry Benefield, John Winfield, Mick Jagger, Nona Hendryx, Siobhan Fahey, Sleepy Stone, Sue Shattock (not all backup singers are on all songs)

"You Talk a Lot"

Vocals, Guitar: Dave Stewart
Keyboards: Bernie Worrell, Terry Disley
Sax: Dave Sanborn
Guitar Solo: Lou Reed
Bass: Bootsy Collins
Drums: Jerome Brailey
Programming: Olle Romo
Backup Vocals: Barbara Tucker, Kristen Gray, Lady Miss Kier, Zhana Sanders, Shara Nelson, Antony Cole, Bootsy Collins, Carrolyn Sanford, Debra Barsha, Gary Mudbeon Cooper, Henry Benefield, John Winfield, Mick Jagger, Nona Hendryx, Siobhan Fahey, Sleepy Stone, Sue Shattock (not all backup singers are on all songs)

"Oh No, Not You Again"

Drums: Ollie Romo
Sax: Dave Sanborn
Voices: Carly Simon, Dave Pacino Sanborn
Vocals, Guitar: Dave Stewart
Bass: Bootsy Collins
Keyboards: Bernie Worrell
Backup Vocals: Barbara Tucker, Kristen Gray, Lady Miss Kier, Zhana Sanders, Shara Nelson, Antony Cole, Bootsy Collins, Carrolyn Sanford, Debra Barsha, Gary Mudbeon Cooper, Henry Benefield, John Winfield, Mick Jagger, Nona Hendryx, Siobhan Fahey, Sleepy Stone, Sue Shattock (not all backup singers are on all songs)

— ☆ —

AXIOM FUNK: 1995

This is probably the most prominent Bill Laswell–produced P-Funk venture. It features a dozen or so members of Parliament-Funkadelic as well as Funkadelic artist Pedro Bell's iconic album art.

Axiom

Funkronomicon

"Order within the Universe"

Backup Vocals: DXT?
Beats, Sound Effects, Bass: Bill Laswell
Organ: Bernie Worrell
Turntable: DXT

"Under the Influence (Jes Grew)"

Lead Vocals: George Clinton
Backup Vocals: Mudbone Cooper, Bootsy Collins, Clip Payne, Deborah Barsha, Zhana Saunders
Drums: Anton Fier
Drum Programming: Sly Dunbar
Bass: Robbie Shakespeare
Guitar: Bootsy Collins
Piano: Herbie Hancock
Congas: Daniel Ponce
Cowbells, Percussion: Aiyb Deng
Tuba: Edwin Rodriguez
Baritone Horn, Euphonium: Joe Daly
Trumpet, Flugelhorn: Ted Daniel
Bassoon: Janet Grice
Tenor Sax, Flute: J. D. Parron
Horns Conductor: Henry Threadgill

"If 6 Was 9"

Lead Vocals, Bass: Bootsy Collins
Guitar: Bucketed, Blackbyrd McKnight, Nicky Skopelitis, Robert Musso
Violin: Lili Haydn

"Orbitron Attack"

Drums: Jerome Brailey
Bass: Bootsy Collins
Guitar: Eddie Hazel
Organ: Bernie Worrell

"Cosmic Slop"

Lead Vocals: Garry Shider
Backup Vocals: Mudbone Cooper
Drums: Sly Dunbar
Bass: Robbie Shakespeare
Guitar: Michael Hampton, Garry Shider, Bootsy Collins
Organ: Bernie Worrell
Fairlight: Nicky Skopelitis
Congas: Aiyb Deng

"Free-Bass (Godzillatron Cush)"

Bass: Bootsy Collins
Guitar: Menace

"Tell the World"

Vocals: Maceo Parker, Bobby Byrd, Sly Stone, Godmoma
Drums, Bass, Guitar: Bootsy Collins
Keyboards: Sly Stone

"Pray My Soul"

Guitar: Eddie Hazel
Organ: Bernie Worrell

"Hideous Mutant Freekz"

Lead Vocals: George Clinton
Backup Vocals: Garry Shider, Mudbone Cooper, Bootsy Collins
Drums: Anton Fier
Bass, Guitar: Bootsy Collins
Synthesizer: Bernie Worrell

"Sax Machine"

Lead Vocals: Maceo Parker, Bobby Byrd, Bootsy Collins
Drums: T-Bone
Bass, Guitar: Bootsy Collins
Keyboards: Bernie Worrell
Sax: Maceo Parker
Trombone: Fred Wesley

"Animal Behavior"

Lead Vocals, Bass: Bootsy Collins
Drums: Brain
Guitar: Bucketed
Keyboards: Bernie Worrell
Samples: Bill Laswell

"Trumpets and Violins, Violins"

Lead Vocals: Abiodun Oyewole
Guitar: Blackbyrd McKnight, Nicky Skopelitis, Robert Musso
Violin: Lili Haydn

"Telling Time"

Drums: Zigaboo Modeliste
Bass: Bill Laswell
Guitar: Nicky Skopelitis
Organ: Amina Claudine Myers
Congas: Guiherme Franco

"Jungle Free-Bass"

Bass: Bootsy Collins, Bill Laswell
Vocals: Torture

"Blackout"

Guitars, Bass, Drums: Dewayne Blackbyrd
McKnight

"Sacred to the Pain"

Lead Vocals: Umar bin Hassan
Guitar: Eddie Hazel
Organ: Bernie Worrell

— ☆ —

BOOTSY'S NEW RUBBER BAND: 1995

This was a revived Rubber Band performing a fresh set of music for the 1990s. It features most of the usual suspects expected on a Rubber Band outing.

P-Vine Records

Blasters of the Universe

"Funk Express Card"

Lead Vocals: Bootsy Collins
Backup Vocals: Gary Mudbone Cooper,
Anthony Goodin, Kristin Gray, Momma
Collins, Pretty Fatt, Robert Peanut Johnson,
George Clinton

Drums, Programming, Bass: Bootsy Collins
Guitar: Catfish Collins, Bootsy Collins,
Keyboards: Joel Johnson

"J.R. (Just Right)"

Lead Vocals: Bootsy Collins
Backup Vocals: Bobby Byrd, Kristen Gray,
Ronni Harris, Pretty Fatt
Drums: Frankie Kash Waddy
Programming, Bass, Guitar: Bootsy Collins
Keyboards, Synth Bass: Bernie Worrell
Trumpet: Richard Griffith, Rick Gardner
Percussion: Frankie Kash Waddy

"Blasters of the Universe"

Backup Vocals: Bootsy Collins, Maceo Parker,
Fred Wesley, Bootsy Fan Club
Drums: Buddy Miles, Bootsy Collins
Bass: Bootsy Collins
Guitar: Bootsy Collins, Catfish Collins, Ron
Jennings
Trumpet: Richard Griffith, Rick Gardner
Trombone: Fred Wesley
Sax: Maceo Parker

"Bad Girls"

Lead Vocals, Drum Programming, Bass:
Bootsy Collins
Backup Vocals: Pretty Fatt, Ronni Harris,
Anthony Cole, Kristin Gray, Bobby Byrd,
Gary Mudbone Cooper
Guitar: Flip Cornett
Keyboards: Joel Johnson

"Back-N-the-Day"

Lead Vocals: Bootsy Collins, Maceo Parker,
Bobby Byrd
Drums: Don Tiger Martin
Synth Bass, Keyboards: David Spradley
Guitar: Catfish Collins
Sax: Maceo Parker

"Where R the Children"

Lead Vocals: Cynthia Girty, Arneta Walker, Carolyn Stanford, Bootsy Collins, Bootsy Fan Club
Drums, Percussion: Bootsy Collins
Synth Bass, Keyboards: Bernie Worrell

"Female Troubles (The National Anthem)"

Lead Vocals, Drums, Bass: Bootsy Collins
Backup Vocals: Kristin Gray, Ronni Harris, Pretty Fatt, Bootsy Collins
Guitar: Catfish Collins, Bootsy Collins
Keyboards: Joel Razor Sharp Johnson

"Wide Track"

Vocals: Fred Wesley, Kristin Gray, Ronni Harris, Pretty Fatt
Drums: Frankie Kash Waddy
Percussion, Bass: Bootsy Collins
Guitar: Mike Mitchell, Vince Campbell
Keyboards: Bernie Worrell
Trombone: Fred Wesley
Sax, Flute: Maceo Parker
Trumpet: Richard Griffith, Rick Gardner

"Funk Me Dirty"

Lead Vocals: Bootsy Collins, George Clinton
Backup Vocals: Robert Peanut Johnson, Gary Mudbone Cooper, Trey Stone, Bootsy Collins
Drums: Trey Stone
Bass: Bootsy Collins
Guitar: Bootsy Collins, Trey Stone
Keyboards: Trey Stone, Wes Boatman
Trombone: Fred Wesley
Trumpet: Richard Griffith, Rick Gardner
Sax: Maceo Parker

"Good Nite Eddie"

Lead Vocals: Bootsy Collins
Backup Vocals: Henry Benefield
Drum Programming, Bass: Bootsy Collins
Guitar: Dee James, Eddie Hazel

Organ: Greg Fitz

"A Sacred Place"

Lead Vocals, Percussion: Bootsy Collins
Organ: Greg Fitz

"Half Past Midnight"

Lead Vocals, Drum Programming: Bootsy Collins
Guitar: Ron Jennings, Dee James
Keyboards: Bernie Worrell, Wes Boatman

"It's a Silly Serious World"

Lead Vocals: Bootsy Collins, Gary Mudbone Cooper
Backup Vocals: Kristin Gray
Drum Programming, Bass: Bootsy Collins
Guitar: Ron Jennings
Keyboards: Bernie Worrell

— ☆ —

A TRIBUTE TO JOHN LENNON (SELECT TRACKS): 1995

George Clinton and P-Funk cover John Lennon's "Mind Games."

"Mind Games"

Strings: Detroit Symphony Orchestra, arranged by Paul Riser
Bass: Billy Bass Nelson
Drums: Gary Mudbone Cooper
Guitar: Dewayne Blackbyrd McKnight
Piano, Keyboards: Amp Fiddler
Vocals: George Clinton, Andre Foxxe Williams, Belita Woods, Michael Clip Payne, Garry Shider, Gary Mudbeon Cooper, Joy Gilliam, Pat Lewis, Patty Walker, Robert Peanut Johnson, Sheila Horne

— ☆ —

FUNKADELIC FTG. GEORGE CLINTON AND BELITA WOODS: 1995

"Black People"

Lead Vocals: George Clinton, Belita Woods
Backup Vocals: George Clinton, Dallas Austin, Belita Woods
Production, Bass, Keyboards: Dallas Austin
Guitar: John Bigham
Sample: Zapp

SOUNDS OF BLACKNESS FTG. BLACK SHEEP: 1995

"We Shall Not Be Moved"

Lead Vocals: Ann Bennett-Nesby, James Q. Wright
Backup Vocals: The Sounds of Blackness
Guitar: Nick Moroch, Jeff Bova
Keyboards: Bernie Worrell, Gerry E. Brown
Percussion: Carol Steele
Samples, Loops: Michael Brown

The above two songs were from the *Panther* movie soundtrack.

BOOTSY COLLINS AND BERNIE WORRELL: 1995

"You Got Me Wide Open"

Drums, Bass, Vocals, Guitar: Bootsy Collins
Keyboards, Synthesizers: Bernie Worrell
Rap: Ice Cube

The above song was from the *Friday* movie soundtrack.

THE GAP BAND (SELECT TRACK): 1995

The Gap Band, founded by the Wilson brothers, Charlie, Robert, and Ronnie, has always been influenced by the P-Funk empire's sound. The Brides' "Disco to Go" was used almost lick for lick, and P-Funk alumni such as Dawn Silva contributed to the Gap Band's material. Since the group has an orbit all its own, however, only one song has been included here for canon.

"Over the Funkin' Hills"

Lead Vocals: George Clinton, Charlie Wilson, Ronnie Wilson, Robert Wilson, Michael Clip Payne

MALLIA FRANKLIN: 1995

Most of this solo album by Parlet cofounder and longtime P-Funk vocalist Mallia "Queen of Funk" Franklin was recorded in Detroit and features the P-Funk All Stars.

P-Vine Records

Queen of Funk Funken Tersepter

"Too Many Fish in the Sea"

Vocals: Mallia Franklin
Backup Vocals: Gary Mudbone Cooper, Garry Shider, Eddie Hazel, Robert Peanut Johnson, Mallia Franklin, Michael Clip Payne, Joe Pep Harris
Drums: Jerry Jones, Land Richards
Bass: Jimmy Ali, Allen McGrier
Keyboards: David Spradley, Ernestro Wilson, Harry Bowens
Guitar: Tony Thomas, Dewayne Blackbyrd McKnight
Horns: Maceo Parker, Fred Wesley, Richard Kush Griffith, Larry Hatcher

"In and Out of Love"

Vocals: Mallia Franklin
Backup Vocals: Gary Mudbone Cooper, Mallia Franklin
Drum Programming: A.J. Sparks, David Scheffler
Bass Keyboards: Tony Stone
Keyboards: Ernestro Wilson
Guitar: Gordon Carlton
Horns: Maceo Parker, Fred Wesley, Richard Kush Griffith, Larry Hatcher

"Buzzards (Don't Let Em Get Me)"

Vocals: Mallia Franklin
Backup Vocals: Junie Morrison, Kimberly Abrams, Mallia Franklin, Conley Abrams, Robert Jordan
Drums, Bass, Keyboards: Junie Morrison
Guitar: Dewayne Blackbyrd McKnight, Junie Morrison
Horns: Maceo Parker, Fred Wesley, Richard Kush Griffith, Larry Hatcher
Trumpet Solo: Tyrone Griffin

"Time to Feel Good"

Vocals: Mallia Franklin
Backup Vocals: Cynthia Girty, Carolyn Stanford, Tony Arnell Carmichael, Steve Boyd, Bobby Franklin, Mallia Franklin
Drums: Bobby Franklin
Drum Programming: David Scheffler, Conley Abrams
Horns: Maceo Parker, Fred Wesley, Richard Kush Griffith, Larry Hatcher
Keyboards: Ernestro Wilson
Guitar: Dewayne Blackbyrd McKnight, Gordon Carlton, Jerome Ali, Rickey Rouse

"Hipnotize (In under the Influence)"

Vocals: Mallia Franklin
Drums, Bass, Keyboards: Kern Brantley
Guitar: Dewayne Blackbyrd McKnight

"Interlude (Of Love)"

Vocals: Mallia Franklin
Backup Vocals: Mallia Franklin, Kimberly Abrams, Teresa Allman, Robert Jordan
Drum Programming: Junie Morrison, Conley Abrams, Mallia Franklin
Bass: Brian Tate
Keyboards, Synth Bass: Junie Morrison
Guitar: Dewayne McKnight, Gary Dee James

"This Must Be Truly Love"

Vocals: Mallia Franklin
Backup Vocals: Mallia Franklin, Kimberly Abrams, Teresa Allman, Robert Jordan
Drum Programming: Junie Morrison, Conley Abrams, Mallia Franklin
Bass: Brian Tate
Keyboards, Synth Bass: Junie Morrison
Guitar: Michael Hampton, Gary Dee Dee James

"Rat-A-Tat-Tat (At My Door)"

Vocals: Mallia Franklin
Backup Vocals: Eddie Hazel, Brian Bellamy, Conley Abrams, Maxsimilliano Marsinelli, Robert Jordan, Mallia Franklin
Drums: Jerry Jones
Drum Programming: Conley Abrams
Bass: Eddie Hazel
Keyboards: David Spradley, Ernestro Wilson
Guitar: Eddie Hazel, Gary Dee Dee James, Ricky Rouse

"Universal Jam "Y'All""

Vocals: Mallia Franklin

Backup Vocals: Shirley Hayden, Janice Evans, Gwen Evans, Jeanette McGruder, Kim Seay, Linda Shider, Sheila Horne, Eddie Hazel, Ray Davis, Ron Ford, Gary Mudbone Cooper, Garry Shider, Belita Woods, Robert Peanut Johnson, Pat Lewis, Larry Hatcher, Joe Pep Harris, Sir Harry Bowen, Steve Boyd, Sandra Feva

Drums: Jerry Jones

Drum Programming: David Scheffler, Conley Abrams, Mallia Franklin

Bass: Jimmy Ali

Keyboards: Ernestro Wilson

Synth Bass: David Scheffler, Mallia Franklin

Guitar: Gordon Carlton, Jerome Ali

Baby Funkers: Andre Foxxe Williams, Tracey Lewis, Steve Parnell, Michael Clip Payne, Patty Walker

"Got My Body Hot"

Vocals: Mallia Franklin

Backup Vocals: Gary Mudbone Cooper, Mallia Franklin, Garry Shider, Shirley Hayden, Janice Evans, Kim Seay, Linda Shider, Gwen Evans, Jeanette McGruder, Robert Peanut Johnson, Val Young

Drums: Kenny Colton, Tony Stone

Bass: Jimmie Ali, Tony Stone

Keyboards: David Spradley, Ernestro Wilson, Tony Stone

Drum Programming: David Scheffler, Tony Stone

Guitar: Dewayne Blackbyrd McKnight, Tony Thomas

— ☆ —

TAL ROSS: 1995

Original Funkadelic rhythm guitarist Tal Ross came out of a 22-year hiatus when he released his 1995 return album. This also features Jerome Brailey on drums.

Coconut Grove

Detrimental Vaseline aka Giant Shirley

"Aint' No Reason"

Lead Vocals, Guitar: Tal Ross

"Green and Yellow Daughter"

Lead Vocals: Tal Ross

Backup Vocals: Peter Wetherbee

Drums: Jerome Brailey

Bass: Wayne Hammond

Guitar: Tal Ross, Jef Lee Johnson

Keyboards: Neil Alexander

Percussion: Aiyb Dieng

"Cry and Show Me"

Lead Vocals: Tal Ross

Backup Vocals: Peter Wetherbee

Drums: Jerome Brailey

Bass: Wayne Hammond

Guitar: Tal Ross, Jef Lee Johnson

Keyboards: Neil Alexander

Percussion: Aiyb Dieng

"Hussein (I'm Lucky)"

Lead Vocals: Tal Ross

Backup Vocals: Peter Wetherbee

Drums: Jerome Brailey

Bass: Wayne Hammond

Guitar: Tal Ross, Jef Lee Johnson

Keyboards: Neil Alexander

Percussion: Aiyb Dieng

"Forget Her"

Lead Vocals: Tal Ross
Backup Vocals: Peter Wetherbee
Drums: Jerome Brailey
Bass: Wayne Hammond
Guitar: Tal Ross, Jef Lee Johnson
Keyboards: Neil Alexander
Percussion: Aiyb Dieng

"Get So Mad"

Lead Vocals: Tal Ross
Backup Vocals: Peter Wetherbee Wayne
  Hammond
Drums: Jerome Brailey
Bass: Wayne Hammond
Guitar: Tal Ross, Jef Lee Johnson
Keyboards: Neil Alexander
Percussion: Aiyb Dieng, Peter Wetherbee

"Keep On Trying"

Lead Vocals: Tal Ross
Backup Vocals: Peter Wetherbee
Drums: Jerome Brailey
Bass: Wayne Hammond
Guitar: Tal Ross, Jef Lee Johnson
Keyboards: Neil Alexander
Percussion: Aiyb Dieng

"Feelin' Good"

Lead Vocals: Tal Ross
Backup Vocals: Peter Wetherbee
Drums: Jerome Brailey
Bass: Wayne Hammond
Guitar: Tal Ross, Jef Lee Johnson
Keyboards: Neil Alexander
Percussion: Aiyb Dieng

"Forever (My Darling Don't Cry)"

Lead Vocals: Tal Ross
Backup Vocals: Peter Wetherbee
Drums: Jerome Brailey
Bass: Wayne Hammond
Guitar: Tal Ross, Jef Lee Johnson
Keyboards: Neil Alexander
Percussion: Aiyb Dieng

"Angry Fire (Intestical Song)"

Lead Vocals: Tal Ross
Backup Vocals: Peter Wetherbee
Drums: Jerome Brailey
Bass: Wayne Hammond
Guitar: Tal Ross, Jef Lee Johnson
Keyboards: Neil Alexander
Percussion: Aiyb Dieng

"Feelin Like Ahh Lover Should"

Lead Vocals: Tal Ross
Backup Vocals: Peter Wetherbee
Drums: Jerome Brailey
Bass: Wayne Hammond
Guitar: Tal Ross, Jef Lee Johnson
Keyboards: Neil Alexander
Percussion: Aiyb Dieng

"Lovin' Toll Man Suite"

Lead Vocals: Tal Ross
Backup Vocals: Peter Wetherbee
Drums: Jerome Brailey
Bass: Jef Lee Johnson
Guitar: Tal Ross, Jef Lee Johnson
Keyboards: Neil Alexander
Percussion: Aiyb Dieng

"It Was (Wars of Armageddon)"

Lead Vocals: Tal Ross
Backup Vocals: Peter Wetherbee
Drums: Jerome Brailey
Bass: Wayne Hammond
Guitar: Tal Ross, Jef Lee Johnson
Keyboards: Neil Alexander
Percussion: Aiyb Dieng

Single

"Message to You (I'm the Captain)"

Vocals, Guitars: Tal Ross
Keyboards: ?
Bass: ?
Drums: ?

— ☆ —

TUPAC SHAKUR (SELECT TRACK): 1996

This 1990s rap music icon featured several songs with P-Funk and Zapp samples and a well-known performance with George Clinton.

Death Row Records

"You Can't See Me"

Lead Vocals: Tupac Shakur
Lead Vocals: George Clinton
Production: Dr. Dre, Larry Chatman

— ☆ —

TOO $HORT (SELECT TRACKS): 1996, 2001–2002

This notorious Oakland, California, rapper featured P-Funk on his albums many times.

Jive Records

"Gettin' It"

Lead Vocals: Too $hort
Backup Vocals: Funkadelic, George Clinton, Parliament, Belita Woods, Gary Mudbone Cooper
Additional Backup Vocals: YZ
Drum Programming: Spearhead X
Keyboards: Amp Fiddler
Lead Guitar: Michael Hampton
Sax: Greg Thomas

"I've Been Watching You (Move Your Sexy Body)"

Lead Vocals: Too Short
Backup Vocals: About Face, George Clinton
Bass, Keyboards: Shorty B
Keyboards: L.A. Dre, Amp Fiddler
Lead Guitar: Michael Hampton
Lead Vocals: Garry Shider
Sax: Greg Thomas

"U Stank"

Lead Vocals: Too $hort
Featuring: Baby D, George Clinton
Additional Vocals: Jerre Manning, Scarface
Production: Taj "Mahal" Tilgham

"The Movie"

Lead Vocals: Too Short
Bass, Guitar, Producer: Shorty B
Vocals: Belita Woods, George Clinton
Producer: Vaughn Wilson
Producer: George Clinton

— ☆ —

STEVE BOYD: 1996, 2002, 2008

These are P-Funk All Stars co-lead vocalist Steve Boyd's solo outings. Boyd was also a member of the singing groups the Five Special and the Dramatics, among others.

Even Steven

"Even Steven"

Lead and Backup Vocals: Steve Boyd
Drums, Bass: Mark Bass
Guitar: Jeff Bass
Keyboards: Amp Fiddler

"Take It Off"

Lead and Backup Vocals: Steve Boyd
Drums: Paul Hill
Bass: Mark Bass
Keyboards: Donnie Rushen

420 Drive Time

"Gangsta Melody"

Lead and Backup Vocals: Steve Boyd
Drums, Bass, Guitar, Keyboards: Anthony Booker

"Ass"

Lead Vocals: Steve Boyd, George Clinton
Backup Vocals: Steve Boyd
Drums, Guitar: Mike Patterson

"Stay"

Lead and Backup Vocals: Steve Boyd
Drums: Kool Ace
Bass: Mark Woodard
Guitar: Anthony Booker
Keyboards: Raymond Johnson

"When I Make You Mine"

Lead and Backup Vocals: Steve Boyd
Drums: Derek Drayden
Bass: Mark Woodard
Guitar: Anthony Booker
Keyboards: Raymond Johnson
Turntables: Sa'D Ali

"On the Grind"

Lead Vocals: George Clinton, Shonda Clinton
Backup Vocals: Steve Boyd
Drums: Sample
Bass, Keyboards: Greg Dokes

The Lost Tapes Vol. 1

"Hit It One More Time"

Lead Vocals: Steve Boyd, RonKat Spearman, Paul Hill, Tracey Lewis, Kendra Foster
Drums, Bass: Steve Boyd
Guitar, Keyboards: El DeBarge

"Can I Baby"

Lead and Backup Vocals: Steve Boyd
Drums, Keyboards: Kenny G
Bass, Guitar: Jeff Bass

"Shawty Know What I Like"

Lead Vocals: Steve Boyd, El DeBarge, RonKat Spearman
Drums: Steve Boyd
Bass, Guitar: RonKat Spearman
Keyboards: El DeBarge

"Issues"

Lead and Backup Vocals, Drums, Keyboards: Steve Boyd

"Cross the Line"

Lead and Backup Vocals, Bass: Steve Boyd
Drums, Keyboards: Jim Wright

"Somethings Strange"

Lead and Backup Vocals: Steve Boyd, Kendra Foster
Keyboards: Jerome Rodgers

"Don't Mess with Me"

Lead and Backup Vocals, Drums, Keyboards: Steve Boyd
Bass: Tony Green
Guitar: Ron Smith

"I'll Do"

Lead Vocals: Steve Boyd
Backup Vocals: Steve Boyd, Michael Clip Payne, Crystal Boyd, Paul Hill, Amp Fiddler
Drum Programming: Michael Clip Payne
Bass: Tony Green
Guitar: Don Davis
Piano: Sidney

"Just Because"

Lead and Backup Vocals, Drum Programming, Keyboards: Steve Boyd

Nothing Really Matters

Lead Vocals: Steve Boyd
Backup Vocals: Steve Boyd, Kendra Foster
Drums: Steve Boyd Jr., Steve Boyd
Synth Bass: Danny Bedrosian
Guitar: Dewayne Blackbyrd McKnight

"Sitting Here"

Lead Vocals, Drums: Steve Boyd
Backup Vocals: Steve Boyd, George Clinton, Joi
Bass, Guitar: Kenny Brazil
Keyboards: Danny Bedrosian

"Varee Is Love"

Lead and Backup Vocals: Steve Boyd
Drums, Bass: The Ohio Players
Horns: The Dramatic Players
Guitar: Anthony Booker
Keyboards: Billy Beck

— ☆ —

FROGG: 1996

This 1990s-era P-Funk rapper featured on the *Dope Dogs* album and other releases from that period.

"Froggisms"

Lead Vocals: Frogg
Vocals: Ali Life
Backup Vocals: Sean Franklin, Kerry Clark, Frogg
Drums: Sean Franklin
Bass, Guitar: Kerry Clark
Embellishments: Mark Bass, Jeff Bass

"What You See"

Lead Vocals: Frogg
Vocals: Ali Life
Backup Vocals: Sean Franklin, Kerry Clark, Frogg
Drums: Sean Franklin
Bass, Guitar: Kerry Clark
Embellishments: Mark and Jeff Bass

"Ruler of the Underground"

Lead Vocals: Frogg
Drums: Sean Franklin
Bass, Guitar: Kerry Clark
Embellishments: Mark and Jeff Bass
Vocals: Ali Life
Backup Vocals: Sean Franklin, Kerry Clark, Frogg

"Bud vs Yayo"

Lead Vocals: Frogg
Drums: Sean Franklin
Bass, Guitar: Kerry Clark
Embellishments: Mark and Jeff Bass
Vocals: Ali Life
Backup Vocals: Sean Franklin, Kerry Clark, Frogg

"Move Dat MC Away"

Lead Vocals: Frogg
Drums: Sean Franklin
Bass, Guitar: Kerry Clark
Embellishments: Mark and Jeff Bass
Vocals: Ali Life
Backup Vocals: Sean Franklin, Kerry Clark, Frogg

"Head Up"

Lead Vocals: Frogg
Drums: Sean Franklin
Bass, Guitar: Kerry Clark
Embellishments: Mark and Jeff Bass
DJ: DJ Flipside
Vocals: Ali Life
Backup Vocals: Sean Franklin, Kerry Clark, Frogg

"You Want It You Got It"

Lead Vocals: Frogg
Drums: Sean Franklin
Bass, Guitar: Kerry Clark
Embellishments: Mark and Jeff Bass
Vocals: Ali Life
Backup Vocals: Sean Franklin, Kerry Clark, Frogg

"Bullet Rash"

Lead Vocals: Frogg
Drums: Sean Franklin
Bass, Guitar: Kerry Clark
Embellishments: Mark and Jeff Bass
Vocals: Ali Life
Backup Vocals: Sean Franklin, Kerry Clark, Frogg

"Bang on the Noggin"

Lead Vocals: Frogg
DJ: DJ Flipside
Drums: Sean Franklin
Bass, Guitar: Kerry Clark
Embellishments: Mark and Jeff Bass
Vocals: Ali Life
Backup Vocals: Sean Franklin, Kerry Clark, Frogg

"Hood Hoppin'"

Lead Vocals: Frogg
Drums: Sean Franklin
Bass, Guitar: Kerry Clark
Embellishments: Mark and Jeff Bass
Vocals: Ali Life
Backup Vocals: Sean Franklin, Kerry Clark, Frogg

"Basehead Rights"

Lead Vocals: Frogg
Drums: Sean Franklin
Bass, Guitar: Kerry Clark
Embellishments: Mark and Jeff Bass
Vocals: Ali Life
Backup Vocals: Sean Franklin, Kerry Clark, Frogg

"Party On!"

Lead Vocals: Frogg
DJ: DJ Flipside
Drums: Sean Franklin
Bass, Guitar: Kerry Clark
Embellishments: Mark and Jeff Bass

"Flytrap"

Lead Vocals: Frogg
Drums: Sean Franklin
Bass, Guitar: Kerry Clark
Embellishments: Mark and Jeff Bass
Vocals: Ali Life
Backup Vocals: Sean Franklin, Kerry Clark, Frogg

"Where Have You Been?"

Lead Vocals: Frogg
Vocals: Louie Kabbabie
Vocals: Ali Life
Backup Vocals: Sean Franklin, Kerry Clark, Frogg
Drums: Sean Franklin
Bass, Guitar: Kerry Clark
Embellishments: Mark and Jeff Bass

"Down Down Baby"

Lead Vocals: Frog
Vocals: Ali Life
Backup Vocals: Sean Franklin, Kerry Clark, Frogg
Keyboards: Arthur Pugh
Drums: Sean Franklin
Bass, Guitar: Kerry Clark
Embellishments: Mark and Jeff Bass

"Mack Pains"

Lead Vocals: Frog
Vocals: Ali Life
Backup Vocals: Sean Franklin, Kerry Clark, Frogg
Keyboards: Arthur Pugh
Drums: Sean Franklin
Bass, Guitar: Kerry Clark
Embellishments: Mark and Jeff Bass

— ☆ —

KYLE JASON (SELECT TRACKS): 1996–

This vocalist from the Public Enemy camp had a brief tenure with the P-Funk All Stars in 1996.

"My World (Interlude)"

Vocals: Kyle Jason
Trumpet: George Fontenette

"Uptown"

Vocals: Kyle Jason
Keyboards: Norman Hurt, Johnny Davis, Kyle Jason
Guitar: Jeff Mahmud
Drums, Guitar: Bootsy Collins

"Life of a Hustler"

Vocals: Kyle Jason
Bass: Brian Hardgroove
Rap: Bobby "B-Wyze" Harding
Guitar: Jeff Mahmud
Keyboards: Kyle Jason

"She Was Mine (Interlude)"

Vocals: Kyle Jason
Trumpet: George Fontenette

"Hush"

Vocals: Kyle Jason, Bootsy Collins, Deborah Williams
Bass, Drums, Guitar: Bootsy Collins
Keyboards: Johnny Davis, Kyle Jason

"Butter Baby"

Vocals: Kyle Jason
Backup Vocals: Carol Johnson, Amp Fiddler, Olivia Ewing, Steve Boyd
Bass: Bubz Fiddler
Drums: Ron Wright
Keyboards: Amp Fiddler

"Matter of Time (Interlude)"

Vocals: Kyle Jason
Trumpet: George Fontenette

"16 Stories"

Vocals: Kyle Jason
Bass: Bubz Fiddler
Keyboards: Amp Fiddler, Kyle Jason

"D Block (Interlude)"

Vocals: Kyle Jason
Trumpet: George Fontenette

"Generations"

Vocals: Kyle Jason
Rap: Chuck D
Bass, Drums, Guitar: Bootsy Collins

"When We Come Around"

Vocals: Kyle Jason
Bass: Bubz Fiddler
Drums: Ron Wright
Keyboards: Amp Fiddler, Kyle Jason

"Butter Baby (Bonus Butter)"

Lead Vocals: Kyle Jason
Backup Vocals: Carol Johnson, Amp Fiddler, Olivia Ewing, Steve Boyd
Bass: Bubz Fiddler
Drums: Ron Wright
Keyboards: Amp Fiddler

— ☆ —

ENEMY SQUAD: 1996–1999

This is the funk rock band of P-Funk drummer Gabe "Undisco Kidd" Gonzalez.

Tufamerica Records

United State of Mind

"Welcome to the Millennium"

Drums: Gabe Gonzalez
Bass: Joseph Hayden
Guitar: Duminie Depores
Keyboards: Gabe Gonzalez
Horn Solos: Fred Wesley Maceo Parker

"Return of the Swamp Thang"

Drums, Keyboards: Gabe Gonzalez
Bass: Kerry Clarke
Guitar: Duminie Depores, Dewayne Blackbyrd McKnight
Vocals: Gabe Gonzalez, Kerry Clarke

"Trick Chick Jane"

Drums: Gabe Gonzalez
Bass: Joseph Hayden
Guitar: Kevin Hagen
Vocals: Gabe Gonzalez, Michael Clip Payne
Backup Vocals: James Anderson, Steffen Bell

"Anti-Prozac Baby"

Vocals, Drums, Bass: Gabe Gonzalez
Guitar: Duminie Depores
Keyboards: Amp Fiddler

"Yeah, the World Is on Drugz" **Drums:** Gabe Gonzalez

Bass: Joseph Hayden
Guitar: Kevin Hagen
Vocals: Dan Harris, Gabe Gonzalez, Belita Woods, Steve Boyd, Louie Kabbabie, Michael Clip Payne, George Clinton, Mark Bass, Robert Peanut Johnson, Steffen Bell

"Love War (Interlude)"

Drums, Keyboards: Gabe Gonzalez
Bass: Joseph Hayden
Guitar: Kevin Hagen, Duminie Depores

"United State of a . . . Mind"

Drums: Gable Gonzalez
Bass: DeWight Blaxton
Guitar: Ron Smith, Duminie Depores
Piano: Amp Fiddler
Vocals: Kerry Clarke, Gabe Gonzalez, Kyle Jason, Belita Woods, Steve Boyd, Michael Clip Payne

"We're on $um Other Shit"

Drum Programming: Michael Clip Payne
Drum Loops: Gabe Gonzalez
DJ: D.J. Lenn Swann
Basses: Kerry Clarke
Guitar: Duminie Depores
Keyboards: Amp Fiddler
Vocals: Gabe Gonzalez, Michael Clip Payne

"Prankster Boogie"

Drums, Keyboards: Gabe Gonzalez
Bass: Kerry Clarke
Guitar: Duminie Depores
Lead Guitar: Piranha Head
Vocals: Gabe Gonzalez, Kerry Clarke

"If It Fits (Do You Swear It?)"

Drums, Keyboards: Gabe Gonzalez
Bass: Kerry Clarke
Guitar: Duminie Depores
Lead Guitar: Piranha Head
Vocals: Gabe Gonzalez, Kerry Clarke

"Sticky Liquid Funk"

Drums: Gabe Gonzalez
Bass: Joseph Hayden
Guitar: Duminie Depores, Ron Smith, Piranha Head
Keyboards: Gabe Gonzalez, James Harris

"Jupiter"

Drums: Gabe Gonzalez
Guitar: Duminie Depores, Dewayne Blackbyrd McKnight
Vocals: Duminie Depores

"Flip the Script (Reprise)"

Drums, Keyboards: Gabe Gonzalez
Bass: Joseph Hayden
Guitar: Duminie Depores
Horn Solos: Fred Wesley, Maceo Parker

Ultraunit: The Angel Dust Theory

"Underground Departure (Prelude)"

Drums: Gabe Gonzalez
Bass: David Johnson
Keyboards: Ron Little
Vocals: An'Kenge Gonzalez

"Kickin' Madd Izms"

Drums: Gabe Gonzalez
Bass: Bubz Fiddler
Keyboards: Amp Fiddler
Vocals: Thyme, Chase (of the Mountain Climbaz), King David's Son, George Clinton

"Mysterious (Duet)"

Drums: Gabe Gonzalez
Bass: Bubz Fiddler
Keyboards: Amp Fiddler
Vocals: Gabe Gonzalez, Olivia Ewing

"Yeah, C'mon Y'all People"

Drum Programming: Michael Clip Payne
Bass: Kerry Clarke
Guitar: Kerry Clarke
Samples: Gabe Gonzalez
Vocals: Steve Boyd, Belita Woods

"Don't You Do That to Me"

Samples: Gabe Gonzalez
Vocals: Dawn Silva

"Still Getting Dogged"

Samples, Synth Bass, Keyboards: Gabe Gonzalez
Guitar: Piranha Head

"Procrastination Reaps Hesitation"

Drum Programming and Music: Gabe Gonzalez

"Hip Hop Time Travel"

Drum Programming and Music: Gabe Gonzalez

"Freaky Deaky Baby"

Drum Loop, Synth Bass, Keyboards: Gabe Gonzalez

"Do What You Do"

Drum Programming: Michael Clip Payne
Bass: Kerry Clarke
Guitar: Ron Smith

"Chocolateshroomininonaenempty-stomach"

Drums, Samples: Gabe Gonzalez
Bass, Guitar: Kerry Clarke

"Up & Down"

Drums: Gabe Gonzalez
Synth Bass, Keyboards, Vocals: Ron Little

"Rollin Wit Thunder"

Drums: Gabe Gonzalez
Synth Bass, Keyboards: Ron Little
Trumpet: John Douglas
Vocals: Kevin Little

"We've Got Style Got, Plenty of Styles"

Drums: Gabe Gonzalez
Upright Bass: Bubz Fiddler
Piano: Amp Fiddler

— ☆ —

LILI HAYDN (SELECT TRACKS): 1997, 2003–2008, 2014–

These are solo albums from the P-Funk violinist, who was on the road with George Clinton and Parliament-Funkadelic from 2003 to 2007 and contributed to studio work with the band starting around 1999.

Light Blue Sun

"Light Blue Sun"

Vocals: Bahar
Violin: Lili Haydn
Bass: Bill Laswell
Drums, Tabla, Percussion: Karsh Kale
Guitar: Corky James
Keyboards, Programming: Steve Nalepa

"Come Here"

Guitar: Chris Bruce
Violin, Vocals, Keyboards, Programming: Lili Haydn
Drums, Tabla, Percussion: Karsh Kale
Tabla: Satnam Singh Ramgotra

"Anything"

Programming: Ted Castro
Violin, Vocals: Lili Haydn
Bass: Bill Laswell
Cello: Gerri Sutyak
Guitar: Corky James
Keyboards, Programming: Steve Nalepa
Viola: Alma Fernandez

"Wounded Dove"

Violin, Vocals: Lili Haydn
Cello: Gerri Sutyak
Drums, Tabla, Percussion: Karsh Kale
Guitar: Corky James
Keyboards, Programming: Steve Nalepa
Tabla: Satnam Singh Ramgotra
Viola: Alma Fernandez

"The Longing"

Violin, Vocals, Keyboards, Programming: Lili Haydn
Bass: Bill Laswell
Drums, Tabla, Percussion: Karsh Kale
Guitar: Corky James

"Denied"

Violin: Lili Haydn, Julianna Klopotic
Cello: Tara Chambers
Viola: Ron Lawrence

"The Chinese Song"

Violin, Vocals, Keyboards, Programming: Lili Haydn
Bass: Bill Laswell
Drums, Tabla, Percussion: Karsh Kale
Guitar: Corky James
Tabla: Satnam Singh Ramgotra

"Sweetness"

Guitar: Geoffrey Moore
Violin, Vocals, Keyboards, Programming: Lili Haydn

"Seek"

Violin, Vocals: Lili Haydn
Bass: Bill Laswell
Keyboards, Programming: Steve Nalepa

"Home"

Guitar: Geoffrey Moore
Violin, Vocals: Lili Haydn
Guitar: Corky James
Keyboards, Programming: Steve Nalepa

"The Promised Land"

Sax: Pharoah Sanders
Vocals: George Clinton
Violin, Vocals: Lili Haydn
Keyboards, Programming: Steve Nalepa

Place between Places

"Memory One"
Violin, Vocals: Lili Haydn

"Strawberry Street"
Violin, Vocals: Lili Haydn

"Can't Give Everything"
Violin, Vocals: Lili Haydn

"Saddest Sunset"
Violin, Vocals: Lili Haydn

"Place between Places"
Violin, Vocals: Lili Haydn

"I Give Up"
Violin, Vocals: Lili Haydn

"Satellites"
Violin, Vocals: Lili Haydn

"The Reverie"
Violin, Vocals: Lili Haydn

"Children of Babylon"
Violin, Vocals: Lili Haydn

"Unfolding Grace"
Violin, Vocals: Lili Haydn

"The Last Serenade"
Violin, Vocals: Lili Haydn

"Powers of Five"
Violin, Vocals: Lili Haydn

"Maggot Brain"
Violin, Vocals: Lili Haydn
Featuring: The Dakah Hip Hop Orchestra

Lililand

"Elephant Trapeze (Welcome to Lililand)"

Violin, Vocals, Keyboards, Programming, Guitar, Kalimba, Percussion: Lili Haydn
Drums: Matt Chamberlain
Guitar: Blake Mills
Piano: Milen Kirov
Trumpet, Flugelhorn: Higai Izraeli

"My My Cross the Line"

Violin, Vocals, Keyboards, Programming, Guitar, Kalimba, Percussion: Lili Haydn
Drums: Matt Chamberlain
Vocals, Additional Drums: Marvin Etzioni

"Sea of Gold"

Violin, Vocals, Keyboards, Programming, Guitar, Kalimba, Percussion: Lili Haydn
Bass, Guitar, Drums: Itai Disraeli
Drums: Matt Chamberlain
Guitar: Woody Aplanalp

"Did Your Mama (Teach You How to Share?)"

Violin, Vocals, Keyboards, Programming, Guitar, Kalimba, Percussion: Lili Haydn
Drums: Matt Chamberlain
Vocals: Miranda Lee Richards

"Tyrant"

Violin, Vocals, Keyboards, Programming, Guitar, Kalimba, Percussion: Lili Haydn
Drums: Matt Chamberlain

"Kashmir"

Violin, Vocals, Keyboards, Programming, Guitar, Kalimba, Percussion: Lili Haydn
Cello: Ginger Murphy, Martin Tillman
Drums: Matt Chamberlain
Tabla: Satnam Singh Ramgotra

"How I Got My Brains Back"

Violin, Vocals, Keyboards, Programming, Guitar, Kalimba, Percussion: Lili Haydn
Cello: Tina Guo
Drums: Matt Chamberlain

"Intro"

Violin, Vocals, Keyboards, Programming, Guitar, Kalimba, Percussion: Lili Haydn
Drums: Matt Chamberlain
Guitar: Toby Pitman

"This Is a Moment of Grace"

Violin, Vocals, Keyboards, Programming, Guitar, Kalimba, Percussion: Lili Haydn
Bass, Guitar, Drums: Itai Disraeli
Drums: Matt Chamberlain
Guitar: Kim Carroll
Piano: Neara Russell

"God Said"

Violin, Vocals, Keyboards, Programming, Guitar, Kalimba, Percussion: Lili Haydn
Cello: Tina Guo
Drums: Matt Chamberlain
Guitar: Blake Mills, Kim Carroll

"Here Is the Rose"

Violin, Vocals, Keyboards, Programming, Guitar, Kalimba, Percussion: Lili Haydn
Drums: Matt Chamberlain
Guitar: Kim Carroll

"I Am a Man"

Violin, Vocals, Keyboards, Programming, Guitar, Kalimba, Percussion: Lili Haydn
Drums: Matt Chamberlain
Piano: Milen Kirov
Vocals: Durga McBroom, Solomon Neara Russell

— ★ —

ROBBEN FORD (SELECT TRACKS): 1997

Blues guitarist Robben Ford had a Grammy-nominated song from the album *Tiger Walk*, which featured P-Funk keyboardist Bernie Worrell.

Blue Thumb Records

Tiger Walk

"In the Beginning"

Drums, Percussion: Steve Jordan
Guitar: Robben Ford
Clavinet, Organ: Bernie Worrell
Bass: Charlie Drayton

"Ghosts"

Drums, Percussion: Steve Jordan
Guitar: Robben Ford
Clavinet, Organ: Bernie Worrell
Bass: Charlie Drayton
Baritone Sax: Ronnie Cuber
Tenor Sax: Bob Malach

"Red Lady W/Cello"

Drums, Percussion: Steve Jordan
Guitar: Robben Ford
Clavinet, Organ: Bernie Worrell
Bass: Charlie Drayton

"Oasis"

Drums, Percussion: Steve Jordan
Guitar: Robben Ford
Organ: Bernie Worrell

"Tiger Walk"

Drums, Percussion: Steve Jordan
Guitar: Robben Ford
Organ: Bernie Worrell

"Comin' Up"

Drums, Percussion: Steve Jordan
Guitar: Robben Ford
Clavinet, Organ: Bernie Worrell
Bass: Charlie Drayton

— ☆ —

THE DAZZ BAND (SELECT TRACK): 1998

This well-known 1970s funk band featured George Clinton on their 1998 album.

Here We Go Again

"Do Poppa Do"

Featuring: George Clinton
Backup Vocals: Keith Haynes Pierre DeMudd
Bass, Keyboards: Nathaniel Phillips
Drums: Raymond Calhoun
Guitar: Marvin McClain
Keyboards: Kevin Kendricks, Michael Norfleet
Vocals: Kenny Pettus, Bobby Harris, Sennie "Skip" Martin III

— ☆ —

THE SIMPSONS (SELECT TRACK): 1998

The TV show *The Simpsons* has been compared to P-Funk by comedian Chris Rock as two phenomena that are still good every time you go back to them. *The Simpsons'* Yeardley Smith (voice of Lisa Simpson) is a fan of P-Funk and is featured on this track with George Clinton and the P-Funk All Stars. Tracey Ullman, whose show first introduced *The Simpsons* shorts, is also a fan.

Geffen Records

The Yellow Album

"She's Coming Out Swingin'"

Lead Vocals: Yeardley Smith (Lisa Simpson), George Clinton
Drums, Bass, Guitar: Dewayne Blackbyrd McKnight
Keyboards: Amp Fiddler
Sax: Yeardley Smith
Backup Vocals: Belita Woods, Tracey Lewis, Ron Ford, Louie "Babblin" Kabbabie, Sheila Horne, George Clinton, Yeardley Smith

— ☆ —

OUTKAST (SELECT TRACK): 1998

This seminal Atlanta hip-hop group had a lot of influence from George Clinton and featured him most notably on the song "Synthesizer."

"Synthesizer"

Lead Vocals: Big Boi, Andre 3000, George Clinton
Backup Vocals: 4.0 b.k.a. the Four Phonics
Bass, Piano, Synthesizer: Earthtone III, Marvin "Chanz" Parkman, Kenneth Wright
Congas: Rajinder "Conga Man" Kala
Guitar: Donny Mathis

— ☆ —

CACOPHONIC FUNK MOB: 1999, 2006

This is one of the three main groups of P-Funk contributor Michael Clip Payne. It featured P-Funk members, French dance musicians, jazz players, and more.

After the Smoke Cleared

"The Journey"

Sax: Jean Gillet
Vocals: Sarah Payne
Bass Station: Gael Barbieri

"Funk History Part 1"

Piano, Keyboards: Amp Fiddler
Man in the Box, Synth, Percussion, Bass Stations: Clip Payne
Bass: Lige Curry
Samples, Cuts: George Clinton

"Suicide"

Guitar: Ron Priesti Smith
Trumpet: Marcus Belgrave
Trombone: Fred Wesley
Sax: Maceo Parker
Backup Vocals: Afro-Knot, P-Wiffy

"Inhale Slowly"

Lead Vocals: Paul Hill
Man in the Box, Synth, Vocals: Clip Payne
Organs, Synthesizer: Amp Fiddler
Guitar Solo: The Flash
Guitar: Chris Bittner

"Shroom!!!"

Guitar: Gael Barbieri
Sax: Jean Gillet
Afro Track Programming: Clip Payne
Percussion: Tony Allen

"I Never Thought That . . ."

Drum Programming, Fender Rhodes, Synthesizer, Backup Vocals: Hamid Saidji
Drums, Backup Vocals: Jean Gillet
Guitar, Backup Vocals, Bass: Gael Barbieri
Rhythm and Solo Guitars: Matthieu Chedid
Lead Vocals: Mudbone Cooper

"F.M. Static"

Man in the Box, Receiver, Music Programming: Clip Payne
Cuts: Slim

"La La Land"

Toy Piano, Vocals: Lucas Gillet

"No Sleep Lullaby"

Sax: Jean Gillet
Synthesizer, Guitar: Gael Barbieri
Drums, Synthesizer, Toy Guitars: Clip Payne

"Make It for You"

Clavinet: Fixi Bossard
Vocals: Clip Payne, Louise Alenius Boserup, Gael Barbieri
Flute: Julia
Tambourine: Clip Payne
Drum Programming, Guitars, Bass: Gael Barbieri

"Say Yeah (Whooa Yeah)"

Drums, Vocals: Jean Gillet
Percussion, Vocals: Hamid Saidji
Bass, Vocals: Gael Barbieri
All Synthesizers: Fixi Bossard
Chorale: Corderie Street Kidz
Vocals: Joann Woodward
Guitars: Matthieu Chedid
Lead Vocals: Mudbone Cooper

"Meltdown"

Keyboards, Bass, Drums: Clip Payne
Bass: Lonnie Motley
Guitar: Ron Priest Smith
Keyboards, Organ: Amp Fiddler
Percussion, Cuts: Gabe Gonzalez

"C'mon Y'all Don't Stop"

Drum Programming, Guitar, Synthesizers: Clip Payne
Vocal Samples: Gabe Gonzalez
Pianos, Keyboards: Amp Fiddler
Guitar: Ron Smith

"Gimme Gimme Gimme"

Vocals: Lige Curry, Fuzzy Haskins, Grady Thomas, Calvin Simon, George Clinton, Ray Davis
Music: Clip Payne

"Summer in the City"

Man in the Box, Percussion, Lead Vocals: Clip Payne
Drums, Percussion: Tony Allen
Sax, Bass: Jean Gillet
Guitar, Wurlitzer, Percussion: Hamid Saidji

"Honey Psychiatry"

Vocals, Guitar, Man in the Box, Loops: Clip Payne
Music Programming, Sax: Jean Gillet
Bass: Gael Barbieri

Fuck Jazz

"Intro"

Tablas, Keyboards: Ted Orr
Samples, Cuts, Guitar: Clip Payne
Trumpet: Deville Edward
Vocals: Gael Barbieri

"Miles Away from Music"

Piano, Electric Piano, Clavinet: Danny Bedrosian
Faux Trumpet, Keyboards, Bass, Guitar: Dave Fruchter
Drums: Clip Payne

"Fuck Jazz"

Trumpet: Paul Henderson
Keyboards, Drum Programming: Clip Payne

"You Take Me There"**Vocals:** Belita Woods, Elizabeth Winters

Keyboards: Étienne de Crécy
Drums, Synth Bass: Clip Payne

"Are You Quiet"

All Vocals and Instruments: Danny Bedrosian

"Homeland Polka"

Moog Synthesizer: Danny Bedrosian
Drums, Samples: Clip Payne
Guitar: Garry Shider, Eric McFadden

"Alive in Spain"

Drums, Samples: Clip Payne
Bass: Lige Curry
Violin, Vocals: Lili Haydn
Horns: Paul Henderson, D'Ville Edward

"Real Love Stories"

Vocals: Elizabeth Winters, Belita Woods, Clip
  Payne
Keyboards, Cuts, Drums: Clip Payne

"Hello?!!"

Vocals: Clip Payne, Elizabeth Winters
Keyboards, Drums, Bass, Sound Effects: Clip
  Payne

"Wake Up Call"

Drums, Samples: Clip Payne
Vocals: Joey Eppard, Clip Payne
Bass: Chris Bittner
Guitar: Joey Eppard

"Hippie Krack"

Moog Synthesizers: Danny Bedrosian
Drums, Samples: Clip Payne

"Cacophony"

Keyboards: Michael Hampton
Drums: Clip Payne
Percussion: Ted Orr
Bass: Lige Curry
Guitar: Michael Hampton, Ted Orr
Trumpet: Chris Young
Sax: Pete Buettner

— ☆ —

ALEX GOPHER (SELECT TRACK): 1999

This French musician worked often with Michael "Clip" Payne as well as Gary "Mudbone" Cooper and others.

Disques Solid

You, My Baby, and I

"Party People"

Vocals: Michael Clip Payne, Gary Mudbone
  Cooper, Hamid Saidji, Gael Barbieri
Mix, Music: Alex Gopher

ARTISTS STARTING IN 2000-2010

ÉTIENNE DE CRÉCY (SELECT TRACK): 2000

This is a French DJ whose *Tempovision* album featured P-Funk's Michael "Clip" Payne, Belita Woods, and others.

Disques Solid

Tempovision

"Tempovision"
Vocals: Michael Clip Payne, Belita Woods
Mix, All Music: Étienne de Crécy

ORIGINAL P: 2000–2001

This contribution is by the original Parliaments sans George Clinton. This album would solidify the live work of the original Parliaments for the 2000s.

What Dat Shakin'

"What Dat Shakin'"
Vocals: Calvin Simon, Fuzzy Haskins, Grady Thomas, Ray Davis, Erica Smith
Guitar: Gene Thomas
Bass: Derrick Davis, Ben Powers Jr., or Milton Price
Keyboards: Gerald Jackson
Drums: Ben Powers Jr. or Milton Price

"35 Years"
Vocals: Calvin Simon, Fuzzy Haskins, Grady Thomas, Ray Davis, Erica Smith
Guitar: Gene Thomas
Bass: Derrick Davis, Ben Powers Jr, or Milton Price
Keyboards: Gerald Jackson
Drums: Ben Powers Jr. or Milton Price

"Funk for You"**Vocals:** Calvin Simon, Fuzzy Haskins, Grady Thomas, Ray Davis, Erica Smith
Guitar: Gene Thomas
Bass: Derrick Davis, Ben Powers Jr., or Milton Price
Keyboards: Gerald Jackson
Drums: Ben Powers Jr. or Milton Price

"Party Down People"

Vocals: Calvin Simon, Fuzzy Haskins, Grady Thomas, Ray Davis, Erica Smith
Guitar: Gene Thomas
Bass: Derrick Davis, Ben Powers Jr., or Milton Price
Keyboards: Gerald Jackson
Drums: Ben Powers Jr. or Milton Price

"Hot Fudge Brownie Girl"

Vocals: Calvin Simon, Fuzzy Haskins, Grady Thomas, Ray Davis, Erica Smith
Guitar: Gene Thomas
Bass: Derrick Davis, Ben Powers Jr., or Milton Price
Keyboards: Gerald Jackson
Drums: Ben Powers Jr. or Milton Price

Hyped Up Westbound Souljaz

"Jump Up in the Air"

Vocals: Calvin Simon, Fuzzy Haskins, Grady Thomas, Ray Davis, Westbound Souljaz
Production: T Money G

"Neva Gonna Tell It 2001"

Vocals: Calvin Simon, Fuzzy Haskins, Grady Thomas, Ray Davis, Westbound Souljaz
Production: T Money G

"One Nation 2001"

Vocals: Calvin Simon, Fuzzy Haskins, Grady Thomas, Ray Davis, Westbound Souljaz
Production: T Money G

"Atomic Dawg 2001"

Vocals: Calvin Simon, Fuzzy Haskins, Grady Thomas, Ray Davis, Westbound Souljaz
Production: T Money G

— ☆ —

FUNKIN 2000

This funk group is made up of brothers and sons of Parliament and Funkadelic members and others. Among them are Garry Shider's brothers and Fuzzy Haskins's son.

"It's On"

Vocals: Tim Shider, Nate Shider, Keith Thomas
Guitar: Nate Shider
Bass: Perk
Keyboards: Tim Shider
Drums: Nowell Haskins

"Off the Hook"

Vocals: Keith Thomas, Nate Shider, Nowell Haskins, Tim Shider
Guitar: Charlie Rivers
Bass, Keyboards: Tim Shider
Drums: Nowell Haskins

"U Don't Have to Cry"

Vocals: Nate Shider, Keith Thomas, Nowel Haskins, Tim Shider, Charlie Rivers, Derek Davis
Guitar: Gene Thomas, Nate Shider
Bass: Derek Davis
Keyboards: Tim Shider
Drums: Nowell Haskins

"Crazy Crush"

Lead Vocals: Keith Thomas, Nate Shider
Backup Vocals: Nowell Haskins, Tim Shider, Charlie Rivers
Guitar: Nate Shider, Gene Thomas
Bass, Keyboards: Tim Shider
Drums: Nowell Haskins

"Funk Done Gone Hip-Hop"

Vocals: Keith Thomas, Derek Davis
Guitar: Nate Shider
Bass: Derek Davis
Keyboards: Tim Shider
Drums: Nowell Haskins

"Lude"

Lead Vocals: Keith Thomas, Nate Shider, Gene Thomas
Backup Vocals: Tim Shider, Charlie Rivers, Nowell Haskins, Billy Spruill
Guitar: Nate Shider, Billy Spruill?, Charlie Rivers?
Bass: Nate Shider
Keyboards: Tim Shider
Drums: Nowell Haskins

"Know about the Funk"

Lead Vocals: Tim Shider, Nate Shider, Nowell Haskins
Guitar, Bass: Nate Shider
Keyboards: Tim Shider
Drums: Nowell Haskins

"Tight Shit"

Lead Vocals: Keith Thomas, Nate Shider, Nowell Haskins
Backup Vocals: Charlie Rivers, Tim Shider, Gene Thomas
Guitar: Nate Shider, Charlie Rivers
Bass: Nate Shider
Keyboards: Tim Shider
Drums: Nowell Haskins

"Rump Shaker"

Vocals: Nowell Haskins, Keith Thomas, Nate Shider
Guitar: Nate Shider
Bass: Perk
Keyboards: Tim Shider
Drums: Nowell Haskins

"Sucker for U"

Vocals: Nowell Haskins
Guitar: Nate Shider
Bass, Keyboards: Tim Shider
Drums: Nowell Haskins

"'Till She Comes Around"

Vocals: Nowell Haskins, Garry Shider, Nate Shider, Gene Thomas
Backup Vocals: Nowell Haskins, Garry Shider, Nate Shider, Craig Staton, Tim Shider, Derek Davis
Guitar: Garry Shider, Nate Shider, Gene Thomas
Bass: Derek Davis
Keyboards: Tim Shider
Drums: Nowell Haskins

"Funk Kin Anthem"

Vocals: Keith Thomas
Guitar, Bass: Nate Shider
Keyboards: Tim Shider
Drums: Nowell Haskins

— ☆ —

RICK GARDNER: 2000, 2009

These are solo albums for P-Funk, Bootsy's Rubber Band, and Horny Horns trumpeter Rick Gardner.

The Gardner of Funk 2

"The Sacred Mound"

Trumpet, Drum Programming, Samples, Keyboards: Rick Gardner

"The Nielsen Rating"

Trumpet, Drum Programming, Samples, Keyboards: Rick Gardner

"Movin On"

Trumpet, Drum Programming, Samples, Keyboards: Rick Gardner

"She's So Fine"

Trumpet, Drum Programming, Samples, Keyboards: Rick Gardner

"Composer of the Earth"

Trumpet, Drum Programming, Samples, Keyboards: Rick Gardner

"Dream Strings"

Trumpet, Drum Programming, Samples, Keyboards: Rick Gardner

"Woo Too Yum Yum"

Trumpet, Drum Programming, Samples, Keyboards: Rick Gardner

"Willow"

Trumpet, Drum Programming, Samples, Keyboards: Rick Gardner

"Genevieve's Clarinet"

Trumpet, Drum Programming, Samples, Keyboards: Rick Gardner

"Alice"

Trumpet, Drum Programming, Samples, Keyboards: Rick Gardner

"Moving On"

Trumpet, Drum Programming, Samples, Keyboards: Rick Gardner

"The Sacred Mound"

Trumpet, Drum Programming, Samples, Keyboards: Rick Gardner

"Vision"

Trumpet, Drum Programming, Samples, Keyboards: Rick Gardner

"Dream Scene"

Trumpet, Drum Programming, Samples, Keyboards: Rick Gardner

"Sex on the Net"

Trumpet, Drum Programming, Samples, Keyboards: Rick Gardner

Mistyblue

"Shame"

Trumpet, Drum Programming, Samples, Keyboards: Rick Gardner

"Rainbow Rider"

Trumpet, Drum Programming, Samples, Keyboards: Rick Gardner

"Mistyblue"

Trumpet, Drum Programming, Samples, Keyboards: Rick Gardner

"Desire"

Trumpet, Drum Programming, Samples, Keyboards: Rick Gardner

"Swimming Up Stream"

Trumpet, Drum Programming, Samples, Keyboards: Rick Gardner

"Breazy"

Trumpet, Drum Programming, Samples, Keyboards: Rick Gardner

"Ridin' Down South"

Trumpet, Drum Programming, Samples, Keyboards: Rick Gardner

Rubber Horn

"Motion"

Trumpet, Drum Programming, Samples, Keyboards: Rick Gardner

"Get Paid"

Trumpet, Drum Programming, Samples, Keyboards: Rick Gardner

"Rapid Fire"

Trumpet, Drum Programming, Samples, Keyboards: Rick Gardner

"Rockin' Rick"

Trumpet, Drum Programming, Samples, Keyboards: Rick Gardner

"Blue Tune"

Trumpet, Drum Programming, Samples, Keyboards: Rick Gardner

"Daylight Saving"

Trumpet, Drum Programming, Samples, Keyboards: Rick Gardner

"Horny Horns"

Trumpet, Drum Programming, Samples, Keyboards: Rick Gardner

"Bewise"

Trumpet, Drum Programming, Samples, Keyboards: Rick Gardner

"Gentle Sex"

Trumpet, Drum Programming, Samples, Keyboards: Rick Gardner

"Wrong Turn"

Trumpet, Drum Programming, Samples, Keyboards: Rick Gardner

"Spaced Out"

Trumpet, Drum Programming, Samples, Keyboards: Rick Gardner

— ☆ —

LARRY SMITH (SELECT TRACKS): 2000

This features several P-Funk alumni.

"Tear It Down"

Vocals: Steve Boyd, Pat Lewis, Garry Shider, Michael Clip Payne, Sandra Feva
Guitar: Eddie Hazel

— ☆ —

LOST IN BASS (SELECT TRACKS): 2000

This bass compilation features Andre Foxxe Williams, Rodney Skeet Curtis, and many more.

AIM Records

"Hangin' Around"Lead Vocals: Andre Williams

Backup Vocals: Andre Williams, Clip Payne, Joe Harris
Bass: Andre Williams, Flea, Ken Williams
Keyboards: Patrick Drummond
Programming: Clip Payne

"Down by the River"

Bass, Vocals: Tony T Green
Guitar: Rickey Rouse
Keyboards: Greg Dokes

"Pretty Girl"

All Instruments: Rodney Curtis
All Vocals: Harry T. Easley

"The Final Frontier"

Bass: Bill Laswell, Jah Wobble, Gabe Katz, Robbie Shakespeare, Bootsy Collins, Jungle Kaos

— ☆ —

DAWN SILVA: 2000

This is a solo outing from cofounder of the Brides of Funkenstein, Dawn Silva. Silva also was a key backup singer with Parliament-Funkadelic, Eddie Hazel, the Gap Band, and others.

All My Funky Friends

"As Long as It's on the One (intro)"

Lead Vocals: Dawn Silva
Backup Vocals, Drum Programming: D'LaVance
Keyboards: Aaron Mason, D'LaVance

"Break Me Off"

Lead Vocals: Dawn Silva
Backup Vocals: Benjamin Mitchell, Jeanette Washington, Dawn Silva, Jackie Simley, D'LaVance
Keyboards, Drum Programming: D'LaVance

"Red Light District"

Lead Vocals: Dawn Silva, Shorty Pimpish
Backup Vocals: Dawn Silva, Quase
Guitar, Drum Programming: D'LaVance
Keyboards: Quase, D'LaVance

"Close to You"

Lead Vocals: Dawn Silva
Backup Vocals: Dawn Silva, D'LaVance
Guitar, Keyboards, Drum Programming: D'LaVance

"Shake It Down"

Lead Vocals: Dawn Silva
Backup Vocals: Dawn Silva, D'LaVance
Guitar, Keyboards, Drum Programming: D'LaVance

"I'd Rather Be with You"

Lead Vocals: Dawn Silva
Backup Vocals: Dawn Silva, Jeanette Washington, SueAnn Carwell, Jackie Simley, Gary Mudbone Cooper
Guitar, Drums: Christopher Troy
Keyboards: Christopher Troy, D'LaVance

"Whole Lotta Game"

Lead Vocals: Dawn Silva
Backup Vocals: Dawn Silva, Jeanette Washington, D'LaVance
Guitar: Aswut Rodriguez, Richard Nance
Keyboards, Drum Programming: D'LaVance

"All My Funky Friends"

Lead Vocals: Dawn Silva
Backup Vocals: Dawn Silva, Jeanette Washington
Guitar, Keyboards, Drum Programming: D'LaVance

"Disco to Go"

Lead Vocals: Dawn Silva
Backup Vocals: SueAnn Carwell, Tommy Jenkins, Jeanette Washington, Jackie Simley, Dawn Silva
Guitar: Christopher Troy and Zack Harmon
Keyboards, Drum Programming, Bass: Christopher Troy
Horns: Fred Wesley, Maceo Parker, Richard Kush Griffith, Rick Gardner

"Calling Out Your Name"

Lead Vocals: Dawn Silva, Aaron Mason
Backup Vocals: Aaron Mason, Dawn Silva
Keyboards, Drum Programming: D'LaVance

"Do You Remember Them"

Lead and Backup Vocals: Dawn Silva
Guitar, Bass, Keyboards, Drum Programming: D'LaVance

"As Long as It's on the One (outro)"

Lead Vocals: Dawn Silva
Backup Vocals, Keyboards, Drum Programming: D'LaVance

— ☆ —

DRUGS: 2000

This was a Funkadelic-inspired band by Michael Clip Payne that also features Garry Shider, bassist Lige Curry, and George Clinton.

The RX for Mis-America

"Brain on Drugs"

Vocals: Clip Payne, Garry Shider
Drums, Bass: Chicken Burke
Guitar: Adam Widoff, Garry Shider, Chicken Burke

"Neva Eva"

Vocals: Clip Payne
Drums: Chicken Burke
Guitar: Adam Widoff, Chicken Burke
Bass: Fred Cash

"Strung Out"

Vocals: Garry Shider
Drums, Bass, Keyboards: Chicken Burke
Guitar: Garry Shider, Adam Widoff, Chicken Burke, Jimmy Eppard

"Jealousy"

Vocals: Garry Shider, Clip Payne
Drums, Bass, Keyboards: Chicken Burke
Guitar: Garry Shider, Chicken Burke, Adam Widoff

"Mis-America"

Vocals: Clip Payne, Joey Eppard, Garry Shider
Drums, Bass, Keyboards: Chicken Burke
Guitar: Garry Shider, Adam Widoff, Chicken Burke

"Daddy's Got a Secret"

Vocals: Clip Payne, Garry Shider Stephanie McKay, Mimi
Drums, Bass: Chicken Burke
Guitar: Adam Widoff, Chicken Burke

"Alabama"

Vocals: Clip Payne, Garry Shider
Drums, Bass: Chicken Burke
Guitar: Chicken Burke, Garry Shider
Lap Steel Guitar, Harp: Jimmy Eppard

"Breathe"

Guitar: Adam Widoff

"Sanitation Engineer"

Vocals: George Clinton

"Deep Down in the Dumps"

Vocals: Clip Payne, George Clinton, Chicken Burke
Drums: Chicken Burke
Guitar: Adam Widoff, Chicken Burke
Bass: Lige Curry
Keyboards: Clip Payne

"Strangest Life"

Vocals: Chicken Burke, Clip Payne
Drums, Bass, Keyboards: Chicken Burke
Guitar: Adam Widoff, Chicken Burke, Jeremy Bernstein

"I Wonder If"

Drums, Bass, Keyboards: Chicken Burke
Guitar: Adam Widoff, Chicken Burke

"Freedom Came"

Vocals: Clip Payne, Stephanie McKay, Garry Shider, Chicken Burke, Joey Eppard
Drums, Keyboards: Chicken Burke
Guitar: Adam Widoff, Garry Shider, Chicken Burke
Bass: Chicken Burke, Fred Cash

"Cold Hearted World"

Vocals: Chicken Burke, Clip Payne, Garry Shider, Joey Eppard
Drums, Bass, Keyboards: Chicken Burke
Guitar: Chicken Burke, Adam Widoff

"Letha Lew Speaks Out"

Vocals: Lew Burke

"Keeps You Runnin'"

Vocals: Chicken Burke, Clip Payne
Drums, Bass, Keyboards: Chicken Burke
Guitar: Adam Widoff, Chicken Burke, Jeremy Bernstein

"Grace"

Vocals: Clip Payne, Chicken Burke
Guitar, Bass: Chicken Burke

— ☆ —

FISHBONE (SELECT TRACKS): 2000

These are select cuts from Fishbone's discography that features Billy "Bass" Nelson, George Clinton, and others.

"Shakey Ground"

Lead Vocals: Angelo Moore
Backup Vocals: Norwood Fisher, Dirty Walt, Bronx Style Bob, Ivan Neville, Donny Osmond
Drums: Chad Smith
Bass: Norwood Fisher, Flea, Billy Nelson
Guitar: Spacey T Singleton, John Frusciante, Jeff Skunk Baxter
Horns: Walt Fowler, Buce Fowler, Albert Wing
Percussion: Lenny Castro
Organ: John McKnight
Theremin: Angelo Moore

"Everybody Is a Star"

Lead Vocals: Angelo Moore, Gwen Stefani, George Clinton, Rick James
Backup Vocals: Perry Farrell, Alexandra Brown, Mona Lisa Young, Portia Griffin, Rose Stone
Drums: Abe Laborial Jr.
Bass: Norwood Fisher
Guitars: Spacey T
Piano: John McKnight
Chamberlin Strings: Patrick Warren
Violin: Lili Haydn
Horns: Angelo Moore, Walt Fowler, Bruce Fowler, Albert Wing
Tambourine: Lenny Castro
Theremin: Angelo Moore

"Dear God"

Lead Vocals: Dirty Walt
Drums, Loops: Abe Laborial Jr.
Bass: Norwood Fisher
Guitars: Spacey T, Billy Nelson
Piano, Organ: John McKnight
Udo: Lenny Castro

Trumpet: Dirty Walt, Walt Fowler
Synthesizer: Steve Lindsey
Chamberlin Strings: Patrick Warren
Theremin: Angelo Moore

— ☆ —

LIGE CURRY/LIGEDELIC/LIGE CURRY BAND: 2000–

These are various projects from P-Funk bassist Lige Curry (the longest-tenured bassist in P-Funk history; tenure: 1979–1986, 1989–2003, 2005–present). They feature dozens of P-Funk members.

4-Track Treasures Vol. 1 and 2

"Welcome (intro)"

Vocals: Garry Shider, Lige Curry

"Pimpin's Been Around"

Production: Bubz Fiddler
Keyboards: Amp Fiddler
Bass: Lige Curry
Guitar: Andre Williams
Vocals: Lige Curry, Amp Fiddler, Bubz Fiddler

"Hihopadelicthang"

Bass, Guitar: Lige Curry
Drum Programming: Sa'D Ali

"New World"

Bass: Lige Curry
Guitar: Dewayne Blackbyrd McKnight
Keyboards: Amp Fiddler

"9/11/01"

Bass, Guitar, Vocals: Lige Curry

"We Ain't Tired"

Bass, Guitar, Vocals: Lige Curry

P-Funk Bassists Rodney "Skeet" Curtis and Lige Curry. Rodney "Skeet" Curtis

"The Cosmic Traveler"

Bass, Guitar: Lige Curry
Vocals: Starr Cullars, Lige Curry

"Shade of Adelic"

Bass, Guitar, Vocals: Lige Curry

"Funk Gets Stronger"

Bass, Guitar, Vocals: Lige Curry

"Be What You Want to Be"

Bass, Guitar, Vocals: Lige Curry

"Only the Strong"

Bass, Guitar, Vocals: Lige Curry

"The Kyle Davis Trip"

Bass, Guitar, Vocals: Lige Curry

"Funkin' Telemarketers"

Bass, Guitar: Lige Curry
Vocals: Starr Cullars, Lige Curry

"Broken Record"

Bass, Guitar, Vocals: Lige Curry

"Bound to Be Boppin'"

Bass: Lige Curry
Guitar: Dewayne Blackbyrd McKnight
Vocals: Lige Curry, Pat Lewis, Sandra Feva, Michael Clip Payne, Shirley Hayden, Janice Evans, Garry Shider, Joe Pep Harris, Lloyd Williams
Keyboards: Amp Fiddler
Drum Programming: Michael Clip Payne

"Greed"

Bass, Guitar, Vocals: Lige Curry

"Home"
Bass, Vocals: Lige Curry
Guitar: Dr. Know
Drum Programming: Michael Clip Payne

"Mike's World"
Guitar: Mike Hampton

"Rock & Roll Me"
Bass, Vocals: Lige Curry
Guitar: Dr. Know
Drum Programming: Michael Clip Payne

"Funk Drunk"
Bass, Guitar, Vocals: Lige Curry

"I'll Kick Yo Motherfunkin Ass"
Bass, Guitar, Drum Machine: Lige Curry
Vocals: Starr Cullars

"Cosmo"
Bass, Guitar, Vocals: Lige Curry

"See You"
Bass, Guitar, Vocals: Lige Curry

"New World"
Bass: Lige Curry
Guitar: Dewayne Blackbyrd McKnight
Keyboards, Drum Machine: Amp Fiddler

"$2500.00 Suit Sucker"
Bass, Guitar, Vocals, Drum Machine: Lige Curry

"Choices"
Bass, Guitar, Vocals, Drum Machine: Lige Curry
Keyboards: Jerome Rodgers

"Burning for Your Love"
Bass, Guitar, Vocals, Drum Machine: Lige Curry

"Funk (Oh It's Got to Be)"
Bass, Guitar, Vocals, Drum Machine: Lige Curry

Introspectives

"Show Biz"
Bass, Guitar: Lige Curry
Vocals: Lige Curry, Star Cullars
Keyboards: Scottie Garner
Drums: Shawn Hill

"Just the Little Things You Do"
Bass: Starr Cullars
Guitar: Lige Curry
Vocals: Lige Curry, Star Cullars
Keyboards: Scott Garner
Drums: Chuck Treece

"If You Want It Go & Get It"
Bass, Vocals: Lige Curry
Guitar: Ron Smith, Garry Shider
Percussion: Anthony Jones

"Visions"
Bass: Lige Curry
Vocals: Lige Curry, Starr Cullars
Drums: Chuck Treece

"Kick Yo Mutha Funkin Ass"
Bass: Lige Curry
Guitar: Lige Curry, Brett Grau
Vocals: Starr Cullars, Mike Harmon
Drums: Shawn Hill

"Visions"

Lead and Backup Vocals, Bass: Lige Curry
Backup Vocals: Starr Cullars
Drums: Chruck Treece

Ligedelic—Funkadelicish

"How Do You Undisco"

Bass, Guitars, Drum Loops, Samples, Sound Effects: Lige Curry

"Mamadelic"

Bass, Guitars, Drum Loops, Samples, Sound Effects: Lige Curry
Keyboards, Synthesizers: Danny Bedrosian

"Hit It on the Verge"

Bass, Guitars, Drum Loops, Samples, Sound Effects: Lige Curry
Keyboards, Synthesizers: Danny Bedrosian

"Mash A Ho Ho"

Bass, Guitars, Drum Loops, Samples, Sound Effects: Lige Curry
Keyboards, Synthesizers: Danny Bedrosian

"Let's Fake It to Get Paid"

Bass, Guitars, Drum Loops, Samples, Sound Effects: Lige Curry
Keyboards, Synthesizers: Danny Bedrosian

"Cold Cuts"

Bass, Guitars, Drum Loops, Samples, Sound Effects: Lige Curry
Keyboards, Synthesizers: Danny Bedrosian

"Bad for You Asshole"

Bass, Guitars, Drum Loops, Samples, Sound Effects: Lige Curry
Keyboards, Synthesizers: Danny Bedrosian

"Super Pussy"

Bass, Guitars, Drum Loops, Samples, Sound Effects: Lige Curry

In & Out of Space

"In and Out of Space"

Bass, Vocals: Lige Curry
Keyboards: Danny Bedrosian
Drum Programming: Nate Oberman

"Don't Stop It"

Bass, Guitar, Vocals: Lige Curry
Drum Programming: M. Scott

"Freedom Road"

Bass, Guitar, Vocals, Drum Programming: Lige Curry
Keyboards: Danny Bedrosian

"Have a Nice Day"

Bass, Guitar, Vocals, Drum Programming: Lige Curry
Keyboards: Danny Bedrosian

"Generations"

Bass, Guitars, Vocals: Lige Curry
Keyboards: Danny Bedrosian
Drum Programming: Nate Oberman

"Life Is What You Make It"

Bass, Guitar, Vocals, Drum Programming: Lige Curry
Keyboards: Danny Bedrosian

"Bass Times Three"

Basses: Lige Curry

"Play to Win"

Bass, Guitar, Vocals, Drum Programming: Lige Curry
Keyboards: Danny Bedrosian

"Girly Girls"

Bass, Guitar, Vocals, Drum Programming:
Lige Curry
Keyboards: Danny Bedrosian

"Sensational"

Bass, Guitar, Vocals, Drum Programming:
Lige Curry
Keyboards: Danny Bedrosian

"Ad Libbin'"

Bass, Guitar, Vocals, Drum Programming:
Lige Curry
Keyboards: Danny Bedrosian

"Stand Strong"

Drum Programming: Lige Curry, P. Tracy
Bass, Guitars, Vocals: Lige Curry
Vocals: Starr Cullars

"A Little Bit of Funk"

Drum Programming, Keyboards: Nate
Oberman
Bass, Guitars, Vocals: Lige Curry

"Long Live Funkadelic"

Bass, Guitar, Vocals, Drum Programming:
Lige Curry
Keyboards: Danny Bedrosian
Vocals: Garry Shider

"Moon in Africa"

Bass, Guitar, Vocals, Drum Programming:
Lige Curry
Keyboards: Danny Bedrosian

"Funk Reward"

Bass, Guitar, Vocals, Drum Programming:
Lige Curry
Keyboards: Danny Bedrosian

"War World Song"

Bass, Guitar, Vocals, Drum Programming:
Lige Curry
Keyboards: Danny Bedrosian

"Cannabis"

Bass, Guitar, Drum Programming: Lige Curry
Keyboards: Danny Bedrosian
Vocals: Starr Cullars

"On the Out"

Bass, Guitar, Vocals, Drum Programming:
Lige Curry
Keyboards: Danny Bedrosian
Guitar Solo: Marc Munoz

"Funkshop"

Bass, Guitar, Drum Programming: Lige Curry
Keyboards, Vocals: Danny Bedrosian

"Nasty Sassy"

Bass, Guitar, Vocals, Drum Programming:
Lige Curry
Keyboards, Vocals: Danny Bedrosian

"Nose Job"

Bass, Guitar, Vocals, Drum Programming:
Lige Curry
Keyboards: Danny Bedrosian
Guitar Solo: Marc Munoz

"Your So Sexy"

Bass, Guitar, Vocals, Drum Programming:
Lige Curry
Keyboards: Danny Bedrosian
Vocals: Starr Cullar

"Computer Curry"

Bass, Guitar, Vocals, Drum Programming:
Lige Curry
Keyboards: Danny Bedrosian

"Woman Glory"

Bass, Guitar, Vocals, Drum Programming:
Lige Curry
Keyboards: Danny Bedrosian

"From Land to Man"

All Instruments: Lige Curry

"The Adventures of Ligedelic"

All Instruments: Lige Curry

Organized Khaos

"Who Stole the Soul"

Bass, Guitars, Vocals: Lige Curry
Drum Programming, Vocals: Clip Payne
Drums: Zachary Alford
Snoring: George Clinton

"Turn On the Lights"

Bass, Guitar, Vocals, Drum Programming:
Lige Curry
Keyboards: Danny Bedrosian

"The Year of the One"

Bass, Guitars, Vocals, Drum Programming:
Lige Curry
Guitar: Chris Sauthoff
Drums: Frankie Kash Waddy
Vocals: Starr Cullars

"Let's Do This"

Bass, Guitars, Vocals: Lige Curry
Keyboards: Danny Bedrosian
Drums: Frankie Kash Waddy

"Push On"

Bass, Guitar, Vocals: Lige Curry
Keyboards: Danny Bedrosian
Guitar: Mike Hampton
Drum Programming: Frankie Kash Waddy,
Lige Curry

"House Play"

Bass, Guitar, Vocals, Drum Programming:
Lige Curry
Keyboards: Danny Bedrosian
Drums: Frankie Kash Waddy

"Whodafunkit"

Bass, Guitar, Vocals, Drum Programming:
Lige Curry
Keyboards, Samples: Danny Bedrosian
Vocals: Starr Cullars
Guitars: Marc Munoz, Brett Grau

"Booty Shakin' Music"

Bass, Guitar, Vocals, Drum Programming:
Lige Curry
Keyboards: Danny Bedrosian
Egg Shakers: Richie Nagan
Vocals: Starr Cullars
Drums: Frankie Kash Waddy

"Last Man Standing"

Bass, Vocals: Lige Curry
Lead Vocals: Paul Hill
Keyboards, Programming: Mel Scott

"Funk Drunk"

Bass, Guitar, Vocals, Drum Programming:
Lige Curry
Keyboards, Vocals: Danny Bedrosian
Horns: HornDogz

"All I Want"

Bass, Guitar, Vocals: Lige Curry
Keyboards: Danny Bedrosian, Andre Foxxe
Williams
Drum Programming: Andre Williams
Vocals, Rap: Rico Lewis

"You Can't Forget Where You Come From"

Bass, Guitar, Vocals, Drum Programming:
Lige Curry
Keyboards: Danny Bedrosian

"Bass in the Hood"

Bass, Guitar, Vocals, Drum Programming:
Lige Curry
Keyboards: Danny Bedrosian

"A Little Help"

Bass, Guitars, Vocals: Lige Curry
Guitars: Freddy Fox
Keyboards: Mel Scott, Rico Lewis
Drum Programming: Mel Scott

"Change Is Now"

Bass, Vocals, Drum Programming: Lige Curry
Keyboards: Danny Bedrosian
Vocals: Starr Cullars

"New Nation"

Bass, Guitars, Vocals, Drum Programming, Samples: Lige Curry

"Speak No Evil"

Bass, Guitar, Vocals, Drum Programming Samples: Lige Curry
Keyboards: Danny Bedrosian

"Move On Through"

Bass, Guitar, Vocals, Drum Programming:
Lige Curry
Keyboards: Danny Bedrosian
Vocals: Starr Cullars

"Hold Those Thoughts"

Sax: Greg Thomas
Keyboards: Danny Bedrosian

— ☆ —

IZM: 2000

This is a funk rock power trio featuring P-Funk guitarist/mandolinist Eric McFadden, P-Funk bassist/guitarist/singer RonKat Spearman, and drummer Kevin Carnes. Live, the drummer would be replaced by P-Funk drummer Ron Wright.

"Superstar"

Guitar: Eric McFadden
Bass: RonKat Spearman
Drums: Kevin Carnes
Vocals: Eric McFadden, RonKat Spearman

"Nappy State of Mind"

Guitar: Eric McFadden
Bass: RonKat Spearman
Drums: Kevin Carnes
Vocals: Eric McFadden, RonKat Spearman

"Can't Help Myself"

Guitar: Eric McFadden
Bass: RonKat Spearman
Drums: Kevin Carnes
Vocals: Eric McFadden, RonKat Spearman

"The Web"

Guitar: Eric McFadden
Bass: RonKat Spearman
Drums: Kevin Carnes
Vocals: Eric McFadden, RonKat Spearman

"Off of My Mind"

Guitar: Eric McFadden
Bass: RonKat Spearman
Drums: Kevin Carnes
Vocals: Eric McFadden, RonKat Spearman

"Dreams"

Guitar: Eric McFadden
Bass: RonKat Spearman
Drums: Kevin Carnes
Vocals: Eric McFadden, RonKat Spearman

"Surviving the Game"

Guitar: Eric McFadden
Bass: RonKat Spearman
Drums: Kevin Carnes
Vocals: Eric McFadden, RonKat Spearman

ALIEN LOVESTOCK: 2000

This is a solo outing by P-Funk's Eric McFadden and also features Belita Woods, George Clinton, and others.

"Warhol's Maze"

Guitars, Lead Vocals: Eric McFadden, Anton Kozikowski
Bass: Charles Gasper
Drums, Percussion: Paul Baldi

"The Trip"

Guitars, Lead Vocals: Eric McFadden, Anton Kozikowski
Bass: Charles Gasper
Drums, Percussion: Paul Baldi

"Make Yourself @Home"

Guitars, Lead Vocals: Eric McFadden, Anton Kozikowski
Bass: Charles Gasper
Drums, Percussion: Paul Baldi
Organ: Chip Roland

"Gone"

Guitars, Lead Vocals: Eric McFadden, Anton Kozikowski
Bass: Charles Gasper
Drums, Percussion: Paul Baldi
Cello: Sam Bass

"Down"

Guitars: Eric McFadden, Anton Kozikowski
Lead Vocals: Storm Large, Eric McFadden, Anton Kozikowski
Bass: Charles Gasper
Drums, Percussion: Paul Baldi

"Alien Love"

Lead Vocals: George Clinton, Belita Woods, Eric McFadden, Anton Kozikowski
Guitars: Eric McFadden, Anton Kozikowski
Bass: Charles Gasper
Drums, Percussion: Paul Baldi

"Room #8"

Guitars: Charles Gasper, Eric McFadden, Anton Kozikowski
Lead Vocals: Eric McFadden, Anton Kozikowski
Bass: Charles Gasper, Ed Ivey
Drums, Percussion: Paul Baldi

"Murphy"

Guitars, Lead Vocals: Eric McFadden, Anton Kozikowski
Bass: Charles Gasper
Drums, Percussion: Paul Baldi

"Lovetractors 4 Sale"

Guitars, Lead Vocals: Eric McFadden, Anton Kozikowski
Backup Vocals: Storm Large
Bass: Charles Gasper
Drums, Percussion: Paul Baldi
Organ: Chip Roland

"Into the Black"

Guitars, Lead Vocals: Eric McFadden, Anton Kozikowski
Bass: Charles Gasper
Drums, Percussion: Paul Baldi

"Waiting"

Guitars, Lead Vocals: Eric McFadden, Anton Kozikowski
Bass: Charles Gasper
Drums, Percussion: Paul Baldi

"Suicide Jack"

Guitars, Lead Vocals: Eric McFadden, Anton Kozikowski
Bass: Charles Gasper
Drums, Percussion: Paul Baldi

— ☆ —

RICHARD "KUSH" GRIFFITH: 2001, 2006

These are solo works by the late trumpeter from P-Funk, Bootsy, the Horny Horns, and the JBs. Griffith has been part of the cornerstone of funk recordings of the 1960s and 1970s.

Blues and Rhythm

"Keep On Calling Me Baby"

Trumpet, Vocals: Richard Kush Griffith
Trombone: John Weigert
Sax: Matt Reynolds, John Zappa, Jimmy Rodriguez
Drums: Tony Byrd
Keyboards: Johnny Davis
Guitar: Craig Mareland
Bass: Donald Payne
Harmonica: Rick Marsberry
Backup Vocals: Kim Seay, Rick Marsberry
Strings: Sylvia and Paul Patterson
Percussion: Fransico Mejias

"The Last Soulman in the Hood"

Trumpet, Vocals: Richard Kush Griffith
Trumpet: Rick Gardner
Sax: Matt Reynolds, John Zappa, Jimmy Rodriguez
Trombone: Fred Wesley
Drums: Bootsy Collins
Keyboards: Joel Johnson
Guitar: Bootsy Collins, Catfish Collins, Garry Shider
Bass: Donald Payne
Harmonica: Rick Marsberry
Backup Vocals: Bootsy Collins, Kim Seay, Rick Marsberry, Garry Shider
Percussion: Francisco Mejias
Strings: Sylvia and Paul Patterson

"That Was Then, This Is Now"

Trumpet, Vocals: Richard Kush Griffith
Trumpet: Rick Gardner
Sax: Matt Reynolds, John Zappa, Jimmy Rodriguez
Trombone: Fred Wesley
Drums: Bootsy Collins
Keyboards: Joel Johnson
Guitar: Bootsy Collins, Catfish Collins, Garry Shider
Bass: Donald Payne
Harmonica: Rick Marsberry
Backup Vocals: Bootsy Collins, Kim Seay, Rick Marsberry, Garry Shider
Percussion: Francisco Mejias
Strings: Sylvia and Paul Patterson

"A Little Bit of Money and a Whole Lotta . . ."

Trumpet, Vocals: Richard Kush Griffith
Trumpet: Rick Gardner
Sax: Matt Reynolds, John Zappa, Jimmy Rodriguez
Trombone: Fred Wesley
Drums: Bootsy Collins
Keyboards: Joel Razor Sharp Johnson
Guitar: Bootsy Collins, Catfish Collins, Garry Shider
Bass: Donald Payne
Harmonica: Rick Marsberry
Backup Vocals: Bootsy Collins, Kim Seay, Rick Marsberry, Garry Shider
Percussion: Francisco Mejias
Strings: Sylvia and Paul Patterson

"How Do You Like Me Now"

Trumpet, Vocals: Richard Kush Griffith
Trumpet: Rick Gardner
Sax: Matt Reynolds, John Zappa, Jimmy Rodriguez
Trombone: Fred Wesley
Drums: Bootsy Collins
Keyboards: Joel Razor Sharp Johnson
Guitar: Bootsy Collins, Catfish Collins, Garry Shider
Bass: Donald Payne
Harmonica: Rick Marsberry
Backup Vocals: Bootsy Collins, Kim Seay, Rick Marsberry, Garry Shider
Percussion: Francisco Mejias
Strings: Sylvia and Paul Patterson

"Captain P's Love Blues"

Trumpet, Vocals: Richard Kush Griffith
Trumpet: Gary Winters, Tony Rodriguez
Sax: Matt Reynolds, John Zappa, Jimmy Rodriguez
Trombone: John Wegert
Drums: Tiger Martin
Keyboards: Johnny Davis
Guitar: Neal Landauer, Sam Mayfield
Bass: Neal Landauer
Harmonica: Rick Marsberry
Backup Vocals: Rick Marsberry, Kim Seay
Strings: Sylvia and Paul Patterson

"Dreamin' Blues"

Trumpet, Vocals: Richard Kush Griffith
Trumpet: Rick Gardner
Sax: Matt Reynolds, John Zappa, Jimmy Rodriguez
Trombone: John Wegert
Drums: Tiger Martin
Keyboards: Joel Johnson
Guitar: Bootsy Collins, Catfish Collins, Garry Shider
Bass: Donald Payne
Harmonica: Rick Marsberry
Strings: Sylvia and Paul Patterson

"Do You Wanna Do a Thang"

Trumpet, Vocals: Richard Kush Griffith
Trumpet: Gary Winters, Tony Rodriguez
Sax: Matt Reynolds, John Zappa, Jimmy Rodriguez
Trombone: John Weigert
Drums: Tony Byrd
Keyboards: Johnny Davis
Guitar: Craig Mareland, Sam Mayfield
Bass: Donald Payne
Harmonica: Rick Marsberry
Backup Vocals: Rick Marsberry, Kim Seay

— ☆ —

RONKAT SPEARMAN: 2001–2005, 2010

These are various solo works by multi-instrumentalist, singer, and songwriter RonKat Spearman (P-Funk tenure: 1999–2011).

Joy to the Funk

"Special Christmas"

All Instruments and Vocals: RonKat Spearman

"Funky Christmas"

All Instruments and Vocals: RonKat Spearman

"Gift"

All Instruments and Vocals: RonKat Spearman

"Joy to the Funk"

All Instruments and Vocals: RonKat Spearman

Little Monsters

"Scary Silent Movie"

All Instruments and Vocals: RonKat Spearman

"Little Monsters with Boo Bass"

Vocals: RonKat Spearman, George Clinton Garry Shider, Kendra Foster, Kim Manning, Linda Shider
All Instruments: RonKat Spearman

"Tears of a Ghost"

Guitar: Dewayne Blackbyrd McKnight
All Other Instruments and Vocals: RonKat Spearman

"Needs Some Love"

All Instruments and Vocals: RonKat Spearman

"Scary Silent Movie Part Two"

All Instruments and Vocals: RonKat Spearman

The Funkectik—Funky Nation

"Sugar Booty"

All Instruments and Vocals: RonKat Spearman
Backup Vocals: Markika

"The Sky Is Falling"

All Instruments and Vocals: RonKat Spearman

"Funky Nation"

All Instruments and Vocals: RonKat Spearman
Backup Vocals: Laritta Norman, Marie Norman, Markika
Keyboards: Lionel
Drums: Beatle Keith Price

"Black Pearl"

All Instruments and Vocals: RonKat Spearman
Backup Vocals: Markika
Guitar: Mark
Drums: Beatle Keith Price

"Fork in the Road"

All Instruments and Vocals: RonKat Spearman

Cheddar

"Intro"

All Instruments and Vocals: RonKat Spearman

"Keep It Wet"

All Instruments and Vocals: RonKat Spearman

"Bounce"

All Instruments and Vocals: RonKat Spearman

"Cheddar"

All Instruments and Vocals: RonKat Spearman
Rap: Moshawn Brown

Dance on the Mothership

"Oh Hi"

Vocals: RonKat Spearman, Pamela Parker, Chi
Trombone: Alan Williams
All Other Instruments: RonKat Spearman

"D.O.T.M.S. (Dance On The Mothership)"

Vocals: RonKat Spearman, George Clinton
Backup Vocals: Chi
Synth Bass, Synthesizer: PTFI Jones
All Other Instruments: RonKat Spearman

"The One"

Vocals: RonKat Spearman, Chi
Drums: Max MacVeety
All Other Instruments: RonKat Spearman

"Rockin' (For a Good Cause)"

Vocals: RonKat Spearman
Drums: Max MacVeety
All Other Instruments: RonKat Spearman

"Change Generation"

Vocals: RonKat Spearman
All Instruments: RonKat Spearman

"(Stop Insulting) My Intelligence"

All Vocals and Instruments: RonKat Spearman

"Love Thyself"

Vocals: George Clinton, RonKat Spearman
Trumpet: Ryan Scott
All Other Instruments: RonKat Spearman

"I'll Wait"

All Vocals and Instruments: RonKat Spearman

"Keep On Loving"

Vocals, All Other Instruments: RonKat Spearman
Sax: David Boyce
Guitar: Michael Cavaseno

"Glow"

Vocals, All Other Instruments: RonKat Spearman
Cello: Sam Bass

"She's Fire"

Vocals, All Other Instruments: RonKat Spearman
Saxes: Alex Baky

"We're Here"

Vocals: Gabby Lala, RonKat Spearman, Chi
All Instruments: RonKat Spearman

"Drive Away"

All Vocals and Instruments: RonKat Spearman

"Mackin' with No Hands"

Vocals, All Other Instruments: RonKat Spearman, Chi
Trumpet: Alan Williams
Synth Bass, Claps: PTFI Jones

"All Is All"

Vocals, Instruments: RonKat Spearman

"Peace to You"

Vocals: George Clinton, Belita Woods, Kendra Foster, Kim Manning, Poo Poo Man, Clip Payne, Chicken, Paul Hill, RonKat Spearman
Slide Guitar: Eric McFadden
Trumpet: Ryan Scott
Cello: Anata
Fiddle: Hooper
All Other Instruments: RonKat Spearman

— ☆ —

REDMAN (SELECT TRACKS): 2001

This celebrated East Coast rapper has been very P-Funk-centric in his career, sampling hits like "Theme from the Black Hole" to great effect. This particular cut features George Clinton.

Def Jam Recordings

Malpractice

"J.U.M.P."

Lead Vocals: Redman, George Clinton
Recorder: Pete Horowitz
Track: Erick Sermon

— ☆ —

FATBOY SLIM (SELECT TRACK): 2001

Big beat and electronic DJ Fatboy Slim had many hit songs in the late 1990s and early 2000s, even sampling the Horny Horns on a couple of his songs. This particular song, which charted as well, was most famous for its music video featuring Christopher Walken and features vocals by Bootsy Collins.

Astralwerks Records

"Weapon of Choice"

Vocals: Bootsy Collins
Production, Samples: Fatboy Slim

— ☆ —

FREEKBASS (SELECT TRACKS): 2001–

Bootsy protégé and bassist Freekbass has developed a consistent solo career over the past almost 30 years.

Body over Mind

"Intro"

Bass, Guitar, Keyboards: Freekbass
Alto and Baritone Saxes, Synthesizers, Flute: Joodi
Drums: Swift (and vocals), John Miracle
Guitar: Sean McGary, Ryan C. Hensley
Additional Horns: New Basics Brass Band
Keyboards, Vocals: Beta-17
Vocals: Big Robb, Bootsy, Mark Chenault, Oui-wey Collins

"Hear Me Play"

Bass, Guitar, Keyboards: Freekbass
Alto and Baritone Saxes, Synthesizers, Flute: Joodi
Drums: Swift (and vocals), and John Miracle
Guitar: Sean McGary, Ryan C. Hensley
Additional Horns: New Basics Brass Band
Keyboards, Vocals: Beta-17
Vocals: Big Robb, Bootsy, Mark Chenault, Oui-wey Collins

"Mission"

Bass, Guitar, Keyboards: Freekbass
Alto and Baritone Saxes, Synthesizers, Flute: Joodi
Drums: Swift (and vocals), John Miracle
Guitar: Sean McGary, Ryan C. Hensley
Additional Horns: New Basics Brass Band
Keyboards, Vocals: Beta-17
Vocals: Big Robb, Bootsy, Mark Chenault, Oui-wey Collins

"Body over Mind"

Bass, Guitar, Keyboards: Freekbass
Alto and Baritone Saxes, Synthesizers, Flute: Joodi
Drums: Swift (and vocals), John Miracle
Guitar: Sean McGary, Ryan C. Hensley
Additional Horns: New Basics Brass Band
Keyboards, Vocals: Beta-17
Vocals: Big Robb, Bootsy, Mark Chenault, Oui-wey Collins

"Sense of Anxiety"

Bass, Guitar, Keyboards: Freekbass
Alto and Baritone Saxes, Synthesizers, Flute: Joodi
Drums: Swift (and vocals), John Miracle
Guitar: Sean McGary, Ryan C. Hensley
Additional Horns: New Basics Brass Band
Keyboards, Vocals: Beta-17
Vocals: Big Robb, Bootsy, Mark Chenault, Oui-wey Collins

"Connect"

Bass, Guitar, Keyboards: Freekbass
Alto and Baritone Saxes, Synthesizers, Flute: Joodi
Drums: Swift (and vocals), John Miracle
Guitar: Sean McGary, Ryan C. Hensley
Additional Horns: New Basics Brass Band
Keyboards, Vocals: Beta-17
Vocals: Big Robb, Bootsy, Mark Chenault, Oui-wey Collins

"Freekbass 2YK"

Bass, Guitar, Keyboards: Freekbass
Alto and Baritone Saxes, Synthesizers, Flute: Joodi
Drums: Swift (and vocals), John Miracle
Guitar: Sean McGary, Ryan C. Hensley
Additional Horns: New Basics Brass Band
Keyboards, Vocals: Beta-17
Vocals: Big Robb, Bootsy, Mark Chenault, Oui-wey Collins

"Baby Baby"

Bass, Guitar, Keyboards: Freekbass
Alto and Baritone Saxes, Synthesizers, Flute: Joodi
Drums: Swift (and vocals), John Miracle
Guitar: Sean McGary, Ryan C. Hensley
Additional Horns: New Basics Brass Band
Keyboards, Vocals: Beta-17
Vocals: Big Robb, Bootsy, Mark Chenault, Oui-wey Collins

"Thang"

Bass, Guitar, Keyboards: Freekbass
Alto and Baritone Saxes, Synthesizers, Flute: Joodi
Drums: Swift (and vocals), John Miracle
Guitar: Sean McGary, Ryan C. Hensley
Additional Horns: New Basics Brass Band
Keyboards, Vocals: Beta-17
Vocals: Big Robb, Bootsy, Mark Chenault, Oui-wey Collins

"Do What You Gotta Do"

Bass, Guitar, Keyboards: Freekbass
Alto and Baritone Saxes, Synthesizers, Flute: Joodi
Drums: Swift (and vocals), John Miracle
Guitar: Sean McGary, Ryan C. Hensley
Additional Horns: New Basics Brass Band
Keyboards, Vocals: Beta-17
Vocals: Big Robb, Bootsy, Mark Chenault, Oui-wey Collins

"Peppermint Leather"

Bass, Guitar, Keyboards: Freekbass
Alto and Baritone Saxes, Synthesizers, Flute: Joodi
Drums: Swift (and vocals), John Miracle
Guitar: Sean McGary, Ryan C. Hensley
Additional Horns: New Basics Brass Band
Keyboards, Vocals: Beta-17
Vocals: Big Robb, Bootsy, Mark Chenault, Oui-wey Collins

"She's Already There"

Bass, Guitar, Keyboards: Freekbass
Alto and Baritone Saxes, Synthesizers, Flute:
  Joodi
Drums: Swift (and vocals), John Miracle
Guitar: Sean McGary, Ryan C. Hensley
Additional Horns: New Basics Brass Band
Keyboards, Vocals: Beta-17
Vocals: Big Robb, Bootsy, Mark Chenault,
  Oui-wey Collins

"Silver 17"

Bass, Guitar, Keyboards: Freekbass
Alto and Baritone Saxes, Synthesizers, Flute:
  Joodi
Drums: Swift (and vocals), John Miracle
Guitar: Sean McGary, Ryan C. Hensley
Additional Horns: New Basics Brass Band
Keyboards, Vocals: Beta-17
Vocals: Big Robb, Bootsy, Mark Chenault,
  Oui-wey Collins

The Air Is Fresher Underground

"Knock the Walls Down"

Bass, Vocals, Guitar: Freekbass
Drums, Vocals: Swift
Guitar: John Hickey or Richard Fortus
Keyboards: Freekbass, Bootsy Collins

"Do We Even Belong Together"

Bass, Guitar: Freekbass
Keyboards: Bernie Worrell
Banjo, Fiddle: Paul Patterson
Drums, Vocals: Swift

"Always Here"

Bass, Vocals: Freekbass
Guitar: Buckethead
Vocals, Keyboards: Bootsy Collins
Drums: Swift

"Invincible Part 1"

Bass, Vocals: Freekbass
Vocals, Keyboards: Bootsy Collins
Drums, Vocals: Swift
Sax: info could not be obtained

"Play"

Bass, Guitar, Keyboards: Freekbass
Vocals, Keyboards, Drum Programming:
  Bootsy Collins
Drums, Vocals: Swift
Guitar: Catfish Collins

"Burnt Cat"

Bass, Keyboards, Vocals: Freekbass
Keyboards: Bootsy Collins
Drums: Swift
Guitars: Catfish Collins, Richard Fortus
Vocals: Carole Walker, Melanie Gregory, Mark
  Chenault
Guitar:

"Gettin' It"

Bass, Guitar, Keyboards: Freekbass
Vocals: Bootsy Collins, Mark Chenault
Drum Programming: Bootsy Collins
Guitar: John Hickey

"Merge"

Bass, Vocals: Freekbass
Guitar: Catfish Collins?, John Hickey?,
  Richard Fortus?
Vocals, Samples: Bootsy Collins
Drums: Swift

"Check It"

Bass, Guitar, Vocals: Freekbass
Sax: info could not be obtained
Keyboards: Greg Fitz
Drums: Swift
Vocals: Carole Walker, Melanie Gregory

"No Regret"

Bass, Vocals, Drum Programming, Keyboards: Freekbass

"Minute to Forever"

Bass, Guitar: Freekbass
Drums: Swift
Samples, Bass: Bootsy Collins

"You"

Bass, Vocals: Freekbass
Keyboards, Melodica: Gregg Fitz
Drums, Vocals: Swift

"Summer"

Bass, Guitar, Drum Programming, Keyboards, Vocals: Freekbass

Grooveyard

"She's Already There Live"

Bass: Freekbass
Drums: Chip Wilson
Guitar: T-Sly

"Milkhunt Live"

Bass: Freekbass
Drums: Chip Wilson
Guitar: T-Sly

"Same Thing Live"

Bass: Freekbass
Drums: Chip Wilson
Guitar: T-Sly

"Mission Live"

Bass: Freekbass
Drums: Chip Wilson
Guitar: T-Sly

"Segue Live"

Bass: Freekbass
Drums: Chip Wilson
Guitar: T-Sly

"Time Live"

Bass: Freekbass
Drums: Chip Wilson
Guitar: T-Sly

"P-Leather Live"

Bass: Freekbass
Drums: Chip Wilson
Guitar: T-Sly

"Up, Up, Up"

Bass: Freekbass
Drums: Chip Wilson
Guitar: T-Sly

"The Overdriven Sun"

Bass: Freekbass
Drums: Chip Wilson
Guitar: T-Sly

Junkyard Waltz

"Get It Go"

Backup Vocals, Rap: DJizzle
Bass Guitar, Talkbox, Lead Vocals: Freekbass
Drums, Backup Vocals: Tobotius
Guitar: T-Sly

"Big Bang Bionic"

Backup Vocals: King Czar, J.B. of O.A.C., Piakhan
Bass Guitar, Lead Vocals: Freekbass
Drums, Turntables, Sequencer: Tobotius
Guitar: Buckethead

"Junkyard Waltz"

Backup Vocals: Gary Mudbone Cooper, Jen Durkin
Bass Guitar: Mike Gordon
Bass Guitar, Lead Vocals: Freekbass
Drums: Chip Wilson
Drums, Percussion: Tobotius

"Higher"

Backup Vocals: Candice Cheatham
Bass Guitar, **Guitar, Lead Vocals:** Freekbass
Drums, Percussion, Turntables, Backup Vocals: Tobotius
Synthesizer, Keyboards: Bernie Worrell

"TV in My Head"

Bass Guitar, Lead Vocals: Freekbass
Drums, Piano, Turntables, Sequencer: Tobotius

"Pretty Heavy Balance"

Bass: Freekbass
Drums: Bootsy Collins
Sequencer: Keith Cheatham
Vocals: Izzy Sherman
Turntables, Sequencer: Tobotius

"X-Ray Vision"

Backup Vocals: Candice Cheatham
Bass, Guitar, Lead Vocals: Freekbass
Drums, Percussion, **Turntables, Backup Vocals:** Tobotius
Guitar: John Hickey
Keyboards: Bernie Worrell

"Ghost of Temptation"

Bass: Freekbass
Drums, Percussion, Turntables, Buckethead Sampling: Tobotius
Guitar: T-Sly
Speech: Josh Seurkamp

"Critical Condition"

Bass, Lead Vocals, Sequencer: Freekbass
Drums, Sequencer: Tobotius
Guitar: Bob Gayol
Vocals: Candice Cheatham

"Body Good"

Bass, Guitar, Vocals: Freekbass
Drums: Chip Wilson
Guitar: T-Sly
Vocals: Gary Mudbone Cooper

"Twilight Zone"

Bass, Lead Vocals, Sequencer: Freekbass
Drums, Turntables, Sequencer: Tobotius
Guitar: T-Sly

Everybody's Feelin' Real

"Rise"

Bass, Vocals: Freekbass
Drums: Chip Wilson
Horns: Skerik
Keyboards, Synthesizer: Joel Johnson
Percussion: David Farris
Vocals: Kim Manning
Vocals, Trumpet: Jennifer Hartswick

"Victoria Thunder"

Bass, Vocals: Freekbass
Drums: Chip Wilson
Horns: Skerik
Keyboards, Synthesizer: Joel Johnson
Percussion: David Farris
Vocals: Kim Manning
Vocals, Trumpet: Jennifer Hartswick

"Everybody's Feelin' Real"

Bass, Vocals: Freekbass
Drums: Chip Wilson
Horns: Skerik
Keyboards, Synthesizer: Joel Johnson
Percussion: David Farris
Vocals: Kim Manning
Vocals, Trumpet: Jennifer Hartswick

"Mama's Like a Cowboy"

Bass, Vocals: Freekbass
Drums: Chip Wilson
Horns: Skerik
Keyboards, Synthesizer: Joel Johnson
Percussion: David Farris
Vocals: Kim Manning
Vocals, Trumpet: Jennifer Hartswick

"Fish a Man"

Bass, Vocals: Freekbass
Drums: Chip Wilson
Horns: Skerik
Keyboards, Synthesizer: Joel Johnson
Percussion: David Farris
Vocals: Kim Manning
Vocals, Trumpet: Jennifer Hartswick

"Never Enough"

Bass, Vocals: Freekbass
Drums: Chip Wilson
Horns: Skerik
Keyboards, Synthesizer: Joel Johnson
Percussion: David Farris
Vocals: Kim Manning
Vocals, Trumpet: Jennifer Hartswick

"Battery"

Bass, Vocals: Freekbass
Drums: Chip Wilson
Horns: Skerik
Keyboards, Synthesizer: Joel Johnson
Percussion: David Farris
Vocals: Kim Manning

Vocals, Trumpet: Jennifer Hartswick

"Go Up"

Bass, Vocals: Freekbass
Drums: Chip Wilson
Horns: Skerik
Keyboards, Synthesizer: Joel Johnson
Percussion: David Farris
Vocals: Kim Manning
Vocals, Trumpet: Jennifer Hartswick

"John"

Bass, Vocals: Freekbass
Drums: Chip Wilson
Horns: Skerik
Keyboards, Synthesizer: Joel Johnson
Percussion: David Farris
Vocals: Kim Manning
Vocals, Trumpet: Jennifer Hartswick

"Fly"

Bass, Vocals: Freekbass
Drums: Chip Wilson
Horns: Skerik
Keyboards, Synthesizer: Joel Johnson
Percussion: David Farris
Vocals: Kim Manning
Vocals, Trumpet: Jennifer Hartswick

All the Way This. All the Way That

"Knuckle Sandwich"

Bass: Freekbass
Guitar: Eddie Roberts
Drums: Rico Lewis
Vocals: Sammi Garrett, Sky White

"You Make Me Wanna Dance"

Bass: Freekbass
Guitar: Eddie Roberts
Drums: Rico Lewis
Vocals: Sammi Garrett, Sky White
Keyboards: Adryon de Leon

"R U Ready"

Bass, Guitar: Freekbass
Drums, Keyboards: Rico Lewis
Vocals: Freekbass, Rico Lewis, Sammi Garrett, Sky White

"Gotta Get Back to You"

Bass: Freekbass
Guitar: Eddie Roberts
Drums: Rico Lewis
Vocals: Sammi Garrett, Sky White

"Blizzard Lizard"

Bass: Freekbass
Guitar: Eddie Roberts
Drums: Rico Lewis
Vocals: Reily Comisar, Sky White

"Fre3kroNomoKon"

Bass, Vocals: Freekbass
Vocals: Lonnie Marshall, Sammi Garrett, Stella Sherman
Keyboards, Synthesizer: Joel Johnson
Drums, Vocals: Rico Lewis
Beats: Charles "Mista Swift" Phillips III
Keyboards, Synthesizers: Itaal Shur

"Your Love Is Always On Time"

Bass, Vocals: Freekbass
Beats: Charles "Mista Swift"
Vocals: Sammi Garrett, Stella Sherman
Keyboards, Synthesizers: Itaal Shur, Joel Johnson

"Steppin' Outta Line"

Vocals, Bass Guitar, Rhythm Guitar: Freekbass
Keyboards, Synthesizers: Joel Johnson
Drums, Vocals: Rico Lewis
Vocals: Sammi Garrett, Lonnie Marshall, Stella Sherman
Keyboards, Synthesizers: Itaal Shur

"Love in Your Pocket"

Vocals, Bass, Rhythm Guitar: Freekbass
Vocals: Sammi Garrett, Lonnie Marshall
Keyboards: Itaal Shur
Drums: Rico Lewis

"Thrust"

Bass Guitar, Vocals, Guitar: Freekbass
Keyboards: Itaal Shur
Vocals: Sammi Garrett
Drums: Chris Donnelly
Beats: Nappy G

— ☆ —

SHEILA HORNE: 2002

These are solo projects from Brides of Funkenstein vocalist Sheila Horne/Brody/Washington. Sheila also goes by the moniker Amuka.

7 Roses

"Got to See Ya"

Vocals: Sheila Horne
Guitar: Michael Hampton

"Mother"

Vocals: Sheila Horne
Guitar: Michael Hampton
Keyboards: Paul G

"Same Damn Thing"

Vocals: Sheila Horne
Backup Vocals: Jenny (a male vocalist as well)

"Tell Me"

Vocals: Sheila Horne
Backup Vocals: Two singer/songwriters, Sheila Horne
Guitar, Bass: Darryl Moon

"Anything"
Vocals: Sheila Horne
Backup Vocals: Jenny

"No Ordinary Man"
Vocals: Sheila Horne
Drums, Guitar, Bass: Kevon

"Garden of Eden"
Vocals: Sheila Horne
Drums: Paul G
Guitar: Michael Hampton
Bass, Keyboards: Paul G

"Turn the Light On"
Vocals: Sheila Horne
Drums, Guitar, Bass, Keyboards: Gabe Gonzalez

"Can't Fall"
Vocals: Sheila Horne
Backup Vocals: Jenny

"You Ainthethe Man"
Vocals: Sheila Horne
Drums, Bass, Keyboards: Paul G
Guitar: Michael Hampton

"Hey Soldier"
Vocals: Sheila Horne
Drums, Bass, Keyboards: Paul G
Guitar: Michael Hampton

"Peace"
Vocals: Sheila Horne
Drums, Guitar, Bass, Keyboards: Antonio Verdi (A&D Music)

"What about You"
Vocals: Sheila Horne
Backup Vocals: Two singer/songwriters, Sheila Horne

FRANKIE "KASH" WADDY: 2002

This is the solo album of drummer Frankie "Kash" Waddy, who played with the JBs, House Guests, Funkadelic, Complete Strangers, Bootsy's Rubberthed, the Brides of Funkenstein, the P-Funk All Stars, and many other groups over his long career.

Kash Up Front

"Funky Drumz and Thangz"
Drum Programming, Keyboards, Vocals: Frankie Kash Waddy

"Stank"
Drum Programming, Keyboards: Frankie Kash Waddy

"Wait 4 Me"
Drum Programming, Keyboards, Vocals: Frankie Kash Waddy

"Get Wild"
Drum Programming, Keyboards: Frankie Kash Waddy

"Wake Up"
Drum Programming, Keyboards: Frankie Kash Waddy

"My Life"
Drum Programming, Keyboards, Vocals: Frankie Kash Waddy

"Desired"
Drums, Keyboards, Vocals: Frankie Kash Waddy

"Stompin'"
Drum Programming, Keyboards: Frankie Kash Waddy

— ☆ —

"Synister"

Drum Programming, Keyboards: Frankie
Kash Waddy

"Struttin'"

Drum Programming, Keyboards: Frankie
Kash Waddy

"Electrofunknastix"

Drum Programming, Keyboards: Frankie
Kash Waddy

"Don't Just Stand Here"

Drums, Keyboards, Vocals: Frankie Kash
Waddy
Guitar: Dewayne Blackbyrd McKnight

— ☆ —

PARLAMACK: 2002

This is solo work by the dancer/contortion-
ist/rapper Carlos McMurray, who had the
Sir Nose D'VoidofFunk role onstage with
George Clinton and P-Funk from 1992 to
2019.

"Sir Nose"

Vocals: Carlos McMurray
Production: G

"Bounce 2 This"

Vocals: Carlos McMurray, George Clinton
Production: Maestro

"Shake Ya Dank"

Vocals: Carlos McMurray
Production: Miestro

"Ridin' Hy"

Vocals: Carlos McMurray, Robert Moss
Production: G

"Keep Fonkin'"

Vocals: Carlos McMurray, Robert Moss
Production: Miestro

"Pimp-Hoe-Duet"

Vocals: Carlos McMurray, Belita Woods
Music: Luther Ingram

"Mercy Mercy"

Vocals: Carlos McMurray, Latonya Morris
Keyboards: Patrick Drummond
Guitar: Stevie Pannell

"Wadadada"

Vocals: Carlos McMurray
Production: Miestro

"Da Club"

Vocals: Carlos McMurray, Jocka, J.Rock
Arsenal, Belita Woods
Production: Miestro

"Fonky Friends"

Vocals: Carlos McMurray
Production: Miestro

"Dr. Bombay"

Vocals: Carlos McMurray
Production: Miestro

"Mr. Feelgood"

Vocals: Carlos McMurray, Latonya Morris
Guitar, Bass: Stevie Pannell

"Ride 2 This"

Vocals: Carlos McMurray, OMAJ
Production: Miestro
Keyboards: Patrick Drummond
Guitar: Stevie Pannell

"Hypnotic Funk"

Vocals: Carlos McMurray, OMAJ
Production: Maestro
Guitar: Stevie Pannell

"AnnonsensicalmusicalHypnotic"

Vocals: Carolos McMurray, Latonya Morris
Production: Carlos McMurray
Guitar: Stevie Pannell

— ☆ —

GARRY "DIAPERMAN" SHIDER: 2002

This is a late-era solo work by Garry "Starchild" Shider, a guitarist/vocalist who was an extremely important part of the P-Funk machine for many decades (1971–2010). He was one of the most important members of the band in terms of sheer output of work and input of ideas. Shider cowrote many hit P-Funk songs and was a master vocal arranger. Always much more of a "team player," he did not do a lot of solo work, as most of his work was incorporated into the larger P-Funk framework. Shider's indelible mark on the music world through his P-Funk contributions is well solidified in the annals of music history.

The Second Coming

"Crazy 'Bout You"

Vocals: Linda Shider, Garry Shider, Marshall Shider, Garrett Shider, Meko Kelly
Guitar: Andre Giles, Garry Shider
Keyboards, Key Bass: Garry Shider
Drum Programming: Ace Boston

"Ghetto Invaders"

Vocals: Linda Shider, Garry Shider
Keyboards: Garry Shider, Dax Greene or Tony Capone
Drum Programming: Ace Boston
Guitar: Ron Rainbow

"The Rainbow"

Vocals: Garry Shider, Linda Shider, Shirley Hayden
Keyboards, Bass, Drums: Dax Greene

"Glory"

Vocals: Garry Shider, Linda Shider
Guitar, Keyboards, Bass: Garry Shider
Drum Programming: Marshall and Garry Shider

"The Light"

Vocals, Keyboards, Bass: Garry Shider

"Side 2 Side"

Vocals: Shirley Hayden, Michael Clip Payne, Garry Shider, Linda Shider
Guitar: Garry Shider, Andre Giles
Keyboards, Drum Programming: Michael Clip Payne
Bass: Cordell Mosson

Diaperman Goes Starchild

"DoDo Wah"

Vocals: Garry Shider, Marshall Shider, Linda Shider
Keyboards, Synth Bass, Drum Programming: Garry Shider

"Funky 1"

Guitar, Bass: Garry Shider
Keyboards: Marshall Shider, Garry Shider, Big George
Drums: Marshall Shider

Garry Shider in front of the Funkadelic Skull on the Motor Booty Affair Tour, 1979. © Diem Jones

"Rough!"

Guitar: Andre Giles, Garry Shider
Keyboards: Tony or Dax Greene, Garry Shider
Bass: Garry Shider

"The Boy's Room"

Guitar: Garry Shider, Mike Hampton
Keyboards: Garry Shider
Bass: Cordell Mosson
Drum Programming: Garry Shider or Ace
   Boston

— ☆ —

BLIND BOYS OF ALABAMA (SELECT TRACKS): 2002–2003

This is one of the only American musical groups with a longer history than P-Funk. It is a gospel group that got its start in the 1930s. The offerings listed below have connections to George Clinton/P-Funk.

"You and Your Folks/23rd Psalm"

Vocals: Clarence Fountain, Jimmy Carter, George Scott, Joey Williams, Ricky McKinnie, Bobby Butler
Pedal Steel Guitar, Guitar: Robert Randolph
Bass: Danyel Morgan
Drums: Marcus Randolph
Keyboards: John Ginty
Percussion: Leon Mobley

"Away in a Manger"

Vocals: George Clinton, George Scott
Organ: John Medeski
Pedal Steel Guitar: Robert Randolph
Guitar: Duke Robillard
Double Bass: Danny Thompson
Drums: Michael Jerome

— ☆ —

THE BROTHERS OF GOSPEL: (SELECT TRACKS): 2003

This gospel group features original Parliaments bassist Richard Boyce.

Vocals: Richard Boyce, James Holmes, Bobby Holmes
Bass: Richard Boyce
Guitar: James Holmes
Additional Musicians:
Vocals: Clarence Boyce, Bob Hunter, Monica Hughes, Ashley Hughes, Brittany Smith, Nikki Jones, Terri Foreman, Daphne Holmes, Andrea Holmes

Keyboards: Jan Dopson Kevin Leonard, Bob Hunter
Guitar: Bob Hunter, Thomas Ryant Jr., Arlander Anthony, Tommy Bush
Bass: Eddie Criminger
Harmonica: Bob Hunter
Drums: Tius Holmes, Ebony King

— ☆ —

YOUNG FUNK: 2003

This solo album is by producer/rapper Young Funk, who is the son of P-Funk vocalist Steve Boyd.

Make My Funk

"American Dream"
Vocals, Beats: Steve Boyd Jr.
Vocal Hooks: Steve Boyd

"Street Code"
Vocals, Beats: Steve Boyd Jr.
Vocal Hooks: Steve Boyd

"Wartime"
Vocals, Beats: Steve Boyd Jr.
Vocal Hooks: Steve Boyd

"Let's Ride"
Vocals, Beats: Steve Boyd Jr.
Vocal Hooks: Steve Boyd

"Bigg Pimpin'"
Vocals, Beats: Steve Boyd Jr.
Vocal Hooks: Steve Boyd

"Bling Bling"
Vocals, Beats: Steve Boyd Jr.
Vocal Hooks: Steve Boyd
Drums: Gabe Gonzalez
Vocals: Jillian

"Feel the Squad"

Vocals, Beats: Steve Boyd Jr.
Vocal Hooks: Steve Boyd

"I Stay"

Vocals, Beats: Steve Boyd Jr.
Vocal Hooks: Steve Boyd

"One Whack Rapper"

Vocals, Beats: Steve Boyd Jr.
Vocal Hooks: Steve Boyd

"Last Seen"

Vocals, Beats: Steve Boyd Jr.
Vocal Hooks: Steve Boyd

"Sittin' Lovely"

Vocals, Beats: Steve Boyd Jr.
Vocal Hooks: Steve Boyd

"Truth and Reality"

Vocals, Beats: Steve Boyd Jr.
Vocal Hooks: Steve Boyd

"Watchin' Me"

Vocals, Beats: Steve Boyd Jr.
Vocal Hooks: Steve Boyd

"Sho Nuff"

Vocals, Beats: Steve Boyd Jr.
Vocal Hooks: Steve Boyd

"Why Do We Live This Way"

Vocals, Beats: Steve Boyd Jr.
Vocal Hooks: Steve Boyd

— ☆ —

SATIVA DIVA: 2003

This rap album is by Shonda Clinton, grand-daughter of George Clinton. It features several P-Funk players.

Jersey Girl

"Something Stank"

Vocals: Shonda Clinton, George Clinton, Tracey Lewis
Bass: Donnie Sterling
Drums: Dennis Chambers
Additional Beats: Gabe Gonzalez
Keyboards: Ernestro Wilson, Manon Saulsby

"Hard as Steel"

Vocals: Shonda Clinton
Backup Vocals: Steve Boyd
Bass: Engineer
Beats: Sa'D Ali
Guitar: Dewayne Blackbyrd McKnight
Keyboards: Engineer

"Envelope"

Vocals: Shonda Clinton
Backup Vocals, Keyboards: Steve Boyd
Guitar: Tracey Lewis
Beats: Steve Boyd, Jr.

"Sativa"

Vocals: Shonda Clinton
Backup Vocals: Steve Boyd
Beats: Steve Boyd Jr.
Keyboards: Danny Bedrosian?

"Greatest"

Vocals: Shonda Clinton
Backup Vocals, Beats: Steve Boyd Jr.
Guitar: Kevin
Keyboards: Steve Boyd

"Otherside (Get the Fuck Out)"

Vocals: Shonda Clinton, Kendra Foster
Guitar: Mike Patterson
Bass, Keyboards: Steve Boyd
Beats: Steve Boyd Jr.

"Keep It Funkin'"

Vocals: Shonda Clinton, Kendra Foster
Guitar: Mike Patterson
Keyboards: Danny Bedrosian
Bass, Keyboards: Steve Boyd
Beats: Steve Boyd Jr.

"Grind"

Vocals: Shonda Clinton, Steve Boyd
Beats, Keyboards: Rico Lewis

"I Do, Do This"

Vocals: Shonda Clinton, George Clinton
Sample: Bop Gun

"Smoke a Lil Bit"

Vocals: Shonda Clinton, Steve Boyd
Guitar: Mike Patterson
Bass, Keyboards: Steve Boyd
Beats: Steve Boyd Jr., Little C

"Figure of Speech"

Vocals: Shonda Clinton
Bass, Keyboards: Steve Boyd
Guitar: Kevin
Beats: Little C

"Denial"

Vocals: Shonda Clinton
Sample: Dr. Dre

"Underground Angel"

Vocals: Shonda Clinton, Steve Boyd
Bass, Keyboards: Steve Boyd
Beats: Mike Bass
Guitar: Dewayne Blackbyrd McKnight

— ☆ —

KENDRA FOSTER: 2003, 2016

This is the solo outing of vocalist/songwriter Kendra Foster, who had a 14-year tenure with George Clinton and later worked with D'Angelo on the *Black Messiah* album, earning her two Grammy Awards.

Myriadmorphonicbiocorpo-melodicrealityshapeshifter

"This World"

Vocals: Kendra Foster
Electric Piano: Whit
Sample, Bass Sample, Drum Programming: Thomas Zulu Simmons
Keyboards: Gary Wright
Additional Production: Gary Wright

"Mrs. Marley"

Vocals: Kendra Foster, Tracey Lewis
Keyboards: Jerome Rodgers
Drum Programming, Guitar: Tracey Lewis

"Road to Nowhere"

Vocals: Kendra Foster
Keyboards, Drum Programming: Gary Wright
Bass:

"We Can Do This"

Vocals: Kendra Foster
Keyboards: Amp Fiddler
Bass: Bubz Fiddler
Drums: Clip Payne

"In Our Minds"

Vocals: Kendra Foster
Keyboards: Paul Determan (Mars Cruiser)
Drum Programming: Paul Determan

"Save Your Love for Me" (redo)

Vocals: Kendra Foster
Keyboards: Jerome Rodgers
Guitar: Tracey Lewis

"Possession Free Philosophy"

Vocals: Kendra Foster
Bass: Dwayne Dungey
Drums: Law Hilson
Guitar: Michael Patterson

"Bounce to This"

Vocals: Kendra Foster, George Clinton, Clip Payne, Garry Shider, Sheila Horne, Belita Woods
Bass: Lige Curry
Drums: Rico Lewis
Guitar: Blackbyrd McKnight, Garry Shider, Eric McFadden, Cordell Mosson

"Happenstance"

Vocals: Kendra Foster
Bass, Drum Programming: Dwayne Dungey
Guitar: Dwayne Dungey, Michael Patterson

"Glass Cage"

Vocals: Kendra Foster
Keyboards: Gary Wright, Kendra Foster
Bass: Tracey Lewis, Kendra Foster
Drum Programming: Gary Wright

"Crush (A Heart Trip)"

Vocals: Kendra Foster
Keyboards: Jerome Rodgers
Guitar: Tracey Lewis
Sound Effects: Gary Wright

Kendra Foster (album)

"Respect"

All Vocals: Kendra Foster
All Instrumentation: Kelvin Wooten

"Promise to Stay Here"

All Vocals: Kendra Foster
All Instrumentation: Kelvin Wooten

"Understand It (Pon Da Phone)"

All Vocals: Kendra Foster
All Instrumentation: Kelvin Wooten

"Sweeta"

All Vocals: Kendra Foster
All Instrumentation: Kelvin Wooten

"A Warning for the Heart"

All Vocals: Kendra Foster
All Instrumentation: Kelvin Wooten

"Fantasize"

All Vocals: Kendra Foster
All Instrumentation: Kelvin Wooten

"Potency"

All Vocals: Kendra Foster
All Instrumentation: Kelvin Wooten

"Far Away"

All Vocals: Kendra Foster
All Instrumentation: Kelvin Wooten

"Just a Memory"

All Vocals: Kendra Foster
All Instrumentation: Kelvin Wooten

"Step into the Light"

All Vocals: Kendra Foster
All Instrumentation: Kelvin Wooten

"Take Our Time"

All Vocals: Kendra Foster
All Instrumentation: Kelvin Wooten

— ☆ —

ERIC MCFADDEN TRIO (SELECT TRACKS): 2003–2009

These are select songs from Eric McFadden's many trio albums.

"Delicate Thing"
Voice, Guitar, Mandolin: Eric McFadden
Double Bass, Voice: James Whiton
Drums: Jeff Cohen

"Catch a Liar"
Voice, Guitar, Mandolin: Eric McFadden
Double Bass, Voice: James Whiton
Drums: Jeff Cohen
Backup Vocals: Gary R. Wertz

"One Bad Reason"
Voice, Guitar, Mandolin: Eric McFadden
Double Bass, Voice: James Whiton
Drums: Jeff Cohen

"Been So High"
Voice, Guitar, Mandolin: Eric McFadden
Double Bass, Voice: James Whiton
Drums: Jeff Cohen

"If I Ever Die"
Voice, Guitar, Mandolin: Eric McFadden
Double Bass, Voice: James Whiton
Drums: Paulo Baldi

"Want Me Too"
Voice, Guitar, Mandolin: Eric McFadden
Double Bass, Voice: James Whiton
Drums: Jeff Cohen

"Ride"
Voice, Guitar, Mandolin: Eric McFadden
Double Bass, Voice: James Whiton
Drums: Jeff Cohen

"Another Day (In a World Betrayed)"
Voice, Guitar, Mandolin: Eric McFadden
Double Bass, Voice: James Whiton
Drums: Paulo Baldi
Backup Vocals: Kevin Meagher

"Are You Happy Now"
Voice, Guitar, Mandolin: Eric McFadden
Double Bass, Voice: James Whiton
Drums: Jeff Cohen

"True Disbeliever"
Voice, Guitar, Mandolin: Eric McFadden
Double Bass, Voice: James Whiton
Drums: Jeff Cohen
Backup Vocals: Gary R. Wertz

"Lie to Me"
Voice, Guitar, Mandolin: Eric McFadden
Double Bass, Voice: James Whiton
Drums: Jeff Cohen

"Bigger Piece of You"
Voice, Guitar, Mandolin: Eric McFadden
Double Bass, Voice: James Whiton
Drums: Jeff Cohen
Keyboards: Bernie Worrell

"Waiting for No One"
Voice, Guitar, Mandolin: Eric McFadden
Double Bass, Voice: James Whiton
Drums: Jeff Cohen

"Come to Me"
Voice, Guitar, Mandolin: Eric McFadden
Double Bass, Voice: James Whiton
Drums: Jeff Cohen

— ☆ —

KIM MANNING (SELECT TRACKS): 2003-2015

These are solo albums by Kim Manning, vocalist with George Clinton and P-Funk from 2000 to 2013.

Kim Manning

"Ripping Fingers"
Lead Vocals: Kim Manning
Vocals: George Clinton
Drums: Frankie Kash Waddy
Bass: Lige Curry
Keyboards: Garry Shider, Nate Oberman
Guitar: Nate Oberman

"Embrace"
Lead Vocals: Kim Manning

"Caught by You"
Lead Vocals: Kim Manning

"Catscratch"
Lead Vocals: Kim Manning

"Flutter"
Lead Vocals: Kim Manning

"A New Day Begins"
Lead Vocals: Kim Manning

"Ashamed"
Lead Vocals: Kim Manning

"Tomorrow"
Lead Vocals: Kim Manning

The Love and Light Activation

"TKO"
Vocals: Kim Manning, Brian Kehew
Keyboards: Kim Manning
Drums: Jason Chang
Bass: Brian Kehew
Guitar: Eric McFadden

"I Stand Alone"
Vocals: Kim Manning
Keyboards: Kim Manning, Jason Chang, Brian Kehew
Bass: Norwood Fisher
Guitar: Brian Kehew, Eric McFadden

"Ganja Street"
Vocals: Kim Manning, George Clinton, ONeal McClure, Bonnie, Brian Kehew
Keyboards: Jason Chang
Drums: Wally Ingram
Bass: Norwood Fisher
Guitar: Eric McFadden

"Love Gone Wrong"
Vocals: Kim Manning
Keyboards: Kim Manning, Brian Kehew
Drums: Joe Russo
Bass, Guitar: Brian Kehew
Cello: Gabe Royal

"I'm Never Gonna Tell It"
Vocals: Kim Manning, George Clinton, Pam Parker, Aradhana Silvermoon, Brian Kehew
Keyboards: Brian Kehew, Stanley Glen, Red Young ·
Drums: Mike Spay
Bass: Thad Jackson
Guitar: Melvin Smith

"Ripping Fingers"

Vocals: Kim Manning, George Clinton
Keyboards: Nate Oberman, Garry Shider
Drums: Frankie Kash Waddy
Bass: Lige Curry
Guitar: Nate Oberman
Sax: Greg Thomas

"2Maro"

Vocals: Kim Manning
Keyboards: Kim Manning, Jason Chang, Brian
  Kehew
Drums: Wally Ingram
Bass: Norwood Fisher
Sitar: Chris Citrus Sauthoff
Guitar: Eric McFadden

"Cat's Scratch"

Vocals: Kim Manning
Keyboards: Jason Chang, Arlan Schierbaum
Drums: Wally Ingram
Bass: Norwood Fisher
Guitar: Eric McFadden
Trombone: Bob Alvarado
Trumpet: Jonas

"Blister in the Sun"

Vocals: Kim Manning
Keyboards: Kim Manning, Marco Benevento
Drums: Joe Russo
Bass, Guitar, Echoplex: Brian Kehew
Banjo Solo: George Clinton

"Two Hookers"

Vocals: Kim Manning
Keyboards: Kim Manning, Marco Benevento,
  Brian Kehew
Drums: Joe Russo

Baked Goods

"Bunny Bear"

Vocals: Kim Manning, Randy Schultz
Keyboards: Eric Levy
Drums: Randy Schultz
Bass: Joseph Buniak
Guitar: Marcos de Fluri

"Morning Star"

Vocals: Kim Manning, Randy Schultz,
Keyboards: Eric Levy, Kim Manning
Drums: Randy Schultz
Bass: Joseph Koniak
Guitar: Marcos de Fluri

"Somewhere in a Tuppa' Ware"

Vocals: Kim Manning, Jerome Rodgers, Lantz
  Laswell, Andrea Wittgens, Meghan Owens,
  Ronnie Sanchez, Steve Manguiat, Mani
  Sanchez
Keyboards: Jerome Rodgers, Kim Manning,
  Lantz Laswell, Andrea Wittgens
Drums: Mani Sanchez
Bass: Ronnie Sanchez
Guitar: Jerome Rodgers, Lantz Laswell,
  Meghan Owens, Steve Manguiat

"Free Myself"

Vocals: Kim Manning

"Basketball"

Vocals: Kim Manning, Jerome Rodgers, Lantz
  Laswell, James Bixler, Randy Schultz
Keyboards: Jerome Rodgers
Drums: Randy Schultz
Bass: Joseph Koniak
Guitar: Jerome Rodgers, Lantz Laswell, Marcos
  de Fluri
Trumpet: Jim Dooley

"Do It"

Vocals: Kim Manning
Keyboards and Other Music: Eric Levy

Good People

"I Am Good People"

Vocals: Kim Manning, Lantz Laswell, Jerome Rodgers, Meaghan Owens, Andrea Wittgens, Mani Sanchez, Clip Payne, Tracey Lewis, Victor de Lorenzo, Ronnie Sanchez, Steve Hamilton
Keyboards: Jerome Rodgers, Ronnie Sanchez, Andrea Wittgens
Drums: Victor de Lorenzo
Bass: Ronnie Sanchez
Guitar: Lantz Laswell, Jerome Rodgers, Meghan Owens, Michael Hampton, Tracey Lewis
Percussion: Steve Hamilton

"Water Below"

Vocals: Kim Manning, Jerome Rodgers, Victor de Lorenzo, Andrea Wittgens, Liv Mueller, Ronnie Sanchez
Keyboards: Jerome Rodgers, Andrea Wittgens, Kim Manning
Drums: Victor deLorenzo
Bass: Ronnie Sanchez
Guitar: Jerome Rodgers

"Morning Star"

Vocals: Kim Manning, Randy Schultz
Keyboards: Eric Levy, Kim Manning
Drums: Randy Schultz
Bass: Joseph Koniak
Guitar: Marcos de Fluri

"Tuppaware"

Vocals: Kim Manning, Jerome Rodgers, Lantz Laswell, Andrea Wittgens, Meghan Owens, Ronnie Sanchez, Steve Manguiat, Mani Sanchez
Keyboards: Jerome Rodgers, Kim Manning, Lantz Laswell, Andrea Wittgens
Drums: Mani Sanchez
Bass: Ronnie Sanchez
Guitar: Jerome Rodgers, Lantz Laswell, Meghan Owens, Steve Manguiat

"Spin"

Vocals: Kim Manning, Lantz Laswell, Steven Manguiat
Keyboards: Kim Manning
Drums: Jamey Clark
Guitar: Lantz Laswell, Steven Manguiat

"Red Hot Mama"

Vocals: Kim Manning, Danny Bedrosian, Clip Payne, Lantz Laswell, Mani Sanchez, Ronnie Sanchez, Steve Hamilton, Meaghan Owens, Andrea Wittgens
Keyboards: Danny Bedrosian
Drums: Mani Sanchez
Bass: Ronnie Sanchez
Guitar: Lantz Laswell, Meaghan Owens

"Steel Bridge Song"

Vocals: Kim Manning Victor deLorenzo, Ronnie Sanchez
Keyboards: Kim Manning
Drums: Victor deLorenzo
Bass: Ronnie Sanchez

"Bunny Bear"

Vocals: Kim Manning, Randy Schultz
Keyboards: Eric Levy
Drums: Randy Schultz
Bass: Joseph Buniak
Guitar: Marcos de Fluri

"Damn"

Vocals: Kim Manning, Jerome Rodgers, Lantz Laswell, Corinna Wanish, Mani Sanchez Steve Manguiat, Ronnie Sanchez
Keyboards: Jerome Rodgers, Kim Manning
Drums: Wally Ingram, Mani Sanchez
Bass: Ronnie Sanchez
Guitar: Jerome Rodgers, Lantz Laswell, Steve Manguiat
Percussion: Wally Ingram

"Basketball"

Vocals: Kim Manning, Jerome Rodgers, Lantz Laswell, James Bixler, Randy Schultz
Keyboards: Jerome Rodgers
Drums: Randy Schultz
Bass: Joseph Koniak
Guitar: Jerome Rodgers, Lantz Laswell, Marcos de Fluri
Trumpet: Jim Dooley

"Path to My Soul"

Vocals: Kim Manning, Meghan Owens, Andrea Wittgens

"Mamma's Haunted House"

Vocals: Kim Manning, Mike Bleck, Jerome Rodgers, Lantz Laswell, Meaghan Owens, Steve Hamilton, Victor deLorenzo
Keyboards: Jerome Rodgers
Drums: Jamey Clark, Victor deLorenzo, Wally Ingram
Melodica: Kim Manning
Guitar: Lantz Laswell, Jerome Rodgers Meaghan Owens
Tuba: Craig McClellan
Percussion: Steve Hamilton, Wally Ingram

Space Queen

"Space Queen"

Vocals: Kim Manning
Keyboards: Billy Triplett
Trumpet: Bennie Cowan
Horns: Ray Gaskins
Percussion: Richie Shakin Nagan, Muruga Booker

"Overboard"

Vocals: Kim Manning
Keyboards: Billy Triplett
Guitar: Jerome Rodgers
Trumpet: Bennie Cowan
Horns: Ray Gaskins
Horns: Craig McLelland
Percussion: Richie Shakin Nagan, Muruga Booker

"Consume"

Vocals: Kim Manning
Keyboards: Billy Triplett, Kim Manning
Bass: Jeff Bunn
Trumpet: Bennie Cowan
Sax: Greg Thomas
Cello: Melanie Jane
Percussion: Richie Shakin Nagan, Muruga Booker

"Tempered"

Vocals: Kim Manning
Keyboards: Billy Triplett, Keith Olsen
Trumpet: Bennie Cowan
Sax: Greg Thomas
Percussion: Richie Shakin Nagan, Muruga Booker

"Baby Please"

Vocals: Kim Manning
Keyboards: Billy Triplett
Bass: Jeff Bunn
Percussion: Richie Shakin Nagan, Muruga Booker

"Peace and Love"

Vocals: Kim Manning, Melanie Jane, Garrett Shider, Marshall Shider, George Clinton, Landon Capelle, Early Thomas, Kory Murphy, Keith Olsen
Keyboards: Billy Triplett
Guitar: Jerome Rodgers
Trumpet: Bennie Cowan
Sax: Greg Thomas
Percussion: Richie Shakin Nagan, Muruga Booker

"Love You Today"

Vocals: Kim Manning
Keyboards: Billy Triplett, Kim Manning
Guitar: Jerome Rodgers
Percussion: Richie Shakin Nagan, Muruga Booker

"Paris"

Vocals: Kim Manning
Keyboards: Billy Triplett
Guitar: Jerome Rodgers
Percussion: Richie Shakin Nagan, Muruga Booker

"Lies"

Vocals: Kim Manning
Keyboards: Billy Triplett
Percussion: Richie Shakin Nagan, Muruga Booker

"Life Is Good"

Vocals: Kim Manning
Keyboards: Billy Triplett
Trumpet: Bennie Cowan
Horns: Ray Gaskins
Percussion: Richie Shakin Nagan, Muruga Booker

"Fireman"

Vocals: Kim Manning
Keyboards: Billy Triplett, Jerome Rodgers
Guitar: Delaney Davidson
Percussion: Richie Shakin Nagan, Muruga Booker

"Bridge of Stars"

Vocals: Kim Manning
Keyboards: Billy Triplett, Kim Manning
Percussion: Richie Shakin Nagan, Muruga Booker

— ☆ —

GENE "POO POO MAN" ANDERSON (SELECT TRACKS): 2004–2005, 2010–2011

These are some of the albums with the closest P-Funk connection to Gene "Poo Poo Man" Anderson, who was a vocalist with P-Funk from 2002 to 2012 but has a storied career in the entertainment industry long before that as well.

Keepin' It Real

"Serious Heavy Drama"

All Instruments and Vocals: Gene Anderson
Bass: Billy Bass Nelson
Guitar: Teenie Hodges

"Don't Fight the Feeling"

All Instruments: John "JT" Thomas
Percussion, All Vocals: Gene Anderson

"Keep It Real"

Keyboards: Mitch Dematoff
Bass: Gene Barrio
Guitar: Chris Mathis
All Vocals: Gene Anderson

"7-24"

Keyboards: Gene Anderson, JT Thomas
Guitar: Big Larry Guitar, Teenie Hodges
Lead Vocals: Gene Anderson
Backup Vocals: Gene Anderson, Paula J and
   Candice of the Mary Jane Girls

"Could I, Would I, Should I?"

All Instruments: Hi Rhythm Band of
   Memphis, Tennessee
Strings, Horns: Lester Shell
Lead Vocals: Gene Anderson
Backup Vocals: Willie Mitchell Singers

"Have You Seen Jesus?"

All Instruments: JT Thomas
Lead Vocals: Gene Anderson
Backup Vocals: International Hook Up Singers

Snot Logical

"Vibe Is Workin"

Vocals: Gene Anderson, George Clinton
Drum Programming, Synthesizers,
   Keyboards, Synth Bass: Gene Anderson
Keyboards: John Thomas
Guitar: Al Ventura, David Dawn

"Yahoo-It's Your Birthday"

Vocals: Gene Anderson, George Clinton
Drum Programming, Synthesizers,
   Keyboards, Synth Bass: Gene Anderson
Keyboards: John Thomas
Guitar: Al Ventura, David Dawn

"Keep 'Em Dancin"

Vocals: Gene Anderson, George Clinton
Drum Programming, Synthesizers,
   Keyboards, Synth Bass: Gene Anderson
Keyboards: John Thomas
Guitar: Al Ventura, David Dawn

"Sprung On"

Vocals: Gene Anderson, George Clinton
Drum Programming, Synthesizers,
   Keyboards, Synth Bass: Gene Anderson
Keyboards: John Thomas
Guitar: Al Ventura, David Dawn

"Poo Poo Strut"

Vocals: Gene Anderson, George Clinton,
   Jessica Cleaves
Drum Programming, Synthesizers,
   Keyboards, Synth Bass: Gene Anderson
Keyboards: John Thomas
Guitar: Al Ventura, David Dawn

"Snot Logical"

Vocals: Gene Anderson, George Clinton
Drum Programming, Synthesizers,
   Keyboards, Synth Bass: Gene Anderson
Keyboards: John Thomas
Guitar: Al Ventura, David Dawn

"Kee Kee Poo"

Vocals: Gene Anderson, George Clinton
Drum Programming, Synthesizers,
   Keyboards, Synth Bass: Gene Anderson
Keyboards: John Thomas
Guitar: Al Ventura, David Dawn

"Club Dub"

Vocals: Gene Anderson, George Clinton
Drum Programming, Synthesizers,
   Keyboards, Synth Bass: Gene Anderson
Keyboards: John Thomas
Guitar: Al Ventura, David Dawn

"Keep on Dancin"

Vocals: Gene Anderson, George Clinton
Drum Programming, Synthesizers,
   Keyboards, Synth Bass: Gene Anderson
Keyboards: John Thomas
Guitar: Al Ventura, David Dawn

"Electro Funk"

Vocals: Gene Anderson, George Clinton
Drum Programming, Synthesizers, Keyboards, Synth Bass: Gene Anderson
Keyboards: John Thomas
Guitar: Al Ventura, David Dawn

"Mama's Baby"

Vocals: Gene Anderson, George Clinton
Drum Programming, Synthesizers, Keyboards, Synth Bass: Gene Anderson
Keyboards: John Thomas
Guitar: Al Ventura, David Dawn

"Zulu Mix"

Vocals: Gene Anderson, George Clinton
Drum Programming, Synthesizers, Keyboards, Synth Bass: Gene Anderson
Keyboards: John Thomas
Guitar: Al Ventura, David Dawn

A Pimp Story

(credits could not be found for this album)

"A Pimp Story"
"Sucka Ducka Ducka Sucka Free"
"If U Really Want a Problem"
"What's Kracalin"
"Ass Kickin' Jones"
"Money"
"You're a Hotty"
"You're My Everything"
"Bounce Dat Booty"

The Blues Diary

(credits could not be found for this album)

"Steal Away"
"The Holiday Inn"
"Time Waits for No One"
"Outside Man"
"Crying in the Chapel"
"The Freakathon"
"Call Le Policeman"
"Take Me Back"
"My O' Lady"
"Passion"
"Lick It B4 U Stick It"

Jumpin' Gene Anderson

"Work It Out"

Lead Vocals: Gene Anderson
Guitar: Dewayne Blackbyrd McKnight
Organ: John JT Thomas
Bass, Synthesizer: Gene Anderson
Horns: Las Vegas Horns
Keyboards: Mike Jackson
Backup Vocals: Sister She She's, Gene Anderson
Guitar: Lonnie Motley

"It's Good"

Guitar, Bass: Lonnie Motley
Piano: Mike Jackson, John JT Thomas
Lead Vocals, Keyboards, Synth Bass, Backup Vocals: Gene Anderson
Backup Vocals: Sister She She's
Horns: Las Vegas Horns

"I Never Will"

Guitar, Bass: Lonnie Motley
Piano: Mike Jackson, John JT Thomas
Lead Vocals, Keyboards, Synth Bass, Backup Vocals: Gene Anderson
Backup Vocals: Sister She She's
Horns: Las Vegas Horns

"There Never Will Be"

Bass: Lonnie Motley
Piano: John JT Thomas
Lead Vocals, Synth Strings, Bass Synth: Gene Anderson
Backup Vocals: Sister She She's
Guitar: J. C. Curtis

"Take Me Back"

Organ: John JT Thomas
Bass, Guitar: Lonnie Motley
Lead Vocals, Backup Vocals: Gene Anderson

"Done Done It"

Guitar, Bass: Lonnie Motley
Piano: Mike Jackson, John JT Thomas
Lead Vocals, Keyboards, Synth Bass, Backup Vocals: Gene Anderson
Backup Vocals: Sister She She's, Lionel Pope
Horns: Las Vegas Horns

"Steppin"

Piano: JT Thomas
Bass: Bass Face
Guitar: J. C. Curtis
All Vocals: Gene Anderson
Horns: Las Vegas Horns

"Busted"

Guitar, Bass: Lonnie Motley
Organ: Money Stone
Lead Vocals, Synth Bass, Synth Guitar: Gene Anderson
Horns: Las Vegas Horns

"Dream Girl"

Synth Strings: Mike Jackson
Guitar, Bass: Lonnie Motley
Piano: Mike Jackson, John JT Thomas
Lead Vocals, Keyboards, Synth Bass, Backup Vocals: Gene Anderson

"She's Mine"

Guitar, Bass: Lonnie Motley
Organ: Mike Jackson, John JT Thomas
Piano: Mike Jackson
Lead Vocals, Keyboards, Synth Bass, Backup Vocals: Gene Anderson
Backup Vocals: Sister She She's, Lionel Pope
Horns: Las Vegas Horns

"Uptown Girl"

Guitar, Bass: Lonnie Motley
Strings, Horns: Mike Jackson
Lead Vocals, Keyboards, Synthesizer, Backup Vocals: Gene Anderson
Horns: Las Vegas Horns

"You Got to Loose It"

Guitar, Bass: Lonnie Motley
Organ, Strings: Mike Jackson
Lead Vocals, Synthesizer, Backup Vocals: Gene Anderson

"Roses & Candy Gram"

Guitar, Bass: Lonnie Motley
Keyboards: Mike Jackson
Lead Vocals, Synth Guitar, Synth Bass, Backup Vocals: Gene Anderson
Backup Vocals: Sister She She's
Horns: Las Vegas Horns

"I Betcha"

Guitar, Bass: Lonnie Motley
Synth Strings: Mike Jackson
Lead Vocals: Gene Anderson
Horns: Las Vegas Horns
Backup Vocals: Lionel Pope

"Slowly"

Guitar, Bass: Lonnie Motley
Piano: John JT Thomas
Lead Vocals, Strings, Synthesizer, Backup Vocals: Gene Anderson
Backup Vocals: Sister She She's
Horns: Las Vegas Horns

"The Time Has Come"

Piano, All Keyboards: JT Thomas
Lead Vocals, Strings: Gene Anderson
Bass: Bill Caruthers

— ☆ —

QUE AND MALAIKA (SELECT TRACKS): 2004

This funk band debuted in 2004 with a track featuring George Clinton and the P-Funk horns

Ernie Green Entertainment

P in the Funk

"P in the Funk" (multiple versions)

Vocals: Que and Malaika
Music: Que and Malaika band
Featuring: George Clinton (also features George Clinton and Gene Anderson)
Horns: Greg Thomas, Bennie Cowan, Scott Taylor

— ☆ —

AMP FIDDLER: 2004, 2008

These are solo albums by P-Funk keyboardist Amp Fiddler (tenure: 1986–1997 and 2016).

Waltz of a Ghetto Fly

"Intro"

Keyboards, Vocals: Amp Fiddler
Guitar: John Arnold

"I Believe in You"

Keyboards, Drum Machine: Amp Fiddler
Vocals: Amp Fiddler, Ihnas Sivad, Marlon Malone, Shante Fiddler

"Dreamin'"

Keyboards: Raphael Saadiq, Amp Fiddler
Vocals, Drum Machine: Amp Fiddler
Bass: Bubz Fiddler

"Superficial"

Keyboards: Amp Fiddler
Vocals: Amp Fiddler, Anetra Wright, Kimberly Chatman
Drum Machine: Only Child

"Possibilities"

Keyboards, Vocals: Amp Fiddler
Drum Machine, Bass: Bubz Fiddler

"Soul Divine"

Keyboards, Drum Machine: Amp Fiddler
Vocals: Amp Fiddler, Anetra Wright

"You Play Me"

Keyboards, Vocals: Amp Fiddler
Drum Machine: J Dilla

"Eye to Eye"

Keyboards: Amp Fiddler
Vocals: Amp Fiddler, Anetra Wright
Bass, Drum Machine: Bubz Fiddler

"Love & War"

Keyboards, Vocals: Amp Fiddler
Trumpet: Dorian Fiddler
Bongos: Lorenzo "Spoons" Brown
Percussion: Efe Best

"If You Can't Get Me Off Your Mind"

Keyboards: Amp Fiddler
Vocals: Amp Fiddler, Ihnas Sivad, Kimberly Chatman, Anetra Wright
Drums: Ron Wright

"Unconditional Eyes"

Keyboards: Amp Fiddler, Marlon Malone
Vocals: Amp Fiddler, Courtney Jackson
Drum Machine: Marlon Malone
Bass: Bubz Fiddler

"This Is How"

Keyboards: Amp Fiddler
Vocals: Amp Fiddler, Anetra Wright

"Waltz of a Ghetto Fly"

Keyboards: Amp Fiddler
Vocals: Amp Fiddler, George Clinton, Anetra Wright
Drum Machine: J Dilla
Bass: Bubz Fiddler
Guitar: John Arnold

Afro Strut

"Faith"

Keyboards: Amp Fiddler, Charles Jones
Lead Vocals: Amp Fiddler
Backup Vocals: Anetria Wright, Amp Fiddler

Programming, Percussion, Drums: Robert Ozuna
Bass: Raphael Saadiq
Guitar: Rob Bacon

"If I Don't"

Keyboards, Lead Vocals: Amp Fiddler
Backup Vocals: Anetria Wright, Garry Shider
Clarinet: Wendell Harrison
Drums: Ron Wright
Guitar: Chris Bruce

"Right Where You Are"

Keyboards, Lead Vocals: Amp Fiddler
Backup Vocals: Amp Fiddler, Mpho Skeef
Drums: Joshua McKenzie
Bass: Tony Bowry
Programming: David Justin Crawford
Strings: Pete Whitfield

"Find My Way"

Keyboards, Vocals, Programming: Amp Fiddler
Guitar: Chris Bruce
Handclaps: Denon Porter

"Empower"

Lead Vocals, Keyboards, Programming: Amp Fiddler
Backup Vocals: Anetria Wright, Amp Fiddler
Percussion: Bruce Cobb
Bass: Bubz Fiddler

"Afro Strut"

Keyboards, Lead Vocals: Amp Fiddler
Tenor Sax: Marko Novachcoff, Michael Carey
Programming: Andy Williams, Amp Fiddler
Guitar: Chas Jankel, Keziah Jones
Sax: Adeboy'e Adegbenro

"I Need You"

Keyboards: Amp Fiddler
Samples, Programming: Andreas Hernandez

"You Could Be Mine"

Keyboards, Programming: Amp Fiddler
Vocals: Amp Fiddler, Ebony Nico Washington
Drums: Collin Dupuis

"Heaven"

Keyboards: Amp Fiddler, James Shelton
Lead Vocals: Stephanie McKay, Amp Fiddler
Drums: Ron Wright
Bass: Paul Randolph
Guitar: Jean-Paul Maunick, Tony Remy
Programming: Amp Fiddler

"Afro Butt"

Keyboards, Programming, Vocals: Amp
    Fiddler
Drums: Tony Allen
Bass, Guitar: Ras Kente Knight

"Seven Mile"

Keyboards, Lead Vocals, Programming: Amp
    Fiddler
Backup Vocals: Amp Fiddler, Anetria Wright
Percussion: Larry Fratangelo
Guitar: Chris Bruce

"Funky Monday"

Keyboards, Lead Vocals, Programming: Amp
    Fiddler
Backup Vocals: Amp Fiddler, Anetria Wright
Drums: Ron Wright
Bass: Kenneth Martin
Guitar: Garry Shider, Rob Bacon

"Ridin'"

Keyboards, Programming, Vocals: Amp
    Fiddler
Programming: David Justin Crawford

"Hustle"

Keyboards, Programming, Vocals: Amp
    Fiddler
Backup Vocals: Charity Grace
Drums: Ron Wright
Percussion: Bruce Cobb
Bass: Kenneth Martin

"Dope"

Keyboards, Vocals: Amp Fiddler
Programming: Adrian Jefferson, Amp Fiddler
Backup Vocals: Lauren Ryder Williams
Percussion: Bruce Cobb
Guitar: Rob Bacon

Rare and Unreleased Album

"The Box"

Keyboards: Amp Fiddler
Drum Programming, Keyboards, Samples:
    Morgan Spacek
Guitar: Rob Bacon

"Pray Together"

Keyboards: Amp Fiddler
Vocals: Nico Redd
Drum Programming: J Dilla
Bass: Chris Bruce

"You Must Be the One"

Keyboards: Amp Fiddler
Drums: Ron Wright
Bass: Bubz Fiddler
Flute: Allan Barnes

"Funky Monday"

Keyboards: Amp Fiddler
Vocals: Anitria Wright
Drums: Ron Wright
Bass: Kenneth Martin
Guitar: Rob Bacon

"Hollywood"

Keyboards: Amp Fiddler
Backup Vocals: Inhos Sivad
Drum Programming: Chrstopher Mohammed

"Hope"

Keyboards: Amp Fiddler
Drum Programming, Samples: OnlyChild

— ☆ —

STOZO THE CLOWN: 2004, 2011

These are late-era solo albums from the visual artist Stozo the Clown, who did artwork on the Parlet and Horny Horns albums, among many others.

DigiDonz

"Ronald Wuzz a Rollin' Stone"

Guitar, Bass, Digital Horns, Keyboards and Shuggie's Original Digital Funk Box: Stozo

"Mashed Potatoes, Peas & Butta"

Digital Horns, Flutes: Stozo
Bass: Brian Vazquez

"She Freaked Me Out"

Vocals: Kenya D.O.G.
Bass: Brian Vazquez
Keyboards, Backup Vocals: Stozo

"Sto Zodiak"

All Music: Stozo

"Guitar in Da Closet"

All Music: Stozo

"Pass Tha Test"

All Music: Stozo and Paul G

"White"

Horns, Percussion, Organ: Stozo

"9/11 Emergency"

Electric Guitar Sounds, Organ: Stozo
Bass: Brian Vazquez

"Ape in Sto"

Digital Horns, Percussion, Bass, Guitar Sounds: Stozo

"Rush to Conclusion"

All Music: Stozo

"What's Yo' Favorite Color?"

Music, Voices: Stozo
Lead Rap: Kenya D.O.G.
Guitar: Metal John
Saxes: Mark!

DigiDonz 2

"Bridge and Tunnel Attack"

Guitar Sounds: Stozo
Bass: Brian Vazquez

"Players Can't Pretend"

All Music: Stozo
Vocals: Lex James

"Give Up the Funk Tonight"

Vocals: Strawberry, Stozo
Drums, Bass, Keyboards: Stozo

"Have Some Fun"

Vocals: Stozo, Pork E. Pine
Drums, Bass, Keyboards: Stozo

"Plainfield Party"

Vocals: Stozo, Pork E. Pine
Drums, Bass, Keyboards: Stozo

"Can You Help Me Wit Some N 2 Eat"

Vocals: Mallia Franklin, Strawberry, Stozo
Drums, Bass, Keyboards: Stozo

"Kook Googa Mooga"

Vocals: Stozo, Batz
Drums, Bass, Keyboards: Stozo
Production, Track: MasterFader

"Dance 2 the Fonk Thanks 2 the Fonk"

Vocals: Buddha Gonzalez, Know 7, Dyce
   Kymura, Stozo
Drums, Bass, Keyboards: Stozo
Guitar: Dyce Kymura

"#1 Love Hogg"

Vocals: Batz, Stozo
Drums, Bass, Keyboards: Stozo

"Upside-Down Brain"

Vocals, Drums, Bass, Keyboards: Stozo
Guitar: Eddie Hazel

"Are You Ready 4 This Thang
2 Go Down"

**Vocals, Drum Machine, Bass, Guitar,
   Keyboards:** Stozo

"Reality Show Hoze"

Vocals: Diggit, Ken Deo, Paul G, Stozo
Drums, Keyboards: Stozo
Bass: Sam Lord

"Stozo Gets Devius"

Vocals: Devius, Stozo
Guitar: Eric Veliotes
Drums, Bass, Keyboards: Stozo

"Make Out"

Vocals, Drums: Stozo
Bass: Sam Lord
Sound Effects: IDX1274

"We're Gonna Make It"

Vocals: Stozo, Strawberry, South Beach Dan
Drums, Guitar, Keyboards: Stozo
Bass: Sam Lord

"Urban Psychodelic Fonk Theme"

Vocals, Drums, Bass, Keyboards: Stozo
Guitar: Mike Tyler

"Shake Yo Butt"

Vocals: Tracey Lewis, Stozo
Guitar: Steve Pannel
Drums, Bass, Keyboards: Stozo

"Make It Alive"

Vocals: Stozo, Mallia Franklin, Gail Mojo
   Nuldrow, Strawberry
All Instruments: Stozo

— ☆ —

CALVIN SIMON: 2004, 2018

These late-era gospel albums are from Parliaments vocalist Calvin Simon. Simon's tenor is a hallmark of several P-Funk classics.

Share the News Past Present and Future

"Share the News"

Vocals: Calvin Simon
Backup Vocals: Calvin Simon, Ray Davis,
   Marty McCarrick, Lisa Brooks, Natasha
   Page, Leah Jones
Drums, Bass: Ben Powers Jr.
Keyboards: Kapp Ivory, William Mims, or
   Calvin Simon
Percussion: Lorenzo Spoon

"No Jesus, No Glory"

Vocals: Calvin Simon
Backup Vocals: Calvin Simon, Ray Davis, Marty McCarrick, Lisa Brooks, Natasha Page, Leah Jones
Drums, Bass: Ben Powers Jr.
Keyboards: Kapp Ivory, William Mims, or Calvin Simon
Percussion: Lorenzo Spoon

"Been Down This Road Before"

Backup Vocals: Calvin Simon, Ray Davis, Marty McCarrick, Lisa Brooks, Natasha Page, Leah Jones
Drums, Bass: Ben Powers Jr.
Keyboards: Kapp Ivory, William Mims, or Calvin Simon
Percussion: Lorenzo Spoon

"In My Father's House"

Vocals: Calvin Simon
Backup Vocals: Calvin Simon, Ray Davis, Marty McCarrick, Lisa Brooks, Natasha Page, Leah Jones
Drums, Bass: Ben Powers Jr.
Keyboards: Kapp Ivory, William Mims, or Calvin Simon
Percussion: Lorenzo Spoon

"Holy"

Vocals: Calvin Simon
Backup Vocals: Calvin Simon, Ray Davis, Marty McCarrick, Lisa Brooks, Natasha Page, Leah Jones
Drums, Bass: Ben Powers Jr.
Keyboards: Kapp Ivory, William Mims, or Calvin Simon
Percussion: Lorenzo Spoon

"He's Coming Back"

Vocals: Calvin Simon
Backup Vocals: Calvin Simon, Ray Davis, Marty McCarrick, Lisa Brooks, Natasha Page, Leah Jones
Drums, Bass: Ben Powers Jr.
Keyboards: Kapp Ivory, William Mims, or Calvin Simon
Percussion: Lorenzo Spoon

"Go for It"

Vocals: Calvin Simon
Backup Vocals: Calvin Simon, Ray Davis, Marty McCarrick, Lisa Brooks, Natasha Page, Leah Jones
Drums, Bass: Ben Powers Jr.
Keyboards: Kapp Ivory, William Mims, or Calvin Simon
Percussion: Lorenzo Spoon

"Squash It"

Vocals: Calvin Simon
Backup Vocals: Calvin Simon, Ray Davis, Marty McCarrick, Lisa Brooks, Natasha Page, Leah Jones
Drums, Bass: Ben Powers Jr.
Keyboards: Kapp Ivory, William Mims, or Calvin Simon
Percussion: Lorenzo Spoon

"Everytime I See Your Face"

Vocals: Calvin Simon
Backup Vocals: Calvin Simon, Ray Davis, Marty McCarrick, Lisa Brooks, Natasha Page, Leah Jones
Drums, Bass: Ben Powers Jr.
Keyboards: Kapp Ivory, William Mims, or Calvin Simon
Percussion: Lorenzo Spoon

I Believe

"Need Someone (It's Not Too Late)"

Vocals: Calvin Simon
Keyboards: Kapp Ivory, Eric Morgeson, Douglas Shepard, Calvin Simon
Bass, Drums: Ben Powers Jr., Denton Whited
Guitars: Mike O'Hara, Melvin Bell
Backup Vocals: Audra Alexander, Beth Griffith, Calvin Simon

"The Holy One"

Vocals: Calvin Simon
Keyboards: Kapp Ivory, Eric Morgeson, Douglas Shepard, Calvin Simon
Bass, Drums: Ben Powers Jr., Denton Whited
Guitars: Mike O'Hara, Melvin Bell
Backup Vocals: Audra Alexander, Beth Griffith, Calvin Simon

"Jesus Is a Friend of Mine"

Vocals: Calvin Simon
Keyboards: Kapp Ivory, Eric Morgeson, Douglas Shepard, Calvin Simon
Bass, Drums: Ben Powers Jr., Denton Whited
Guitars: Mike O'Hara, Melvin Bell
Backup Vocals: Audra Alexander, Beth Griffith, Calvin Simon

"Sorrow Street"

Vocals: Calvin Simon
Keyboards: Kapp Ivory, Eric Morgeson, Douglas Shepard, Calvin Simon
Bass, Drums: Ben Powers Jr., Denton Whited
Guitars: Mike O'Hara, Melvin Bell
Backup Vocals: Audra Alexander, Beth Griffith, Calvin Simon

"A Soldier's Story"

Vocals: Calvin Simon
Keyboards: Kapp Ivory, Eric Morgeson, Douglas Shepard, Calvin Simon
Bass, Drums: Ben Powers Jr., Denton Whited
Guitars: Mike O'Hara, Melvin Bell
Backup Vocals: Audra Alexander, Beth Griffith, Calvin Simon

"Power of Love"

Vocals: Calvin Simon
Keyboards: Kapp Ivory, Eric Morgeson, Douglas Shepard, Calvin Simon
Bass, Drums: Ben Powers Jr., Denton Whited
Guitars: Mike O'Hara, Melvin Bell
Backup Vocals: Audra Alexander, Beth Griffith, Calvin Simon

"In My Fathers House"

Vocals: Calvin Simon
Keyboards: Kapp Ivory, Eric Morgeson, Douglas Shepard, Calvin Simon
Bass, Drums: Ben Powers Jr., Denton Whited
Guitars: Mike O'Hara, Melvin Bell
Backup Vocals: Audra Alexander, Beth Griffith, Calvin Simon

"I Am a Soldier"

Vocals: Calvin Simon
Keyboards: Kapp Ivory, Eric Morgeson, Douglas Shepard, Calvin Simon
Bass, Drums: Ben Powers Jr., Denton Whited
Guitars: Mike O'Hara, Melvin Bell
Backup Vocals: Audra Alexander, Beth Griffith, Calvin Simon

— ☆ —

THE CLINTON ADMINISTRATION: 2004

This is a cover album of P-Funk music by several great musicians, notably JB's drummer Clyde Stubblefield and DJ Logic.

Magna Carta Records

One Nation Under a ReGroove

Personnel (All Tracks):
Turntables, Sound Effects: DJ Logic
Sax: Skerik
Keyboards: Robert Walter
Bass: Melvin Gibbs
Drums: Clyde Stubblefield
Guitar: Phil Upchurch
Percussion: Chuck Prada

— ☆ —

JOHN HICKEY: 2004

This is solo work by Woo Warriors guitar player John Hickey, who was also a onetime technician for Bernie Worrell.

Down with the Ship

"The Means of Production"

Vocals: Gregg Fitz, Anthony Lyles, John Hickey
Guitar, Bass, Keyboards, Drums: John Hickey

"What I Want to Do"

Vocals: Carol Thomas, John Hickey
Guitar, Bass, Keyboards, Drums: John Hickey

"Down with the Ship"

Vocals, Guitar, Bass: John Hickey
Keyboards: Gregg Fitz, John Hickey
Drums: Garry Sullivan

"Rub and Tug"

Vocals, Guitar, Bass: John Hickey
Keyboards: Bernie Worrell, John Hickey
Drums: Garry Sullivan

"See an N"

Vocals, Guitar, Bass, Keyboards: John Hickey
Drums: Garry Sullivan

"Lost"

Vocals: Alex Lyles, John Hickey
Guitar, Bass, Keyboards: John Hickey
Drums: Alex Posilkin

"Know Me Better"

Vocals, Guitar, Keyboards: John Hickey
Bass: T. M. Stevens
Drums: Garry Sullivan

"On the Water"

Vocals, Guitar, Bass, Keyboards, Drums: John Hickey

"Dead Beat"

Vocals: Gregg Fitz, John Hickey
Guitar, Keyboards: John Hickey
Bass: Freekbass
Drums: Garry Sullivan

"Brokedown"

Vocals: Carol Thomas, John Hickey
Guitar, Keyboards: John Hickey
Bass: Donna McPherson
Drums: Garry Sullivan

"Pot Top"

Vocals: Carol Thomas
Guitar, Bass, Keyboards, Drums: John Hickey

"Only Time"

Vocals, Guitar, Bass, Keyboards, Drums:
John Hickey

— ☆ —

JEROME RODGERS: 2004

This is a solo album by P-Funk keyboardist Jerome Rodgers (tenure 1979–1984, 2000–2002, 2004–2006, and 2008–2015).

Character Disorder

"Dance (NuJack '04)"

Vocals, Keyboards, Guitar: Jerome Rodgers
Scream: Linda Agresti
Drum Programming: Mr. Boskoff

"Ghost Lover"

Vocals, Keyboards, Synth Bass: Jerome Rodgers
Drum Programming: Mr. Boskoff
Guitar: Rudy Fletcher

"Overload"

Vocals: Jerome Rodgers, Steve Boyd, Geroge Clinton, George E. Clinton III, Kendra Foster
Drum Programming: George E. Clinton III
Guitar: Jerome Rodgers

"Hold On"

Vocals: Jerome Rodgers, Rob Manzoli
Keyboards: Jerome Rodgers
Drum Programming: Sue Brooks
Guitar: Rob Manzoli

"P.M.S. Monkeys"

Vocals, Keyboards, Guitar: Jerome Rodgers
Drum Programming: Mr. Boskoff

"Come On in This House"

Vocals: Jerome Rodgers, Mickey Rodgers
Keyboards: Jerome Rodgers
Drum Programming: Steve Boyd
Guitar: Jerome Rodgers, Eric McFadden

"All of My Friends Are Laid Back"

Vocals, Keyboards, Guitar: Jerome Rodgers
Drum Programming: Steve Boyd Jr.

"Be Ready"

Vocals, Keyboards: Jerome Rodgers
Drum Programming: Mr. Boskoff
Guitar: Rudy Fletcher

— ☆ —

DANNY BEDROSIAN/SECRET ARMY (SELECT TRACKS): 2005–

This is solo work by George Clinton and P-Funk keyboardist Danny Bedrosian (tenure 2003 to the present). It also features his work with Secret Army, a band made up of several P-Funk members over the years.

Som'n Fierce

"Incompetence"

Keyboards, Synth Bass, Vocals: Danny Bedrosian
Drum Programming: Jon Picken

"Speed Bump (Hey Sugarcane)"

Vocals: Danny Bedrosian
Track: Deryl Spielman

"New Clone on the Block"

Vocals: Danny Bedrosian, Garry Shider, Jerome Rodgers
Keyboards, Synth Bass, Guitar: Jerome Rodgers
Drum Programming: Danny Bedrosian

"Corn"

All Vocals and Instruments: Danny Bedrosian
Voice: Lisa Toney

"Soul Mate"

Vocals: Danny Bedrosian, Jerome Rodgers
Drums: Deryl Spielman
Bass: Lige Curry
Guitar: Jerome Rodgers

"Long Division"

Vocals, Keyboards, Synth Bass: Danny Bedrosian
Drums: Seth Ceders

"Cop This"

Keyboards, Synth Bass, Synthesizers: Danny Bedrosian
Drums: Clip Payne

"Bump N' Da Nite"

Vocals, Keyboards, Synth Bass, Synthesizers: Danny Bedrosian
Drum Programming: Danny Bedrosian, Marc Munoz
Bass: Ral Bryant
Guitar: Mike Maloney

"Miss Sarah Tonin's Waltz"

All Instruments: Danny Bedrosian

"My Country Life"

Vocals, Keyboards: Danny Bedrosian
Drums, Bass, Guitar: Deryl Spielman

"Retain Grace"

Vocals, Synth Bass, Keyboards, Synthesizers: Danny Bedrosian
Drums: Clip Payne

"Co-Writer"

All Vocals and Instruments: Danny Bedrosian

"Don't Be Sore at Me"

All Vocals, Synthesizers, Synth Bass, Keyboards: Danny Bedrosian
Drums: Deryl Spielman
Guitar: Marc Munoz

"Lisa's Lullaby"

All Instruments and Vocals: Danny Bedrosian

"Yestermorrow"

All Vocals and Keyboards: Danny Bedrosian
Bass: Troy Normandin
Shakers: Richie Nagan

Secret Army

"Busy Signals"

Vocals, Synth Bass, Synthesizers, Keyboards: Danny Bedrosian
Guitars: Blackbyrd McKnight, Marc Munoz

"The Battle for Sophene"

Vocals, Keyboards: Danny Bedrosian
Drums: Danny Bedrosian, Chris Monty
Percussion: Danny Bedrosian, Mike Blancato
Bass: Lige Curry, Sean Carmichael
Guitar: Blackbyrd McKnight, John Deming, Josh Baribeau
Trumpet: Adam Trull, Mike Ricci
Sax: Matt Soucy
Violin: Carolyn Kokko

"Chosen"

Vocals, Keyboards: Danny Bedrosian
Drums: Danny Bedrosian, Seth Ceders
Bass: Lige Curry
Guitar: Marc Munoz

"Cloudy Processional"

Keyboards, Synthesizers, Synth Bass: Danny
 Bedrosian
Guitars, Bass: Marc Munoz

"Sun Comes Up (Like You Do)"

Vocals, Keyboards, Synth Bass, Drums:
 Danny Bedrosian
Bass: Ral Bryant
Guitar: Blackbyrd McKnight

"Tune for the Toons"

Vocals: Danny Bedrosian, Josh Baribeau, Chris
 Monty, Josh Maldonado, Elise Bedrosian
Keyboards, Percussion: Danny Bedrosian
Drums: Chris Monty
Bass: Troy Normandin
Guitar: Blackbyrd McKnight, Marc Munoz,
 Josh Baribeau
Trumpet: Adam Trull
Trombone: Larry Ngyuen

"Bitter"

Vocals: George Clinton, Danny Bedrosian, Clip
 Payne
Keyboards, Drum Programming: Danny
 Bedrosian
Drums: Chris Monty
Bass, Guitar: Lige Curry

"Drive"

Vocals: Danny Bedrosian, Josh Baribeau
Keyboards, Synth Bass: Danny Bedrosian
Drum Programming: Danny Bedrosian, Seth
 Ceders
Drums: Seth Ceders
Bass: Jeff Bonhag
Guitar: Blackbyrd McKnight, John Deming
Mandolin: Josh Baribeau
Violin: Carolyn Kokko

"Survival"

All Instruments: Danny Bedrosian

"I Was There"

Vocals, Keyboards, Synthesizers: Danny
 Bedrosian
Bass, Guitar: Duane Day

"Euphrates Babies"

Vocals, Keyboards: Danny Bedrosian
Drums: Chris Monty
Percussion: Mike Blancato
Bass: Lige Curry, Sean Carmichael
Guitar: John Deming
Mandolin: Josh Baribeau
Violin: Carolyn Kokko

"Bird Flu"

All Vocals and Instruments: Danny Bedrosian

"Committee of Onions & Failure"

All Vocals and Instruments: Danny Bedrosian

"A Secret Army"

All Vocals and Instruments: Danny Bedrosian

"Stupifying Times"

Vocals, Keyboards, Drum Programming:
 Danny Bedrosian
Bass: Lige Curry

Parliament-Funkadelic keyboardist Danny Bedrosian. Mikiodo

"Shake, Stoopid!"

Vocals: Danny Bedrosian
Crowd Noises: Seth Ceders, Jeff Bonhag, Josh Baribeau, John Deming, Elise Bedrosian, Andrea Quigley, Ken Wilk, Adam Trull, Nick Winslow, Matt Soucy, Matt Lemieux, Marc Munoz
Keyboards: Danny Bedrosian
Drums: Seth Ceders
Bass: Jeff Bonhag
Guitar: Josh Baribeau, John Deming, Marc Munoz, Matt Lemieux
Trumpet: Adam Trull, Nick Winslow
Sax: Matt Soucy

"90 Years"

All Vocals and Instruments: Danny Bedrosian

"O Perfect Love"

All Vocals and Instruments: Danny Bedrosian

The Sleaziest of the Greaze

"Radio Flyer"

Vocals: Danny Bedrosian, Teresa Jimenez
Keyboards, Synthesizers: Danny Bedrosian
Drums: Jon Picken
Bass: Lige Curry
Guitar: Marc Munoz

"Don't Insult Me"

Vocals: Danny Bedrosian, Elise Bedrosian, Andrea Quigley, Steve Robidoux, Ken Wilk
Keyboards, Synthesizers: Danny Bedrosian
Drums: Seth Ceders
Bass: Jeff Bonhag
Guitar: Josh Baribeau, Marc Munoz, John Deming, Matt Lemieux
Trumpet: Adam Trull, Nick Winslow
Sax: Matt Soucy

"Gaseous Thunder"

Vocals, Keyboards: Danny Bedrosian
Drums: Jon Picken
Bass: Lige Curry

"Harvey CreamFrame"

Vocals, Keyboards: Danny Bedrosian
Drums: Jon Picken
Bass: Lige Curry
Guitar: Marc Munoz, Mike Maloney

"CookyMonztah"

Vocals, Keyboards, Synthesizers, Drum Programming: Danny Bedrosian
Bass: Lige Curry

"Butt Medicine"

Vocals, Keyboards, Synthesizers: Danny Bedrosian
Drums: Rico Lewis
Bass: Lige Curry
Guitar: Brett Grau

"Lightly Soaring"

Vocals, Keyboards: Danny Bedrosian
Drums: Jon Picken
Bass: Lige Curry
Guitar: Marc Munoz

"Har-Hippie-Hump-High"

Vocals, Keyboards, Drum Programming: Danny Bedrosian
Bass: Lige Curry
Guitar: Mike Maloney

"Sleaze Sonata"

All Vocals and Instruments: Danny Bedrosian

"Miss Goody Two Shoes"

Vocals: Danny Bedrosian, Lige Curry
Keyboards: Danny Bedrosian
Drums: Jon Picken
Bass: Lige Curry
Guitar: Marc Munoz

"Sloppy Rider"

Vocals, Hammond B-3, Keyboards: Danny Bedrosian
Crowd Noises: Danny Bedrosian, Marc Munoz, Seth Ceders
Drums: Seth Ceders
Bass: Lige Curry
Guitar: Marc Munoz
Banjo: Duane Day

"Sleaze Sonata Reprise"

Keyboards, Synthesizers: Danny Bedrosian
Drum Programming: Seth Ceders, Danny Bedrosian

"Games Are Fun"

All Vocals and Instruments: Danny Bedrosian

"Sway Songs"

Vocals, Bass, Keyboards: Danny Bedrosian
Guitars: Marc Munoz, Brett Grau

"Hometown Zero"

Vocals, Keyboards: Danny Bedrosian
Drums: Seth Ceders
Bass: Lige Curry
Guitar: Mike Maloney

"Miss Fortune"

Vocals: Danny Bedrosian, Teresa Jimenez
Keyboards, Bass: Danny Bedrosian
Drums: Jon Picken
Guitar: Marc Munoz

"Sweet Nothings"
Vocals, Keyboards: Danny Bedrosian
Drums: Jon Picken

"Living for a Time"
Vocals: Danny Bedrosian, Elise Bedrosian
Keyboards: Danny Bedrosian
Drums: Chris Monty
Bass: Troy Normandin
Guitar: Josh Baribeau, Marc Munoz

"Front Door"
Vocals, Keyboards: Danny Bedrosian
Drums: Jon Picken
Bass: Lige Curry

"Incompetence II"
Vocals, Keyboards: Danny Bedrosian
Drums: Rico Lewis
Man in the Box: Clip Payne
Bass: Lige Curry
Guitar: Blackbyrd McKnight

"The Brightest Star"
Vocals: Danny Bedrosian, Teresa Jimenez
Keyboards, Bass: Danny Bedrosian
Guitar: Marc Munoz

"Infiniti"
Vocals, Keyboards: Danny Bedrosian
Drums: Jon Picken
Bass: Lige Curry
Guitar: Mike Maloney

"All Alone"
Vocals: Danny Bedrosian
Keyboards: Danny Bedrosian, Clip Payne
Drums: Clip Payne
Bass: Lige Curry

"Wrong Dimension"
All Instruments: Danny Bedrosian

"Have"
Vocals, Keyboards, Synthesizers, Synth Bass:
Danny Bedrosian
Drum Programming: George E. Clinton III
Bass: Lige Curry
Guitar: Marc Munoz

"Mista Lil' Strangah"
Vocals, Keyboards, Synthesizers: Danny
Bedrosian
Drums: Jon Picken
Bass: Lige Curry
Guitar: Marc Munoz

Muzzle Moosick

"Cherry Pie"
Vocals, Grand Piano, Keyboards: Danny
Bedrosian
Drums: Jon Picken
Bass: Lige Curry

"Detka/Regenerator"
Vocals: Garry Shider, Danny Bedrosian,
Natasha Pavlova, MC Panda, Sasha Melnik
Keyboards, Synthesizers: Danny Bedrosian
Drums: Sasha Melnik
Bass: Roman Grinev
Guitar: Alexander Staroverov, Pavel
Martynenko
Violin: Felix Lahuti

"Rebel Keys"
Keyboards, Synthesizers: Danny Bedrosian
Bass and Drum Samples: Lige Curry
Guitar: Marc Munoz

"Incompetence III"
Vocals, Keyboards: Danny Bedrosian
Drums: Rico Lewis
Man in the Box: Clip Payne
Bass: Lige Curry
Guitar: Blackbyrd McKnight

"Dusty Basement"
Vocals, Keyboards: Danny Bedrosian
Drums: Jon Picken
Bass: Lige Curry

"Do Thangs"
Vocals: Danny Bedrosian
Keyboards: Danny Bedrosian, Rico Lewis
Drum Programming: Rico Lewis

"Morning Freak"
Vocals, Keyboards, Synthesizers: Danny Bedrosian
Drums: Seth Ceders
Bass, Synth Bass: Troy Normandin
Guitar: Marc Munoz

"FDNA"
Vocals: Danny Bedrosian, Teresa Jimenez, Jon Picken, Mike Maloney
Keyboards: Danny Bedrosian
Drums: Jon Picken
Bass: Lige Curry
Guitar: Marc Munoz

"Tanyel of Anzitene"
Keyboards, Synthesizers: Danny Bedrosian
Drums: Danny Bedrosian, Jon Picken
Bass: Lige Curry
Guitar: Marc Munoz

"Lightning"
Vocals: Danny Bedrosian, Elise Bedrosian, Mike Maloney, Teresa Jimenez
Keyboards, Synthesizers, Drums: Danny Bedrosian
Bass: Lige Curry

"Royal"
Vocals, Keyboards, Drums: Danny Bedrosian
Bass: Lige Curry
Guitar: Mike Maloney

"Invention"
Keyboards, Synthesizers: Danny Bedrosian
Drums: Jon Picken

"Bingey"
Vocals: Danny Bedrosian, Teresa Jimenez
Keyboards, Synthesizers, Synth Bass, Drum Programming: Danny Bedrosian
Guitar: Marc Munoz

"Double Turpentine"
Vocals, Keyboards: Danny Bedrosian
Bass: Lige Curry

"Sasounasar"
All Vocals and Instruments: Danny Bedrosian

MonsterPeace

"Five (Monsterpeace)"
Vocals, Keyboards: Danny Bedrosian
Drums: Sasha Melnik
Bass: Lige Curry

"Reaction Time"
All Vocals and Instruments: Danny Bedrosian

"Reaction Time Live (Sleezgreezkeez)"
Vocals: Kendra Foster
Keyboards, Synthesizer: Danny Bedrosian
Drums: Rico Lewis
Bass: Lige Curry
Guitar: Marc Munoz

"Locksmith (Getnel Ev Tesnel)"
Vocals, Keyboards, Synthesizers, Synth Bass: Danny Bedrosian
Drums: Sasha Melnik

"Torgom the Giant"
All Vocals and Instruments: Danny Bedrosian

"Set the T.V. On Fire"

Vocals: Danny Bedrosian, Teresa Jimenez
Keyboards: Danny Bedrosian
Drum Programming: Rico Lewis
Bass: Lige Curry

"Nasterio (Vocal Version)"

All Vocals and Instruments: Danny Bedrosian

"I Dissolve in You"

Vocals, Keyboards: Danny Bedrosian
Drums: Sasha Melnik
Bass: Roman Grinev
Guitar: Alexander Staroverov, Pavel
   Martynenko

"Solar Disk"

All Vocals and Instruments: Danny Bedrosian

"UMightBN22"

Vocals, Keyboards, Synthesizers: Danny
   Bedrosian
Drum Programming: Rico Lewis
Bass: Lige Curry

"Funk across the Water"

Vocals: Danny Bedrosian, Teresa Jimenez, Lige
   Curry, Elise Bedrosian
Keyboards: Danny Bedrosian
Drums: Sasha Melnik
Bass: Lige Curry

"Yerkar Bazhanum"

Vocals: Kendra Foster
Keyboards, Synthesizer: Danny Bedrosian
Drums: Rico Lewis
Bass: Lige Curry
Guitar: Marc Munoz, Mike Maloney

"The Piatek"

All Vocals and Instruments: Danny Bedrosian

"As I Slowly"

Vocals, Keyboards: Danny Bedrosian
Bass: Lige Curry
Guitar: Marc Munoz, Mike Maloney

"Makes Me Believe"

Vocals: Kendra Foster, Danny Bedrosian
Keyboards, Synthesizers: Danny Bedrosian
Drum Programming: Rico Lewis
Bass: Lige Curry

"Binge"

All Vocals and Instruments: Danny Bedrosian

"Nasterio"

All Instruments: Danny Bedrosian

Seri Mistik

"Hurrian Hymn"

All Vocals and Instruments: Danny Bedrosian

"Puru Kuzzi"

All Vocals and Instruments: Danny Bedrosian

"Eyes"

All Vocals and Instruments: Danny Bedrosian

"Anahid"

All Vocals and Instruments: Danny Bedrosian

"Now I Know"

All Vocals and Instruments: Danny Bedrosian

"You Know I Gotcha"

All Vocals and Instruments: Danny Bedrosian

"Here Is the Water (Habousi)"

All Vocals and Instruments: Danny Bedrosian

"Remote Control"
All Vocals and Instruments: Danny Bedrosian

"Vahagn"
All Vocals and Instruments: Danny Bedrosian

"My Daytime"
All Vocals and Instruments: Danny Bedrosian

"Tondurak"
All Vocals and Instruments: Danny Bedrosian

"Mer Tan Etev"
All Vocals and Instruments: Danny Bedrosian

"Organ Donor"
All Vocals and Instruments: Danny Bedrosian

"Hurrian Hymn (second verse)"
All Vocals and Instruments: Danny Bedrosian

Lost Froth

"Grass Chamber"
Vocals, Drums: Rico Lewis
Keyboards, Synthesizers: Danny Bedrosian
Bass: Lige Curry

"Torgom the Giant Live"
Keyboards: Danny Bedrosian, Elise Bedrosian
Drums: Rico Lewis
Bass: Lige Curry
Guitar: Mike Maloney

"Nasterio Live"
Vocals: Danny Bedrosian, Kendra Foster, Elise Bedrosian, Steve Robidoux
Keyboards: Danny Bedrosian
Drums: Rico Lewis
Bass: Lige Curry
Guitar: Marc Munoz

"Reaction Time Live"
Vocals: Danny Bedrosian, Lige Curry
Keyboards, Synthesizers: Danny Bedrosian
Drums: Rico Lewis
Bass: Lige Curry

"Two Three Nasty"
Keyboards, Synthesizers: Danny Bedrosian
Drums: Rico Lewis
Bass: Lige Curry

"Five Live"
Vocals: Kendra Foster
Keyboards, Synthesizer: Danny Bedrosian
Drums: Rico Lewis
Bass: Lige Curry
Guitar: Marc Munoz

"Too Far Removed"
Vocals, Keyboards: Danny Bedrosian
Drums: Rico Lewis
Bass: Lige Curry

"Set the T.V. On Fire Live"
Vocals, Keyboards: Danny Bedrosian
Drums: Rico Lewis
Bass: Lige Curry

"Rooster Riot!"
Vocals, Keyboards, Synthesizers: Danny Bedrosian
Drums: Rico Lewis
Bass: Lige Curry

"Dog-A-Doux Live"
Vocals: Danny Bedrosian, Steve Robidoux, Rico Lewis, Kendra Foster
Keyboards: Danny Bedrosian, Elise Bedrosian
Drums: Rico Lewis

"Teaction Rhyme"

Keyboards, Synthesizers, Drum Programming: Danny Bedrosian
Bass: Lige Curry

"Sway Songs Live"

Vocals, Keyboards, Synthesizers: Danny Bedrosian
Drums: Rico Lewis
Bass: Lige Curry

Single

"Sunny Side Up"

Vocals, Drums, Keyboards: Danny Bedrosian
Bass Guitars: Lige Curry
Arrangement: Appalachee Trio

Songs for a Better Tomorrow

"Better Tomorrow"

All Vocals and Instruments: Danny Bedrosian

"P-Ramids"

Vocals, Keyboards, Synth Bass: Danny Bedrosian
Drums: Deryl Spielman
Guitar: Marc Munoz

"Bardez"

Vocals, Keyboards, Synthesizers, Synth Bass: Danny Bedrosian
Track, Additional Keyboards: Steve Boyd Jr.

"The Bozfonk Hump"

Vocals, Grand Piano, Keyboards, Drums: Danny Bedrosian
Bass, Guitar: Lige Curry

"Urha"

All Vocals and Instruments: Danny Bedrosian

"Azadoom"

All Vocals and Instruments: Danny Bedrosian

"Snot from the Duck's Bill"

Vocals, Keyboards: Danny Bedrosian
Drums: Rico Lewis
Bass: Dwayne Dungey
Guitar: Chris Sauthoff

"Clam Dunk"

Vocals: Danny Bedrosian
Keyboards: Danny Bedrosian, Clip Payne
Drums: Clip Payne
Bass: Lige Curry

"Closer to the End"

All Vocals and Instruments: Danny Bedrosian

"Snack"

All Vocals and Instruments: Danny Bedrosian

"Meet Me There Sometime"

All Vocals and Instruments: Danny Bedrosian

"Walking in the Rain"

Vocals, Keyboards: Danny Bedrosian
Drums: Dave Kelsay
Upright Bass: Sean Gorman

"No One In the World"

Vocals, Keyboards: Danny Bedrosian
Drums: Jon Picken
Bass: Lige Curry
Guitar: Mike Maloney

"Deuces Pig-Sow"

All Vocals and Instruments: Danny Bedrosian

"Karmir Tsagik"

All Vocals and Instruments: Danny Bedrosian

Single

"Azadoom Kessab"

All Vocals and Instruments: Danny Bedrosian

Endangered

"Mudsy"

Vocals, Keyboards: Danny Bedrosian
Drums: Benjamin Cowan
Bass: Lige Curry

"Seasonal Fruit"

Vocals, Keyboards, Synth Bass: Danny Bedrosian
Drums: Benjamin Cowan

"I-Detective"

Vocals, Keyboards: Danny Bedrosian
Drums: Benjamin Cowan
Bass: Lige Curry

"Endangered"

Vocals, Keyboards: Danny Bedrosian
Drums: Benjamin Cowan
Bass: Lige Curry

"Robots Don't Die"

Vocals, Keyboards, Synthesizers: Danny Bedrosian
Drums: Benjamin Cowan
Bass: Lige Curry

"Infiniti III"

Vocals, Keyboards: Danny Bedrosian
Drums: Rico Lewis
Bass: Lige Curry
Guitar: Marc Munoz

"Ayo"

All Vocals and Instruments: Danny Bedrosian

The Clock

"Da-dadn-da-Da"

All Instruments and Vocals: Danny Bedrosian

"Super McGilp Bros."

Keyboards, Synth Bass, Synthesizers, Percussion: Danny Bedrosian
Drum Programming: Adam Trull
Guitar: John Deming

"Carry Me (And I'll Carry You)"

All Instruments and Vocals: Danny Bedrosian

"Lemme Lemme"

Synthesizers, Keyboards, Vocals: Danny Bedrosian
Drum Programming: Trazae Lewis-Clinton

"Instilled (In Me)"

All Instruments: Danny Bedrosian

"Siirt Ev Ughegh (Heart & Brain)"

Synthesizers, Keyboards, Vocals: Danny Bedrosian
Drums, Keyboards, Synth Bass: Steve Boyd Jr.

"Busy Blast"

All Instruments: Danny Bedrosian

"One Last Time"

All Instruments and Vocals: Danny Bedrosian

"The Clock"

Synth Bass, Synthesizers: Danny Bedrosian
Drums: Adam Trull

"The Merrimack River"

Piano: Danny Bedrosian

"Tub Thumpin'"
All Instruments: Danny Bedrosian

"Set the T.V. On Fire" (original version)
All Instruments and Vocals: Danny Bedrosian

"Dosey Dough"
Vocals, Synthesizers, Piano: Danny Bedrosian
Drums, Synth Bass, Samples, Keyboards:
  Dan Forberg

"Thumb Tappin'"
All Instruments: Danny Bedrosian

"That Mambo"
All Instruments and Vocals: Danny Bedrosian

"Ani"
Electric Piano: Danny Bedrosian

Solo Piano Improvariations (whole album)

All Songs
All Piano and Vocals: Danny Bedrosian

My Oldest Friend

"In Times of Trouble"
All Instruments: Danny Bedrosian
Vocals: Michael Clip Payne

"The Ire of a Vamp"
All Instruments: Danny Bedrosian

"Miser, the Minstrel, and the Monster"
All Instruments and Vocals: Danny Bedrosian

"Not Squeamish"
All Instruments: Danny Bedrosian

"Miss Maybe"
All Instruments and Vocals: Danny Bedrosian

"My Oldest Friend"
(instrumental version)
All Instruments: Danny Bedrosian

"Head over Heels"
All Instruments and Vocals: Danny Bedrosian

"Tamzara"
All Instruments: Danny Bedrosian

"Wildfire"
Drums, Piano, Vocals: Danny Bedrosian
Bass: Lige Curry
Guitars: Garrett Shider

"Do the Alligator Elevator"
All Instruments: Danny Bedrosian

"Eye Saw an Eye"
All Instruments and Vocals: Danny Bedrosian

"In and Around"
All Instruments: Danny Bedrosian

"My Oldest Friend"
All Instruments and Vocals: Danny Bedrosian

"Nor Piano"
Piano, Electric Piano: Danny Bedrosian

Eightfinity

"Outside the Lines"
Vocals, Keyboards: Danny Bedrosian
Bass: Lige Curry
Drums: Benjamin Cowan

"Baba & Baby"

Vocals: Ani Bedrosian, Danny Bedrosian, Clip Payne
Keyboards, Bass, Drums: Danny Bedrosian

"Nor Ashoog"

Vocals, Keyboards, Synthesizers, Synth Bass: Danny Bedrosian
Drums: Benjamin Cowan

"Rehearse This"

Vocals: Steve Boyd, George Clinton
Keyboards: Danny Bedrosian
Bass: Dwayne Dungey
Drums: Deryl Spielman

"Eightfinity"

Vocals, Keyboards: Danny Bedrosian
Bass: Lige Curry
Drums: Benjamin Cowan

"Funky Tools"

Vocals: Natasha Pavlova, Arif Akimov, Danny Bedrosian
Keyboards, Synthesizers: Danny Bedrosian
Bass: Slava Bubbles
Drums: Sasha Melnik

"Danzel"

Keyboards, Synthesizer, Synth Bass: Danny Bedrosian
Drums: Benjamin Cowan

"Orbeli-ani"

All Vocals and Instruments: Danny Bedrosian

"Baroque Hoy"

Vocals: Elise Bedrosian
All Instruments: Danny Bedrosian

"Sans Genes"

Vocals: Elise Bedrosian
All Instruments: Danny Bedrosian

Gifteh!

"Gifteh!"

Keyboards, Drums, Vocals: Danny Bedrosian
Guitars, Bass: Sean Gorman

"Tribe Called Home"

Keyboards, Drums: Danny Bedrosian
Guitars, Bass: Sean Gorman

"Hunter's Redux"

Keyboards, Drums: Danny Bedrosian
Guitars, Bass: Sean Gorman

"Thirty One (Skip Skap Skallywap)"

Keyboards, Drums, Vocals: Danny Bedrosian
Guitars, Bass: Sean Gorman

"This Doesn't Have A"

Piano, Strings: Danny Bedrosian
Guitars, Bass, Cello: Sean Gorman

"Lyric Piece"

Keyboards, Drums, Vocals: Danny Bedrosian
Guitars, Bass: Sean Gorman

"An Exploration of Acceleration"

Keyboards, Drums: Danny Bedrosian
Guitars, Bass: Sean Gorman

"Swak!"

Keyboards, Drums: Danny Bedrosian
Guitars, Bass: Sean Gorman

"Slender Strut"

Keyboards, Drums, Percussion: Danny
  Bedrosian
Guitars, Bass: Sean Gorman

"Water and Space"

Keyboards, Synthesizers, Percussion: Danny
  Bedrosian
Guitars, Bass: Sean Gorman

"Nanny Says Hi"

Keyboards, Synthesizers, Drums, Vocals:
  Danny Bedrosian
Guitars, Bass: Sean Gorman

"Marching 1 by 1"

Keyboards, Drums: Danny Bedrosian
Guitars, Bass: Sean Gorman
Vocals: Lige Curry

"Syntheseizeya"

Keyboards, Drums, Vocals: Danny Bedrosian
Guitars, Bass: Sean Gorman

"Little Prelude in Cello"

Piano, Strings, Harpsichord: Danny Bedrosian
Contrabass, Cello: Sean Gorman

Lusine and Arev

"Ballad"

All Instruments and Vocals: Danny Bedrosian

"Bar"

All Instruments: Danny Bedrosian

"Storm"

All Instruments and Vocals: Danny Bedrosian
Vocals: Patavian Lewis

"Gratitude"

All Instruments: Danny Bedrosian

"Melik"

All Instruments and Vocals: Danny Bedrosian

"Earth"

All Instruments: Danny Bedrosian

"Home"

All Instruments and Vocals: Danny Bedrosian

"Mher"

All Instruments: Danny Bedrosian

"Lusine"

All Instruments and Vocals: Danny Bedrosian

"Soldiers"

All Instruments: Danny Bedrosian

"Promenade II"

All Instruments and Vocals: Danny Bedrosian

"Bouree"

All Instruments: Danny Bedrosian

"Promenade I"

All Instruments and Vocals: Danny Bedrosian

"Oror"

All Instruments and Vocals: Danny Bedrosian
Voice: Ani Bedrosian

Exaltation

"Grail Disgusting Fire"

All Instruments and Vocals: Danny Bedrosian

"Sarabande"

All Instruments: Danny Bedrosian

"Exaltation"

All Instruments and Vocals: Danny Bedrosian

"On Time"

Keyboards, Synthesizers, Synth Bass, Sound Effects: Danny Bedrosian
Drums: Gabe Gonzalez

"Because I'm in Your Face"

All Instruments: Danny Bedrosian
Vocals: Thirteen

"Armo Funk"

All Instruments: Danny Bedrosian

"Dark N' Dirtay"

All Instruments: Danny Bedrosian
Vocals: Trazae Lewis, George Clinton

"Crinkly"

All Instruments: Danny Bedrosian

"I Still Stand"

Piano, Bass, Keyboards, Synthesizers, Melodica, Vocals: Danny Bedrosian
Drums: Gabe Gonzalez
Guitar: John Deming

"Olives"

Electric Piano, Bass, Guitar: Danny Bedrosian
Drums: Gabe Gonzalez

"Accustomed"

Drums, Vocals, Piano: Danny Bedrosian
Bass Guitars: Lige Curry

"St. Pete Swang"

Bass, Organ, Piano, Synthesizers: Danny Bedrosian
Drums: Rico Lewis

"My Country Life Live"

Vocals, Electric Piano, Synthesizer: Danny Bedrosian
Drums: Benjamin Benzel Cowan
Bass: Lige Curry
Guitar: Dewayne Blackbyrd McKnight

"Robinsonville Roost"

All Instruments: Danny Bedrosian

"Clam Dunk Live"

Clavinet, Vocals, Synth Bass: Danny Bedrosian
Bass Guitar: Lige Curry
Sax, Vocals: Greg Thomas
Guitar: Dewayne Blackbyrd McKnight
Drums: Benjamin Benzel Cowan

"Days Past"

Drums, Piano, Electric Piano: Danny Bedrosian
Bass Guitars: Lige Curry

"Moment for the Privy"

All Instruments and Vocals: Danny Bedrosian

"Clanny & Dip"

Piano, Electric Piano, Bass, Strings: Danny Bedrosian
Drums, Pads: Michael Clip Payne

Garmir Caramel

"My Songbook"
"Why You Wanna"
"Restless"

"Hydrogen Primate"

"Garmir Caramel"

"Moon & Sun"

"Jelly Bean"

All songs feature Danny Bedrosian on vocals and keyboards and the Brothers Nalbandyan on production.

— ☆ —

DANNY BEDROSIAN ASSORTED PRODUCTIONS (SELECT TRACKS)

The Soular System (select track): 2006

"RU Receiving Me?"

Vocal: Desmond D'Angelo
Drums: Jes Bradley
Bass: Ral Bryant
Guitars: Mike Maloney, Cordell Mosson
Keyboards, Moog: Danny Bedrosian
Trumpet: The Damn Diz
Trombone: Sir Rothenberg
Sax: Pedro Pizzarro

— ☆ —

Teresa Jimenez (select tracks): 2008

"Mostly Happy"

Keyboards, Piano, Backup Vocals: Danny Bedrosian
Drum Programming: Jon Picken
Bass Guitar: Lige Curry
Guitar: Mike Maloney
Electric Violins: Felix Lahuti
Lead/Backup Vocals: Teresa Jimenez

"Adelic"

Drum Programming, Bass Guitar, Keyboards, Synthesizers, Piano, Backup Vocals: Danny Bedrosian
Guitar: Marc Munoz, Mike Maloney
Lead/Backup Vocals: Garry Shider
Lead/Backup Vocals: Teresa Jimenez

"Risk Part 1"

Drums: Rico Lewis
Piano, Keyboards Backup Vocals: Danny Bedrosian
Bass Guitar: Lige Curry
Lead/Backup Vocsls: Teresa Jimenez

"Little Sherry"

Drum & Percussion Programming: Jon Picken
Synthesizers, Synth Bass, Grand Piano, Keyboards, Kalimba, Backup Vocals: Danny Bedrosian
Bass Guitars: Lige Curry
Flute: Chris Rothenberg

— ☆ —

Chris Cornwell (select track): 2009

"Drifting Beyond the Clouds"

All Vocals: Kendra Foster
Drums, Keyboards: Danny Bedrosian
Bass Guitar: Chris Cornwell

— ☆ —

Tugboat (select track): 2011

"Cousin Slick"

Guitar: John Deming
Keyboards: Danny Bedrosian
Bass Guitar: Lige Curry

— ☆ —

Nick Groff (select track): 2011

"Ghost Killer"

Drums, Keyboards, Vocals: Danny Bedrosian
Baby Bass: Sean Gorman
Guitars: Garrett Shider
Vocals: Nick Groff

— ☆ —

Moonchild (select track): 2014

"Truth Part 1"

Drum Programming, Keyboard: Michael Clip Payne
Bass Guitar: Lige Curry
Keyboards, Piano, Vocals: Danny Bedrosian
Lead/Backup Vocals: Elise Bedrosian

— ☆ —

CHILDREN OF PRODUCTION: 2005

This album is by the hip-hop group C.O.P., made up of P-Funk's younger members in the early 2000s. It features Shonda "Sativa" Clinton, Jason Drennen, Rico Lewis, Steve Boyd, Kendra Foster, Danny Bedrosian, Chris "Citrus" Sauthoff, and Steve "Young Funk" Boyd Jr.

"Intro"

Organ: Danny Bedrosian
Vocals: George Clinton
Guitar: Chris Sauthoff

"Children of Production"

Vocals: Shonda Clinton, Jason Drennen, Rico Lewis, Steve Boyd Jr., Steve Boyd, Kendra Foster
Track: Signature

"Gettin Paid"

Vocals: Shonda Clinton, Jason Drennen, Kendra Foster, Steve Boyd, Steve Boyd Jr.
Guitar: Ron Smith
Track: Steve Boyd

"New Day"

Vocals: Steve Boyd, Jason Drennen
Guitar: Blackbyrd McKnight
Beats: Steve Boyd Jr.
Bass: Billy Nelson
Keyboards: Joel Johnson
Organ: Danny Bedrosian
Violin: Lili Haydn

"Blazin'"

Vocals: Ric Lewis, Shonda Clinton, Kendra Foster, Belita Woods
Track: Rico Lewis

"Sittin' Lovely"

Vocals: Steve Boyd, R. Phillips, Steve Boyd Jr., Kendra Foster
Bass: Steve Boyd
Track: Steve Boyd Jr., Steve Boyd

"Get It Back"

Vocals: Shonda Clinton, Kendra Foster
Track: Signature

"On the Scene"

Vocals: Rico Lewis, Jason Drennen, Kendra Foster, Steve Boyd Jr., Shonda Clinton, Garry Shider
Track: Rico Lewis

"Hotel Room Skit"

Vocals: Shonda Clinton, Jason Drennen, Danny Bedrosian, Kendra Foster, Steve Boyd, Steve Boyd Jr., Chris Sauthoff

"Roll Up"

Vocals: Kendra Foster, Shonda Clinton, Jason Drennen, Steve Boyd Jr., Steve Boyd
Track: Signature

Street Code

Vocals: Steve Boyd, Steve Boyd Jr., Jason Drennen, Michael Shae
Track: Steve Boyd, Steve Boyd Jr.

"No Secret"

Vocals: Belita Woods, Shonda Clinton, Shock G, Kendra Foster, George Clinton
Track, Bass: Steve Boyd
Keyboards: Shock G

"Grudge"

Vocals: Jewell, Kendra Foster, Shonda Clinton
Track: Signature

"What's Poppin'"

Vocals: George Clinton, Jason Drennen, Tracey Lewis, Steve Boyd Jr., Kendra Foster
Tracks: George Clinton III
Guitar, Bass: Cordell Mosson

"Outro"

Vocals: George Clinton
Keyboards: Danny Bedrosian
Guitar: Chris Sauthoff

— ☆ —

BLACKALICIOUS (SELECT TRACK): 2005

The hip-hop group Blackalicious featured George Clinton, among others, on their 2005 album *The Craft*.

The Craft

"Lotus Flower"

Vocals: Blackalicious, George Clinton, Joy King, Kween

— ☆ —

STEFANIE KEYS (SELECT TRACKS): 2005

Keys is the sister of Original P keyboardist Peter Keys. These songs feature the P-Funk Horns, Clip Payne, and others.

"Walk with Me"

Drums: Terry Les Perance
Bass: Dan Ingenthron
Guitar: Stefanie Pisarczyk, Alan Hall, Dave Shul
Keyboards: Peter Keys
Vocals: Stefanie Pisarczyk
Horns: Bennie Cowan, Greg Thomas

"Try (Just a Little Bit Harder)"

Drums: Todd Glass
Bass: Mike Bertrand
Guitars: Bobby East
Keyboards: Peter Keys
Vocals: Stefanie Pisarczyk, Clip Payne, Chris Breest
Percussion: Todd Glass, Stefanie Pisarczyk
Horns: Bennie Cowan, Greg Thomas

— ☆ —

US PIPE AND THE BALLS JOHNSON DANCE MACHINE (SELECT TRACKS): 2005–2008

This is a Colorado band from P-Funk stage manager and COP guitarist Chris "Citrus" Sauthoff. These songs feature contributions from several P-Funkers.

"Get Up"

Lead Guitar, Vocals: Chris Sauthoff
Bass: Kurt Rosenbecker
Drums, Vocals: Chris Murphy
Sax: Mike Chiesa, Scott Osborne
Trumpet: Rick Gardner
Trombone: Jonathan Braddy
Vocals: Missy Gutreuter, Azma Holiday, Natalie Millican

"Hooker"

Lead Guitar, Vocals: Chris Sauthoff
Bass: Kurt Rosenbecker
Drums, Vocals: Chris Murphy
Sax: Mike Chiesa, Scott Osborne
Trumpet: Rick Gardner
Trombone: Jonathan Braddy
Vocals: Missy Gutreuter, Azma Holiday, Natalie Millican

"Smokescreen"

Lead Guitar, Vocals: Chris Sauthoff
Bass: Kurt Rosenbecker
Drums, Vocals: Chris Murphy
Sax: Mike Chiesa, Scott Osborne
Trumpet: Rick Gardner
Trombone: Jonathan Braddy
Vocals: Missy Gutreuter, Azma Holiday, Natalie Millican

"Enjoy Life"

Lead Guitar, Vocals: Chris Sauthoff
Bass: Kurt Rosenbecker
Drums, Vocals: Chris Murphy
Sax: Mike Chiesa, Scott Osborne
Trumpet: Rick Gardner
Trombone: Jonathan Braddy
Vocals: Missy Gutreuter, Azma Holiday, Natalie Millican

"Bad Mutha"

Lead Guitar, Vocals: Chris Sauthoff
Bass: Kurt Rosenbecker
Drums, Vocals: Chris Murphy
Sax: Mike Chiesa, Scott Osborne
Vocals: Missy Gutreuter, Azma Holiday, Natalie Millican

"Shookie"

Lead Guitar, Vocals: Chris Sauthoff
Bass: Kurt Rosenbecker
Drums, Vocals: Chris Murphy
Sax: Mike Chiesa, Scott Osborne
Trumpet: Rick Gardner
Trombone: Jonathan Braddy
Vocals: Missy Gutreuter, Azma Holiday, Natalie Millican

"Writa' Man"

Lead Guitar, Vocals: Chris Sauthoff
Bass: Kurt Rosenbecker
Drums, Vocals: Chris Murphy
Sax: Mike Chiesa, Scott Osborne
Trumpet: Rick Gardner
Trombone: Jonathan Braddy
Vocals: Missy Gutreuter, Azma Holiday, Natalie Millican

"Woo"

Lead Guitar, Vocals: Chris Sauthoff
Bass: Kurt Rosenbecker
Drums, Vocals: Chris Murphy
Sax: Mike Chiesa, Scott Osborne
Trumpet: Rick Gardner
Trombone: Jonathan Braddy
Vocals: Missy Gutreuter, Azma Holiday, Natalie Millican

"Super Stupid"

Lead Guitar, Vocals: Chris Sauthoff
Bass: Kurt Rosenbecker
Drums, Vocals: Chris Murphy
Sax: Mike Chiesa, Scott Osborne
Vocals: Missy Gutreuter, Azma Holiday, Natalie Millican

"Funky Family"

Lead Guitar, Vocals: Chris Sauthoff
Bass: Kurt Rosenbecker
Drums, Vocals: Chris Murphy
Sax: Mike Chiesa, Scott Osborne
Trumpet: Rick Gardner
Trombone: Jonathan Braddy
Vocals: Missy Gutreuter, Azma Holiday, Natalie Millican

MUDBONE: 2005

This is a solo album from longtime P-Funk vocalist/drummer/songwriter Gary "Mudbone" Cooper. Cooper has one of the largest discographies in this book, appearing on albums by scores of bands listed herein. He contributed heavily to Parliament, Funkadelic, Bootsy's Rubber Band, Parlet, the Brides of Funkenstein, and many others. His session work continued to be extremely vast through the 1980s and beyond, garnering hits with George Clinton, Sly Fox, and others.

Fresh Mud

"Make the Devil Mad"

Lead Vocals, Synth Bass: Gary Mudbone Cooper
Backup Vocals: Mudbone Cooper and Beverly Skeete
MC: Nadirah X
Guitar: Dave Stewart
Programmer: Ned Douglas
DJ: R.Kidz

"Karma"

Lead and Backup Vocals, Acoustic Drums, Bass: Gary Mudbone Cooper
MC: Nadirah X
Guitars: Dave Stewart
Programming: Ned Douglas
DJ: R.Kidz

"Evil"

Lead and Backup Vocals, Synth Bass: Gary Mudbone Cooper
MC: Nadirah X
Guitars: Dave Stewart
Programmer: Ned Douglas
DJ: R.Kidz

"Heaven"

Lead and Backup Vocals: Gary Mudbone
  Cooper
MC: Nadirah X
Guitar: Dave Stewart
Programming: Ned Douglas

"This Old World"

Lead Vocals: Gary Mudbone Cooper, Camar
Backup Vocals: Mudbone, Camar, Tami Chin,
  Nadirah X
MC: Nadirah X
Guitar: Dave Stewart
Programming: Ned Douglas
DJ: R.Kidz

"Boy from Baltimore"

Lead Vocals: Gary Mudbone Cooper
MC: Nadirah X
Programmer: Ned Douglas
DJ: R.Kidz

"Freedom's Coming"

Lead Vocals: Gary Mudbone Cooper, Dave
  Stewart
Backup Vocals: Mudbone, Beverly Skeete,
  Samantha Smith
MC: Nadirah X
Programmer: Ned Douglas
Harmonica Solo: Antonin Bastian
DJ: R.Kidz

"Come Together Now"

Lead Vocals: Gary Mudbone Cooper
Backup Vocals: London Community Choir
  Featuring Samantha Smith
MC: Nadirah X
Guitar: Dave Stewart
Programming: Ned Douglas
Keyboards: Jools Holland

"Where the Wind Lives"

Lead and Backup Vocals: Gary Mudbone
  Cooper
MC: Nadirah X
Guitar: Dave Stewart
Harmonica: Antonin Bastian
Programming: Ned Douglas

"Walking on Air"

Vocals: Gary Mudbone Cooper, Tami Chin
Backup Vocals: Gary Mudbone Cooper, Tami
  Chin, Camar
MC: Nadirah X
Guitar: Dave Stewart
Synth Bass: Gary Mudbone Cooper
Programming: Ned Douglas

"Rest of My Life"

Lead and Backup Vocals: Gary Mudbone
  Cooper
MC: Nadirah X
Guitar: Dave Stewart
Programming: Ned Douglas
DJ: R.Kidz

"Pray"

Lead Vocals: Gary Mudbone Cooper
Backup Vocals: Mudbone, Tami Chin, Camar
MC: Nadirah X
Guitar: Dave Stewart
Programming: Ned Douglas

"Stranded for Life"

Lead Vocals, Acoustic Drums: Gary Mudbone
  Cooper
MC: Nadirah X
Guitar: Dave Stewart
Harmonica: Antonin Bastian
Programming: Ned Douglas

"Life Can Be the Greatest Thing"

Lead and Backup Vocals: Gary Mudbone
Cooper
Guitar: Dave Stewart
Sax: Candy Dulfer
Programming: Ned Douglas
DJ: R.Kidz

"Home"

Lead and Backup Vocals: Gary Mudbone
Cooper
Guitar: Dave Stewart
Piano: Bob Dylan
Programming: Ned Douglas

DAZ DILLINGER: 2005

Prominent Dogg Pound member Daz goes
solo, featuring George Clinton and others,
replete with samples and interpolations of
G-Funk's favorite P-Funk song: "(Not Just)
Knee Deep."

Gangsta Advisory Recordingz

Tha Dogg Pound Gangsta LP

"Nothing Can Stop Us Now"

Vocals: Daz Dillinger, George Clinton
Producers: Daz Dillinger, Ivan Johnson

ELECTROFUNKADELICA: 2006

This is a solo outing from P-Funk engineer,
technician, and rhythm guitarist Shaunna
Hall (tenure 2005–2011).

E3+Funk nth=Music for the Body

"Good Thoughts, Bad Thoughts"

Vocals, Guitar, Synthesizer, Loops, Tracks:
Shaunna Hall
Drums: Kevin Carnes
Bass: Christa Hillhouse

"Second Wind"

Guitar, Loops, Tracks: Shaunna Hall
Vocals: RonKat Spearman
Moog Synthesizer: Jerome Rodgers
Rhythm Guitar: Marc Munoz

"Sweet Leaf 2006"

Heavy Guitar, Loops, Tracks, Backup Vocals:
Shaunna Hall
Vocals: Michael Clip Payne, Shonda "Sativa
Diva" Clinton
Intro Guitar: Citrus Sauthoff
Solo Guitar: Eric McFadden
Funky Guitar: Cordell Mosson
Bass: Lige Curry

"Naughty"

Guitar, Bass, Vocoder, Tracks, Loops:
Shaunna Hall
Vocals: Lisa Cash, Shonda "Sativa Diva"
Clinton, Kendra Foster

"Nebula Star"

Guitar, Tracks, Loops: Shaunna Hall
Vocals: Belita Woods, Kendra Foster, Michael
Clip Payne

"Stellar Evolution"

Guitar, Vocals, Synthesizers: Shaunna Hall
Drums: Kevin Carnes
Bass: Lige Curry

"Beauty Sleeps"

Guitar, Loops, Tracks: Shaunna Hall
Saw: Janis Tanaka
Drums: Kevin Carnes
Contrabass: Paula O'Rourke
Cello: Sam Bass
Violin: Benjamin Barnes

"Horsey"

Guitar, Bul Bul Tarang, Loops, Tracks: Shaunna Hall

"Loop Station"

Guitar, Loops, Tracks: Shaunna Hall

"Save Myself"

Guitar, Vocals, Bass, Keys, Loops: Shaunna Hall

"The Third Eye"

Guitar, Loops, Tracks: Shaunna Hall
Featuring: Paul Hill, Michael Clip Payne

"Details"

Guitar, Vocals, Synthesizer: Shaunna Hall

— ☆ —

BELITA WOODS (SELECT TRACKS): 2006

Important 1990s-era P-Funk vocalist Belita Woods contributed to many George Clinton and P-Funk All Stars releases. Originally from the disco group Brainstorm, Belita joined P-Funk in the studio in the late 1980s and was a featured vocalist with the All Stars by the early 1990s.

The Voice

"Over Emotional"

Vocals: Belita Woods
Music: Shawn

"Take a Great Escape"

Vocals: Belita Woods
Music: Shawn

"Love Games"

Vocals: Belita Woods
Music: Shawn

"Symphony"

Vocals: Belita Woods
Music: Trenita Womack

"If You Want Some Love"

Vocals: Misty Love, Belita Woods, Toney Diamond

"Rockin' the Club"

Vocals: Belita Woods
Music: Ed Harris, Shawn

"This Must Be Heaven"

Vocals: Lamont Johnson, Belita Woods, Chuck Overton
Music: Brainstorm

"Diamond Ring"

Vocals: Belita Woods
Rap: Many styles

"Take Me with You"

Vocals: Belita Woods
Music: Blackbyrd McKnight

"You Take Me There"

Vocals: Belita Woods
Music: Clip Payne

"Lovin' Is Really My Game"

Vocals: Belita Woods, Trenita Womack
Music: Brainstorm

— ☆ —

MR. KANE AKA KOKANE (SELECT TRACKS): 2006

G-Funk vocalist Kokane stylistically is very influenced by the P-Funk sound. Several P-Funkers show up on his albums.

Circle Music

Pain Killer'z

"Thugs Meet"

Vocals: Kokane, Mallia Franklin
Music: Josef Leimberg

"Hard as Steel"

Vocals: Kokane, George Clinton
Additional Music: Quaze, Kokane

— ☆ —

WU-TANG CLAN (SELECT TRACK): 2007

Hip-hop supergroup Wu-Tang Clan sampled "Man's Best Friend" and featured George Clinton on their *8 Diagrams* album.

Universal Motown

8 Diagrams

"Wolves"

Lead Vocals: U-God, Method Man, Masta Killa
Backup Vocals: George Clinton
Horns: Uncle John

— ☆ —

DIEM JONES: 2007, 2011

These albums are from P-Funk photographer Diem Jones, whose book *#1 Bimini Road* showed off some of his visually stunning photography of the band from the mid-1970s to the mid-1980s.

Equanimity

"Nomaad"

Poet: Elmaz Abinander, Suheir Hammad, Quincy Troupe, or Fladimir MS Woo
Featuring: Gabriel Powers

"Skatalogical Politricks"

Poet: Elmaz Abinander, Suheir Hammad, Quincy Troupe, or Fladimir MS Woo
Featuring: Tony Khalife

"Life & Love"

Poet: Elmaz Abinander, Suheir Hammad, Quincy Troupe, or Fladimir MS Woo
Featuring: Frank Colon, Eddie Gale, Luci Murphy

"Spirit Out the Dark"

Poet: Elmaz Abinander, Suheir Hammad, Quincy Troupe, or Fladimir MS Woo
Featuring: Eddie Gale, David Lee Spradley

"Rhythm of the Slave"

Poet: Elmaz Abinander, Suheir Hammad, Quincy Troupe, or Fladimir MS Woo
Featuring: Luci Murphy

"Mind Time"

Poet: Elmaz Abinander, Suheir Hammad, Quincy Troupe, or Fladimir MS Woo
Featuring: JD Parran, Gabriel Powers

"It's Anew"

Poet: Elmaz Abinander, Suheir Hammad, Quincy Troupe, or Fladimir MS Woo
Featuring: JD Parran

"Finale"

Poet: Elmaz Abinander, Suheir Hammad, Quincy Troupe, or Fladimir MS Woo
Featuring: Eddie Gale, Gabriel Powers

"Cachet"

Poet: Elmaz Abinander, Suheir Hammad, Quincy Troupe, or Fladimir MS Woo
Featuring: Kathryn Bostic

"Strut"

Poet: Elmaz Abinander, Suheir Hammad, Quincy Troupe, or Fladimir MS Woo
Featuring: Daniel Figueiredo

"HipHo"

Poet: Elmaz Abinander, Suheir Hammad, Quincy Troupe, or Fladimir MS Woo
Featuring: Gabriel Powers, Len Wood

"Sahara Nights"

Poet: Elmaz Abinander, Suheir Hammad, Quincy Troupe, or Fladimir MS Woo
Featuring: Gabriel Powers

"Dance"

Poet: Elmaz Abinander, Suheir Hammad, Quincy Troupe, or Fladimir MS Woo
Featuring: Eddie Gale, Gabriel Powers

"Triumph Of The Spirit"

Poet: Elmaz Abinander, Suheir Hammad, Quincy Troupe, or Fladimir MS Woo
Featuring: JD Parran, Chuck Cuyjet

A Spirit of Qui

"Dance Remix"

Lead Vocals: Diem Jones, Sheila "Amuka" Brody
Music Programming, Backup Vocals: D. Baloti Lawrence
Guitar: Len Wood
Trumpet: Eddie Gale

"Love Bug"

Lead Vocals: Diem Jones, George Clinton, Sheila "Amuka Brody, David Spradley
Keyboards: David Spradley
Music Programming: Amp Fiddler
Guitar: Len Wood
Tablas: Frank Colon
Backup Vocals: Debra Barsha, Susanna Peredo

"Everyday"

Backup Vocals, Arrangements: Garry Shider
Lead Vocals: Diem Jones and Susanna Peredo
Additional Vocals: Garry Shider
Music Programming: D. Baloti Lawrence
Keyboards, Vocoder: David Lee Spradley
Bass: Ray Burton
Guitar: Len Wood
Flute, Soprano Sax: JD Parran
Cello: Mechelle Djokic
Backup Vocals: Moy Eng, Susanna Peredo, Linda Shider, Garry Shider, David Spradley

"Do Oui Do"

Lead Vocals: Diem Jones, Zuri "Universe Soul" Moore
Music Programming, Backup Vocals, Arrangement: David Spradley
Guitar: Len Wood
Congas: Frank Colon
Bass Sax: JD Parran

"Spirit Speak"

Lead Vocals: Diem Jones
Guitar: Tony Kalife
Keyboards: David Spradley
Cello: Michelle Djokic

"Useless Education"

Lead Vocals: Diem Jones, Slaira Shawn Harris,
 Brandon 1 OAK McFarland, Ashley Bizell,
 Liezel Rivera
Drums: Bob Walter
Bass: Jason Fifield
Piano, Flutes, Percussion: Byard Lancaster
Guitars, Synthesizers: G-Koop

"Spirit of Doo"

Lead Vocals: Diem Jones, Susanna Peredo
Music Programming, Timbales: Frank Colon
Guitar: Len Wood

"Life"

Lead Vocals: Diem Jones, Suheir Hammad
Keyboards: D. Baloti Lawrence
Guitar: Len Wood
All Winds: JD Parran
Percussion: Diem Jones

"Haiti Rebuild: Amen to You"

Lead Vocals: Diem Jones, Moy Eng
Guitar: Len Wood

"Collibri de Amor"
(Love Bug Spanish Version)

Music Programming: Amp Fiddler
Keyboards: David Spradley
Guitar: Len Wood
Tablas: Frank Colon
Backup Vocals: Debra Barsha, Susanna Peredo

— ☆ —

SCIENCE FAXTION: 2008

This funk rock outing is from the Bootsy camp
and also features Gary Mudbone Cooper.

Living on Another Frequency

"Sci Fax Theme"

Samples, Programming, Drums: Bootsy
 Collins
Turntables, Programming: Tobe Tobotius
 Donohue

"Lookin' for Eden"

Bass, Guitars, Vocals: Bootsy Collins
Vocals, Guitars: Greg Hampton
Guitars: Buckethead
Drums, Programming: Bryan Brain Mantia

"At Any Cost"

Bass, Vocals: Bootsy Collins
Vocals, Guitars, Bass: Greg Hampton
Backup Vocals: Gary Mudbone Cooper, Greg
 Hampton
Guitars: Buckethead
Drums, Programming: Bryan Brain Mantia

"Chaos in Motion"

Bass: Bootsy Collins
Vocals, Guitars, Bass: Greg Hampton
Guitars: Buckethead
Drums, Programming: Bryan Brain Mantia
Backup Vocals: Greg Hampton, Kyle Jason

"Famous"

**Bass, Drums, Vocals, Guitars, Keyboards,
 Drums, Synthesizers, Programming:**
 Bootsy Collins
Guitars: Buckethead, Catfish Collins
Keyboards: Bernie Worrell
Turntables, Programming: Tobe Tobotius
 Donohue
Vocals: Candice, Gary Mudbone Cooper

"L.O.A.F. (Living On Another Frequency)"

Bass, Guitars, Vocals: Bootsy Collins
Vocals, Guitars: Greg Hampton
Guitars: Buckethead
Bass, Drum Programming: Dan Monti
Drums, Programming: Bryan Brain Mantia

"Gone Tomorrow"

Vocals, Guitars, Bass, Keyboards: Greg Hampton
Bass, Drum Programming: Dan Monti
Drums, Programming: Bryan Brain Mantia

"Life-IS IN-Deliver"

Vocals, Bass: Bootsy Collins
Vocals, Guitars, Drums: Greg Hampton
Backup Vocals: Candice
Guitar: Keith Cheatham

"Take You Down"

Vocals, Guitars, Bass, Keyboards: Greg Hampton
Drums: Bryan Brain Mantia

"What It Is"

Vocals: Chuck D
Bass: Brian Hardgroove
Bass, Guitars, Vocals: Bootsy Collins
Guitar: Larry Mitchell
Backup Vocals: Kyle Jason, Brad Hardgroove, Candice
Drums, Programming: Bryan Brain Mantia
Turntables: DJ DQ
Turntables, Programming: Tobe Tobotius Donohue

"Fatally Flawed Flesh"

Bass: Bootsy Collins
Vocals, Guitars: Greg Hampton
Guitars: Buckethead
Drums, Programming: Bryan Brain Mantia

"I See Rockets"

Bass, Keyboards, Vocals, Programming: Bootsy Collins
Bass, Programming: Dan Monti
Guitars: Buckethead
Turntables, Programming: Tobe
Drums, Programming: Bryan Brain Mantia

"ZIONPLANET10"

Bass, Guitars, Keyboards, Programming: Bootsy Collins
Vocals: Zion Planet 10
Keyboards, Backup Vocals: Steve Ferlazzo
Turntables, Programming: Tobe Tobotius Donohue

— ☆ —

LIGE CURRY AND THE NAKED FUNK: 2008, 2013

This is the San Diego–based funk jazz band of Lige Curry.

Naked Funk

"Spread the Funk"

Bass, Guitar: Lige Curry
Drums, Keyboards: Ed Fletcher
Vocoders, Synthesizers: Sean Hart
Trombone: Andy Geib
Flute: Harold Todd
Guitar Solo: Dave Carrano

"El Conquistador"

Bass: Lige Curry
Drums: Ed Fletcher
Horn Patches: Lynn Willard
Saxes: Harold Todd
Guitar: Joe Serrano
Congas: Tim Pacheco

"Hot Bald Peanuts"

Basses: Lige Curry
Drums, Keyboards: Ed Fletcher
Dub Treatments: Sean Hart
Flute: Harold Todd

"Filter 3000"

Bass: Lige Curry
Drums, Keyboards: Ed Fletcher
Synthesizers: Sean Hart
Trombones: Andy Geib
Keyboard Solo: Eric Gabriel

"Pour Gas on the Fire"

Bass, Guitar: Lige Curry
Drums, Keyboards: Ed Fletcher
Synthesizers, Guitar: Sean Hart
Saxthesizer: Harold Todd
Spoken Word: Al Howard

"Foolin' the Mind's Ear"

Bass: Lige Curry
Drums, Keyboard, Steel Drums: Ed Fletcher
Synthesizers: Sean Hart
Hammond Organ: Lynn Willard
Saxthesizer: Harold Todd
Guitar Solo: Jimi Lewis

"The Meat and Potatoes"

Bass: Lige Curry
Drums, Wurlitzer: Ed Fletcher

"Kick It Up a Notch"

Bass: Lige Curry
Drums, Percussion: Ed Fletcher
Wurlitzer: Lynn Willard
Guitar: Dave Carrano
Saxthesizer: Harold Todd

"Well Swung"

Bass: Lige Curry
Drums: Ed Fletcher

Synthesizer: Sean Hart
Wurlitzer: Lynn Willard
Flute, Saxes: Harold Todd
Guitars: Jose Serrano

"Wanka War"

Bass, Guitar: Lige Curry
Drums, Keyboards, Harmonium: Ed Fletcher
Synthesizers, Fauxbots, Guitar: Sean Hart
Keyboard Solo: Eric Gabriel
Steel Pan Solo: Tom Gates

Lige Curry Presents the Naked Funk

"Naked Trip"

All Instruments: Sean Hart

"Mr. Cho-Kin"

Bass: Lige Curry
Drums: Ed Fletcher
Guitar: Garry Shider, Dave Corona
Keyboards: Eric Gabriel, Danny Bedrosian
Vocals: Lige Curry, Danny Bedrosian, Garry Shider, Ed Fletcher, Eric Gabriel
Tenor Sax: Robert Helm

"Funky and True"

Bass: Lige Curry
Drums: Ed Fletcher
Guitar: Lige Curry, Jose Sorrano
Keyboards: Eric Gabriel
Trumpet: Christofer Kaye Welter, C.Money
Vocals: Lige Curry, Ed Fletcher

"Sexy Sexy Sexy"

Bass: Lige Curry
Drums: Ed Fletcher
Keyboards: Eric Gabriel, Sean Hart
Effects: Sean Hart
Vocals: Lige Curry, Ed Fletcher

"I Got a Secret"

Bass, Guitar, Vocals: Lige Curry
Drums: Rico Lewis
Keyboards: Danny Bedrosian

"Sensational"

Bass, Vocals: Lige Curry
Drums: Ed Fletcher
Other Instruments and Effects: Sean Hart
Keyboards: Eric Gabriel

"Lige Naked Bass Solo"

Bass: Lige Curry
Percussion: Ed Fletcher
Other Instruments: Sean Hart

"Shake It"

Bass, Guitar: Lige Curry
Drums: Ed Fletcher
Keyboards: Eric Gabriel
Vocals: Lige Curry, Ed Fletcher, Eric Gabriel

"Alien Head Babies (Talkin Shit)"

Voice Effects: Sean Hart

"Capital Defence"

Bass, Vocals: Lige Curry
Drums: Ed Fletcher
Keyboards: Eric Gabriel
Effects: Sean Hart

"One Joint (Island Funk)"

Bass, Vocals: Lige Curry
Drums, Percussion: Ed Fletcher
Guitar: Dave Corona
Keyboards: Eric Gabriel, Ed Fletcher

"Because I Use to Love You"

Bass, Vocals: Lige Curry
Drums: Ed Fletcher
Keyboards: Danny Bedrosian

"Super Stupid 57"

Bass, Guitar, Vocals: Lige Curry
Drums: Ed Fletcher
Keyboards, Effects: Sean Hart

— ☆ —

THE PLAINFIELD ADMIRATIONS INTO BAGS PRESENTED BY RICHARD BOYCE: 2008

This compilation of music is from the group Bags, from Plainfield, New Jersey, featuring several P-Funk–related contributors.

"Stone to the Bone"

Lead Vocals: Gregg Fitz
Backup Vocals: Richard Boyce, Gregg Fitz, Jeff Dudley, Gary Knight
Bass: Richard Boyce
Keyboards: Gregg Fitz, Gary Knight
Guitar: Jeff Dudley
Drums: Damon Mendes
Percussion: William Winky Sykes
Sax: Darryl Dixon
Trumpet: Wally Zelinsky
Trombone: Clarence Clay Lawrey

"I See a Cloud"

Lead Vocals, Guitar: James "Frankie" Boyce
Backup Vocals: Richard Boyce, James "Frankie" Boyce, John "JoJo" Boyce, Rochelle Eure
Bass: Richard Boyce
Drums: Michael Lewis
Piano: Jerry Ragovoy
Keyboard Strings: Kevin Leonard

"Funky Rock"

Lead and Backup Vocals: Richard Boyce
Guitar: Garry Shider
Keyboards: Kareem Hinds
Sax: Ronald Adams
Drums: Excel Lewis

"Soul Soldier"

Lead Vocals: Richard Boyce
Backup Vocals: Richard Boyce, Melinda
    Morrow
Keyboards: Kevin Leonard
Drums: David "A1" Kirkland
Lead Guitar: Jimmy Paschal

"It's Heavy"

Lead Vocals: Glenn Goins
Backup Vocals: Richard Boyce, Glenn Goins,
    Gary Brunson, Richard "Shaidi" Banks,
    Larry Dicks
Drums: Gary Brunson
Bass: Richard Boyce
Guitar: Glenn Goins
Keyboards: Richard Shaidi Banks
Tambourine: Ronald Robinson

"Get on Time"

Vocals: Gregg Fitz, Richard Boyce, Jeff Dudley,
    Gary Brunson
Bass: Richard Boyce
Keyboards: Gregg Fitz
Guitar: Jeff Dudley
Drums: Gary Brunson
Sax: Darryl Dixon
Trombone: Clarence "Clay" Lawrey
Trumpet: Wally Zeminsky

"Hey Girl"

Lead Vocals, Guitar: Glenn Goins
Backup Vocals: Richard Boyce, Glenn Goins,
    Richard "Shaidi" Banks, Larry Dicks
Bass: Richard Boyce

Drums: Gary Brunson
Keyboards: Leon Pendarvis, Richard "Shaidi"
    Banks

"Feel Like Gettin Down"

Bass: Richard Boyce
Guitar: Glenn Goins, Deno "Moe Dene" Wynn
Keyboards, Organ: Gregg Fitz
Keyboards, Clavinet: Richard "Shaidi" Banks
Drums: Gary Brunson
Sax: Darryl Dixon
Trombone: Clarence Lawrey
Trumpet: Wally Zelinsky

"Until Then (love theme from _Grazia_, the movie)"

Lead and Backup Vocals: Richard Boyce
Bass, Guitar, Music Arrangement: James
    Holmes

"Beautiful Birds"

Lead Vocals, Guitar: Glenn Goins
Backup Vocals: Richard Boyce, Glenn Goins,
    Gary Brunson, Richard "Shaidi" Banks, Lou
    Courtney, Peanut Shider, Carl Hall, Larry
    Dicks, Ms. Floyd, Diane Green
Bass: Richard Boyce
Tambourine: Ronald Robinson
Drums: Gary Brunson
Keyboards: Richard "Shaidi" Banks

"Funky Rock"

Bass: Richard Boyce
Guitar: Garry Shider, Richard Boyce
Keyboards: Kareem Hinds
Sax: Ronald Adams
Drums: Excel Lewis

— ☆ —

N.A.S.A. (SELECT TRACK): 2009

This is funky hip-hop from the group N.A.S.A. featuring George Clinton.

Anti -

The Spirit of Apollo

"There's a Party"

Featuring: George Clinton, Chali2NA
Music: N.A.S.A.

DEWAYNE "BLACKBYRD" MCKNIGHT: 2009

This is the long-awaited solo debut from long-time P-Funk guitarist Dewayne "Blackbyrd" McKnight (tenure: 1978–1986, 1989–2007, 2016–2020), who, in addition to being at various times a member of Herbie Hancock's Headhunters, the Red Hot Chili Peppers, and the Miles Davis Band, was also a band director for P-Funk in the 1990s and 2000s.

'Bout Funkin' Time

"Funkarockaholic"

All Instruments and Vocals: Blackbyrd McKnight

"Joke of the Butt"

All Instruments and Vocals: Blackbyrd McKnight

"Funk the Phone Bill"

All Instruments and Vocals: Blackbyrd McKnight

"#6"

All Instruments and Vocals: Blackbyrd McKnight

"Funkin Where You Belong"

All Instruments: Blackbyrd McKnight
All Vocals: Danny Bedrosian

"#3"

Drums, Bass, Guitars: Blackbyrd McKnight
Organ, Piano: Danny Bedrosian

"Smoosh"

All Instruments and Vocals: Blackbyrd McKnight

"On Down the Line"

All Instruments and Vocals: Blackbyrd McKnight

"The Mad Hit"

All Instruments and Vocals: Blackbyrd McKnight

"Graffiti"

All Instruments and Vocals: Blackbyrd McKnight

PAUL HILL: 2009

This is some of the solo work from Detroit-born P-Funk vocalist Paul Hill, who was a contributor and member of the P-Funk All Stars from the late 1980s up through 2014.

Same

"Destiny"

Lead and Backup Vocals: Paul Hill
Keyboards: Amp Fiddler
Bass: Bubs Fiddler
Drums: Larry Tucker
Guitar: Anthony Booker
Trumpet: Marcus Belgrave
Sax: Mark Kierne
Trombone: Ron Kishchuck
Additional Backup Vocals: Peila, Paula

"Need Me Some U"

All Vocals and Arrangement: Paul Hill
Programming: Terrence Fleming

"These Issues"

All Vocals and Arrangement: Paul Hill
Organ: Amp Fiddler
Guitar: Louis Brantley, Mike Puwal
Programming: Terrence Fleming

"Miles Away"

All Vocals and Arrangement: Paul Hill
Organ, Keyboards, Programming: Amp Fiddler
Drums: Ron Wright
Guitar: Anthony Booker

Ur Thoughts

"Ur Thoughts"

Lead Vocals: Paul Hill, George Clinton
Backup Vocals: Paul Hill

"Clone"

Lead Vocals: Paul Hill

"Tha 1"

Lead Vocals: Paul Hill

"After Affects"

Lead Vocals: Paul Hill

"Sexy Voice"

Lead Vocals: Paul Hill

"4 Life"

Lead Vocals: Paul Hill

"Mama Proud"

Lead Vocals: Paul Hill

"3Ology"

Lead Vocals: Paul Hill

"Til We Meet Again"

Lead Vocals: Paul Hill

— ☆ —

SOCIALYBRIUM: 2010

This funk metal band contained P-Funk's Bernie Worrell and Blackbyrd McKnight and toured heavily around the period of the release of their debut album.

For You

"Swamp"

Keyboards: Bernie Worrell
Guitar: Dewayne Blackbyrd McKnight
Bass: Melvin Gibbs
Drums: J. T. Lewis

"Glory Story"

Keyboards: Bernie Worrell
Guitar: Dewayne Blackbyrd McKnight
Bass: Melvin Gibbs
Drums: J. T. Lewis

"He-Then Holiday"

Keyboards: Bernie Worrell
Guitar: Dewayne Blackbyrd McKnight
Bass: Melvin Gibbs
Drums: J. T. Lewis

"Rockin' Uptown"

Keyboards: Bernie Worrell
Guitar: Dewayne Blackbyrd McKnight
Bass: Melvin Gibbs
Drums: J. T. Lewis

"Another Day"

Keyboards: Bernie Worrell
Guitar: Dewayne Blackbyrd McKnight
Bass: Melvin Gibbs
Drums: J. T. Lewis

"BQE"

Keyboards: Bernie Worrell
Guitar: Dewayne Blackbyrd McKnight
Bass: Melvin Gibbs
Drums: J. T. Lewis

"Free Your Mind"

Keyboards: Bernie Worrell
Guitar: Dewayne Blackbyrd McKnight
Bass: Melvin Gibbs
Drums: J. T. Lewis

"We Painted It Colors"

Keyboards: Bernie Worrell
Guitar: Dewayne Blackbyrd McKnight
Bass: Melvin Gibbs
Drums: J. T. Lewis

"Momma Told Me"

Keyboards: Bernie Worrell
Guitar: Dewayne Blackbyrd McKnight
Bass: Melvin Gibbs
Drums: J. T. Lewis

"Over There"

Keyboards: Bernie Worrell
Guitar: Dewayne Blackbyrd McKnight
Bass: Melvin Gibbs
Drums: J. T. Lewis

— ☆ —

BIG BOI (SELECT TRACK): 2010

One-half of the rap group Outkast strikes out on his own with this 2010 offering featuring George Clinton.

Def Jam Recordings

Sir Lucious Left Foot: The Son of Chico Dusty

"Fo Yo Sorrows"

Vocals: Big Boi, George Clinton, Sam Chris, Too $hort
Backup Vocals: Debra Killings
Drum Programming: Organized Noize
Guitar: Billy Odum, David Whild
Keyboards: Kevin Kendricks

— ☆ —

FUNKSCRIBE AND STARRCHILD: 2010

Seattle-area producer/keyboardist's album features Garry Shider.

"Keep the Funk Alive"

Keyboards, Vocals: Anthony Warner
Lead Vocals: Garry Shider
Saxes: Mike Theiss
Bass: Lawrence Hightower
Backup Vocals: Fysah Thomas, Wuddha

"I Remember"

Keyboards, Vocals: Anthony Warner
Lead Vocals: Garry Shider
Saxes: Mike Theiss
Bass: Lawrence Hightower
Backup Vocals: Fysah Thomas, Wuddha

"Keep On Keepin' On"

Keyboards, Vocals: Anthony Warner
Lead Vocals: Garry Shider
Saxes: Mike Theiss
Bass: Lawrence Hightower
Backup Vocals: Fysah Thomas, Wuddha

"Robotrippin'"

Keyboards, Vocals: Anthony Warner
Lead Vocals: Garry Shider
Saxes: Mike Theiss
Bass: Lawrence Hightower
Backup Vocals: Fysah Thomas, Wuddha

"Booty for Days"

Keyboards, Vocals: Anthony Warner
Lead Vocals: Garry Shider
Trumpet: Chris Littlefield
Bass: Lawrence Hightower
Backup Vocals: Fysah Thomas, Wuddha

"Twisted"

Keyboards, Vocals: Anthony Warner
Lead Vocals: Garry Shider
Bass: Lawrence Hightower
Backup Vocals: Fysah Thomas, Wuddha

"Caramel Queen"

Keyboards, Vocals: Anthony Warner
Lead Vocals: Garry Shider
Saxes: Mike Theiss
Bass: Lawrence Hightower
Backup Vocals: Fysah Thomas, Wuddha

"When It Rains, It Pours"

Keyboards, Vocals: Anthony Warner
Lead Vocals: Garry Shider
Bass: Lawrence Hightower
Backup Vocals: Fysah Thomas, Wuddha

"Keep the Funk Alive (Bernie & Garry Mixapella)"

Keyboards, Vocals: Anthony Warner
Lead Vocals: Garry Shider
Bass: Lawrence Hightower
Backup Vocals: Fysah Thomas, Wuddha

— ☆ —

WAYMAN TISDALE (SELECT TRACKS): 2010

This jazz and rhythm-and-blues singer released a funk album in 2010 featuring George Clinton.

Rendezvous Music

The Fonk Record

Lead Vocals: Wayman Tisdale, George Clinton, Garry Shider
Drums, Percussion: Arthur Thompson
Guitar: Perry Hardin

ARTISTS STARTING IN 2011-2021

GARY AND GARRY (REISSUE YEAR): 2011

These are some of the songs from Gary Mudbone Cooper and Garry Shider's duo album originally slated for a release in the mid-1980s.

"Dance Rocket"

Vocals: Garry Shider, Gary Mudbone Cooper
Drum Programming, Synth Bass, Keyboards: David Lee Spradley
Percussion: Gary Mudbone Cooper
Guitar: Eddie Hazel

"Satisfied"

Lead Vocals: Gary Mudbone Cooper, Garry Shider
Backup Vocals: George Clinton, Mallia Franklin
Drum Programming, Synth Bass, Keyboards: David Lee Spradley
Guitar: Garry Shider

— ☆ —

GABE "UNDISCO KIDD" GONZALEZ: 2011

This is a solo outing for P-Funk drummer Gabe Gonzalez (tenure: 1994–1996).

A Negative Nuisance

"Maggot Brain"

Drums: Gabe Gonzalez
Guitar: Spacey T

"Enter The Life of Da' Kid Pre-Lude"

Drums, Keyboards: Gabe Gonzalez
Bass: Tony Green

"Kredit Kard"

Drums, Keyboards, Bass, Guitars, Vocals: Gabe Gonzalez
Backup Vocals: Terese Rose

"You'll Regret It (Never Should Have Said It)"

Drums, Synth Bass, Keyboards: Gabe Gonzalez
Guitar: Michael Hampton
Vocals: Gabe Gonzalez, Shirley Hayden

"A Whole Lotta Love"

Drums: Gabe Gonzalez
Guitar, Bass: Spacey T
Vocals: Jim Wright

"Theme from the Black Troll"

Drums, Bass, Keyboards: Gabe Gonzalez
Guitars: Michael Hampton, Garry Shider
Vocals: Gabe Gonzalez, Samples

"Slow Down & Get Low Down"

All Instruments and Vocals: Gabe Gonzalez

"One Nation Deep Under a Dog"

Drums, Bass, Keyboards: Gabe Gonzalez
Guitar: Michael Hampton

"Pounce on This"

Drums, Other Instruments: Gabe Gonzalez

"We Won't Go Away"

Drums, Bass, Keyboards: Gabe Gonzalez
Guitar: Ron Priest, Tracey Lewis
Vocals: Tracey Lewis, Gabe Gonzalez

"Streets Don't Fail Me Now"

All Instruments and Vocals: Gabe Gonzalez

"Booty Pie (Honey Buns Make Me Feel So Good)"

Drums, Synth Bass: Gabe Gonzalez
Guitar: Mike Hampton, Ron Smith
Keyboards: Gabe Gonzalez, Mike Hampton

"Funky Eenuff"

Drums, Synth Bass, Keyboards: Gabe Gonzalez
Guitar: Mike Hampton
Vocals: Gabe Gonzalez, Shirley Hayden

"7 Up"

Drums, Synth Bass, Keyboards: Gabe Gonzalez
Guitar: Ron Smith, Spacey T

"R U on the One?"

Drums, Guitar, Synth Bass, Keyboards: Gabe Gonzalez
Vocals: Sheila Horne

"Still Freakn' Out over You"

Drums, Vocals: Gabe Gonzalez
Guitar: Mike Hampton
Bass: Lige Curry

"Maggot Brain (Reprise)"

Drums: Gabe Gonzalez
Guitar: Spacey T

— ☆ —

JOE SMOOTH FEATURING GEORGE CLINTON AND SCREAMING RACHAEL: 2011

Chicago house DJ Joe Smooth did this track along with George Clinton and Screaming Rachael. The song was recorded several years before this compilation was released.

Trax Records

Trax Records: The 25th Anniversary Collection

"Our House Is Funkdafied"

Vocals: George Clinton, Screaming Rachael
Mix: Joe Smooth

— ☆ —

RALPH MYERZ (SELECT TRACK): 2011

This hip-hop artist features George Clinton, Snoop Dogg, Nipsey Hussle, and more.

"Do the Damn Thang" (multiple versions)

Vocals: Ralph Myerz, Snoop Dogg, George Clinton, Nipsey Hussle, Da Youngfellaz

Alternate versions also feature Noelle, Ciscoe, and others.

— ☆ —

THE BIG OL NASTY GET DOWN (SELECT TRACKS): 2012

This Jam Band compilation features more than half a dozen P-Funk members.

"The Big Ol' Nasty Getdown"

Vocals: Clip Payne
Drums: Terrence Higgins
Bass: John Heintz
Guitar: Ian Neville
Keyboards: Dave Grissom
Trumpet: Effrem Towns
Trombone: Robert Andrews, Derrik Johnson
Sax: Roger Lewis, Kevin Harris, Greg Hollowell
Percussion: Frank Mapstone, John Paul Miller

"Include Me"

Vocals: Belita Woods, Garry Shider, Kendra Foster, Laura Reed
Drums: Alvin Ford Jr.
Bass: John Heintz
Guitar: Garry Shider, Ian Neville, Elliot Cohn
Keyboards: Brandon Butler, Frank Mapstone
Trombone: Derrik Johnson
Sax: Greg Hollowell

"I Will Wait for You"

Vocals: Laura Reed, George Clinton, Sidney Barnes, Garry Shider, Belita Woods
Drums: Terrence Higgins
Bass: Robert Mercurio
Guitar: John Paul Miller
Keyboards: Tyler Simmons, Frank Mapstone
Pedal Steel Guitar: Roosevelt Collier
Trombone: Derrick Johnson
Sax: Greg Hollowell

"College Funk"

Drums: Terrence Higgins
Bass: Robert Mercurio
Guitar: Matt Grondin, John Paul Miller
Keyboards: Frank Mapstone, Tyler Simmons
Trumpet: Efrem Towns
Trombone: Derrick Johnson, Revert Andrews
Sax: Roger Lewis, Kevin Harris, Greg Hollowell
Pedal Steel Guitar: Roosevelt Collier
Percussion: John Paul Miller
Shekre: Justin Hunnicut

"Wake Me Up"

Vocals: Ralph Roddenbery, Belita Woods, Frank Mapstone, Sidney Barnes, Derrick Johnson, Laura Reed, Molly Rose Reed, Eleanor Underhill, Mich'ele Barrington, Sherwood Brown, Angela Moss Pool, Andrew White
Drums: Alvin Ford Jr.
Bass: Lil' Alvin Cordy
Guitar: Ralph Roddenbery, Alvin Lee
Keyboards: Frank Mapstone
Pedal Steel Guitar: Roosevelt Collier

"Platinum"

Vocals: Kendra Foster
Drums: Terence Higgins
Bass: John Paul Miller
Guitar: Matt Grondin
Keyboards: Frank Mapstone, Tyler Simmons
Pedal Steel Guitar: Roosevelt Collier
Trombone: Derrick Johnson
Sax: Kevin Harris, Greg Hollowell

"Room 2012"

Vocals: Desmond D'Angelo, George Clinton, Sidney Barnes, Kendra Foster, Laura Reed, Garry Shider, Belita Woods
Drums: Terence Higgins
Bass: John Paul Miller
Guitar: Matt Grondin
Keyboards: Frank Mapstone
Trombone: Derrick Johnson
Sax: Greg Hollowell

"Away from the World"

Vocals: Laura Reed, Kendra Foster, Sidney Barnes
Drums: Alvin Ford Jr.
Bass: John Heintz
Guitar: Derrick Johnson
Keyboards: Frank Mapstone
Flute: Kofi Burbridge

"The Beauty of Pretty"

Vocals: George Clinton, Sidney Barnes
Drums: Alvin Ford Jr.
Bass: John Heintz
Guitar: John Paul Miller
Keyboards: Danny Bedrosian
Trombone: Derrick Johnson
Sax: Greg Hollowell

"It's So Hard to Go"

Vocals: George Clinton, Derrick Johnson, Belita Woods, Laura Reed, Kendra Foster, Garry Shider, Robert Peanut Johnson, Sidney Barnes, Desmond D'Angelo, Ralph Roddenbery, John Heintz, Greg Hollowell, John Paul Miller, Arieh Samson, Clella Ann Zvat, Kara Demtry, Kellie Meadows
Drums: Terence Higgins
Bass: John Heintz
Guitar: Roosevelt Collier
Keyboards: Frank Mapstone, Tyler Simmons
Trombone: Derrick Johnson
Sax: Greg Hollowell

"Amplify"

Vocals: Kendra Foster, Agent 23, Gift of Gab, George Clinton
Samples: Agent 23
Keyboards: Danny Bedrosian

— ☆ —

REBEL TONGUE: 2012

Thus Colorado band features Lige Curry and Danny Bedrosian.

"Lose Hope"

Bass: Justin Francoeur
Vocals: Azma Holiday
Keyboards: Danny Bedrosian
Drums: Chris Murphy
Guitar: Scott Rolfs
Trumpet: James Chiesa
Sax: Michael Chiesa
Trumpet Solo: Rick Gardner
Percussion: Damon Scott

"Bad Mutha F*#%"

Bass: Justin Francouer
Vocals: Azma Holiday
Keyboards: Danny Bedrosian
Drums: Chris Murphy
Guitar: Scott Rolfs
Trumpet: James Chiesa
Sax: Michael Chiesa
Percussion: Damon Scott
Six-String Bass: Lige Curry

"Tell Them Why"

Keyboards: Danny Bedrosian
Drums: Chris Murphy
Bass: Justin Francouer
Vocals: Azma Holiday
Guitar: Scott Rolfs
Trumpet: James Chiesa
Sax: Michael Chiesa

"Writa Man"

Bass: Justin Francouer
Vocals: Azma Holiday
Keyboards: Danny Bedrosian
Drums: Chris Murphy
Guitar: Scott Rolfs
Trumpet: James Chiesa
Sax: Michael Chiesa

"Do for Love"

Bass: Justin Francouer
Vocals: Azma Holiday
Keyboards: Danny Bedrosian
Drums, Handclaps: Chris Murphy
Guitar: Scott Rolfs
Trumpet: James Chiesa
Sax, Handclaps: Michael Chiesa
Six-String Bass: Lige Curry
Percussion: Ido Ziv
Handclaps: Sarah Polvogt

"Can't Say No"

Bass: Justin Francouer
Vocals: Azma Holiday
Keyboards: Danny Bedrosian
Drums: Chris Murphy
Guitar: Scott Rolfs
Trumpet: James Chiesa
Sax: Michael Chiesa
Percussion: Damon Scott, Ido Ziv

"Spotlight"

Keyboards: Danny Bedrosian
Drums: Chris Murphy
Bass: Justin Francouer
Vocals: Azma Holiday
Guitar: Scott Rolfs
Trumpet: James Chiesa
Sax: Michael Chiesa
Percussion: Damon Scott, Ido Ziv

— ☆ —

BENNIE COWAN AND THE REAL BRASSTAXX: 2013

This is a solo album from trumpet player for P-Funk Bennie Cowan. Along with Greg Thomas, Michael Clip Payne, and Lige Curry, Cowan has one of the longest tenures in P-Funk history (tenure: 1978–1986, 1989–present). He makes up one-third of the P-Funk Horns, also known as the Baltimore Connection (along with saxophonist Greg Thomas and trombonist Greg Boyer), who all appear on this album, along with Bennie's son Benzel, the current drummer for P-Funk; George Clinton; Kendra Foster; and others.

P-Funk Horns trumpeter Bennie Cowan. Mikiodo

It's a Horn Thing "G"

"Arm & Hammer"
Trumpet: Bennie Cowan, Ron Rolling
Sax: Greg Thomas, Scott Taylor
Trombone: Greg Boyer
Drums: Benjamin Cowan
Bass: Jeff Bunn
Keyboards: Gary Hudgins
Guitar: Guy Curtis

"Olympic Theme"
Trumpet: Bennie Cowan, Ben Frock
Sax: Greg Thomas, Scott Taylor
Trombone: Greg Boyer
Drums: Benjamin Cowan
Bass: Greg Deanda
Keyboards: Gary Hudgins
Guitar: Guy Curtis

"Bennie & the Jets"
Trumpet: Bennie Cowan, Ben Frock
Sax: Greg Thomas, Scott Taylor
Trombone: Greg Boyer
Drums: Ju-Ju
Bass: Glenn Ellis
Keyboards: Greg Rice
Guitar: Guy Curtis
Vocals: George Clinton, Llewelyn "Hondo" Scruggs, Greg Deanda
Congas: Foxy Rob

"My Last Spliff"

Trumpet: Bennie Cowan, Ron Rolling
Sax: Greg Thomas, Scott Taylor
Trombone: Greg Boyer
Drums: Benjamin Cowan
Bass: Jeff Bunn
Keyboards: Bennie Cowan, Gary Hudgins
Guitar: Guy Curtis
Vocals: Kendra Foster, Llewelyn "Hondo" Scruggs

"Scott a Go-Go"

Trumpet: Bennie Cowan, Ben Frock
Sax: Greg Thomas, Scott Taylor
Trombone: Rufus Roundtree .
Drums: Benjamin Cowan
Bass: Jeff Bunn
Keyboards: Guy Curtis, Bennie Cowan
Guitar: Guy Curtis

"Ocean"

Trumpet: Bennie Cowan, Ben Frock
Sax: Greg Thomas, Scott Taylor
Trombone: Greg Boyer
Drums: Benjamin Cowan
Bass: Rodney Curtis
Keyboards: Ernie McNair
Guitar: Guy Curtis

"Hornicopia/Loopit"

Trumpet: Bennie Cowan, Ron Rolling
Sax: Greg Thomas, Scott Taylor
Trombone: Rufus Roundtree
Drums: Benjamin Cowan
Bass: Jeff Bunn
Keyboards: Gary Hudgins
Guitar: Guy Curtis
Vocals: George Clinton, Bennie Cowan

P-Funk drummer Benjamin "Benzel Baltimore" Cowan. Mikiodo

"Wichita Lineman"

Trumpet: Bennie Cowan, Ron Rolling
Sax: Scott Taylor
Trombone: Rufus Roundtree
Drums: Benjamin Cowan
Bass: Greg Deanda
Keyboards: Gary Hudgins
Guitar: Guy Curtis

"Straight"

Trumpet: Bennie Cowan, Ben Frock
Sax: Greg Thomas, Scott Taylor
Trombone: Greg Boyer
Drums: Benjamin Cowan
Bass: Rodney Curtis
Keyboards: Gary Hudgins
Guitar: Guy Curtis

"Ironman"

Trumpet: Bennie Cowan, Ben Frock
Sax: Scott Taylor
Trombone: Rufus Roundtree
Drums: Benjamin Cowan
Bass: Jeff Bunn
Keyboards: Gary Hudgins
Guitar: Guy Curtis

— ☆ —

SOUL CLAP (SELECT TRACKS): 2013

These are DJs with one foot in the funk who have worked with George Clinton and company in recent years.

"The Hourchild Introduces"

All Mixes: Soul Clap
Featuring: Sa'D Ali (the Hourchild)

"Feature for Love"

All Mixes: Soul Clap
Bass: Billy Bass Nelson
Featuring: Nick Monaco

"Numb"

All Mixes: Soul Clap
Featuring: Ebony Houston

"Elevation"

All Mixes: Soul Clap
Featuring: Dayone Rollins, Freeky Neek, Ricky Tan

"Funk Bomb"

All Mixes: Soul Clap
Bass: Billy Bass Nelson

— ☆ —

GRAND SLAM (SELECT TRACKS): 2013

This German funk band features Gary Mudbone Cooper, Lige Curry, and many more.

"Recipe"

Vocals: Mudbone Cooper, Lige Curry, Oliver Allwardt, Palmer Murphy, Eric Rohner, Robert Collins, MC Man-E-Faces, Michael Deml
Guitars, Drum Programming, Bass, Synth Bass, Keyboards: Machael Dandorfer
Synth Solo, Vocoder: Toby Mayerl
Drums: Frank Holderied
Turntables: RPM

"Long Term Ticket"

Vocals: Eric Rohner, Mudbone Cooper, Oliver Allwardt, Robert Collins, Palmer Murphy, MC Man-E-Faces
All Guitars, Synth Bass, Programming: Michael Dandorfer
Sax, Keyboards: Erick Rohner
Piano, Organ, Synth Bass: Toby Mayerl
Bass: Lutz J. Mays
Drums: Frank Holderied

"Chillin' with My People"

Vocals: Olvier Allwardt, Palmer Murphy, Robert Collins
Guitars: Michael Dandorfer
Synthesizer, Organ: Toby Mayerl
Drums: Frank Holderied
Bass: Lutz J. Mays
Turntables: RPM

"You Can't Nickname the Truth"

Vocals: Mudbone Cooper, Palmer Murphy, Oliver Allwardt, Robert Colins, Eric Rohner
Guitar: Michael Dandorfer
Electric Piano: Toby Mayerl
Sax: Eric Rohner
Drums: Frank Holderied
Bass: Lutz J. Mays
Turntables: RPM
Handclaps: Grand Slam Family

"Elemelemel"

Vocals: Palmer Murphy, MC Man-E-Faces, Oliver Allwardt, Robert Collins
Guitar: Michael Dandorfer
Piano, Synthesizer, Synth Bass: Toby Mayerl
Bass: Lutz J. Mays
Drums: Frank Holderied
Turntables: RPM

"Camp Down"

Vocals: Robert Collins, Mudbone Cooper, Oliver Allwardt, Palmer Murphy, MC Man-E-Faces
Guitars: Michael Danddorfer
Clavinet, Synthesizer, Vocoder: Toby Mayerl
Bass: Lutz J. Mays
Drums: Frank Holderied
Turntables: RPM

"Funky Juices"

Vocals: Mudbone Cooper, Palmer Murphy
All Instruments: Michael Dandorfer

"The Fog"

Vocals: Palmer Murphy, Robert Collins, Oliver Allwardt
Guitar: Michael Dandorfer
Wurlitzer: Toby Mayerl
Harp: Palmer Murphy
Bass: Lutz J. Mays
Drums: Frank Holderied

"Streets of Harlem"

Vocals: Robert Collins, Oliver Allwardt, Palmer Murphy
Guitars: Michael Dandorfer
Synthesizer, Clavinet, Electric Piano: Toby Mayerl
Bass: Lutz J. Mays
Drums: Frank Holderied
Turntables: RPM

"Dancing in Bavaria"

Vocals: Lige Curry, Eric Rohner, MC Man-E-Faces, Oliver Allwardt, Robert Collins, Palmer Murphy
All Basses: Lige Curry
Synthesizer, Clavinet, Electric Piano: Toby Mayerl
Guitars, Drum Programming: Michael Dandorfer
Drums: Frank Holderied

— ☆ —

KILLAH PRIEST: 2013

Killah Priest's 2013 album featured George Clinton and some Funkadelic-inspired tracks.

The Psychic World of Walter Reed

"Tonite We Ride"

Vocals: Killah Priest, George Clinton
Producer: Jordan River Banks

— ☆ —

GOD'S WEAPON: 2013

This heavy metal group is led and founded by George Clinton's grandson Trafael.

The Light & the Darkness

"My Last Regret"

"Dirty Queen"

"Wormtail Tongue"

"Annhilation"

"The Other Side"

"Darkest before the Dawn"

"Ambrosia"

"Sing!!!"

"Until Undone"

"Love Is Strength"

All songs by Trafael Lewis & God's Weapon
Guitar, Drums, Vocals, Bass, efx.]

— ☆ —

FREEKBOT METAL FACE: 2014

This album features Freekbass and Tobotius.

"Mars Attacks"

Bass, Vocals, Keyboards, Guitar: Freekbass
Turntables, Programming, Drums, Additional Sequencing, Keyboards: Tobotius

"Get Up and Dance"

Bass, Vocals, Keyboards, Guitar: Freekbass
Turntables, Programming, Drums, Additional Sequencing, Keyboards: Tobotius

"Metal Face"

Bass, Vocals, Keyboards, Guitar: Freekbass
Turntables, Programming, Drums, Additional Sequencing, Keyboards: Tobotius

"Food, Beauty, Fashion, Toys"

Bass, Vocals, Keyboards, Guitar: Freekbass
Turntables, Programming, Drums, Additional Sequencing, Keyboards: Tobotius

"Grinder"

Bass, Vocals, Keyboards, Guitar: Freekbass
Turntables, Programming, Drums, Additional Sequencing, Keyboards: Tobotius

"Wana Dance"

Bass, Vocals, Keyboards, Guitar: Freekbass
Turntables, Programming, Drums, Additional Sequencing, Keyboards: Tobotius

God's Weapon: Trafael Lewis. Mikiodo

"Black Market Death Wish"

Bass, Vocals, Keyboards, Guitar: Freekbass
Turntables, Programming, Drums, Additional Sequencing, Keyboards: Tobotius

GORANGUTANG (SELECT TRACKS): 2014–

Gorangutang features hip-hop with a didjeridoo and was founded by Trazae Lewis-Clinton (George Clinton's grandson) and didjeridoo player and photographer William Thoren.

Sounds from the Gorabitat

"Sleep No More"

Vocals, Keyboards, Beats: Trazae Lewis-Clinton
Vocals, Didgeridoo, Mandolin, Keyboards, Beats: William Thoren

"Country Swag"

Vocals, Keyboards, Beats: Trazae Lewis-Clinton
Vocals, Didgeridoo, Mandolin, Keyboards, Beats: William Thoren

"Yam"

Vocals: George Clinton
Vocals, Keyboards, Beats: Trazae Lewis-Clinton
Vocals, Didgeridoo, Mandolin, Keyboards, Beats: William Thoren

Gorangutang: Trazae Lewis-Clinton and William Thoren. William Thoren

"Gold Pen"

Vocals, Keyboards, Beats: Trazae
   Lewis-Clinton
**Vocals, Didgeridoo, Mandolin, Keyboards,
   Beats:** William Thoren

"Watch You Dance"

Vocals, Keyboards, Beats: Trazae
   Lewis-Clinton
**Vocals, Didgeridoo, Mandolin, Keyboards,
   Beats:** William Thoren

"Water and Oil"

Vocals, Keyboards, Beats: Trazae
Lewis-Clinton
**Vocals, Didgeridoo, Mandolin, Keyboards,
Beats:** William Thoren

"Mojo Jojo"

Vocals, Keyboards, Beats: Trazae
Lewis-Clinton
**Vocals, Didgeridoo, Mandolin, Keyboards,
Beats:** William Thoren

"Smokey Tha Bear"

Vocals, Keyboards, Beats: Trazae
Lewis-Clinton
**Vocals, Didgeridoo, Mandolin, Keyboards,
Beats:** William Thoren

"Dragon"

Vocals, Keyboards, Beats: Trazae
Lewis-Clinton
**Vocals, Didgeridoo, Mandolin, Keyboards,
Beats:** William Thoren

"Oh Yeah"

Vocals, Keyboards, Beats: Trazae
Lewis-Clinton
**Vocals, Didgeridoo, Mandolin, Keyboards,
Beats:** William Thoren

"Sheep"

Vocals, Keyboards, Beats: Trazae
Lewis-Clinton
**Vocals, Didgeridoo, Mandolin, Keyboards,
Beats:** William Thoren

"If the World Ends"

Vocals, Keyboards, Beats: Trazae
Lewis-Clinton
**Vocals, Didgeridoo, Mandolin, Keyboards,
Beats:** William Thoren

"Turnip"

Vocals, Keyboards, Beats: Trazae
Lewis-Clinton
**Vocals, Didgeridoo, Mandolin, Keyboards,
Beats:** William Thoren

"Bell Bottoms"

Vocals, Keyboards, Beats: Trazae
Lewis-Clinton
**Vocals, Didgeridoo, Mandolin, Keyboards,
Beats:** William Thoren

Funky Monkey

"Wyoming"

"Funky Monkey"

"Tres"

"Glistnin"

"Shake"

By William Thoren and Trazae Lewis-Clinton

Singles

"WorldStar"

Who I Be (featuring Scottie Clinton)

— ☆ —

HORNDOGZ (SELECT TRACKS): 2014

This French funk horn section features Clip Payne, Lige Curry, and others.

"Prelude"

Vocals: Clip Payne
Harmonica: Antonin Bastian
Bass: Lige Curry
Guitar: Rico Kerridge
Keyboards: Stephane Lenavelan
Sax: Eric Rohner
Trumpet: Gilles Garin

"Paris"

Rap: Mike Larry, Jude Kidsude Pericles
Turntables: DJ Myst
Programming, Guitars, Bass: Rico Kerridge
Keyboards: Stephane Lenavelan
Sax: Eric Rohner
Trumpet: Gilles Garin

"Movin' On"

Vocals: Peeda
Rap: Ty, Breis
Guitars: Rico Kerridge, Adam Bastard
Bass: Mounir Messaoud
Keyboards: Stephane Lenavelan
Sax: Eric Rohner
Trumpet: Gilles Garin
Drums: Lawrence Clais

"Rocksteady"

Vocals: Mary Griffin
Rap: Breis
Turntables: DJ Dee Nasty
Drums, Bass: Rico Kerridge
Keyboards: Jay Murphy
Sax: Eric Rohner
Trumpet: Gilles Garin

"People"

Trombone: Fred Wesley
Guitar, Bass, Programming, Vocals: Rico Kerridge
Sax, Rap, Vocals: Eric Rohner
Trumpet: Gilles Garin

"Got to Blow"

Rap, Programming, Guitars, Bass: Rico Kerridge
Keyboards: Stephane Lenavelan
Saxes, Vocals: Eric Rohner
Trumpet: Gilles Garin

"I Know"

Lead Vocals: Blitz the Ambassador
Cheerleader: Laura Laurens
Programming, Guitars, Bass: Rico Kerridge
Additional Bass: Lige Curry
Sax: Eric Rohner
Trumpet: Gilles Garin
Trombone: Greg Boyer, Simon Andrieux

"In My DNA"

Lead Vocals: Juan Rozoff
Trombone: Fred Wesley, Simon Andrieux
Backup Vocals: Juan Rozoff, Rico Kerridge, Eric Rohner
Guitar, Bass: Rico Kerridge
Keyboards, Programming: Fab Lerigab
Trumpet: Gilles Garin
Sax: Eric Rohner

"Take My Heart"

Vocals: Jee Williams
Guitar: Rico Kerridge
Flugelhorn, Sounds, Noises: Gilles Garin

"Move On Up"

Vocals, Bass: Bibi Tanga
Vocals: Peeda
Drums, Percussion: Lawrence Clais
Guitar: Rico Kerridge
Sax: Eric Rohner
Trumpet: Gilles Garin

"All about You"

Vocals: Sadiq Bey
Synthesizer, Tweaking: Amp Fiddler
Programming, Guitars, Bass: Rico Kerridge
Saxes, Vocals: Eric Rohner
Trumpet: Gilles Garin

"La Trompeta O Yo"

Voice: Candela Montero Martin
Programming, Guitars, Bass: Rico Kerridge
Keyboards: Stephane Lenavelan
Trumpets: Gilles Garin

"City of Love"

Vocals: Mary Griffin
Programming, Guitar: Rico Kerridge
Bass: Mounir Messaoud
Drums: Fab Lerigab
Keyboards: Stephane Lenavelan
Percussion: Gerald Bonnegrace
Trumpet: Gilles Garin
Saxes: Eric Rohner
Trombone: Simon Andrieux

"P Is the People"

Vocals: Clip Payne
Harmonica: Antonin Bastian
Guitars: Rico Kerridge
Bass: Bibi Tanga
Keyboards: Stephane Lenavelan
Drums: Lawrence Clais
Sax: Eric Rohner
Trumpet: Gilles Garin

— ☆ —

KENDRICK LAMAR (SELECT TRACK): 2015

The progressive hip-hop force hit paydirt with the 2015 album *To Pimp a Butterfly*, which defied conventions, featuring Terrace Martin, Thundercat, Robert Glasper, and P-Funk mastermind George Clinton.

Aftermath Entertainment

To Pimp a Butterfly

"Wesley's Theory"

Sax: Terrace Martin
Trumpet: Josef Leimberg
Lead Vocals: Kendrick Lamar, George Clinton
Backup Vocals: Anna Wise, Ash Riser, Dr. Dre, Josef Leimberg, Whitney Alford
Producers: Flying Lotus, Ronald "Flip" Colson, Sounwave, Thundercat

— ☆ —

COOP DEVILLE (SELECT TRACKS): 2015

This Australian funk guitarist's album features Danny Bedrosian, Lige Curry, Benzel Cowan, the Baltimore Connection, Rodney Skeet Curtis, Steve Boyd, and others.

Bat Funk Crazy

"Intro"

Vocals: George Clinton
Guitar: Ishan Cooper

"Bad Larry Jones"

Synthesizer, Keyboards, Piano: Danny
   Bedrosian
Bass: Lige Curry
Drums: Benjamin Cowan
Sax: Greg Thomas
Trumpet: Bennie Cowan
Trombone: Greg Boyer
Guitar: Ishan Cooper

"Science of Pants"

Vocals: Angelo Moore
Synthesizer, Keyboards, Piano: Danny
   Bedrosian
Bass: Lige Curry
Drums: Benjamin Cowan
Sax: Greg Thomas
Trumpet: Bennie Cowan
Trombone: Greg Boyer
Guitar: Ishan Cooper

"Keep My Head Up"

Vocals: Kokane
Drums: Graeme Pogson
Bass: Pat Moevasa Sili
Keyboards: Gideon Priess
Guitar: Ishan Cooper

"Bat Funk Crazy"

Vocals: Steve Boyd, Sueann Carwell
Synthesizer, Keyboards, Piano: Danny
   Bedrosian
Bass: Lige Curry
Drums: Benjamin Cowan
Sax: Greg Thomas
Trumpet: Bennie Cowan
Trombone: Greg Boyer
Guitar: Ishan Cooper

"Faded & X-Rated"

Vocals: George Clinton
Synthesizer, Keyboards, Piano: Danny
   Bedrosian

Bass: Lige Curry
Drums: Benjamin Cowan
Sax: Greg Thomas
Trumpet: Bennie Cowan
Trombone: Greg Boyer
Guitar: Ishan Cooper

"Ears for Your Funkhole"

Vocals: Steve Boyd, Sueann Carwell
Synthesizer, Keyboards, Piano: Danny
   Bedrosian
Bass: Lige Curry
Drums: Benjamin Cowan
Sax: Greg Thomas
Trumpet: Bennie Cowan
Trombone: Greg Boyer
Guitar: Ishan Cooper

"Tallahassee Dreaming"

Guitar: Ishan Cooper
Keyboards: Danny Bedrosian

"Round & Round"

Vocals: Kokane
Guitar: Ishan Cooper
Bass: Rodney Curtis
Synthesizer, Keyboards, Piano: Danny
   Bedrosian
Drums: Benjamin Cowan
Sax: Greg Thomas
Trumpet: Bennie Cowan
Trombone: Greg Boyer

"One Time Spacesuit"

Vocals: Angelo Moore
Drums: Graeme Pogson
Synthesizer, Keyboards, Piano: Danny
   Bedrosian
Bass: Lige Curry
Sax: Greg Thomas
Trumpet: Bennie Cowan
Trombone: Greg Boyer

"Outro"

Voice: George Clinton
Guitar: Ishan Cooper

— ☆ —

SPACE BUGS (SELECT TRACKS): 2015

This Italian funk band features Danny Bedrosian.

Party of the P-Brains

"The Final Funktier"

Drums, Vocals: Alessandro Cavallaro
Bass, Rhythm Guitar: Fabio Gabbianelli
Keys, Grand Piano, Synthesizers, Vocals: Danny Bedrosian
Guitar Solo: Marco Zitelli
Saxes: Fabio Tullio
Backup Vocals: Francesca Ngoc Lan Tran, Heidi Li, Mary Ginn

"Unsleeping Booty"

Drums, Vocals: Alessandro Cavallaro
Bass, Rhythm Guitar: Fabio Gabbianelli
Lead Vocals, Keys, Grand Piano: Danny Bedrosian
Guitar Solo: Marco Zitelli
Saxes: Fabio Tullio
Rap: Avi the Most III

"Black Orange"

Drums: Alessandro Cavallaro
Bass, Rhythm Guitars: Fabio Gabbianelli
Guitar Solo: Marco Zitelli
Keyboards, Grand Piano: Danny Bedrosian

"Eskimo"

Drums, Backup Vocals: Alessandro Cavallaro
Lead Vocals, Keyboards, Grand Piano, Synthesizer: Danny Bedrosian
Bass, All Guitars: Fabio Gabbianelli
Saxes: Fabrio Tullio
Rap: Avi the Most III
Backup Vocals: Flaviano Pizzoli

"Upside West Side"

Drums: Alessandro Cavallaro
Bass, Rhythm Guitar: Fabio Gabbianelli
Arpeggiator: Marco Zitelli
Keys, Grand Piano, Synthesizers, Vocals: Danny Bedrosian
Vocals: Francesca Ngoc Lan Tran
Rap: Avi the Most III

"P-Cock Fever"

Drums: Alessandro Cavallaro
Bass: Fabio Gabbianelli
Guitar: Leandro Fiacco
Guitar: Marco Zitelli
Keys, Grand Piano, Synthesizers, Vocals: Danny Bedrosian
Vocals: Francesca Ngoc Lan Tran

"Natural Essence"

Drum Programming, Vocals: Alessandro Cavallaro
Bass, Rhythm Guitar: Fabio Gabbianelli
Lead Vocals, Keyboards, Grand Piano, Synthesizers: Danny Bedrosian
Guitar: Marco Zitelli
Saxes: Fabio Tullio
Rap: Avi the Most III
Backup Vocals: Francesca Ngoc Lan Tran, Heidi Li

"Street Lights"

Drums, Vocals: Alessandro Cavallaro
Bass, All Guitars: Leandro Fiacco
Vocals, Keyboards, Grand Piano, Synthesizers: Danny Bedrosian
Backup Vocals: Francesca Ngoc Lan Tran, Heidi Li, Flaviano Pizzoli

"One Is All Is One"

Electronic Drums: Alessandro Cavallaro
Bass: Fabio Gabbianelli
All Guitars: Marco Zitelli
Vocals, Keyboards, Grand Piano: Danny Bedrosian
Psychedelic Guitar: Daniele De Sapio
Rap: Avi the Most III

"Collision Course (I Don't Want to Feel It)"

Drums, Vocals: Alessandro Cavallaro
Bass: Fabio Gabbianelli
Lead Vocals, Keys, Grand Piano: Danny Bedrosian
Guitar, Vocals: Marco Zitelli
Saxes: Fabio Tullio

— ☆ —

SLIGHT RETURN (SELECT TRACK): 2016

This Detroit funk/rock/rap group featured a song and music video with George Clinton.

Welcome to the D

"Funky People"

Featuring: George Clinton, Pat Lewis, Tony Green
Music: Slight Return

— ☆ —

LIGE CURRY AND RAS MANOS PRESENT: TRANSFONKATION: 2016

This is a Lige Curry project with German/Greek rapper Ras Manos and features Danny Bedrosian, Trazae Lewis-Clinton, Benzel Baltimore Cowan, and more.

"The Word"

Vocals: Lige Curry
All Keyboards: Danny Bedrosian

"Transfonkation"

Bass, Guitars, Vocals: Lige Curry
Vocals: Trazae Lewis-Clinton, Starr Cullars
Keyboards: Danny Bedrosian
Drums: Benjamin Cowan
Guitar, Vocals, Djembe: Ras Manos

"Universal Funk"

Bass, Guitars, Vocals: Lige Curry
Keyboards: Danny Bedrosian
Guitar, Vocals, Djembe: Ras Manos
Sax: Eric Rohner
Drums: Frankie Kash Waddy

"Dirty Funk"

Bass, Guitars, Vocals: Lige Curry
Keyboards: Danny Bedrosian
Drums: Benjamin Cowan
Guitar, Vocals, Djembe: Ras Manos
Vocals: Flowin Immo
Guitars, Vocals: Boo Boo
Vocals, Guitar: Garrett Shider
Vocals: Starr Cullars

"Step It Up"

Bass, Guitars, Vocals: Lige Curry
Keyboards: Danny Bedrosian
Drums: Benjamin Cowan
Guitar, Vocals, Djembe: Ras Manos
Vocals: Flowin Immo

"4 in the Floor"

Bass, Guitars, Vocals: Lige Curry
Keyboards: Danny Bedrosian
Drums: Benjamin Cowan
Guitar, Vocals, Djembe: Ras Manos
Vocals: Flowin Immo, Trazae Clinton, Clip Payne

"Together Now"

Bass, Guitars, Vocals: Lige Curry
Keyboards: Danny Bedrosian
Drums: Benjamin Cowan
Guitar, Vocals, Djembe: Ras Manos
Guitars, Vocals: Boo Boo
Vocals: Starr Cullars

"The Real Deal"

Bass, Guitars, Vocals: Lige Curry
Keyboards: Danny Bedrosian
Drums: Benjamin Cowan
Guitar, Vocals, Djembe: Ras Manos
Vocals: Flowin Immo
Guitars, Vox: Boo Boo
Vocals: Starr Cullars

"P on It"

Bass, Guitars, Vocals: Lige Curry
Keyboards: Danny Bedrosian
Drums: Benjamin Cowan
Guitar, Vocals, Djembe: Ras Manos
Vocals: Flowin Immo
Sax: Eric Rohner
Vocals: Clip Payne

— ☆ —

DETROIT RISING: 2017

This funk album, recorded in Detroit, New York City, and Tallahassee, Florida, features 10 or more members of Parliament-Funkadelic.

DownJazz Records

"Lashing Out"

Vocals: Tonysha Nelson, Danny Bedrosian
Piano, Synth Bass, Synthesizers, Strings: Danny Bedrosian
Drums: Benjamin Cowan
Bass: Lige Curry
Sax: Greg Thomas

"Little Bit"

Vocals:
Keyboards, Piano, Synthesizer: Danny Bedrosian
Drums: Benjamin Cowan
Bass: Lige Curry
Guitar: Blackbyrd McKnight
Sax: Greg Thomas

"My Heart Is Frozen"

Vocals, Guitar: Duminie Depores
Keyboards: Amp Fiddler
Drums: Gabe Gonzalez
Bass: Kern Brantley

"Rocket Love"

Vocals, Guitar: Duminie Depores
Keyboards: Amp Fiddler
Drums: Gabe Gonzalez
Bass: Kern Brantley

"What's That You Heard?"

Vocals: Steve Boyd, Sueann Carwell
Keyboards, Piano: Danny Bedrosian
Drums: Benjamin Cowan
Bass: Lige Curry
Guitar: Blackbyrd McKnight
Sax: Greg Thomas

"Our World"

Vocals: Tonysha Nelson, Danny Bedrosian
Keyboards, Synthesizers, Synth Bass, Organ,
   Piano: Danny Bedrosian
Drums: Benjamin Cowan

"Gorgeous"

Vocals, Guitar: Duminie Depores
Keyboards: Amp Fiddler
Drums: Gabe Gonzalez
Bass: Kern Brantley

"With Peace & Harmony"

Vocals: Steve Boyd, Sueann Carwell
Keyboards, Piano: Danny Bedrosian
Drums: Benjamin Cowan
Bass: Lige Curry
Guitar: Blackbyrd McKnight
Sax: Greg Thomas

"Fly to Freedom"

Vocals: Steve Boyd, Sueann Carwell
Keyboards, Piano: Danny Bedrosian
Drums: Benjamin Cowan
Bass: Lige Curry
Guitar: Blackbyrd McKnight
Sax: Greg Thomas

— ☆ —

GARRETT SHIDER: 2017–

These are solo outings from vocalist/guitarist (and son of Garry Shider) Garrett Shider and also feature several P-Funk members.

Hand Me Down Diapers

"Sugar Rush"

Vocals: Garrett Shider, Trazae Lewis-Clinton
Guitar: Garrett Shider
Bass: Lige Curry

Keyboards: Danny Bedrosian
Drums: Benjamin Cowan

"Bop Gun '17"

Vocals, Guitar: Garrett Shider
Bass: Lige Curry
Keyboards: Danny Bedrosian
Drums: Benjamin Cowan

"Hard Pill"

Vocals, Guitar: Garrett Shider
Bass: Lige Curry
Keyboards: Danny Bedrosian
Drums: Benjamin Cowan

"Jamnastics"

Vocals: Garrett Shider
Guitar: Garrett Shider, another
Bass: Lige Curry
Keyboards: Danny Bedrosian
Drums: Benjamin Cowan

"Nightcap"

Vocals, Bass: Garrett Shider
Keyboards: Danny Bedrosian

"Raw Life Theme (On One)"

Vocals: Garrett Shider, George Clinton
Guitar, Bass, Drums: Garrett Shider
Keyboards: Danny Bedrosian, Garrett Shider

"Stuck in the Middle"

Vocals, Guitar: Garrett Shider, Tracey Lewis
Bass: Lige Curry
Keyboards: Danny Bedrosian
Drums: Benjamin Cowan

"Hand Me Down Diapers"

Vocals, Guitar: Garrett Shider
Bass: Lige Curry
Keyboards: Danny Bedrosian
Drums: Benjamin Cowan

P-Funk Vocalist Garrett Shider works a crowd. William Thoren

Regurgitated Youth

"We Are Here"

Vocals: Garrett Shider, Lance Reynolds
Guitar: Garrett Shider
Bass: Doug Wimbush
   Keyboards: Ali Sankoh
Drums: Benzel Cowan
Trumpet: Chris Brouwers
Tenor Sax: Greg Sanderson
Baritone Sax: Josh Schwartz

"Fun with A K"

Vocals: Garrett Shider, Lance Reynolds, Keith Marshall
Guitar, Bass, Drum Programming: Garrett Shider
Keyboards: Ali Sankoh

"I'm a Funkadelic"

Vocals, Guitar, Bass: Garrett Shider
   Keyboards: Ali Sankoh
Drums: Benzel Cowan

When Freaks Fall in Love

Vocals, Guitar, Bass: Garrett Shider
Keyboards: Ali Sankoh
Drums: Benzel Cowan

"Pretty Eyes"

Vocals, Guitar, Bass, Drum Programming: Garrett Shider
Keyboards: L'John Epps

"Toasted (A Stone's Autobiography)"

Vocals, Guitar, Keyboards: Garrett Shider
Bass: Lige Curry
Drums: Benzel Cowan

"Addicted to Your Reality"

Vocals, Guitar: Garrett Shider
Bass: Lige Curry
  Clavinet: DeAnna Hawkins
Drums: Benzel Cowan
Horns: The Horn Dogz

"Omarosa"

Vocals, Guitar, Keyboards, Drum
  Programming: Garrett Shider
Bass: Doug Wimbush

""Jive Time Johnny""

Vocals, Guitar, Stand-Up Bass Sample,
  Organ: Garrett Shider
Drums: Benzel Cowan
Sax Solo: Eugene Chapman

"Nosey"

Vocals, Guitar, Bass: Garrett Shider
Keyboards, Flute Sample: Ali Sankoh
Drums: Benzel Cowan

"Painstrain"

Vocals: Garrett Shider, Keith Marshall, India
  Reynolds, Roy Patton
Guitar: Garrett Shider
Bass: Norwood Fisher
  Clavinet: Chris Rob
Drums: Benzel Cowan

"It Don't Come Easy"

Vocals: Garrett Shider, the Amores
Guitar, Bass, Synthesizers: Garrett Shider
Drums: Benzel Cowan

"Regurgitated Youth"

Guitar: Garrett Shider
Bass: Flea
  Keyboards: DeAnna Hawkins
Drums: Benzel Cowan

Pandemic

"Pandemic"

Bass: Doug Wimbush
Vocals, Drum Programming, All Other
  Instruments: Garrett Shider

"Cabin Fever"

Vocals: Garrett Shider, Season Shider
Drum Programming, All Instruments: Garrett
  Shider

"Bi-Polar"

Organ: Ali Sankoh
Vocals, Drum Programming, All Other
  Instruments: Garrett Shider

"Like Pac-Man"

Vocals, Drum Programming, All Instruments:
  Garrett Shider

"Fly"

Bass: Josh Hartzog
Vocals, Drum Programming, All Other
  Instruments: Garrett Shider

"That Blows (Hydrochlorophunk)"

Guitar: Olu Ramsey
Vocals, Drum Programming, All Other
  Instruments: Garrett Shider

"San Mateo"

Vocals, Drum Programming, All Instruments:
  Garrett Shider

"When We Have Love"

Bass: Lige Curry
Vocals, Drum Programming, All Other
  Instruments: Garrett Shider

"Loose My Nut"

Vocals: Garrett Shider, Norwood Fisher
Drums: Andy Kravitz
Bass, Guitar, Synthesizer: Garrett Shider

"I Ain't Mad at It"

Vocals, Guitar, Piano: Garrett Shider
Drums: Andy Kravitz
Bass: Norwood Fisher

Singles

"Fly"

All Instruments and Vocals: Garrett Shider

"Lucky Star"

Guitars: Garrett Shider

— ☆ —

GARRY SHIDER AND LINDA SHIDER: 2017

This compilation of work was done by Linda and Garry Shider and released posthumously with reference to the latter.

"Take It to the Stage"

Lead Vocals, Guitar: Garry Shider
Backup Vocals: Ishmael Hart, Kareem Hart, Mann Hart

"I Remember"

Lead Vocals: Garry Shider, Linda Shider
Backup Vocals: Anthony MacMillan, Ron Rainbow
All Instruments: Garry Shider

"It Don't Come Easy"

Lead Vocals: Linda Shider, Garry Shider
Backup Vocals: Thomas Robinson
Guitar: Earnest Jackson, Grady Gambrell, Thomas Robinson
Keyboards: Graham Jackson, Linda Shider
Bass: Kenny Gambrell
Drums: Rick Owens

"Knockin'"

Lead Vocals: Garry Shider
Backup Vocals: Anthony McMillan, George Hancock, Ron Rainbow

"Glory of Love"

Lead Vocals: Linda Shider
Guitar, Instrumentation: Garry Shider

"Funkin' Around"

Lead Vocals: Linda Shider, Garry Shider
Rap: Kareem Dennis, Marshall Shider
All Instrumentation: Garry Shider

"High Drama"

Lead Vocals, All Instrumentation: Garry Shider

"Street Sounds (Are You a Legz Man?)"

Lead Vocals: Linda Shider, Garry Shider
Backup Vocals: Thomas Robinson
Guitar: Earnest Jackson, Grady Gambrell, Thomas Robinson
Keyboards: Linda Shider
Bass: Kenny Gambrell
Drums: Rick Owens

"The Ghost"

Lead Vocals: Garry Shider, Garrett Shider
Keyboards, All Instrumentation: Tim Shider

Mike Judge Presents:
Tales from the Tour Bus

Second season. Produced by Mike Judge. Theme music created and performed by George Clinton and Parliament-Funkadelic

"Tales from the Tour Bus Theme"

Drums: Benjamin Cowan
Bass: Lige Curry
Piano, Keyboards, Synths: Danny Bedrosian
Lead/Rhythm Guitars: Dewayne Blackbyrd McKnight
Lead Vocals: George Clinton

"12 Instrumentals"

Drums: Benjamin Cowan
Bass: Lige Curry
Piano, Keyboards, Synths: Danny Bedrosian
Lead/Rhythm Guitars: Dewayne Blackbyrd McKnight

"Doing It in the Mud"

Vocals: George Clinton, Patavian Lewis, Tonysha Nelson, Scottie Clinton, Thirteen, Garrett Shider
Drums: Benjamin Cowan
Bass: Lige Curry
Piano, Keyboards, Synths: Danny Bedrosian
Lead/Rhythm Guitars: Dewayne Blackbyrd McKnight
Trumpet: Bennie Cowan
Sax: Greg Thomas

KANDY APPLE REDD: 2018–

This female rhythm-and-blues vocal group was founded by two of Clinton's granddaughters: Patavian Lewis and Tonysha Nelson.

Kandy Apple Redd: Tonysha Nelson and Patavian Lewis. William Thoren

Singles

"This Club"

Vocals: Patavian Lewis, Tonysha Nelson
Track: Trazae Lewis-Clinton

"All I Want"

Vocals: Patavian Lewis, Tonysha Nelson
Track: Tim Shider, Jupiter

"Do Things"

Vocals: Patavian Lewis, Tonysha Nelson
Track: Jupiter, Constance Hauman
Arrangement: Paul Hill

— ☆ —

WILL SESSIONS AND AMP FIDDLER FEATURING DAMES BROWN (SELECT TRACKS): 2018

This Detroit-style soul and funk band features P-Funk Keyboardist Joseph "Amp" Fiddler on keyboards and vocals.

Sessions Sounds

The One

"What It Is"

Vocals: Amp Fiddler
Organ, Fender Rhodes, Piano, Synthesizer: Amp Fiddler
Synthesizer: Sam Beaubien
Synthesizer, Bass: Tim Shellabarger
Vocals: Athena Johnson, Lisa Cunningham, Teresa Marbury
Guitar: Ryam Gimpert
Percussion: Eric Kacir
Drums: Jason Bonaquist
Trombone: Matt Martinez
Trumpet: Jimmy Smith, Eric Beaubien

"Lost without You"

Vocals, Piano, Synthesizer: Amp Fiddler
Guitar: Ryan Gimpert
Fender Rhodes: Sam Beaubien
Percussion: Eric Kacir
Drums: Brian Arnold
Vocals: Athena Johnson, Lisa Cunningham, Teresa Marbury

"Belle Isle Drive"

Guitar: Ryan Gimpert
Bass: Tim Shellabarger
Cello: Andrea Yun
Flugelhorn: Jimmy Smith
Vocals, Piano: Amp Fiddler
Violin: Eliot Heaton, Melody Wootton, Molly Hughes, Ran Cheng
Percussion: Eric Kacir
Drums: Jason Bonaquist

"Rendezvous"

Cello: Andrea Yun
Vocals, Talkbox: Amp Fiddler
Guitar: Ryan Gimpert
Bass: Tim Shellabarger
Synthesizer: Sam Beaubien
Violin: Eliot Heaton, Melody Wootton, Molly Hughes, Ran Cheng
Trombone: Matt Martinez
Trumpet: Jimmy Smith, Eric Beaubien
Drums: Jason Bonaquist

"Reminiscin'"

Cello: Andrea Yun
Vocals, Synth Bass: Amp Fiddler
Guitar: Ryan Gimpert
Bass: Tim Shellabarger
Synthesizer: Sam Beaubien
Violin: Eliot Heaton, Melody Wootton, Molly Hughes, Ran Cheng
Trombone: Matt Martinez
Trumpet: Jimmy Smith, Eric Beaubien
Percussion: Eric Kacir
Drums: Jason Bonaquist

"Seven Mile"

Vocals, Piano: Amp Fiddler
Bass: Tim Shellabarger
Synthesizer: Sam Beaubien
Violin: Molly Hughes
Drums: Brian Arnold
Guitar: Ryan Gimpert
Percussion: Eric Kacir

"Who I Am"

Clavinet, Piano, Vocals: Amp Fiddler
Guitar: Ryan Gimpert
Synthesizer: Sam Beaubien
Bass, Bells: Tim Shellabarger
Vocals: Athena Johnson, Lisa Cunningham, Teresa Marbury
Percussion: Eric Kacir
Drums: Jason Bonaquist

"Reconcile"

Cello: Andrea Yun
Drums: Jason Bonaquist
Bass: Tim Shellabarger
Guitar: Ryan Gimpert
Piano, Clavinet: Amp Fiddler
Percussion: Eric Kacir
Violin: Eliot Heaton, Melody Wootton, Molly Hughes, Ren Cheng
Trombone: Matt Martinez
Trumpet: Jimmy Smith, Eric Beaubien

— ☆ —

MANOU GALLO (SELECT TRACKS): 2018

This African funk bassist featured Bootsy Collins on her 2018 album.

Contre-Jour

Afro Groove Queen

"ABJ Groove"

Featuring: Bootsy Collins

"Leve-Toi Et Move"

Featuring: Bootsy Collins, Lene Norgaard Christensen, Sabine Kabongo

"Come Together"

Featuring: Blvck Seeds, Bootsy Collins, Chuck D

"Dalla"

Featuring: Bootsy Collins

— ☆ —

KALI UCHIS (SELECT TRACK): 2019

This Colombian American vocalist and multi–Grammy Award nominee had a single featuring Bootsy, Tyler the Creator, and others.

"After the Storm"

Lead Vocals: Kali Uchis, Tyler The Creator, Bootsy

— ☆ —

STARR CULLARS (SELECT TRACKS): 2019

Rock bassist Starr Cullars was in the P-Funk All Stars in the early 1990s. This album features Lige Curry on guitar.

Living Galaxy

"Red Alert"

Lead Vocals, Bass: Starr Cullars
Backup Vocals, Guitar: Lige Curry
Drums: Shawn Hill

"Never Was Lover"

Lead Vocals, Bass: Starr Cullars
Backup Vocals, Guitar: Lige Curry
Drums: Shawn Hill

"Harmony"

Lead Vocals: Starr Cullars
Backup Vocals, Guitar: Lige Curry
Bass: Starr Cullars, Lige Curry
Drums: Chuck Treece

"Starr Gazing"

Lead Vocals, Bass: Starr Cullars
Backup Vocals, Guitar: Lige Curry
Drums: Shawn Hill
Keyboards: Scott Garner

"Soul Mate"

Lead Vocals, Bass: Starr Cullars
Backup Vocals, Guitar: Lige Curry
Drums: Shawn Hill

"Tonight"

Lead Vocals, Bass: Starr Cullars
Backup Vocals: Lige Curry
Guitar: Lige Curry, Michael Hampton, Mike Tyler
Drums: Chuck Treece

"Emerging from the Galaxy"

Bass: Starr Cullars
Drums: Shawn Hill

"Let Your Star Shine"

Bass, Vocals: Starr Cullars
Guitars: Lige Curry
Drums: Sandro Feliciano

"I See the Freedom"

Bass, Vocals: Starr Cullars
Guitars: Lige Curry
Drums: Sandro Feliciano

"Amazon Warrior"

Bass, Vocals: Starr Cullars
Guitars, Vocals: Lige Curry
Drums: Sandro Feliciano

"I'll Kick Your Muthafunkin' Ass"

Bass: Starr Cullars
Guitars: Lige Curry
Drums: Shawn Hill
Vocals: Starr Cullars, Lige Curry

"Femme Fatale"

Bass, Vocals: Starr Cullars
Guitars: Lige Curry
Drums: Sandro Feliciano

"Seduce Me"

Bass, Vocals: Starr Cullars
Guitars: Lige Curry
Drums: Sandro Feliciano

"Revolution/Living Galaxy"

Bass, Vocals: Starr Cullars
Guitars: Lige Curry
Drums: Kattaway Kiss

"The Mirror"

Bass: Starr Cullars

"Diabolical Done"

Bass, Vocals: Starr Cullars
Guitars: Lige Curry
Drums: Kattaway Kiss

"I'm Still Standing"

Bass, Vocals: Starr Cullars
Guitars: Lige Curry
Drums: Frankie Kash Waddy

— ☆ —

SCOTTIE CLINTON: 2019–

This solo work is by P-Funk/3GP vocalist Scottie Clinton. Scottie is George Clinton's stepdaughter.

Scottie Clinton of P-Funk and 3GP. William Thoren

Singles

"12 Roses"

Vocals: Scottie Clinton
Track: Trazae Lewis-Clinton

"Breezy"

Vocals: Scottie Clinton
Track: Chris Severe

"Break Right NOW"

Vocals: Scottie Clinton
Track: Chris Severe

"Hit and Run"

Vocals: Scottie Clinton
Track: Chris Severe

"The Answer Is Love"

Vocals: Scottie Clinton
Track: Chris Severe

OCTAVEPUSSY (FTG. GEORGE CLINTON AND PARLIAMENT-FUNKADELIC) (SELECT TRACKS): 2019

This Dutch funk band features a dozen or so members of P-Funk.

"Straight from #1 Bimini Road"

Vocals: Clip Payne, Garrett Shider, Danny Bedrosian, Steven van Rijn, Ismael Johannis
Keyboards: Joris van Rijn
Drums: Patrick Jordens
Bass: Billy Nelson
Guitar: Michael Hampton
Sax: Greg Thomas
Trumpet: Bennie Cowan

"If the Funk Don't Fit"

Vocals: George Clinton, Mary Griffin, Garrett Shider, Steven van Rijn, Remy Britsemmer
Keyboards: Joris van Rijn
Drums: Patrick Jordens
Bass: Erwin Latuheru
Guitar: Joris van Rijn

"Unfunky UFO"

Vocals: Fred Wesley, Steven van Rijn, Erwin Latuheru, Ismael Johannis, Remy Britsemmer, Justine de Jong, Ebi van Slooten, Katell Chevalier
Keyboards, Guitar: Joris van Rijn
Drums: Patrick Jorden
Bass: Erwin Latuheru
Trombone: Fred Wesley

"My Profession Is Funk"

Vocals: Robert Peanut Johnson, Kim Manning, Gene Anderson, Remy Britsemmer, Steve Boyd, Erwin Latuheru, Jennifer Schuler
Keyboards: Joris van Rijn
Drums: Patrick Jordens
Bass: Erwin Latuheru
Guitar: Angelo Schifano, Joost Borgonjen
Sax: Jim Verschelden
Trumpet: Mark Mulder
Percussion: Femke Krone

"Let's Get Funky"

Vocals: George Clinton, Mudbone Cooper, Steven van Rijn
Keyboards: Joris van Rijn
Drums: Patrick Jordens
Guitar: Blackbyrd McKnight, Edwin Konings

"Come On with Yer Come On"

Vocals: Steven van Rijn, Remy Britsemmer, Justine de Jong, Erwin Latuheru, Travis Rolfes
Keyboards: Joris van Rijn
Drums: Patrick Jordens
Bass: Erwin Latuheru
Guitar: Michael Hampton
Sax: Greg Thomas

"Long Live the Funk"

Vocals: Kendra Foster, Steven van Rijn, Garrett Shider, Erwin Latuheru
Keyboards: Joris van Rijn
Drums: Patrick Jordens
Bass: Erwin Latuheru
Guitar: Erwin Latuheru, Jean-Paul Pino

"The Funkshipz Captain"

Vocals: George Clinton, Mudbone Cooper, Steven van Rijn, Garry Shider, Robert Peanut Johnson, Edwin Konings, Arno Konings, Yolanda Andriesen
Keyboards: Joel Johnson, Joris van Rijn
Drums: Patrick Jordens
Bass: Jan Sanda
Guitar: Michael Hampton, Edwin Konings
Sax: Greg Thomas

"Keep Your Head Up and Hold Your Head High"

Vocals: Ismael Johannis, Justine de Jong, Steven van Rijn, Erwin Latuheru, Travis Rolfes
Keyboards: Danny Bedrosian
Drums: Patrick Jordens
Bass: Lige Curry
Guitar: Ricky Rouse
Sax: Greg Thomas
Trumpet: Bennie Cowan

"Grooves from the Deep"

Keyboards: Joris van Rijn
Drums: Patrick Jordens
Bass: Billy Nelson
Guitar: Michael Hampton, Joris van Rijn

"Blackbyrdelic"

Keyboards: Joris van Rijn
Drums: Patrick Jordens
Guitar: Blackbyrd McKnight

— ☆ —

FSQ (FUNK STYLE QUALITY) (SELECT TRACKS): 2019

This group was founded by contributor Chuck Fishman and features George Clinton, Billy Nelson, and others.

"Reprise Tonight"

Original Mix by DJ Ayres
Lead Vocals: Denise King
Guitar: Neal Landauer
Bass Guitar: G Koop, Neal Landauer
Drum Programming, Keyboards: DJ Ayres, G Koop, Neal Landauer

"Vibe Out Now"

Lead Vocals: Sarah Finchum
Keyboards: Chuck Fishman
Albeton Programming: Loose Shus
Guitar, Bass, Keyboards, Drum Programming, Mix: G Koop

"Dancefloor Democracy"

Lead Vocals: Trey Lewd
Vocals: George Clinton
Bass Guitar: Billy Bass Nelson, One Era
Keyboards: Chuck Da Fonk Fishman, One Era, G Koop
Drum Programming: One Era, G Koop, Loose Shus

"The Infinite Reprise"

Drum Programming: Joe Caserta
Strings: Lauren Avery
Flutes, Baritone and Soprano Saxes: Lincoln
  Adler
Tuba, Sousaphone: Mike Rinta
Trumpet, Trombone: Dave Richards
Percussion: Scott Brian aka Reno

"Peel Back"

Lead Vocals: Nona Hendryx
Backup Vocals: Kiki Hawkins, Asa Arnold,
  Keith Fluitt, Darien Dollinger, Ramona
  Dunlap, Jack Fuller, Dave "D" Bellevue,
  Ashmy KI Bellevue
**Keyboards, Guitars, Drum Programming,
  Bass:** G Koop
Piano, Keyboards: Graham Richards
Keyboards, Programming: Chuck Fishman
Additional Drums: Neal Landauer

"What They Don't Know"

Lead Vocals: Dolette McDonald
**Keyboards, Guitar, Drums, Drum
  Programming:** One Era
Keyboards, Guitar, Drum Programming:
  Chuck Da Fonk Fishman, Michael the Lion
Bass: Rodney Curtis

"11:00 A.M."

Lead Vocals: Fonda Rae
Keyboards, Guitar, Drum Programming:
  Chas Bronz
Keyboards: Chuck Da Fonk Fishman
Guitar, Bass: Billy Bass Nelson
Drums, Percussion: Andrew Marsh

"Reprise Tonight Disco Remix"

**Bass, Guitar, Keyboards, Drum
  Programming:** G Koop
Sax: Lincoln Adler

— ☆ —

MISS VELVET AND THE BLUE WOLF (SELECT TRACK): 2019

This New York City–based funk rock band opened up for George Clinton and Parliament-Funkadelic live heavily from 2019 to the present and after several personnel shake-ups is currently known as Blue Eye Extinction.

Feed the Wolf

"Phat Blunt"

Lead Vocals: Miss Velvet, George Clinton
Drums: Nick Carbone
Bass: James Jones
Guitar: Henry Ott
Trumpet: John Williams
Trombone: Timothy Robinson
Keyboards: Constance Hauman

SMUDGE ALL-STARS (SELECT TRACKS): 2019

This new funk group features appearances from George Clinton, Fred Wesley, Pee Wee Ellis, and more.

"Up Is Just a Place to Come Down From"

Featuring: George Clinton
Vocals: Mary Pearce?, others

"Headache"

Featuring: George Clinton
Vocals: Mary Pearce?, others

— ☆ —

BABY SWEET (SELECT TRACKS): 2019

Atlanta-based rapper Baby Sweet had a few songs and skits featuring George Clinton, Kool Ace, and more.

Stack 'em Entertainment

Geeked Up Album Hosted by Fabo

"Congo"
Featuring: Baby Sweet, George Clinton, Kool Ace, Skinny Pimp

"My Pockets Stay Full"
Featuring: Baby Sweet, George Clinton

"Crack Pipes (Skit)"
Featuring: George Clinton

GEORGE CLINTON AND PARLIAMENT-FUNKADELIC FTG. MARY J. BLIGE AND ANDERSON .PAAK: 2020

RCA Records

Trolls World Tour Soundtrack

"Atomic Dog (Dogs of the World Unite Remix)"
Drums: Anderson .Paak, Mudbone Cooper, Dennis Chambers, Zachary Frazier
Synth Bass, Keyboards, Synthesizers: David Spradley, Danny Bedrosian
Lead Vocals: George Clinton, Anderson .Paak, Mary J. Blige

Backup Vocals: Patavian Lewis, Tonysha Nelson, Brandi Scott, Gary Mudbone Cooper, Garry Shider, Eddie Hazel, Mallia Franklin, Michael Clip Payne, Robert Peanut Johnson, Sheila Horne, Ron Ford

YOUNG POPPI: 2020–

These are solo outings for rapper and George Clinton's grandson Young Poppi.

Singles

"Savage Girl"
Vocals: Young Poppi
Guitar: Benjamin LePage
Track: TeShawn

"Bad Luck"
Vocals: Young Poppi

"Hoodie"
Vocals: Young Poppi
Track: Trazae Lewis-Clinton

Blood of a Legend 2

"Trap Today"
Vocals: Young Poppi

"Hope"
Vocals: Young Poppi

"Haters around Me"
Vocals: Young Poppi
Track: TeShawn

"Life"
Vocals: Young Poppi

"Star Power"

Vocals: Young Poppi, Trazae Lewis-Clinton

"Skin Hair"

Vocals: Young Poppi, Trazae Lewis-Clinton,
Patavian Lewis

"Get Money"

Vocals: Young Poppi

"Hands Up"

Vocals: Young Poppi
Track: Trazae Lewis-Clinton

"Daydreams"

Vocals: Young Poppi

"Wassup"

Vocals: Young Poppi

"Ok"

Vocals: Young Poppi, Trazae Lewis-Clinton,
Tonysha Nelson, Patavian Lewis
Track: Kool Ace

New Jersey Drive

"Yea"

Vocals: Young Poppi
Track: Vando

"Average"

Vocals: Young Poppi, Ivan X

"280"

Vocals: Young Poppi, Pvso Paid

"2 Eyes"

Vocals: Young Poppi
Track: Vando

"Save Me"

Vocals: Young Poppi

Singles

"Downtime"

Vocals: Young Poppi
Track: Jupiter

"Occasional Friends"

Vocals: Young Poppi, Lil Goat
Track: Matrix

Preeminent

"Survival of the Fittest"

"Black Mayo"

"Best Behavior (Ftg. Thirteen)"

"Turn Up King"

"Pornstart (Ftg. WorldWideMaro)"

"What You Know about It (Ftg. Trazae)"

"Live from the Bottom
(Ftg. Kandy Apple Redd)"

"Compatable"

"Got It One Me"

"Loyalty (Ftg. Dakoda Rollins)"

All lead vocals and lyrics: LuShawn Clinton
Jr,, aka Young Poppi

— ☆ —

THURTEEN: 2020–

These are solo works from P-Funk/3GP
vocalist Thurteen.

"Knock Em Out the Box"

Vocals, Track: Thurteen

P-Funk and 3GP Vocalist/Contributor Thurteen.
William Thoren

"Stars & Stripes"
Vocals, Track: Thurteen

— ☆ —

TRAZAE LEWIS-CLINTON: 2020–

These are solo works from George Clinton's grandson and P-Funk contributor Trazae Lewis-Clinton (tenure: 2010–2020).

Single

"Play Too Much"
Vocals, Track: Trazae Lewis-Clinton

Single

"Trazzberry"
All Vocals: Trazae Lewis-Clinton
Production: Tikki Tavi

Influenced

"Yo Body"
Vocals, Track: Trazae Lewis-Clinton

"Squat It (And Pop It)"
Vocals, Track: Trazae Lewis-Clinton

"Share Wit Yo Friends"
Vocals, Track: Trazae Lewis-Clinton

"Reverse"
Vocals, Track: Trazae Lewis-Clinton

"Bad Words"
Vocals, Track: Trazae Lewis-Clinton

"Wassup Tho"
Vocals, Track: Trazae Lewis-Clinton

"Need Me"
Vocals, Track: Trazae Lewis-Clinton

"Funny Feelings"
Vocals, Track: Trazae Lewis-Clinton

"The Most"
Vocals, Track: Trazae Lewis-Clinton
Guitar: Stevie Pannell

West Dat Smell

"Walk Wit Me"
Vocals, Track: Trazae Lewis-Clinton

"ADD"

Vocals, Track: Trazae Lewis-Clinton
Keyboards, Synthesizers: Danny Bedrosian
Guitar: Ishan Cooper

"Da Guy"

Vocals, Track: Trazae Lewis-Clinton

"On My Block"

Vocals, Track: Trazae Lewis-Clinton

"Zae Area"

Vocals, Track: Trazae Lewis-Clinton

"Bad Bitch Goodies"

Vocals, Track: Trazae Lewis-Clinton
Guitar: Brad Foutch
Vocals: Cleome Bova

"Playas Ball"

Vocals: Trazae Lewis-Clinton
Track: Jamial White

"Yayzer"

Vocals: Trazae Lewis-Clinton, Jenna Gaines, Saquarius Gomez
Track: Trazae Lewis-Clinton

"Tonight Is the Night"

Vocals, Track: Trazae Lewis-Clinton
Vibe: Tat

Trazombipulation

"Lolly Pop Man"

Vocals, Track: Trazae Lewis-Clinton
Drums: Sample Some of Disc Drums

"On the One"

Vocals: Trazae Lewis-Clinton, Hazel Lewis
Track: Trazae Lewis-Clinton

"Tra'zombipulation"

Vocals, Track: Trazae Lewis-Clinton

"Disco"

Vocals: Trazae Lewis-Clinton, Garrett Shider
Track: Trazae Lewis-Clinton
Piano, Synthesizer: Danny Bedrosian

"The Girl Is Bad"

Vocals: Trazae Lewis-Clinton, Keith Smith, Thirteen, Brandy Ogden and family
Track, Guitar: Trazae Lewis-Clinton

"Together"

Vocals: Trazae Lewis-Clinton, Alana, George Clinton, Steve Boyd, Garrett Shider
Drum Stem Arrangements: G-Koop Rob Mandell
Bass: Doug Wimbush
Synthesizers: Danny Bedrosian
Rhodes: O-Man

"Just Do It"

Vocals, Drum Track, Keyboards: Trazae Lewis-Clinton

Sample of *Hydraulic Pump*

"Soul Tra'zae"

Vocals: Trazae Lewis-Clinton, Margaret Atayants, Brandi Scott
Track: Trazae Lewis-Clinton
Guitar: Ishan Cooper

"Testifly"

Vocals: Trazae Lewis-Clinton, Garrett Shider
Track: Sample of Testify
Drum Track, Synth Bass: Trazae Lewis-Clinton

Electra'Zonic Parts I and II

"Play"

"Tennis Racket"

"Hour Child"

"Teledrone"

"Trobot"

"Galaxy"

"Gelectra'zonic"

"Grunk"

"Witches Brew"

"Wendy"

All Vocals and Instruments: Tracey Lewis-Clinton

Time 4 U

"Give It to You"

Vocals, Production: Tracey Lewis-Clinton
Drums, Pads: Cymatics

"Honeyz"

Vocals, Production: Tracey Lewis-Clinton
Vocals: Big ScuD

"Changed My Life"

Vocals, Production: Tracey Lewis-Clinton

"Tell Me"

Vocals, Production: Tracey Lewis-Clinton

"Origins"

Vocals, Production: Tracey Lewis-Clinton
Vocals: Steve Boyd

"Rub You Down"

Vocals, Production: Tracey Lewis-Clinton
Vocals: Flo

"Angelz"

Vocals, Production: Tracey Lewis-Clinton
Vocals: Big ScuD, Balance

"Had To"

Vocals, Production: Tracey Lewis-Clinton
Vocals: Bouvier Richardson

"When I See You"

Vocals, Production: Tracey Lewis-Clinton

Junie Bug

"Bernie's Bus Start Intro"

Vocals, Production: Tracey Lewis-Clinton

"Funk Within"

Vocals, Drums, Synthesizers, Organs: Tracey Lewis-Clinton
Vocals, Guitar: Garrett Shider

"Junie Bug"

Vocals, Drums, Bass Synth, Synthesizers: Tracey Lewis-Clinton
Guitars: Ishan Cooper, Benjamin LePage

"Nice 2 Funk"

Vocals, Pianos, Synthesizers: Tracey Lewis-Clinton
Vocals: Brandi Scott
Guitar: Brad Fouch

"Funk Bus"

Vocals, Drums, Piano, Synthesizers, Guitar: Tracey Lewis-Clinton
Bass: Indigo
Guitar: Benjamin LePage

"On the 1 (interlude)"

Synthesizers, Strings, Organ: Tracey Lewis-Clinton

"Wellington Wigout"

Vocals, Drum Loop, Synthesizers, Piano, Organ: Tracey Lewis-Clinton
Guitar: Stevie Parnell, Benjamin LePage

"Hit Me Band"

Vocals, Drums, Organs, Synthesizers: Tracey Lewis-Clinton
Vocals: Margaret Atayants, Cleome Bova
Bass: Chaz, Indigo

"Bernie's Bus Stop"

Vocals, Drums, Guitars, Synthesizers: Tracey Lewis-Clinton
Flute: Tristano
Guitars: Henry Ott

"Bernie's Journey"

Vocals, Synthesizers, Drums: Tracey Lewis-Clinton
Vocals, Synthesizers: Danny Bedrosian
Vocals: Scottie Clinton

Just Like Dat

"Just Like Dat"

Vocals, Drums, Synthesizers: Tracey Lewis-Clinton
Guitar: Stevie Parnell

"Bridge boy"

Vocals, Drums, Synthesizers, Strings: Tracey Lewis-Clinton

"White Russian"

Vocals, Drums, Piano, Strings, Synthesizers: Tracey Lewis-Clinton
Vocals: Tanganyika

"Foolieyo"

Vocals, Drums, Synthesizers: Tracey Lewis-Clinton
Vocals: 81 Soundz

"Eye Rub"

Vocals, Drums, Piano, Synthesizers: Tracey Lewis-Clinton

"Hella Talk"

Vocals, Drums, Synthesizers: Tracey Lewis-Clinton
Vocals: Bouvier Richardson, Frank Nobil

"To Each"

Vocals, Drums, Piano, Synthesizers: Tracey Lewis-Clinton
Vocals: Big ScuD

"EBT"

Vocals, Drums: Tracey Lewis-Clinton
Piano: Cymatics
New Califlorida
Vocals, Drums: Tracey Lewis-Clinton
Strings: Jay'anna Lewis-Clinton
Sample: Jamial White
Vocals: Young Poppi, Big ScuD

Single

"No Joke"

All Instruments and Vocals: Tracey Lewis-Clinton

Black Father

"My Fault"

"Black Father"

"Dear Baby"

"Keep Going"

"City Life"

All Songs, Instruments, and Vocals: Tracey
 Lewis-Clinton

N.E.W.S.

"Gangsta Trap"

"N.E.W.S."

"Bang Bang (Sheeit Cheauh)"

"Cowded"

All Songs, Instruments, and Vocals: Tracey
 Lewis-Clinton

Cous Cous: The Collection

"Cous Cous"

"Bumpy"

"Howl Eye Phil"

"Ripplez"

"Wizdumb"

All Songs, Instruments, and Vocals: Tracey
 Lewis-Clinton

Singles

"No Slack"

All Instruments and Vocals: Tracey
 Lewis-Clinton

Single

"Get Rich"

All Instruments and Vocals: Tracey
 Lewis-Clinton

"Burkin Boy"

All Instruments and Vocals: Tracey
 Lewis-Clinton

"Basco"

All Instruments and Vocals: Tracey
 Lewis-Clinton

"Backboardz"

All Instruments and Vocals: Tracey
 Lewis-Clinton

Wild Child

"Sand Castle"

"Elephunk"

"Hot Air Balloon"

"Fuzzy Feather"

"Funk U 4RM Da Bak"

"Akward Oasis"

"Zap Me Up"

"Sunset Safari"

All Instruments and Vocals: Tracey
 Lewis-Clinton

"N2U"

"I Just Wanna"

"Up on Me"

"Right for You"

"Speechless"

"No Smoke"

"Signals"

"Vibrations"

"Desires"

All Instruments and Vocals: Tracey
Lewis-Clinton

"9D2"

"Party Hard (Hosted by Kasino)"

"Pamona"

"Sandbox"

"So Icy"

"Rain Man (Hosted by Kasino)"

"Death on Skid Row"

"2 Braidz"

"Get High (Hosted by Kasino)"

"Downtown"

All Songs, Instruments, and Vocals: Tracey
Lewis-Clinton (except where noted)

Singles

"You're the Only One I Trust"

All Vocals and Production: Tracey
Lewis-Clinton

"Snoopin'"

All Vocals and Production: Tracey
Lewis-Clinton

— ☆ —

BUSTY AND THE BASS (SELECT TRACK): 2020

Busty and the Bass put out this very "Bootsy-esque" track with George Clinton in 2020. This album was executive produced by Earth, Wind & Fire bassist Verdine White.

Eddie

"Baggy Eyed Dopeman"

Music, Vocals: Busty and the Bass
Featuring: George Clinton

SILKSONIC (SELECT TRACKS): 2021

This funk throwback supergroup, founded by modern music superstars Bruno Mars and Anderson .Paak, features Bootsy Collins and many more. Only songs featuring Collins are featured below.

Aftermath Entertainment

An Evening with Silk Sonic

"Silk Sonic Intro"

Alto Sax: Kirk Smothers
Backup Vocals, Bass, Organ, Piano, Keyboards: D'Mile
Drums: Anderson .Paak
Guitar: Bruno Mars, D'Mile, Ella Feingold
Trombone: Kameron Whalum
Trumpet: Marc Franklin
Vocals: Anderson .Paak, Bootsy Collins, Bruno Mars, James King, Kameron Whalum

"After Last Night"

Bass: Thundercat
Cabasa: Alex Resoagli
Cello: Glenn Fischbach
Drums: Anderson .Paak
Flute: Ron Kerber
Guitar: Ella Feingold, Bruno Mars (solo), D'Mile
Piano: D'Mile
Percussion: Charles Moniz, Jeremy Reeves
Viola: Jonathan Kim, Yoshihiko Nakano
Violin: Blake Espy, Chris Jusell, Emma Kummrow, Luigi Mazzocchi, Natasha Colkett, Tess, Varley
Vocals: Anderson .Paak, Bootsy Collins, Bruno Mars, Thundercat, Krystal Miles

"Smokin' Out the Window"

Alto and Baritone Saxes: Kirk Smothers
Bass, Piano: D'Mile
Cello: Glenn Fischbach
Drums: Homer Steinweiss
Guitar, Percussion: Bruno Mars
Tenor Sax: Lannie McMillan
Trombone: Kameron Whalum
Trumpet: Marc Franklin
Vibraphone: Ella Feingold
Viola: Jonathan Kim, Yashihiko Nakano
Violin: Blake Espy, Chris Jussell, Emma Kummrow, Luigi Mazzocchi, Natasha Colkett, Tess Varley
Vocals: Anderson .Paak, Bootsy Collins, Bruno Mars

"Put On a Smile"

Alto Sax: Kirk Smothers
Backup Vocals: Babyface
Backup Vocals, Bass, Piano: D'Mile
Cello: Glenn Fischbach
Drums: Anderson .Paak
Guitar: Bruno Mars
Percussion: Bruno Mars, D'Mile
Tenor Sax: Lannie McMillan
Trombone: Kamerson Whalum

Trumpet: Marc Franklin
Viola: Jonathan Kim, Yashihiko Nakano
Violin: Blake Espy, Chris Jussell, Emma Kummrow, Luigi Mazzocchi, Natasha Colkett, Tess Varley
Vocals: Anderson .Paak, Bootsy Collins, Bruno Mars

— ☆ —

DAFONK/BONE MAGNET: 2021

This features Greg Boyer and others.

"Bone Magnet"

Bass, Guitars, Drum Programming, Keyboards, Synthesizers: DaFonk
Keyboards, Synthesizers: Jay Murphy
Sax: Eric Rohner
Trumpet: Gilles Garin
Trombone: Greg Boyer

— ☆ —

P-UNION (SELECT TRACKS): 2021

This West Coast P-Funk band features Binky Womack, Treylewd, Donnie Sterling, and others.

"P-Funk City"

Featuring: George Clinton, Binky Womack, Chris Parker, Uncle Funk, Treylewd, Donnie Sterling, Lady Z, Lisa Love Omega, Donnie Sterling, Mark Payne, Mustafa Womack, Stonetone the Clone

"Party Me Up"

Featuring: George Clinton, Binky Womack, Chris Parker, Uncle Funk, Treylewd, Donnie Sterling, Lady Z, Lisa Love Omega, Donnie Sterling, Mark Payne, Mustafa Womack, Stonetone the Clone

ARTISTS STARTING IN 2022-2023

BLK ODYSSY (SELECT TRACK): 2022

This new hip-hop from BLK Odyssy features George Clinton.

BLK Vintage: The Reprise

"Benny's Got a Gun"

Vocals: BLK Odyssy, featuring Benny the Butcher and George Clinton

— ☆ —

TONYSHA NELSON: 2022

This solo album is by P-Funk vocalist and George Clinton's granddaughter Tonysha Nelson (joined 2014).

Gemini Vibes

"On Love"

Vocals: Tonysha Nelson
Production: Ricky Tan
Backup Vocals: Ebony

"Midnight"

Vocals: Tonysha Nelson
Production: Roc (Adrian Brunson)
Backup Vocals: Ebony

"Go Up"

Vocals: Tonysha Nelson
Production: Demetrius Walter, Bakari Hines

"Compatible"

Vocals: Tonysha Nelson
Backup Vocals: Ebony
Production: Roc (Adrian Brunson)

"Black Hole"

Vocals: Tonysha Nelson
Production: Trazae Lewis-Clinton

"Come To Me"

Vocals: Tonysha Nelson
Backup Vocals: Ebony
Production: Ricky Tan

— ☆ —

CIMA FUNK (SELECT TRACK): 2022

Cuban funker Cima Funk had a successful breakout album featuring George Clinton and others.

Terapia Productions

El Alimento

"Funk Aspirin"

Vocals: George Clinton, Adriana Pimienta Quinones
Bass, Drum Programming, Percussion, Organ, Moog, Backup Vocals: Jack Splash
Guitars: Hector Quintana, Raul nibal Venegas
Bass: Bejuco, Dr. Zapa
Percussion: Adel Gonzalez
Piano, Keyboards: Juan Marcos Rodriguez Faedo, Andy Garcia
Trombone: Charlie Gonzalez

— ☆ —

KLAK (DANNY BEDROSIAN AND TRAZAE LEWIS-CLINTON): 2022

These songs were produced by Trazae Lewis-Clinton and Danny Bedrosian and feature George Clinton and a dozen members of P-Funk.

"Klak (intro)"

All Instruments and Vocals: Danny Bedrosian
Do This
Lead Vocals: George Clinton, Young Poppi, Trazae Lewis-Clinton, Garrett Shider, Thirteen

Backup Vocals: Michael Clip Payne, Danny Bedrosian, Trazae Lewis-Clinton, Thirteen, Garrett Shider
Piano, Synthesizer Poly Leads, Faux String Instrument, Synth Bass 1: Danny Bedrosian
Drum Programming, Synth Bass 2, Synthesizer: Trazae Lewis-Clinton

"Shavesharan"

All Vocals: Danny Bedrosian
Drum Programming, Synthesizers, Pads, Sounds: Trazae Lewis-Clinton
Synth Bass, Synth Lead, Other Synthesizers: Danny Bedrosian

"This Club (Klak Mix)"

Vocals: Patavian Lewis, Tonysha Nelson
Drum Programming: Trazae Lewis-Clinton
Synth Bass, Synthesizers: Danny Bedrosian

"Next to You"

Lead Vocals: Pvso Paid, Young Poppi
Backup Vocals: Trazae Lewis-Clinton, Gary Mudbone Cooper, Scottie Clinton
Organ, Piano, Electric Piano, Synth Bass, Melodica: Danny Bedrosian
Drum Programming, Keyboards: Trazae Lewis-Clinton

"Watch Out! (Superbad)"

All Vocals: Danny Bedrosian
Drum Programming, Faux Guitar, Faux Horns: Trazae Lewis-Clinton
Synth Bass, Synthesizer Leads, Clavinet, Piano: Danny Bedrosian

"Backwoods (Klak Mix)"

All Vocals: Trazae Lewis-Clinton
All Instruments: Danny Bedrosian

"One Wish"

Vocals: Trazae Lewis-Clinton, Danny
  Bedrosian, Young Poppi
**Electric Piano, Synth Bass, Strings, Other
  Keyboards:** Danny Bedrosian
Drum Programming: Trazae Lewis-Clinton

— ☆ —

420 FUNK MOB: 2023

This P-Funk alumni band is performing mostly
live and focuses largely on unperformed or
underperformed P-Funk cult classics as well
as some newer material. It features many
past and present P-Funk members and is led
by Michael Clip Payne, who has the longest
tenure of any P-Funk band member, past or
present, other than George Clinton.

WeFunk Records

Single

"Flirt"

Vocals: George Clinton, Michael Clip Payne,
  Lige Curry, Garry Shider, Garrett Shider,
  Iwan Traeger-Payne
Drums: Zachary Alford
Bass: Lige Curry
Keyboards, Synthesizers: Danny Bedrosian,
  Michael Clip Payne
Guitars: Michael Hampton, Ted Orr

— ☆ —

MONONEON (SELECT TRACK): 2023

Former Prince bassist MonoNeon struck out
on his own with an extremely unique style
and a series of collaborations with, among
others, George Clinton and members of
P-Funk.

Single

"Quilted!"

Vocals, Bass: MonoNeon
Vocals: George Clinton
Drum Programming, Keyboards: Davy
  Nathan

*MonoNeon jamming live with George Clinton and
P-Funk.* Mikiodo

LIVE RELEASES

The live albums associated with P-Funk have been put into their own section. Rather than listing song by song, these releases, with some exceptions, have been listed concert by concert, with the full live personnel at that particular show listed. And rather than doing every bootlegged live album from every iteration and side project, mainly the essential core P-Funk groups are listed here for their commercially released live concert albums, with the exception of groups who have only live albums; those were included here as well with some exceptions. These are all live albums that were professionally packaged and sold, not including bootlegs and independent pressings. The following albums are listed alphabetically and then chronologically by band or artist.

STEVE BOYD

Live in Austin, Texas, 2015

Vocals: Steve Boyd, Paul Hill, Michael Clip Payne, Kendra Foster, Lige Curry, George Clinton, Danny Bedrosian
Drums: Rico Lewis
Bass: Lige Curry
Keyboards: Danny Bedrosian
Guitar: Michael Hampton
Trumpet: Bennie Cowan
Sax: Greg Thomas

BRIDES OF FUNKENSTEIN

Live, 1979

Vocals: Lynn Mabry, Dawn Silva
Drums: Frankie Kash Waddy
Bass: Jeff Cherokee Bunn
Guitar: Dewayne Blackbyrd McKnight
Keyboards: Joel Johnson
Trumpet/MD: Richard Kush Griffith
Trumpet: Rick Gardner
Sax: Maceo Parker
Trombone: Fred Wesley
Comedian: James Wesley Jackson

GEORGE CLINTON

The Mothership Connection, 1976

Vocals: George Clinton, Calvin Simon, Fuzzy Haskins, Ray Davis, Grady Thomas, Garry Shider, Glenn Goins, Debbie Wright, Jeanette Washington, Gary Mudbone Cooper
Drums, Percussion: Jerome Brailey
Bass: Cordell Mosson
Keyboards, Synthesizers: Bernie Worrell
Guitar: Michael Hampton, Garry Shider, Glenn Goins
Trumpet: Richard Griffith, Rick Gardner
Congas: Calvin Simon
Guest Vocals, Percussion (Encore): Bootsy Collins, Gary Mudbone Cooper, Robert Peanut Johnson, Sly Stone, Dawn Silva, Lynn Mabry

GEORGE CLINTON AND PARLIAMENT-FUNKADELIC

Mothership Connection Newberg Sessions

1976 (released in 1995) P-Vine Records
All songs:
Vocals: George Clinton, Calvin Simon, Fuzzy Haskins, Ray Davis Grady Thomas, Garry Shider, Glenn Goins, Debbie Wright, Jeanette Washington
Keyboards & Synthesizers: Bernie Worrell
Bass: Cordell Mosson
Guitar: Michael Hampton, Garry Shider, Glenn Goins
Trumpet: Richard Kush Griffith, Rick Gardner
Saxophone: Maceo Parker
Trombone: Fred Wesley
Drums: Jerome Brailey

The State Theater, Portland, Maine, 2004

Vocals: George Clinton, Garry Shider, Steve Boyd, RonKat Spearman, Poo Poo Man, Cordell Mosson, Greg Thomas, Shonda Clinton, Kendra Foster, Kim Manning, Jerome Rodgers, Paul Hill, Michael Clip Payne, Robert Peanut Johnson
Drums: Frankie Kash Waddy, Rico Lewis
Bass: Billy Nelson, RonKat Spearman
Guitar: Garry Shider, Michael Hampton, Blackbyrd McKnight, Cordell Mosson, Billy Nelson, Citrus
Keyboards: Bernie Worrell, Jerome Rodgers, Danny Bedrosian
Trumpet: Bennie Cowan
Sax: Greg Thomas

Music Midtown Festival, 2004

Vocals: George Clinton, Garry Shider, Steve Boyd, RonKat Spearman, Poo Poo Man, Cordell Mosson, Greg Thomas, Shonda Clinton, Kendra Foster, Kim Manning, Jerome Rodgers, Paul Hill, Michael Clip Payne, Robert Peanut Johnson
Drums: Frankie Kash Waddy, Rico Lewis
Bass: Billy Nelson, RonKat Spearman
Guitar: Garry Shider, Michael Hampton, Blackbyrd McKnight, Cordell Mosson, Billy Nelson, Citrus
Keyboards: Bernie Worrell, Jerome Rodgers, Danny Bedrosian
Trumpet: Bennie Cowan
Sax: Greg Thomas

P-Funk guitarist Kevin Oliver, P-Funk and American Idol *vocalist Uche, and ringleader George Clinton.* Mikiodo

Coming to Funktify Your Soul, Sweden, 2004

Vocals: George Clinton, Steve Boyd, RonKat Spearman, Poo Poo Man, Greg Thomas, Shonda Clinton, Kendra Foster, Kim Manning, Michael Clip Payne, Robert Peanut Johnson
Drums: Frankie Kash Waddy, Rico Lewis
Bass: Billy Nelson, RonKat Spearman
Guitar: Michael Hampton, Blackbyrd McKnight, Billy Nelson, Citrus
Keyboards: Bernie Worrell, Danny Bedrosian
Trumpet: Bennie Cowan
Sax: Greg Thomas
Violin: Lili Haydn

Live at Montreux, 2004

Vocals: George Clinton, Steve Boyd, RonKat Spearman, Poo Poo Man, Greg Thomas, Shonda Clinton, Kendra Foster, Kim Manning, Michael Clip Payne, Robert Peanut Johnson
Drums: Frankie Kash Waddy, Rico Lewis
Bass: Billy Nelson, RonKat Spearman
Guitar: Michael Hampton, Blackbyrd McKnight, Billy Nelson, Citrus
Keyboards: Bernie Worrell, Danny Bedrosian
Trumpet: Bennie Cowan
Sax: Greg Thomas
Violin: Lili Haydn

George Clinton and Parliament-Funkadelic live during the finale of a concert, when audience members are invited onstage with the band. William Thoren

Live at the Billboard Live, 2013, Tokyo

Vocals: George Clinton, Steve Boyd, Greg Thomas, Shonda Clinton, Kendra Foster, Kim Manning, Michael Clip Payne, Danny Bedrosian, Garrett Shider, Paul Hill, Michael Hampton, Mary Griffin

Drums: Foley

Bass: Lige Curry

Guitar: Michael Hampton, Rickey Rouse, Garrett Shider

Keyboards: Danny Bedrosian, Jerome Rodgers

Trumpet: Bennie Cowan

Sax: Greg Thomas

Chocolate City Live at Metropolis, London, 2014

Vocals: George Clinton, Steve Boyd, Greg Thomas, Lige Curry, Kendra Foster, Michael Clip Payne, Danny Bedrosian, Garrett Shider, Mary Griffin, Joss Stone

Drums: Benjamin Cowan, Foley

Bass: Lige Curry

Guitar: Michael Hampton, Rickey Rouse, Garrett Shider

Keyboards: Danny Bedrosian

Trumpet: Bennie Cowan

Sax: Greg Thomas

GEORGE CLINTON AND THE P-FUNK ALL STARS

Funk Um Again . . . For the First Time: Live in LA, 1989

Vocals: George Clinton, Gary Mudbone Cooper, Greg Boyer, Lige Curry, Eddie Hazel, Robert Peanut Johnson, Tracey Lewis, Blackbyrd McKnight, Cordell Mosson, Michael Clip Payne, Garry Shider, Greg Thomas, Robert Wilson

Drums: Tony Thomas

Bass: Rodney Curtis, Lige Curry

Keyboards: Amp Fiddler, David Spradley

Guitar: Michael Hampton, Eddie Hazel, Blackbyrd McKnight, Cordell Mosson, Garry Shider

Trumpet: Bennie Cowan

Sax: Greg Thomas

Trombone: Greg Boyer

Percussion: Leland Zales

Live from Atlanta's House of Blues, 1996

Vocals: George Clinton, Garry Shider, Grady Thomas, Robert Peanut Johnson, Michael Clip Payne, Lige Curry, Mallia Franklin, Dawn Silva, Belita Woods, Sheila Horne, Steve Boyd, Paul Hill, Kyle Jason, Louie Kabbabie, Silk, Andre Williams

Drums: Frankie Kash Waddy

Bass: Rodney Curtis, Lige Curry

Guitar: Michael Hampton, Blackbyrd McKnight, Garry Shider, Billy Nelson, Cordell Mosson, Andre Williams

Keyboards: Amp Fiddler

Man in the Box (Keyboards): Clip Payne, Ron Wright, Billy Nelson

George Clinton and Parliament-Funkadelic. Mikiodo

George Clinton and P-Funk. L–R: Greg Boyer, Danny Bedrosian, Greg Thomas, Kevin Oliver, Bennie Cowan, Thurteen, Tonysha Nelson, George Clinton, Young Poppi, Benjamin "Benzel" Cowan, Pvso Paid, Scottie Clinton, Tracey "Treylewd" Lewis, Uche, Michael "Clip" Payne, Garrett Shider, and Lige Curry. Mikiodo

GEORGE CLINTON AND THE P-FUNK ALL STARS

Live in France, 2005

Vocals: George Clinton, Garry Shider, Steve Boyd, RonKat Spearman, Poo Poo Man, Greg Thomas, Shonda Clinton, Kendra Foster, Kim Manning, Michael Clip Payne, Robert Peanut Johnson
Drums: Frankie Kash Waddy, Rico Lewis
Bass: Lige Curry, RonKat Spearman
Guitar: Michael Hampton, Garry Shider, Blackbyrd McKnight, Billy Nelson, Citrus
Keyboards: Bernie Worrell, Jerome Rodgers, Danny Bedrosian
Trumpet: Bennie Cowan
Sax: Greg Thomas
Violin: Lìli Haydn

HyBurn Shwagstock, 2005

Vocals: George Clinton, Garry Shider, Steve Boyd, RonKat Spearman, Poo Poo Man, Greg Thomas, Shonda Clinton, Kendra Foster, Kim Manning, Michael Clip Payne, Robert Peanut Johnson
Drums: Frankie Kash Waddy, Rico Lewis
Bass: Lige Curry, RonKat Spearman
Guitar: Michael Hampton, Garry Shider, Blackbyrd McKnight, Billy Nelson, Citrus
Keyboards: Bernie Worrell, Jerome Rodgers, Danny Bedrosian
Trumpet: Bennie Cowan
Sax: Greg Thomas

HyBurn Long Beach, 2005

Vocals: George Clinton, Garry Shider, Steve Boyd, RonKat Spearman, Poo Poo Man, Greg Thomas, Shonda Clinton, Kendra Foster, Kim Manning, Michael Clip Payne, Robert Peanut Johnson
Drums: Frankie Kash Waddy, Rico Lewis
Bass: Lige Curry, RonKat Spearman
Guitar: Michael Hampton, Garry Shider, Blackbyrd McKnight, Billy Nelson, Citrus
Keyboards: Bernie Worrell, Jerome Rodgers, Danny Bedrosian
Trumpet: Bennie Cowan
Sax: Greg Thomas
Violin: Lili Haydn

BOOTSY'S RUBBER BAND

Live in Oklahoma, 1976

Vocals: Bootsy Collins, Gary Mudbone Cooper, Robert Peanut Johnson, Maceo Parker
Drums: Frankie Kash Waddy
Bass: Bootsy Collins
Guitar: Catfish Collins
Keyboards: Joel Johnson
Sax, Flute: Maceo Parker
Trumpet: Richard Griffith, Rick Gardner
Trombone: Fred Wesley

Live in Louisville, 1978

Vocals: Bootsy Collins, Gary Mudbone Cooper, Robert Peanut Johnson, Maceo Parker
Drums: Frankie Kash Waddy
Bass: Bootsy Collins
Guitar: Catfish Collins
Keyboards: Joel Johnson
Sax, Flute: Maceo Parker
Trumpet: Richard Griffith, Rick Gardner

BOOTSY COLLINS AND BOOTSY'S NEW RUBBER BAND

Keepin' the Funk Alive 4, 1995

Vocals: Bootsy Collins, Gary Mudbone Cooper, Henry Benifield, Michael Gaitheright
Drums: Frankie Kash Waddy
Lead Guitar: Gary James
Rhythm Guitar: Flip Cornett, Bootsy Collins
Bass: Bootsy Collins, Flip Cornett
Keyboards: Bernie Worrell, Joel Johnson, Gregg Fitz
Horns: Vince Calloway, Reggie Calloway, Larry Hatcher, Don Bynum, Rick Gardner

FUNKADELIC

Live at Meadowbrook, 1971

Vocals: George Clinton, Fuzzy Haskins, Calvin Simon, Ray Davis, Grady Thomas, Billy Nelson, Eddie Hazel, James Wesley Jackson
Drums: Tyrone Lampkin
Bass: Billy Nelson
Guitar: Eddie Hazel, Harold Beane
Keyboards: Bernie Worrell
Percussion: Ray Davis, Grady Thomas, Fuzzy Haskins, Calvin Simon

420 FUNK MOB

420 FM Live on the Off Days, 2002

Balance, Still Tight, Naked, Maggot Brain
Vocals: Clip Payne, Lige Curry, Gregg Fitz
Drums: Gabe Gonzalez
Bass: Lige Curry
Guitar: Michael Hampton, Billy Nelson, The Flash
Keyboards: Gregg Fitz, Ron Stozo Edwards

Nuthin before Me but Thang, the Goose, Baby I Owe You Something Good

Vocals: Clip Payne, Lige Curry, Garry Shider, Andre Foxxe, Gregg Fitz
Drums: Gabe Gonzalez
Bass: Lige Curry
Guitar: Andre Williams, Ron Smith, Ted Orr, The Flash
Keyboards: Gregg Fitz

Funky Dollar Bill

Vocals: Clip Payne, Lige Curry, Garry Shider, Andre Foxxe, Gregg Fitz, George Clinton, Sheila Brody
Drums: Gabe Gonzalez
Bass: Lige Curry
Guitar: Andre Williams, Ron Smith, Ted Orr, the Flash
Keyboards: Gregg Fitz

Inhale Slowly

Vocals: Clip Payne, Lige Curry, Garry Shider, Andre Foxxe, Gregg Fitz
Drums: Gabe Gonzalez
Bass: Lige Curry
Guitar: Andre Williams, Ron Smith, Ted Orr, the Flash, Stanley Jordan
Keyboards: Gregg Fitz

Don't Mess with Me, Moonshine Heather, West Woody Jam

Vocals: Clip Payne, Julia Nichols, Joey Eppard
Drums: Chicken Burke
Guitar: Adam Widoff, Ted Orr, the Flash, Joey Eppard
Sax: Dave Castiglione
Trumpet: Chris Young

Red Hot Mama

Vocals: Clip Payne, Iwan 10, Ras T
Drums: T Ixes
Guitar: Dr. Know, the Flash
Bass: Daryl Jenifer

Cold Hearted World, Deep Down in the Dumps

Vocals: Clip Payne, Garry Shider, Lige Curry, Joey Eppard, Toshi Reagan
Drums: Chicken Burke
Bass: Lige Curry
Guitar: Adam Widoff, Joey Eppard, Andre Williams, Garry Shider

Live in Spain 2004, Zaragoza, Spain

Vocals: Mike Clip Payne, George Clinton, Garry Shider, Lige Curry, The Law, Kendra Foster, Lili Haydn, Avalon, Danny Bedrosian, Jeremy Bernstein
Drums: Gabe Gonzalez, Zachary Alford
Guitar: Garry Shider, Jeremy Bernstein, Ted Orr, Shaunna Hall
Keyboards: Peter Keys, Danny Bedrosian
Horns: Shane Kirsch, Dean Jones
Percussion: Man in the Box, Richie Nagan
Violin: Lili Haydn
Bass: Lige Curry

Jacksonville, Florida

Vocals: Mike Clip Payne, George Clinton, Kendra Foster, Cordell Mosson
Drums: Gabe Gonzalez
Guitar: Michael Hampton
Bass: Derrik Davis
Keyboards: Danny Bedrosian
Man in the Box: Mike Clip Payne

Universal Church of Love & Music

Vocals: Mike Clip Payne, George Clinton, Garry Shider, Cordell Mosson, Avalon, the Law, Lige Curry, Danny Bedrosian
Drums: Gabe Gonzalez
Bass: Lige Curry, Rodney Curtis, Billy Nelson
Guitar: Garry Shider, Ted Orr, Billy Nelson, Cordell Mosson, the Wolf
Keyboards: Peter Keys, Danny Bedrosian
Percussion: Man in the Box, Richie Nagan

"Coast to Coast" Mateel Center, 2010

Vocals: Mike Clip Payne, Garry Shider, Lige Curry, Greg Thomas, George Clinton, Danny Bedrosian
Drums: Gabe Gonzalez
Bass: Lige Curry
Guitar: Garry Shider, Jen Leigh, Rickey Rouse, Ted Orr, Michael Hampton
Keyboards: Danny Bedrosian, Greg Thomas
Sax: Greg Thomas
Percussion: Man in the Box, Richie Nagan

Children of Production Greek Theatre

Vocals: Raphael Saadiq, Amp Fiddler, Clip Payne, Joi Gilliam, Keisha Jackson
Drums: Steve Perkins
Bass: Cat Daddy
Keyboards: Amp Fiddler
Guitar: Rob Bacon
Horns: Daryl Dixon, Dave Watson

Bearsville Theater

Vocals: Joey Eppard, Stephanie McKay, Garry Shider, Law, Jeremy Bernstein, Clip Payne
Drums: Chris Gartmann, Ross Rice
Guitar: Joey Eppard, Adam Widoff, Garry Shider, Tedd Orr, Jeremy Bernstein, Michael Hampton
Bass: Fred Cash, Alana Orr
Percussion: Man in the Box

Sirius Satellite Radio

Vocals: Michael Clip Payne, George Clinton, The Law, Danny Bedrosian, Lige Curry, Garry Shider
Drums: Gabe Gonzalez
Bass: Lige Curry
Guitar: Michael Hampton, Garry Shider
Keyboards, Synthesizers: Danny Bedrosian
Tablas: Ted Orr

GOV'T MULE

GOV'T MULE LIVE . . . WITH A LITTLE HELP FROM OUR FRIENDS (SELECT TRACKS): 1999

"Soulshine"

Guitar, Vocals: Warren Haynes
Bass, Backup Vocals: Allen Woody
Drums: Matt Abts
Organ: Bernie Worrell
Guitar: Derek Trucks
Wurlitzer Electric Piano: Chuck Leavell

"Devil Likes It Slow"

Guitar, Vocals: Warren Haynes
Bass, Backup Vocals: Allen Woody
Drums: Matt Abts
Organ: Bernie Worrell
Guitar: Jimmy Herring

"Afro Blue"

Guitar, Vocals: Warren Haynes
Bass, Backup Vocals: Allen Woody
Drums: Matt Abts
Guitar: Jimmy Herring, Derek Trucks
Organ: Bernie Worrell
Percussion: Yonrico Scott
Tenor Sax: Randall Bramblett

MICHAEL HAMPTON

Kidd Funkadelic Live in San Francisco, 2004

Lead Guitar: Michael Hampton
Vocals: Steve Boyd
Guitar: Dewayne Blackbyrd McKnight, RonKat Spearman, Carlos Hernandez
Bass: T-Bone
Drums: Rocko

LIGEDELIC

Live & in Concert 2012, 9:30 Club Washington, D.C.

Bass, Vocals: Lige Curry
Guitar: Michael Hampton, Garry Shider
Vocals: Michael Clip Payne, Kendra Foster, George Clinton, Cordell Mosson, Tracey Lewis, Garry Shider
Drums: Rico Lewis
Keyboards: Jerome Rodgers
Sax: Greg Thomas
Trombone: Greg Boyer
Trumpet: Bennie Cowan

House of Blues, Houston, Texas

Bass, Vocals: Lige Curry
Guitar: Michael Hampton, Andre Williams
Vocals: Michael Clip Payne, Kendra Foster, Danny Bedrosian, Andre Williams, Shonda Clinton, Sa'D Ali, Carlos McMurray, Tracey Lewis, Steve Boyd, Greg Thomas, Garry Shider, George Clinton
Keyboards, Synthesizers: Danny Bedrosian
Drums: Rico Lewis
Sax: Greg Thomas
Trumpet: Bennie Cowan

MACEO PARKER

Live on Planet Groove, 1992

Alto Sax: Maceo Parker, Candy Dulfer, Vincent Henry
Vocals: Maceo Parker, Pee Wee Ellis, Fred Wesley, Kym Mazelle
Tenor Sax, Flute: Pee Wee Ellis
Trombone: Fred Wesley
Organ: Larry Goldings
Bass: Vincent Henry
Guitar: Rodney Jones
Drums: Kenwood Dennard

Maceo Soundtrack

"Cold Sweat"

Alto Sax, Vocals: Maceo Parker
Tenor Sax, Vocals: Pee Wee Ellis
Trombone: Fred Wesley
Bass: Jerry Preston
Drums: Jamal Thomas
Guitar: Bruno Speight
Organ: Will Boulware

"Knock on Wood"

Alto Sax, Vocals: Maceo Parker
Tenor Sax, Vocals: Pee Wee Ellis
Trombone: Fred Wesley
Bass: Jerry Preston
Drums: Jamal Thomas
Guitar: Bruno Speight
Organ: Will Boulware

"New Moon"

Alto Sax, Vocals: Maceo Parker
Tenor Sax, Vocals: Pee Wee Ellis
Trombone: Fred Wesley
Bass: Jerry Preston
Drums: Jamal Thomas
Guitar: Bruno Speight
Organ: Will Boulware

"House Party"

Alto Sax, Vocals: Maceo Parker
Tenor Sax, Vocals: Pee Wee Ellis
Trombone: Fred Wesley
Bass: Jerry Preston
Drums: Jamal Thomas
Guitar: Bruno Speight
Organ: Will Boulware

"New Song"

Alto Sax, Vocals: Maceo Parker
Tenor Sax, Vocals: Pee Wee Ellis
Trombone: Fred Wesley
Bass: Jerry Preston
Drums: Jamal Thomas
Guitar: Bruno Speight
Organ: Will Boulware

"Do Right Woman Do Right Man"

Alto Sax, Vocals: Maceo Parker
Tenor Sax, Vocals: Pee Wee Ellis
Trombone: Fred Wesley
Bass: Jerry Preston
Drums: Jamal Thomas
Guitar: Bruno Speight
Organ: Will Boulware

"Chameleon"

Alto Sax, Vocals: Maceo Parker
Tenor Sax, Vocals: Pee Wee Ellis
Trombone: Fred Wesley
Bass: Jerry Preston
Drums: Jamal Thomas
Guitar: Bruno Speight
Organ: Will Boulware
Other Horns, Drums: Rebirth Brass Band

"Make It Funky-Funky Good Time-There Was a Time"

Alto Sax, Vocals: Maceo Parker
Tenor Sax, Vocals: Pee Wee Ellis
Trombone: Fred Wesley
Bass: Jerry Preston
Drums: Jamal Thomas
Guitar: Bruno Speight
Organ: Will Boulware

"C Jam Funk"

Alto Sax, Vocals: Maceo Parker
Tenor Sax, Vocals: Pee Wee Ellis
Trombone: Fred Wesley
Bass: Jerry Preston
Drums: Jamal Thomas
Guitar: Bruno Speight
Organ: Will Boulware
Vocals: George Clinton, Kym Mazelle

PARLIAMENT

Live P-Funk Earth Tour, 1977

Vocals: George Clinton, Calvin Simon, Fuzzy Haskins, Ray Davis, Grady Thomas, Garry Shider, Glenn Goins, Debbie Wright, Jeanette Washington, Gary Mudbone Cooper
Drums, Percussion: Jerome Brailey
Bass: Cordell Mosson
Keyboards, Synthesizers: Bernie Worrell
Guitar: Michael Hampton, Garry Shider, Glenn Goins
Trombone: Fred Wesley
Trumpet: Richard Griffith, Rick Gardner
Sax: Maceo Parker

PARLIAMENT-FUNKADELIC

Live 1976–1993 4 Disc, San Diego Arena, San Diego, California, 1977

Vocals: George Clinton, Calvin Simon, Fuzzy Haskins, Ray Davis, Grady Thomas, Garry Shider, Glenn Goins, Debbie Wright, Jeanette Washington, Gary Mudbone Cooper
Drums, Percussion: Jerome Brailey
Bass: Cordell Mosson
Keyboards, Synthesizers: Bernie Worrell
Guitar: Michael Hampton, Garry Shider, Glenn Goins
Trombone: Fred Wesley
Trumpet: Richard Griffith, Rick Gardner
Sax: Maceo Parker

Howard Theatre, Washington, D.C., 1978

Vocals: George Clinton, Ray Davis, Garry Shider, Ron Ford, Larry Heckstall, Dawn Silva, Lynn Mabry, Babs Stewart, Sheila Horne, Jeanette McGruder, Junie Morrison
Drums: Tyrone Lampkin
Percussion: Larry Fratangelo
Bass: Rodney Curtis
Keyboards, Synthesizers: Bernie Worrell, Junie Morisson
Guitar: Michael Hampton, Garry Shider, Eddie Hazel, Cordell Mosson
Trombone: Greg Boyer
Trumpet: Bennie Cowan
Sax: Greg Thomas

Denver, Colorado, 1976

Vocals: George Clinton, Calvin Simon, Fuzzy Haskins, Ray Davis, Grady Thomas, Garry Shider, Glenn Goins, Debbie Wright, Jeanette Washington, Gary Mudbone Cooper
Drums, Percussion: Jerome Brailey
Bass: Cordell Mosson
Keyboards, Synthesizers: Bernie Worrell
Guitar: Michael Hampton, Garry Shider, Glenn Goins

Hampton Coliseum, Hampton, Virginia, 1978

Vocals: George Clinton, Ray Davis, Garry Shider, Ron Ford, Larry Heckstall, Dawn Silva, Lynn Mabry, Babs Stewart, Sheila Horne, Jeanette McGruder, Junie Morrison
Drums: Tyrone Lampkin
Percussion: Larry Fratangelo
Bass: Rodney Curtis
Keyboards, Synthesizers: Bernie Worrell, Junie Morisson

Guitar: Michael Hampton, Garry Shider, Eddie Hazel, Cordell Mosson
Trombone: Greg Boyer
Trumpet: Bennie Cowan
Sax: Greg Thomas

Howard Theatre, Washington, D.C, 1978

Vocals: George Clinton, Ray Davis, Garry Shider, Ron Ford, Larry Heckstall, Dawn Silva, Lynn Mabry, Babs Stewart, Sheila Horne, Jeanette McGruder, Junie Morrison
Drums: Tyrone Lampkin
Percussion: Larry Fratangelo
Bass: Rodney Curtis
Keyboards, Synthesizers: Bernie Worrell, Junie Morisson
Guitar: Michael Hampton, Garry Shider, Eddie Hazel, Cordell Mosson
Trombone: Greg Boyer
Trumpet: Bennie Cowan
Sax: Greg Thomas

Hara Arena, Dayton, Ohio, 1981

Vocals: George Clinton, Ron Ford, Garry Shider, Ray Davis, Clip Payne, Mallia Franklin, Larry Heckstall, Robert Peanut Johnson, Lige Curry, Maceo Parker, Greg Thomas
Drums: Dennis Chambers
Percussion: Larry Fratangelo
Bass: Rodney Curtis
Guitar: Michael Hampton
Keyboards, Synthesizers: Jerome Rodgers
Trumpet: Bennie Cowan
Sax: Greg Thomas
Trombone: Greg Boyer

Beverly Theatre, Los Angeles, 1983

Vocals: George Clinton, Maceo Parker, Garry Shider, Gary Mudbone Cooper, Robert Peanut Johnson, Ron Ford, Lige Curry, Clip Payne, Cordell Mosson
Drums, Percussion: Dennis Chambers
Bass: Rodney Curtis
Guitars: Garry Shider, Michael Hampton, Eddie Hazel, Cordell Mosson
Keyboards, Synthesizers: Jerome Rodgers, Bernie Worrell
Trumpet: Bennie Cowan
Sax: Greg Thomas
Trombone: Greg Boyer

Monroe Civic Center, Monroe, Louisiana, 1978

Vocals: George Clinton, Lynn Mabry, Dawn Silva, Jeanette Washington, Debbie Wright, Ray Davis, Ron Ford, Garry Shider, Larry Heckstall
Drums: Jerome Brailey
Bass: Rodney Curtis
Keyboards, Synthesizers: Bernie Worrell
Guitars: Michael Hampton, Garry Shider, Cordell Mosson
Sax: Greg Thomas
Trumpet: Bennie Cowan
Trombone: Greg Boyer

Tokyo, 1993

Vocals: Garry Shider, Ray Davis, Steve Boyd, Paul Hill, Greg Thomas, Robert Peanut Johnson, Lige Curry, George Clinton, Gary Mudbone Cooper, Clip Payne
Drums: Frankie Kash Waddy
Guitar: Blackbyrd McKnight, Andre Williams, Michael Hampton, Garry Shider
Keyboards: Amp Fiddler

Bass: Jeff Bunn, Lige Curry
Trumpet: Bennie Cowan
Sax: Greg Thomas
Trumpet: Bennie Cowan
Trombone: Greg Boyer
Tambourine: Gary Mudbone Cooper, Robert Peanut Johnson, Michael Clip Payne

Chicago, 1993

Vocals: George Clinton, Gary Mudbone Cooper, Lige Curry, Garry Shider Belita Woods, Linda Shider, Michael Clip Payne, Robert Peanut Johnson, Tracey Lewis,
Drums: Guy Curtis
Bass: Lige Curry, Jeff Bunn
Guitar: Blackbyrd McKnight, Michael Hampton, Garry Shider, Andre Williams
Keyboards: Gary Hudgins
Trombone: Greg Boyer
Trumpet: Bennie Cowan
Sax: Greg Thomas
Percussion: Muruga Booker

Sugar Shack, Boston, 1972

Vocals: George Clinton, Calvin Simon, Grady Thomas, Ray Davis, Fuzzy Haskins
Drums: Frankie Kash Waddy
Bass: Bootsy Collins
Guitar: Catfish Collins, Harold Beane
Keyboards: Bernie Worrell
Trumpet: Chicken Gunnells, Ronnie Greenway
Sax: Robert McCullough

Kawasaki Citta, Tokyo, 1993

Vocals: Garry Shider, George Clinton, Clip Payne, Louie Kabbabie, Sheila Horne
Drums: Barry Chenault
Bass: Lige Curry
Percussion: Muruga Booker

Memphis, Tennessee, 1993

Vocals: George Clinton, Michael Clip Payne, Lige Curry, Garry Shider, Robert Peanut Johnson, Gary Mudbone Cooper, Tracey Lewis
Drums: Tony Thomas
Bass: Lige Curry
Guitar: Blackbyrd McKnight, Michael Hampton, Garry Shider, Andre Williams
Keyboards: Amp Fiddler, Gary Hudgins
Percussion: Muruga Booker
Trumpet: Bennie Cowan
Sax: Greg Thomas
Trombone: Greg Boyer

Lifted (Live)

Vocals: George Clinton
Drums: Dennis Chambers
Bass: Rodney Curtis
Guitar: Blackbyrd McKnight
Percussion: Muruga Booker

PARLIAMENT 3GP BANGERZ 2019

First Ya Gotta Shake the Gate Medley

Drums: Benzel Cowan
Bass: Lige Curry
Keyboards, Synthesizers: Danny Bedrosian
Guitars: Dewayne Blackbyrd McKnight, Garrett Shider, Trafael Lewis
Vocals: George Clinton, Tracey Lewis, Trazae Lewis-Clinton, Tonysha Nelson, Patavian Lewis, Michael Clip Payne, Thurteen, Scottie Clinton

P-FUNK ALL STARS

Live at the Beverly Theater, 1983

Vocals: George Clinton, Maceo Parker, Garry Shider, Gary Mudbone Cooper, Robert Peanut Johnson, Ron Ford, Lige Curry, Clip Payne, Cordell Mosson
Drums, Percussion: Dennis Chambers
Bass: Rodney Curtis, Lige Curry
Guitars: Garry Shider, Michael Hampton, Eddie Hazel, Cordell Mosson
Keyboards, Synthesizers: Jerome Rodgers, Bernie Worrell
Trumpet: Bennie Cowan
Sax: Greg Thomas
Trombone: Greg Boyer
Flute: Maceo Parker

BERNIE WORRELL AND THE WOO WARRIORS

Live, 1998

Keyboards: Bernie Worrell, Gregg Fitz
Bass: Donna McPherson
Lead Vocals: Bernie Worrell, B. J. Nelson
Guitar: Michael Moon Reuben
Drums: Van Romaine
Backup Vocals: Gregg Fitz, Michael Moon Reuben, Van Romaine

True DAT!!, 2002

Keyboards: Bernie Worrell, Gregg Fitz
Bass: Donna McPherson
Lead Vocals: Jen Durkin, Bernie Worrell
Guitar: Flash, John Hickey, Brett Grau
Drums: Garry Sullivan

George Clinton leading the P-Funk. William Thoren

OTHER IMPORTANT SOURCE MATERIAL

Bronson, Fred, and Adam White. *Billboard Book of Number One Rhythm & Blues Hits.* Billboard Books, 1993.

Mills, David. *For the Record: George Clinton and P-Funk: An Oral History.* Harper Collins, 1999

Thompson, Dave. *Funk.* Backbeat Books, 2001

Vincent, Rickey. *Funk: The Music, the People, and the Rhythm of The One.* St. Martin's Press, 1996

Visser, Marcel, and Arno Konings. *George Clinton & P-Funk.* BBNC Publisher, 2013

INDEX OF ARTISTS, GROUPS, AND BANDS

INDEX OF
FEATURED SONGS

ABOUT THE AUTHOR

Daniel Bedrosian has been the keyboardist for George Clinton and Parliament-Funkadelic for more than 20 years. He is now the longest-tenured keyboard player in the band's touring history. In his time with the band, he has played all over the world—180 to 300 days a year on average—on all six livable continents, in scores of nations worldwide, and across the United States, including some of the biggest festivals and concerts in the world. He has appeared on *25 Strong: The BET Silver Anniversary Special*, *The Tonight Show with Jay Leno*, *The Carson Daly Show*, *I'm with Rolling Stone*, *The Late Show with David Letterman*, *The Late Late Show with Craig Ferguson*, *The Mo'Nique Show*, *The Tonight Show with Jimmy Fallon*, and *Later. . . with Jools Holland*, *Tales from The Tour Bus* as well as on MTV in several nations and other international televised events. In addition to his work with the multifaceted Clinton and company, Bedrosian has collaborated with a veritable who's who in the world of popular music, including Snoop Dogg, Chuck D and Flavor Flav of Public Enemy, Bow Wow, Scarface, Ice Cube, Shavo Odadjian (from System Of A Down), Fishbone, Kendrick Lamar, the Red Hot Chili Peppers, Erykah Badu, Queen Latifah, T-Pain, Noel Gallagher, Mumford & Sons, RZA, Sly Stone, Steve Arrington, Chris Dave, Flying Lotus, Thundercat, CeeLo, Sheila E., DJ Battlecat, Wu-Tang Clan, EarthGang, MonoNeon, Kamasi Washington, MuzikMafia, Ivan Neville, the Roots, Paul Schaffer, Wiz Kalifa, and many more. All the while, he has continued recording, touring, and producing his own music—now up to 23 albums—as well as more than 37 albums for other artists and bands.

.